A CHILD IN TRUST

THE REPORT OF THE
PANEL OF INQUIRY
INTO THE CIRCUMSTANCES
SURROUNDING THE DEATH OF
JASMINE BECKFORD

Published by
LONDON BOROUGH OF BRENT
Brent Town Hall
Forty Lane, Wembley
Middlesex HA9 9EZ

ISBN 0-9511068-0-5

Printed by
THE KINGSWOOD PRESS
9-19 Palmerston Road
Wealdstone, Harrow,
Middlesex

A CHILD IN TRUST:

the Report of the Panel of Inquiry into the circumstances surrounding the death of
Jasmine Beckford

Presented to Brent Borough Council and to Brent Health Authority by the members
of the Panel of Inquiry:

Dr. John Beal

Mr. Louis Blom-Cooper Q.C.
(in the Chair)

Mr. Ben Brown

Mrs. Pat Marshall

Miss Mary Mason J.P.

Adviser to the Panel of Inquiry:

Mr. Russell Profitt

Secretary to the Panel of Inquiry:

Miss Rosamond John-Phillip

CONTENTS

PREFACE   1

PART I   INTRODUCTION

A   *General*

    Chapter 1.   Historical background to contemporary child abuse   9
    Chapter 2.   Law and practice relating to Care Orders   17
    Chapter 3.   Our Inquiry   23

B   *Specific*

    Chapter 4.   Dramatis personae   41
    Chapter 5.   Chronological summary of events, 2 December 1979
                    – 2 December 1985   57
    Chapter 6.   Demographic profile of Brent   61
    Chapter 7.   Medical evidence of child abuse.   65

PART II   FACTS AND COMMENTS ON THE EVENTS

A   *The Events, August 1981 – July 1984*

    Chapter 8.   The making of the Care Orders, August/September
                 1981.   77
    Chapter 9.   Fostering and thriving, September 1981-April 1982.   105
    Chapter 10.   Home on trial, post-April 1982.   115

B   *Social agencies' response to events*

    Chapter 11.   Social Services Department of Brent Borough Council   129
    Chapter 12.   Brent Health Authority   139
    Chapter 13.   Law and Administration Department of Brent
                 Borough Council   149
    Chapter 14.   Education Department of Brent Borough Council   155
    Chapter 15.   Metropolitan Police   159
    Chapter 16.   The Juvenile Court   167
    Chapter 17.   National Society for the Prevention of Cruelty to
                 Children   175

PART III   POST-MORTEM EVENTS

    Chapter 18.   Political complexities of Brent Borough Council   179
    Chapter 19.   Responses of Brent Borough Council   181

PART IV   GENERAL ISSUES

Chapter 20.   Training   197
               (a)   Social Workers
               (b)   Health Visitors
               (c)   Magistrates
               (d)   Lawyers
Chapter 21.   Supervision: 215
               (a)   Social workers
               (b)   Key workers
               (c)   Health Visitors
Chapter 22.   Documentation   223
Chapter 23.   General Practitioners   235
Chapter 24.   Area Review Committees   239
Chapter 25.   Case Conferences and Statutory Case Reviews   245
Chapter 26.   Guardians ad Litem   253
Chapter 27.   Place of Safety Orders   255
Chapter 28.   Court Officers   259
Chapter 29.   Options on placement: residential, fostering or home
               on trial.   263
Chapter 30.   Fostering   269
               (a)   general − selection and management
               (b)   trans-racial

PART V   CONCLUSIONS AND RECOMMENDATIONS

Chapter 31.   Conclusions   287
Chapter 32.   Summary of Recommendations   299

Appendices

A: Representation of Parties   i

B: List of Witnesses   ii

C: Documents relating to Care Proceedings on 9 September 1981 and
    22 June 1983   iv
    1. Dr. Levick's report
    2. Miss Joan Court's report
    3. Mr. Thompson's note of Magistrates' Statement on making Care Order.
    4. Magistrates' Q & A to Panel of Inquiry.

D: Proceedings before the Central Criminal Court, March 1985   xix
    1. Charges against Morris Beckford and Beverley Lorrington.
    2. Questioning by the Common Serjeant, Judge Pigot QC, of officers of
        Brent Borough Council

E: Relevant Child Care Law   xxiv

F: Miss Alix Causby's guardian ad litem report of 18 September 1984.   lxix

G: Case Conferences and Statutory Case Reviews   lxxxii
    1. 6 August 1981
    2. 20 August 1981
    3. 9 December 1981
    4. 5 April 1982
    5. 25 May 1982
    6. 30 September 1982
    7. 9 November 1982
    8. 18 April 1983
    9. 6 December 1983

H: Brent Borough Council's Green Book (1977).   cxxii

I: Dr. Iain West's post-mortem report on Jasmine Beckford.   cxxxi

J: Chief Executive's report on complaint re advertisement to find a
    foster-home for Louise and Chantelle Beckford.   cxxxvii

K: Selected bibliography   cxxxix

INDEX   cxliii

PREFACE

On 28 March 1985 we were appointed by the Council of the London Borough of Brent, and subsequently in conjunction with the Brent Health Authority, to inquire into and report on the events leading up to, and the circumstances surrounding the death of Jasmine Christina Beckford who was born on 21 December 1979 and died on 5 July 1984.

Terms of reference

Our terms of reference were as follows:

(a) To investigate all the circumstances surrounding the death of Jasmine Beckford, a child who was in the care of Brent Council.

(b) To determine what action had been taken by the Directorate of Social Services in the period preceding the circumstances (events) and what support had been given to the family, and the adequacy thereof.

(c) To determine whether any immediate steps should be taken arising from the Inquiry, and to advise what action relating to staffing issues should be taken and/or followed if necessary, and to recommend accordingly.

(d) To inquire into the co-ordination of services to the family by the relevant Local Authority and Health Services and any other persons or agencies involved and the liaison between them, and to make appropriate recommendations.

We have interpreted our terms of reference not merely in the letter but in their spirit. Although, for example, we were not specifically called upon to examine the twin issues of trans-racial fostering and of employment of a white social worker with the Beckford family, which was Afro-Caribbean in ethnic origin, we could hardly fail to notice the importance attached to these aspects of our Inquiry by the inclusion of Mr. Russell Profitt (who is Principal Race Relations Adviser to the London Borough of Brent) as our adviser. (We mention this aspect of the Beckford case later in this chapter). Other topics did not, on the face of them, appear to concern us, but we were soon made aware of their relevance. It could not have been anticipated that the proceedings before the Willesden Magistrates would be so central to the issues we had to examine. Again, on 4 July 1985 the Department of Health and Social Security issued a consultative paper on Child Abuse Inquiries. Our experience of conducting the inquiry in public, during which many of the thorny procedural matters relating to child abuse inquiries were exposed, provided a unique opportunity to add our thoughts to an important aspect of our task.

Furthermore we were conscious throughout our work that an Interdepartmental Working Party, serviced by the Department of Health and Social Security, was undertaking a thorough review of Child Care Law. (It reported on 4 October 1985). Here again we considered that we had something to offer in the course of the continuing debate about the protection of children in care. We were also alive to the recent creation of a Social Services Inspectorate within the Department, which prompted us to look rather more closely into the structure of the local authority child protection service than would otherwise have been the case.

1

These examples are not exhaustive. We cite them merely to indicate the reasons why we have interpreted our remit in a more extensive and expansive way than a strict reading of our terms of reference would indicate. In any event, as we shall indicate in our chapter on inquiries (Chapter 3), a major justification for such a large expenditure of public funds is the seizing of an opportunity to go beyond an examination of the events that surround the fatality of a particular child in care, and to examine some of the broader issues that provide the framework, both statutory and in practical application, of the law of child care. Part IV of this report reflects what some critics might describe unkindly as a half-baked exegesis on the management of the child abuse system. We hope the description is inapt.

The Circumstances Leading to the Inquiry

Jasmine Beckford died at the age of 4½, in Kensal Rise, North-West London, at the home of Mr. Morris Beckford (her step-father) and Miss Beverley Lorrington (her mother) of cerebral contusions and subdural haemorrhage as a direct result of severe manual blows inflicted on the child's head shortly before death. At the time of her death, and for some months (if not years) before, Jasmine was a very thin little girl, emaciated as a result of chronic undernourishment. When she was discharged from hospital after being taken into care she weighed 18 lbs. 14 ozs. Seven months later, when she was reunited with her parents after being fostered, she weighed 25 lbs. 5 ozs. She died, 27 months later, weighing 23 lbs. Apart from her stunted development, she had been subjected to parental battering over a protracted period, multiple old scars appearing both to the pathologist who conducted the post-mortem and to the consultant orthopaedic surgeon who gave evidence to us, as being consistent with repeated episodes of physical abuse, to say nothing of the psychological battering she must have undergone.

Morris Beckford was convicted of Jasmine's manslaughter at the Central Criminal Court on 28 March 1985, and was sentenced by the Common Serjeant, Judge Pigot QC, to 10 years' imprisonment. Earlier in the trial Beverley Lorrington changed her plea to guilty of child neglect; she was sentenced to 18 months' imprisonment (For the full list of charges and verdicts, see Appendix D:1).

From 17 August 1981 until her death, Jasmine and her sister, Louise (then two and a half months old) were the subject of Care Orders in favour of the London Borough of Brent, for the earlier part of which they had been boarded-out with foster-parents, and subsequent to April 1982 had been physically in the care and control of their parents, Morris Beckford and Beverley Lorrington. Those bare facts and circumstances leading up to Jasmine's violent and unnatural death, which were not publicised until the newspaper reports of her parents' criminal trial, aroused a considerable volume of public disquiet as reflected in the extensive treatment accorded to the case by both national and local press and by radio and television.

Throughout our Inquiry we have been acutely aware of the time it has taken to set up the Panel of Inquiry, for us to conduct a thorough investigation of the events and to ensure a fair hearing to all those whose involvement has inevitably come under the public searchlight, and of the need to report expeditiously. We have thought it helpful to re-mind all those entrusted with the task of deciding when and how to hold a child abuse inquiry, of the first such inquiry in modern times – namely, the inquiry conducted in 1945 by Sir Walter Monckton (later Viscount Monckton of Brenchley) into the cir-

2

cumstances which led to the boarding-out of Dennis and Terence O'Neill, and the steps taken to supervise their welfare*.

Dennis O'Neill was boarded out at Bank Farm, Minsterley, Shropshire on 28 June 1944 by Newport Borough Council, to whom he had been committed on 30 May 1940 as a "fit person" within the meaning of sections 76 and 96 of the Children and Young Persons Act 1933 (Dennis O'Neill was joined by his brother, Terence, on 5 July 1944). Dennis O'Neill died, shortly before his 13th birthday, on 9 January 1945 as a result of acute cardiac failure following violence applied to the front of the chest and back, while — be it noted — in a state of undernourishment due to neglect. The foster-parents, Mr. and Mrs. Gough, were charged with his manslaughter. On 19 March 1945 at Stafford Assizes, Reginald Gough was found guilty of manslaughter and sentenced to 6 years' penal servitude (by that time indistinguishable in practice from ordinary imprisonment): Esther Gough was found not guilty of manslaughter, but guilty of child neglect, and sentenced to 6 months' imprisonment, sentences which bear comparison with the severer penalties inflicted on Morris Beckford and Beverley Lorrington. The two relevant authorities, Newport Borough Council and Shropshire County Council asked the Home Secretary to order a public inquiry. This he did on 28 March 1945. Nowadays the relevant local authority is normally expected to set up the requisite inquiry. **Where (as here) the inquiry is, exceptionally, one of enormous public interest and likely to involve such large financial cost that it is unreasonable for local government to bear, we think that the Secretary of State should initiate the inquiry under his statutory powers given in section 98, Children Act 1975. And we so recommend.**

Sir Walter Monckton's one-man inquiry sat for four days in mid-April 1945, when 22 witnesses were called and 7 parties were legally represented. Sir Walter reported on 8 May 1945, four months after Dennis O'Neill's death which had attracted widespread attention both in and out of Parliament, and led to the setting up of the Curtis Committee on the Care of Children (H.M.S.O., Cmd. 6922) on 25 March 1945; it reported in September 1946 (The Children Act 1948 was the direct legislative response).

In the other famous modern inquiry, into the death of Maria Colwell, the dates are not uninformative. Maria died on 7 January 1973; her step-father was convicted of murder on 16 April 1973, but his conviction was reduced to manslaughter by the Court of Appeal on 19 July 1973 and a sentence of 8 years' imprisonment substituted. On 17 July 1973 the Secretary of State appointed an inquiry. The Inquiry sat in public for 41 days between October and December 1973, hearing 70 witnesses with 7 parties represented, and reported (with a partial dissent from Miss Olive Stevenson) in April/May 1974*.

We allude in a later chapter to the methods of conducting child abuse inquiries which we think could materially expedite the time taken in reporting to the initiating authorities. But one matter that is to be elicited from both the O'Neill and Colwell Inquiries immediately strikes us. The criminal proceedings in respect of a child in care or under supervision of a local authority (where it is apparent that an inquiry will inevitably follow

---

* see H.M.S.O. Cmd. 6636.

---

* The report of the majority, Mr. T.G. Field-Fisher QC and Alderman Mrs. Davey, was dated 23 April, and Miss Stevenson's dissent, 3 May.

the criminal process, if any) could, and should be given the highest priority in criminal investigation by the police, in the prosecution by the relevant prosecutor (which in future will be the national independent prosecuting service) and in the Crown Court's calendar of criminal business. While we have not felt it necessary to examine why it took so long for Morris Beckford and Beverley Lorrington to be brought to trial, we can see no reason why it took nearly nine months. (About the same delay occurred in the recent cases of Tyra Henry, a child who was killed while in care of Lambeth Borough Council, and of Reuben Carthy who was killed by his mother in Nottingham, both taking more than six months to come to trial). The arrests were made instantaneously; there were damning admissions from Morris Beckford at his first interrogation; and the prosecution evidence was limited both in scope and volume; the trial lasted only three days. The delay appears to us to have been inexcusable. Whatever may be the explanation for this inordinate delay in the criminal process, **we strongly recommend that in future in all child abuse prosecutions involving children in care of a local authority, where the public is almost certain to express disquiet about the handling of the case by social services and other relevant agencies, suggestive of fault by social workers and other professional people, the criminal trial should, other than for exceptional reasons, take place within 3-4 months of the homicidal event, and certainly not beyond six months.** In both the *O'Neill* and *Colwell* cases, the trial took place inside 3-4 months. The Home Secretary has recently acquired the statutory power under the Prosecution of Offenders Act 1985 to place time limits within which criminal trials must take place. Child abuse cases represent a classic instance of the type of prosecution where the exercise of this power would be entirely appropriate.

The procedure for an Inquiry

The Panel of Inquiry sat for a preliminary hearing at Brent Town Hall on 15 April 1985 (just over a fortnight after our appointment) to determine the procedure for the forthcoming taking of evidence and to entertain applications for legal representation. At that hearing we decided to sit in public session throughout the Inquiry wherever it was possible to do so, consistent with the dictates of confidentiality and propriety. We devote hereafter a part of Chapter 3 to the question of appropriateness of the mode of an inquiry into a case of child abuse, since we recognise this as an issue of acute contemporary debate.

Our Inquiry began its oral hearings at Brent Town Hall on 29 April 1985 and completed hearing evidence from 93 witnesses (including 16 who were expert witnesses) nine weeks later on 28 June 1985. We had hoped to conclude the proceedings on that day, since one of us (MM) had a long-standing commitment to an exercise with the Health Advisory Service of the DHSS. We were forced to adjourn, until the first week of September, to hear final speeches from the representatives of the parties appearing before us by counsel or solicitor. (We took the opportunity of the adjournment to recall one witness and to hear from one witness who had returned from abroad only in the last days of June). The break in our proceedings extended the length of time taken to report only by a few weeks, something less than the period of the two months' adjournment. (We attach in Appendix A and B the representation of the parties and the list of witnesses respectively). As we have said, we have been conscious throughout of the need for expedition in producing our report, and we have done our best to produce this lengthy report without unnecessary delay. Any defects in the style and shape of the report may be partly attributable to some haste in production.

4

Although conspicuously we had no statutory or other legal powers to compel the attendance of witnesses before us, all those from whom we considered it necessary to hear evidence, and who were available in this country, agreed to assist us. We would like to put on record our sincere gratitude to all these witnesses, without qualification, for the spirit in which they came forward and in some instances knowingly exposed themselves to the searchlight of public examination, never a pleasant experience at the best of times. For those professionally engaged as social workers in the events under public scrutiny at our inquiry who were conscious of the potential criticism coming their way, the giving in public session of oral testimony against a background of often virulent press hostility must have been an ordeal. Their foregoing of the right to claim silence in the face of such an unfriendly atmosphere is a testimony to their regard for professional responsibility to stand up and be publicly accountable for their statutory obligations. They were all not merely co-operative in attending for oral questioning and cross-examination; without their ready response to be subjected to a unique − we trust, non-repetitive − experience we would have failed to do our task with the thoroughness vital to any unravelling of often highly complex factual situations. We would not ordinarily wish to single out any individual witness, for to do so is always invidious. But we do wish to mention Ms. Gun Wahlstrom, for it was she who conspicuously bore the brunt of unbridled media coverage of an unpleasant, harassing nature outside and far beyond the committee room. Yet before us she bore herself with a dignity that does her great credit. We told her so at the conclusion of her testimony. But now that we must be highly critical of her social work with Jasmine Beckford − in which, of course, we are at pains to point out, she is not alone − we wish to say that her behaviour as a spectator in the weeks before she gave evidence and in the testing days of giving her evidence was exemplary. If her answers to searching questions often failed to convince us, she never lost her composure. And her distress over the death of Jasmine Beckford, as with all her colleagues in the Social Services Department, was unqualifiedly genuine.

Additional to the days of hearing and testimony we were supplied unstintingly with all the relevant documents from Brent Borough Council and from Brent Health Authority. These authorities never sought any immunity from disclosure of information, often of a sensitive nature, being clinical records of professional staff. They were content to leave it to us to determine the extent to which the veil of confidentiality should, if at all, be pierced. We hope that we have faithfully fulfilled the trust reposed in us, and that we handled the documentary material with the degree of delicacy consistent with both public and private interests.

We appointed counsel to appear and conduct the inquiry on behalf of the panel. Miss Presiley Baxendale and Mrs. Helen Helston performed the arduous task of picking their way through the thickets of disparate documentation, of collating the diverse material from the various agencies, and of presenting the evidence with a professionalism that was of the highest quality. When the Director of Social Services told us that, while initially apprehensive about the effect on her staff of an inquiry in the glare of publicity, she thought our Inquiry had been "very well managed", she no doubt thought she was paying us a compliment. We accepted it in that spirit. But in reality the compliment was due to our counsel. Only those who know what happened behind the scenes can testify to whom the credit is due. In so saying, we are not simply recording the traditional words of gratitude. The role of counsel for an Inquiry such as ours is a vital cog in a wheel that is bound to encounter some bumpy passages, if only because there is no well-settled procedure to guide one, as there is in a court of law or in an administrative tribunal. This is particularly so where the Inquiry is devoid of powers to compel anyone to do anything. Only the manifest respect that the Inquiry can evoke in those who appear before it can sustain the ordered process. Such manifestation is immeasurably enhanced by the way in which counsel for the Inquiry orchestrates the evidential material and obtains the collaboration of all the other legal representatives. Miss Baxendale and Mrs. Helston steered us through the traffic on smooth and bumpy roads with such consummate skill that our task was relatively an easy one. The smooth management of our sessions allowed us to relax and listen attentively, and without diversion, to the witnesses.

Leave to be legally represented was granted to all parties who sought representation. Witnesses were examined in chief either by counsel for the Panel or, where they were legally represented, by their own counsel or solicitor. All witnesses were open to cross-examination by the other parties' legal representatives. We describe some of the problems of conducting our Inquiry in Chapter 3.

Witnesses before the Inquiry

We have noted that everyone who could assist us came at our request. We felt at an early stage that we should, if at all possible, hear from Jasmine's parents who had the children exclusively in their custody for more than two years before her death. We were afforded every facility from the Director General of the Prison Service and his staff both at headquarters and at H.M. Prison, Wandsworth and H.M. Prison Cookham Wood to take evidence from Morris Beckford and Beverley Lorrington. In the event, the former was unwilling to see us, but Mrs. Helston on two separate occasions interviewed him and obtained two signed written statements that filled some of the gaps in our knowledge about his relationship with the social workers, and about other matters related to the home on trial from April 1982 to July 1984. Miss Lorrington, in the company of her solicitor, agreed to see the Panel, together with Mr. Profitt and Miss Baxendale, at H.M. Prison, Cookham Wood. A transcript of her evidence was taken and circulated to the parties' representatives. This excursion did not add much to our factual knowledge, but it did at least give us some insight into the human alchemy of the Beckford household.

The Willesden Juvenile Court

The only persons who declined an invitation to come before us were the Magistrates who heard the care proceedings on 9 September 1981 and the application on 22 June 1983 for revocation of the Care Orders on Jasmine and Louise Beckford (Of the four Magistrates involved, two, including the Chairman, were common to both hearings). This was not because they personally were unwilling to assist in any way they could, but because they were advised by the Lord Chancellor not to appear before a public inquiry such as ours. The reason was that the Lord Chancellor took the view that it would be constitutionally improper for those who exercised judicial powers to be accountable to anyone other than an appellate or judicially reviewing court. But we were permitted to administer such questions to the Magistrates as they were willing to answer about any matter that related to what took place in the courtroom. We were not allowed to ask questions that were designed to elicit answers revealing any of the decision-making process. It was not, and is not for us to question the propriety of the constitutional rule or convention. We merely note its effect in a case where a good deal turned on the legal proceedings in our determination of any fault that existed in the decision to restore the Beckford children to their battering (and themselves battered) parents. The questions and answers (where given) are included in Appendix C:4. While these answers failed to resolve all the conundra of the care proceedings, and on occasions served only to confound an already confusing picture of what took place, we are grateful to the Willesden Magistrates for the assistance they provided on some of the issues we had to determine.

But at the end of the day we found ourselves stymied by the absence of any articulation of the Magistrates' decision to make the Care Orders and then to add a rider to their decision. Magistrates enjoy an immunity conferred by constitutional convention that uniquely screens what Lord Devlin describes as "the zenana of the [English] judiciary"* from accountability by way of oral examination at a public enquiry, an immunity made doubly unfortunate by the absence of reasons. On the giving of reasons, we are clear that in future in all care proceedings full reasons must be given. We deal with this topic fully in Chapter 16.

Miscellany

Two of us (LB-C and MM) attended a week-end seminar on Child Care Law, organised by the Department of Health and Social Security and held at the Civil Service College, Sunningdale from 9-11 May 1985. We were grateful to the Department for inviting us and allowing us to imbibe many ideas relevant to our Inquiry. We have all informed ourselves from the considerable body of literature on the subject of child abuse; and we include in Appendix K a selected bibliography. Not all of us have read all the works listed, but all the works listed have been read by one or more of us. We supplemented our reading of relevant literature by calling a number of expert witnesses on the various aspects of child abuse. They are listed in Appendix B:2. We are very grateful to them for compressing into a short time a wealth of professional knowledge and experiences that immeasurably enhanced our comparatively inexpert and often meagre knowledge.

We cannot conclude our prefatory remarks without acknowledging the assistance of certain persons. Mr. Russell Profitt, Principal Race Relations Adviser of Brent Council, was appointed as adviser to the Panel.

It appeared at the outset of our Inquiry, exceptionally among the many recent inquiries into cases of child abuse, that there was a discrete racial dimension to the case of Jasmine Beckford (although in the end it played little or no part in our consideration of the issues for determination). The placement for fostering of an Afro-Caribbean child with an Anglo-Indian foster-father and English foster-mother provoked debate about the propriety and efficacy of trans-racial fostering. And the employment of a key social worker of Swedish origin and Anglo-Swedish educational background, supervised by a white American-trained senior social worker, and assisted by a family aide of Afro-Caribbean origin, aroused comment among the black community on the paucity of black social workers in social service departments in inner-city areas. Throughout our Inquiry we have found Mr. Profitt's advice invaluable. He never stepped outside his allotted task of adviser, by intruding into our deliberations; yet he was always to hand with sound guidance whenever we turned to him, or he thought we needed his advice, which he proffered judiciously. Indeed we quickly came to respect his judgment, not just on racial issues but on other aspects of our Inquiry where we were insufficiently informed. The political background to the events after Jasmine's death was peculiar to Brent Borough Council. Mr. Profitt's inside knowledge of the machinery of this corner of London local

* *Easing the Passing: The Trial of John Bodkin Adams*, Bodley Head (1985) 93.

7

government was of great help to our understanding of the interaction between members and between members and officers of Brent Borough Council. Not to be accused of making a poor pun, we have not said that we have profited enormously from Mr. Profitt's wise counsel. To say so, however, would be entirely apt.

Second, we have a particular debt to our Secretary, Miss Rosamond John-Phillip. Plucked from her life as an articled clerk to the Director of Law and Administration, she adapted cheerfully and with great facility to her unusual task of servicing the demands of the five of us. (We were delighted to hear, in October, of her appointment as an Assistant Solicitor with Brent Borough Council) She materially assisted Miss Baxendale and Mrs. Helston in marshalling the documentation and in contacting the witnesses. She further provided a helpful link between the Inquiry and the administrators at Brent under the gently guiding hand of Mr. Bill Graham. Throughout the long weeks we were made constantly aware of her cool efficiency.

We wish to add that the preparatory work before we began the hearings substantially smoothed the path of our task. For this we are indebted to Mr. Stephen Forster, Director of Law and Administration for Brent Council. Once he had laid the sure foundations of our Inquiry he quietly slipped into the distance and detached himself from our work, save for coming and giving evidence on Day 34. His attitude was characteristic of all the officers of the Council and most of the members. They were determined to ensure that our Inquiry was independent, and seen to be so. We have to say, however, that the attitude was not universal. The Labour Group on the Council did not desist from communicating with us in order to indicate how we should be conducting our Inquiry and by pointing to issues that the Group considered important for us to cover. We have not overlooked any of the Group's suggestions, but we did think it was unseemly of the Group to appear to be influencing our work. We mention this matter in order to point to the desirability of the authorities which set up an independent panel of inquiry distancing themselves from the tribunal once they have set the inquiry up to investigate a child abuse case. In this instance there were allegations from members of Brent Council of an attempted cover-up by officers of the Social Services Department. We should have preferred to come to our conclusion unembarrassed by private communications from those making the allegations. Since we have rejected the allegations, no harm has been done.

We add one word of explanation about our use of gender in this report. We are acutely aware that nowadays there are many people in our society (both men and women) who actively oppose the use of any grammatical classification roughly corresponding to the two sexes, and who demand the use of a sexless word. Thus they demand that the person who takes the chair at a meeting should be described as "chair" or "chairperson". We agreed, not without some animated discussion, to adopt throughout our report the traditional approach of using the male gender to include the female, at the same time acknowledging that in so doing we will offend some of our readers. Stylistically at least, we think that "chairman" still sounds better than "chair" or "chairperson", while recognising that in time the reverse may become true.

Finally, a word of sincere gratitude to Joost and Madeline Cohen of Textpertise and to Mr. Malcolm Jellows of Kingswood Press for having translated our manuscript via the word-processor into print with such speed and efficiency.

CHAPTER 1

Historical Background to Contemporary Child Abuse*

> He argued that the principal duty which a parent owes to a child
> was to make him happy.
>
> (Trollope, Doctor Thorne, 1858)

> Child abuse is not a black problem, a brown problem, or a white
> problem. Child abusers are found in the ranks of the
> unemployed, the blue-collar worker, the white-collar worker
> and the professional. They are Protestant, Catholic, Jewish,
> Baptist and atheist.
>
> (Fraser, 1976-1977)

Historical Background

Some parents abuse, even kill their children. Throughout history, they always have, and they always will. What is new about child abuse has been the increased and still increasing public awareness of this socially unpalatable, endemic phenomenon. Realisation that the deliberate abuse of children not only occurs but is also by no means a rare occurrence is profoundly shocking both to the individual and to the body politic. It is hardly surprising, therefore, that acknowledgement of child abuse, with the corollary that social intervention is required in an attempt both to prevent children from suffering at the hands of their parents and to reduce the risk of repetition of disclosed abuse, has been slow in coming to the fore of the public consciousness.

Interest – initially in the United States in the immediate post-war years – among radiologists in the bone fractures, bruising and other physical injuries to children produced the medical base from which, in turn, paediatric, psychological, social and legal interest in the problem developed. It is now only a quarter of a century ago since Dr. Caffey, a paediatric radiologist, and subsequently Dr. Kempe, a paediatrician (both of them working in the United States) described injuries in infants which they strongly suggested could be traced to deliberate acts of violence on the part of parents or other persons responsible for looking after children. The disinclination, even among the medical profession, to acknowledge the truth of these assertions was challenged by the seminal publication in 1962 of Dr. Kempe's studies in which he explored with his colleagues in Denver, Colorado the physical abuse of children. Their studies were enlightening. If they failed, however, to illumine the path of future action, they did at least make the darkness of the past more visible.

At first, it was thought that to call a phenomenon "child abuse" might make people wary of social intervention, since it tended to emphasise the legal liability and social deviance aspects of the problem. Dr. Kempe, therefore, renamed the phenomenon the "Battered-Child Syndrome". The revised label proved crucial in helping to gain the at-

---

* For the early part of this chapter we have drawn heavily upon Mr. Nigel Parton's fascinating work, *The Politics of Child Abuse*, Macmillan, 1985.

tention of the medical profession generally to the problem. While it was distinctly emotive, it did at least play down the legal and socially deviant aspects, and it alerted social policy-makers to the need to encourage legislators and administrators to take action. It defined it as an illness, a syndrome. Today, there will be no need to find an alternative to the title, "child abuse", so long as it acknowledges that it can take the form of physical, psychological and sexual abuse.

The initiative in this country was centred on the medical profession. In 1963, two orthopaedic surgeons were the first to describe the condition in England. But the main impetus came from forensic pathologists, such as the late Professor Francis Camps at the London Hospital Medical School and the late Professor Keith Simpson, Professor of Forensic Medicine in the University of London. Members of the legal and social welfare agencies became involved only gradually, primarily because at that time — the mid 1960s — although they saw cases of child abuse, they rarely recognised them as such, and the emphasis was being placed on the need to work with whole families and to prevent delinquency. Doctors, moreover, reflected the general public attitude. Working in casualty departments of hospitals, they were unaware, or unwilling to believe that parents could deliberately harm their children. They also adhered to the principle of client-confidentiality and rarely reported cases to the police or to social workers. There was also a reluctance to become involved in the criminal justice system, because of the time involved and the loss of their ability to control the outcome of the criminal process. By contrast, the forensic pathologists, closely allied to the court system and sensitive to the role of agencies other than the health services, were prepared to bridge the gap between medicine, Social Services and the law.

By the late 1960s, stimulated by the work of the widely respected National Society for the Prevention of Cruelty to Children, medical auxiliaries and social workers had begun to study the problem. According to the NSPCC Annual Report for 1969, the objectives of the Battered Child Research Unit, set up two years earlier, were "to carry through a comprehensive programme of study and treatment of families where a child has been battered, and to help build up an informed body of opinion on the 'Battered-Child Syndrome'." The unit's most important function was to publicise the problem and educate the professionals concerned. Miss Joan Court, whom we have heard as a witness, was a prominent member of that unit. Between 1969 and 1973, members of the unit published 17 articles in a variety of journals, of which Miss Court wrote 10. The unit was recognised as the main repository of knowledge on child abuse. The problem and its control was at that time being described as a "medico-social" one, in which the emphasis was on early identification of abuse and society's non-punitive response to those committing abuse. Social workers were being told not to ascertain whether the criminal law had been broken and whether the parents were legally responsible: Rather the objective was to form a "consistent, trusting, professional relationship", and there was early recognition that authority had little or no part to play in restoring the equilibrium of family life that had experienced a breakdown. Thus the legal system — the lawyers, the police and the courts — were seen as significant partners in handling child abuse cases only when the law was regarded as part of a more general rehabilitative or treatment programme. The police, in particular, were kept at arm's length. The courts were invoked in care proceedings under the Children and Young Persons Act 1969 to protect children at risk. The police were generally excluded from access to juvenile courts by virtue of the provisions of section 47 (2), Children and Young Persons Act 1933.

By the early 1970s a number of local authorities, reorganising under the generic Social Services departments, following the Seebohm Report and the resultant legislation of 1970, were setting up warning systems or coordinating committees as part of the management of what was fast becoming the child abuse system. In 1974 and 1976, two circulars were issued from central government encouraging local action. Both circulars stressed the preventive aspect of the work. Child protection was seen as the prime objective, but it was to be achieved generally in terms of rehabilitation of the whole family. The 1974 circular recommended the establishment of area review committees and case conferences; and the 1976 circular indicated a favourable response from local authorities to the earlier circular. While the framework was multi-professional, consultant paediatricians were top dogs, and the nascent Social Services departments became merely the field workers and managers of the Care Orders introduced under the 1969 legislation. The police were rarely included on the committees and were regarded, at best, as peripheral to the management of the child abuse system. It is that background of medical-orientated work and a low profile in Social Services against which one needs to assess the impact of the Maria Colwell case in 1973.

The Maria Colwell Case

Maria Colwell was killed by her stepfather on the night of 6/7 January 1973, 11 weeks short of her eighth birthday. She was the fifth and youngest child of her mother's first marriage. Within weeks of her birth, Maria's father left home and a few weeks later died. At the age of four months, Maria, while in care of the local authority, was placed by her widowed mother with Maria's paternal aunt and uncle, with whom she was happily fostered for more than five years. In October 1971, Maria was taken back to live with her mother and step-father, whom she had been visiting regularly for some time before. Maria's mother then sought the revocation of the Care Order. In spite of forebodings about the wisdom of Maria's removal from the foster-home back to her mother's home, and because the Social Services − East Sussex County Council − were apprehensive that the magistrates would favour the reuniting of Maria with her mother, the application to revoke the Care Order was not opposed. Instead, the local authority supported the move, subject to the substitution of a Supervision Order. One of the criticisms made subsequently by the majority of the Committee of Inquiry was that the Social Services had decided not to oppose revocation of Maria's Care Order "on insufficient evidence". Social Services were also criticised for having rushed to judgment about the child's rehabilitation. Whether those criticisms were justified or not, the fact was that the local authority ceased to exercise parental powers over Maria and was under a duty only to "advise, assist and befriend" Maria under the terms of the Supervision Order. Apart from that exceedingly general provision, the legislation is silent as to the supervisor's powers. But one thing is clear. A Supervision Order does not empower the supervisor to give legally effective directions about the upbringing or conduct of the child. Everything that Miss Lees, the key social worker for Maria, did thereafter had to be judged against the backcloth of the absence of any legal sanctions, short of returning to court for the reinstatement of the Care Order, which had little or no prospect of success in the short term.

Three further criticisms of the social work activity with Maria Colwell were directed at failures to supervise. The local authority failed to monitor the result of Maria's return home "with sufficient care"; it had failed to react with due sense of urgency to the first signs of physical injury; and it had entirely failed to supervise Maria in the six months prior to death. The pattern of visiting and seeing Maria in those last months was not dissimilar from that exhibited in the case of Jasmine Beckford, although on occasions Miss Lees did at least take Maria out on her own and talk to her, always being reassured that nothing untoward was happening in her mother's household. A month before Maria died, Miss Lees saw the girl. She thought Maria was a little taller but very thin, rather pale and listless; she was impressed that Maria had lost "a tremendous amount of weight".

11

At death Maria weighed 36 lbs., whereas she should have been anything between 46 and 50 lbs. Since last being weighed, in August 1971, she had lost 5 lbs. Supervision had demonstrably failed. But it was as much a failure in the lack of provision of legal powers as it was the supervisor's failure to protect Maria: Not so, this case.

In retrospect, it now appears that, apart from the specific issues over supervision, the Committee of Inquiry found itself ensnared by a public preoccupation with the fundamental question of the nature of the relationship between social work and society, social work and the State. The interest of the public and of the media in the case of Maria Colwell – not underestimating the importance of the tragedy itself – was fanned by a widespread feeling of a need to reassess the role of social workers in the community, and their role vis-à-vis some of the moral issues that are powerful factors in any culture – natural parenthood, fostering, adoption, child protection, delinquency and crime, deprivation and freedom of the individual. Since 1974, there has been significant progress in achieving clarification in these areas, so that it has been possible in the later child abuse inquiries to concentrate on specific aspects of organisational efficiency and effectiveness, on professional competence or responsibility, and on aspects of the multidisciplinary approach, without the deflection of the "moral panic" that pervaded the scene in 1973. We have been conscious that over the Jasmine Beckford case there has been some recrudescence of the moral arguments.

The Maria Colwell inquiry itself was conducted at a time when the social work profession had not yet come to terms with its relationship with the public. Writing in *Social Work Today**, six years after Maria's death, Miss Ann Shearer graphically depicted the pain, the bewilderment and the air of injured innocence that social workers expressed whenever the events of 1973 to 1974 were being recalled. She wrote: "It was bizarre, remembers Jeanne Wall (an area director in East Sussex at the time): 'It was so beyond one's experience to be a sort of pawn or puppet, pushed and pulled. It felt so totally unreasonable, so totally unjust .... It [the inquiry] was so unprofessional – Olive Stevenson apart – and so sensational, which was beyond our experience, because until that time nothing had been more private than social work'."

The telling phrase, "nothing more private than social work" reflected the major impact of the Maria Colwell case on the social work profession and its practitioners. A whole generation of social workers, senior social workers, area managers and directors of Social Services were suddenly brought face to face with the fact that they were publicly accountable for their actions in sensitive areas of human behaviour, to an extent that hitherto had not been fully appreciated by many of those appointed in an era of rapid expansion in Social Services. The academic origins of modern social work in the 1950s casework literature had led many to believe that the one-to-one therapeutic relationship was at the heart of professional social work practice. This approach, on the medical model, paradoxically went hand in hand with a strong dislike among many social workers for the authoritarian role inherent in the concept of social control. Since then, despite some continuing resistance, social workers have begun to grapple with the fact that Social Services operate within a statutory framework and that the administration is performed, as Professor Timms aptly describes, "under social auspices". We are strongly of the view that social work can, in fact, be defined *only* in terms of the functions required of its practitioners by their employing agency operating within a statutory framework. We would endorse some wise words spoken in the course of a dissenting judgement (but not on this point) by Lord Justice Donaldson (now Sir John Donaldson, the Master

* "The Legacy of Maria Colwell", Vol. 10, No. 19, 9 January 1979

of the Rolls) in *R* v. *Birmingham City Council ex parte O* [1982] 1WLR 679 at 688G-689C:

> The work done by social workers is not new, but until modern
> times was undertaken by voluntary organisations, family doc-
> tors, the clergy and neighbours. The change to paid and train-
> ed workers and the growth of their professionalism are of recent
> origin. In many ways this is all to the good, particularly the
> professionalism. Every profession has to develop its own ethics
> and those ethics must take full account of the circumstances
> in which the member is working. In the case of the social work
> professions, the development is taking place, but in some
> respects it is going astray ..... The social workers' recognition
> of their own professionalism has led them to speak and think
> of those whom they seek to help as their 'clients'. This, in turn,
> has led some to equate their relationship with their 'clients' to
> that of doctor, lawyer or accountant with their patients or clients
> ..... I do not criticise this. Indeed, I applaud the professional
> instinct which engenders it. But I think that it is to some extent
> misguided. The fundamental fallacy is to regard a local authority
> social worker as being in the same position as a general practi-
> tioner operating under the National Health Service. One is not
> more professional than another. It is just that they are different.
> It is no part of the National Health Service to treat patients.
> It function is to provide doctors who will do so. The resulting
> relationships are (a) employer and employed doctor and (b) doc-
> tor and patient. By contrast, it is the duty of a local authority
> to care for children *and to play a part in the process* (emphasis
> supplied). For this purpose, local authorities employ social
> workers. The resulting relationships are (a) local authority and
> employed social workers, and (b) local authority, social workers
> and the 'clients/patients' of both.''

This tripartite role imposes a form of professionalism that may mean that social workers
must exercise control, never more so than in the care and protection of children. It may
militate against treating the child and its family as an indivisible unit, and even require
intervention by the social worker to protect the child from its parents.

The development of professionalism in social work has not been helped by the publicity
given to it and to the work of its practitioners. Throughout the 1960s and 1970s it was
perhaps inevitable that the media should publicise the problems, particularly of child
abuse, faced by social workers. An early, isolated example was the Dorset County Council
case in 1966 (HMSO). When the Maria Colwell case burst upon an unsuspecting and
unprepared public, the press indulged in simplistic answers for the phenomenon. Since
then, social workers have become the butt of every unthinking journalist's pen whenever
a scapegoat was needed to explain a fatality or serious injury to a child in care or under
supervision of Social Services Departments of local authorities. It is the height of absur-
dity for the media, or indeed the public, to castigate social workers. Likewise, it is neither
sensible nor wise to canonise them. Social workers perform a difficult professional task,
and their professional work should be judged by the standards appropriate to the requisite professionalism. When they fall below those standards, they deserve public cen-
sure. The local authority and its employees are subjected to a wide range of specified

13

statutory duties in respect of children taken into care; the local authority is both accountable to its electorate and liable in law for breach of any statutory duty. It and its employees are also legally liable if they fail to take such care as was reasonable in all the circumstances to protect a child from abuse.*

The Lessons of the Maria Colwell Case

The report of the Committee of Inquiry into the Maria Colwell case, with its product of hurt and anger among social workers, was a catalyst. Both the Department of Health and Social Security and Social Services Departments of local authorities have implemented its recommendations to good effect, and subsequent child abuse inquiries have built on those foundations. We note three principal factors of the child abuse system which have undergone significant change.

(1) *Decision-making*

All decisions being taken in relation to children in care have become more formalised, more rigorously recorded, and more open to investigation and assessment by administrative officers and politicians in local government. As a direct result of the Maria Colwell case, for example, East Sussex County Council produced large volumes of operational instructions which distinguish between *procedures* – "they must be followed" – and *guidance* – "if you depart from this, make sure that you have good reasons and that you record them". Other local authorities followed suit. In 1980, after another widely publicised child abuse case involving Wirral Metropolitan County Council (Paul Brown), East Sussex County Council resolved that Councillors, and not officers, should henceforth have the final say on whether any child in care should be returned home permanently or not (This practice has not been adopted in Brent). Thus, in the area of decision-making, the joint impact of case conferences and of the intervention of committee members has meant a significant diminution in the power of the key social worker working at grass roots. He or she remains responsible for making assessments and for putting forward recommendations. Research suggests that such recommendations are likely to be acted upon. But the formality of a committee decision, properly minuted, has gone a long way towards counteracting the concern of the civil liberties lobby which has argued vigorously that administrative decisions about child placements and their variation have been too private, too informal, and too little open to challenge. We know of no up-to-date public information that would enable us to say whether such arrangements for decision-making in child placements are universally satisfactory throughout England and Wales. **We recommend that a review be carried out by the Social Services Inspectorate of the Department of Health and Social Security to evaluate the processes of decision-making in the management of child abuse cases.**

(2) *Risk-taking*

Social Services Departments of local authorities have undoubtedly come to terms with the fact that they have to take into account the contemporary wishes and feelings of society in implementing their child care policies. In that respect, it seems clear that fewer risks have been taken in the recent past than might have been the case previously. Emphasis has been increasingly placed on the importance of social workers "covering themselves" by ensuring that they have gone through all the

---

* *Leeds City Council* v. *West Yorkshire Metropolitan Police* [1983] A.C. 29.

14

necessary procedures and have acted quickly whenever neighbourly or other concerns were reported to them. On the other hand, there has also been a process of learning by the media and the public. There is probably a more general awareness now that the issues involved are rarely simple, and that the choice facing the social worker is often not between a wholly unsatisfactory family setting and an idyllic alternative, but that the choice is between two imperfect and uncertain options. There is a body of evidence in the literature of criminology and psychiatry to lead social workers to a recognition that council-provided care can be as damaging in its long-term effects as is the experience of incompetent parenting at home. We are confident that the majority of social workers work hard at holding the balance between effectively preventing child abuse and striving not to deprive natural parents unnecessarily of the privilege, if not right, of bringing up their children in the normal way. The situation still involves critical decision-making and involves, therefore, a degree of risk, a risk which is particularly present at an early stage in any referral before overt evidence of cruelty has emerged. We trust that our report and its recommendations will not in any way disturb the balance that social workers must endeavour constantly to strike between parental rights, limited as they are when those rights have been abused, and child protection.

(3) *Policing/Surveillance*
This remains a critical area for exploration. Society and its representatives (including the media) undoubtedly demand a policing function from social work. We give just one recent example: When a 13-month-old child died of hypothermia after being found by ambulance-men on a urine-soaked mattress, covered in sores and suffering from gangrene, the judge commented critically that the social worker called 51 times "but didn't go to the right part of the house"*. In the instant case, Judge Pigot adversely commented on Ms. Wahlstrom's ineffective visiting during 78 calls to the Beckford household over two and quarter years.

Social workers have felt apprehensive about the implications of such comments. They are uneasy and anxious about the much more formalised response that is being demanded in cases of child abuse suspected or actual. And underlying the unease is the fact that when child abuse is suspected, there may follow a radical change in the one-to-one relationship with the client: what was seen as a helping, supportive role may now be perceived as punitive and authoritarian, and in extreme cases the client may feel that his trust in the social worker has been betrayed, and may react accordingly.

When a child is already in care and is known to be "at risk", only two social work options are possible. Either the child is removed as long as it is thought to be necessary, or the child is left with, or returned to his/her parents, and the social worker is required to work with them intensively, supportively, encouragingly, while still keeping a watch-out for further violence. Can the social worker fulfil a policing role, firmly and efficiently, if he has also to gain the family's confidence, and to convey the personal warmth and genuineness necessary for him to provide the support which will enable them to become better parents?

The evidence from pre-Seebohm models of child care and of probation practice is that the duality of approach is by no means impossible to achieve, providing that the worker is crystal clear about the nature of the job. It is essential that the worker recognises that he owes allegiance both to the agency (and society) which

* The Guardian, 2 February 1980

15

requires him to be a child protector, and at the same time to the parent on whose trust he can build a relationship. There is evidence from client-perspective studies that clients value openness in the social worker, and that they are neither deceived nor impressed by the worker who appears uncertain of his central responsibility for ensuring child protection.

Conclusion

Forty years ago, in his report on the Dennis O'Neill case, Sir Walter Monckton, K.C. (later Viscount Monckton of Brenchley) wrote:

> "The 'fit person' must care for the children as his own; the relation is a personal one. The duty must neither be evaded nor scamped (para 46) ..... I cannot escape the conclusion that there was in neither authority [in that case, Newport Borough Council and Shropshire County Council] a sufficient realisation of the direct and personal nature of the relationship between a supervising authority and boarded-out children, that there was too great a readiness to assume that all was well without making sure (para 50) ..... The personal relation in which the public authority, which has undertaken care and protection, stands to the children should be more clearly recognised (para 54)."

Mutatis mutandis, those words could be ours. We gratefully adopt them. But they do not stand alone; they have not been wholly ignored over the last forty years. The Curtis Committee in its report, *The Care of Children** in 1946 said: "Throughout our investigations we have been increasingly impressed by the need for the personal element in the care of children, which Sir Walter Monckton emphasised in his report of the O'Neill case." Thereafter, until the absorption of children's departments in the new unified Social Services departments, it would have been unnecessary to stress the personal relationship. One of the recent (1980) child abuse inquiry reports, *The Committee of Inquiry into the Case of Paul Steven Brown*** stated in bold type: "We would wish to draw attention to the rights of children to be protected from those parents who, for whatever reason, expose their children to influences which impair their proper development." In an adjournment debate in the House of Commons on 26 July 1985 on child abuse, Mrs. Virginia Bottomley MP pointed out that it was impossible for social workers to work only through the parents: "Direct contact must be made with the child."*** And on the first day of oral submissions before us – 2 September 1985 – Mr. John Trotter, appearing on behalf of the British Association of Social Workers, said that it was the Association's "clear and unequivocal view that in any child abuse case the primary client for the social worker is the child. In practice, child abuse cases are complex and conflicts of interest will inevitably arise. The many conflicts are easier to resolve if social workers always bear in mind who is the primary client." We agree. Throughout this report we too are at pains to underscore the personal relationship between the local authority as the trustee-parent of the child and the child in its care. That personal relationship of trusteeship is, we think, the legal and practical effect of a Care Order.

* Cmd. 6922, para 441, p. 146
** Cmnd. 8107, para 155, p. 43
*** Hansard, HC, Vol.83, No. 164, Col. 1424

16

CHAPTER 2

Law and Practice Relating to Care Orders

General

The leitmotif of modern child care law is preventive action. To that end, a general duty is imposed on a local authority to provide support for a child in his family and thereby avoid the child being received or taken into the care of the local authority: section 1, Child Care Act 1980 imposes a general obligation on the local authority "to make available such advice, guidance and assistance as may promote the welfare of children" by lessening the need either to receive or keep children in care, or to bring children before the juvenile court. The local authority, in exercising its powers has a complete discretion and must not limit its discretion as to the manner in which it discharges its duty. The decision on any child must depend entirely on the different circumstances of each child being individually considered by the local authority. By the Local Authority Social Services Act 1970 the local authority must operate its powers through a social services committee. It must also appoint a Director of Social Services, and "shall secure the provision of adequate staff for assisting" the Director in the exercise of statutory functions.

Voluntary Care

By section 2 (1), Child Care Act 1980 a duty is imposed on the local authority to receive a parentless child into its care if it appears that certain grounds for reception exist – parentless, in the sense that the child is an orphan or has been deserted, or where the parent is permanently or temporarily incapacitated by mental or physical illness from providing the child with proper accommodation, maintenance and upbringing. In either case the local authority's intervention must be necessary in the interests of the child's welfare, and the child must be kept in care so long as the child's welfare requires it and the child has not attained the age of 18. The voluntary nature of care under this section is demonstrated by the duty being placed on the local authority to secure the resumption of parental care if a parent desires it and such resumption of parental care is consistent with the child's welfare (there is a limitation on this where the child has been in care under this section for the preceding six months: section 13 (1) and (2).)

Section 3 (1), Child Care Act 1980 confers on a local authority a *power* to pass a resolution vesting in the authority "the parental rights and duties with respect to that child", subject only to certain specified exceptions. The expression, "parental rights and duties" means "all the rights and duties which in law the mother and father have in relation to a legitimate child and his property". It includes a "right of access and any other element included in a right or duty". The statutory definition is not particularly helpful in explaining precisely what *is* encompassed by the concept of parental rights or duties, but we think it unnecessary to overload our discussion by an indulgence in determining the finer points of family law.* The parental rights and duties which the law specifically provides do not vest in a local authority are a) the right to agree to the making of an adoption order, an order authorising adoption abroad, or an order freeing a child for adoption; and b) the right to determine the religious creed of the child. The child's parents are specifically not relieved of any liability to maintain, or to contribute towards the maintenance of the child. On the contrary, there are elaborate provisions to regulate the liability of the parent to contribute to the cost of the child's maintenance and the enforcement of that liability. In practice, only a small proportion of the cost of keeping a child in care is recovered from parents. The local authority has the power to complain

---

* see Cretney, Principles of Family Law, 4th ed. (1984) pp. 299-310

to a juvenile court if the parent serves a counter-notice in response to the local authority's notice to the parent of its resolution to receive the child into care. The juvenile court may affirm the resolution if it is satisfied that the grounds for the resolution are made out and the grounds still pertain. A resolution may be rescinded if rescission appears to be for the benefit of the child. The juvenile court also has the power to determine a local authority's resolution. Appeals lie to the High Court only from decisions of the juvenile court.

These provisions impose on a local authority a duty to *receive* a child into care, known as "voluntary care"; no power is conferred on a local authority to *take* a child into care*. That can be done only under a parallel piece of legislation. The compulsory taking into care of a child stems from the provisions of the Children and Young Persons Act 1969, to which we now turn. Before doing so, we should make one or two general observations.

Whenever a child is in the care of a local authority, whether voluntarily or compulsorily, the local authority assumes in general the mantle of a parent. So long as the child remains in care, the local authority is under a duty, in arriving at any decision about the child, to give "first consideration" to the need to safeguard and promote the welfare of the child throughout childhood. A local authority is further required to make reasonable use, in providing for children in its care, of facilities and services available for children in the care of their own parents. Every child in care must have its case reviewed at least once every six months. On that review consideration must be given whether a Care Order in force in respect of him or her should be discharged. We shall discuss later the precise effects of, what we call, institutional parenthood.

Compulsory Care

The Children and Young Persons Act 1969 imposes, by section 2, a duty upon a local authority to make enquiries into any case in which it has received information suggesting that there are grounds for bringing care proceedings with a view to taking the child into care, unless it is satisfied that such enquiries are unnecessary. This is a duty exclusive to local authorities. While a local authority, a constable or an authorised person (the NSPCC) may bring a child before a juvenile court, only a local authority has the duty to bring care proceedings. If it appears to a local authority that there are grounds for bringing care proceedings the local authority has a duty to exercise its powers to bring the child before the juvenile court unless satisfied that it is neither in the interest of the child "nor in the public interest to do so, or that some other person is about to do so or to charge him with an offence." Both these legal duties are subject to a proviso giving the local authority a discretion not to make enquiries or bring care proceedings. The general duty under section 1, Child Care Act 1980 and the duties under section 2 of the 1969 Act are not expressly correlated. **We recommend that future legislation should make it clear whether it is intended or not that preventive work has to be exhausted before care proceedings are initiated.** We would think that it was unnecessary to exhaust preventive action before taking care proceedings.

The juvenile court has power to make a Care Order if two conditions are satisfied. The primary condition may be established by any one of seven grounds. The main ground, and the one that will be most appropriate in any case of child abuse, is that the child's development is being avoidably prevented or neglected, or his health is being avoidably impaired or neglected, or he is being ill-treated. The ill-treatment is not restricted to

---

* *Lewisham London Borough Council* v. *Lewisham Juvenile Court* [1980] A.C. 273, 395-396

physical injury, but may include emotional or psychological deprivation.* The secondary condition that must be satisfied is that the child is in need of care or control which he is unlikely to receive unless the court makes an order. Frequently, juvenile courts deal with the two conditions in two distinct stages, although, not surprisingly, some of the evidential material is likely to overlap. The local authority's report on the need for care or control will invariably be referable only to the secondary condition. A Care Order can be made only in favour of the local authority, and generally to that local authority in whose area the court thinks that the child is resident.

Analysis of the Care Order

Once a Care Order is made, the local authority is under a duty to receive the child into its care and to "keep" the child in care "notwithstanding any claim by his parent". So long as the child is in care, whether the child comes into care via the compulsory or voluntary process, the local authority has the same powers and duties with respect to the child as his parent would have had over him, subject to the specific exceptions relating to adoption and religious upbringing. These provisions relating to the compulsory process do not indicate how the local authority should administer the Care Order. It certainly does not mean that the child has to be kept in detention. The child may be kept in a residential home, or may be boarded out with foster parents. The local authority may make "such other arrangements as seem appropriate", which may, and often does, include allowing the child to be under the physical care and control of its parents. The decision whether to leave the child with its parents or, where the child has been removed from home, whether the child should be re-united with his family, is a matter entirely for the local authority to decide.

We conclude from these statutory provisions the following propositions. Parental rights and duties are not *transferred* to the local authority. They are in suspended animation during the currency of the Care Order. The parental rights and duties vested in the local authority are statutorily created, and do not arise from any concept of transfer from the parents. Parental rights and duties in strict law thus exist in parallel with the institutional parenthood, but since the House of Lords' decision on 17 October 1985 in *Gillick* v. *West Norfolk and Wisbech Area Health Authority and another* it can be confidently stated that in any event parental rights cannot be insisted on where the parent has abused those rights. The principle underlying the legislation is that the local authority, as parent of the child, is in total control of that child during the subsistence of the Care Order. The courts, moreover, have no general power to review or control the local authority in the proper exercise of its discretionary powers. In particular, the courts have no say whatsoever in the decision to reunite the family or, if so, the phased return of the child to its family. If the child is reunited with its family, to that extent the local authority delegates its powers to the parents, such delegation being terminable at the will of the local authority, which remains the parent of the child. The only other limitation on the exercise of the local authority's powers is that if it wishes to deny access to the parents, it is required to issue a formal notice of termination of access, against which the parent can appeal to the juvenile court. That court may then make an Order for access.

We think that the "Care Order" is at best a misnomer and at worst a deception on the public. If (as is frequently the case) the child is actually being cared for, day in and day out, by its parents, it is, to say the least, quaint to describe the child as being "in care" of the local authority. The ordinary man in the street would scratch his head in

* *F* v. *Suffolk County Council* (1981) 2 F.L.R. 208

19

bewilderment at such grimgribber nonsense; he would say that the child is in care of its parents and not in the local authority's care. We observe that the Report on the Review of Child Care Law recommends that the terminology of the order by a juvenile court giving a local authority the like parental rights and duties to those of the parents should be altered, and suggests "parental responsibility order". Our preference would be for "parental control order" or "child protection order." Either terminology would signify the reality that the law would be handing the decision of control over the child's pattern of life to the local authority for it to determine by whom and where the protection of the child should be effected.

Nature of Institutional Parenthood
The legislation with regard to the execution of a Care Order is almost entirely unspecific. There are no statutory regulations prescribing minimum standards, save for those dealing with the boarding-out of children in care, to foster parents who have been approved for the child. Rules 21 and 28, Boarding-Out of Children Regulations 1955, for example, lay down the frequency of visiting children in a foster-home. Rules 6, 7 and 8 deal with the requirements for medical examination and arrangements for medical and dental treatment. Good practice would seem to dictate the application of these rules to the placement of children in the home of their parents who have abused them in the past. We shall deal with the aspects of monitoring the parents' handling of such children on a home on trial, in the course of this report. There are the restrictions imposed by section 21A, Child Care Act 1980 and the Secure Accommodation (No. 2) Regulations 1983 with regard to placing a child in secure accommodation.

The legislation simply gives the local authority an unfettered discretionary power to decide how it will manage the Care Order in the best interests of the child. To the question, what criterion should a local authority establish, the simple answer would be, act as a reasonable parent would towards his/her child. We think this answer is too simplistic and inadequate, at least when applied to the situation where the child is in care and on the child abuse register, but is home on trial as part of the process of rehabilitation. We give two examples.

A child under the age of compulsory education may − and many do − go to nursery school. Jasmine Beckford, on 20 April 1982 when she was only just two years old, was sent to the Mortimer Road Day Nursery which is part of the Social Services Department; she ceased attending on 2 November 1982 and on 10 January 1983 was transferred by her mother to the nursery section of Princess Frederica Primary School (which is run by Brent Education Authority) but failed to attend after 9 September 1983. Jasmine's mother, in the ordinary family situation, was perfectly entitled not to send Jasmine to school. Any reasonable parent could properly decide that matter either way. But Jasmine had another parent, the local authority which had control over her life. Given the background of severe child abuse, no local authority, however, could properly decide other than to send Jasmine to a nursery. It would be bound to exercise its discretionary power in that way, not because that is what a reasonable parent would do but because the local authority has a higher duty to ensure the protection of the child. It would send the child to a nursery, not so much for its educational or social value as for its monitoring effect on the child's physical and emotional well-being. The nursery authorities would be able, for the time that they had the child on the school premises, to learn a great deal about how a child was being treated at home.

Another example relates to the question of medical examinations. No reasonable parent would normally take a child for a medical examination unless the child was ailing in some way. Apart from the statutory provisions relating to a new-born baby, parents, however, may or may not decide to take their child for a medical examination every six months as a precautionary measure, until the child goes to school, when the education authorities are required to provide a check on all schoolchildren's health and development. But in the case of a child in care, the local authority must insist, or at the very least as a matter of good practice, require that the child is taken for regular medical examinations. It does so, not because that is what a reasonable parent might do, but because the local authority is bound to protect the child from possibly suffering any harm like that which initially led to the child coming into care.

We have concluded that the nature of the local authority's responsibility for a child in care, whether received into care voluntarily or taken in compulsorily, is one of trust. The local authority is a trustee-parent on behalf of the community which demands that the child be protected. Although the analogy of trust is imperfect, there is an equivalent expectation from the law. A trustee of property has a higher duty in the administration of such property than does the property-owner himself. The latter may be as profligate with his possessions as he will; the trustee, on the other hand, is not permitted to be other than prudent with other people's money impressed with the trust. So too the position of a local authority which has by law assumed parental rights and duties. The local authority is bound by the trust reposed in it by society, through the agency of the juvenile court, to safeguard and promote the interests of the child in its care. To do so, it may have to take steps that go beyond mere sound parenting, and may even have to take action which denies the real parents any exercise of their parental rights.

We do not think there is anything revolutionary in our interpretation of the Care Order. The High Court, when exercising its parallel jurisdiction in wardship, does much the same. The ancient and special jurisdiction arises from the Sovereign's obligation as *parens patriae* to protect the person and property of all of her subjects and particularly those who cannot look after themselves, notably children. The legal significance of this is reflected in the limitations on the exercise of parental rights. In a case in 1981, the mother of an 11-year-old mentally handicapped girl was concerned about the possibility that her daughter might be seduced and, as a result, give birth to a mentally defective child. Acting on professional medical advice, the mother arranged for the daughter to be sterilized. Before the operation took place, an educational psychologist made the child a ward of court. The court determined whether the operation should go ahead by reference to the fundamental principle that the welfare of the child had to be considered "first, last and all the time". Applying that test, the court held that it was not in the child's interests that she should be irrevocably deprived of the basic human right to procreate. The operation was stopped.* The mother was by ordinary standards not acting unreasonably, but the court overrode her parental decision on the grounds that society had all children in its trust, and trusteeship demanded intervention in the parental decision.

The Care Order is the device whereby the Sovereign's universal parenthood has been delegated statutorily to local authorities. Even if our analysis of the legal effect of a Care Order is jurisprudentially unsound, **we would want the law to state that a child in care is a child in trust, and we so recommend.** The nature of a trustee's duty towards such a child will undoubtedly vary according to the circumstances in which the child came into care and the conditions in which it was being kept in care. A child who has been taken into care should always be regarded as being in trust to the local authority. Every decision made about the child, short of revocation of the Care Order by the juvenile court, should be tested against the concept of trust, a test that imposes a higher duty than that of the reasonable parent.

* *Re D (a minor) (Wardship: Sterilisation)* [1976] FAM. 185. In *Re B (a minor) (Wardship: Medical Treatment* [1981] 1 W.L.R. 1421 the Court of Appeal reversed the decision of the trial judge who had declined to interfere with a parental decision not to submit a Downs Syndrome baby to surgery that would prolong the child's life.

CHAPTER 3

Our Inquiry

Since 1974, child abuse inquiries have burgeoned roughly at the rate of two to three cases a year. Some of the inquiries were set up locally, others by central government. While central government has tendered informal advice to local authorities, there have been no formal guidelines and no concerted policy as to how local authorities should respond to public disquiet about individual cases of child deaths (or near deaths) caused by their parents or other persons responsible for looking after children.

There have been various approaches to the persistent problems as to which governmental or other agency should set up the inquiries, whether such inquiries should be conducted in public or in private, and what procedures and practices should be adopted. Many approaches have been tried. No agreed policy has emerged out of them, until the proposals of the Department of Health and Social Security's consultative paper on 4 July 1985, which pointed in the direction of a local framework and basic general guidelines, with central government standing in the wings, to be resorted to only as a fall-back when local initiatives either were not forthcoming or had failed.

The *fons et origo* of contemporary child abuse inquiries was the case of Maria Colwell in 1974, a public inquiry set up by the Secretary of State for Social Services and chaired by a Queen's Counsel*. Since that traumatic experience for the social work profession and for many social workers, all kinds of inquiries have been tried: a private inquiry by review panel of five members and a county area review committee, chaired by a local government solicitor and Deputy Chief Executive, in the case of Wayne Brewer (1977);* an itinerant team of investigators from the Social Work Service of the Department of Health and Social Security, in the case of Stephen Menheniott (1978);** an independent inquiry set up jointly by a local authority and an Area Health Authority and conducted in private by a professor of law, aided by assessors, in the case of Karen Spencer (1978);*** an independent statutory inquiry set up by the Secretary of State for Social Services and chaired by a Queen's Counsel after two false starts by non-statutory panels, in the case of Paul Brown (1980);**** an independent inquiry of five members, chaired by a former Chief Executive of a London borough and set up jointly by another London borough together with a London Area Health Authority (T) and the Inner London Probation and After-Care Committee, in the case of Maria Mehmedagi (1981);***** and an independent panel of inquiry sitting in private, on which the Queen's Counsel-Chairman issued the dissenting report to that of his four members, after a year-long deliberation, in the case of Lucy Gates (1982).******

We only recently received a report of the Standing Inquiry Panel to Nottinghamshire Area Review Committee into the case of Reuben Carthy. The striking features of that inquiry were threefold: First, the speed with which the Panel reported. The child (a boy not quite 3 years old) died on 4 February 1985; the Panel completed its 42-page report,

---

* London HMSO

* Somerset Area Review Committee for Non-Accidental Injuries of Children
** London HMSO
*** Derbyshire Social Services
**** HMSO, Cmnd. 8107
***** London Borough of Southwark
****** London Borough of Bexley

with a summary of 17 recommendations, on 17 September 1985; the trial of the child's mother for murder was heard at Nottingham Crown Court on 20 September 1985 before Mr. Justice Hodgson. Second, the Panel was able to complete its task without the assistance of the police, the main consequence of which was that the forensic pathologist who conducted the post-mortem was unable to appear before the Panel and produce the x-rays showing the extent and timing of bone injuries. Third, the general practitioner who had seen the child only a few days before death when his body revealed a fracture of a rib and did not alert the social welfare agencies, was advised by the Medical Defence Union not to appear before the Panel. We are in no position to make any judgment about this Inquiry, but we commend the existence of a Standing Inquiry Panel, established by Nottinghamshire Area Review Committee in June 1982, and we strongly favour the expeditious inquiry, even though completeness of such inquiry is hampered by the pending criminal proceedings.

Which of these multiform inquiries, if any, has proved satisfactory as an instrument of investigation, both thorough, but nevertheless expeditious in its examination and exposition of the events, and scrupulously fair to those whose professional work came under scrutiny, demonstrating in its report the cogency of analysis and of its critique of professional work and service, and culminating in the utility of its recommendations? We do not pretend to give any answer to that question. But at a time when there is a vigorous and continuing debate, evidenced if only by the DHSS consultative paper on child abuse inquiries, we offer a description of our Inquiry and some reflections on our experience and study of the patterns of child abuse inquiries.

There are three components in the normal social responses to child abuse cases; they cause unhappiness and disequilibrium within the family (both nuclear and extended); they create distress and anxiety for professional workers involved in the case; and they not infrequently arouse acute, and even lingering concern among the immediate community and the wider public. Those publicly accountable and responsible for the management of serious cases of child abuse, resulting in death or serious physical or emotional harm, need to allay the consequences of these responses both quickly and positively. The need is in part to preserve the quality of service to the public and not to allow it to be undermined by the single incident; and in part to allay public concern, if not to assuage private and public anger, often heightened by the outpourings of an often not too scrupulous press.

The initial approach

The DHSS Consultative Paper stresses that in all cases involving the death of, or serious harm to a child, where child abuse is confirmed or suspected, a case review by each of the relevant agencies should be instigated. An inquiry by a review panel may, or may not need to follow. If the initial case review reveals no cause for any concern, and no public disquiet is disclosed, case reviews will suffice. If case reviews disclose shortcomings in procedures and practices, the individual agencies will need to take remedial action. In the residue of a handful of cases, an independent inquiry will be indicated, either because the public perception of what went wrong demands a review outwith the relevant agency, or because the shortcoming revealed by the case review cannot be quickly or easily put right. That much is received wisdom, with which only the unreasonable will cavil. It is upon the nature and conduct of the independent inquiry that informed opinion is sharply divided. We would add, parenthetically, that neither criminal proceedings (if any) against the abusing parents, nor the Coroner's Inquest is appropriate to deal with other than limited aspects of the death of a child who has been abused by its parents.

Public or Private?

Since most of the debate about procedure and practice depends on what basic form the inquiry takes, we deal with the core of the discussion: a public or private inquiry? The DHSS consultative paper states that the "inquiry should normally be conducted in private" (Para 4.2) but, of course, with a published report. While it contemplates that the relevant agencies may consider that the inquiry should be in public, it clearly advocates only a rare departure from the norm (Para 4.3). Anticipating our reasoned argument, we would make two observations. First, we think that the norm should be reversed, at least where there is a volume of demand from the public, when the presumption should be in favour of a publicly conducted inquiry. We say this, not only from our own experience but from the intention of Parliament. In giving the Secretary of State power to set up a statutory inquiry, Parliament further provided, in Section 98(2), Children Act 1975 that he "may direct that it shall be held in private. Otherwise the person holding the inquiry may, if he thinks fit hold it or part of it in private", a statutory recognition of the presumption of publicity. It should be observed that whereas the Secretary of State or his Department will rarely, if ever, be involved in the management of a child abuse case, a local authority will almost invariably be the object of public criticism. Hence, the presumption of publicity in the case of a statutory inquiry by the Secretary of State is reinforced by the need for a local authority to have its responsibilities exposed to public scrutiny.

Second, in the case of a local authority instituting a non-statutory inquiry – there is no statutory power other than in the case of the Secretary of State – we think it is best left to those appointed as the independent panel to decide in the particular case whether it should be in public or not. We were not directed by Brent Borough Council or Brent Health Authority how we should conduct our Inquiry, although we gained the distinct impression that both authorities favoured the Inquiry in public.

At the preliminary hearing to determine procedure the panel should entertain any application by any of the parties or their legal representatives before finally deciding the matter. This we did on 15 April 1985. We were then addressed by Mr. John Trotter, on behalf of the Director of Social Services and the British Association of Social Workers, supported by Miss Barbara Beaton on behalf of three social work members of NALGO, with cogent and powerful arguments, attractively presented, why it was undesirable and even harmful to the morale of the staff of Brent to ask them to be exposed to further publicity in addition to that which had been displayed in the media in an absurdly hostile and hurtful manner during the preceding weeks. Mr. Trotter has had considerable experience in a number of recent child abuse inquiries and his advocacy, therefore, had added point to it. Two of us (J.B. and M.M.) have had previous experience of child abuse inquiries either as member or assessor (one of us as chairman in one inquiry) and were hesitant about any departure from what had become a regular practice of conducting these inquiries in private. But the two of us acknowledged that this case had peculiarly attracted an inordinate amount of publicity reflecting public disquiet, encapsulated in the critical remarks of the Common Serjeant, Judge Pigot QC, when he was sentencing Morris Beckford and Beverley Lorrington at the Central Criminal Court on 28 March 1985. Hence the two of us agreed with our colleagues, but not without certain misgivings, that this Inquiry had to be in public. Nothing less than a public inquiry, with the witnesses giving oral evidence and subject to close questioning in front of the other affected parties, could hope to satisfy a demanding public, and at the same time maintain the credibility for our Inquiry. As we stated at the outset, we were determined to ensure that the Inquiry would be neither a witch hunt nor a whitewash. We could demonstrate that determination only by exposing our conduct of the Inquiry to full view of the public.

For reasons additional to those we have already given, we rejected Mr. Trotter's submission. Except for two occasions involving very peripheral issues, which we decided should be heard in camera, we have throughout held our sessions in public. Apart from the preliminary hearing, we did not allow cameras or tape recorders into the committee room. This was part and parcel of our desire to protect witnesses against the immediate glare of publicity, a matter to which we shall allude later. We experienced no untoward incident, save for one case of a single remonstrator who was quietly removed after a few minutes' disturbance, and very occasionally by interjections from one or two members of the public who were quickly silenced by a sharp reminder that the public could be excluded at any time.

We have been much comforted by the reactions to our Inquiry being held in public. On Day 28 – 14 June 1985 – the Director of Social Services herself, in the course of her impressive evidence, said that she was very circumspect at the outset about the effect instant publicity would have on the morale of her staff. She was particularly fearful that giving evidence in public would put great stress on them. She was also seriously concerned about the cost of the Inquiry, particularly when measured against the other pressing needs of Social Services. Before us, she expressed the unsolicited testimony that she thought that "this Inquiry has not been disadvantageous" (We should add that we too have been acutely conscious of the cost factor in child abuse inquiries, a matter to which we shall return). In *The Guardian* for 29 June 1985, Miss Sarah Boseley reported that our Inquiry had undermined the professional social workers' case in anticipating their criticisms of public inquiries, by their conceding that the "panel has been scrupulously fair, considerate, and even protective of the witnesses", and she quoted Mr. David Storr of BASW as saying that the professional social workers' fear now was that all Boroughs unfortunate enough to have a child abuse death on their doorstep "will want an inquiry like this". We gratefully accept this testimonial. But we add our hope and anticipation that local authorities will seek a public inquiry only when the dictates of openness and overt unfolding of the facts of a particular case strongly indicate it. To repeat, where the public disquiet is absent or insufficiently strong, the inquiry can safely be held in private.

The main arguments against holding these inquiries in public were put forcefully by Mr. Alan Bedford, the chairman of BASW's study project whose draft report we have studied. The thrust of his evidence was that there is no need for a public hearing to uncover the sequence of events and discover what can be done better by the multi-disciplinary agencies handling a child abuse case. Public hearings put the workers of those agencies in a defensive role. What needs to be done in the future to ensure that the tragedy does not happen again can be revealed without the panoply of an expensive, lengthy and potentially harmful process akin to a piece of litigation unfolded in the courtroom setting. He characterised the purpose of a child abuse inquiry as an exercise in "learning" rather than "looking at public accountability."

We see the force of these arguments. But we think they overlook certain important factors. First and foremost, the publicly acceptable exposition of the events will often be achieved only if the inquiry retains public credibility. The publication of the ultimate report may go a long way towards establishing that credibility, but it can never satisfy the severest critics so long as the findings are uncheckable against the evidence publicly tested. There will always be some people who will suspect the suppression or distortion of unpublicised testimony. Second, we think that a child abuse inquiry is, in part at least, a way of demonstrating accountability publicly. It is not just a learning exercise. While child abuse inquiries are not trials or disciplinary proceedings against named individuals, they are expected to point to fault, where appropriate, and to indicate who, if anyone, has acted negligently. It is for others to say whether such pinpointing should lead to disciplinary or other action. But an inquiry would be less than useful if it did not accept responsibility for making judgments of human and social conduct.

Clearly the learning implications of the inquiry are important. But learning is not to be evinced exclusively from the fact-finding process as elicited in private examination and public reporting. The public exercise itself is a learning process. We were struck by something Miss Adeline Martin said to us. She had given instructions to all her health visiting staff that they should take time off to attend some part of our hearings as a most valuable educational tool. We have not kept any record of those who attended in the audience at Brent Town Hall, but were not unaware that numbers of social workers from other London Boroughs and of health visitors came and listened to witnesses from the respective disciplines. We applaud Miss Martin's initiative and other senior managers who did likewise. Additionally, ordinary members of the public had a rare opportunity of seeing and hearing professional people describe how they go about performing their public service. We think that this aspect of a public inquiry cannot be underrated. It provides an insight into social welfare services that will have a lasting impact that can only be for the good of public understanding of what is being done in the name of the public.

The Director of Social Services made an additional point that deserves to be answered. She expressed a commonly-held view that witnesses will be franker about their evidence if they can give it in the sanctuary of the private inquiry. We think that this is one of those unproved and unprovable assertions of logic. Our experience during this Inquiry at least makes us feel that a question mark needs to be put upon the assertion. Doubtless the person who does not have to face his adversary may feel less inhibited. But that assumes that the adversary is not present, in private session, to hear any allegation. If, as we assume even in the privately-conducted inquiry the parties will all be present to hear and cross-examine another witnesses, we think that there will be the same inhibitions. If, as in some child abuse inquiries, the panel merely conducts an investigation in the absence of any party other than the witness being questioned, we regard such practice as the negation of fairness. It transgresses the basic precept that anyone against whom allegations are made has proper knowledge of them and the evidence on which they are based, and has ample opportunity to refute them and put his own case fully to the inquiry. This can be done, with difficulty, by calling witnesses sequentially out of hearing of the other. But it is far from satisfactory, because the evidence of one has to be relayed by the panel; and if a later witness makes allegations, earlier witnesses may have to be recalled. Alternatively, if the practice of seeing witnesses sequentially is adopted, the panel must ensure that every party has an opportunity of seeing and commenting upon the report in draft.

But there is a more important point to be made. It sounds plausible to say that evidence in private is likely to be more candid, and inferentially reveal more nearly the truth, even though the evidence in public is likewise tested for its veracity and credibility. There is another side, however, to the coinage of testimony. A witness is more likely to be cautious about any allegation that he makes in the forensic arena than he might be in private. And caution in accusation is to be encouraged, and not discouraged. We had an example of this, which would be invidious to detail. A highly respectable witness, when being interviewed by our counsel preparatory to giving evidence, was much more bullish about a piece of his testimony than he was in the witness box. Giving evidence has a moderating effect which may approximate to the truth, while an exaggeration may deviate or divert from the essence of the testimony. At all events we conclude that the point made by the Director of Social Services is at least of dubious validity. Even if we agreed with it, we would think that, put into the scales, it is only one of a number of factors that would weigh against a decision to conduct the inquiry in public. An associated argument is that witnesses will be less forthcoming if they have to give their evidence in the full glare of publicity. And non-statutory inquiries have no powers to compel witnesses to attend to give evidence. The only answer we can give is based upon our experience. Not one of the persons whom we wanted to come before us, except the Willesden Magistrates, in fact declined. In the end we sense that the public mood favours our approach. We are reminded of what Lord Salmon, the Chairman of the Royal Commission on Tribunals of Inquiry (1966)* wrote. (Lord Salmon and his colleagues were, of course, concerned only with tribunals set up by Parliamentary resolution under the Tribunal of Inquiry (Evidence) Act 1921, an instrument of public investigation that is infrequently resorted to nowadays). He wrote** that it was important to hold the tribunals in public, "for it is only when the public is present that the public will have complete confidence that everything possible has been done for the purpose of arriving at the truth....Unless these inquiries are held in public they are unlikely to achieve their main purpose, namely that of restoring the confidence of the public in the integrity of public life." Such has been the innate hostility of some sections of the public towards social workers that only a public inquiry has the remotest chance of maintaining public confidence in the social services. Even if (as we are) highly critical of Brent Social Services and their agencies in the management of the child abuse system in the handling of the Beckford case, the position would be the same as and when our report was published following private sessions. What the public nature of our Inquiry has done is to demonstrate that social workers, warts and all, are caring, professional people who do not have horns and tails, and are not murderers (as they have been monstrously described in some writings we have seen) but are dedicated workers who sometimes get things wrong, even wildly wrong.

Who should set up the inquiry?

In almost all cases of child abuse it will be the local authority in whose area the child lived and died that will order the requisite inquiry. Increasingly it is recognised that, while the local authority social services will have been primarily responsible for the child's welfare, other agencies will have been involved. Joint promotion of the inquiry will often be the case. This reflects not merely the multi-disciplinary approach, but means that the burden of the costs will be shared. The alternative would be to place the responsibility for deciding to hold an inquiry and for setting it up on the relevant Area Review Committee. While we have no doubt that the Area Review Committee ought to be apprised of every child abuse case which causes concern about the quality of professional work it received, we do not think that it is the appropriate forum for the inquiry. Although it is a body independent of the agencies, frequently its chairman is the Director of Social Services (as in this case) and will not be perceived as sufficiently independent. As we describe in Chapter 2, we favour a Standing Inquiry Panel. The Area Review Committee could be an appropriate body to set up an independent inquiry – and was in the case of Wayne Brewer (1977) – were it not for the fact that it has no funds to finance an inquiry. Some consideration might be given to the possibility of specific funding from central and/or local government, together with the relevant health authorities. We return to this topic when we discuss the question of costs.

The Composition of an Independent Panel

The tendency has been to appoint a lawyer, usually a Queen's Counsel, to take the chair of the panel. All child abuse inquiries are likely to involve the legal processes in the

---

* Cmnd. 3121
** Tribunals of Inquiry, Lionel Cohen lectures (1967), O.U.P., p. 18.

management of the child abuse system, but the main focus of any such inquiry is much more likely to be the social services and the health services. While there are some advantages in having legal acumen from the chair – in particular, it is perhaps inevitable that in a public inquiry the lawyer's expertise in conducting the procedure and in handling both witnesses and legal and other representatives of the parties is almost a prerequisite – we think there is no absolute rule that a practising lawyer, or even a legally-qualified person should take the chair. What we do think is, that there ought to be some legal expertise readily available, preferably in one or more of the panel members, but possibly through the appointment of counsel to the inquiry of appropriate seniority, experience and, if possible, specific knowledge of child care law. We note that the inquiry set up by the Department of Health and Social Security into the recent outbreak of legionnaire's disease is being chaired by Sir John Badenoch, a distinguished medical practitioner, with a practising lawyer as Deputy Chairman, and a Queen's Counsel who is a trained scientist and a specialist in patent law, acting as counsel for the panel.

We have observed that none of the inquiries since 1974 contained anyone who did not specifically possess an expertise in either social services, health visiting, community medicine, adoption and fostering agencies or the administration of local government. Where the panel is composed of five members (and we think it should never be larger in numbers) we think it both wise and sensible to include someone who is not qualified in any of the directly relevant agencies, but who is broadly representative of the public.

Our Inquiry reflected in its membership the main agencies – a former Director of Social Services, a director of community nursing, an assistant divisional director of Dr. Barnardo's, a community medicine specialist and a Queen's Counsel in the chair. We also had uniquely an adviser, who is the Principal Race Relations Adviser to the local authority setting up the inquiry. One of us (JB) was one of the assessors in the Karen Spencer case (1978) and did not find his status entirely satisfactory. If the inquiry needs some expert input, it is best achieved either by having a panel-member with the requisite expertise or by calling such expert as a witness. The status of an assessor can be obscure in the process of conducting an inquiry, depending on the chairman's perception of, and reliance on such expertise. The status is distinctly ambiguous to the observing public. We were made conscious that outsiders were puzzled whether Mr. Profitt was there to advise us only on race relations or generally, and whether he took part in our deliberations. We have had no hesitation in acknowledging the enormous help that we received from our adviser, but at the same time we did not feel easy about the public perception of his role; neither did Mr. Profitt. **We recommend that all child abuse inquiries should incorporate in their membership all the major professional disciplines, and should not have advisers or assessors.** If, for example, it is thought that race relations or local government administration needs to be represented on the panel, such expert should be a panel-member, and no less.

We have been troubled by the various labels attached to those who have participated in child abuse inquiries other than as members of the Panel or Committee. We were given Mr. Profitt as our adviser, ostensibly only on matters pertaining to race relations. But we did not so limit the scope of his advisory role. There was no restriction on his asking questions of the witnesses other than his own self-denying ordinance. But while we have made full use of our ability to consult him and to hear unsolicited advice from him, he did not participate in the decision-making process. We are not clear how that role differs from that of assessors, who have been appointed in some child abuse inquiries. Strictly speaking, the primary meaning of an assessor is a person who sits as adviser to a judge. One of us (JB), who was one of the assessors in the Karen Spencer inquiry (1978) told us that he acted as adviser to the one-man tribunal, Professor McClean. We think that in the context of child abuse inquiries "assessor" and "adviser" are interchangeable terms, and comment on the role of the one, accordingly, includes the other.

From time to time the Department of Health and Social Security has nominated an observer to a panel of inquiry. We did not officially have an observer, but we were aware that throughout most of our hearings a member of the Social Services Inspectorate was present in the audience. If there is to be an observer, we think that he should be officially acknowledged by being seated to one side of the bench containing the members of the panel.

Our procedure

An inquiry is not a trial, with its predetermined rules of evidence or of practice and procedure. Given the fact, nevertheless, that professional and other persons may have their reputations, not to say their jobs at risk, it is still necessary for an inquiry to observe the fundamental principle of fairness. The tablets of stone in inquiry matters have been inscribed in the report of the Royal Commission on Tribunals of Inquiry (the Salmon report),* the White Paper giving the government's reactions to that report published in May 1973 [Cmnd 5313] and the note, at the end of the Crown Agents Inquiry Report, on "Procedure and the Royal Commission on Tribunals of Inquiry.** We have found no better statement of the basic aims and procedures of inquiries than Lord Scarman's statement at the preliminary hearing of the Red Lion Square Inquiry (1974) which we append as a footnote.*** We proceed to indicate those aspects of our procedure where we have modified the established procedure and where we think we have some valuable comment to make on existing practices.

It is, in our view, imperative that at the preliminary hearing of the inquiry the panel should be explicit about the procedure it is proposing to adopt. There may be occasions for variation at a later stage, but these should be avoided as far as possible. We were conscious that in the Lucy Gates Inquiry (1982) the inquiry had to adjourn after a few days of taking oral evidence to discuss its procedure. It was an unhappy augury of things

---

* Cmnd 3121
** Parliamentary Paper HL149, HC364 at p. 569.
*** I shall refer briefly both to the character of the Inquiry that it is my duty to hold and also to the terms of reference. First of all — and I stress it — this is an Inquiry not a piece of litigation. It is not the sort of adversary-type confrontation between parties with which we English lawyers are familiar in the criminal and civil trials of our country. This Inquiry is to be conducted — and I stress it — by myself.

This means that all the decisions have to be taken by me. Let me indicate now so that there need be no misunderstanding, what are the implications of what I have just said. First of all, it is I, and I alone, who will decide what witnesses will be called. I also decide to what matters their evidence will be directed. There is, in an Inquiry of this sort, no legal right to cross-examination, but I propose, within limits, to allow cross-examination of witnesses to the extent that I think it helpful to the forwarding of the Inquiry, but no further. I also have to determine how witnesses will be examined, bearing in mind the inquisitorial rather than the adversarial nature of the Inquiry. All witnesses will first be examined by Tribunal Counsel. An opportunity will then be afforded to those persons who have been granted representation to cross-examine the witnesses called. The cross-examination will be subject, of course, to the limits that I impose, and it should be directed to eliciting matters that affect those who are represented. No witness will be called to give evidence unless he or she has first given to the Tribunal a written statement of evidence. It is from the written statements of evidence submitted to the Tribunal that I shall make my selection as to the witnesses to be called. The only criterion that I propose to observe in exercising this power of selection will be the extent to which, in my judgment, the witness can help the Inquiry.

to come. The tenor of any inquiry will be determined by how it sets out on its task.

If we had to start again there is one thing at least that we would do differently. We provided only a fortnight between the preliminary hearing and the commencement of oral evidence. This time-lag was too short. We began our task almost immediately after our appointment on 28 March 1985 and set about collating the documentary material, deciding on those persons whom we wanted to call as witnesses, and arranging for them to be interviewed preparatory to taking witness statements. When we held the preliminary hearing on 15 April 1985 we were poised to distribute the first, major set of documents, and we had perused their contents for ourselves. We could discern the broad outlines of our oral hearings. But the period of time for the parties to receive the material, assimilate its contents and take instruction from their clients and prepare for the forensic exercise was, to coin the phrase we adopt for describing a document prepared for the meeting of the Cases Sub-Committee of Brent Borough Council, "woefully inadequate". We apologise to the parties for the inconsiderate treatment that we accorded them. We note it here for future inquiries. **We strongly recommend that sufficient time must be allowed for the parties to be able to prepare their respective cases for the hearing.** How much time that should be will depend on the nature of the case under inquiry.

A good start to the oral hearings will be reflected in the opening speech by the inquiry's counsel. Miss Baxendale's brilliant exposition did much to soften the blow inflicted by the inadequate time given for the parties' perusal of the documentary material. Everyone who is to take part needs to know at the outset what broadly is to be the inquiry's ambit of investigation. Terms of reference provide a framework; they do not sufficiently indicate the precise areas of concern. We gave the represented parties the opportunity to make an opening statement. A few took the opportunity; others declined, on the grounds that they were uncertain at that stage what precisely they would have to deal with. One unusual feature of our procedure that might strike the connoisseurs of inquiries as quaint, if not eccentric was that we invited the represented parties to suggest any avenues of inquiry to which the panel should address itself. Normally, the panel keeps (or tries to keep) the subject matter and direction of the inquiry firmly in its own hands. Lord Scarman's statement is an example of an assertion of control by the inquisitor. But we were conscious that there might be subjects about which the represented parties would like guidance in the Inquiry's report. We give one example. Mr. Bond, on behalf of Mr. Bishop, asked that our report should deal with the remarks made by the Common Serjeant, Judge Pigot QC, in the criminal proceedings, where he attached blame to the social workers. We thought that the request was reasonable, and at the end of this chapter we have expressed our views on judges at criminal trials commenting on the work of Social Services.

The procedure for the examination and cross-examination of witnesses followed closely that recommended in the Salmon report. We varied the order of cross-examination so that the party most directly affected by the particular witness' evidence was the penultimate cross-examiner, followed only by our counsel and questions from the panel. But even this was flexible, and we departed from it whenever we thought that fairness demanded a variance. Occasionally when the panel's questioning raised a fresh point, we invited further questioning by a relevant party. But at all times we made it clear that we controlled the questioning, both as to length and scope. We also gave a represented party the right to ask that certain witnesses be called. Only a handful of our 93 witnesses came before us as a result of such a request. Such requests normally relate to expert testimony that a represented party desires to call. Where witnesses were represented, their own legal representative led them in examination-in-chief. Otherwise our counsel performed the examination.

Three features of the conduct of our inquiry deserve mention.

Hindsight

First, there is the issue of hindsight. Mr. Pitt, who appeared for the health visitors, sharply reminded us that, in analysing the part played by the various persons in providing the services to the Beckford family, we are possessed of the incalculable benefit of hindsight. Many things which now look like flashing amber lights might have seemed of little significance today had Jasmine been alive and well, the implication being that when Jasmine was alive – in 1981, 1982, 1983 and half-way through 1984 – those who were around at those times could not reasonably be held to have seen them as warning signals. Mr. Pitt goes on to support his cautionary note of relying on hindsight, with a quotation from the report of the inquiry into the death of Malcolm Page (1981, paras 1.10 and 1.12). That committee said:

> "We have spent a lot of time in examining and analysing this case and in doing so we were not subject to the pressing every-day and often equally important and urgent problems confronting the individuals and agencies involved with helping the Page family. Looking back it is very easy to ask the question: 'Why didn't you do this or that?' There can be no certainty that the 'this or that' would have made any difference. In our view the only proper criterion is to look at decisions and actions within the context in which they were made or taken and this context must necessarily encompass the knowledge and experience of the individuals involved and the pressures on the agencies for which they worked."

Mr. Pitt's submission was echoed by several of the other advocates before us. We think that there is a danger that "hindsight" is being used to indicate a limiting factor in the proper judgment of past conduct. We, therefore, state here what our approach has been. We do not dissent from what was said by the Committee of Inquiry in the Malcolm Page case, but we think it does not deal adequately with the matter. We repeat the essence of the forensic caution. Actions of social workers and health visitors, it is suggested, may easily be seen as wrong when judged at a later date after more detailed knowledge of all relevant facts and circumstances has become available. Those looking back at past events (as we have done) possess knowledge which those whose past actions are being judged did not know, and could not have known. Therefore, it is at least hinted, if not asserted positively, that hindsight may be a handicap to any sound or fair judgment by us.

In our view, in arriving at a sound judgment of past conduct we are helped, rather than hindered by hindsight, so long as we remind ourselves (as we do) of certain basic principles. In judging the actions of social workers or health visitors as at a particular time, we should ask ourselves what such a person did know, ought to have known, did foresee and ought to have foreseen at that time, bearing in mind all relevant circumstances. We are entitled to judge a person's actions by reference to what was and should, reasonably, have been in his or her mind at the relevant time. We are not entitled to blame him or her for not knowing, or not foreseeing what a reasonable person would neither have known nor foreseen. In assessing whether a reasonable person would have known or foreseen an event, we are entitled to have regard to what actually happened, though, of course, the fact that an event occurred does not mean that a reasonable person would necessarily have known that it would occur or would have foreseen its occurrence. But the fact that it *did* occur (and was not an Act of God but the result of human action or inaction) gives rise to a presumption – either that there was knowledge that it would occur, or that foresight would have indicated its likely occurrence.

32

As long as we remain mindful (as we do) of these principles, we believe that hindsight is of assistance to us in our task, being no more than reasonable foresight, with the additional benefit of knowledge of what has actually occurred. Hindsight enables us to appreciate the consequences of the acts or omissions upon which we are concerned to adjudicate. It is only with the aid of hindsight that those acts and omissions can be analysed in their full context. It is for this reason that courts every day judge people with the aid of hindsight. They do so aware of the advantages of hindsight, properly applied on the principles we have explained above. Indeed, out of court everyone of us judges each other's actions as friends, colleagues and acquaintances, on similar principles. We see no reason why we should not apply the like approach to the matters before us in this Inquiry.

The second feature is that there is no magic about the order of witnesses. But we laid down two principles for ourselves. One was that the social workers who were on the face of the case the most likely candidates for public criticism were to be heard towards the end, on the footing that they should hear all the evidence which tended to substantiate allegations against them. Fairness to them demanded no less. Hence Mr. Bishop, Mrs. Dietmann and Ms. Wahlstrom gave evidence on, respectively, Days 25, 26 and 27; Days 33,34 and 35; and Days 29, 30 and 32. We decided when witnesses should come, and modified our wish to the extent that we were prepared to accommodate the convenience of those witnesses who were fully occupied in employment. We were forced in only one respect to call a witness on terms dictated to us. Councillor Sealy said that he was not prepared to give his evidence *before* he had the opportunity of hearing the evidence of the social workers. We had originally wanted to hear on one occasion all the councillors who were present at the two meetings of the Cases Sub-Committee. On Day 25 Councillors Rees-Hughes and Haftel kindly accepted our invitation, but Councillors Sealy and Cribben declined. They both came eventually on Day 31 (after Mr. Bishop and the bulk of Ms. Wahlstrom's evidence, but before Mrs. Dietmann). Councillor Stone, who was Chairman of the Social Services Committee, came on the same day, as invited by us. We subsequently heard Councillors Coleman and Crane on Day 35, but their late appearance was due to a later invitation from us to appear and give evidence. Their appearance at the tail-end bore no significance. We add one word about the order of witnesses. Ideally the value of expert witnesses is enhanced if they are heard at the end, so that their generalised comments can be related to the specific factual issues of the case. But we did not feel that we lost anything by fitting in our expert witnesses as and when it was convenient to them. Professor Greenland, for example, was visiting England from Canada only for a few weeks in May. He gave up a whole day (and probably more in preparation) to come at an early stage. His evidence early on in fact led us to consider what he said about the "rule of optimism" (see Chapter 21) and apply it to the evidence of the social work practitioners. We would have found it less valuable if we had grasped it only at the end of our hearings. Some experts we did hear last of all − namely, those four who guided us through the brambles of trans-racial fostering and adoption.

The third feature of our Inquiry was the role of the chairman vis-à-vis his members. Our chairman throughout the inquiry regarded himself as *primus inter pares*. While it is always necessary for one of a panel of members to be the spokesman and to control the ebb and flow of the forensic process, it is wrong, in our view, that his colleagues (who have an equal voice in every decision of substance, as opposed to immediate decisions on procedure) should appear to be mere book-ends, propping up their chairman. Consequently, we all participated in asking questions without first consulting or deferring to the chairman. Our only guide was to exercise the restraint that is demanded in order not to disrupt the flow of the proceedings. Members of a panel in a child abuse inquiry are there primarily for their special expertise. It is absurd that they should be stifled in ferreting out the answers to questions which they alone perceive, by any rule that requires that they put their questions only after permission from the chairman. That practice, which we know has been adopted in earlier child abuse inquiries is, in our view, to be deprecated. We are confident in our belief that, whatever the intrinsic merits of each panel member being free to ask questions (and we think they are considerable) the legal representatives at our Inquiry much appreciated the direct involvement of all panel members in the process of eliciting answers to questions. We utter only one word of caution. There is a danger of the process getting out of hand, by the panel members usurping the function of their own counsel and of the parties' legal representatives. It is for the chairman quietly and discreetly to exercise the role of controller of the proceedings. He must not allow the reins to be taken out of his hands for more than a few minutes at any one time.

There is no firm practice about the circulating of the statements of potential witnesses in advance of their giving evidence. Some inquiries do it, and some do not. We made it our practice that we would not in general call any witness until we were in possession of a statement. We think that for key witnesses at least, it is only fair that the represented parties should know in advance what the witnesses are going to say. We relaxed the practice only when we thought that no unfairness would ensue. Quite how far in advance statements are circulated has been a bone of contention in inquiries. Time, the need for continuity and the availability of witnesses have meant that in some instances statements were available only just before the witness gave evidence. Each inquiry must, we think, do its best to get the statements out as soon as possible.

A general problem with any inquiry is that it is an inquiry. Its object is to find out what, if anything, people have done wrong or omitted; and if anything has been done wrong, or omitted. As the inquiry's function is to *find out*, it is not wholly compatible with that function to fling round fully-fledged sets of allegations. In the V & G case (1968) the Tribunal was asked to particularise with greater precision the shortcomings alleged against the participants. The Tribunal refused to do so, on the grounds that it was conducting the inquiry to find out just exactly what officials had failed to do, and could not give a detailed description of what it was trying to discover. We are in no position to criticise that decision. All we would say is that, while each inquiry is different and calls for different response from the inquisitors, child abuse inquiries should adopt a procedure of full and early disclosure.

But one thing we were emphatic about. Some form of prior disclosure of evidence should always be made to parties who are likely to be criticised as a consequence of that evidence. In this regard we followed one of the stronger recommendations of the Salmon report. When allegations are made, the person against whom they are made must be given an opportunity to answer them. Even if witnesses' statements are circulated early enough, the represented party whose conduct is being called into question will be shown the evidence against him and the allegations that spring from it. But sometimes the allegation may be made against someone not then represented. We had a number of witnesses where representation occurred during the course of the nine weeks' hearings. We have been careful to ensure that particulars of allegations (known as "Salmon letters") were sent. We take the view that if an individual's conduct is being called into question, and especially those cases where the nature of the allegations or the likely findings are of some sophistication, it is not merely wise but sensible to reduce the allegation to writing, and not just leave witnesses to pick up the drift of the allegations in some other way. A formula for a Salmon letter might be: "You should be aware that your conduct may be called into question in the following respects:-.......". There would need to be annexed to such a letter, or forwarded at a later date, the evidence (in the form of statements and documents) relating to the allegations. We administered a number of Salmon letters and in this case indicated the lines of questioning a witness that could be taken by our counsel. We did not find it necessary to issue a Salmon letter to any public body. The servants of the local authority and of the health authority were capable of dealing with any allegations that might affect their employer.

Brent Health Authority was represented from Day 15 onwards, and we were glad that the Authority thought that representation was appropriate. Quite apart from the responsibility of the health services for their work with the Beckford family, Miss Goodrich, who appeared on its behalf, was quite exceptionally helpful in extracting and collating the documentation. The Commissioner of the Metropolitan Police was represented from the outset. Since no blame whatever attaches to the conduct of any of his officers, the representation was merely precautionary. Miss James and Mr. Coupland, however, assisted the Inquiry in a number of small ways.

Brent Borough Council was not represented. We think this was a mistaken attitude on its part. But we fully appreciate that anyone who had to hold a brief for the Council might have found his role peculiarly difficult, in view of the political components of the Council. We have been very conscious of the deep divisions in this "hung" Council. Whatever the political complexities, we think that a local authority which holds a Care Order for a child who has died as a result of abuse from its parents or other persons responsible for looking after children should invariably be represented before the inquiry. We only hope that our conclusions on the response of Brent Borough Council to Jasmine Beckford's death are not lopsided, due to any imbalance of political views communicated in the hearings.

Representation

In the end, 18 barristers and solicitors appeared on behalf of 22 individuals and 4 organisations or public bodies. With one exception, all those individuals and bodies played some part or had some interest in the events under inquiry. None could have been legitimately denied the right to be heard by the counsel of their choice. The exception was the representation accorded to the Brent Young People's Law Centre. Its director, Mr. Courtnay Abel, applied to us at the preliminary hearing for his organisation, which had played no part in the Beckford case at any time before April 1985, nevertheless to be represented. He added, grandiloquently, that it would be absurd not to allow him to appear. His claim was that the voice of young people in Brent should be clearly heard and listened to. We saw the force of this.

We think that it should be rare for any individual or organisation to be represented in a child abuse inquiry, unless that person or body was directly affected by the evidence to be given in the inquiry. To allow a party, interested but unaffected by the evidence, to have a say is to introduce an element into the proceedings that is not warranted. The prime reason is that such representation invites a roving commission; and, although the inquiry can properly control the ambit of any questioning, the need to cover matters that are, for whatever reason, not covered by the other represented parties should properly be left for counsel to the inquiry. Since he or she is in direct communication with the panel members, any issue that the inquiry wants to explore can be investigated perfectly well by the neutral role of such counsel. We were grateful to Mr. Abel for having sometimes put his forensic finger on some highly pertinent issue by a penetrating question. But his introduction in our Inquiry sometimes unhelpfully lengthened the hearings. If there is a role to be played by some individual or organisation in such inquiries – and we readily concede there may be – it calls for a high degree of self-discipline.

Costs

From the outset of our inquiry, we have been acutely conscious of the financial burden placed both upon public funds and on those who were legally represented before us. We entirely sympathise with the Director of Social Services who expressed to us considerable dismay that such a large amount of money was being spent on the Inquiry, at a time when resources for Social Services were being squeezed. We trust that the changes in the management of the child abuse system that we are recommending will bring a lasting benefit to her department and the public whom she and her staff serve. If so, the cost may be justified. We deal with the two items – costs of the inquiry and costs to the parties – separately.

Costs of the inquiry

Once it has been determined that there should be a full independent inquiry, there is no escape from the fact that there will be an expenditure of substantial sums of money. There is the major cost of paying for the members of the panel. The Chairman is likely to be a Queen's Counsel who will be taken away from his daily practice for a lengthy period and will expect to be paid a fee commensurate with what he would be earning at the Bar. The other members are likely to be either retired, and will need to be suitably remunerated, or will be in full time employment, in which case the employers will expect to be wholly or partially reimbursed for their employees' salaries. Additionally, there will be appropriate fees for counsel to the inquiry. Over and above these disbursements, there will be the costs of servicing the panel of inquiry, witnesses' expenses, the cost of a daily transcript and the costs of preparing and publishing the report. We have been informed by the local authority that the total cost of all these items will be approximately £250,000, to be shared by it and Brent Health Authority.

It is our view that such a large bill of costs can be justified only if the inquiry deals with issues of general public importance and will, by its recommendations and educative function, make a major contribution to the development of the management of the child abuse system, nationally as well as locally. We have taken special note of Professor Olive Stevenson's reflections in 1979 as a member of the Committee of Inquiry into the death of Maria Colwell. She observed: "We must at least acknowledge that the launching of an inquiry is like casting a huge stone in a pond. The ripples spread outward, often involving many who did not expect it and, more important, in ways they did not anticipate. The emotional cost is very, very high and can only be justified if the inquiries appear to play a constructive part in protecting the lives of other children." Given that the costs of child abuse inquiries have been literally as well as figuratively very high, we trust that it will only be the cynical who would deny that substantial progress has been made in at least articulating the procedures for the management of the child abuse system. We think that earlier inquiries have led to a consensus about the nature and size of the problem and what needs to be done about it. We would like to think that our Inquiry – the latest in a long line since Maria Colwell – has added a new dimension to society's attitude towards the problem of managing the "high risk" cases of child abuse. We leave it to others to record their verdict on the Inquiry into the death of Jasmine Beckford.

Since the assumed benefit of such an inquiry as ours goes far beyond the boundaries of Brent, it is not unreasonable to expect the financing of the Inquiry not to be wholly borne by the local authority and health authority. Had Brent Borough Council declined to set up an independent inquiry, either for reasons of cost or for some other reason, we understand that the Secretary of State would have stepped in and exercised his statutory power to order an inquiry, with the consequence that the financial burden would have been borne by central government. We do not think it sensible to discourage local authorities from accepting the primary responsibility for child abuse inquiries and so shuffling off that responsibility onto central government. We have recommended in the Preface that exceptionally child abuse inquiries like ours should be set up by the Secretary of State. If the Minister declines to use his statutory powers, then alternative machinery is required. It is our view that some financial support to local authorities for the administration of child abuse inquiries should be arranged for the future. While there is some merit in financing Area Review Committees, they are not answerable to any electorate but only advisory to the two main agencies, the local authorities (through social service departments) and health authorities. The Department of Health and Social Security should consider the machinery of financing child abuse inquiries in the course of its current consultative process.

Cost to the Parties
Persons who are likely to be affected by an inquiry, and organisations which have a direct interest in the subject matter under inquiry, will often desire to be legally represented. If they have to bear the costs of that representation themselves, the conferment of the privilege of legal representation − it cannot be a right − may be an empty gesture. In our Inquiry, all but four of the twenty-two individuals granted legal representation were backed by a trade union or a professional association. The social workers had the full backing of either the National and Local Government Officers Association or the British Association of Social Workers, which itself was separately represented. The Health Visitors' Association, the Royal College of Nursing and the Medical Defence Union lent their support, in some form or other, to the medical and health service personnel who appeared before us. Only the foster parents, Mr. and Mrs. Probert and the court officers, Mr. Thompson and Mr. Hobbs, were unable to find any organisation to finance their legal representation. Brent Borough Council readily acceded to our request at the outset of our Inquiry to pay the reasonable legal costs of the foster parents. Only Mr. Thompson and Mr. Hobbs have been left to foot their own solicitors' costs. (We deal with that one exception in Chapter 18).

We were told by Mr. Bond that the National and Local Government Officers' Association's legal disbursements for the union's five members (Mr. Simpson, Mr. Bishop, Mrs. Dietmann, Miss Rogers and Ms. Wahlstrom) amounted to £50,000. The British Association of Social Workers expended £35,000 on direct legal costs of the representation for itself and its two members (Miss Howarth and Mrs. Ruddock). The legal costs of other parties who were legally aided by professional organisations have probably been a good deal less, but would still represent a considerable item in their accounts. We think it is hard on organisations that their strained resources should be depleted by the outlay of legal disbursements. **We recommend that earnest consideration be given by both central and local government to the question of whether the parties to a child abuse inquiry should not be funded out of public funds.** We note that in the inquiry by Lord Scarman into the Brixton Disorders, 10 to 12 April 1981* Lord Scarman informed the parties concerned at the preliminary hearing that, on the invitation of the Home Secretary, he intended to recommend that the reasonable costs, taxed on the common fund basis, of any party granted leave to be represented be met from the Police Fund, except where he considered that the person representing the party had wasted the time of the inquiry. He would expect and hope to be able to give a warning if and when he considered that point was about to be reached, and would not make any adverse recommendation as to costs without giving the party concerned an opportunity to make representations to

* Cmnd. 8427, page 141, paras 15-17

him. The power of the Home Secretary to meet those costs was contained in section 35(2), Police Act 1964. **We recommend that a similar statutory power should be given to the Secretary of State and to local authorities to direct that the whole or part of the costs incurred by any party to a local inquiry should be defrayed out of some specified fund.**

Remarks of the Common Serjeant
After he had passed sentence on Morris Beckford and Beverley Lorrington, the Common Serjeant of London, Judge Pigot QC, called into the witness box the then Assistant Director of Social Services in Brent Borough Council, Mr. Dennis Simpson, and personally examined him on oath. (Why he was sworn, we are at a loss to understand). Having noted that the local authority had instituted an inquiry, and proposing therefore to limit his remarks so as not to prejudice the deliberations of that inquiry, Judge Pigot nevertheless proceeded to relate the salient facts, as he saw them, from September 1983 leading up to the visit by Ms. Wahlstrom to the Beckford household on 12 March 1984: "When she [Jasmine] was seen then, there was nothing to arouse anxiety", a fact with which we profoundly disagree. Mr. Simpson was asked whether there was "any mechanism now to ensure that when a child is not produced by those in whose custody it is, it can be produced for your authority?", to which Mr. Simpson said that two steps had been taken – a) to review the local authority's child abuse procedures; and b) to amend those procedures to ensure that the social worker will physically see the child. Judge Pigot then went on to say that he hoped that in future there would be more scepticism about excuses for not producing the child, because it appeared that the social worker "was fobbed off time and time again by excuses which would not then have deceived a child." He asked no questions about the work of the health visitor. Judge Pigot further questioned Mr. Simpson about the link of social services with the educational authorities and asked what went wrong, to which Mr. Simpson said that he thought that was "a matter for the external inquiry to assess". Judge Pigot then called Mr. Risley, an officer in Brent Education Department. After questioning him (on affirmation), the Common Serjeant expressed the view that "it is quite clear that no blame whatsoever can be attached to the school authorities", a conclusion again with which we disagree. (We include in Appendix D:2 a transcript of the exchanges between Judge Pigot and the two officers of Brent Borough Council).

Mr. Simpson was disturbed and distressed by what seemed to him to be an inappropriate experience of himself and his departmental colleagues being put on trial without the benefit of a full examination of all the complexities of three years' social work involvement with the Beckford family and without the benefit of legal representation. The Director of Social Services echoed Mr. Simpson's perturbation and stated (or rather, understated) that she found the exercise in court "extraordinarily difficult to understand." Quite clearly, the personnel of the Social Services Department found the public display of judicial criticism, with little or no opportunity of defending themselves, very distasteful. We have been much troubled by the Common Serjeant's extra-judicial utterances about the subject matter of an imminent, independent inquiry. Throughout our extended hearings we have been conscious that witnesses came before us voluntarily, and might at any time have declined to assist the Inquiry. We were fearful that the excessively hostile press accorded at the outset of our Inquiry to the social services personnel of Brent, which quoted repeatedly from the words of Judge Pigot – in particular, the remark made in the course of sentencing Beverley Lorrington, that Miss Wahlstrom had shown "a naivete almost beyond belief" – might induce in potential witnesses to the Inquiry such a sense of public persecution that they would not be willing to be subjected to written or oral examination, whether in public or in private. Such has been the experience of previous child abuse inquiries, even when held in private: ours being in public, we were all the more anxious about our ability to conduct a thorough enquiry.

We would hope that what we have said here will lead any judge in similar circumstances simply to note the setting up of an inquiry as a satisfactory response to a socially disturbing event, and to say that he hopes that everyone who is asked to assist the inquiry will readily do so.

On 4 July 1985, in answer to a parliamentary question, the Parliamentary Secretary for Health, Mr. John Patten MP, stated that local authorities should inform the public of the outcome of any child abuse review and "subsequently, authorities will be able to describe to the court, if necessary, the action taken both in terms of inquiry and of changes to procedures and services." We think that, in conformity with that suggested practice, the Common Serjeant was entitled to be told, either privately or in the face of the court, that an inquiry had been instituted and that procedures had been reviewed. That should have sufficed.

CHAPTER 4

Dramatis Personae

For the purpose of understanding our exposition of the events under inquiry, together with our interpretation and critique of the various services (and their personnel) and of the private individuals involved in the case, the reader of this report needs to know something of the personal background, training and experience of the main actors participating in the events. Rather than interpose, in the course of this lengthy and unavoidably discursive account of those events, the personal details of the individuals as and when they first come into the story, we concluded that it would make for easier reading and better appreciation of what we have to say if at the outset we included vignettes of 58 of our witnesses (including Morris Beckford, from whom we received two written statements). These character sketches do not include our expert witnesses, for the obvious reason that their evidence was extrinsic to the events: Their qualifications appear in Appendix B:2. We have also not included in the list of characters those who played only a walk-on part and whose minor role would, therefore, not be likely to arouse any breath of criticism, or indeed commendation. The disparity in the style and length of the vignettes reflects no more than the particular relevance of the individual's known personal details to the part he or she played in the happenings that we are directed by our terms of reference to investigate. For the individuals in the various social agencies the emphasis is on their qualifications, training and experience related to the highlights of their involvement in the process of child protection; for those who are the objects of social agency activity the sketches are personalised, and partake of thumbnail portraits rather than of professional vignettes.

The Beckford/Lorrington family

Jasmine Beckford: born 2 December 1979 at Hammersmith Hospital under the name of Jasmine Lorrington, the daughter of Beverley Lorrington. Shortly after her birth her records were changed to Jasmine Beckford, since Morris Beckford who was then cohabiting with Beverley Lorrington acknowledged the child, and registered himself as the father, although he knew that he was not. Admitted to St. Charles Hospital on 4 August 1981 with broken femur. Made subject of a Place of Safety Order on 5 August 1981; interim Care Order in favour of Brent Borough Council on 17 August 1981; full Order on 9 September 1981. Contemporaneously placed on the Non-Accidental Injury Register until removed in November 1982. Discharged from hospital on 14 September 1981 to foster parents. Home on trial, April 1982. Attended irregularly at Mortimer Road Day Nursery, run by Brent Social Services from April 1982 until November 1982. Removed from nursery register in January 1983. Attended at Princess Frederica Primary School (Nursery) (run by Brent Education Authority) in January 1983 spasmodically until June 1983 and again in September 1983. Last attended school on 9 September 1983. Died, aged 4½, on 5 July 1984.

Louise Beckford: born 27 May 1981 to Morris Beckford and Beverley Lorrington. Admitted to St. Charles Hospital on 1 August 1981 with broken arm and eye haemorrhages; considered by doctors as a case of non-accidental injury. Made subject of Place of Safety Order on 5 August; interim Care Order on 17 August; full order 9 September 1981. Removed from NAI register in November 1982. Discharged from hospital on 26 August 1981 to foster parents. Joined there by Jasmine on 14 September 1981. Home on trial, April 1982. On 5 July 1984 stayed with maternal grandparents; the following day removed by Social Services Department of Brent to foster parents. On 18 December 1984 application for access to parents refused.

Chantelle Beckford: born 8 December 1983 to Morris Beckford and Beverley Lorrington. On 5 July 1984 stayed with maternal grandparents; following day removed to foster parents. Made subject of Place of Safety Order. Interim Care Order made on 1 August 1984. Care Order made on 24 October 1984. Application for access to parents refused on 18 December 1984.

Morris Beckford: born June 1959 in Jamaica, where he spent the first 9 years of his life. He was the third child of a family of eight. His mother and father came to England, leaving him and two sisters in the care of his maternal grandmother. When he and his two sisters came to this country in 1968 and were reunited with their parents, there were other siblings in the family. In May 1972 he and his sister were accused of stealing from their own home. This led to Morris being severely beaten by both parents and to intervention by both NSPCC and the police. The parents were prosecuted on charges of ill-treatment and neglect of Morris and one of his sisters. The ill-treatment and neglect included the two children having to sleep in an outhouse without a bed and sharing only one blanket between them. Morris and his sister were taken into care of Brent Borough Council. Morris and Beverley Lorrington were both pupils at the same time at Woodfield Special School in Kingsbury, a school run by Brent Education Authority. Although he was classified as educationally subnormal, his subnormality was educational and not intellectual. His later work record at a scaffolding and access equipment company near his home was exemplary. He worked there for ten years from the time he left school, being described as "an excellent employee, very hard-working, very reliable." He worked long hours and had in addition to his labouring work a responsible job as key-holder at the company's premises which he unlocked every morning. He was boisterously jolly and very well-liked by his fellow workmen; he caused no problem at all to his employers. At the time of Jasmine's death he was earning £12,000 a year.

In 1979 when Beverley was pregnant with Jasmine he began cohabiting with her, and at the time of Jasmine's birth acknowledged her as his daughter. In November 1981 he was convicted of assaulting Louise (his own child) occasioning her actual bodily harm, for which he received, in November 1981, a sentence of 3 months' imprisonment suspended for two years and a fine of £250, with legal costs of £100, to be paid by weekly instalments of £15 a week. He paid £50 at court that day. The suspension lapsed just before the birth of Chantelle (also his own child) in December 1983.

On 28 March 1985 he was convicted of the manslaughter of Jasmine and was sentenced to 10 years' imprisonment. (Full details of the charges and verdicts are contained in Appendix D:1)

Beverley Lorrington: born on 2 November 1959 in England of Jamaican parents. Her mother deserted the family when Beverley was only six months old. She claimed that she was the scapegoat of the family and was beaten by both her stepmother and her own father. Resulting from this treatment, she ran away from home when she was 17; she had very little contact with the extended family who lived in Perivale, Middlesex.

She met Morris Beckford at Woodfield Special School, Kingsbury, a school run by Brent Education Authority. She was described by an educational psychologist as having a "significant degree of intellectual handicap". She presented a pathetic figure being emotionally flat in her responses to those who saw her both during and after her trial. Descriptions of her by witnesses to this inquiry were not substantially different, although the evidence indicated that at times she appeared to cope with the problems of two children under the age of 4. She was much less able to cope once she became pregnant in the Spring of 1983. She had previously cohabited with a man who, she said, was violent to her. She began to live with Morris Beckford in the autumn of 1979 when she was several months pregnant with Jasmine. She told the health visitor, Miss Hindle, in December 1979 that Morris was not the father of Jasmine, but, apart from her stepsister, Carol, she told no-one that Morris was not the father, until she took the deceased Jasmine in her arms to St. Mary's hospital on 5 July 1984. At Jasmine's birth, the midwife recorded that Beverley had had two previous abortions.

Carol Lorrington: stepsister of Beverley Lorrington, with one child born in September 1979. Is an office manager with a computer firm. Was a regular week-end visitor to the Beckford household before Jasmine and Louise were taken to hospital in August 1981. Knew from the time of Beverley's pregnancy in 1979 that Morris Beckford was not Jasmine's father. After the children returned home from foster parents in April 1982 she visited the family once or twice a month. Recalled marital differences between Morris and Beverley in November 1982, and suggested that Beverley and children come to live at maternal grandparents' home, where she lived. Last time she saw children was at the time of Chantelle's birth in December 1983. Thereafter (on 2 or 3 occasions) when visiting, Beverley (usually) and children (always) were not at home. Kept in touch with Beverley by telephone during 1984. Took telephone call at maternal grandparents' home from Ms. Wahlstrom on afternoon of 5 July 1984 asking for Beverley.

Social Services personnel of Brent Borough Council

Mr. Harry Whalley: Director of Social Services of Brent Borough Council from 1971, and Chairman of Brent Area Review Committee from its inception in 1974 until retirement on 18 June 1982. After war service, admitted as an associate (1949) and fellow (1966) of the Institute of Chartered Secretaries; obtained Diploma in Sociology (University of London) in 1959. 1946-1948 general administrator with Lancashire County Council. 1948-1950 chief administrative officer of Children's Department of Gloucestershire County Council. 1950-1965 staffing officer and then chief administrative officer (1955) (and occasionally deputising for Children's Officer) of Middlesex County Council. From 1964 Children's Officer in charge of Children's Department of London Borough of Brent until reorganisation of social services, and becoming first Director of Social Services. Department's budget for 1981-1982 was £23 million, with staff of 1800.

Apart from one instance, he had no direct personal knowledge of the Department's responsibility for Jasmine and Louise Beckford. He personally authorised the expenditure of monies on equipment for Jasmine at the home of the foster parents. He was told in a memorandum of 10 September 1981 from Mr. Jeremy Burns, head of the Adoption and Foster Care section, that "subject to any development in the future it is hoped that the first placement of these children will be *a permanent placement for the rest of their childhood.*" (This was explained a fortnight later in a memorandum from Mr. Burns to Mrs. Diane Dietmann as intended only to be read in conjunction with original request from Area 6, and did not pre-empt any decision made for rehabilitation, following the care proceedings).

Specifically he was not sent the minutes of the Case Conferences of 6 and 20 August 1981; he was not made aware of the Willesden Justices' rider to the Care Orders of 9 September 1981; nor was he aware of the refusal of the social services department to allow Miss Joan Court access to departmental files, in accordance with his general directive relating to independent social workers. He had no knowledge of differences between Area 6 and the Adoption and Foster Care Section. And he was not told of the letter handed by Mrs. Probert to Mr. Jeremy Burns on April 10 1982.

Miss Valerie Howarth: Director of Social Services, Brent Borough Council, and Chairman of Brent Area Review Committee, from June 1982 up to the present time. Obtained Diploma in Social Studies (1962) and certificate in Applied Social Studies (1963) from the University of Leicester, and Certificate in Child Care (1968) from North London Polytechnic. From 1963 to 1968 employed as a social worker with Family Welfare Association in Leicester. (During professional qualification, trained in Family Service Unit part-time and partly in practical work in Child Guidance). From 1968 to 1971 employed as a Senior Social Worker/Assistant Training Officer in the Children's Department of Lambeth Borough Council. On reorganisation of social services, became successively Area Officer, Social Work Coordinator, and Assistant Director of Lambeth Social Services Department, until her appointment as Director in Brent in June 1982. (Had been Chairman of Lambeth Area Review Committee). In April 1985 she withdrew her candidature for the Directorship of Social Services for Cambridgeshire County Council in the light of the impending independent inquiry into the circumstances surrounding the death of Jasmine Beckford, which would involve her department at Brent.

The Department has a budget of £27 million revenue and £2.5 million capital. It has 144 cases of children on the "at risk" register and 358 children in care. The Department has a staff of about 2000. It has 13 establishments for the elderly, 17 for the disabled, ten for children and 15 day nurseries.

She had not been consulted or informed about the Beckford family until she was told on 6 July 1984 of the death of Jasmine. That morning she met with the Assistant Director, Mr. Dennis Simpson, Area Manager, Mr. David Bishop, the senior social worker, Mrs. Diane Dietmann, the key social worker, Ms. Gun Wahlstrom, and the Court Officer, Mr. William Thompson. A further meeting of those except Ms. Wahlstrom (who had gone on holiday) was held on 10 July when a synopsis of events was presented to the meeting. On 6 July Miss Howarth informed the Chief Executive, Mr. Michael Bichard, and about the same time the Chairman of the Social Services Committee (Councillor Stone) but not the shadow chair (Councillor Sealy). She was on leave from 16-30 July inclusive. A further meeting took place on 31 July, without Mr. Simpson who was on leave. On his return from leave, Miss Howarth on 9 August instructed him to prepare the department's report for presentation to the Cases Sub-Committee meeting on 29 October at which Miss Howarth was unable to be present. The Cases Subcommittee required a fuller and more detailed report for a meeting fixed for 26 November. Miss Howarth held a meeting of staff in mid-November to prepare for that meeting, and attended the meeting personally on 26 November.

Mr. Dennis Simpson: Director of Social Services, London Borough of Southwark, April 1985. Assistant-Director (Field Services Division) London Borough of Brent from November 1981 to April 1985. Obtained in 1970 Certificate of Qualification in Social Work at Leicester University and MA in Social Services Planning from Essex University. Employed from 1970-1974 by London Borough of Lambeth as a social worker (subsequently team leader). From 1975-1978 Principal Planning Officer, London Borough of Lambeth. 1978-1981 Assistant-Director of Social Services, London Borough of Newham.

Apart from one instance he had no knowledge or involvement with the case of Jasmine Beckford until he heard on 6 July 1984 of her death. On 15 April 1982 he received a memorandum from Mr. David Bishop, Manager of Area 6, seeking authority for certain payments to Jasmine's parents and was told of arrangements for Jasmine and Louise to be transferred from the foster parents to the Beckford household via Green Lodge, with a view to the children "going home on trial in the near future". Mr. Simpson wrote on the memorandum: "Why can't it take place from the foster home?"

Unconnected with the Beckford case, he initiated in 1982 a review of the department's child abuse procedures, which led to amendments of the Policy Memorandum of 1977. In the absence of the Director of Social Services he arranged in August 1984 the preparation of the report for, and attended at the subsequent meeting of, the Cases Sub-Committee on 29 October 1984. He was present at the meeting of the Cases Sub-Committee on 26 November 1984. He attended before the Common Serjeant, Judge Pigot QC, on March 28 1985 to answer questions about the work of Brent Social Services with the Beckford family.

Mr. David Brian Bishop: Area Manager, Area 6, Brent Social Services, 1976 to present day. Qualified as a registered mental nurse, in 1961, and obtained the Certificate of Qualification in Social Work in 1968. A regular soldier serving in the Royal Army Medical Corps as a student mental nurse, 1957-1960. From 1960-1963 employed by the Bristol group of mental hospitals as a staff mental nurse and, later, charge nurse. Mental Welfare Officer, Essex County Council, 1963-1965; Senior Mental Welfare Officer (1965-1970) and Senior Social Worker (1970-1973) London Borough of Barking; Deputy Area Manager, London Borough of Newham (1973-1976).

Chairman of Case Conferences of 6 and 20 August 1981 on non-accidental injuries to Jasmine and Louise Beckford. On 27 August 1981 approved Mr. and Mrs. Probert temporarily as foster parents. On 16 September 1981 received memorandum from Mr. Thompson, Principal Court Officer of Social Services Department, informing him of the magistrates' decision of 9 September 1981 to make Care Orders, together with their rider expressing hope that social services will carry out a rehabilitation programme to unite children with their parents. Thereafter, intermittently involved with social worker (Ms. Wahlstrom) and her superior (Mrs. Dietmann) in Area 6 about placement of Beckford children. Signed statutory form pursuant to review on 9 December 1981. Chairman of Case Conference of 5 April 1982, approving plan to return children to parents and to supply intensive casework with family. Did not attend case review of 30 September 1982, or Case Conference of 9 November 1982, at which it was agreed to remove Jasmine and Louise from the non-accidental injury register. Not present at case review of 18 April 1983 at which it was decided to apply for revocation of Care Orders. Not present at case review of 6 December 1983.

Learned on evening of 5 July 1984 of Jasmine's death. Reported next day to Director of Social Services and heard for the first time that Morris Beckford was not Jasmine's father. Arranged for fostering of Louise and Chantelle. Helped to prepare report for Cases Sub-Committee and attended its meeting of 29 October 1984. At that meeting he is recorded as saying that magistrates had "directed us to make every effort to rehabilitate children with their parents... We are obliged to try to do that, though it seemed unrealistic."

Mrs. Diane Dietmann: Senior Social Worker, Team Leader, Area 6, Brent Social Services, 1978 to present day. Born in New Jersey and brought up in Chicago, Illinois. Wife of John Dietmann, also an American, also employed by Brent Social Services. Obtained a degree of B.A. in Sociology and Psychology, Western Reserve University, Cleveland, Ohio (1969); M.A. in Social Work, University of Chicago (1971). Latter curriculum contained no course on child abuse (No practical experience of child abuse while working in the United States). Came to England in 1972 and worked for London Borough of Brent for a year as a generic social worker in Area 2. (Experienced one case of sexual abuse of a child and a few cases of child neglect,but no case of child ill-treatment). Returned to the United States, 1972-1976 and worked with old people at Senior Centre of Metropolitan Chicago. Employed, 1976-1978, by Warwickshire County Council as a Senior Social Worker; encountered child abuse cases but, after initial assessment, cases were allocated to a long term team. Attended a number of courses from 1981 onwards on social work management, old age, housing problems and mental health, but none on child abuse.

Became supervisor of Ms. Wahlstrom on the Beckford case shortly before first case conference on 6 August and attended both that case conference and that of 20 August 1981. Did not attend magistrates' court on 9 September 1981, but thereafter attended all case conferences and case reviews except for the one of 9 December 1981, and took the chair at meetings of 30 September and 9 November 1982 (agreeing to take the children off the non-accidental injury register); 18 April 1983 (at which it was decided to apply for revocation of the Care Orders); and case review of 6 December 1983. Supervised every stage of placement of Jasmine from August 1981 until her death on 5 July 1984, with the exceptions of periods of leave, notably from 27 April to 19 November 1983 when she was herself on maternity leave.

As supervisor, discussed all cases on social workers' case load every two or three months for half a day and particular cases as and when they were to be dealt with at case conferences or case reviews.

On 13 April 1982 went with a locum family aide to the foster parents' home and assisted in the removal of Jasmine and Louise to Green Lodge. Had previously met the foster parents on only one occasion. Thereafter relied on Ms. Wahlstrom to inform of developments with the Beckford family. Accompanied Ms. Wahlstrom on 5 July 1984 to Beckford house for purpose of arranging for forthcoming review preparatory to a renewed application to magistrates' court for revocation of Care Orders. Frantic search for Morris Beckford and Beverley Lorrington at home, at Morris' workplace and at the maternal grandparents' home at Greenford, Middlesex. Without managing to trace the parents, arranged to go to Greenford the next day, but told of Jasmine's death when arriving at office on 6 July.

Ms. Gun Ann-Marie Wahlstrom: Born and educated in Sweden. Obtained a degree in Pedagogics, Sociology and English from the University of Stockholm (1974) and a Certificate of Qualification in Social Work at the North London Polytechnic (1979), of which first year had a "children at risk programme", a small proportion on child abuse. Employed by Brent Borough Council since 1974, except for secondment for training, 1977-1979. Worked for eighteen months in an hostel for boys and girls aged 14-17, and from 1975-1977 in a children's home for age group 5-12. No further training in child abuse, except for a two-day multi-disciplinary course in Brent at the end of 1983. Took up post as social worker in Area 6 in February 1980.

The case of Jasmine Beckford was her first child abuse case as field social worker. As a generic social worker in Area 6, caseload varied from 20 to 32 cases at any one time, including 8 to 11 child care cases, but no more than two families with a child or children in care, and only one case at any time of a child on the non-accidental injury register. The rest of the caseload was made up of elderly and handicapped adults. Additionally she ran a playscheme and support group for parents of handicapped children. Other duties included being on a duty rota as mental welfare officer. For three months, May-July 1983, when Mrs. Dietmann was on maternity leave and there was no locum for the latter, she acted as a Senior Social Worker supervising field social workers.

The Beckford case was allocated to her by the Case Conference on 6 August 1981. As the key social worker operating the Care Orders on Jasmine and Louise Beckford she had the prime responsibility for the protection of the two children throughout the three years of the Orders. Her files on the Beckford family contained a Social Worker's Report which ran to nearly 100 pages of meticulous notes detailing 78 official visits to the family, 37 of them in the period from 19 April 1982 (when the children returned to the Beckford household) until 12 November 1982 (when the children were removed from the non-accidental injury register). There were 18 visits from November 1982 until 22 June 1983 (when the application for the revocation of the Care Orders was unsuccessfully made). There were 5 visits from June 1983 to 9 September 1983 (the last day that Jasmine attended school) and thereafter until 5 July 1984, there were 18 visits. (Not all those visits resulted in Ms. Wahlstrom seeing Jasmine). On 13 of those last visits Ms. Wahlstrom received no reply at the house. On five occasions she did gain entry to the house. In addition, Ms. Wahlstrom had recorded in her personal diary a number of intended and actual visits to the Beckfords, including one around Christmas time when she heard Jasmine and her two sisters playing upstairs.

46

The last time she saw Jasmine was on 12 March 1984. Subsequent to that last sighting of the child, Ms. Wahlstrom made six unsuccessful visits. In the period May-July 1984, she wrote five letters attempting to make an appointment, almost exclusively for the purpose of arranging the review preparatory to renewing the application to the magistrates' court for a revocation of the two Care Orders. On 5 July 1984 she and her supervisor, Mrs. Dietmann, went, for the first time together, to make contact with Morris Beckford and Beverley Lorrington. Her entry for "5.7.84 1 p.m." was: "Home visit to have the Review--- No reply--- left card."

Mrs. Dorothy Ruddock: Family Aide attached to the long-term team in Area 6, July 1981-September 1983, when she was seconded by Brent Borough Council to study for the Certificate of Qualification in Social Work. Born in Jamaica, she came to England in 1960. Before starting a family she was a nurse, and returned to work as a nursing auxiliary after having three children and fostering a mentally handicapped child. Did part-time secretarial and administrative work after the youngest child was born.

She was specifically allocated to work with the Beckford family under Ms. Wahlstrom as a family aide, first at Tree Tops, when parental access was effected, and later at the new house at College Road, Kensal Rise when the children were reunited with their parents. Mrs. Ruddock continued to visit the Beckford home until 15 August 1983, but her visits for the last year, since September 1982, had been voluntary and not as part of the social work input from Area 6.

Mr. William Thompson: Principal Court Officer, Social Services Department, Brent Borough Council since February 1977. Had served for eleven years as a police officer with the Norfolk Constabulary. In 1968 became Probation Officer with Hampshire Probation and After-Care Service, and prior to joining Brent Social Services was the Crown Court Liaison Officer at Knightsbridge Crown Court.

Conducted case for Brent Borough Council in its application for the Care Orders in respect of Jasmine and Louise Beckford before Willesden Magistrates' Court on 9 September 1981, and communicated to the Area Manager on 16 September 1981 the Court's Orders, together with the rider expressing the hope that social services would initiate programme of rehabilitation with a view to reuniting the children with their parents. Appeared before the same Court on 22 June 1983 to seek revocation of the two Care Orders.

Mr. James Hobbs: Assistant Court Officer, Social Services Department, Brent Borough Council, since March 1976. Previously served with the Metropolitan Police, and for the last five years of police service held the rank of Sergeant in the local Juvenile Bureau. Had known both Morris Beckford and Beverley Lorrington during their schooldays. Attended the two Case Conferences of 6 and 20 August 1981. Attended Case Conference of 5 April 1982 at which it was decided to reunite the children with their parents. Did not attend Case Conference of 9 November 1982, when children taken off NAI register, but Mr. Gadsten, another Court Officer from the Court Section attended. Attended Case Review of 18 April 1983 when it was decided to apply to the court for revocation of the Care Orders.

Mr. Robert Jeremy Falcon Burns: Independent Social Worker since April 1985. Appointed in 1981 Principal Social Worker, Adoption and Foster Care Section, London Borough of Brent. Qualified as a probation officer, having obtained the Home Office Certificate in Probation, 1965/1966. Prior to taking up appointment as head of the Adoption and Fostering Section, he had been Assistant Director of the British Association of Social Workers. Appointed in 1985 member of the panel of *guardians ad litem* for Inner London.

Was responsible for the assessment of Mr. and Mrs. Probert as foster parents, and for the placement of Jasmine and Louise with the Proberts in August and September

1981. Considered at that time that this was to be a permanent placement for the rest of the children's childhood. Throughout the period of fostering, September 1981 to April 1982, he was the main link between the Proberts and Area 6. This was his first experience of assessing foster parents.

Miss Carol Ann Rogers: Acting Principal Officer, Adoption and Foster Care Section, London Borough of Brent since 17 April 1985. From 1980 until April 1985, team leader in Adoption and Foster Care Section under Mr. Jeremy Burns. Holder of Certificate of Qualification in Social Work. Before joining Brent Borough Council, employed by the City of Westminster for three years as Intake Social Worker, and four years Team Leader with London Borough of Harrow.

First involvement with the Beckford case was the receipt in early August 1981 from Area 6 of a request for a foster placement. Attended Case Conference of 20 August 1981, when she indicated what might be available by way of fostering, short term or long term. Visited the Proberts on 13 November 1981 to prepare documentation for presentation to Divisional Fostering Group. Noted difficulties of Proberts vis-à-vis parental contact, future reuniting of the children with parents, and communication with staff of Area 6. Had no further contact with the Proberts, except that she met Mrs. Probert at Foster Parents' Social Evenings occasionally from 1983-1985. At a meeting of the Adoption and Fostering Panel on 5 November 1982 an application from the Proberts to be considered for other fostering was considered, but discussion deferred to await comments from Area 6.

Miss Marjorie Proudlock: Day Nursery Officer, Mortimer Road Day Nursery, London Borough of Brent. Joined as Deputy Officer in charge 1970, became Officer in charge, July 1972. Previously, since 1968, Nursery Officer at Kilburn Day Nursery.

Jasmine was given a part-time place at the Day Nursery on 22 April 1982, shortly after being reunited with parents. Nursery informed that Jasmine was in care of the local authority and was on the non-accidental injury register. Attendance erratic at end of 1982, finally leaving on 2 November. Miss Proudlock attended Case Conference of 9 November 1982 (at which decision to remove children from NAI register taken). Told in January 1983 that Jasmine was to be taken off Day Nursery register. No signs of child abuse during Jasmine's attendance at Day Nursery.

Miss Pamela Gordon: Completed a two-year course at Kilburn Polytechnic in Home Management and Family Care. Worked in a residential unit for disturbed adolescents. Took up employment with Brent Borough Council as a residential worker at Green Lodge in May 1981. Left October 1984. Represented Green Lodge as the Senior Residential Worker at the Case Conference on 5 April 1982 when it was decided that the Beckford children should be admitted to Green Lodge for a short time on their way home.

Education Department of Brent Borough Council
Miss Gwenneth Margaret Rickus: Retired. Director of Education, London Borough of Brent, October 1971-March 1984. B.A. (University of London); a qualified teacher, with teaching and administrative experience. Responsible for issuance of Green Book in 1977 outlining procedures for heads of schools to take in case of non-accidental injuries to children. This was the direct result of the recommendation of the Maria Colwell inquiry report in 1974 that there should be direct and frequent communications between the social workers and education welfare officers beyond matters of regular school attendance.

Mr. Adrian John Frederick Mark Parsons: Director of Education, London Borough of Brent from April 1984. University graduate and holder of diploma in public administration. Started in teaching in 1967 for six years. Educational administrator for twelve years. Previous appointment was Deputy Director of Education, Manchester City Council.

Miss Elizabeth Valerie Mead: Assistant Education Officer, London Borough of Brent since 1971. B.A. in English, teacher's certificate, nine years' teaching experience and three years as an educational adviser. Member of the Brent Area Review Committee from inception until recently. (No longer in schools division of the Department of Education). Responsible for ensuring that chief education welfare officer discusses procedures laid down in Green Book of 1977 with heads of schools.

Mrs. Pamela Scafardi: Chief Education Welfare Officer, London Borough of Brent since September 1978. Supervised education welfare officers; in particular reminded them of child abuse cases, and sent memorandum on 3 August 1984, unprompted by Beckford case. Not responsible for detection of child abuse in relation to children under compulsory school age in nursery schools.

Miss Frieda Elsie Florence Cowgill: Retired. Head Teacher, Princess Frederica C. of E. J.M. and I. School from 1972 until April 1983. Had no knowledge of the existence of the Green Book. Not told that Jasmine was under a Care Order and had been removed from NAI register in November 1982, when she first attended school in January 1983. Received a telephone call from Ms. Wahlstrom on 11 January 1983 leaving her name and asking "school to contact Area 6 if there is a problem." Miss Cowgill had made a note on the inside cover of her diary: "Social worker re Jasmine Beckford, Miss Wahlstrom", a fact that never got transferred on to any school record or passed on to nursery staff.

Mr. Sean Francis McErlean: Deputy Head, Princess Frederica C. of E. J.M. and I. School. Acting Head, March-September 1983. Been at school for fifteen years. Had no knowledge that Jasmine Beckford was under a Care Order. Had never seen the Green Book. Never had an occasion to contact the Social Services Department about a child at school.

Mrs. Eris Felix: Nursery teacher at Princess Frederica C. of E. J.M. and I. School. Jasmine's teacher from January 1983-September 1983. Was unaware that Jasmine was under a Care Order or had a social worker. Would have reacted differently had she known of Care Order. Once Jasmine came to school with bruises, successfully explained by mother. Jasmine was "rather quiet really, very, very thin."

Miss Ashley Caroline Player: Nursery Assistant at Princess Frederica C. of E. J.M. and I. School January 1983-1984. Did not know that Jasmine was under a Care Order, or that she had a social worker connected with her. Noted contemporaneously that Jasmine's attendance at school was "very poor".

Mr. John Michael Barry: Education Welfare Officer, London Borough of Brent. University graduate, holder of diploma in education, and teacher for eight years. Knew nothing of Jasmine's social or educational history. On 14 July 1983 was asked by Princess Frederica C. of E. J.M. and I. School to inquire of Beckford parents whether Jasmine would be returning to school in September. Visited Beverley Lorrington and learnt that Jasmine had not been well, but would be taking her place at infant school in September, 1984.

Officers of Brent Borough Council other than social services or educational personnel
Mr. Michael George Bichard: Chief Executive Officer, London Borough of Brent. Obtained LL.B. and M.Soc.Sc. Received news of Jasmine's death from Director of Social Services on 6 July 1984, before which no involvement with Beckford case. Informed Leaders of Conservative and Labour groups on the council at briefing meetings with each. Relayed message from Director of Social Services that information at that time "would not have been such as to have raised undue concern in their mind." Did not state that social services department work with the Beckfords had been "exemplary". During the independent inquiry he investigated a complaint from the Leader of the Labour

group regarding the placing of an advertisement seeking a home for Louise and Chantelle Beckford. (Mr. Bichard's report, which we endorse, is contained in Appendix J).

Mr. Stephen Robert Forster: Director of Law and Administration, London Borough of Brent since 1981. Solicitor of the Supreme Court. Chief Solicitor to Brent Borough Council, 1973-1981. Department not involved at any stage of obtaining Care Orders, or executing them. First involvement with Beckford case came with the meeting of the Cases Sub-Committee on 29 October 1984. Attended Old Bailey at the conclusion of the trial of Morris Beckford and Beverley Lorrington, when the Assistant Director of Social Services was questioned by the Common Serjeant, Judge Pigot QC.

Mr. Martin Damms: Principal Assistant Solicitor, Walsall Borough Council from January 1985. Previously Senior Solicitor, London Borough of Brent. Represented Director of Law and Administration at the Cases Sub-Committee meetings on 29 October and 26 November 1984.

Members of Brent Borough Council

Mr. Martin Andrew Coleman: Lecturer in law, Brunel University, Councillor, Leader of the Labour group on Brent Council. Informed orally of Jasmine's death by Chief Executive shortly after 6 July 1984. No involvement with case until Cases Sub-Committee met in October/November 1984. Considered that the Chief Executive should have given information in writing. A protagonist for an independent inquiry in public.

Mr. George Edward Crane: Production manager, 14 years a Labour Councillor, member of the Cases Sub-Committee since its formation in 1982. Heard of the death of Jasmine only when he received the documents for the Sub-Committee's meeting on 29 October 1984. Showed dissatisfaction at the paucity of information given by officers. Never doubted that officers of Social Services department expected full inquiry. Strongly supported internal, and subsequently, independent inquiry; thought initially that inquiry under auspices of Area Review Committee was a good compromise.

Miss Mary Patricia Cribbin: Assistant Accountant, Labour Councillor since May 1982. Member of the Cases Sub-Committee since it was set up in 1982. Attended the Cases Sub-Committee meeting on 29 October 1984. Heard of Jasmine's death at the time from a colleague at work but did not know that Jasmine had been in care of Brent Borough Council until told officially by Councillor Coleman, just before the October meeting of the Cases Sub-Committee, in her capacity as shadow-chair of the Under-Fives Committee. Supported an inquiry, but thought it would reveal no criticism of social services department. Did not attend later Sub-Committee meeting on 26 November. Consented to Councillor Sealy substituting for her. Attended meeting of Social Services Committee on 8 January 1985. Favoured independent inquiry, with preference for it to be held under auspices of Area Review Committee.

Mr. Mark Haftel: Company Director, Justice of the Peace, Conservative Councillor since May 1982. Promoter of the setting up of a Cases Sub-Committee in 1982, and member thereafter. Initiator of demand at Cases Sub-Committee meeting of 29 October 1984 for more and better information from social services department. Backed Councillor Sealy's proposals at meeting of 26 November for an immediate internal inquiry. Attended Social Services Committee meeting on 8 January 1985 and reluctantly accepted reference to the Area Review Committee. Surprised but pleased to learn subsequently of independent inquiry.

Mrs. Frances Rees-Hughes: Retired civil servant. Conservative Councillor since May 1982. Chairman of the Cases Sub-Committee. Was told about the death of Jasmine soon after 6 July 1984 by Councillor Stone, chairman of the Social Services Committee. Was satisfied at the meeting of 29 October with the information supplied, but required further information. At meeting of 26 November appeared not to favour inquiry, but on tied vote cast vote in favour of an internal inquiry. Present at Social Services Committee meeting of 8 January 1985 where decision reversed.

Mr. Philemon Alexis Caroline Sealy: State Registered Nurse (1959) Registered Mental Nurse (1961); Diploma in Social Administration from London School of Economics (1966). Past chairman of the national branch of ASTMS. Principal Race Relations Adviser, London Borough of Lambeth. Justice of the Peace since 1977. Labour Councillor on Brent Borough Council since May 1978. Member of the Social Services Committee 1984/5. Spokesman of Labour group on Social Services affairs. Was unaware of death of Jasmine Beckford until the recommendation of the Cases Sub-Committee came before the Social Services Committee on 31 October 1984. Attended Cases Sub-Committee meeting of 26 November, Vice Councillor Cribbin. Was a forceful proponent of an internal inquiry which would include considering disciplinary action against social services staff found to be at fault. Moved resolution for an internal inquiry, accepting deletion of references to disciplinary action. On holiday when the Social Services Committee met on 8 January 1985 and reversed Case Sub-Committee recommendation for internal inquiry. Spoke volubly at preliminary hearing of Panel of Inquiry on 15 April 1985 in favour of independent inquiry being held in public.

Mr. Roger Douglas Stone: Retired. Ended career as management accountant with Brent Health Authority. Conservative Councillor since April 1964. Chairman of Social Services Committee in 1984/5. Present Mayor of Brent Borough Council. Informed by Director of Social Services on or about 6 July 1984 of the "death of a child in care, that the parents had been charged with murder and that a full report would be going to the Cases Sub-Committee." Assumed from conversation with Councillor Rees-Hughes that she knew about Jasmine's death and would be convening a meeting of the Cases Sub-Committee. Chaired Social Services Committee meeting on 8 January 1985 when recommendation by Cases Sub-Committee for internal inquiry was set aside in favour of reference to Area Review Committee.

Brent Health Authority
Miss Adeline Rosemary Martin: Director of Nursing Services, Primary Health Care Unit, Brent Health Authority since September 1983. M.A. in Public Health (Dundee), Diploma in Advanced Nursing Studies, Registered Nurse, Registered Fever Nurse, qualified in Midwifery, holds certificate for Health Visitors. Member of Brent Area Review Committee since October 1983. No direct involvement in Beckford case.

Mrs. Joyce Margaret Brown: Senior Nurse, Health Visiting (formerly post of Nursing Officer) with special responsibility for child abuse cases, Brent Health Authority, since May 1983. Qualified as a Registered Nurse and Health Visitor. Employed initially in 1971 by London Borough of Brent and subsequently Brent Health Authority. Until 1980 had been responsible for Mortimer Road Clinic. Supervisor to Miss Leong from May 1983.

Miss Mary Jane Tyler: Senior Nurse, Health Visiting, Brent Health Authority. Qualified as a Registered Nurse, a State Certified Midwife and Health Visitor. Employed by the London Borough of Brent since 1973 and subsequently by Brent Health Authority. Until late 1983 Nurse Manager for the Mortimer Road Clinic. Was Miss Leong's supervisor from February 1980 to December 1983.

Miss Savitrie Baichoo: Health Visitor for the elderly, Bloomsbury Health Authority. Senior Nurse, Health Visiting, Brent Health Authority, between December 1983 and December 1984 (in succession to Miss Tyler) with special responsibility for ethnic minorities and health education. Between 1975 and 1983 Health Visitor, City and Hackney Health Authority. Qualified as a Registered Nurse, Registered Midwife, Family Planning Nurse. Diploma in Health Visiting (1975) and a Diploma in Health Education (1983).

Highly critical of methods of supervision in Brent and of documentation kept and filed by health visitors.

Mrs. Nadani Vivekanandan: Health Visitor, Brent Health Authority since 1977. Health Visitor to Louise and Chantelle Beckford after Jasmine's death on 5 July 1984. Qualified as Registered Nurse and Health Visitor. Obtained certificates in Health Education and Family Planning. Critical of supervision of health visitors in Brent: "I do not think there is enough support" for health visitors.

Miss Judith Elizabeth Knowles: Health Visitor, Brent Health Authority, 1979-July 1982. Succeeded Miss Hindle as health visitor for Beckford family in October 1980. Consistently recorded weight of Jasmine. On 24 October 1980 recorded, inaccurately, Jasmine's "weight below 25th percentile", whereas it was below 3rd percentile. On 17 March 1981 weight recorded as 8.21 kgs, which is further below the third percentile. On 8 June 1981 Miss Knowles, on a health visit, described Jasmine as "thin, miserable looking child". Repeated this information at Case Conference of 6 August 1981: "Jasmine was of normal development mentally but that her weight was low." Attended second Case Conference on 20 August and suggested returning children to parents "with support". Invited to Case Conference of 5 April 1982 (when decision to reunite family was made) but did not attend. Restarted visiting after children reunited with parents. On 6 June 1982 Miss Knowles recorded: "Jasmine rather pathetic child ... still looks pinched and [word illegible]." Handed over case to Miss Leong in July 1982, on going abroad. Returned to U.K. in June 1985.

Miss Yeng Lai Leong: Health Visitor, Brent Health Authority, 1979 onwards, operating out of Mortimer Road Clinic. Qualified as Registered Nurse (1974) and Health Visitor (1979). Attended two-day multi-disciplinary course on child abuse (1982). Health Visitor to the Beckford family from July 1982 to July 1984. Invited to Case Conference of 9 November 1982. Ill on day and unable to attend. Subsequently noted that children were removed from non-accidental injury register, and accordingly, on own initiative, removed children from replica register. Visited Beckford family throughout 1983 but did not see Jasmine (who had been attending nursery school) after 22 April 1983. Saw Beverley Lorrington on 20 and 30 December 1983 following birth of Chantelle. Told on latter occasion that Jasmine was staying with grandparents, in breach of Care Order. Visited five times between February and May 1984, but got no reply.

Mrs. Gillian Hindle (née Boyle): Health Visitor, Barnet Health Authority since 1984. Qualified as a State Registered Nurse and passed Part I Midwifery training. Degree in Law and Politics, Brunel University (1983). Health Visitor, Brent District Health Authority from September 1977, completing training in September 1978; member of full-time health visitor staff until 1980. First saw Beverley Lorrington on 13 December 1979, following birth of Jasmine; told on first or second occasion that Morris Beckford was not Jasmine's father. Handed over to Judy Knowles in September 1980 as health visitor to Beckford family.

Legal representatives appearing before the Willesden Justices on 9 September 1981
Mr. Charles McLain Cochand: Barrister. Instructed by Paddington Law Centre to appear on behalf of Beverley Lorrington (Morris Beckford was present at Court) in the care proceedings relating to Jasmine and Louise Beckford. Recalls from notes made contemporaneously that Dr. Levick's report was held admissible by the court under section 26, Children and Young Persons Act 1963 and read out as part of the evidence given by Dr. John Warner. Certain that he "must have seen it and read it at the time of the hearing", although he did not retain a copy of it, shown to him by counsel for the children, Miss Szwed. Recollects that substance of report was to the effect that both children had suffered multiple injuries on separate occasions.

Mr. Simon Keith Pollard: Solicitor of the Supreme Court. Principal in the firm of Alexander & Partners. In August 1981 received a legal aid order from Willesden Magistrates' Court to act on behalf of Jasmine and Louise Beckford in relation to proceedings for interim (17 August) and full Care Orders (9 September). Obtained a report from an independent social worker, Miss Joan Court, dated 8 September 1981; obtained a report from a paediatric radiologist, Dr. Levick, dictated on 4 September over the telephone, and signed report sent on 7 September; and had arranged (never fulfilled) for parents to be seen by child psychiatrist at Great Ormond Street Hospital at the end of September. Briefed counsel to appear for the children, sent articled clerk to attend court, and was present at latter part of proceedings on 9 September 1981. Arranged for copies of Dr. Levick's unsigned report to be available at court. In November 1981 wrote to Brent Social Services querying frequency of access.

Miss Petula Lorraine Smith: Solicitor of the Supreme Court. In September 1981 articled clerk with Alexander & Partners. Made detailed notes of the proceedings before the Willesden justices on 9 September 1981 when instructing counsel on behalf of the Beckford children. She had no recollection of having seen Dr. Levick's report, although her notes confirm that it was referred to in the course of Dr. Warner's evidence.

Miss Elizabeth Maria Szwed: Barrister. Founder and secretary of *Justice for Children* and co-author of a book, *Justice for Children* (1980) and co-editor (with Mr. Hugh Geach) of, and contributor to, a book of essays, *Providing Civil Justice for Children* (1983). Instructed as counsel for the Beckford children at care proceedings before Willesden justices on 9 September 1981. Recollects cross-examining Dr. Warner about Dr. Levick's report and, without recalling having a copy of the report in her hand, "must have done, in order to put the matters to him." Also recollects having handed a copy of the unsigned report to other parties and to the Bench of justices.

Medical practitioners involved in the Beckford case

Dr. John Oliver Warner: MD Sheff. 1979, MB ChB 1968; MRCP (U.K.) 1972; DCH Eng. 1970; (Sheff.); Consultant (Paediatrics) Brompton Hospital London and St. Charles Hospital London: Fellow Royal Society of Medicine; Member British Paediatric Association. Author, papers and chapters on Respiratory Disease and Allergy in Childhood. Consultant Paediatrician at St. Charles Hospital, Paddington in August 1981 when the Beckford sisters were brought to hospital with suspected non-accidental injuries. Attended Case Conferences of 6 and 20 August 1981 and confirmed fractures on both children. Expressed view that injuries were so serious that it was unlikely children should be rehabilitated with their parents. Gave evidence before Willesden Justices on 9 September 1981 in support of application for Care Orders. Saw both children a month after they went to foster parents, and reported to Dr. Mallik on 5 October 1981 that "Jasmine is now walking normally. Her vocabulary has blossomed and she appears very happy." Was not invited to attend any subsequent Case Conferences or Case Reviews. Never saw children again.

Dr. Ganesan Supramaniam: MB, BS (Ceylon) MRCP DCh (London). Consultant Paediatrician, Watford General Hospital. In August 1981 was senior Registrar in Paediatrics at St. Charles Hospital. Did not see Louise Beckford (brought into hospital on Saturday 1 August 1981) until Monday 3 August. Assumed that consultant might have been called in over the weekend. Attended Case Conference on 6 August, but left it to Dr. Warner to attend subsequent Case Conferences.

Dr. Hosaima Kavarana: MB, BS (Bombay) medical practitioner in Kilburn area of London. Temporary registration of Beverley Lorrington and two children in April 1982. Saw Jasmine on 20 April 1982. Invitation on 20 October 1982 to Case Conference for November declined. Saw Beverley in Spring 1983 when pregnant with Chantelle.

Dr. Jeffrey Gordon Christopher Peiris MB BS (Ceylon) DCH (Ceylon) Qualified in 1959 and practised in Sri Lanka for fifteen years. Since 1975 medical officer at Mortimer Road Clinic. Responsible for medical care of children in all schools in catchment area. Saw Jasmine on a number of occasions following birth in December 1979. Exhibited no concern over Jasmine's weight throughout 1980 and first half of 1981. Had no notification of child abuse on Jasmine in August 1981; was not invited to any Case Conference; and only knew of Care Orders in November 1981 when children with foster parents. Was not informed of Case Conference of 5 April 1982. While Jasmine attending Mortimer Road Day Nursery in 1982 she was produced to Dr. Peiris on 26 October 1982 for a medical examination. She was not weighed on that occasion. Was due to be examined at Princess Frederica C. of E. J.M. and I. School on 29 November 1983, but visit was postponed.

Other professionals involved in Beckford case
Miss Susan Elizabeth Knibbs: Senior Social Worker, Royal Borough of Kensington and Chelsea, working in social services department of St. Charles Hospital since 1976. Holds Certificate of Qualification in Social Work. Saw Louise Beckford at hospital on Monday 3 August, interviewed Beverley Lorrington that day, and arranged for further interview with both parents the following day. Jasmine brought to casualty by parents on that day (4 August) before interview. Applied that evening for a Place of Safety Order in respect of both Beckford children. Obtained Order from Magistrate of Inner London Juvenile Panel for 14 days. Arranged for Case Conference to be held at St. Charles Hospital. Attended personally both conferences of 6 and 20 August 1981. No further contact with Beckford case.

Miss Janet Bowden: Health Visitor, Harrow Health Authority. Qualified as a State Registered Nurse, State Qualified Midwife, Health Visitor, Field Work Teacher and Family Planning Nurse. Obtained diplomas in Sociology and in Social Studies. Health Visitor since 1969. Health Visitor to Beckford children while fostered with Proberts from September 1981 to April 1982. Recorded weight increase of Jasmine from August 1981 to April 1982. Invited to attend Case Conference of 5 April 1982 to consider reuniting children with parents; declined to attend, supplying information orally three days earlier about children prospering with foster parents.

The Proberts
Mr. Peter Duncan Probert: born of Anglo-Indian parents, married Gabrielle Hilary Probert in 1957.

Mrs. Gabrielle Hilary Probert: Born 1938 at Weston-super-Mare, the youngest of seven children. After her father died in 1947 the family moved to London, living in Ealing and Greenford. After marriage she and her husband continued to live in north-west area of London, ultimately in Hillingdon, which is not in the Borough of Brent but in Harrow. Through Harrow Borough Council she and her husband applied to adopt a baby of mixed racial origin. The first child, of mixed Indian and West Indian parentage, was born in March 1962 and placed with the Proberts six weeks after birth. The second adopted child, of West Indian origin, was born in 1967 and likewise placed early in life. In early 1981 Mr. and Mrs. Probert answered an advertisement placed by Brent Borough Council seeking a foster home for two sisters aged ten. Interviewed by Mr. Jeremy Burns in June and on 7 August 1981 (the day after the Case Conference on Louise and Jasmine Beckford) with a view to formal application to become foster parents. The Proberts were interested only in long-term fostering. Before they had been assessed and formally approved, Mr. Jeremy Burns asked the Proberts whether they would be willing to take Jasmine (then 21 months) and Louise (4 months) for fostering. They met Mr. Jeremy

Burns with Ms. Gun Wahlstrom on 24 August 1981, following which Louise was discharged from hospital and placed with them on 26 August 1981 and Jasmine on 14 September. Both children flourished while in the foster home, Jasmine dramatically putting on seven pounds in weight in seven months. Pursuant to the decision of 5 April 1982 to place the children home on trial, the Beckford sisters were removed from the Probert home on 13 April 1982.

CHAPTER 5

Chronological Summary of Events
2 December 1979 – 2 December 1985

1979

2 December   Jasmine Beckford born; Morris Beckford registered as father. Miss Gillian Hindle, health visitor, visits Beckfords.

1980

24 October   Miss Judy Knowles, health visitor, weighs Jasmine and starts recording on percentile chart.

1981

27 May   Louise Beckford born. Miss Judy Knowles, health visitor, visits Beckfords.

8 June   Visit by Health Visitor, Miss Judy Knowles, who described Jasmine as a "thin, miserable-looking child."

1 August   Louise taken to hospital with broken arm, retinal haemorrhage.

4 August   Jasmine taken to hospital with broken femur. Place of Safety Order on each child granted for 14 days.

6 August   Case conference held at St. Charles' Hospital. Both children placed on Non-Accidental Injury Register. Brent Social Services to apply for interim Care Order. Ms. Gun Wahlstrom appointed as key worker.

17 August   Interim Care Orders made by Inner London Juvenile Court. Brent Borough Council ordered to bring both children before the Willesden Juvenile Court.

20 August   Case conference held at St. Charles' Hospital. Area 6, Brent Social Services takes over full responsibility for Beckford case.

26 August   Louise discharged from hospital and placed with foster-parents, Mr. and Mrs. Probert.

9 September   Willesden Juvenile Court makes Orders committing both children into care of Brent Borough Council. Magistrates add rider expressing the hope that children will be re-united with parents.

14 September   Jasmine discharged from hospital and placed with the same foster parents, Mr. and Mrs. Probert. Weekly access to parents.

16 September   Health Visitor notes transfer to foster parents "following Care Order. This probably will be contested by parents!"

17 September   Mrs. Dorothy Ruddock, Family Aide with Brent Social Services, introduced to Miss Lorrington.

19 November   Morris Beckford convicted of assault occasioning actual bodily harm to Louise, and sentenced to 6 months' imprisonment, suspended for two years, and a fine of £250 plus costs.

26 November   Foster parents, Mr. and Mrs. Probert, informed that they were approved as "long-term foster parents for Jasmine and Louise". `

9 December   Review by Brent Social Services. Decision to step-up parental contact at parents' home.

1982

22 March	Morris Beckford and Beverley Lorrington re-housed by Brent Borough Council at 57 College Road, Kensal Rise.
5 April	Case Conference: decision to return children to parents: key worker to organise "intensive visiting when children return home".
13 April	Jasmine and Louise transferred to Green Lodge Residential Day Nursery.
19 April	Children taken home. Daily visiting by social workers begins.
20 April	Jasmine begins attending at Mortimer Road Day Nursery.
25 May	Case Review by Brent Social Services. Visiting reduced to five days a week.
6 June	Health visitor, Miss Knowles, records Jasmine looking "pinched...."
15 July	Miss Leong takes over health visiting to Beckford family.
30 September	Case Review by Brent Social Services.
2 November	Jasmine ceases attending Mortimer Road Day Nursery.
9 November	Case Conference: Both children to be removed from child abuse Register.
12 November	Both children taken off child abuse register.
29 November	Health visitor, Miss Leong, receives notification of removal from child abuse register.

1983

11 January	Jasmine starts attending Princess Frederica C. of E. J.M. & I. School (Nursery).
18 April	Case Review by Brent Social Services: decision to apply for revocation of Care Order.
7 June – 22 July	Jasmine fails to attend nursery school.
22 June	Application for revocation of Care Orders refused by Willesden Juvenile Court.
15 August	Family Aide, Mrs. Dorothy Ruddock, makes last visit (unofficial) to Beckford household; due to go on CQSW course.
5-7 September	Jasmine attends nursery school.
8 September	Home visit by Ms. Gun Wahlstrom when both children seen.
9 September	Jasmine attends nursery school. Never again attends school.
6 December	Case Review by Brent Social Services.
11 December	Chantelle Beckford born.

1984

13 and 17 February	Health Visitor visits Beckford home: no reply on either occasion.
12 March	Home visit by Ms. Gun Wahlstrom: "All three children appeared well and happy". Beverley Lorrington admits that she no longer takes Jasmine to nursery school.
16 May	Ms. Gun Wahlstrom contacts Princess Frederica Primary School on telephone. Discovers officially that Jasmine has not attended nursery school since September 1983.
22 May	Six-monthly review by Brent Social Services due to take place: postponed.
24 May	Ms. Gun Wahlstrom visits home: sees Morris Beckford and Beverley Lorrington.
30 May	Ms. Gun Wahlstrom visits: only Morris Beckford seen

4 June	Ms. Gun Wahlstrom visits: Morris Beckford and Beverley Lorrington seen.
11 June	Ms. Gun Wahlstrom visits: No reply; note left.
28 June	Ms. Gun Wahlstrom visits: Morris Beckford and Beverley Lorrington seen.
3 July	Ms. Gun Wahlstrom delivers letter by hand, announcing visit by her and Mrs. Dietmann at 1 p.m. on 5 July 1984 to start review procedure.
5 July	1.00 p.m. Ms. Gun Wahlstrom and Mrs. Diane Dietmann visit: no reply: leave note.
	2.00 p.m. They return to Beckford home: still no reply.
	3.00 p.m. Ms. Gun Wahlstrom telephones Beverley Lorrington's parents: told Beverley expected, but not yet back.
	5.30 p.m. Jasmine taken to St. Mary's Hospital: dead on arrival.
6 July	Director of Social Services informed of Jasmine's death: 28-day Place of Safety Order made on Chantelle Beckford. Louise and Chantelle transferred from maternal grandparents' home to foster-home.
6 July	Around midnight Morris Beckford and Beverley Lorrington were charged with the murder of Jasmine
9 July	Synopsis of events, August 1981-July 1984 prepared by Area 6.
10 July	Meeting of Director of Social Services and Staff.
12 July	Case Conference held: Louise and Chantelle to be put on child abuse register.
18 July	DHSS informed by Assistant Director of Social Services of Jasmine's death.
2 October	Case Conference: Gun Wahlstrom to be key worker.
29 October	Meeting of Cases Sub-Committee of Social Services Committee of Brent Borough Council; report from Director of Social Services.
26 November	Meeting of Cases Sub-Committee: recommends setting up of internal inquiry.
18 December	Care Order made on Chantelle. Application for parental access to Louise and Chantelle refused.

1985

8 January	Social Services Committee of Brent Borough Council decides internal inquiry not to proceed, but that external inquiry under auspices of Area Review Committee should be instituted.
10 January	Review by Area 6 on cases of Louise and Chantelle Beckford. Decision: so long as access denied, children to come off child abuse register.
12 February	Policy and Resources Committee of Brent Borough Council decide on independent inquiry.
28 March	At Central Criminal Court, Morris Beckford convicted of the manslaughter of Jasmine Beckford and sentenced to 10 years' imprisonment: also convicted of cruelty to children, and sentenced concurrently to 8 years' imprisonment. Miss Beverley Lorrington convicted of wilful neglect, and sentenced to 18 months' imprisonment.
15 April	Independent Panel of Inquiry holds preliminary hearing to announce its procedure and to receive applications for legal representation.
29 April	Independent Panel of Inquiry begins its hearings.

28 June	Inquiry adjourns to 2 September, having completed hearing evidence after 37 days.
6 September	Inquiry completes oral hearings after 4 days of oral submissions.
2 December	Panel of Inquiry submits its report to the two authorities, Brent Borough Council and Brent Health Authority.

CHAPTER 6

Demographic Profile of Brent

To describe the conditions of life for the population of the London Borough of Brent is to tell in broad terms the tale of two Boroughs. Brent, even more markedly today, reflects the marriage at the time of London government reorganisation in 1965 of two boroughs, Wembley and Willesden, the former as prosperous as the latter was poverty-stricken. The Borough is bisected horizontally by the North Circular Road; to the south there are in abundance the social ills associated with inner city areas, to the north, the affluence that reflects the comparison of the South-East of England to the rest of the country. The politics of Brent collide at the North Circular Road, providing a chronic instability that we describe shortly in chapter 18. The Beckford family lived in the deepest south of the Borough, where the major social problems literally tumble over each other.

Brent's population of 250,000 has the highest proportion of black ethnic communities of any local authority, many of whom unquestionably suffer disproportionately from poor housing, unemployment and lack of community facilities. An analysis of the results of the 1981 census prepared by the Department of the Environment reveals Brent (even with its affluent segment) as the eighth poorest local authority in England in terms of various indices of disadvantage. Three of the eight most deprived wards in London are in Brent. There are 1200 homeless families, the highest number in any local authority. These bare statistics of poverty show a high concentration of social problems at the "inner city" end of the Borough serviced by Area 6 of Brent Social Services Department.

According to figures from the 1981 Census, Brent has a larger New Commonwealth and Pakistani (NCW and P) population, numerically and proportionately, than any other Borough in the Greater London Area. Over 83,000 people (or 33% of Brent's population in 1981) were of NCW and P origin. This figure is generally recognised as an underestimate of the position at that time, and has probably even increased since then.

Table 1 – Brent's Population by Ethnic Group

Ethnic Group	Numbers	Percentages
UK and Eire	142,703	57.5%
Afro Caribbean	35,620	14.4%
Asian	40,890	16.5%
Other	28,560	11.5%

Brent's Population by age and Social Services Area
Figures prepared by Brent's Social Services Department, based on the 1981 Census, in the light of the age-group 0-4, strongly suggest the proportion of Brent's total population of NCW and P origin is nearer 40% than the 33% of the Census.

Population by Ethnic Groups
Estimates prepared by Brent's Development Department based on the 1981 Census indicate the distribution of the ethnic groups in the Areas of Social Services

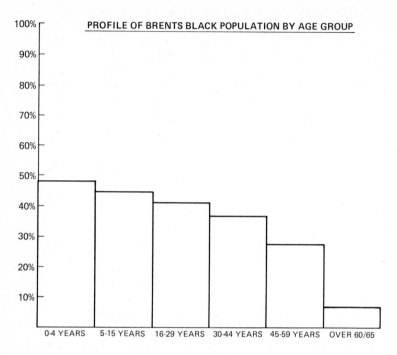

PROFILE OF BRENTS BLACK POPULATION BY AGE GROUP

100% — 90% — 80% — 70% — 60% — 50% — 40% — 30% — 20% — 10%

0-4 YEARS 5-15 YEARS 16-29 YEARS 30-44 YEARS 45-59 YEARS OVER 60/65

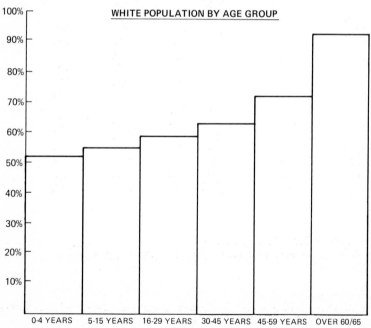

WHITE POPULATION BY AGE GROUP

100% — 90% — 80% — 70% — 60% — 50% — 40% — 30% — 20% — 10%

0-4 YEARS 5-15 YEARS 16-29 YEARS 30-45 YEARS 45-59 YEARS OVER 60/65

Table 2 — Brent's Ethnic Population — by Age and Social Services Area

	0-4	5-15	16-29	30-44	45-59/60	60/65+
Area 1	39%	32%	33%	29%	17%	5%
Area 2	56%	48%	48%	45%	30%	8%
Area 3	55%	48%	45%	40%	32%	7%
Area 4	36%	38%	28%	24%	21%	5%
Area 5	36%	38%	28%	24%	21%	5%
Area 6	47%	45%	44%	36%	36%	8%
Overall	48%	45%	41%	37%	28%	7%
Total Pop.	15,366	35,960	62,128	47,681	47,722	39,222
Total Ethnic Pop.	7,413	16,130	25,561	17,748	13,466	2,712

Table 3 — Number of Children Boarded Out in Brent 1973-1985

31st March	Boarded Out	% of total	At Home	% of total	Total in Care
1973	153	22%	104	15%	693
1974	183	25%	96	13%	726
1975	174	25%	86	23%	709
1976	190	27%	105	15%	707
1977	192	29%	105	16%	666
1978	216	31%	123	17%	707
1979	213	31%	126	18%	688
1980	212	34%	116	19%	622
1981	185	36%	87	17%	518
1982	196	39%	87	17%	509
1983	205	45%	93	20%	455
1984	240	58%	79	19%	416
1985*	214	60%	73	20%	358

Source: DHSS Children in Care Statistics
*Source: Brent Social Services Statistics Bulletin March Quarter

These statistics need to be interpreted with care; in particular they need to be compared with the rest of the country.

Children in care
In recent years there has been a sharp decline in the numbers of children received or taken into care by local authorities, resulting from the drop in the national birth rate and changes in social policy. Brent has been no exception. The number of children in care of Brent in 1985 is half of that in the years 1973-1979. The percentage of children in care residing at home with their parents has remained fairly constant. The highly significant percentage increase has been in respect of the children in care who have been boarded-out with foster-parents. Whereas in the 1970s less than one-third of children in care were boarded-out, today it is approaching two-thirds.

CHAPTER 7

Medical Evidence of Child Abuse

August 1981: Beckford sisters in hospital

During June and July 1981 social workers from Brent Borough Council and the Health Visitor from Brent Health District (after reorganisation in 1982, Brent Health Authority), Miss Judy Knowles, were expressing anxieties about the living conditions of the Beckford family; and Miss Knowles had expressed her deep concern about Jasmine's health, and pointedly about her development. The family of four occupied a double bed-sitting room in a house in Harrow Road, Kensal Green, London N.W.10., from which all the other tenants had moved out, reputedly because of infestation with mice. The family ate and slept in the same room, but had exclusive use of the kitchen, toilet and bath from which they and the tenants, who had earlier shared the facilities, were said to have picked up infectious diseases. The severe restriction on space is evident in the fact that Jasmine (then 18 months old) was confined to the landing and stairs for her play area. On 27 July 1981 Miss Dulcie Joseph, a social worker, wrote to the Housing Manager of Brent Housing Department requesting an early visit to the family. She wrote: "I visited the family recently and have reason to feel anxious about the children's health, safety and development . . . If the children are to thrive it is important that they transfer to larger accommodation. It is for their well-being that I request an urgent assessment visit by your department." Miss Joseph's anxieties were more than amply justified; indeed they were instantly prophetic. Contemporaneously with the letter of 27 July 1981, the younger of the Beckford sisters, Louise (aged 2 months) was subjected to a "yanking, twisting action" of her arm which on examination showed a spiral fracture of the left humerus; further examination disclosed haemorrhages in the right eye caused by violent shaking of the baby.

Louise's mother said that she had noticed on 29 July the swelling of the arm and had bathed it in cold, salt water. When, by Saturday 1 August, the swelling had not subsided, she took the child to St. Charles' Hospital, Exmoor Street, London W.10. There was no doubt in the minds of the doctors and nurses at St. Charles that Louise's injuries were non-accidental, no plausible explanation being offered for the fracture (other than a lame suggestion that the child had "slept on it badly") or for the ocular haemorrhages, for which Morris Beckford alone admitted being responsible.

Neither the senior registrar nor the consultant on call that week-end was contacted by the junior medical staff. While we have not seen the specific guidelines operative for St. Charles' Hospital (which is under Kensington and Chelsea Health Authority) we were told by Dr. Supramaniam, then senior registrar at the hospital, that very similar guidelines to those framed by Brent Area Review Committee were in operation. And Dr. Warner, the consultant paediatrician at the same hospital, told us that the senior house officer resident in the hospital would normally contact the registrar or senior registrar and, if necessary, the consultant on call that weekend. Dr. Nicola Wood, the responsible doctor on duty, has gone abroad and has not been traced; we are unable to say that any individual is to blame for the serious omission to get in touch immediately with the senior registrar or consultant. The seriousness of the omission lies in the fact that Miss Knibbs, the senior social worker at the hospital, was not at that time alerted and hence not in a position to apply on the day of Louise's admission for a Place of Safety Order in respect of both Louise and Jasmine, which might have had the effect of protecting Jasmine from the physical abuse she suffered over that weekend at home.

Three days after Louise's admission to St. Charles hospital — on Tuesday, 4 August

65

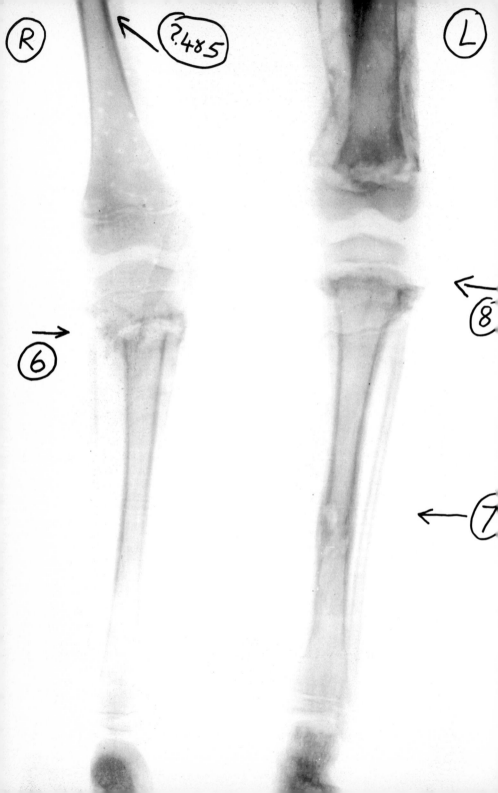

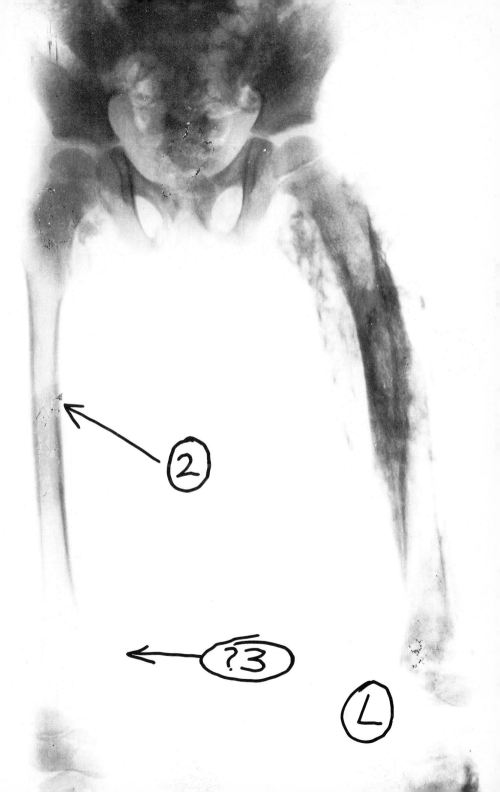

1981 — Jasmine was brought to the same hospital with a fracture of her left upper leg. She could stand, but not walk. This injury had been diagnosed by the local general practitioner, Dr. Mallik, who immediately referred Miss Lorrington to St. Charles' Hospital, where she reluctantly took Jasmine. Her reluctance stemmed from a, not unnatural, fear that the hospital authorities would again suspect child abuse.

The initial diagnosis of Jasmine's injury, by way of x-rays taken in the hospital's radiology department, was of a subtrochanteric fracture of the left femur with bruising over the site of the injury, but none elsewhere. The fracture was the result of considerable force having been applied. The mother offered the explanation that Jasmine had fallen downstairs. She herself did not suggest that she had then fallen on top of the child, an explanation that might have been forthcoming to substantiate an accidental injury; such an occurrence might have supplied the greater impact necessary to cause a fracture of that nature. Since it was highly unusual for siblings to be admitted to hospital contemporaneously, with injuries that had all the hallmarks of child abuse, it was not surprising that Miss Knibbs, on 5 August 1981, applied for, and obtained Place of Safety Orders for 14 days from Mrs. Katherine Porteous, a Magistrate of the Inner London Juvenile Panel. The doctors at St. Charles at that time, and subsequently at the Case Conferences of 6 and 20 August, felt unable conclusively to rule out the possibility that Jasmine's injury was accidental, and hence hesitated to say positively that she had been the subject of non-accidental injury. The medical input to the management of the child abuse case was focused entirely on the orthopaedic condition of both children and the ophthalmic condition of Louise. There was an absence of information relating to child development. Since the records have been mislaid, we do not even know whether the children had whole body x-rays or straight skull x-rays, or whether the doctors ever considered a CAT scan.

It was not until the hearing of the application for a Care Order in respect of each child on 9 September 1981 at Willesden Juvenile Court that the full nature of Jasmine's injuries was revealed. A solicitor, Mr. Simon Pollard, of Alexander & Partners, had been appointed by the court under a legal aid certificate to represent the children, and Miss Joan Court, an independent social worker, renowned for her outstanding studies on child care over twenty years, was in turn asked by the solicitor to make a report. The solicitor also sensibly sought the opinion of Dr. Richard Levick, a consultant paediatric radiologist from Sheffield. Dr. Levick concluded, in a written report relating to both Louise and Jasmine, that was in evidence before the Magistrates, in circumstances we shall discuss fully in Chapter 8, that not only was there a fracture of Jasmine's left femur, which had occurred within 4 or 5 days as a result of the application of considerable force, but that there was also a periosteal reaction on the lateral aspect of the right tibia which was probably between 7 to 10 days old. Dr Levick's report clearly suggested two separate incidents on each of the two children. With a deft touch of disarming disbelief, Dr. Levick concluded that the evidence of injury to Jasmine on two separate occasions "must be carefully matched with the account given by the parents or other persons in charge as to how bone damage was sustained." Had those who treated and nursed Jasmine at the hospital, and who at the subsequent Case Conferences had to consider the cause of her injuries, assimilated the information that was tantalisingly available on and after 9 September 1981, it cannot be doubted that they would have had no hesitation in stating that Jasmine too had been the victim of a non-accidental injury. We shall have to consider hereafter what impact, if any, Dr. Levick's specialist report had on the decisions of the Magistrates' Court and of the social workers. We pause only to say that expert radiological opinion is vital in suspected child abuse cases so that the full extent and timing of bone injuries can be properly assessed, which in turn will promote sound decisions by those who become responsible for the welfare of such children.

Further Fractures on Jasmine: September 1983 — July 1984

The post-mortem examination on 6 July 1984 on Jasmine continued to show traces of the subtrochanteric fracture of the left femur suffered in August 1981. There was additionally a well-healed long spiral fracture of the centre of the shaft of the left femur which had united in excellent position; there was evidence that considerable re-modelling of this fracture had taken place. There was a more recent injury of the lower femoral epiphyses, together with a mass of partially organised callus surrounding the entire shaft of the left femur. The spiral fracture was probably older than six months; the epiphyseal injury was more recent, probably 2-3 months old, but could have been inflicted more than six months before death. We attach a diagram of Jasmine's thigh and leg, with numbered injuries, as demonstrated to us by Mr. Geoffrey Walker, a consultant orthopaedic surgeon. He expressed his opinion that the order of injuries was probably 2,7,8,6 and 3, the earliest being placed between September 1982 and September 1983, and No. 3 around early March 1984. We will refer at length to the earliest injury — No. 2 — in Chapter 10 in the context of events around November 1982. With regard to the latest of the injuries — No. 3 — Mr. Walker told us:

> This is obviously a very crucial point, really relating to the question of limping after fractures of the lower limb in children, and one never ceases to be surprised the way children react differently to the same injury. We all react differently to the same injury but one sees this particularly with limping after lower limb fractures, either significant major ones, such as this child had, or very minor greenstick fractures. Some children will get out of bed and walk normally within a week. Other children with the same fracture will still be limping at a year. There is no way of knowing and there is nothing that you or I or the parents can do about it. Nature will cure it. So I think this is possibly relevant to the visit — to pre-empt presumably your next question. If there had been significant bone injury within the six weeks before this child was visited, it is quite likely that she would either not have walked or would have limped. If there had been significant bone injury in the period before six weeks before she was visited, there is really no reason that I know why she should not have been able to walk a few steps quite well, and I notice she had trousers on. I think if a child of that age gets up and walks a few steps one is not going to take a great deal of notice about her gait anyway. But this is guesswork.

Our guess is that on 12 March 1984, the last time Ms. Wahlstrom saw the child, Jasmine was able to stand up and could have moved a short distance with a limp that, on a superficial sighting, would not necessarily have been noticed.

Failure to thrive, June 1981-July 1984

Throughout the intense publicity given to the death of Jasmine Beckford there has understandably been a heavy concentration on the appalling physical injuries suffered by Jasmine, first in August 1981 and again in the months leading up to her death in July 1984. Stripped of the multiple physical abuse, there remained, however, the underlying and continuing problem of Jasmine's lack of development. The failure on the part of those responsible for Jasmine's health and welfare to stop and ask themselves the

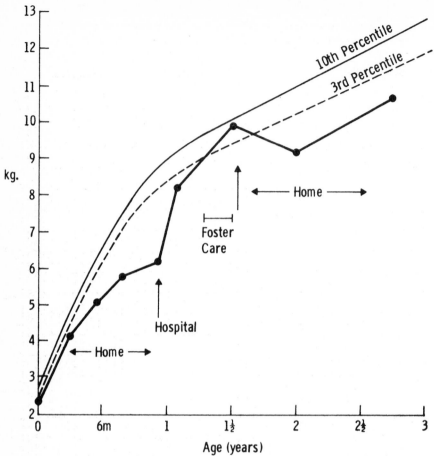

question which any normal parent would ask – namely "is this child passing the milestones of babyhood and childhood?" – is hard to explain. The simplest test in the world is to put the child on a pair of scales. From April 1980 until September 1981, and from then onwards till her death, excluding the period of the dramatic improvement during the seven months with the foster-parents, Jasmine was worryingly abnormal in weight. This factor was readily discoverable from any study of a percentile chart of Jasmine's weight.

Percentile charts have been constructed by the medical profession, at least since 1959, as a result of examination of a very large number of children of different ages, in order to get an idea of the average height, weight and head circumference for a child at any particular age. The data are recorded on lines, the middle of which is the average known as the 50th centile, where 50% of children are heavier and 50% are lighter. The two lines either side are known as the 10th and 90th centiles. The lower one means that 90% are heavier and 10% of the population are lighter, and vice-versa. The charts give the 3rd, 10th, 25th, 50th, 75th, 90th and 97th percentiles. As a rough guide, children outside the area of the 10th to 90th percentile range should be regarded with slight suspicion. And those outside the 3rd to 97th range as unhealthy, until proved otherwise. This is not merely *our* view. It is extracted from the notes on the reverse side of the percentile

70

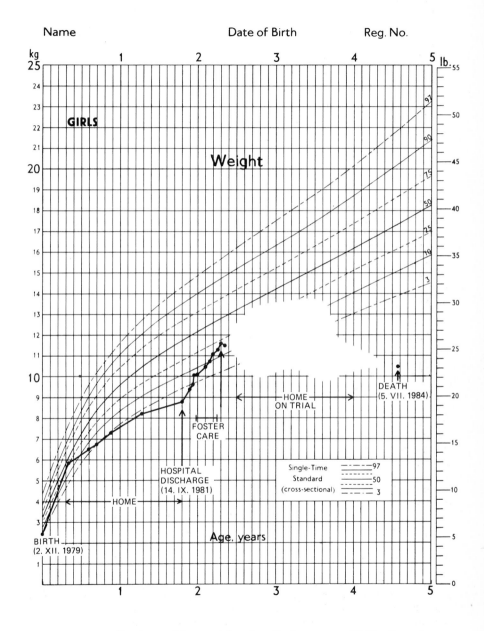

Name   Date of Birth   Reg. No.

GIRLS

Weight

HOME ON TRIAL

DEATH (5. VII. 1984)

FOSTER CARE

HOSPITAL DISCHARGE (14. IX. 1981)

Single-Time ----97
Standard ------50
(cross-sectional) ---.--- 3

HOME

Age, years

BIRTH (2. XII. 1979)

Jasmine's percentile chart of her weight, described at pages 72-74. Opposite an anonymous percentile chart, referred to at the top of page 74.

chart used by Miss Knowles. In the Consultation Record for Children, 0-5 years, used in health clinics and known as the MCW46, there is normally a percentile chart with a marked line known as the 3rd centile. These charts are available in all children's clinics and are regularly filled in and examined to see that the child is keeping within the appropriate acceptable norm, and that his or her growth is following a normal pattern. Once the child has reached the age of 4 months and has established a pattern of growth, he is likely to remain on the centile. If the chart then shows that the child's weight or height is falling away from the centile formerly followed, alarm bells should start ringing. If there is no disease to explain the drop in weight, there is a strong probability that the child is, physically and/or emotionally, deprived. We have had prepared a growth chart for Jasmine based on the chart kept by Miss Knowles and other data available in the documentation from Brent Health Authority, none of which was ever seen by social services. The data are plotted on the weight chart. Since there are no data to chart after Jasmine reached 2 years and 3 months, the last two years of her life are a blank. At birth Jasmine, a full term normal delivery by forceps, weighed 2.6 kg (5 lbs. 11½ ozs). Thereafter she gained weight rapidly, so that by the age of four months her weight was close to the 50th centile. Although of relatively low birth weight she had reached a very satisfactory weight, near to the average for the population. During the following six months her weight gain slowed down, and fell to the 3rd centile. On 24 October 1980 her weight was below the 3rd centile, but the health visitor, Miss Knowles, noted (in error) her concern because Jasmine's "weight below 25 percentile." On 17 March 1981 Miss Knowles recorded the weight as 8.21 kgs (18lbs. 6 ozs), indicating a further fall away below the 3rd centile. By the time that Jasmine, aged 20 months, was taken into hospital with a broken femur she was well below the 3rd centile.

Miss Knowles had kept the percentile chart on Jasmine during 1980 and 1981. She had recorded the weights in her health visitors' cards and on the visit of 8 June 1981 had noted that Jasmine was a "thin, miserable-looking child." Jasmine had by then fallen further away from the 3rd centile. While Miss Knowles is to be applauded for having done the right thing up to that stage, she failed to translate her initiative into further appropriate action. The percentile chart lay in the files of Mortimer Road Clinic; she had no discussion with (a) the clinic's medical officer, (b) the child's general practitioner, or (c) her supervisor, the nursing officer, and the chart was not made available to St. Charles' Hospital, either for hospital purposes or for the attention of participants at the Case Conference. Although Miss Knowles observed at the Case Conference on 6 August 1981 that Jasmine's weight was not normal, the fact was noted, but not followed up either by the doctors present or by Social Services. It is clear from the two Case Conferences, and from the proceedings before the Magistrates on 9 September 1981, that Dr. Warner was looked to by Social Services for his paediatric opinion on the orthopaedic and ophthalmic conditions of the two children, and was never asked about any developmental aspects of Jasmine's health. We accept that Dr. Warner did not state in his evidence to the Magistrates on 9 September 1981 that Jasmine's "height and weight were normal", despite the justices' clerk's note to the contrary. Indeed he could not have said anything about her weight, since the health visitors' records had not been disclosed to him and Jasmine was in traction from the moment of admission until a few days before discharge from hospital on 14 September. It would have been very unusual to weigh a patient in traction, since to carry out the exercise would either be very painful or complicated. There is the further point that Dr. Warner's concern in August 1981 was to provide evidence to ensure the making of the Care Order. For reasons we shall explain, Dr. Warner did not see the children after they had been discharged from hospital, other than on 5 October 1981 when the two children were thriving in their foster home. Had he known that the two children would be returning on a home on trial in April

1982 he would, without question, have wished to be consulted about monitoring the children's development. He was never invited to any of the Case Conferences or Statutory Case Reviews after 20 August 1981. We conclude that it was a serious omission on the part of Area 6 not to involve Dr. Warner once again, after the children's return to the Beckford household in April 1982.

During the time that Miss Bowden was the health visitor for the children (i.e. from September 1981 – April 1982, when the children were being fostered) Jasmine was frequently weighed, as the chart indicates. No one thereafter looked at, let alone appreciated the significance of the dramatic improvement in Jasmine's weight. Miss Knowles, on 6 June 1982, just prior to handing over her case-load to Miss Leong, had recorded that Jasmine was a "rather pathetic child, little speech or concentration although [Miss Knowles] tried to go through books with her. [Jasmine] not interested if mother showed her either. .... Jasmine still looks pinched and [the next word was rendered illegible on account of being either altered or crossed out, but our reading of it would indicate the word 'worried']." Even more inexplicable is the fact that Jasmine was never weighed after April 1982, not even when Dr. Peiris conducted a developmental health check at Mortimer Road Clinic in October 1982.

Before us Dr. Hugh Jolly stated emphatically that had he been shown the percentile chart as at August 1981 he would have exhibited considerable concern about Jasmine's development. Had the evidence of the percentile chart for Jasmine's first 20 months of life been seen by those present at the Case Conference – more particularly at the Case Conference or Statutory Case Reviews after August 1981 – another important factor about Jasmine's treatment at the hands of her parents would have been weighed in the balance of decision-making about the extent of child abuse Jasmine had undergone. The future placement of the two children, moreover, would have been materially affected, had Jasmine's failure to thrive been properly recorded and noted.

This is not the end of the story so far as any future decision about Jasmine that had to be made. From the age of 20 months her growth in weight took a significant upturn; she gained weight steadily until the age of 27 months, by which time she was nearly at the 25th centile. This development strongly indicated a period of "catch-up" growth, highly suggestive of a dramatic change in her well-being and of something radically wrong with her earlier development. Recent research indicates that where children show substantial catch-up growth in foster homes it is doubtful whether early return to the natural parents is appropriate. Anybody at the Case Conference on 5 April 1982, when the decision to return the children to the Beckford home was taken, and in the absence of Miss Knowles with her unique knowledge about Jasmine's failure to thrive, should have called for a medical examination which would have unearthed the tell-tale of the percentile chart, then updated. (Miss Knowles, for some unexplained reason, did not receive the invitation to attend that Conference). There was only a note in the minutes of that Case Conference to the health visitor, who it was then appreciated would be Miss Leong, to "encourage" Beverley Lorrington to take Jasmine to the clinic.

The path of Jasmine's development is thereafter uncharted, but the trend overall was downwards. She died weighing something alarmingly below the 3rd centile. Whether the drop to that disastrous level was gradual, or whether it improved and dropped sharply in the last months of life, cannot now be calculated. If Miss Knowles' observation of 6 June 1982 is accurate there could hardly have been any upward trend six weeks after leaving the foster home. The most likely trend is a gradual dropping away from the 3rd centile, with the weight remaining almost constant until the end. But we conclude that, for at least the last six months of her life, Jasmine was below the 3rd centile and, therefore, ought to have been the subject of profound concern to those responsible for her welfare. In those months she would have begun to appear, if not actually to be, emaciated. We attach the diagram of Jasmine's percentile chart; we have "fogged out" the chart for the period April 1982 to July 1984 during which there were no recordings.

It is not as if the fact of failure to thrive has not been singled out by authors on child abuse, making a special mention of weight as an index of child abuse, as well as disclosing child neglect. In a book, *Understanding Child Abuse*, published in June 1982 and edited by Mr. David Jones, now General Secretary of the British Association of Social Workers, it is stated that "included in the spectrum of child abuse is the grossly neglected child who shows evidence of inadequate feeding, stunted growth, poor hygiene." The book adds that it is often possible to reach a decision about child abuse, and demonstrates the point by including (at p. 75) a diagram of a percentile chart, prepared by Dr. Peter Barbor, strikingly similar to that which depicted Jasmine's failure to thrive. (Diagram attached). Abnormally low weight was a factor in both the leading cases of child abuse – Dennis O'Neill (1945) and Maria Colwell (1973). Yet no one in Area 6 seems to have been even faintly aware of this material in the literature of child abuse. **We recommend that whenever social workers are engaged in a child abuse case, they must re-acquaint themselves with the Policy Memorandum and the procedures to be applied as well as consult any relevant literature on the subject.**

On her visit to the Beckford family on 8 June 1981 Miss Knowles, the health visitor had described Jasmine in graphic terms: "A thin miserable-looking child. Does not eat well, understimulated...". Anyone observing Jasmine, even with an inexpert eye, in the summer of 1981 must have echoed Miss Knowles' description. (Miss Court's observation on her visit to St. Charles' Hospital confirmed the picture). Yet the fact of failure to thrive was overlooked, if not ignored. The startling improvement in Jasmine's development during the seven months with the Proberts should have not only been welcomed but also have alerted social and health services to what had gone on before and what happened subsequently. Even in June 1982 Miss Knowles was observing the "pathetic" child with signs of developmental failure. At least by the end of 1982 Jasmine was reverting to "the miserable-looking child" of eighteen months before. In Chapter 10 we conclude that she had been physically abused around this time. By the Autumn of 1983, when Jasmine ceased going to school, she was being subjected to fresh abuse. Anyone with half an eye on the child could hardly have failed to notice the pointers to impending tragedy. By the Spring of 1984 the die was cast. The pitiable picture that Jasmine must have presented to her parents – and the local authority was also her parent – calls to mind the part of Cardinal Spellman's prayer:

> "Somewhere – the place it matters not
> ---somewhere
> I saw a child, hungry and thin of face ---
> Eyes in whose pool life's joys no longer
> stirred,
> Lips that were dead to laughter's eager
> kiss,
> Yet parted fiercely to a crust of bread"

Prayers for Children 1944
Francis Joseph, Cardinal Spellman

We conclude that, while the fact of Jasmine's weight did not go entirely unnoticed until April 1982, it was never properly taken on board by the doctors or the health visitors, and never at all by social workers. Weight is, of course, an important aspect of physical development. Development, in its wider sense, however, barely gets a mention in the records: at what age did Jasmine sit up, walk, and, more importantly, develop her vocabulary and language? (Some concern was shown about Jasmine's speech; she was seen by a speech therapist.) Above all, there is barely a whisper of community child health practice. If (as was the case) Miss Knowles was worried about Jasmine's development, why did she not refer Jasmine in June 1981, or June 1982 for that matter, to a senior clinical medical officer, or to a community paediatrician for investigation and a full developmental report, and not leave it to the perfunctory check by Dr. Peiris that took place in October 1982? It is blindingly clear what needs to be done, and we are confident it will be done now that Dr. Bridget Edwards has taken up her post as Consultant Paediatrician for the Community in June 1985.

A case of severe child abuse, as was presented to the statutory agencies in August 1981 in respect of Louise and Jasmine Beckford, invariably calls for the very full involvement of community child health, and not just hospital consultants and registrars whose specialties (even if they are paediatricians) might not touch child abuse.

Part II: Facts and Comments on the Events

A. The Events, August 1981-July 1984

CHAPTER 8

The Making of the Care Orders, August/September 1981

Beckford sisters abused

Sometime during the last days of July 1981 – probably in the morning of Wednesday 29 July – Louise Beckford, then a baby two months old, was physically abused by her own father in the cramped conditions of their home. Since Morris Beckford alone was later convicted of assaulting Louise, we must assume that he was solely responsible for that injury. But we find that Beverley Lorrington at least connived at the concealment of this criminal offence, even if she was not guilty of collusion. Louise's left arm had been subjected to a "yanking, twisting action" of some severity, producing a spiral fracture of the left humerus. The inevitable swelling of the upper arm did not respond to the mother's bathing of it in cold salt water. Given no perceptible lessening in the swelling over three days, the mother finally took the baby to Dr. Mallik's surgery on the morning of Saturday, 1 August 1981. The doctor instantly suspected a fracture and directed Beverley Lorrington to St. Mary's Hospital, whence she was re-directed to St. Charles' Hospital, arriving around 8 p.m. Louise was admitted by the Senior Hospital Officer in Paediatrics, Dr. Nicola Wood (who has since gone abroad and has not been traced).

Brent Area Review Committee's guidelines for professional agencies involved in child care, entitled *Non-Accidental Injury to Children*, issued in 1977 – and we are told that a similar booklet has emanated from the Paddington and North Kensington Area Review Committee – is emphatic in its direction to hospital staff. Under the heading ACCIDENT UNIT DOCTORS, it states "RECORD precise description of injuries and how they are said to have been caused. Illustrate all injuries and clinical findings on charts. CONSULT a Paediatric Consultant immediately and directly." Under the next rubric, ALL OTHER HOSPITAL STAFF (NURSING, MEDICAL, ADMINISTRATIVE AND ANCILLARY) the guidelines stress the need to "CONSULT a Paediatric Consultant or a Hospital Senior Paediatric Social Worker immediately and directly." More detailed instructions along the same lines are set out for "members of a paediatric unit." Neither Dr. Supramaniam, the senior registrar under the consultant paediatrician, Dr. John Warner, nor Dr. Warner himself, saw Louise until Monday, 3 August 1985. Miss Knibbs, the Senior Social Worker at St. Charles, was likewise not apprised of the admission of a battered baby until the Monday morning. We have indicated in Chapter 7 that we are unable to point to any individual responsible for this serious omission that delayed the application for a Place of Safety Order in respect of both children that might have prevented the physical abuse of Jasmine Beckford. Had such an Order been obtained on that Saturday evening, and no later, Jasmine might have been spared the fracture of her left femur. At the very least, prompt action was demanded from the hospital authorities as a preventive measure.

On Sunday, 2 August, Louise's godmother, Miss McLean, visited the flat at Harrow Road and saw Jasmine sitting down, but in evident pain with her left leg, whenever she moved. Beverley Lorrington supplied the explanation that was oft-repeated, that Jasmine had fallen down the stairs. On the Monday, Beverley contacted Miss McLean by telephone, asking her to visit the following day with a view to having Jasmine while Beverley went to visit Louise in hospital. Beverley expressed her intention to take Jasmine to the evening surgery, to which Miss McLean responded by volunteering to take Jasmine that very morning. Miss McLean, in her statement to the police on 19 August 1981, said that she went alone, finding Beverley at home and telling her that Jasmine had a suspected fracture and should be taken to hospital. In a statement of the same date, Dr. Mallik confirmed to the police what Miss McLean had said, but before us he said that two women had brought in the limping Jasmine. Dr. Mallik particularly recalled Beverley being present at his surgery — she had been registered with him for some 18 months; he had seen her, only 3 days before, with the injured Louise; and, unlike Miss McLean, she was well known to him. It was she, he remembered, who was so volubly insistent on not taking Jasmine to St. Charles (Dr. Mallik had suggested St. Charles because he thought it was important that the sisters should be together). Dr. Mallik recalled Beverley saying that the hospital staff at St. Charles had asked so many questions when she had brought Louise in three days earlier: ("That lot there think we are baby bashers"). Could she not, she asked Dr. Mallik implicitly, put Jasmine in a hospital that would not ask awkward questions about possible child abuse?

Beverley Lorrington's desire to avoid being accused of child abuse was never followed up. Dr. Mallik was unable to attend either of the two Case Conferences of 6 and 20 August, to add his voice to those others confidently concluding that Jasmine's injury was not accidental. Had the personnel of Area 6 contacted Dr. Mallik between the two conferences with a view to determining the cause of Jasmine's injury, they might have obtained a useful piece of evidence to remove the question mark that hung over the cause of Jasmine's fractured thigh. Mrs. Diane Dietmann did telephone Dr. Mallik on 7 August (Ms. Wahlstrom appears to have called the day before only to find the doctor unobtainable). But when she did so, the conversation was strictly confined to the social workers' worry about Beverley Lorrington's depression. Dr. Mallik was reassuring that he was not concerned about her mental health, and indicated that he would try to attend the next Case Conference. This episode is an early instance of unbroken concentration of impressive social work input. But it is also characteristic of the attitude of Mrs. Dietmann (and Ms. Wahlstrom) in which all the social workers' attention was focused on the needs of the Beckford parents and was totally oblivious to their role as agents of a child protection service, other than as a spin-off or spill-over of casework with the parents. If Jasmine, as well as Louise, had initially been categorised a child abuse case, the inclination towards any future reuniting of the children with their parents would have been that much weaker. The failure to investigate this aspect of the child abuse on the Beckford sisters was one of the many, little instances where social workers in Area 6 denied to themselves information cumulatively, if not individually, invaluable towards the compilation of the profile of child abuse on the Beckford sisters and towards constructing the psychopathology of the Beckford parents.

A similar example of turning a blind eye to important reaction to a case of child abuse occurred on 3 August. Miss Knibbs, based at St. Charles, had on that Monday morning, asked the health visitor to visit Jasmine at home, and informed Area 6 of Louise's admission to hospital and Jasmine's exposure to risk at home. The matter was discussed and a social worker went to the flat at Harrow Road unavailingly. There was no sense of urgency at Area 6, since it was thought that seeing Jasmine could wait. Before us, Mr. David Bishop candidly conceded that he would not now wait a second before taking preventive action. He acknowledged that such a situation demanded "action first and talk afterwards," instead of vice-versa. Fortunately the omission to find Jasmine and seek immediately a Place of Safety Order in respect of her had no ill-effect. Had someone seen Jasmine on that Monday they would have discovered a child with a broken thighbone. The only effect would have been an earlier admission to hospital. **We recommend that child abuse procedures should emphasise that where a child has been admitted to hospital as a result of abuse by its parent(s), immediate steps must be taken to protect any sibling in the household that may be at risk.**

Miss Knibbs had, not unnaturally, assumed that Brent Social Services would have acted on this information urgently, and if found to be necessary would have themselves gone for a Place of Safety Order. (There was no need for urgency in respect of Louise who was already in a place of safety for the time being). In the meantime Miss Knibbs, together with Dr. Supramaniam, interviewed Beverley Lorrington on the Monday and arranged for her to return the following day with Morris Beckford for further interviewing. The late arrival of the Beckfords was due to the fact that they were ultimately induced by Dr. Mallik's advice to take Jasmine to St. Charles, driven there by Mr. Philip Bennett, regional manager of the scaffolding company that employed Morris Beckford. Faced with the facts of two very serious injuries inflicted contemporaneously on two very small children in the same family, and of knowledge gleaned from Mr. Raymond Jenkins of the NSPCC that Morris Beckford himself as a child had been physically abused by his parents, Miss Knibbs did not pause to inquire further. She went that evening to the home of a Magistrate of the Inner London Juvenile Panel and obtained a 14-day Place of Safety Order in respect of the children.

Miss Knibbs, who could not be faulted in any respect for her actions and decisions, set in train, in consultation with Mr. Bishop, the preparation for convening a Case Conference to be held at St. Charles' Hospital on 6 August. She reported fully to that Case Conference, including the odd remark that "Miss Lorrington was brighter than Mr. Beckford and ... that Miss Lorrington probably manipulated him", a fact that we find was quite the reverse, and in any event called for verification subsequently, along with other data that needed to be garnered. Mr. David Bishop, the Area Manager of Area 6, who chaired both Case Conferences, had on 5 August 1981 nominated Ms. Gun Wahlstrom as the key social worker, and thereafter she took over under the supervision of the Senior Social Worker, Mrs. Diane Dietmann, a team leader in Area 6. Miss Knibbs formally handed over the case to Brent Social Services at the Case Conference. She attended the second Conference on 20 August, but thereafter bowed out of the case. Her secretary took the minutes of the Case Conferences.

Into Care — and beyond
The immediate task of the first Case Conference on 6 August 1981 was to determine the causes of the injuries to the two children, and to discuss what action should be taken (We include the minutes of that Case Conference in Appendix G:1). Not surprisingly, the Conference agreed that Care Orders should be sought, and interim Orders were obtained on 17 August 1981 from Kensington & Chelsea Juvenile Court, with a direction from that Court that the case should come before Willesden Juvenile Court on 9 September 1981. Time to prepare the case for a full hearing was short. There had been some expectation that the Magistrates at Willesden might adopt a common practice of splitting the hearing, concluding first, that one of the primary conditions had been satisfied and leaving the issue of need of care or control to a later stage, but that did not materialise.

Before we turn to the procedures adopted at the Case Conferences and any decisions made at them, it is well at the outset of the exposition of the events to dispose of some confusion of terminology. We heard a great deal about short-term and long-term placements of children under Place of Safety Orders who will be taken into the care of a local authority. Without dilating upon much conflicting and confusing, if not confused evidence, we arrived at the following conclusion. Short-term fostering means the temporary placing of a child while a suitable plan is worked out for its future; the period is generally thought to be between 2 and 3 months, but not longer than 3 months. It is very much an emergency, stop-gap provision. Long-term fostering can be anything from 3 months to several years, even including the rest of childhood. It does not envisage anything more permanent than fostering for an indefinite period, stretching possibly into adolescence. Long-term fostering *with a view to adoption* alone envisages permanence, in the sense that the foster-parents may reasonably expect to convert a fostering into an extinction of the rights of natural parents and a transfer in law of all rights and duties to them as adopters. (We do not pause to consider the new order of custodianship which, later this month, will for the first time vest the legal custody of a child in a custodian. Before then, short of adoption and excepting wardship proceedings, no procedure has existed whereby foster-parents and others who have long-term care of a child can obtain formal legal recognition of their relationship with the child. More important, there is generally no procedure for protecting the foster-parent against a claim of a natural parent.) **We recommend that in all the policy statements and guidelines for procedure in child abuse cases the definitions that we have arrived at should become standardised.** Much misunderstanding, leading to acerbic statements from the Proberts, would have been avoided if everyone had understood what was meant by long-term fostering.

The Case Conference of 6 August 1981 was decisive in a number of respects. It had no hesitation in concluding that an interim Care Order should be obtained; that the children should forthwith be placed on Brent's child abuse register; that the police would further interview the parents; and that the Case Conference would be re-convened on 20 August. The two children were to remain in hospital pending further investigations, and Beverley Lorrington would be encouraged to live in hospital with the children, so that medical and nursing staff could observe her relationship with her children. Beyond these aspects, the Case Conference was wholly and understandably indecisive about the future placement of the children. By that time Ms. Wahlstrom had had only one meeting with Beverley Lorrington, the previous day. She found her emotionally flat and unconcerned about her children. Rehousing seemed to be her preoccupation.

We have heard 12 out of the 16 persons who attended the Conference. We did not think it necessary to hear the two Senior House Officers, one in paediatrics the other in orthopaedics (both of them in any event had gone abroad) since the Consultant and Senior Registrar were present at the Case Conference and gave evidence before us. We did not hear the Ward Sister in Peter Pan Ward at St. Charles, where the children were placed, since the doctors were quite able to convey any nursing information. Sister Ritchie is, however, recorded as having received the verbal report from the radiologist, saying that there was no sign of any bone injury to Jasmine other than the one to the left femur. (We shall have to comment later on this aspect of radiological paediatrics). And she noted that Beverley Lorrington's visits to hospital were not very frequent, of short duration, but that she had a good relationship with Jasmine. Miss Muriel Broad, who was a Nursing Officer/Health Visitor at Cranford Avenue Health Clinic, did not appear to us to be able to assist.

Of the twelve present at the Case Conference, there was inevitably a spectrum of opinion expressed at the meeting and of impression of a possible consensus of view. The medical personnel were, on the whole, hawkish in thinking that reuniting the Beckford family was a non-starter, compared with those among the social workers who did not rule out the possibility, in the not-too-distant future, of a programme of rehabilitation. Indeed, the decision to encourage the mother to live in the hospital was a faint indication of a move towards access after the children left hospital, with a view to monitoring the capacity of the parents to look after their children. Generally, the various participants did not discern at that stage any firm view about the future of the children. That was to be left as the main topic for the reconvened meeting when, expectantly, fuller and more adequate information would be available. We conclude that Mr. Bishop's summary to us of the situation accurately reflects the outcome of that Case Conference. That summary is encapsulated in this way: apply for interim Care Orders, move the children to a fostering situation on discharge from hospital; the children would decidedly not go home; neither to a residential nursery; nor to any member of the Beckford's extended family. They would remain firmly in local authority care, looked after in a foster-home for as long as it was going to be necessary. In short, the Conference was definitely not making any decision about any permanent residence. Despite sustained cross-examination by Miss Scotland, on behalf of Mr. and Mrs. Probert, we do not think that there was any hint of any firm attitude, let alone decision that this was a case of "fostering with a view to adoption", although no doubt one or two people at the meeting entertained the thought that that might well be the ultimate destination for the children. Hence, any subsequent communication between 6 and 20 August to any third party to suggest fostering with a view to adoption would have been wholly erroneous. In broad terms, the Case Conference of 6 August did the job assigned to it under the terms of Brent's policy memorandum. But there are features of that meeting that we think were less than satisfactorily handled. We proceed to deal with them at this stage, but we defer discussion of the invitations to attend Case Conferences to Chapter 25. We observe only of this Case Conference that there was a failure to invite Dr. Bridget Edwards, then Principal Physician in Community Health in Brent, although her name had been inserted in handwriting on the Policy Memorandum on Non-Accidental Injury to Children, 1977, a document which Mr. Bishop had at his elbow and instinctively reaches for whenever he is arranging a Case Conference on child abuse.

Radiological expertise
At the Case Conference there was an x-ray report from the radiology department of St. Charles on Louise's injuries and an oral report on Jasmine's injuries, communicated to the meeting by Sister Ritchie. Mr. Bishop pointedly sought an answer to the question whether Louise had suffered her injuries to the arm and the eyes on the same or separate occasions. Dr. Supramaniam thought it was on one occasion since there was no other evidence of bruising. Mr. Raymond Jenkins, with his long experience in the employ of NSPCC, demurred. He told us that he had a difference of opinion with Dr. Supramaniam about the coincidence in time of a bone fracture and retinal haemorrhage,* the latter produced by a violent shake as opposed to a severe blow. We do not criticise Dr. Supramaniam. What we do say is that the issue whether Louise's injuries were a "one-off" episode, or part of a pattern of battering, was so important as to demand further radiological investigation. This was the more necessary when one came to consider Jasmine's case. The subsequent report from Dr. Levick clearly indicated multiple child abuse on both children. That report was obtained at the initiative of Mr. Simon Pollard, the solicitor acting for the children in the juvenile court proceedings. We accept that his initiative was prompted by Dr. Warner, but we conclude that it ought to have been initiated by St. Charles and the results made available to the reconvened Case Conference, or if time did not permit such expedition, it ought to have been provided by the medical authorities to Brent Social Services and not left, hazardously, to the lawyers involved in care proceedings. **We recommend that in future the specialism of a radiological**

---

* We allude to this episode in Chapter 17.

paediatrician, capable not merely of discerning the more obscure bone and other injuries but also of dating the various injuries, should invariably be sought by the relevant hospital authorities whenever serious non-accidental fractures occur.

Failure to thrive

Miss Judy Knowles was the sole participant at the Case Conference who had any recent knowledge of the Beckford family before 1 August 1981. She had been the Health Visitor to the family since she succeeded Miss Gillian Hindle in the summer of 1980. It was she who, on a visit of 8 June 1981, had recorded in her Health Visitor's Continuation Card that Jasmine was a "thin, miserable-looking child". While we conclude that she expressed empathy for the Beckford parents and was implicitly an advocate for a reunion of the family as and when the children were discharged from hospital, she nevertheless possessed information that pointed strongly against the prospect of rehabilitation. She had started the percentile chart disclosing the worrying information. Her supervisor, Miss Tyler, who attended the Second Case Conference, should have discussed this matter preparatory to attendance on 20 August 1981. The percentile chart never did surface from the health visitors' files. Miss Knowles was simply recorded at the meeting of 6 August 1981 as saying that "Jasmine was of normal development mentally but that her weight was low and she felt that the child was under-stimulated." She also noticed that Beverley was very impatient with both Morris Beckford and on occasions with Jasmine: "She did not seem to have much idea on how to handle the child emotionally." Miss Knowles' contribution was either disregarded, or not properly appreciated by both the doctors and the social workers.

In the case of the doctors, we conclude that it was disregarded, not wilfully but unthinkingly. Dr. Warner was present at both Case Conferences and made no response, directly or indirectly to Miss Knowles' invaluable information. That, in itself, would be excusable, if (as we think was the case) he was concentrating on the physical injuries to the two children. But he is a paediatrician and not an orthopaedic specialist, and should have been alerted to the implications for Jasmine's developmental health, as well as to the immediate fact of child abuse. After all the Case Conference was called to consider what future action would need to be taken beyond the obtaining of the Care Orders. Faced with that knowledge on 6 August 1981 Dr. Warner should instinctively have responded by requesting the compilation of a percentile chart on Jasmine, a matter that could so easily have been provided on the basis of the chart already in existence and prepared by Miss Knowles, and other documentary material then available to the health authorities and from which we have been able to construct the chart, in diagrammatic form referred to in Chapter 7. We hesitate to conclude that the reason for such disregard of Miss Knowles' information was the inferior status accorded to health visitors by a doctor. But we cannot help feeling that throughout our Inquiry the worth and status of health visitors are not always given the credit that they deserve. In Dr. Warner's case we conclude that he was not dismissive of Miss Knowles but that he simply was not asked to comment on what she had said. We think nevertheless he ought to have initiated a discussion about the children's development. Like social workers who forget their primary task of child protection as opposed to social work with parents, doctors are apt to see their function in strictly medical terms instead of utilising their medical skills in the wider context of social policy and practice that demands a broader focus of child protection. Where physicians are trained in a psycho-social context, medical people are more likely to perceive themselves as co-equals and colleagues of nurses, health visitors, social workers and occupational therapists, rather than being top-dogs in a professional hierarchy, or as head of a team. In traditional medical schools physicians are trained to be in charge. Emphasis tends to be placed on being in charge, taking decisions, hearing and even listening to other professional views, but still taking decisions based upon their own best medical judgment. This function is substantially different from arriving at a consensus view on a model of inter-disciplinary team-work. It is an aspect of enquiry that calls for attention by those working in social medicine and by those responsible for community health.

In the absence of any appropriate response from the doctors to a health visitor's contribution to a child abuse case, the social workers may be forgiven for failure to appreciate the significance of Miss Knowles' information. Mr. Bishop considered the suggestion, that he paid insufficient attention to what Miss Knowles had been saying, by interpreting it merely as a description of the Beckford family not substantially different from what he regularly heard about families which came within the purview of social services in Area 6. We accept that this was how Mr. Bishop interpreted Miss Knowles' information, particularly so because she was saying it in the context of sympathetic understanding of the family's housing and social problems. He now appreciates that the combination of a physically abused child's abnormally low weight, understimulation and the general lack of competent parenting are the indicia of predictive child abuse. His failure to appreciate that at the time is no more than a commentary on the absence of knowledge about child abuse generally among social workers. The yawning gap in that knowledge should now be filled by the publicity given to this case during the public hearings and, we trust, by the publication of our report.

Battered parents
The other background information about the Beckford family came from Mr. Raymond Jenkins of the NSPCC. From his files he was able to run through the cases that had come to the notice of his organisation. As a result he was able to alert Miss Knibbs and, later, the Case Conference to the severe maltreatment Morris Beckford received at the hands of his parents in 1972, to which we have alluded in the thumbnail sketch in Chapter 4. He clearly regarded the fact that a battering parent had been battered as a child as highly significant, and to be a very important consideration when taking decisions about the future of the children, particularly when deciding to return them to their parents. Here again, little if any attention was paid to an important feature of child abuse. While Mr. Jenkins did not criticise the fact that he was not invited to the re-convened Case Conference – he might have been listened to more attentively had he possessed the opportunity of underlining the childhood experience of both Morris Beckford and Beverley Lorrington – he did expect to be invited to any Case Conference where the reuniting of the children with their parents or their removal from the child abuse register was being contemplated. Area 6 did not invite Mr. Jenkins to either the Case Conference of 5 April 1982 or 9 November 1982. In that respect there was an omission of no little significance. In those parts of the country where the NSPCC has set up special units for dealing with child abuse we think that NSPCC officers working in these units should as a matter of good practice be invited to, and if possible attend Case Conferences. It may be that in the areas there are NSPCC officers whose contribution would be valuable.

The missing information
To pick up the narrative, we look at the activity in preparation for the Case Conference on 20 August. The provision of a foster-home was an urgent consideration – and it got it. On 10 August the application to the Adoption and Foster Care Section was made. To the question, for how long is the placement for a foster-home needed, the answer was "probably long term", thus negativing a short term placement but giving no hint of a placement envisaging adoption. On 12 August Mr. and Mrs. Probert filled in an application form for "acceptance as Foster/Adoptive Parents". While they indicated

that in 1962 and 1967 they had successfully applied to adopt, they merely indicated that their reason for applying to Brent was that "we would like to give some children a chance to enjoy a normal family life." They assented to any child placed with them being under supervision of the local authority. On 12 August Ms. Wahlstrom had a discussion with the Adoption and Foster-Care Section which recorded that the children would need long-term care, "quite possibly adoption, but decisions cannot be made until more information is available." At that stage adoption was a remote option; the immediate view was simply long-term fostering.

Ms. Wahlstrom was busy monitoring the parental visits to St. Charles' Hospital and seeing Beverley Lorrington at home. She either visited or telephoned the hospital on six occasions: 11, 12, 13, twice on 14, and 17 August (before that day's hearing at court for the interim Care Order). She visited the Beckford home on 10 August (when she talked to both parents) and on 14 August to hand Beverley Lorrington the court summons. She was contacted on 11 August by the solicitors, Alexander and Partners, informing her that the parents had been interviewed by the police, and agreed to make contact at court on 17 August. She spoke to Mr. Hobbs, the Deputy Court Officer, on 13 August, following which Mrs. Dietmann sensibly asked the Principal Court Officer, Mr. Thompson, to try and arrange "unbiased representation for the children". Mr. Thompson promised to talk to the Justices' Clerk. Alexander & Partners were about that time given a legal aid certificate for the children's separate representation. A note made by Mr. Thompson at that time of a conversation with Ms. Wahlstrom does not indicate any further inquiries by Social Services or Health Services about the nature of the children's injuries, or information about the social and medical history of the Beckford family. Indeed, his note gives a distinct hint that the two social workers were even at that early stage contemplating the option of a reuniting of the family. Mr. Thompson's undated note ambiguously records: "Does term of placement or disposal rest with you. Decision. Rehabilitation when." On 18 and 19 August, Ms. Wahlstrom was meeting with the personnel of the Adoption and Foster Care Section about finding a suitable foster-home. A family in Harlesden was mentioned, but was found inappropriate at the Case Conference on 20 August. In the short amount of time, a fortnight, between the two Case Conferences, no attention was paid to finding out more about the nature and extent of child abuse. We have mentioned already the obtaining of further radiological examination of the x-rays, the evidence from Miss Knowles of the failure to thrive, and the NSPCC information about the battering of the Beckford parents as children. We point to two other gaps in the knowledge of Social Services that could, and should have been instantly filled.

Jasmine's parentage
From the moment of the involvement of social services with the Beckford family it had been assumed that Morris Beckford was the natural father of Jasmine as well as of Louise. To be fair, Beverley Lorrington never told anyone after August 1981 that Morris was not the father, until she told the hospital staff at St. Mary's on 5 July 1984 as she carried the dead child in her arms, a fact picked up by Miss Alix Causby in her *guardian ad litem's* report in September 1984 in the court proceedings relating to Louise and Chantelle Beckford. Miss Causby told us that a step-parent has a higher statistical average of battering his or her step-child. In the case of the Beckford children, all three had been abused, but Jasmine as the one step-child was probably singled out for more severe and more frequent abuse. Miss Causby added that it was extremely important when a social worker is beginning to work with a family to go through in very fine detail their history and relationships.

Beverley Lorrington told us — and we believe her — that all her family knew that

Morris was not the father, but neither her limited circle of friends and acquaintances (with one exception) nor any social workers had been told by her that Jasmine was not Morris's daughter. Beverley's step-mother told us that she and the family always knew of Jasmine's true parentage, and her step-sister, Carol Lorrington, echoed her mother's statement and confirmed the one exception among Beverley's friends. The two witnesses from Morris Beckford's place of work, Mr. Bennett and Mrs. Goban, had, on the other hand, no thought other than that Jasmine was Morris's child. Likewise, the staff at Princess Frederica Primary School were told that Jasmine's surname was Beckford, and assumed accordingly that Morris was her father.

Ms. Wahlstrom always believed Morris to be Jasmine's father, because he had registered himself as her father at birth. Ms. Wahlstrom had herself, at the end of August 1981, filled in a form applying for a copy of a certificate of birth in which she named Morris as the father. Morris Beckford had never said anything to indicate the contrary; and Jasmine and Louise had always looked like sisters to Ms. Wahlstrom. We have concluded that this is yet another example of Ms. Wahlstrom's inability at that time to adopt a healthy scepticism towards any information emanating from the Beckford parents. It was that inability by a trained social worker to be on guard against deception by a parent who had seriously abused his two children (and declined to acknowledge his responsibility) that in part led her to being fobbed off with implausible excuses on almost every occasion of her visiting the house, about the whereabouts of Jasmine from September 1983 until July 1984, and which led the Common Serjeant at the Old Bailey trial in March 1985 to say, with ample justification, that her behaviour in that respect was "naive almost beyond belief."

The evidence about the true paternity of Jasmine was present for anyone to glean with an inclination to uncover it, particularly for the purpose of a full assessment of the family. Neither Ms. Wahlstrom nor, perhaps more significantly, her supervisor, Mrs. Dietmann, had the wit to follow up two separate avenues of inquiry. The first line of inquiry would have been to the extended family of the Lorringtons. They all knew the truth, and we do not doubt that if they had been asked the one simple question they would have given a simple, truthful answer. But they never appeared to have been seen by social workers from Brent. There was knowledge that the Lorringtons lived in Greenford, because from time to time Beverley mentioned going there. The lack of any approach by Social Services, over three years of contact with the Beckfords, to their extended family is tellingly illustrated by an incident on the last day of an evolving tragedy. On 5 July 1984 – the day Jasmine died – Ms. Wahlstrom, for the first time with Mrs. Dietmann, was frantically searching for the Beckfords in circumstances we describe in great detail at the end of Chapter 10. Having failed to trace the family at home, Mrs. Dietmann had the bright idea of ringing the home of the Lorrington grandparents in Greenford. For that purpose it was found necessary to consult a telephone directory to discover the telephone number, 998 7605, as is recorded in Ms. Wahlstrom's entry for that day in her Social Worker's Report. It says everything about the importance which these two social workers attached to the place of an extended family in a child abuse case that they had never before felt any reason to contact them or to have ready to hand their address or telephone number for purposes of contact, even though Ms. Wahlstrom had been told by Morris Beckford that Beverley and the children were actually staying with the maternal grandparents. We say no more than that it is incredible how neglectful these two workers could have been of information relating to child protection, even if they had correctly ruled out any question of a placement with grandparents, or uncles and aunts.

The second route to the knowledge of Jasmine's true paternity was no less obvious and direct, and more likely to produce a ready and verified answer. Ms. Wahlstrom, in re-examination, for the first time said that she thought she had acquired the information about Jasmine's parentage from conversation with Miss Knibbs and "from the conversations with the Health Visitor", meaning no doubt Miss Knowles. Although this evidence has all the marks of an afterthought, we accept that Ms. Wahlstrom did talk to those two persons about Morris Beckford's parenthood, but we think that it was a piece of knowledge acquired less by an inquiring mind than one that was receiving unsolicited information. Had Ms. Wahlstrom been interested in verifying the fact of Jasmine's paternity, she would, and could so easily have gone to the health visitor or midwife who attended Beverley Lorrington in December 1979 at Jasmine's birth.

A simple search of the health records at the time of Jasmine's birth would have revealed what was disclosed to us. A document headed "Brent and Harrow Area Authority: Brent Health District: *First Visit Record*" shows that on 13 December 1979 Miss Gillian Hindle, the Health Visitor who preceded Miss Knowles, saw the mother and child at home. Her record showed that she entered the name of Lorrington, later crossed out and replaced by the name of Beckford. Either at that visit or a subsequent one, Miss Hindle recalls being told that the man Beverley was then living with was not the father of the child. Miss Hindle probed the matter, and was told that Jasmine's father was somebody with whom Beverley Lorrington had no further contact. Miss Hindle did not record the fact that Morris Beckford was not the father, because Beverley Lorrington did not wish it to be public knowledge. Confidentiality demanded that a veil of secrecy should be drawn over it. But, if a colleague or a social worker had sought the information in the context of a child abuse investigation, Miss Hindle would unhesitatingly have divulged the information. Likewise, if the Area Health Authority's Notification of Birth form, filled in and signed by the midwife, Miss Ratnam, on 2 December 1979, had been consulted, Ms. Wahlstrom would have seen, not one but three important pieces of information. The baby girl's name was filled in as Lorrington; the form indicated that Beverley had had two previous abortions (a fact never picked up in the whole course of Social Services involvement); and, to suggest doubt about paternity, it had been noted that this was a "one-parent family." It would have been the simplest of tasks for Ms. Wahlstrom to go to Mortimer Road Clinic and consult the health visitors. From them she would have been able to verify the fact from Miss Hindle or Miss Ratnam that Morris was not the father of Jasmine. That fact was never retrieved from the records, and hence was not available to the Case Conference on 20 August. It should have been.

We would add only this one comment. Ms. Wahlstrom's failure to consult health visitors at the local clinic may be another reflection of the lack of collaboration between social and health services, a topic to which we shall have occasion to return. Even if collaboration on a personal level is, for one reason or another, absent, there should never be any disinclination on the part of one service, in circumstances of a child abuse case, to allow an allied service access to its documentation. We do not suggest that Brent Health Authority did, or would deny access. It was just the fact that access was never sought.

Psychopathology of child abuse
Even before the Case Conference of 6 August took place, some significant information about the Beckford parents had been discovered. Morris Beckford had undergone an horrendous experience as a cruelly beaten child at the hands of both parents. Beverley Lorrington too had described an unhappy childhood, running away from home after school-leaving age. There was also the bald statement that both Morris and Beverley had attended a special school for ESN children, run by Brent Education Authority. Yet none of these pointers to a cycle of deprivation, predictive of child abuse, was ever followed up.

When Mr. Pollard started acting in mid-August as the legal representative for the children, he approached Dr. Levick for a second radiological opinion on the children's bone injuries, a matter to which we have already alluded as being within the province of the hospital authorities. But he also sought the assistance of an independent social worker, Miss Joan Court. It was she, as a person of national renown in child abuse, who suggested that a psychiatric assessment on the Beckford parents ought to be obtained; and to that end Mr. Pollard had arranged for them to be interviewed by a consultant psychiatrist at the Institute of Child Health, at Great Ormond Street hospital. That appointment was ultimately fixed for the end of September, after the court proceedings were in fact concluded, and so became ineffective. But there was no reason why the social workers in Area 6, who should have been thinking along similar lines to Miss Court, did not themselves arrange such an appointment at any time, before or after the care proceedings. More important than perhaps obtaining a report for the initial Case Conferences, it was vital to obtain some psychiatric profile of the Beckford parents as soon as it was ever contemplated returning the children to the Beckford home.

Professor Greenland told us that a psychiatric assessment of parents who had abused their children was helpful both for establishing the psychopathology of past abuse – a thorough analysis of how and why the injuries were caused – and for the purpose of judging how far they would be able to cope with children in the future. He qualified his answer only by saying that the assessor would have to be someone experienced in forensic work; it could not be assumed that all psychiatrists, or psychologists, had sufficient knowledge of child abuse. A psychiatrist inexperienced in child abuse would not be very valuable. When we put this point to Mr. Bishop, he was hostile to the idea, doubtless induced by his contact with psychiatry during his earlier career in mental health. Mr. Bishop was unpersuaded of the value of psychiatric assessment, either at the time or even in 1985 when faced with expert opinion to the contrary.

We agree that any value to be derived from a psychiatric assessment will depend upon the quality of the psychiatrist. But to have available on your doorstep a consultant psychiatrist working in one of the most famous children's hospitals in the world and not to seek that advice and opinion is to deny assistance of an important kind. Dr. Taitz believes that within his children's hospital in Sheffield there were psychiatrists and psychologists who had, working alongside himself, considerable experience in child abuse. If, moreover, Miss Court thought it was valuable, so should Area 6, Brent Social Services. We do not suggest that in every case of child abuse, the battering parents should be hauled off to the psychoanalyst's couch or the psychiatrist's consulting room. But we do say that in some cases where (as here) there had been a pattern of battering on two small children in the same family by two parents who themselves had had unhappy childhood experiences, everything pointed to doing what a mere solicitor had thought sensible to do. We cannot excuse the Social Services from their failure to have the Beckfords psychologically assessed. At the very least the Beckfords should have been told in April 1982 that before they could have their children back it would be necessary for them to be seen by a psychiatrist selected by Social Services. That requirement should have been made a part of a protection plan in reuniting the family, an aspect of the placement of children "home on trial" to which we refer in Chapter 10.

As long ago as the landmark article of 1962 by Dr. Kempe and his American colleagues, *The Battered Child Syndrome*, it was noted that although the knowledge of the psychiatric factors in child abuse was limited, they were probably of prime importance in "the pathogenesis of the disorder." The authors thought that parents who inflict abuse on their children do not necessarily have psychopathic or socio-pathic personalities or come from some borderline socio-economic groups, although most publicised cases have fallen into one of those categories. But they averred that in most cases some defect in character structure was probably present: "Often parents may be repeating the type of child care practised on them in their childhood''. We observe that when Dr. Jolly compiled his report in December 1984 on Louise and Chantelle Beckford he reported the foster-mother as saying that Louise got on well with her baby sister, but that when Chantelle cried Louise "would hit her, put her fingers in her eyes and tell her foster-mother to hit and kick her''. As one member of the Denver programme under Dr. Kempe observed in 1976, child abuse is "an infectious disease whose carrier is the parent and whose victim is the child'' (Child Protection Report 1976).

Discussion, Conclusion and Decision

The structure of Case Conferences in Brent (and we assume elsewhere) are uniformly divided into three sections: a general discussion about the present situation; conclusions; and decisions. The discussion at the meeting of 20 August 1981 on the present situation did little more than update the information revealed a fortnight earlier. It ended up with Miss Carol Rogers from the Adoption and Foster-Care Section stating that both children could be fostered [long-term] in Harlesden almost immediately [moving on to adoption in due course].'' The words in square brackets were tippexed out by Mr. David Bishop when he received the minutes prepared by Miss Knibbs' secretary. In Chapter 22 on documentation we comment on the practice, not uncommon we understand, of chairmen of case conferences deleting or amending parts of the minutes. Even if Miss Rogers said (as we find she did say) what was originally recorded by the minute-taker, it did no more than indicate what her section could at that time provide. It did not reflect any kind of decision to provide a permanent residence for the Beckford children. Adoption was naturally mentioned in the course of the meeting, but it was no more than a passing remark about the possible outcome for the Beckford sisters. The conclusions of the Case Conference were that Louise, followed by Jasmine, would be discharged from hospital into a foster-home − not the Harlesden foster-home − on a "long-term basis''. The section on decisions was meagre and did not relate to any plans for the children at all. It stated that Ms. Wahlstrom would acquaint the parents with "decisions of today's meeting'', whatever that could conceivably involve beyond indicating that the children would not be going home straight from hospital. It directed Area 6 to organise future Case Conferences of a smaller number of persons attending, limited to those that it was in fact necessary should attend. And it alluded to future orthopaedic surveillance of the two children. The meeting was deliberately indecisive about the placement, beyond the immediate future, because no one imagined that it could at that stage be otherwise. Again, nobody could have come away from that meeting with the idea that the case was being pointed in any particular direction. All options were left wide open.

Brent's Policy Memorandum states that the Case Conference should have as one of its objectives "agreement on the foundation and broad outline of the 'long-term' treatment plan (where appropriate).'' Clearly the Case Conference of 20 August thought it inappropriate to agree on the long-term treatment plan. And rightly so. At that stage it was quite impossible to take anything other than the most tentative steps towards securing the future welfare of two seriously abused children. BASW's report, *Child Abuse Policy*, a draft of which has been supplied to us, and its contents expounded by the chairman of the Project Group, Mr. Alan Bedford, which prepared it, expresses the view that Case Conferences should not make *decisions* (apart from deciding that the child should go on or off the child abuse register and to nominate the key worker) since it has no power greater than that of its constituent agencies. Case Conferences should merely make *recommendations* to the constituent agencies. It is they who must decide whether to invoke the legal process to protect children and how to execute any legal powers they may possess. We agree with BASW that the true function of the Case Con-

88

ference is advisory and not executive. But we would go further in restructuring the Case Conference (a topic to which we shall return below and in Chapter 25).

If (as we shall be recommending in Chapter 27) the Place of Safety Order is to be treated as an emergency procedure for only a very limited time – say, no more than 72 hours – it will be necessary for the local authority Social Services (or other initiating agency, such as the NSPCC) to decide immediately without the assistance of other agencies, whether to take care proceedings and to apply for the interim Care Order on the lapsing of the Place of Safety Order. The value of the Case Conference is in advising the local authority as to its proper attitude to the hearing of the full care proceedings. The two Case Conferences of 6 and 20 August in this case would have been just as effective for that purpose if they had been a single meeting after the interim Order of 17 August. The then Director of Social Services, Mr. Whalley, before us said that looking at the documentation now - he had not been provided with copies at the time – he regarded them as one meeting split into two. The prime importance of the Case Conference before the hearing of the care proceedings is that it will assist those representing the local authority at court to know what tentative proposals are being made in the eventuality of the court making either a Care Order, a Supervision Order (with or without conditions) or refusing to make any Order. Mr. Bishop acknowledged that it was important for the Case Conference to make a positive statement about the case which the local authority's legal representative could present, if necessary, to the court. **We recommend that the second Case Conference should take place only as and when the Magistrates' Court has conferred legal powers on the local authority.** Nowadays it is common for parents to be legally represented in the Care proceedings, for a *guardian ad litem* to be appointed to provide separate representation for the children, and for the hearings to be a good deal more thorough than they were a decade ago. This case occupied Willesden Magistrates' Court the whole of an extended morning. Given this much more significant, lawyerly ingredient in the process of child care, the essential function of the Case Conference is to take on board all the material adduced before the juvenile magistrates and, together with the information supplied from extra-forensic sources, to indicate the direction that the constituent agencies – in particular, the agency in whom the execution of a Care Order is legally vested – should go.

The Beckford case exemplifies the point we are making. After 20 August 1981 no Case Conference took place for eight months until 5 April 1982 when the decision was taken to return the Beckford children to their parents on a home on trial. We shall have a good deal hereafter to say about the conduct and result of that Case Conference. Suffice it to say here, there was no one present at that meeting who was from any agency other than Brent Social Services. Had that Case Conference, composed of those who collectively attended the two meetings of 6 and 20 August, been convened and met in the Autumn of 1981, after the making of the Care Orders, to consider the situation in the light of the court proceedings, it would have been in a sound position to perform its real function of steering the local authority, armed with its legal powers and with the children by then discharged from hospital into a foster home, towards a soundly-based, rational programme of social work action, suitably supported by health and education services. Such a conference would have had the opportunity of considering the valuable report of Miss Joan Court, an *independent* social worker's view, and it would have had Dr. Levick's radiologist's report that negatived any possible suggestion that Jasmine was not the subject of non-accidental injury. We will deal with the fate of Dr. Levick's report at and after the court hearing. (It was not seen by anybody on the Staff of Area 6 until our Inquiry began). But had a Case Conference taken place in the autumn of 1981 (immediately after the Care proceedings), we would have expected the whole file in the Social Services Department's Court Section to have been taken out, and a copy of Dr. Levick's unsigned report to have been uncovered from the place where we found it three and a half years later. Even more significant would have been the attendance of Dr. Warner with his forensic experience of having expounded to the Magistrates the substance of Dr. Levick's report. Such a Case Conference would have been in an incomparably better position to pronounce upon any question of the future placement of the children. It would also have been able to discuss both the propriety and the effect of the Magistrates' Order and the rider to their decision supposedly endorsing the hope that the children would be reunited with their parents. Miss Court expressed to us the view that the Case Conference should have been reconvened to consider what the Magistrates had said. She also told us that she was horrified at their remarks. Given the amplified material and any other information that should, as we have indicated, been additionally provided, we are confident in concluding that such a Case Conference would have recommended – and rightly so – against any attempt to reunite the Beckford family in the near future, and that Area 6 would have endorsed that view.

Why do we think that, contrary to what happened, the Beckford children should, and would never have been returned to their parents? Two main reasons prompt the answer. One is that the preponderant view at the Case Conference in support of removal to a foster home, but little prospect of a reuniting of the family, would have won the day. And, second, we think that the impact of the Magistrates' rider to their decision would have been reduced in significance, if not wholly negatived, by the Case Conference's proper appreciation of the total situation, in which re-uniting the family was out of the question for at least the near future. (We include the text of Mr. Thompson's memorandum of 16 September 1981 to Mr. Bishop, setting out the remarks of the Magistrates, at Appendix C:3). Properly informed and sensibly advised, Area 6 would have concluded that returning the children would be, as Dr. Taitz described the case to us, "bonding with barbed wire."

Disparate pessimisms
All those at the Case Conference, with the exception of Miss Knowles and the two social workers, Mrs. Dietmann and Ms. Wahlstrom, were gloomy about the prospect of the children going home. Dr. Warner reflected a generally held view among social work practitioners that if there was to be any rehabilitation, it had to take place at once. A policy of drift was at all costs to be avoided. Because of the severity of the injuries and their eventual discharge from hospital to a foster home, he did not envisage the children ever going back to their parents. The police officers present took a similarly hawkish view, that it would not be in the interests of the children to be brought up by their parents. If they came near to ruling out rehabilitation as a possible option, few of the others were much more sanguine about the prospect. Miss Knibbs, Miss Rogers, Miss Tyler and Mr. Hobbs all said that the question of rehabilitation would need to be looked at, but they were not optimistic about its likelihood. Miss Knowles, who knew the Beckfords and showed evident sympathy with them hoped, that there might be a home on trial, but it would have to be backed by massive casework with the family. She was not alone in her expressed sadness at the personal plight of the Beckfords. Dr. Warner, too, was sorry for the parents, but he commented that "bad parents produce bad parents", and he saw the chances of rehabilitation being effective as relatively low "without an enormous amount of effort" on the part of Social Services. Such prospects as there were for a successful reuniting of the family came from the social workers, imbued no doubt with their background training and perception of public opinion that strongly supported retaining natural parents' rights and reflecting the bond of the blood tie. Mrs. Dietmann averred before us that she, Mr. Bishop and Ms. Wahlstrom shared a like pessimism in thinking that rehabilitation would probably not work. Both her colleagues before us

frequently referred to their pessimism. But we conclude that while Mrs. Dietmann and Ms. Wahlstrom were of one mind, Mr. Bishop's pessimism was of a wholly different order.

Mr. Bishop's pessimism was directed solely to the question of embarking on a home on trial. He told us: "I did not think that it was likely that the children would ever be returned to their parents." Mrs. Dietmann's and Ms. Wahlstrom's pessimism, on the other hand, was about the likelihood of success of a rehabilitation programme. They were committed, we think, at least to trying it. And we are convinced that they held that view at, or shortly after the care proceedings on 9 September 1981. On 21 September 1981, Ms. Wahlstrom composed a memorandum addressed to the Director of Housing from the Director of Social Services, asking for urgent consideration to be given to providing suitable accommodation "for a family with two young children." The letter went on to say that it was stressed at the hearing before the Magistrates "by counsel* and the Bench that all efforts should be made to return the children to the care of the parents as soon as possible. Our Department has *implemented* [emphasis supplied] a concentrated treatment plan involving social work, family aide and developmental worker support, to work towards reuniting this family. Unfortunately the family and some who have been involved with them, feel that the housing situation was a major contributing factor to family breakdown and a stumbling block to effective rehabilitation. Therefore, I hope that your Department can work in conjunction with our efforts with this family and that they can be rehoused on a priority basis."

Stripped of the hyperbole of language in which the memorandum was couched, appropriate to arouse the maximum response from the Housing Department, the letter nevertheless disclosed an absolute commitment on the part of Ms. Wahlstrom – and, we think, Mrs. Dietmann – to return the children to their parents as soon as the Beckfords were re-housed in suitable accommodation. It was a commitment that was not of recent origin; it had been there in their minds since they became involved with the case. Mr. Bishop associated himself with the memorandum in that he put his initialled signature to it. His interpretation before us of the memorandum was that it would have been daft not to have dealt with the appalling housing situation of the Beckfords if the children were ever to be returned to their parents. It was sensible to get the housing department geared up to providing the housing, and in any event they could always have put the process into reverse. But whatever else might be said, it did not "imply that we had made a decision; by no means was that the case."

We accept that no decision to reunite the family had been taken. Only the Case Conference which took place on 5 April 1982 did that. But we do think that the two workers were pointing themselves firmly, if not decisively, in that direction. To the extent that Mr. Bishop was being led along the same route as his two social workers, we are convinced that his willingness to consider rehabilitation – even as a viable proposition – was of very recent origin. We do not think he contemplated any return of the children to their parents until 16 September. It was on that day that Mr. Thompson, the Court Officer, had reported to Mr. Bishop by memorandum the remarks of the Magistrates, and subsequently discussed the matter with him. Faced with the intervention of the Magistrates with their rider to the Care Orders, Mr. Bishop, with unfeigned reluctance, acceded to the blandishments of his two social workers that they should engage upon the task of the intensive and extensive process of rehabilitating the Beckford family. It is in that sense that we understand Mr. Bishop's acceptance of the memorandum to

---

* Ms. Wahlstrom interpreted that as meaning the legal representative for both the parents and the children

the Director of Housing, and not to his, frankly, strained interpretation of what it actually meant. Mr. Bishop's interpretation is inconsistent with the phrase, "our department has *implemented* [emphasis supplied] a concentrated treatment plan ... to work towards reuniting the family."

Preparing for Court
Three lines of activity preceded the hearing before the Willesden Magistrates on 9 September 1981. Ms. Wahlstrom was in regular contact with the Beckfords to arrange meetings with them and to effect access to Louise following her discharge from hospital on 26 August. There was no hint in Ms. Wahlstrom's activities that she was probing further the capacity of the Beckfords to parent the children. Since access was being arranged, the assumption was that the disrupted bonding during hospitalisation should be resecured instantly. On 26 August 1981 Mr. and Mrs. Probert signed the statutory form of undertaking required by foster-parents. We shall comment later on the inappropriateness of some of the undertakings, in particular the one that says that the foster-parents will bring up the child "as I would a child of my own". The following day Ms. Wahlstrom noted the provisional approval of the Proberts as foster-parents for both Louise and Jasmine, and sought Mr. Bishop's authority to pay the Proberts double boarding-out rate for Jasmine, since she would require extra amounts of care and stimulation for this very "understimulated" child. The approval of the foster-parents was to be for a period of eight weeks pending the general approval. Ms. Wahlstrom expressed her belief in the suitability of the foster-parents – she had met them on 24 August with Mr. Jeremy Burns who was due to complete his assessment of them by 19 October. The only investigative activity of the Beckford parents was the receipt from St. Charles' Hospital of a monitoring of parental visits to the children. The record disclosed unimpressive parental concern,and should have added to the pessimism about reuniting the family. Between the time of the second Case Conference and 6 September Jasmine was not visited on six out of 18 days, four of them after Louise had left hospital for the foster-home. No explanation was sought from the Beckfords as to why they had not maintained daily contact, let alone why Beverley had not been living at the hospital. One of the decisions at the Case Conference of 6 August had been that Ms. Wahlstrom and Sister Ritchie should encourage Beverley to live in hospital with the children so that her relationship with them could be assessed. Ms. Wahlstrom did not appear to follow up that decision to the full.

This failure to investigate was compounded by an apparent absence to talk to Miss Joan Court or Sister Ritchie about an occasion when the former visited the hospital. Jasmine was playing on the floor with Sister Ritchie, "having a whale of a time." The parents arrived to put her to bed. This they did competently, but Miss Court noticed how Jasmine became watchful and completely quiet, in a state of "frozen watchfulness" of her mother. Miss Court was so struck by this incident that she recorded it in her court report. She told us that it at least indicated the need for a thorough assessment (including a psychiatric assessment) at one of the units specialising in child psychiatry before any decision was made to return Jasmine to her parents. Miss Court was more worried about Beverley Lorrington than about Morris Beckford. She recognised that Beverley had parent-craft, i.e., changing nappies, washing the child and so forth. But she lacked parent-skill; interaction between parent and child was palpably lacking. This again was an index of child abuse, in this case possibly at the hands of the mother. It too failed to strike any chord in those involved in protecting Jasmine. We would simply observe that if it is thought sensible – as indeed it was – to observe the mother with her children 24 hours a day in hospital, the parent living at the hospital should have been made a precondition to the parents ultimately having their children returned to them. In short, it should be made contractual, and not left, at best, to gentle persuasion.

The day after Louise had arrived at the Proberts, and they had signed the normal undertaking, Miss Joan Court, having been asked by Mr. Pollard to prepare an independent social worker's report on 24 August, went to the offices of Area 6. She met Mrs. Dietmann, Ms. Wahlstrom and Mr. Thompson. She was not permitted to talk with Ms. Wahlstrom on her own, an unprecedented experience and never repeated in her experience as an independent social worker. Nor was she permitted access to the files of the Social Services Department, although she was given a copy of the Case Conference minutes and, later, Ms. Wahlstrom's report to the court. Miss Court asked if she might visit Louise and Mrs. Probert before the court hearing, but was told by Mr. Thompson that this was not possible.

The coming onto the child care scene of the independent social worker in the early 1980s not unnaturally caused Social Services Departments some initial problems. Were they bound to give free access to confidential records and information generally held within their departments? The policy at Brent, along with other Social Services Departments, was that as a general rule access should be denied. Mr. Whalley, who was then Director of Social Services, had laid down such a policy in oral direction to his Assistant Directors, but it was not a blanket prohibition and could be departed from on authority from him or an Assistant Director. He was not consulted at the time. Knowing of Miss Court's high standing in the field of child abuse, he would have given authority to reveal to her any information she needed. The policy became obsolete with the introduction of the *guardian ad litem* system after May 1984. We do not, therefore, need to make any recommendation about the confidentiality of information in the future. But we find it necessary to consider the impact of the policy as it applied in August/September 1981.

Area 6 personnel referred the question to Mr. Thompson who discussed the question at a Principal Officers' meeting chaired by the Assistant Director who was Mr. Simpson's predecessor in post. We have not thought it necessary to call him. It appears that there was a misunderstanding at that time about the extent of the policy. Contrary to what Mr. Whalley indicated to us, Mr. Thompson seemed to think that the policy was inflexible. He, moreover, did not know of Miss Court or her outstanding reputation, and hence did not contemplate the possibility of any variation in applying the policy. We do not blame him for that. But it is surprising that no one in Area 6 realised that Miss Court's request might provide an exception to any hard-and-fast rule. The failure to appreciate her standing in the field of child abuse reinforces our general conclusion of how meagre was the knowledge of anyone in Area 6 about the problems of handling a child abuse case. Had there been in post a child-abuse coordinator, with the required specialisation in that area of social work, the problem would have been readily solved. Again, the approach might have been different had a solicitor from the Law and Administration Department been consulted. The extent of confidentiality might have been canvassed and the problem resolved in favour of giving Miss Court the access she sought and was entitled to expect. Whatever else may be said about an unhappy episode as between co-professionals, the inability of Miss Court to see the files, to talk uninhibitedly with Ms. Wahlstrom, and to visit Mrs. Probert and see Louise in the foster-home seriously detracted from the value of her report. We were somewhat perturbed by both Mrs. Dietmann and Ms. Wahlstrom (who saw the report at court on 9 September) telling us that they did not think very highly of Miss Court's report, when they themselves were in part responsible for its depreciation. We were surprised to hear from Mr. Bishop that he too was unimpressed with Miss Court's report when he saw it sometime after the court proceedings. The social workers' disparagement of her report, rendered defective as it was by inaccessibility to valuable information, does not lie in their mouths. Miss Court, as we shall demonstrate, was pointing cautiously to the possibility of rehabilitation, which is exactly what we find was the attitude, with somewhat less cautiousness, of the two social workers. The fact that they took little or no notice of what Miss Court was saying only goes to show how perfunctory was the subsequent assessment made by Area 6 of the prospects of reuniting the family, and how committed Mrs. Dietmann and Ms. Wahlstrom were to returning the children home, as soon as they had solved the crucial problem of adequate housing. We do not find their attitude to Miss Court and her independent social worker's report as indicating an appropriate professional approach. Unlike Miss Court, who kept child protection very much as the focus of her report, the two social workers were already directing their thoughts, and preparatory work on the Beckford parents, to the virtual exclusion of protection of two seriously abused children.

The Court report

It is convenient at this stage to state our conclusions on Miss Court's report (reproduced in full at Appendix C:2) and to indicate what (if any) impact it had on the Magistrates. Her report was dated 8 September, the day before the court hearing, when she had a telephone conversation with Mr. Pollard. He discussed with her the import of Dr. Levick's radiological opinion on the children's injuries. We digress here to note the fate of Dr. Levick's report (reproduced in Appendix C:1) since much turns on it, both at the Magistrates' Court and subsequently, in the sense that it disappeared from human sight until April 1985.

On Friday, 4 September Dr. Levick telephoned to Mr. Pollard and dictated his report, which was then transcribed in the solicitor's office, the unsigned report being the one used thereafter at court and which found its way into the files of Brent Social Services Department. Mr. Pollard talked to Miss Court that day about the report, but in insufficient detail for her to take it on board in writing her report. The details of the report were communicated to her only during the subsequent telephone conversation on 8 September. Mr. Pollard sent the transcription of the dictated report back to Dr. Levick that day, but sent copies to no-one else. Dr. Levick responded by sending the signed report, with some textual amendments, under cover of a letter dated 7 September (Monday). Whatever happened to the signed report – whether it reached Mr. Pollard on or after Tuesday 8 September, we have been unable to discover – it was never put into circulation. Dr. Levick produced to us a carbon copy of his letter of 7 September with a photocopy of his signed report, undated. The immediate onset of an expeditious court hearing may have been responsible for a good deal of confusion about Dr. Levick's report at court on Wednesday, 9 September.

Mr. Pollard did telephone Mr. Thompson, the Court Officer of Brent Social Services on 8 September. It is not at all clear who was asking whom, whether Dr. Warner could see Dr. Levick's report. Presumably, since Dr. Warner was a witness called by Brent Social Services and Dr. Levick's report was initiated by those representing the children, Mr. Pollard was either giving notice of it in advance to Mr. Thompson, or Mr. Thompson was insisting that Dr. Warner should see it before he gave evidence. It matters not to resolve this conundrum. Suffice it to say, it is clear from the notes taken by counsel and by the justices' clerk that Dr. Warner had at his elbow a copy of the unsigned report and referred throughout his evidence in both examination-in-chief and in cross-examination to its contents. Anybody listening to the evidence could not have failed to appreciate Dr. Levick's findings of multiple injuries to both children on separate occasions, thereby confirming Louise's injuries as non-accidental and finally dispelling any remaining doubt about Jasmine also having undergone a non-accidental injury. The

Magistrates have informed us, by written answer, that they "cannot recollect what understanding they reached as to Dr. Levick's report." This somewhat startling statement is explicable because, as we find, they were not supplied with copies of the report. Why that was so, we fail to understand. Mr. Cochand, for the parents, said that he must have seen it in order to be in a position to cross-examine Dr. Warner about Dr. Levick's findings. When we showed him a copy he said that it had a familiar look about it. Miss Szwed, for the children, could not remember seeing any copy, but accepted that she must have had a copy because she too could not have cross-examined Dr. Warner without having the text in front of her. And to this day Mr. Pollard has spare copies of Dr. Levick's unsigned report in his files, which he showed us.

The Court Officer and Dr. Levick's Report

How did the one copy of Dr. Levick's unsigned report find its way into the "court file" on the Beckford case, which was held in the Court Section of Brent Social Services Department? There can be only one answer. At some point in the court proceedings, Mr. Thompson, the Court Officer conducting the case for Brent Borough Council, had that one copy physically in his possession. Initially, Mr. Thompson, in his evidence to us did nothing to soften the angularity of his position, that he had never seen Dr. Levick's report. But, faced with the blindingly obvious fact that he must have both seen and handled the document, he eventually maintained that he had no recollection of having seen it. He went on to describe to us how, in the courtroom, all his papers would be spread out in front of him and, at the end of the case, they would all be gathered up and put into a brown folder. He would then take the brown folder back to his office where his clerical staff would sort out the papers, send any duplicates to the relevant Area Team and file the rest. He said that he did not see Dr. Levick's report among the papers which he took away from Willesden Magistrates' Court at the conclusion of the Beckford case on 9 September 1981, and offered the suggestion that someone might subsequently have posted the report to his office, where it was filed without reference to him. There is no evidence that that was how the report came to be in the file, and we find accordingly.

Our belief is that a copy of Dr. Levick's report was in front of Mr. Thompson in Court on 9 September 1981, and that he swept it up into his folder, along with all his other papers and took it back to his office where it was filed by his clerical staff. Like many other people in court, Mr. Thompson totally failed to recognise the significance of Dr. Levick's report, with its clear indication that both Jasmine and Louise had suffered at least two sets of bone injuries at different times. This information, showing that the abuse of the children was not a "one-off" episode, should have been important to those both planning the children's future and considering the possibility of their returning home to their parents. The report should certainly have been sent to Area 6 immediately after the court hearing.

Mr. Pollard, as the solicitor representing the children, must be given credit for his initiative in obtaining Dr. Levick's report, but he must bear some responsibility for failing to recognise that the information which it contained should have been conveyed to the area team to assist them in planning for the future of the children. He was assertive enough in November 1981, to write complaining of the amount of access, yet insufficiently assertive on behalf of the children to point out the implications of Dr. Levick's report.

The person who was primarily to blame for failing to inform Area 6 about the content of the Levick report was, without any doubt, Mr. Thompson. (No blame can attach to Ms. Wahlstrom, since she was not present in court while Dr. Warner was giving his evidence and discussing the Levick report. She had not given her evidence at that

95

stage, and was therefore kept out of the courtroom. We think that this was an error, since as the key social worker in applying for Care Orders on behalf of her employer, Brent Borough Council, she was the person to give instructions (if needed) to Mr. Thompson, and to that end was entitled to be in court throughout the proceedings.) Mr. Thompson's failure was particularly blameworthy, in that he was not only the Social Services Department's Court Officer (with a status comparable to that of an Area Manager), but was also the custodian of the Brent Child Abuse Register. He was, as he told us in evidence, very experienced in the work of the Juvenile Courts and he was also a qualified social worker (an ex-probation officer). He and his colleagues constantly attended case conferences and he also regularly attended meetings of the Area Review Committee. Among his duties was the preparation and delivery of "lectures on Non-Accidental Injury training for professional groups in conjunction with Training Sections of Social Services Departments, Police and Probation". At one time he had been responsible for providing "supervision and support to the Specialist Social Worker in non-accidental injury both on specific high risk cases as well as borough-wide referrals."

Yet, in spite of all this involvement and expertise in the field of child abuse, Mr. Thompson entirely failed to recognise that the information contained in Dr. Levick's report should have been of vital importance in the subsequent handling of the case. Indeed, he took so little notice of it that he literally "did not see" the report, either in the courtroom or subsequently, when it was filed in his office. His handwritten notes, made at the court hearing did, in fact, include the words, "diagnosis − fractures of different ages in different sites", but he told us that, while he was aware that this information had not been available at the Case Conferences prior to the court hearing, "I was really considering totally getting a Care Order on these children and that is what I was looking at and I thought that that confirmed my case." Clearly, he saw his responsibility for the Beckford children as restricted to the obtaining of Care Orders, and it never occurred to him that it might be important to them that the information about previous injuries should be conveyed to Area 6. To quote his own words to us: "My role at that time was in the obtaining of the Care Orders and I had carried out my instructions and in fact I got the two Care Orders." Later, on 16 September 1981, when he wrote to Mr. Bishop about the Magistrates' rider to the making of the Care Orders, he did not refer to his own file on the case which, we find, by then contained Dr. Levick's report. More surprisingly, he did not refer to his file on the case when he was asked, in June 1983, to apply to the court for the revocation of the Care Orders.

Throughout Mr. Thompson's handling of the Beckford case, Dr. Levick's report remained invisible to him. The aphorism, that "there is none so blind as he who goes about his business blinkered", fits Mr. Thompson to a T. The tragedy is that Mr. Thompson's blinkered approach infected others. It deprived all the other people in the Social Services Department, who were involved in the case, of the vital information that the child abuse in the Beckford household had started well before the admission of Louise and Jasmine to hospital in August 1981, and had been going on for some time before. Had they known this, the question of returning the children to their parents might have been more critically examined. While we think that it may not have deflected Mrs. Dietmann and Ms. Wahlstrom from their commitment to reuniting the family, we are inclined to think that it would have influenced Mr. Bishop in his opposition to the children being returned home on trial.

Why the Magistrates never saw a copy, we are at a loss to understand. There is no evidence that the justices' clerk was handed one by Miss Szwed, acting for the children. But the Magistrates ought not to have sat expectantly, for copies to be handed up. They saw and heard Dr. Warner referring to it. Either they thought that it had no relevance to what they were adjudicating upon; or, if they had the faintest notion that it was relevant — and it was highly pertinent both to the primary conditions of a Care Order as well as the secondary requirement to find the need for care and control — they should have demanded to have sight of a copy of Dr. Levick's report. We conclude it is the former, if only for the reason that they themselves now say that they cannot recollect their understanding of its contents. They were further alerted to the existence of Dr. Levick's report by the simple fact that it was not, under the ordinary rules of evidence, admissible in law. From Mr. Cochand's note of the proceedings and from Miss Petula Smith's very helpful, full note, that there was an actual ruling by the Magistrates that it should be admitted under Section 26, Children and Young Persons Act 1963. That section provides that "in any proceedings... before a juvenile court.... any document purporting to be a certificate of a fully registered medical practitioner as to any person's medical or mental condition" may be admitted in evidence. Having admitted Dr. Levick's report, why did the Magistrates not ask to be provided with a copy? Their apparent lack of interest about the injuries is reflected in the fact that their justices' clerk's notes of evidence discloses that no questions were asked of Beverley Lorrington about the children's injuries when she gave evidence as the last witness. Everything seems to have been concentrated on her inability to cope in poor housing. The whole episode depicts a lapse — we hope only an aberration — in acceptable judicial conduct in proceedings that so materially and emotionally affect the lives of parents and children.

Our finding that Dr. Levick's unsigned report was not generally circulated in the courtroom is supported by Miss Court's statement that, although she does not recollect seeing it, she fully imbibed its contents as it was expounded by Dr. Warner in his evidence. She was quite firm in asserting that Dr. Levick's findings convinced her that she had been wrong in thinking at first that the injury to Louise may have been a "one-off episode". She added, with like firmness, that the totality of the medical evidence adduced before the Magistrates disclosed a classic textbook case of non-accidental injury in respect of children, both of whom had received more than one serious injury on separate occasions. The whole represented a "high-risk case", were the children to be reunited with their parents. When she read the Case Conference minutes at the end of August she told us she regarded the case as a weak one for possible rehabilitation. It was weaker still on 9 September before the Magistrates. Yet, when we first read her report at the outset of our Inquiry, we regarded her report as being mildly advocating a programme of early rehabilitation. Miss Court, however, re-interpreted her report in a way we will describe, but we think that such re-interpretation has been powerfully induced by what she heard in court on 9 September 1981 and by what she has learnt since. We do not think that anyone reading her report — and we invite our readers to judge for themselves by looking at Appendix C:2 — could feel that she was indulging in anything other than a partisanship of natural parents' rights. Miss Court, in that respect, was only reflecting the social pressures that have been coming from public opinion and professional social workers. There is in fact an amalgam of lay attitude and professional preaching that concludes that there is some kind of impermeable bond between natural parent and child. This is translated by the more sophisticated person into a principle that young children should ideally be reared by their own parents. By definition, however, the child that has been abused has demonstrably not bonded with its abusing parents. Dr. Taitz told us, and we echo it, that the elemental feeling that there is some magical, invisible elastic between a mother and her child, simply because it is the natural child, is totally untrue. Bonding can be achieved with non-natural parents. Adoption, by and large, has proved to be a highly successful social institution for rearing healthy and happy children.

The feature in Miss Court's report that struck us most as conveying an advocate's voice in favour of rehabilitation is the phrase, "but I consider the parents to have many strengths." The strengths were not spelt out in the report. But before us it appeared that they were factors that were personal to the Beckford parents and not to their qualities as parents. Miss Court listed them as follows: Morris Beckford had an impressive work record, and most abusing parents were unemployed. There were no serious delinquency problems. Neither parent was ostensibly using drugs, other than mild indulgence in cannabis. And they were capable of managing their little flat in difficult circumstances. Miss Court may thus have misled the Bench into thinking that there were positive parental skills at play, and that a pattern of child abuse could not be inferred.

We think that Miss Court has in effect re-written her report, understandably in the light of the evidence of Dr. Levick and the inadequacy of her investigation due to the limitations imposed on her in respect of access to confidential material. We endorse what Mr. Bond, counsel for Mr. Bishop and Ms. Wahlstrom put to Miss Court, and we reject her answers. He suggested to her that she took "a very much more serious view of the case now than appears from your reports and your evidence in the autumn of 1981," to which Miss Court replied: "I would not agree with you, because if you read the report carefully it is full of red lights and danger signals, especially to a professional social worker who read it carefully." Mr. Bond pressed home the point that we think was valid: "I suggest again to you that the thrust of your evidence in court and the nature of your report rather suggest you were taking an almost critical view of the way the Social Services were dealing with the case, almost saying, 'you are being too much in favour of non-rehabilitation'", to which Miss Court answered: "I am surprised you should feel, reading my report, it is not very negative, particularly the description of the interactions between the parents and the children." We share Mr. Bond's feeling. We do not think Miss Court was merely alerting Brent Social Services to the need to keep open the options of rehabilitation while they assessed the case over the next three or four months. She was, perhaps unwittingly, adopting the attitude, which we find existed just as strongly in Mrs. Dietmann and Ms. Wahlstrom, of favouring experimental rehabilitation as soon as the housing problem was solved.

From the answers given to our questions administered to the Magistrates it does not appear that they regarded Miss Court's report as having particular potency for favouring rehabilitation. They considered her report as being in support of the welfare of the children, unrelated to parental rights. They seemed not to have appreciated the handicap from which Miss Court suffered in limited access to information, and the timing of her report and the reception of Dr. Levick's report. To the extent that we conclude that Miss Court was mildly favouring a reunion of the Beckford family, we do not think it played a significant part in the decision-making process of the Magistrates' Court.

The Willesden Magistrates' rider
We have already briefly noted the impact which the pronouncement of the Magistrates had upon the thinking of the members of Area 6 about how they would handle the Beckford case, once they had obtained the Care Orders in respect of the two children. We deal now with the circumstances which led up to the pronouncement by the Magistrates, and the practical consequences that followed it. But we defer our more general consideration of the propriety and wisdom of such pronouncements emanating from the Bench in Chapter 16 until we discuss the role of juvenile courts in care proceedings.

It is common ground that at the conclusion of the hearing on 9 September 1981 the Magistrates made certain comments which, although throughout our Inquiry have been termed as recommendations, we think can be more aptly described as a rider to the two Care Orders. We have seen three contemporary versions of what the Magistrates said, the amplest being that recorded by Mr. Thompson in the memorandum of 16 September 1981 sent to Mr. Bishop. Since it is that memorandum which was the material document acted upon by Area 6, we would in any event have regarded it as the one pertinent to our task. As compared with the notes taken separately by Miss Szwed, counsel appearing for the children, and by Miss Petula Smith, the articled clerk in the solicitors' firm of Alexander & Partners instructing Miss Szwed, Mr. Thompson's note is the only one of the three that is explicit about a rehabilitation programme for the Beckford family. The Magistrates are recorded as having said, and their answers to our questions do not demur as to its accuracy, the following words: "In making these Orders it is our earnest hope that the Social Services Department will do it's [sic] utmost to carry out a rehabilitation programme to unite these children with their parents." The Chairman is recorded as having directed comments to the parents that "the Social Services will do everything to help you both and get your children back to you...."

The Magistrates have told us that "the only recommendation in the proceedings was made to the Court by Miss Gun Wahlstrom, the social worker, in terms that the Care Orders be made with a view to both being made for the children to see their parents, to encouragement being given by the local authority for these visits to take place, to access being envisaged as one day a week at first, and to put the family back together again hopefully in the future; all of which the Bench reiterated on making the Care Orders." In answer to a further question which we posed, the Magistrates said they did not accept that they made a recommendation, only that they declared "an expression of hope following on the recommendation made to it by Miss Gun Wahlstrom," which they had accepted. The Magistrates' answers reflect Ms. Wahlstrom's evidence-in-chief, as recorded by the Justices' Clerk that "the intention is to put the family back together again hopefully in the future." In cross-examination on behalf of the parents, Ms. Wahlstrom was cautious about, if not averse to the idea of, a re-uniting, when she is recorded as saying that she was "convinced that a Care Order is required. I do not feel that we could give sufficient support in the home to enable them to take the children back. I agree that our arrangement is not ideal but supervision is not enough."

Had the Magistrates relied rather upon Miss Court as favouring an immediate programme of rehabilitation − she is recorded as saying that she felt "that they could now be reunited" − we might have had more sympathy for so ready an acceptance of the view of so distinguished an independent social worker who was called on behalf of the children and who might be regarded as having their best interests uppermost in her mind. But the Magistrates have indicated that all they were endorsing was the local authority's intention to reunite in the future. Mr. Thompson's memorandum of 16 September indicates that the Magistrates were doing more than just endorsing what they perceived was the local authority's intentions, by noting the remarks made by Ms. Wahlstrom. Reading Mr. Thompson's memorandum, we think that the Magistrates were going way beyond the message that Ms. Wahlstrom was conveying, which was no more than an indication that at that stage no decision had been reached. Given that a reunion of the family was still one of the options, but in practice only a remote possibility, Miss Petula Smith's contemporaneous note strikes us as the verisimilitude of the tale before the Magistrates. Her version of the last recorded words of Ms. Wahlstrom's evidence-in-chief is: "We will consider rehabilitation in due course." The fact that the Magistrates specifically told the parents that Social Services "will do everything to help you both and get your children back to you" demonstrates that they themselves strongly favoured a reunion. In so thinking, the Magistrates were utterly misguided. Any idea of a reunion of the Beckford family, at least for the foreseeable future, could not be envisaged by anyone who studied the evidence then before the Magistrates.

The Magistrates sat to hear evidence from Dr. Warner (including his exposition of Dr. Levick's unsigned report) and Ms. Wahlstrom on behalf of Brent Borough Council. They heard Miss Court as the independent social worker, called by counsel for the children. They also heard Beverley Lorrington, none of whose testimony (including cross-examination by the Magistrates) was directed to the question of how the children had suffered their injuries. The evidence occupied three hours, and the Magistrates retired to consider their verdict for 25 minutes. We naturally assume that their deliberations included a composition of their decision with its rider, and that in so composing their statement they acted on the evidence heard in court in order to arrive at their judgment. Since we have concluded that no Bench of Magistrates could reasonably have included any rider to the making of the Care Orders, we suggest that there are three possible explanations for the Willesden Magistrates' rider.

The first possibility is that they were given incorrect or inadequate evidence. On this score we had initially some sympathy with the Magistrates. To the extent that their minds were directed not merely to the physical injuries caused to the children, but were also concerned about Jasmine's failure to thrive, the Magistrates appeared to have been misled by Dr. Warner's evidence. He is recorded by their clerk as telling the Magistrates that "Jasmine is of normal height and weight ... the development of both is normal." Having heard Dr. Warner on his recall to give evidence on Day 38 (2 September 1985) we find that he did not say anything about Jasmine's height and weight. But we do think that there was some misunderstanding, and that the Magistrates thought that Dr. Warner had said something that indicated normality in Jasmine's weight.

The second possibility is that the Magistrates were given incomplete evidence that would have dissuaded them from favouring a reunion of the children with their parents. Neither Mr. Thompson nor Miss Szwed appears to have conceived it as their duty to elicit from Beverley Lorrington any explanation for the non-accidental injuries. The Magistrates cannot be blameless in this regard. They too seemed to display no interest in what is a vital aspect of a child abuse case, if there is any thought of reuniting abused children with abusing parents. Moreover, there was no psychiatric assessment of the Beckford parents. If (as was the case) Mr. Pollard, the solicitor, thought it was wise to have one, surely the Bench should have desisted from expressing a favourable view of the parents, at least until they had seen a report that explained the psychopathology of battering parents.

The third possibility is that the Magistrates simply misunderstood or misinterpreted the evidence. We have already indicated our view that they misinterpreted what Ms. Wahlstrom was saying to them. We think that, like most people who have seen Morris Beckford and/or Beverley Lorrington, the Magistrates found the Beckford parents very appealing, and were understandably sorry for them in their plight of having to live in appalling housing conditions and with a background of unhappy childhood. But those who sit judicially must not permit their human emotions to outweigh their professional duties – in this case to protect two abused children as well as to have proper regard to parental rights. But what is much more disturbing is the Magistrates' apparent failure to appreciate the significance of Dr. Levick's report. Earlier in this chapter we have dealt with this aspect of the care proceedings. We add only the remark that the Magistrates, consistent with their whole approach to this case, were less concerned with the medical evidence about child abuse than with the issue of the housing accommodation and the need to satisfy parental desires to have their own children back with them. If social workers are, rightly in our view, criticised for ignoring their role as a child protection service, Magistrates who do not recognise the known characteristics of child abuse, and do not protect such children, should likewise be publicly upbraided.

Whatever objectively the investigators of this episode in the Beckford Case may conclude about the Magistrates' rider, there is no doubt how it was perceived by everyone in court, in particular by those in Social Services who had to operate the two Care Orders against the background of what took place in court. Even Miss Court who favoured experimenting with reuniting the family was very surprised to hear the rider, because it "pushes social workers into unbalancing their own professional assessment." All the legal representatives in some way thought it surprising, although Miss Szwed, who is very experienced as counsel in child care cases and is an author of recognised legal literature on the topic, did not express disapproval. She did, however, acknowledge that its impact might be unfortunate. Mr. Alan Bedford, giving expert evidence on behalf of the British Association of Social Workers, thought that the Magistrates' rider would have caused confusion in the activities of social workers. He thought that such a rider meant that Social Services "lost therapeutic control." He envisaged that the reaction of a good social worker would be that the parents would threaten to go back to court for a revocation, in which case the Care Order was in jeopardy. Better, therefore, to adopt the lesser of two evils and engage in a home on trial under the protection of an extant Care Order. And that was precisely the attitude adopted by Mr. Bishop.

Mr. Bishop was astonished that the Magistrates found it possible to add their rider, given the evidence of multiple child abuse. And he thought that, without having seen or known of Dr. Levick's report. With Dr. Levick's findings in mind, Mr. Bishop's astonishment of 1981 turned into incredulity in 1985. What perturbed him more, in practical terms, was the effect it would have on the parents. While Mrs. Dietmann and Ms. Wahlstrom seemed less perturbed by the Magistrates' rider (for the reason we have already given) both of them were concerned at the fact that Ms. Wahlstrom would constantly have the parents pestering her to reunite the family, an aspect of "losing therapeutic control." Mr. Bishop, with whose reaction we entirely sympathise, was asked what he would have done in the absence of the Magistrates' rider. While not wanting to hypothesise, he said it would have meant that he and his colleagues would have had one less factor to consider when assessing the case in the future. But he was more emphatic on the positive side, in concluding that what the Magistrates had indicated did powerfully influence at least his ultimate decision concur in a programme of rehabilitation.

Conclusions

Whatever else may be said about the Magistrates' rider, it was not sought, either actively or passively, by Brent Social Services. Mr. Thompson told us that his instructions were to apply for a Care Order in respect of both children, and to that end he ensured his objective by establishing, through the medical evidence of Dr. Warner, the primary condition under section 1(2)(a), Children and Young Persons Act 1969; and, subsequently, through the evidence of Ms. Wahlstrom, the need for care or control which the children were unlikely to receive in the absence of Care Orders. He himself thought that under a Care Order rehabilitation of the children with their parents was a possibility, certainly not a probability. Once the Care Orders were made, however, Mr. Thompson remained silent. He said he had no hint that the Magistrates would add the rider, and he made no comment or objection. He told us that he complied fully with his job description, "to advise Magistrates on possible action to be taken by the Social Services Department when a child is committed to care...." He thought that that duty arose only when the child in care is going home, in which case it was departmental policy so to inform the court. We think that the spirit of the Court Officer's job description is that whenever a Care Order is pronounced it is the Court Officer's invariable duty to tell the court what plans, if any, the local authority has. It is a means of informing both the court and the parties what conclusions have come out of the Case Conference(s) and any subsequent review, statutory or otherwise. It is also a way of heading-off the Magistrates from involving themselves in the exclusive decision-making function of the local authority. Mr. Thompson's silence was tantamount to acquiescence in the pronouncement of the rider, in breach of his terms of employment and contrary to good sense as an advocate for a local authority that wishes to avoid the encumbrance of judicial interference in exercise of its statutory powers.

Counsel for the parents had no interest in deflecting the Magistrates from doing or saying anything that promoted his clients' desire to have the children back home. Short of failure to persuade the court not to make Care Orders, any hint that the local authority should take steps towards reuniting the family would be a welcome bonus. The stance adopted by those representing the child is much harder to understand. Suffice it to say, the Magistrates' rider did not appear unwelcome to counsel, or to the solicitors instructing her.

Miss Court's report, on the face of it, favoured the reunion of the children with their parents. The Magistrates were fully entitled to treat it as such. Before us Miss Court re-interpreted her own report to indicate that she was cautioning Brent Social Services against too hasty a dismissal of the possibility of reunion. Miss Court clearly anticipated much further investigation into the Beckford parents before any decision was arrived at. To that extent her commitment to a programme of reuniting the family was circumspect and qualified. The overall impression was that she did focus on the welfare of the children. She did not see her role as providing an expert's objective view of the case either for or against the making of Care Orders, but as an expert providing an initial, necessarily provisional (because it was rendered incomplete through lack of access to files and to persons) psycho-social assessment of the Beckford family. In so approaching her task, she took into account the possibility of rehabilitation in the interests of the children; hence the emphasis on adequate access by the parents to their children while being fostered, so as not to pre-empt the possibility of reunion. If any reader of her report was misled into thinking that Miss Court positively favoured reunion – and they may be forgiven for so reading it – Miss Court was much less enamoured with the Beckford parents than others appear to have been, or so readily captivated by their appealing nature.

What we find most puzzling is Mr. Pollard's approach to the problem. While he deserves credit for engaging the services of both Miss Court and Dr. Levick, and for arranging for a psychiatric assessment of the Beckfords, his performance causes us to doubt seriously whether he saw himself as acting either exclusively or predominantly in the interests of the children. He had originally been instructed to act for the parents. But when he became in receipt of a legal aid certificate to act on behalf of the children he correctly arranged for the parents to be separately represented. His behaviour subsequently indicates that he never shook off that earlier representation. We say this for two main reasons.

When Mr. Pollard had Dr. Levick's report transcribed from what was dictated over the telephone on Friday 4 September, he ought to have realised the immense significance of the radiological report. Had he grasped the importance of what Dr. Levick was saying, he would (or should) have asked Dr. Levick to appear at court the following Wednesday to give evidence on behalf of the children, and not simply have it tacked on to Dr. Warner's evidence. Miss Court clearly recognised the great significance of Dr. Levick's report when she spoke with Mr. Pollard on Tuesday, 8 September. By then it was probably too late to get Dr. Levick down from Sheffield to London the following day. Failing that, if Mr. Pollard had really been considering the children's interests, he would have made certain that the Social Services Department got a copy of Dr. Levick's report. It was insufficient for him simply to talk to Mr. Thompson about it. And even if that comes near to a counsel of perfection, there was no reason at all why Ms. Wahlstrom should not personally have been handed a copy of the report at court that day, or as a last resort that a copy of Dr. Levick's signed report, sent to Mr. Pollard under cover of letter of 7 September, should not have been immediately sent by post to the Director of Social Services or the Area 6 manager. It is not as if Mr. Pollard regarded his legal services as being at an end, once the Care Orders were made. He continued to busy himself in the case, although hardly in the cause of his clients, the children, whom he incidentally never saw. Parenthetically, **we recommend that any solicitor acting for children in care proceedings must see, and if possible talk to or play with, those whose interests he is hired to protect and to promote.**

Two months after the hearing before Willesden Magistrates' Court, Mr. Pollard wrote to the Director of Social Services at Brent, in which he enclosed a typescript of Miss Szwed's endorsement on her brief, noting briefly the Magistrates' rider to the making of the Care Orders. The letter, dated 9 November 1981, inexplicably unanswered until 25 February 1982, took up the cudgels of the parents (as represented to Mr. Pollard by Paddington Law Centre, acting for the Beckford parents) about the paucity in the amount of access. The letter went on to say – we think wrong-headedly – "that parenting should be done by the natural parents themselves." It went on to say that, as solicitors for the children who called Miss Court, they might be over-influenced by her report, and concluded: "That report sees the parents being reunited with the children in the future, in better housing and after counselling support and with the eldest in a day nursery. This was no doubt the opinion of the Court, as their comments show." The letter offered the writer as an attender at the forthcoming, December review. We do not think it was for Mr. Pollard as the children's legal representatives to assume the role of advocate for the parents. And even if it could be said that where the interests of the children and of the parents coalesce, such advocacy would be permissible, by no stretch of the imagination could it be said in the case of the Beckfords that the interests of Jasmine and Louise were instinctively the same as their parents'. The view of any reasonable legal adviser to the children was that their interests pointed, not in the direction of life with their parents, but in an opposite direction for at least their childhood and probably adolescence. Mr. Pollard significantly made no reference in his letter of 9 November 1981 to Dr. Levick's report languishing in his files as well as in the files of the Court Section of Brent Social Services.

From almost every point of view, the forensic process was little short of disastrous. The Magistrates received no evidence of Jasmine's developmental health; they misunderstood the crucial findings from Dr. Levick's report on the pattern of child abuse; they read more into Ms. Wahlstrom's evidence about reuniting the family than was warranted; they translated what they perceived to be the right course for Brent Social Services to adopt into a programme of increased access leading to reunion in better housing; and by their unrestricted rider to the Care Orders, they powerfully influenced the decision about the children's placement, in a way that interfered with the exclusive statutory function of Social Services. Had the proceedings been conducted in a way that elicited all the available evidence, properly understood and applied, no reasonable Bench of Magistrates could have done other than make the Care Orders *simpliciter*. Like the social workers, they could not have done more than hint at the possibility of reunion – that is, even if it was wise and sensible to say anything beyond making the Care Orders and explaining in clear and simple language what the legal effect and consequences of such Orders were. That, and no more, was required.

The Magistrates were assisted neither by the testimony from Dr. Warner, limited – as we find it was – to the children's orthopaedic condition, nor by the mishandling of the case respectively by Mr. Thompson and Mr. Pollard. But the Magistrates must bear the prime responsibility for having indulged their whim to encourage the Beckford parents in the expectation of early reunion with their children. In so doing, the Magistrates sped the case on its way to ultimate fatality for Jasmine Beckford. The impact of the Magistrates' rider might not have been so compelling, had its legal effect been duly appreciated by Brent Social Services. At the meeting of Social Services staff on 6 July 1984 in the confidential note prepared for the meeting it was stated that the Magistrates' Court had "instructed that rehabilitation should take place with the protection of a Care Order". And when Mr. Bishop appeared before the Cases Sub-Committee on 29 October 1984 he explained to the questioning Councillors that the Court had "directed us to make every effort to rehabilitate the children with their parents", and that "we were obliged to try to do that, though it seemed unrealistic." Mr. Thompson's note to his colleagues in the Social Services Department in November 1984 stated that "on making the Orders the Magistrates requested positive steps to move towards rehabilitation." In his memorandum of 16 September 1981 communicating the Magistrates' rider to Mr. Bishop, Mr. Thompson had ended the quoted words of the Magistrates by saying: "I hope you find this report of adjudication of help." Nowhere did he state that the Magistrates' remarks had no legal effect, and that Social Services were absolutely entitled to ignore the rider. He told us that when Mr. Bishop spoke to him on receiving the memorandum, he did say just that. Mr. Bishop denies that he was given any such advice. We are inclined to believe him. Had Mr. Thompson stated any such emphatic legal opinion, we do not doubt that Mr. Bishop would have sought advice from a qualified lawyer in the Law and Administration Department. In any event we think that, on such a crucial matter as ignoring a considered statement from Magistrates, Mr. Thompson would himself have checked his understanding of the law with a lawyer, since he had no legal qualification, although he possessed vast practical experience of juvenile justice. And even if he felt competent to give such an unequivocal legal advice, he would have recorded that in his memorandum of 16 September 1981.

There are two serious aspects of this treatment of the Magistrates' rider. One is the lack of any reliance by social services, and by Mr. Thompson in particular, on the services of the Law and Administration Department. We comment on this at some length in Chapter 13 below. The second matter is the true legal position of the Magistrates' rider which, as we have indicated already, we defer to Chapter 16.

CHAPTER 9

Fostering and Thriving, September 1981 – April 1982

When Mr. and Mrs. Probert fetched Louise Beckford from St. Charles' Hospital and took her to their home on 26 August 1981, to be joined by Jasmine Beckford on 14 September 1981, they had not been fully assessed as foster-parents, let alone approved. In fact the assessment of them by Mr. Jeremy Burns, head of the Adoption and Foster Care Section of the Social Services Department, was much less advanced than Area 6 had been led to believe. On 21 August 1981 Ms. Wahlstrom had recorded Mr. Burns as saying that "he was in the process of assessing" the Proberts. It was not until 16 November 1981 that the Proberts were approved for Brent, and then *only* in respect of Jasmine and Louise.

No thought appears to have been given by Area 6 to any question of residential care for the Beckford sisters on their discharge from hospital, even though the Proberts were the only prospective foster-care resource on offer. The instinctive response of Social Services to the severe child abuse was long-term fostering, meaning (as we have described in chapter 8) a period of time in a foster-home of more than 2 to 3 months, while a fuller consideration was given to the question of a permanent placement. In chapter 29 we consider the options for placement of children in care, and suggest that there is a place for residential care within the child abuse system, an option that was available and ought at least to have been discussed as a possible short-term solution in August 1981 while approved foster-parents were being sought. We do not criticise Area 6 for not using the residential care which Brent could have provided, because then – as now - the distinctly preferred option, where there is a suitable family for the children to go to (even one unapproved) is foster-care. The Proberts certainly qualified as such.

Ms. Wahlstrom had met the Proberts for the first time, with Mr. Burns, at their home in South Harrow on 24 August 1981 and recorded that the "family appears very suitable – sensitive and sensible caring family ... Confirmed with Jeremy Burns that placement is suitable." We accept the accuracy of Ms. Wahlstrom's first impression of the Proberts. But their suitability could never have been – and never was intended to be – a substitute for a full assessment leading to approval. It could, therefore, never have been contemplated by Ms. Wahlstrom and Mrs. Dietmann (with whom Ms. Wahlstrom had a discussion on the day of her visit to the Proberts' home) that the placement of the Beckford sisters was anything but a temporary, even stop-gap, arrangement pending further assessment and decision about a permanent solution. It was always a possibility, of course, that as and when the Proberts became approved foster-parents the placement might be converted into one of permanency, assuming, of course, that the fostering of the Beckford sisters continued beyond the completion of the assessment and approval. Mr. Burns appears, not unreasonably at that time, to have assumed some degree of permanency. Ms. Wahlstrom had had on 21 August a telephone conversation with Mr. Burns. She recorded in her social worker's report: "They [meaning the Adoption and Foster Care Section] understand that long term plans cannot be arranged at this stage." In his evidence to us Mr. Burns said that by 10 September 1981 (the day after the Care Orders had been made) he believed that the placement with the Proberts was unambiguously to be "a permanent placement for the rest of the children's childhood." We shall consider later in this chapter why it was that Mr. Burns, alone among social services personnel, thought the placement was unequivocally permanent, and what effect (if any) it had on the Proberts in their subsequent behaviour. His deputy, Miss Rogers, who had attended the Case Conference of 20 August 1981, was much less sanguine about the future of the Beckford children with the Proberts, appreciating that Area 6 was contemplating rehabilitation. This reflects perhaps her closer collaboration with Area 6 than was the case of Mr. Burns. We repeat here our concluded view, expressed in chapter 8, that by the middle of September 1981 Mrs. Dietmann and Ms. Wahlstrom were committed to the experiment of a home on trial and, consistent with that commitment, could never have given any hint, direct to the Proberts or indirectly through Jeremy Burns, that the Proberts had been selected as long term foster-parents with a view to adoption. We find that neither of them at any time conveyed to Mr. Burns their intention of using the Proberts' home as anything other than long-term fostering *simpliciter*.

Misleading the Proberts?

The Adoption and Foster-Care Section (AFCS) was a resource agency within the Social Services Department. The Principal Officer (AFCS) was equivalent in status to an Area Manager, being directly answerable to an Assistant Director. Since the staff of AFCS work with children, foster-parents and prospective adopters, rather than with natural parents, they are inevitably concerned more with the appropriateness of a proposed or existing foster placement than with the aptness of returning a child to the natural family household. It is indeed not for AFCS to influence decisions about re-uniting children with their families, but to be ready to respond to requests for foster placement. There was the added complication in this case that, quite exceptionally, the principal officer of AFCS (Mr. Burns) was acting simultaneously as a basic grade social worker with the Proberts. Not only did this ally Mr. Burns to his clients, the Proberts, and so lead him not unnaturally on occasions to champion their cause; it also affected his professional relationship with Ms. Wahlstrom in a way that detracted from her independent judgment as the key social worker in the Beckford case. We accept Ms. Wahlstrom's evidence that she found it difficult having a principal officer assessing the family and they being linked with him: "I did not feel I could question what he was doing" in the process of assessment and approval. Over and above the awkwardness of this unusual professional relationship, there was a personal clash between Mrs. Dietmann and Mr. Burns, which had to be contended with by all those working on the Beckford case. (We consider hereafter what effect, if any, this had on the decisions in the case.) We think that Ms. Wahlstrom was compromised by the fact of Mr. Burns' dual role in the case. She is not in any way to blame for the difficulties that infected both the relationship between Area 6 and AFCS and between Area 6 and the Proberts. We similarly do not blame Mr. Burns. By his desire personally to carry out the assessment of the Proberts (surprisingly for a principal officer in an adoption and fostering section, but he had never done one before, his previous career being in probation and, most recently, as Assistant Secretary of BASW) he put himself in relation to the Beckford case in an invidious position. It was inevitable that, in the process of assessment and working generally with the Proberts during the period of the placement, he buoyed up their hopes that the Beckford sisters would remain for a long time, in which case adoption might easily become a legitimate expectation. But we conclude that Mr. Burns never told the Proberts in so many words that the children would never return to their parents, and that, therefore, they would be in their custody for the rest of their childhood, although at one stage in his evidence before us he went close to conceding as much. We do not think he meant to. What he said by way of encouragement of long-term stay, shading off into permanency, no doubt fed the Proberts' hopes and desires, but he did no more than that. To have done so would have been very unprofessional, and we adjudge him to have high professional standards. We find that the Proberts had all along deluded themselves into thinking that they were being treated as prospective adopters, partly because they regarded themselves in that light, having gone through the adoption process twice in the 1960s, and partly because they chose to ignore the reality of a rehabilitation programme that was implicit in the plans for access that Area 6 was making for the Beckford parents.

Mr. Burns told us that he never suggested that Area 6 was in any way misleading the Proberts about the nature of the placement. We agree. And we do not think that he misled the Proberts either, although he might have been more cautious in reinforcing their hopes for permanent fostering and adoption.

The arrangements for access were the clearest possible indication that the Beckford parents, throughout the months of fostering, retained a distinct chance of having their children back, although we have concluded that that chance should have been only of the remotest kind. The Proberts must also have been aware of the encouragement to the parents by what the Magistrates had said when making the Care Orders about the need for adequate access. So that the reader of this report can judge for himself the effect of access arrangements, we detail them here.

During the time that the children were in hospital the Beckford parents were encouraged to visit; we have alluded to this aspect of the case in chapter 8. On the day Louise left hospital and was placed with the Proberts, Ms. Wahlstrom saw the Beckfords and told them that they would not be able to visit Louise at the foster-home, but that arrangements would be made for Louise to be brought to them on 3 September 1981. That took place. A locum Family Aide went to the Proberts, took Mrs. Probert to see Jasmine in hospital and then picked up Ms. Wahlstrom who took Louise to the Beckfords' home. On 7 September 1981 Louise was again, unexpectedly, taken to the Beckford's home. Jasmine left hospital a week later.

On 15 September 1981 Mrs. Dietmann and Ms. Wahlstrom made their plans for parental contact with the children – a deliberate first step towards a programme of reuniting parents and children. Beverley Lorrington was to meet Jasmine and Louise at Treetops, the Social Services Family Centre, on Tuesdays 11-12 noon, with Dorothy Ruddock supervising. Morris Beckford was to meet the children from 12-1 p.m., with either Dorothy Ruddock or Ms. Wahlstrom to supervise. Beverley Lorrington was also to spend about an hour at Treetops on Thursdays to help Dorothy Ruddock with play sessions and for Beverley to learn how to respond and communicate with children. This arrangement for weekly access was communicated by Ms. Wahlstrom to Mrs. Probert the next day, 16 September 1981. (It was about this time that Mrs. Probert indicated her desire to visit her dying sister in the United States, a matter that aroused some concern by Social Services about the quality of fostering that Jasmine and Louise were receiving). The weekly access took place at Treetops on 22 September 1981, the day after Mrs. Probert left for the United States. The access was repeated on 29 September 1981. On 5 October 1981 the children were taken to see Dr. Warner at St. Charles' Hospital, and the following day the weekly access took place. Mrs. Probert returned from the United States that day.

On 13 October 1981 the parents had a further access to the children at Treetops. On 20 October 1981 the visit again took place; on this occasion Beverley Lorrington was complaining of the shortness of the stay with the children. Later that day Ms. Wahlstrom spoke to the Proberts and told them that the uncertainties of the placement might last for a long time "and [they] are quite realistic about the future." After the next visit, on 27 October 1981, Beverley Lorrington actively sought a meeting with the children more than once a week. But there was no immediate change. The visits took place on 3, 10, 17 and 24 November and on 2, 8, 10 and 15 December 1981. On 9 December 1981 the statutory case review took place.

Increased access

The statutory case review was attended only by Social Services personnel. It had been intended to hold the review in two parts, the first part at the home of the Proberts and the second in the offices of Area 6, with the Beckford parents present. Because of the inclement weather and the shortage of staff on that day, it was impossible for the meeting to be held in Harrow. Both the Beckfords turned up at Area 6 office, but Morris Beckford did not stay, having to go to work. Miss Bowden, the health visitor from Harrow, had been invited to attend, but did not do so. The review was concentrated heavily on the outcome of the access visits. There was only one mention of the development of the children with the Proberts: "Jasmine and Louise are very well settled with the foster-parents, Mr. and Mrs. Probert. The children have developed well." The Review recommended the continuation of parental contact once per week, but the venue was to be changed from Treetops to the Beckfords' home, and the visits were to last for four hours, with Ms. Wahlstrom or Mrs. Ruddock supervising. Beverley Lorrington was to spend two mornings a week at Treetops under Mrs. Ruddock's tuition in developing skills "in parenting as well as relationships with other adults."

On 22 December 1981 Jasmine and Louise made their first visit to see their parents at home. On that day Ms. Wahlstrom talked to Mrs. Probert about the new arrangements for the four-hour visits at home once a week. Ms. Wahlstrom recorded that "Mrs. Probert suggested that if the children are rehabilitated, the Department should remove them soon as she would suffer to see them go. However, Mrs. Probert said she did not really mean what she said as she wanted the best for the children." Whatever else might be said of this conversation, we do not doubt that Mrs. Probert was fully acknowledging the uncertainties about the children's future. She could not, on any view, have thought that the placement was permanent.

The fact of an increase in the amount and quality of access, to four hours a week at the Beckford household, could only mean a further step towards a home on trial. Area 6 was giving practical expression to the need to retain the bond between parent and child. It represented the antithesis of a movement towards a permanent placement with the Proberts. Thereafter, there was no turning back, leading to the removal in April 1982 of the Beckford sisters from the Proberts. Meanwhile, the further visits to the Beckford household continued almost weekly, on 30 December 1981, 5, 12, 19, 26 January, 2, 9, 23 February, 2, 3 and 18 March 1982, when the children made the last home visit to 1030 Harrow Road. The Beckfords moved into the house at College Road on 25 March 1982. That chronology of almost uninterrupted access was no more than a continuous reflection of the plan, hatched in the autumn of 1981, to experiment with a home on trial.

Before we consider the difficulties that arose between Area 6 and the Proberts during the operation of the continuing and effective access, we digress to say only a few words about the relationship between Mrs. Dietmann and Mr. Burns, and its effect on the management of the case. Miss Dodson, on behalf of Mrs. Dietmann, submitted that her client was familiar with the staff of AFCS, other than Mr. Burns who had arrived in post only in 1981, and felt able to rely on their experience and skill. She claimed that it was reasonable, therefore, for her to place similar reliance on Mr. Burns, "although she now considers that reliance to have been misplaced and questions the quality of his assessment of the foster-parents, of his ongoing work with them and of his co-operation with Area 6 staff." We have heard from both Mrs. Dietmann and Mr. Burns. But we have, we think, only scratched the surface of a profound personality clash about which we are quite incapable of determining where the truth lies. And we thought it unnecessary and unhelpful to delve any deeper. We concluded that their clash of personalities rendered collaborative effort between Area 6 and AFCS impossible. We do not think that Mr. Burns' qualities as an assessor of foster-parents or head of AFCS could properly be called in question. He certainly lacked training and experience in foster-care, and he may have exacerbated those limitations by a certain brusqueness of manner. But we do not think his work added more complications to an otherwise complex situation. The only possi-

108

ble fault was in the dilatoriness in assessing the Proberts. Doubtless his antipathy to Mrs. Dietmann may have reinforced his alliance to the Proberts, but it did no more than give that impression. Mr. Burns was rather more decorous in his view about Mrs. Dietmann. We detected in his evidence that he reciprocated her coolness, not to say hostility to her professional work. But he refrained from saying as much. At the end of the day we find that this unseemly squabble did not affect the management of the case. It merely added a personal dimension that Area 6 and AFCS could well have done without. Even without such squabbles, the Beckford children would still have been reunited with their parents. The case would have followed the same path, but without the cacophonous background of personal bickering between professionals.

Friction in fostering

From very early days in the fostering of the Beckford children there were complaints from the Proberts about the state in which the children were being returned from the weekly access to their parents. The complaints started when the visits took place at Treetops, but were stepped up when the visits took place after December 1981 at the Beckfords' home. There were complaints that the children came back wearing clothes that were much too big. Beverley Lorrington had purchased new clothes – particularly for Louise – that apparently were too big. But Mrs. Ruddock told us that the complaint was unjustified. The size of the clothes could have been a matter for comment, but no more. There were also frequent complaints about the clothes often being dirty and smelly, and about the greasing of the children's hair. It is a normal practice to grease and plait Afro-hair. Mrs. Probert complained that their hair was "dripping" with grease. Again, Mrs. Ruddock told us that the hair was greased, but not abnormally. We accept Mrs. Ruddock's evidence unhesitatingly. And we do not think the children were ever dirty or smelly. Morris Beckford was fastidious, to the point of obsession, about cleanliness, a feature of his relationship with Beverley Lorrington that had repercussions in November 1982. These and other complaints, directed at the Beckfords, increased in intensity over the months. On 22 December 1981, after the first access visit of the children to their parents' home, Ms. Wahlstrom had a telephone call from Mrs. Probert listing various complaints. Ms. Wahlstrom "explained *yet again* that this was part of the exercise for the parents to do 'ordinary' activities with their children in order to learn how to cope." We find that these complaints were not justified; that they reflected the Proberts' recognition that the children would very likely be going back to their parents' home on trial; and the Proberts' inability, at least in 1981, to appreciate the importance of foster-parents working in partnership with Social Services.

On 12 January 1982 Mrs. Probert told Ms. Wahlstrom that Jasmine "was wearing her out, waking up early in the morning and not sleeping throughout the day." Jasmine was "very demanding and attention-seeking." Ms. Wahlstrom said that Mrs. Probert sounded very depressed over the telephone. On 14 January 1982 there was a discussion between Ms. Wahlstrom and Mr. Burns about "possible move of Jasmine and Louise." She also mentioned the possibility of rehabilitation. Later that day Ms. Wahlstrom visited the Proberts, by arrangement, following the telephone conversation of 12 January. Mr. and Mrs. Probert said that they were not sure if they could manage increased parental contact. They agreed to think about it. On 10 February 1982 Mrs. Probert offered to teach the parents about the children's likes and dislikes "if this will help the children to settle in with their parents again," the first recognition by the Proberts that their fostering of the children was going to end shortly. On 11 March 1982 Ms. Wahlstrom told the Proberts that the Beckfords were going to be rehoused and that rehabilitation was likely. The Proberts expressed concern about the risks involved.

There is no doubt in our minds that, while rehabilitation was on the cards from the early days of fostering in September 1981, there was an increasing awareness that the Proberts in any event were turning out to be not a suitable placement for the Beckford children. Three factors contributed to the Social Services' view of the Proberts. First, there was the perturbation over Mrs. Probert's visit to her sister in the United States at the outset of the foster-placement. Second, there were the frequent, unjustified complaints about the children's appearance on return from parental access, which simply made Ms. Wahlstrom's task of laying the foundation of a home on trial that much more difficult. Third, there was the unwillingness of the Proberts, until March 1982, to come to terms with the reality that the children were going back to their parents. Some of the tension between Area 6 and the Proberts was due to the lack of preparation in August 1981 to render the process of fostering a smooth and leisurely affair. Because the placement was rushed, initial preparation and understanding of what was involved in fostering (in contradistinction to adoption, of which the Proberts had experience and failed to distinguish from fostering) the placement was unsatisfactory. The lack of cooperation from the Proberts served only to create difficulties and ultimately friction.

Decision to rehabilitate

On 5 April 1982 a Case Conference was held which was, in our view, little more than a rubber-stamp to a decision, made many months before, to rehabilitate the children with their parents. The purpose of the Case Conference was stated to be "to review the situation regarding the children. *Given agreement re the degree of success of the rehabilitation programme*, plan return home and input on return" [emphasis supplied]: see Appendix G:4. The Case Conference was defective in a number of important respects. Mr. Bishop was in the chair and took the minutes of the meeting. In Chapter 25 we give our reasons for disapproving the use of line-management in chairing case conferences and the chairman having to take the minutes of the meeting. The health visitor, Miss Knowles, was not present at the meeting. A letter had been sent inviting her, but it never reached her. Miss Bowden, who was the health visitor in Harrow while the children were with the Proberts had as her last entry in her records for 2 April 1982: "Message received re Case Conference with Social Services." Apologies for absence came from the Adoption and Foster Care Section. There was no invitation to Dr. Warner, the consultant paediatrician, which there should have been. All six persons present were from the Social Services Department, four of them being part of the Area 6 team responsible for handling the case. The other two were Mr. Hobbs from the Court Section and Miss Gordon from Green Lodge. There was, thus, no independent voice to question, let alone to prevent the plan to return the children home.

The meeting was taken up almost entirely with Ms. Wahlstrom reflecting the high optimism about the future, on the basis of improved handling by their parents of the children during seven months of access visiting. Mrs. Dietmann, when asked at the Case Conference if she entertained any reservations about a home on trial, said, "they do not have the kids 24 hours per day, 7 days per week so their behaviour cannot be predicted", but she went on to say "rehabilitation to continue with adequate safeguards." The meeting went on to discuss the details of the plan, which was a transfer from the Proberts to Green Lodge residential day nursery where Beverley Lorrington would come for the day.

The Case Conference concluded six matters. The children would remain on the child abuse register, to be reviewed one month after their return home. Ms. Wahlstrom and Mrs. Ruddock were to organise intensive visiting when the children came home. Miss Knowles, who would shortly be transferring the case to Miss Leong, would "continue to liaise with" Ms. Wahlstrom and "Beverley to be encouraged to attend clinic monthly and HV to visit about fortnightly." Since no health visitor was present, and no com-

110

munication seems to have been made, it is not surprising this became a dead letter. **We recommend that whenever there is a decision to reunite abused children with their parents, there should be a requirement as part of a protection plan that, *inter alia*, parents take children under five to the clinic at least monthly.** We commend to local authorities the contractual document drawn up by the Rochdale Unit of the NSPCC as a model. Finally, the Case Conference made a contingency plan, should the reuniting of the Beckford family fail. The children would go, short-term, to foster-parents with a view to a long-term placement with foster-parents which may lead to adoption "(Not present foster-parents)."

The Proberts' riposte

On 10 April 1982 Mrs. Probert personally handed to Mr. Burns at Brent Town Hall a typewritten statement, signed by Mr. and Mrs. Probert. We find that the statement was not intended by the Proberts to be acted upon, but to serve as a record of the Proberts' view of the Beckford case. We set out the statement in full.

> 12a Primrose Close
> South Harrow, Middlesex
> 01-422-7213
> 10th April, 1982

> *Jasmine Beckford and Louise Beckford*

> As foster parents of the above named children, we wish to have the following statement placed on their case histories.

> We wish to state our concern at the manner in which the entire case has been handled. In August 1981 we were asked by a senior social worker to foster these two babies who were then 3 months and 18 months old. They were in St. Charles Hospital and everyone concerned was anxious to have them removed. Although we had not then been assessed as foster parents, we willingly agreed and gave these children the same care and attention in our home as we had given our two adopted daughters. We were assured this was to be a long-term fostering, i.e. for the remainder of their childhood. This point was emphasised to us and we were advised that there was no way in which they could be returned to their natural parents in view of the previous history.

> Earlier this year, we rang the social worker for advice regarding the sleeping pattern of the elder child. We hoped for some constructive help, but within days we were visited and told there was a place for the children at Green Lodge. We were astounded and very upset. The social worker appeared surprised when we said we wanted to keep the children. After this we were informed the children were going to be returned to their parents.

The social worker and her senior had agreed to get the parents re-housed and then put the children in Green Lodge for a month so the parents could get to know them. We confirmed that we wanted to keep them until they went back to their parents, to save them the upset of going into the children's home. We were told this was impossible as it was too far for the children to travel. We still live in the same house and live no further away now than when we were asked to take the girls out of hospital. Even so, we were willing to take the children to see their parents.

Every suggestion we have made, every offer, has been totally ignored. We requested on numerous occasions to meet the parents, to try to make the handing over of the children easier but all our pleas have been in vain. The social workers had made their decision and were not prepared to discuss the situation. We have been totally left out of any rehabilitation schemes and in fact, have been unaware of what has been taking place regarding the children's future apart from unconfirmed statements. Any comments we have made, however, have been duly noted.

We were advised there would be a case conference on 5th April 1982. By this time the parents had already been rehoused and when we asked who would be present at this meeting, we were surprised to learn there would be no General Practitioner present and concerned that our health visitor was not informed nor asked for a report. We could only assume the meeting would result in a foregone conclusion. Our views were not requested, which we feel is grossly unfair as we must know the children more intimately than anyone else having had them with us continuously since last summer.

We were told the result of the meeting was that the children would be taken to Green Lodge on Tuesday 13th April. We requested that we be allowed to escort them, to at least settle them in, but this request was denied. We feel most strongly that if these schemes were handled with more thought for the children, the innocent parties, and their feelings, there would be fewer maladjusted children in the world. To these tiny tots we are their Mother and Father and to be taken abruptly away shows a complete lack of appreciation of their feelings.

We have never been asked for any details about the children's day to day habits or likes and dislikes, which surely would help settle them into a new environment. We have been advised that if the children did come into care again, they would not be able to return to us since it is too far for them to travel. We have also been told it would be too embarrassing for the social worker.

112

Surely the return to a loving home in familiar surroundings would be of considerable help to them in their plight? By the time the younger of these two babies is a year old, she will have had five homes. This must be detrimental to future well-being. We feel the social worker's concern should be for the children in all cases: these children have not been considered.

We must emphasise that this statement is being made because of our concern for these children and the unfeeling way in which the next stage of their lives is being handled. Gentle transition from one home to another is surely less stressful to them.

....

P.D. Probert   G.H. Probert

Although the statement ended with a general observation of "concern for these children", there was no mention of the Proberts' fear of further abuse of them by Morris Beckford. We mention this because subsequently the Proberts made great play of the fact that they had continually warned Social Services of renewed child abuse. The statement also makes allegations against Social Services which we find are untrue. It states that "we were assured this was to be a long-term fostering, i.e. for the remainder of their childhood. This point was emphasised to us and we were advised that there was no way in which they could be returned to their natural parents, in view of the previous history." We find that Mrs. Dietmann and Ms. Wahlstrom never gave the slightest indication that the children would be remaining permanently with the Proberts. We think it plausible, however, that Mr. Burns went along with the Proberts, or at the very least did not disabuse them of their impression that the placement of the Beckford sisters was permanent. The statement went on to say that "we have been totally left out of any rehabilitation schemes and in fact have been unaware of what has been taking place regarding the children's future apart from unconfirmed statements." Given the facilities for access, in which the Proberts were always involved in releasing and receiving back the children, this statement is a gross distortion of the fact that preparations for reuniting the family were palpably being made.

We think that it is a thousand pities that an immediate refutation of the contents of this statement was not undertaken. While the Proberts did not treat the statement as a complaint, requiring to be investigated, we think it was a piece of maladministration on the part of Brent Borough Council not to have treated it as a complaint. For this act of maladministration we blame Mr. Burns. It was up to him, in consultation with Area 6, to deal with the matter urgently. After Jasmine's death, the Proberts were saying publicly that Social Services had, not to put too fine a point on it, acted with gross professional impropriety, not promoted the welfare of the children, and paid scant regard to the services of foster-parents. Had Mr. Burns reacted promptly to the statement of 10 April 1982, some, if not all of these allegations could have been scotched, instead of fermenting. The most serious allegation, that social workers had "snatched the children screaming" from the Proberts, was withdrawn only by the Proberts' counsel at the inquiry.

While we sympathise with the Proberts in their sincere concern for the children −

they had looked after them physically with loving care for 7 months in which Jasmine actually thrived – we strongly deprecate their social behaviour. They were unhelpful in the process of providing foster-care, in the sense of collaborating in the maintenance of the parental bond, and they hindered the orderly transition of the children back to their parents as soon as it became clear, at the latest after Christmas 1981, that the children were being prepared for a return home.

The hand-over

On 13 April 1982 Mrs. Dietmann and the locum Family Aide went, by arrangement to the Proberts' home to fetch the children. When they arrived at the house, the bags were packed ready for departure. Mr. and Mrs. Probert and their younger, adopted daughter, who was fondly playing with Jasmine, were all in the front room. There was some inconsequential chatter. The locum Family Aide, with Jasmine, Mr. Probert and the Proberts' daughter, moved out to the car, leaving Mrs. Dietmann and Mrs. Probert behind. Mrs. Probert was understandably upset, and Mrs. Dietmann sought to comfort her by describing the nature of supervision that Social Services would be undertaking. To avoid any distressing scene, Mrs. Dietmann picked up Louise from Mrs. Probert and went to the car. As she was preparing to leave, she noticed the evident distress of Mrs. Probert; she said something soothing, and left. On the journey Jasmine played with her toys happily. Louise cried for a while. Mrs. Dietmann later rang Mr. Burns to ask him to plan a visit to the distressed Mrs. Probert.

What we have described in outline is a scene fraught with sincerely expressed emotions. Nothing untoward happened. There was no "snatching", no "screaming", no act of unkindness, let alone callousness. We are confident in concluding that a delicate operation was handled with evident care and sympathy. There was no basis for any suggestion of improper conduct by Mrs. Dietmann. The ultimate picture, purveyed by the press, of some unprofessional activity by social workers is entirely unfounded.

During the seven months that the Beckford children were living with the Proberts, Jasmine's failure hitherto to thrive took a dramatic upturn. Miss Bowden, the Harrow Health Visitor, said that both children did very well: "They made a good weight gain which is seen by the weight charts." Jasmine was weighed at the clinic almost every fortnight, moving from below the 3rd centile (at 18 lbs 14 ozs) on 17 September 1981, to just below the 25th centile (25 lbs 5 ozs) on 1 April 1982 before returning home. (See diagram in chapter 7). She had been alerted by Ms. Wahlstrom to Jasmine's previous underweight, in a conversation in September 1981 just before Jasmine's discharge from hospital; and Miss Bowden knew about, but did not attend, the December 1981 Statutory Case Review. Although invited by Ms. Wahlstrom, she did not attend the Case Conference of 5 April 1982. No one at that Case Conference seemed to know about the dramatic improvement that had taken place in Jasmine's weight and emotional development, and hence drawn the inference from the previous, likewise dramatic failure to thrive. Ms. Wahlstrom was clearly alive to the weight problem, but seems not to have continued her concern about it. At no time after April 1982 was Jasmine weighed. She died, weighing 23 lbs, and way below the 3rd centile. The failure of Area 6 to take particular note of Jasmine's weight over the three years of ε Care Order is perhaps the most striking, single aspect of child abuse that was fatally neglected. It is a failure for which the social workers and health visitors alike must share the blame. Social workers may refer to a child's weight, but we gain the impression that rarely do they draw the proper inferences from it in monitoring cases of child abuse. We suspect that this is true of some health visitors, and even some doctors.

CHAPTER 10

Home on Trial, Post-April 1982

The protection plan

Following the children's short stay at Green Lodge, Ms. Wahlstrom and Mrs. Ruddock spent the whole of the first week during daytime at the Beckford's new home at 57 College Road. On 26 April 1982, a week after the Beckford sisters had been reunited with their parents, Mrs. Dietmann, Ms. Wahlstrom and Mrs. Ruddock held a "progress discussion" of the case. Ms. Wahlstrom recorded the substance of the "progress discussion" in her Social Worker's Report:

> "Beverley beginning to get a routine for herself and the children, but will still need regular support. Agreed to withdraw weekend visits unless Beverley contacts Dorothy. Dorothy to visit Mondays, Wednesdays and Fridays, afternoons/evening. Myself to visit on Tuesdays and Thursdays, mornings or lunchtime."*

By any standards, that disclosed an impressive input of social work service. Indeed, the intensive and extensive casework did not taper off until six months later. But it was clear from the outset (and it remained more and more markedly so over the next two years) that that casework was pronouncedly focused on the Beckford parents. It reflected the local authority's responsibilities for a child in care, resulting from severe abuse by a parent, only in the sense that the two Beckford girls were part and parcel of that family unit. The social workers' "progress discussion" gave no practical expression to the essential requirement that the Beckford children should be visited and seen regularly in order to ensure their safety and well-being. We are unyielding in our assertion that a child should never be reunited with its family unless such visits can be ensured. Everyone should realise that that is the first priority in a home on trial. Furthermore, it should be clear in everyone's mind that the parents must not alter the child's residence – even overnight – without the express agreement of the local authority, through its social workers. The parents should understand that any failure by them to cooperate in any respect of child protection will entail the removal of the child from its parents.

However commendable and impressive the initial (and continuing) casework on the Beckford family was, the paramount consideration should have been the welfare of the Beckford children, instead of their needs being subsumed under the casework to the Beckford parents, necessary and desirable as that was. Instead of engaging in a "progress discussion" centred on the family, the three social workers should, on that day at the latest, have been working out a protection plan, which, quite properly, would have incorporated casework with the parents. **We recommend that whenever a child, who has been abused by its parents, is returned to its family home on trial there must be in existence a protection plan.** It will be convenient if that is done, with the parents present, at the case conference that is recommending the actual return. The protection plan should contain the contractual elements a) of regular visits to see (and talk to) the children on their own; b) of regular medical examinations at the clinic; c) depending

---

* Throughout this Chapter, we have quoted extracts from Ms. Wahlstrom's Social Worker's Report. We have not included the Report in the Appendices, for to have done so would have lengthened considerably our already very lengthy report. But we think consideration might be given by Brent Borough Council to limited circulation of the Report as a teaching tool for social workers.

on the age of the child, of attendance at a nursery, or nursery section of a primary school; and d) the requirement of notification by the parents to the local authority if they wish the child to stay away from home overnight. Any breach of those contractual terms may involve the termination of the home on trial.

Bonding with barbed wire

Throughout the first month of the trial at home, Ms. Wahlstrom and Mrs. Ruddock amply monitored the daily lives of the Beckford family. In the early stages, Miss Knowles was requested to stay away "until the situation has calmed down a bit more" – a reference to the irritation being displayed to the social workers by both Morris Beckford and Beverley Lorrington in their handling of an intensely supervised pattern of life by public authority. (Miss Knowles restarted visiting at the end of May 1982). It is fair to say that Ms. Wahlstrom did at least keep contact with Mortimer Road Day Nursery about Jasmine's erratic attendance there, but she appears always to have accepted Beverley Lorrington's excuses for not having taken Jasmine to the nursery. This expression of trust in what she was told by Beverley Lorrington, both about herself and the children, permeated every aspect of Ms. Wahlstrom's social work. She was, fatally, much too willing to believe everything "her clients" (the Beckford parents) told her.

On 25 May 1982 there took place the statutory case review (Appendix G:5). The three social workers and Morris Beckford alone attended. The itemised topics under review did not allude directly to the issue of child protection; indeed the fourth item talked of "procedure regarding revocation of the Care Order." We conclude that it was much too early even to contemplate, let alone discuss, revocation. The summary of the discussion was principally about Morris Beckford's resentment at the intrusion of social workers in his private life. The final sentence recorded in the discussion was to the effect that there was no concern over the care of the children, "nor is it felt that they are at risk in their home on trial." The long-term objective was to be "revocation of the Care Order", the short-term being to help the Beckford parents "to make rational decisions rather than emotional reactions." Items 25a, 26 and 27 on the review form, which related to the children specifically, merely had "N/A" recorded against them. All this was wildly optimistic. There had by then been barely any opportunity for, let alone actual observance of the children's welfare. To give only one example of the lack of any sign of the risk of child abuse dissipating: Had Jasmine's spurt in weight-gain while with the Proberts been maintained? No one gave a thought to that factor, and no one even noted the erratic school attendance. The observations of Miss Proudlock at the Mortimer Road Day Nursery were not fed into the case review. Had there been a protection plan, the fulfilment of contractual arrangements would have been at the forefront of the statutory case review. Outwith any focus on the children, the social workers blithely observed what they perceived, perhaps correctly, as the real improvement in parental behaviour. They assumed that such improvement (if it was sustained) could only be reflected advantageously in the children. They were never aware that the bonding process they were promoting was, to use Dr. Taitz's telling phrase, "bonding with barbed wire."

The next statutory case review took place on 30 September 1982. Again it was composed only of the three social workers, together with Beverley Lorrington, who brought Louise with her (Appendix G:6). The review followed much the same pattern. Only this time, more emphasis was placed on moving towards revocation of the Care Orders via removal of the children from the child abuse register (to be discussed at a forthcoming case conference), on the basis that there had been "positive changes that have occurred in this family." Item 30 on the review form called for action on a number of matters, one of them requiring that "Jasmine's school to be looked at". Those who were to perform that important aspect of monitoring were Mrs. Ruddock (the Family Aide) and

Beverley Lorrington. There was no discussion about Jasmine's attendance at the nursery. Miss Proudlock's handwritten note, which was produced before us, showed that Ms. Wahlstrom was alerted on 7 occasions between the week ending 7 May 1982 and 22 October 1982. While Ms. Wahlstrom recorded most of those alerts, the only reference to Jasmine's education was a remark that Louise should be found a day nursery place, as and when Jasmine "goes to school." A discussion took place about putting Jasmine on a waiting list. No adverse conclusion was drawn from the record of attendances.

On 21 October 1982, Miss Proudlock, Dr. Khan and Miss Leong were all invited to attend the Case Conference convened for 9 November (Appendix G:7). Miss Leong was ill on that day and did not attend; Dr. Khan indicated non-attendance, but asked for the minutes to be sent. The meeting went ahead, therefore, without any input from the health visitor or the general practitioner. Mrs. Dietmann took the chair. As the senior social worker involved in the management of the case this meant that there was no objective assessment available at the meeting which was to remove the children from the child abuse register. It reduced significantly an element of child protection. There are two crucial features of that Case Conference that we deal with here.

Miss Proudlock told us that she mentioned Jasmine's attendance record, but nothing appears to that effect in the minutes of the meeting. It records baldly the fact that Jasmine in April 1982 had been "given a part-time Day Nursery place at M.R.D.N." A week before the meeting of 9 November 1982 Jasmine was recorded as having "left" the nursery. She in fact never returned; she started at Princess Frederica Primary School (Nursery) only on 11 January 1983. On 20 October 1982 Ms. Wahlstrom was told by Beverley Lorrington that she had found a place for Jasmine there. Ms. Wahlstrom's notes record "Jasmine to start in December when she is three years. Beverley no longer taking Jasmine to the Day Nursery!! [sic] However, she takes the children out and talks to them at home." For two months, therefore, Jasmine was out of sight of the one daily monitoring provision. We regard that as highly significant, because we have concluded that the first repetition of child abuse on Jasmine took place around the time of the November 1982 Case Conference. We conclude this primarily as a result of the evidence of the earliest of the bone fractures reported by Mr. Walker from the x-rays taken at the post-mortem in July 1984. Mr. Walker was asked by Miss Baxendale at the Inquiry:

> "So we now have the major injury that we know about, the evidence we have got so far is that it probably happened about September 1983, and that would be No. 2,* the one that was kept with the weights?"**

Mr. Walker:

> "Yes. You are being too specific, with respect. You cannot say September 1983 is that thing (pointing to No. 2 on the x-ray). I am saying it did not happen after September 1983. It may have happened in September 1982."

* The earliest of the bone fractures
** Morris Beckford subsequently told the police that he had applied weights to Jasmine's fractured thigh.

We find eloquent support for our view that Jasmine suffered a bone fracture around the first week of November in another important piece of evidence that was not merely alluded to at the Case Conference on 9 November 1982 but about which the meeting was dis-informed by Ms. Wahlstrom.

On 1 November 1982 Ms. Wahlstrom made a home visit to the Beckfords. She saw only Morris Beckford, who indicated that he did not want to attend the forthcoming Case Conference. On the morning of 4 November 1982, Ms. Wahlstrom again visited the Beckfords. She recorded that "Morris and Beverley at home with Jasmine and Louise," but there is no entry indicating that she saw either of the children. Morris Beckford left for work, leaving Beverley talking to Ms. Wahlstrom. Beverley then indicated that she was extremely unhappy in her relationship with Morris Beckford: "Beverley talking about leaving him and taking the children with her." Ms. Wahlstrom returned the next day to find Beverley "more relaxed." Jasmine and Louise are recorded as having been at home, but again there is no indication that Ms. Wahlstrom saw the children. Ms. Wahlstrom felt reassured: "Beverley confident that she will be able to talk to Morris about the situation." On the day before the Case Conference Ms. Wahlstrom received a message from Mortimer Road Day Nursery that "Jasmine was not in to-day." At the Case Conference it is recorded that the parents have "improved their marital relationship and communication" and that "there are no longer any signs of ongoing stress in the family." Since there was no "cause for concern about the physical or emotional care of the children and the parents were continuing full co-operation with this department", it was agreed to remove the children from the register "as they are no longer at risk."

Parental disharmony is a major indicator of risk of child abuse. Even if Ms. Wahlstrom was unaware of that single aspect of child abuse, she was palpably blameworthy in allowing the participants at the Case Conference to proceed on the assumption that all was well between the Beckford parents. If, on 4 November, the Beckfords had really patched up a relationship that was clearly fragile, if not on the point of disruption, Ms. Wahlstrom at least should have given an account of what she had learned about that relationship. She was also at fault in not at least observing what impact the parental bickering was having on Jasmine. If Ms. Wahlstrom had for a moment thought about child protection, she would have made it her business to see and talk with Jasmine (Jasmine was by then 3 years old and able to talk sensibly).

The combination of 1) Jasmine's non-attendance at the nursery after 2 November; 2) the disharmony between the Beckford parents disclosed to Ms. Wahlstrom on 4 November; 3) the fact that Jasmine had not been seen for some time by Ms. Wahlstrom and not by Miss Leong from October 1982 to mid-January 1983; and 4) absence of information from the general practitioner and the health visitor about Jasmine's health and development — all these would have led any reasonable bunch of social workers to question what they were about to do. There was no basis whatsoever for taking the children off the child abuse register. The primary blame for so doing must rest with Mrs. Dietmann who both as the supervisor was in duty bound to ask pertinent questions of Ms. Wahlstrom, and as chairman of the Case Conference should not have allowed the participants to act blindly and blameworthily.

Health Visiting, April-November 1982
On 6 June 1982 Miss Knowles made her last visit to the Beckford family before handing over the case to Miss Leong. She described Jasmine as "rather a pathetic child" and "still looked pinched and [the word is illegible]." That alarming description never seemed to be appreciated by Miss Leong when she took over, and it was never fed into the Social

Services' pool of knowledge. It is surprising that during her extensive work with the Beckford family in April and May 1982 Ms. Wahlstrom also did not come to a like conclusion about the picture Jasmine was presenting to Miss Knowles. But then Ms. Wahlstrom was not looking at Jasmine as a child to be protected, even if she averted her glance from the Beckford parents to the children.

Miss Leong took over on 9 July 1982. She first saw Jasmine on 20 August 1982 and reported her looking well. She visited a month later but Jasmine was in nursery. She saw her again on 6 October 1982. She did not see Jasmine again until 21 January 1983 when Jasmine was reported as a "friendly girl." Miss Leong had made two attempts to visit on 29 and 30 November but there was no reply on either occasion. Miss Leong left her card on the first occasion. She did not attend the Case Conference on 9 November 1982, due to ill health. When she received the notice of 12 November from Ms. Wahlstrom of removal from the child abuse register, in which it was stated that there were "no signs of stress in the family" and the reasons for removal were that there was "no concern about the physical or emotional care of the children," she repeated verbatim those words when automatically removing the children from the Health Visitors' replica Child Abuse Register. Miss Leong's report went to Miss Bateman and Miss Tyler, but no discussion of the case took place with her.

The visiting by Miss Leong came nowhere near compliance with the request made at the Case Conference of 5 April 1982 that the health visitor should "visit about fortnightly." Neither was there the "liaison with key workers" that was also indicated. Miss Knowles had been in touch with Ms. Wahlstrom on 7 July 1982 and obtained details of the "family making good progress." Apart from the invitation to attend the Case Conference on 9 November 1982 and receiving the minutes of that meeting, Miss Leong's records show no contact with Social Services at all during this period. (The next contact was 5 April 1983). Ms. Wahlstrom's records indicate a conversation with Miss Leong on 27 September 1982 when Miss Leong told her that she had recently seen the children "both at home and in the clinic", although Miss Leong could not recall the conversation. Ms. Wahlstrom's note indicates some concern about Beverley Lorrington's handling of Louise. An entry in Miss Leong's notes for 6 October 1982 supports the substance of that conversation.

During the crucial period of the first six months home on trial, Miss Leong carried out her health visitor's role in almost total detachment from the social workers. There never was any exchange of notes and Miss Leong's absence from the Case Conference of 9 November 1982 meant that the parallel paths taken by health visitor and social worker were persisted in. Even if Miss Leong had nothing to contribute to the discussions on 9 November 1982, there would at least have been an opportunity to check with her how far she had been carrying out the expressed wishes of the Case Conference of 5 April 1982. This whole period is characterised by a failure to operate a bi-disciplinary approach to child protection and a complete absence of any surveillance by the respective supervisors to ensure that both health visitor and social worker did cooperate in providing a child protection service. Indeed, Miss Tyler told us: "It is not the health visitor's responsibility to go into the family for the prime purpose of monitoring child abuse."

We have already stated that we think that Jasmine suffered an assault, resulting in a bone fracture, in the first week of November 1982. The fact that it happened, and that it went undetected by social workers or health visitor is a lamentable failure in operating a child protection service at a time of great risk to the child. While Ms. Wahlstrom and Miss Leong must take some responsibility for this failure, we think that their superiors, Mrs. Dietmann and Miss Tyler must take the major blame. (We deal in Chapter 21 with the question of supervision generally, and in particular with child abuse cases).

Loosening the bonds of care
Once the Beckford children had been taken off the child abuse register in November 1982 it was inevitable that the input of social work would be substantially reduced. And so it was. Mrs. Ruddock was officially taken off the case in November 1982, although she continued to visit occasionally on a purely informal basis until August 1983, just before she started her CQSW training. Ms. Wahlstrom continued visiting, but by the Spring of 1983 her visits had been reduced to about one a month. Unconnected with any social work activity, Miss Leong continued her visits to check the family's health. She saw Jasmine only twice after Christmas 1982 – on 21 January and 22 April 1983. On that latter occasion, not by design, Ms. Wahlstrom was also visiting. It was the last time that Ms. Leong saw Jasmine.

On 22 November 1982 Ms. Wahlstrom visited the Beckford home, but did not see Jasmine. She was told on that day by Miss Proudlock that Jasmine had not been to the nursery for the past two weeks. Beverley Lorrington had said that she was unable to send Jasmine to the day nursery "as she has not got the dinner money." Ms. Wahlstrom's note added an exclamation mark and a question mark. Although it was a palpable lie, Ms. Wahlstrom did not pursue her exclaiming and questioning. On her next visit on 3 December 1982 Ms. Wahlstrom learnt that Jasmine was due to start at Princess Frederica Primary School. And when she visited on 11 January 1983 she learned that Jasmine had that day started attending during the afternoon session. Ms. Wahlstrom telephoned the school. She spoke to the Headmistress, Miss Cowgill, who wrote a pencilled note on the inside cover of her diary: "Social Worker re Jasmine Beckford, Ms. Wahlstrom." Miss Cowgill was told to contact Area 6 if there was any problem. She received no written confirmation, although Ms. Wahlstrom wrote to Miss Proudlock on the following day, informing her that the place at the Mortimer Road Day Nursery was no longer required as Jasmine had started part-time at Princess Frederica Primary School. From her attitude to the lax attendance at the nursery during 1982 and the failure to communicate formally that Jasmine was the subject of a Care Order, Ms. Wahlstrom clearly indicated that she did not regard Jasmine's attendance at Princess Frederica Primary School as a device for monitoring Jasmine's welfare. She saw it only positively as a part of Jasmine's educational and social training. She was at fault in not perceiving it as another way of protecting the child from the risk of further abuse. **We recommend that whenever a child in care is attending any educational establishment the local authority which has the child in its care must formally notify not only the local education authority but also the school or institution which the child is attending, and the notice should ask for information about non-attendance and any other relevant matter pertaining to the child's health and welfare.**

Miss Cowgill was not even told that there was in existence a Care Order in respect of Jasmine, or that she had only recently been taken off the child abuse register. Unfortunately, Miss Cowgill's pencilled note was never transferred into any school document, such as the child's registration card held in the administrative office. Hence no member of staff at Princess Frederica Primary School knew of Jasmine's background. Miss Cowgill must bear some responsibility for the staff's ignorance of the Care Order. The situation was compounded by the fact that Brent's Green Book, which provides guidance on non-accidental injury to children, was unknown to the staff. A copy had been sent in 1977, when it was published, but it was not uncovered from the headmistress's room until the Inquiry. We trust that that situation will not recur. **We recommend that the Director of Education should periodically check that the Green Book (updated) should be known and made readily available to every member of staff.**

Two consequences flowed from the ignorance of Jasmine's status as a child in care. The first related to her erratic attendance. For the first three weeks she came to school.

In February she hardly ever attended. From the beginning of March to the end she came to school on most days. She began coming in the Easter term, but apart from early May and one week at the end of that month she never again attended during the summer term. She attended during most of the first week of the new school year, but never again attended after 9 September 1983. On 14 July 1983 Mr. John Barry, an Education Welfare Officer for Brent, was asked by the school secretary to find out from Jasmine's parents whether she would be coming back for the September term. He went to the Beckford household, and was told by Beverley Lorrington that Jasmine had not been very well but that she certainly wanted the place kept for her in September. Since Mr. Barry knew nothing of Jasmine's history, he reported back to the school that the parents wanted to keep the place. Jasmine did attend for the first four days until 9 September 1983, but never to return thereafter. The new headmistress, Mrs. Baines, wrote a letter to the Beckfords at the end of September pointing out the non-attendance and asking if they still wanted Jasmine to go to school, otherwise the place would be taken up by another child. In October, Morris Beckford went to the school and explained that Beverley was pregnant with their third child. He also said that as a result of Beverley having a difficult pregnancy Jasmine had gone to stay with the maternal grandparent (which could not be done lawfully without the local authority's agreement). Beverley Lorrington saw the nursery teacher after Chantelle was born in December 1983 and told her that she would not be bringing Jasmine. She did, however, ask for admission to the infant school – i.e., compulsory education - for September 1984, which would have been just before Jasmine's fifth birthday. Had Mrs. Baines known of the Care Order, once again the Social Services would have been alerted to a grave situation. In fact, as we shall observe, the child abuse started up again around September 1983 and never wholly desisted up until Jasmine's death.

The second matter was minor, but indicative of what can go wrong if the various agencies involved in the welfare of a child are unaware that a child is at risk from parental abuse. Mrs. Felix, a nursery teacher at Princess Frederica, told us of an incident which, had she known that there was a Care Order in existence, she would have treated seriously. She said:

> "...she came with some bruises once, after being away for a few weeks. Her mother brought her then and we asked why she was away, and the mother said, well, she was playing with a bicycle and fell off. And we looked at the bruises, there were scars there, but it was healed. And if I knew that she was in care, we would either see our School Welfare Officer and then the headmistress or someone. But we knew nothing."

A nursery assistant, Mrs. Ashley Player, confirmed Mrs. Felix's evidence. She described the bruising down Jasmine's face: "We asked the mother about it and she just said that she had fallen off a bicycle, so we just believed that." Mrs. Player said that if she had known about the Care Order she would have "contacted the social worker straight away." We do not blame the staff at Princess Frederica for having taken no action after the mother's explanation, although they might reasonably have put two and two together – the very poor record of attendance and the physical injury – and told the headmistress. It might have led to Social Services being alerted. Their decision to accept the mother's explanation would never have deterred them reporting, had they known of Jasmine's background. That they were ignorant of it was the fault of the educational authorities and Social Services.

Fresh stresses

Ms. Wahlstrom did accompany Beverley Lorrington once – on 11 April 1983 - to Princess Frederica Primary School to fetch Jasmine. She did so "to find out from Jasmine's teachers how she has progressed since she started in January." Ms. Wahlstrom recorded that the two teachers she spoke to were happy with Jasmine's progress, and there were no problems. None of the teachers – all of whom gave evidence before us – can remember the occasion. We accept Ms. Wahlstrom's account that she had spoken to someone at the school. But at that time Jasmine's non-attendance had at school had been only sporadic, and the bruising incident occurred almost certainly later in that year.

A week later – on the day of the statutory case review preparatory to applying for revocation of the Care Order – Ms. Wahlstrom had known that Beverley Lorrington had been referred by the General Practitioner to St. Mary's Hospital for a pregnancy test on the following day (19 April). No mention was made of this at the case review. It ought to have been, and Ms. Wahlstrom was negligent in not telling the meeting. Likewise on 9 May 1983, no mention was made of the fact of the pregnancy when Mr. Bishop signed the form requesting Mr. Thompson to apply to the Court for revocation. He was not to blame. Ms. Wahlstrom had failed to tell him, so that the court could be properly informed. For any normal mother – and, whatever else, Beverley Lorrington had enormous difficulties in exhibiting maternal care – to have to cope with three children under the age of four is a daunting task. The ordinary stresses of home life would tax the most redoubtable mother. Throughout the summer and autumn of 1983 Social Services knew of the forthcoming birth of a third child. Yet they did not for one moment recognise what this event meant in terms of the additional risk to Jasmine and Louise, or indeed to the new baby. No one in Area 6 seems to have given a thought to obtaining a Care Order in respect of Chantelle. That failure was consistent with what was being prepared on 18 April, the revocation of the existing Care Orders. But once they failed to obtain a revocation on 22 June 1983, Chantelle should similarly have been made the subject of a Care Order, alongside her sisters.

Willesden Magistrates' Court refused to revoke the Care Orders. There is a strong conflict of recollection between Mr. Thompson and the Magistrates about what took place in court. The contemporaneous notification of the court's decision simply stated "Appn. refused. Try again in 10 months' time." At the meeting of the departmental staff on 6 July 1984 it was recorded that "we approached the Court to suggest the revocation of the Care Order. The Court acknowledged the excellent progress being made but said that they thought it was too short a time and that the Area should come back in two [sic] months' time." This statement accords broadly with what Mr. Thompson told us. He said that in roughly 5-10 minutes in court he outlined the background to the application. This is in flat contradiction to the answers supplied to us by the Willesden Bench: see Appendix C:4. We are quite unable to resolve this conflict of recollections, particularly in the absence of any contemporary documentation from the Magistrates' Court. Since the issue is of no material consequence to our findings, we have left it unresolved. We make only one observation. It is clear from what happened afterwards that Area 6 treated the Care Order as if it was no longer extant. The social work activity thereafter was barely consistent even with the operation of a Supervision Order.

After the court hearing, which was not attended by Ms. Wahlstrom who was on leave, the Beckfords were visited by Ms. Wahlstrom on 24 June 1983 and told of the court decision. There was discussion about the forthcoming birth. She visited again on 12 July 1983, and on 15 August 1983 Mrs. Ruddock made her last (unofficial) visit to the Beckford household. Ms. Wahlstrom visited again on 24 August, when both Jasmine and Louise were seen: "all cheerful and relaxed." Ms. Wahlstrom visited once more on 8 September 1983. Jasmine was there, "not at school this afternoon as Beverley forgot this time and she would have been late." Ms. Wahlstrom showed no concern about this non-attendance, which had special significance because the following day was the last time Jasmine attended school. There then begins the evasive action by the Beckfords, and we conclude that the child abuse restarts about that time. We give a sample of Ms. Wahlstrom's activities as disclosed in her Social Worker's Report.

> "28.9.83 T/C to Beverley – no reply
> 7.10.83 T/C to Beverley – no reply
>   T/C to Miss Leong, H.V.; has not visited for
>   some time but occasionally sees Beverley in the
>   area.
> 17.10.83 Home Visit – no answer; left my card
> 20.10.83 T/C to Beverley – girlfriend Claudia informed
>   me that Beverley was out, would be back in ½
>   hour.
> " 3pm   T/C to Beverley – no reply."

On 21 October a home visit was effected. Beverley Lorrington told Ms. Wahlstrom that "Jasmine and Louise are spending a couple of weeks with her mother in Perivale ... Beverley quick to inform me that she informed the school why Jasmine is away." Ms. Wahlstrom appeared not to have appreciated that Brent Borough Council's agreement was needed for a change in placement. And she does not pursue Jasmine's absence from school over the last 6 weeks. Although Ms. Wahlstrom made an arrangement to visit on 2 November at lunchtime, she in fact visited on 22 November without getting a reply. She visited effectively on 23 November. Jasmine was not there, "out shopping." The visit was taken up with discussion about the expected birth on 16 December and with the statutory case review of 6 December. Ms. Wahlstrom had not seen Jasmine since 8 September 1983. Ms. Wahlstrom visited the Beckfords on the morning of 6 December to find Morris Beckford and Louise there. Beverley Lorrington "at the hospital for check up. Jasmine with Beverley."

The statutory case review repeated the absence of any cause for concern and added that "we feel strongly that *this family* [our emphasis] ought to be relieved of any legal ties to Social Services and will reapply to the court in the Spring, when the children have been at home 2 years." Under Item 30, "What action must now be taken?" it was stated: "Review [in April 1984] to include Court Section and School: Statutory Visits: Revocation of Care Order." Ms. Wahlstrom made a home visit that afternoon, but got no reply. She did get a reply the following day, but Jasmine was not there. She again saw Morris Beckford on 13 December and was told of Chantelle's birth two days earlier. Ms. Wahlstrom left Christmas presents for Jasmine and Louise.

In her evidence at the Central Criminal Court on 25 March 1984 Ms. Wahlstrom said at first that on 13 December she could hear both children in the front room, but later said that she was mistaken. She remembered Morris Beckford saying that the two children were staying with the maternal grandparents in Perivale. Whether she did hear them in the house or not, she said she certainly "did not see them." Before us, she said that "Jasmine was in the front room, but the door was open, ajar, and she was inside there looking for Louise." Ms. Wahlstrom said that she did not notice "anything odd about her". We conclude that she saw Jasmine, but only fleetingly.

Ms. Wahlstrom made a visit on 18 January 1984, but again did not see Jasmine: "Beverley informed me that Jasmine was upstairs in bed with a bad cold." There was a visit on 2 February 1984 when there was no reply. On 3, 15 and 27 February Ms. Wahlstrom's personal diary contained on each occasion an entry, "Beverley – intended to visit." She made an ineffective visit on 28 February. On 7 March Ms. Wahlstrom wrote as follows:

> "Dear Beverley and Morris,
> I have tried to contact you several times but you seem to be out when I call. I would like to see you *and* the children so that we can start planning the Review.
> I will visit you on Monday 12th March at about noon.
>
> Yours sincerely,
> Gun Wahlstrom
> Social Worker"

A missed opportunity

On 12 March 1984 Ms. Wahlstrom saw Jasmine alive for the last time. Before we describe in detail what happened on that occasion, we digress to express our views about the visits by social workers to children in the care of a local authority. The local authority has the powers and duties of a parent, which we have discussed in chapter 2. A decision to return a child to the family must always be the prime, positive ingredient in any planned process to reunite the family, and not merely the consequence of a return to the parents of their child. It must include a protection plan. The plan must include sufficient oversight to confirm that the child is likely to flourish, and that its welfare will continue to be promoted by a permanent return to the family. There are no specific legislative provisions concerning the frequency of visiting such children. A conscientious discharge of the local authority's duties and of good professional practice demands regular, frequent and effective contact between the responsible worker and the child. The frequency of visiting should be no less than that prescribed by Regulation 21 of the Boarding-Out of Children Regulations 1955 (see Appendix E). A circular letter from the Chief Inspector, Social Services Inspectorate, to all Directors of Social Services, dated 9 April 1985, states:

> Local authorities have a statutory duty to review the cases of all children in their care at least every six months. I recommend that, where a child in care is placed with its family, the placement be reviewed by a social services manager or appropriate professional officer within 2-4 weeks and thereafter as necessary. This review and subsequent reviews should examine all aspects of the child's well-being and should include first-hand reports by the social worker of visits to the family with particular reference to the physical and emotional development of the child so that the authority can take an informed decision as to whether or not the child should remain with its family. The review might also wish to consider if there is a need for additional support to the family.
> Social workers who have day to day responsibility for such children should be provided with the necessary support,

guidance, supervision and management. You may wish to consider in addition administrative procedures to ensure that effective mechanisms exist to arrange for the removal of a child if necessary."

We thoroughly endorse these recommendations. But we would go further.

First, we wish to stress that the visits are to the children, and not to the parents. We would refer to what Sir Walter Monckton said in his report in 1945 on the Dennis O'Neill case, which we have cited at the end of chapter 1. The relationship of the local authority to a child in care is a personal one: "The duty must neither be evaded nor scamped." There are other wise words to be extracted from Sir Walter Monckton's classic report that deserves to be read and re-read by all those concerned with the protection of children in care. Referring to the visitor in that case, he said: "Her visit was inadequate in certain respects. It is admittedly not advisable for obvious reasons to notify foster-parents – [the same goes for natural parents with children in care, home on trial] – of supervisory visits in advance. The Goughs were notified of her visit in advance ... More important still she only saw the children in the presence of the Goughs."

Ms. Wahlstrom very seldom visited the Beckford family unannounced. Indeed, on one occasion, on 28 September 1982, when she did visit unannounced, Beverley berated her for having come on the wrong day. Beverley was placated by the news that Ms. Wahlstrom had come to arrange for the review which would lead to the removal of the children from the child abuse register. The letter of 7 March 1984 (supra) was an example of a series of letters Ms. Wahlstrom wrote between then and 3 July 1984. We have, moreover, found that on no occasion over two and a quarter years of the home on trial did Ms. Wahlstrom take Jasmine out on her own for a walk; that she recorded no conversation with Jasmine; and that virtually all the entries in her Social Worker's Report which mentioned Jasmine were related to matters that occurred in the presence of one or both of the Beckford parents. Ms. Wahlstrom demonstrated with eloquent testimony the negation of any sense of the personal relationship between her and the two children. The visit of 12 March 1984, to which we now turn, exemplified what we have said.

Ms. Wahlstrom's own entry for this occasion is headed: "*Home Visit as arranged.*" Beverley Lorrington opened the front door and showed Ms. Wahlstrom into the downstairs front room. Ms. Wahlstrom enquired about the children, and Beverley took her upstairs. We have seen a drawing of the room, which was sparsely furnished. It shows the positioning of the furniture and children. We have also seen photographs of this room and other rooms in the house, including the kitchen, taken by the police on 5 or 6 July. They were spotlessly clean, reflecting Morris Beckford's obsessive cleanliness that he ruthlessly imposed on Beverley Lorrington. Jasmine (dressed in jeans) and Louise were both sitting on the floor watching "Jungle Book" on a hired video. Chantelle was sitting in the baby-sitter. When Ms. Wahlstrom came into the "playroom", Jasmine did get up but took only a step or two towards the bedstead, upon which she probably used to prop herself. She did not walk across the room and was not heard to say anything. She remained in that position for some moments and then continued watching the film. Ms. Wahlstrom proceeded to have a conversation with Beverley Lorrington in which she admitted that she no longer took Jasmine to nursery class, the reason given being that she had been "off school for a while with a bad cold and got out of the habit of going to school." There was talk of Miss Leong visiting the family, of Chantelle going to the clinic for an injection, and Beverley inquiring about a playgroup vacancy for Louise. There was mention of putting Jasmine's name down for full-time education in September

1984. Morris Beckford returned home and the three adults went downstairs. Altogether Ms. Wahlstrom was in the playroom for 20 minutes and in the home for 45 minutes. The rest of the conversation with the Beckfords was about furnishings for the house and talk about the dangers of a Calor gas heater without a guard. The visit ended with discussion about a further statutory case review in the Spring and plans to return to court to have the Care Orders revoked.

Ms. Wahlstrom's record of the children's health and welfare was that "all three appeared well and happy." Before us, she amended that phrase to "calm and collected." The grounds for those generalised words are not apparent. We have stated in Chapter 7 that we find that on that day Jasmine was recovering from a fracture of her thigh and would have walked with an abnormal gait. Since she did not perform any purposeful act of mobility, her healing bone fracture would not have been noticed. Ms. Wahlstrom also explained to us – and we accept her description – that Beverley Lorrington was waving her arm about so that Jasmine was partially obscured from sight, Miss Lorrington standing between the two of them in the playroom. If Ms. Wahlstrom had carried out only the elementary task of walking with Jasmine, or talking to her, even in her mother's presence, the fact of child abuse would have been all too apparent. We think Ms. Wahlstrom was gravely in error in doing no more than have a cursory glance at the children in front of the television set. Her visit did not accord with the basic requirement of ensuring the welfare of the children. She was grossly negligent. We conclude, moreover, that the visit was stage-managed by the Beckford parents who had been given 5 day's notice of the impending visit and thus had ample opportunity to arrange the siting of the children and the unrevealing clothing worn by Jasmine. Indeed, Morris Beckford said as much in his written statement to the Inquiry. Ms. Wahlstrom should have been alive to such parental ruses to conceal the effects of child abuse.

Terminal care

Ms. Wahlstrom's concern for the welfare of the children was aroused not a scintilla. She did not visit for another two months. On 14 May 1984 she visited the Beckford home. There was no reply, so she left a card to say that she would visit the following day "at about 3 p.m.". On that day she received a message from Morris Beckford cancelling her visit. He said that Beverley was staying with her father for two weeks because he was seriously ill. She telephoned that day and the next, but there was no reply on either occasion. Ms. Wahlstrom did telephone Princess Frederica Primary School, to learn that Jasmine had not attended there since September 1983, "but her name is on for full-time ed. in September 84." Ms. Wahlstrom wrote two letters on 16 and 24 May indicating her desire for contact, and on the latter date she arranged to visit on 30 May. She saw Morris Beckford who told her that Beverley Lorrington was staying with all three children at her parents' home. There was further talk of the impending case review. Ms. Wahlstrom indicated that she would see Beverley Lorrington the following Monday either at home or at her parents' home. On 4 June 1984 Ms. Wahlstrom got a message to say that Beverley Lorrington could not see her that week. Later that day Ms. Wahlstrom wrote an urgent letter saying how imperative it was that she saw Beverley and the children before the Review. There was no answer. A visit to the house on 11 June was ineffective. Ms. Wahlstrom left a note. The following day Beverley Lorrington telephoned in an angry mood about the note. She said she would be at her parents' home for the next fortnight and would contact Ms. Wahlstrom after that to arrange a meeting.

On 28 June Ms. Wahlstrom wrote another letter suggesting that she visited the next week. She added that she would be on leave from 9 July, "and we wish to have the Review next week to be able to apply to the Court as soon as possible." By that time Social Services were way out of time. 6 June was the deadline for the statutory case review.

On 3 July 1984 Ms. Wahlstrom wrote the following letter which we reproduce:

3rd July 1984

"Dear Morris and Beverley,
As I have not yet heard from you this week I am writing to inform you that Diane Dietmann and I will *visit you* on Thursday 5th July at 1 p.m. so that we can have the Review and hopefully apply to the Court for the Care Order to be discharged.

Yours sincerely,
Gun Wahlstrom
Social Worker"

We reserve our comments on it until we have described what happened on 5 July 1984, the day Jasmine was killed by her step-father. Mrs. Dietmann and Ms. Wahlstrom duly arrived at the Beckford house at 1 p.m. for "Home visit to have the Review — no reply — left card." The two social workers went to Morris Beckford's place of work and found that, quite exceptionally, he had failed to report for work. They returned to the house; there was still no reply. At 3 o'clock the two were becoming quite frantic. They went to the Public Library to find the maternal grandparents' telephone number (it is astonishing that they did not know it) and called. They were told that Beverley Lorrington was not in. The person at the other end put the telephone down. There was then a telephone call to Morris Beckford's employer who said that Morris Beckford had not been at work that day. A message was left for him to contact the social workers "urgently to-morrow."

It has been assumed, as indeed the Panorama programme of 21 October 1985 on this case did assume, that Mrs. Dietmann and Ms. Wahlstrom had been searching desperately for Jasmine and Louise. Not a bit of it. As the letter of 3 July 1984 says, the desperate need of the social workers was to hasten the process for the case review preparatory to going back to court for the revocation of the Care Orders. The letter did not even mention the children. At the very moment that the two social workers were banging on the Beckford's front door, Jasmine, whom they had the responsibility of protecting against child abuse, was dying, if not dead. If ever in this saga of a home on trial there was a vivid expression of a failure to protect a child it was when Jasmine was *in extremis*.

Stripped of the inessential details of social work activity, the picture is one of unrelieved focusing on the parents. In short, Mrs. Dietmann and Ms. Wahlstrom had been saying, at least since May 1982: "We can rehabilitate this family if we work hard enough on defective parents. Improvement in their parental handling of the children will ensure that there is no repetition of the earlier child abuse." Once the Beckfords were rehoused in March 1982, the social workers' earlier pessimism about rehabilitation quickly changed to a *genuine* attempt at rehabilitation. As soon as the social workers thought they saw the first signs of improved conduct on the part of Morris Beckford and Beverley Lorrington, an overweening optimism took hold. The prime focus on the parents was never adjusted — indeed it was sharpened as the home on trial appeared, month by month to be working. Jasmine thus became the victim of persistent disfunctioning social work while the law demanded, above all, her protection.

127

Part II: Facts and Comments on the Events

B. Social Agencies' Response to Events

CHAPTER 11

Social Services Department of Brent Borough Council

We have thought it helpful if, at the outset of this part of our report dealing with the response of social services and the auxiliary agencies in the management of the child abuse system, we set out at some length the structure of the Social Services Department of Brent throughout the period, August 1981 to date. At the time when Jasmine Beckford's welfare became the direct responsibility of Brent Borough Council, the Director of Social Services was Mr. Harry Whalley. He retired in June 1982 and was succeeded by Miss Valerie Howarth, who has remained in that post. Of the Assistant Directors, Mr. Denis Simpson was responsible for Family Services from November 1981 until he left in March 1985 to become Director of Social Services in Southwark. Area 6 was under his management. Throughout the whole of the relevant period Mr. David Bishop was the Area Manager for Area 6.

Management Team
Since its inception in 1971 Brent Social Services Department has been structured on a functional basis, with Assistant Directors responsible to the Director for various functional duties. Under Mr. Whalley the management team consisted of:-
a) *The Director*
b) *The Assistant Director, Residential and Day Care* — responsible for all the Council's residential and day care establishments, e.g., Old People's Homes, Day Centres for Handicapped People, Children's Homes, Day Nurseries, Meals Kitchen, etc.
c) *The Assistant Director, Development* — responsible for training, research, forward planning, liaison with voluntary organisations, development of new projects.
d) *The Assistant Director, Family Services* — responsible for all services to clients in their own homes and in hospitals; for adoption and fostering work; for court liaison; for three neighbourhood centres; and for an intermediate treatment centre.
e) *The Chief Administrative Officer* — responsible for administrative support to the other divisions and for staffing and finance.

Following the appointment of the present Director, the post of Chief Administrative Officer was deleted from the establishment. Principal Administrative Officers were appointed in the Residential and Day Care and Family Services Divisions, and the Assistant Director, Development and Resources, became responsible for finance and staffing, with some restructuring of his division. At about this time, a Race Relations Adviser was added to the Management Team, which now consists of:-
a) The Director
b) The Assistant Director, Residential and Day Care
c) The Assistant Director, Family Services
d) The Assistant Director, Development and Resources
e) The Race Relations Adviser
Under both Directors there have been regular weekly meetings of the Management Team and, in addition, the Director sees individual Assistant Directors, informally, almost daily, on specific matters.

This functional type of structure is very common in Social Services Departments, although many County Councils and some large Borough Councils have adopted geographical structures, with each Assistant Director undertaking responsibility for all the services within a geographical area. The structure operating in Brent, however, seems appropriate for a relatively small and densely populated Borough.

Each Assistant Director has a substantial number of third-tier officers directly responsible to him, and no-one could accuse Brent Social Services Department of being "top-heavy". The present Director's statement to us that "the Department's senior management is extremely stretched" is entirely understandable. From what we have observed, it is also justified.

The Family Services Division

In this Division, there are 13 Principal Officers (including the Principal Court Officer) directly accountable to the Assistant Director. They are:-

a) *Six Area Managers*, based in offices away from the Department's headquarters at Brent House. These are responsible for providing social services – social work, home help, aids and adaptations, etc. – to clients in their own homes, and for developing community resources within their areas.

b) *Two Hospital Social Work Managers*, based in hospitals and responsible for providing social work for clients in hospital.

The remaining specialist and staff officers are based at Brent House:-

c) *Principal Assistant*, responsible for dealing with staffing issues; reviewing procedures; preparing and presenting reports for the Social Services Committee and Cases Sub-Committee; reviewing service changes and developments.

d) *Principal Administrative Officer*

e) *Intermediate Treatment Co-ordinator*, responsible for arranging "intermediate treatment" facilities for juveniles and advising area teams on these.

f) *Principal Social Worker, Adoption and Foster Care and Community Assessment*, responsible for recruiting and assessing foster-parents and for advising area teams on suitable placements for individual children. Staff in this section also offer social work support to foster parents, but are *not* responsible for the case management of children placed with foster parents; this is the duty of Area team staff. This section is also responsible for adoption work.

g) *Principal Court Officer*, responsible for:

   i) Collation of Social Inquiry Reports, school reports, psychiatric reports, etc., for production at juvenile courts

   ii) Preparation and presentation of care cases in juvenile courts, on behalf of the local authority

   iii) Compilation of statistics relating to the court work of the Department

   iv) Advising the staff of the Social Services Department on matters relating to current legislation and trends in court work, penal policy, etc.

   v) Advising juvenile courts on Council policy relating to juveniles, and on the facilities provided by the Social Services Department

   vi) Acting as custodian of the Child Abuse Register, and co-ordinating policies adopted by the Brent Area Review Committee

   vii) Organisation and supervision of the Night Duty Social Work Team.

These 13 officers, together with the Assistant Director, Family Services, form the Divisional Management Group and meet weekly to deal with relevant policy and practice issues in the Division. Individual principal officers also meet the Assistant Director frequently to discuss specific problems.

We were told that, although the Principal Court Officer advises staff of the Social Services Department on legal matters relating to Child Care, he does not consult the legal officers of the Council's Law and Administration Department, unless he judges this to be necessary, or where he is bound to do so, because he cannot himself conduct the case in court, e.g., wardship cases in the High Court. We were also told that there is no member of the Law and Administration Department who handles legal cases exclusively, or even mainly for Social Services.

The Director of Social Services told us that she would welcome the allocation of a solicitor in the Law and Administration Department who would take part in case conferences, if appropriate, represent the Social Services Department in care cases in court, and, generally, advise her and her staff on points of law. We discuss the question of nominating of such a legal adviser in our section on legal services.

There is no member of staff specifically concerned with child abuse,although such a post existed for three or four years in the late seventies, funded in collaboration with the NSPCC. This officer worked on some of the more difficult child abuse cases and, although technically responsible to the Principal Court Officer, had close contact with the Assistant Director. The post ceased to exist when NSPCC involvement was withdrawn. The Director of Social Services told us that she regarded the establishment of a post of Principal Social Worker as a high priority. Such an officer would, inter alia, take the chair at difficult case conferences, act as custodian of the Child Abuse Register and give professional advice to social work staff. As an alternative, bearing in mind financial restraints, **we recommend that Brent Borough Council discuss with Brent Health Authority the establishment, under joint financing arrangements, of a post of Child Abuse Training Coordinator.** Such a post is held in the City of Westminster by one of our expert witnesses, Miss Alix Causby, who sets up training programmes, and is a trainer about child abuse for all professionals, both in the Health Authority and in the Social Services Department, who come into contact with families and children. Such an appointment would have the cosmetic, if not actual advantage of acknowledging the joint involvement of both authorities in cases of child abuse, and would, indeed, be a reflection of our own Inquiry which was set up jointly by Brent Borough Council and Brent Health Authority.

Area 6 Team
Area Managers are required to deploy the staff available to them in such a way as to provide the optimum level of service to the local community. They can structure their teams as they see fit, in order to meet the needs of their areas.

When the Beckford case started, Area 6 social workers were divided into four teams, each under the leadership of a Senior Social Worker. The teams were

a) *Intake Team,* consisting of the senior social worker; 3 social workers for reception and short-term case work; one health social worker who liaised with the Health Visitors in the area; one social worker specialising in mental health cases; one homefinding officer for adults. This team dealt with new referrals and short term cases.

b) *Home Care Team,* consisting of the senior social worker; 2 generic social workers; one social worker attached to a general practice; one occupational therapist; one family aide; one home care organiser; two assistant home care organisers; 30 home helps. This team was responsible for all long term work with elderly, physically handicapped or mentally handicapped clients in the area; the social workers, however, spent only about half of their time on such clients, the remainder being spent on a variety of clients, including children in care.

c) *Long Term Team,* consisting of the senior social worker; 4 generic social workers;

131

one family aide; one social work assistant. This team was responsible for working with children in long term care.

d) *Family Care Team*, consisting of the senior social worker; 4 generic social workers; one childminding development worker; one under-fives development worker and one playworker employed at Treetops under-fives centre; one Asian specialist social worker. This team was responsible for work with families and children.

Although these four teams were organised broadly according to types of client, there was some flexibility in allocating cases to them. The four senior social workers would meet weekly, the leader of the Intake Team would describe the cases which had come in during the week, and the senior social workers would allocate these among themselves. Occasionally, as with the Beckford children, who were allocated to Ms. Wahlstrom, a member of the Home Care Team, the allocation of a case was made by the Area Manager, in consultation with the senior social workers. Flexibility was further illustrated by the "borrowing" of a Family Aide (Mrs. Ruddock) by the Home Care team from the Long Term Team to work specifically with the Beckford family.

The advantage of this type of structure is that some expertise in working with a particular category of client is developed within the social work team. Although the Home Care team included workers such as the Home Help Organisers who dealt almost entirely with the elderly and with handicapped adults, the social workers had, however, to be diverted from work with such clients in order to spend some 50% of their time on child care cases. This preponderance of social workers' time spent on children and families, as opposed to other clients, is usual in social services departments, although not necessarily desirable.

In addition to the four social work teams, Area 6 in 1981 had a *Neighbourhood Centre* staffed by two neighbourhood workers and one clerk/receptionist.

These teams were supported in the Area by an *Administrative Section* consisting of a senior administrative officer; an assistant administrative officer; 7 clerical staff; one typist; one receptionist; three cleaners; one driver; one escort. Additional typing support was provided by the central typing pool at Brent House, but this was wholly unsatisfactory, since the typing pool was some miles from Area 6 office and was unable to return typing in less than a week or ten days.

In January 1984, after lengthy discussion and careful planning, the structure of Area 6 was changed to a "Patch" system, with each social work team being responsible for all services to clients living in a small geographical patch. The new teams were:-

a) *Chamberlayne Patch* – consisting of the senior social worker; 3 generic social workers; 1/2 (whole-time equivalent) Family Aide; one Asian specialist social worker; one mental health specialist social worker; one childminding development worker; 1½ (WTE) clerks.

b) *Kensal Rise Patch* – consisting of the senior social worker; 4½ (WTE) generic social workers; one social work assistant; ½ (WTE) family aide; one clerk. The Neighbourhood Centre with a staff of 2 neighbourhood workers, and one clerk/receptionist was included in this team.

c) *Manor Patch* – consisting of the senior social worker; 3½ (WTE) generic social workers; one family aide; one clerk.

d) *Queens Park Patch* – consisting of the senior social worker; 3 generic social workers; one social work assistant; one G.P. attached social worker; one clerk.

Social services officers, other than social workers and their assistants and family aides, ceased to be attached to the social work teams, but were formed into separate professional units, covering the whole area and directly responsible to the Area Manager. These units were:-

a) *Home Care* – consisting of the home care organiser, 2½ (WTE) assistant home care organisers, 80 home helps and one clerk. One or ½ (WTE) assistant home care organiser worked with each patch team to ensure satisfactory liaison with the social workers.

b) *Occupational Therapy* – consisting of the senior occupational therapist, one occupational therapist and one clerk.

c) *Treetops* – This centre for the under-fives ceased to be attached to a social work team. The officer-in-charge became directly responsible to the Area Manager and was assisted by a senior playworker, two playworkers, a driver and an escort.

d) *Homefinding for Adults* – The number of workers involved in this task was increased from one to four, and these officers formed a separate unit.

e) *The under fives development worker*

As in the former structure, the *Administrative Section* provided support to the professional teams. The staffing of this section was increased by one clerk and 7½ (WTE) of the 8 clerks, although still accountable to the senior administrative officer, were attached to the professional teams. Similarly, the driver and escort were based at Treetops.

We were told that, since January 1984, additional staff had been appointed to Area 6 to work in two Homeless Persons Units (2 social workers, one family aide, one playworker, one clerk); also an additional part time family aide to work on mental health with the Asian specialist social worker.

"Patch Teams" of social workers are becoming increasingly common in social services departments. Mr. Bishop, the Area Manager of Area 6, explained to us that two or three social workers, confining their cases to a small geographical patch, should become a part of the life of that neighbourhood, in close touch with school staff, health visitors, GPs, shopkeepers and the community in general. He felt that if such a system had been in operation from 1981 onwards, the Beckfords' social worker might have received indications from various sources in the community about what was happening in the family during 1983 and 1984.

In practice, the change to the Patch System did not affect the Beckford case because, in order to avoid a change of social worker for the family, Ms. Wahlstrom retained the case, although she and her senior, Mrs. Dietmann, were working in the Manor patch and the Beckfords lived in Kensal Rise patch. Ms. Wahlstrom did not, therefore, have the opportunity to become closely involved in the neighbourhood surrounding the Beckfords' home.

In general, we believe that there is merit in the patch system, provided that the social workers are prepared to involve themselves fully in the life of the community in which they are working. This is easier if the team's office is situated in the patch; unfortunately this could not be achieved in Area 6, where staff have to work from their very inadequate Area office on the periphery of the area, and far from most of the patches.

We have very little, if anything to say critically about the structure of Brent Social Services Department, save what we have interspersed in the course of this descriptive section of the report. But we do have one concern that we think needs urgent attention. We consider that the provision of typing services to an Area team from a central typing pool several miles away is highly inefficient. Much time is wasted in conveying manuscript or typed material for typing from the Area Office to the typing pool and, because of staff shortages there, Area staff cannot rely on important reports being typed in time to meet deadlines, e.g. for court. Professional staff have to produce less important reports in handwriting, which is a waste of their time. Mr. Bishop told us that, owing to lack of clerical support he had to take the minutes of meetings and case conferences which he was chairing, as did his senior social workers — not an efficient practice, as they all recognised.

We strongly recommend that adequate typing support should be provided in each Area office.

Resource Constraints

The Director of Social Services told us that Brent was seriously under-resourced, by comparison with similar London Boroughs. However, while accepting her evidence, we do not consider that shortage of resources was a significant factor in this case, save in respect of the continuing deficiency of senior social workers in Area 6. Indeed, we were favourably impressed by the large amount of staff time which was devoted to the Beckford family, from the day when Place of Safety Orders were obtained for Jasmine and Louise until the day of Jasmine's death, nearly three years later.

Three members of Area 6 staff and a Social Services Court Officer attended the initial case conference on 6 August 1981 and during the next five weeks, Ms. Wahlstrom saw the family ten times. There was also intensive work by her seniors, by the Adoption and Fostering Care Section which had been searching for foster parents for the children, and by the Court Section which was preparing the case for the juvenile court.

After the Care Orders were made on 9 September 1981, a programme was established to maintain the link between the children and their parents. This entailed fortnightly counselling sessions with the parents by Ms. Wahlstrom, weekly sessions at Treetops for Beverley Lorrington with Mrs. Ruddock, the Family Aide, "borrowed" from another Team, and weekly visits by the children to their parents at Treetops, which involved a driver and an escort to convey them from their foster home.

This programme, which must have cost the equivalent of about two full-time staff days per week, continued until December 1981, when it was intensified. Parental contact was to be increased from two to four hours per week, and was to be at the parents' own home under supervision; also Miss Lorrington was to spend two half days, instead of one, with Mrs. Ruddock at Treetops.

Throughout this period, in addition to intensive work with the parents, staff time was also being spent with the foster parents. Ms. Wahlstrom visited them at least 14 times and had many telephone conversations with them. Mr. Burns was also a frequent visitor.

Shortage of resources was not a problem in the Social Services Department's dealings with the Proberts. Not only did they receive the standard boarding-out allowances but the allowance was doubled for Jasmine because of the extra work involved in caring for her after the injury to her leg. Also some £600 was given to them for equipment for the children.

In March 1982, the Beckford parents were offered a Council tenancy and during the period of their removal, Ms. Wahlstrom visited them frequently. On 5 April 1982, it was decided that the children should be moved to Green Lodge for daily contact with their parents and thence, if all went well, home on trial. The move took place on 13 April 1982 and, during the following week, Mrs. Ruddock spent all her time with the Beckfords, and Ms. Wahlstrom also spent three days with them.

On 19 April 1982, the children were returned to their parents, and after a week during which they were visited daily it was arranged that Mrs. Ruddock would visit on 3 days and Ms. Wahlstrom on 2 days each week. Also Jasmine would attend Mortimer Road Day Nursery on 5 mornings each week. Thus, although the Social Services were no longer having to pay for the maintenance of the children in the foster home, substantial resources in terms of staff time were still being spent on the Beckford family. Also some £300 was given to the Beckfords under Section 1, Child Care Act 1980, for essential equipment.

[In this connection, it is worth noting that financial constraints were less pressing for the Beckfords than for many clients of the Social Services Department, since Mr. Beckford had always been in regular employment and was able and willing to work overtime to increase his income].

On 25 May 1982 it was decided that visiting could be reduced to once a week by Mrs. Ruddock and once a fortnight by Ms. Wahlstrom, but it is clear that this decision was based on a belief that the family did not need, and would prefer not to have more frequent visits, rather than on a shortage of resources.

In September 1983 Mrs. Ruddock left to go on a professional training course, and it was decided that she need not be replaced. We are satisfied that this decision was based on the mistaken belief of Mrs. Dietmann and Ms. Wahlstrom, expressed as early as April 1982, that the family no longer needed the kind of help which Mrs. Ruddock had been giving. (Mrs. Ruddock continued to support and befriend the Beckford family on a voluntary basis thereafter until September 1983). Had they felt it to be necessary, they could have provided, if not a Family Aide, at least a Home Help. Once again, shortage of resources was not a significant factor. Ms. Wahlstrom continued to visit the family frequently but, unfortunately, the time which she devoted to them was ineffective, in that she failed to see what was happening to Jasmine.

We are satisfied that, whatever resource constraints existed in the Social Services Department, there was no shortage of finance either for the foster parents or for the parents of Jasmine and Louise. Also, the staff in charge of the case were able to make use of facilities provided by the Department's establishments — Tree Tops, Green Lodge and Mortimer Road Day Nursery. Above all, a great deal of staff time was spent on this case.

The problem was not lack of staff time spent with the family, but a faulty appraisal of what was happening in the Beckford household and faulty decision-making at several stages in the case. Could these faults be attributed to lack of resources?

We recognise that both Mrs. Dietmann and Ms. Wahlstrom lacked experience of child abuse cases, but they were both qualified and experienced social workers of several years' standing. We note that the Social Services Department did provide many training courses for staff; indeed Ms. Wahlstrom had obtained her CQSW in 1979 and had attended a multi-disciplinary course on child abuse in December 1983, but she seems not to have related any of this training to her daily practice with the Beckford family. We do not think that shortage of resources was ever a cause of her failure to see what was happening in the Beckford household in the months preceding Jasmine's death.

Regarding the quality of decision-making throughout the case, we have stated our view that it is undesirable for case conferences to be chaired by the officer supervising the social worker directly involved in a case. An Area Manager, either from the Area concerned or from another Area, would be a more suitable chairman. However, we recognise that the very serious shortage of senior social workers in Area 6 from September 1981 to October 1983 made it impossible for Mr. Bishop to undertake this task in all cases. Furthermore, this shortage put him under severe pressure, not only because he had to undertake many of the duties of the missing seniors but also because he had to maintain the morale of the remaining staff in the face of these shortages and the constant shortage of clerical and administrative assistance. The burdens of administration in Area 6 were exacerbated by the appalling physical conditions in which Mr. Bishop and his staff had to work. **We recommend that the local authority should give urgent attention to the question of accommodation.** Had Area 6 been fully staffed, we believe that Mr. Bishop could, and probably would have taken a more active part in decision-making over the Beckford case and also monitored more closely the work being done by Mrs. Dietmann and Ms. Wahlstrom.

The shortage of senior social workers was largely due to circumstances beyond the

Council's control, but we do note that in August 1983 the Chairman of Finance and General Purposes Committee, Councillor Sealy, and the Chairman of the Establishment Sub-Committee, Councillor Hansen, imposed a three-month delay on the advertising of one of the vacant posts. We regret that, when Mr. Bishop succeeded in recruiting a locum to take the place of Mrs. Dietmann during her maternity leave, Councillor Sealy would not allow him to implement the appointment for the first three months of Mrs. Dietmann's absence. This meant that Ms. Wahlstrom was not only without supervision of her work but that she herself also had to undertake some of Mrs. Dietmann's supervisory duties over other members of the Team.

We have recorded elsewhere our view that a specialist in child abuse would be a valuable addition to the staff of the Social Services Department. Such an appointment was made in the late 1970s by Mr. Whalley, the former Director of Social Services, and was funded by arrangement with the NSPCC, but the post disappeared when that funding ceased to be available.

The present Director of Social Services told us that a new post of Principal Social Worker in the Department would be one of her highest priorities at this stage. She would like such a person to be responsible for the child abuse register, to take the chair at difficult case conferences and to look at and monitor social work activities in general. We note that although she has made a number of recommendations to the Social Services Committee about staffing, since her appointment in 1982, she has not mentioned such a post. However, although she has made, and the Council has accepted, some recommendations for increased staffing of Central Support Services, most of her recommendations have been for the development of family and community centres, for more services for the elderly (care assistants, home helps, meals on wheels staff, etc.) and for resources for mentally handicapped people – a salutary reminder that the Social Services Committee has to provide for the needs of many, many people other than children at risk.

Mortimer Road Day Nursery

At the Case Conference on 5 April 1982, when it was decided to return Jasmine and Louise Beckford to their parents' home, Mrs. Diane Dietmann is recorded as having stated that plans had been made for Jasmine to attend five mornings a week at Mortimer Road Day Nursery (it was to be part-time) and that Jasmine would be seen by the speech therapist there. Miss Proudlock, the day nursery officer in charge (or matron) apologised for her absence from that Case Conference. Nothing appeared in the documentation to indicate the purpose of Jasmine's attendance at nursery school (In Chapter 22 we refer generally to the need for all documentation to indicate clearly the objectives and purposes of social work action in child abuse cases).

At our Inquiry, Ms. Wahlstrom was asked by her own counsel whether the place at the nursery had been designed to secure a means of monitoring the child. She answered: "It was to help Beverley so that she did not have the care of both children all day and also to give Jasmine the opportunity to play with other children and to help Jasmine with her speech." In cross-examination, Ms. Wahlstrom reluctantly conceded that attendance at the nursery had some monitoring content, although she was quite unaware that she saw school attendance generally as a monitoring process in child abuse cases. Mrs. Dietmann also did not envisage the plan, as detailed to the Case Conference, as having a monitoring effect. It is manifest that neither Ms. Wahlstrom, nor Mrs. Dietmann appreciated the significance of the monitoring element in a child, who is at risk, of attending at school.

There was no hitch in the channel of communication between Ms. Wahlstrom and Miss Proudlock. The latter knew in March of Jasmine's impending arrival at the nursery and that Jasmine was on the non-accidental injury register, although, again, monitoring was at best given no priority, because Miss Proudlock was told "not to put any pressure" on the Beckfords and to contact the social workers only if there were problems and anxieties.

It says much for the effect of monitoring in child abuse that Miss Proudlock's keen observations of Jasmine's welfare did not reveal any sign of bruising during her stay at the nursery, and we have concluded that no child abuse occurred during that period. Miss Proudlock in fact discerned an improving relationship between Beverley Lorrington and Jasmine; she rarely saw Morris Beckford deliver or pick up his step-daughter. Miss Proudlock kept a record, but not a contemporary one, of Jasmine's attendances and noted that they became erratic — "out for a week, in for a week and out again", her attendance ceasing altogether at the beginning of November 1982. Miss Proudlock actually took Jasmine off the nursery register only in January 1983 when she was notified to do so. After 9 November 1982, when the children were taken off the non-accidental injury register, Miss Proudlock treated Jasmine as being no longer at risk, but had she been attending the nursery after November 1982 she would still have kept a weather-eye open for signs of physical abuse. (We observe that, according to Mr. Walker's expert evidence, the earliest of Jasmine's bone injuries may well have occurred around that time, and we have so found: see Chapter 9.) Miss Proudlock, in our view, did regard attendance as having a distinct monitoring purpose.

At the Case Conference of 9 November 1982 which was chaired by Mrs. Dietmann, who also took the minutes of the meeting — a disastrous combination of line-management chairing and minute-taking — Miss Proudlock attended. She told us — and we believe her — that she mentioned to the conference her unease at Jasmine's nonattendance in the autumn of 1982. That important fact, however, wholly escaped the attention of Mrs. Dietmann. Even if she can justifiably claim that chairing and taking the minutes means that the record is inevitably skimpy, we think that the omission is of a piece. It is entirely consistent with the tenor of the work with the Beckfords — that everything was going smoothly with the process of rehabilitation, and nothing that could detract one iota from that rosy picture should be allowed to intrude to question the decision to remove the children from the register, or to appear as a question-mark on the record of that decision-making process.

The minutes of that Case Conference refer specifically to Jasmine's speech having improved. Given that in April 1982 the referral to the speech therapist has been in the context of attendance at Mortimer Road Day Nursery, one might have expected some note of how Jasmine had performed at the nursery, including the record of attendance. The Case Conference is deafeningly silent on one important aspect of child abuse. We conclude, however, that the failure to take on board this aspect of child abuse played only an insignificant part in the process of a flawed service in child protection.

CHAPTER 12

Brent Health Authority

The period of Jasmine Beckford's life, from December 1979 to July 1984, was punctuated by the reorganisation of the National Health Service in 1982, whereby a tier of authority was removed, so that Brent Health Authority (previously Brent Health District) came directly under the North-West Thames Regional Health Authority. We mention that fact to indicate that reorganisations do sometimes cause upheaval. We have in this instance discerned no adverse effect of the changes on the quality of health visiting in Brent during the relevant period. But there was one change in the structure of the management of community nursing — namely, the removal of one tier of management, the Senior Nursing Officer — which had a direct, but still not significant impact on the supervision of health visitors involved in the child abuse system.

The three Nursing Officers for Health Visiting were in 1982 upgraded to Senior Nurses, one of them having specific responsibility, among other things, for child abuse. Prior to reorganisation, the Senior Nursing Officer had responsibility as Child Abuse Coordinator. To that end she kept two lists — one, which was kept for administrative purposes, coinciding with the Child Abuse Register held by the Area Review Committee or the Social Services Department of the local authority; the other was called the Health Visitors Concern List.

The Health Visitors Concern List consisted of a list of children who were not on the Child Abuse Register, but, in the view of the Health Visitor, were giving cause for concern as to health or potential risk of physical injuries. The Health Visitor had, as a matter of routine, to submit four-monthly reports on any child who was on Tier 2 of the Health Visitors Concern List. Tier 1 cases, which included children not on the Child Abuse Register but were nevertheless of concern to the Health Visitor, had to be reported half-yearly.

There were three Health Visitors in the Brent community nursing services who were involved with the Beckford family during Jasmine's lifetime. Together with the community health doctor, they worked from Mortimer Road Clinic. (During the seven months that Jasmine was boarded-out with foster-parents, September 1981-April 1982, she was regularly visited by Miss Bowden, a Health Visitor from Harrow Health Authority. We note only that during this period Jasmine was weighed regularly, disclosing a dramatic reversal of her earlier failure to thrive, a fact that never seemed to dawn on anyone as significant of persistent child abuse long before the hospitalisations of August 1981).

Resource constraints
There was no indication in the evidence before us that the service provided by the community nursing service to the Beckford family, and especially to Jasmine and Louise Beckford, was adversely affected by any constraint consequent upon the available resources. It is convenient, in indicating our reasons for so concluding, to outline the actual input of health visiting during the relevant periods by the three health visitors, even though we are aware that much of it is repetitious of facts related in chapters 8 and 10.

December 1979 — September 1980
Miss Gillian Hindle made seven visits to the family during the period, but actually saw Jasmine and her mother on only four occasions. Jasmine attended the Mortimer Road Clinic on three occasions for developmental assessment, as well as for immunisations

by the Clinic Medical Officer, who had worked continuously at the Clinic since 1975.

During the first six months from birth, Jasmine's weight gain was satisfactory and there were no indications that Jasmine should have been placed on either the Child Abuse Register or on the Health Visitors Concern List. Although Jasmine was healthy, there were social problems which were recorded and seen as indicators of potential difficulties, but not dissimilar from other children in the neighbourhood.

September 1980 – August 1981 and April – July 1982

Miss Judy Knowles took over when Miss Hindle left the Authority in September 1980. She made three home visits in the period to July 1981 and during that period Jasmine was also seen at Mortimer Road Clinic on three occasions for further assessment and immunisations. In October 1980 Miss Knowles began the percentile chart which was to lie unseen after July 1982 in the files of the Mortimer Road Clinic.

The first Case Conference on Jasmine on 6 August 1981 was attended by Miss Knowles, accompanied by a Nursing Officer, and with apologies received from the Child Health Specialist. At that Case Conference Miss Knowles is recorded as having said that Jasmine was of normal development mentally, but that her weight was low. Miss Knowles also observed that Jasmine was under-stimulated; that Miss Lorrington was impatient with her boyfriend, Mr. Beckford, and also with Jasmine; and that Miss Lorrington did not have much idea of how to handle the child emotionally. The Case Conference decided that the two Beckford sisters should be placed on the Child Abuse Register. At the second Case Conference on 20 August 1981, Miss Knowles attended, accompanied by a Nursing Officer. On 5 April 1982 a Case Conference was held to discuss a plan to return the children home on trial. Although an invitation was sent to Miss Knowles, neither she nor the Nursing Officer attended. However, they did receive the minutes of the Case Conference. The Case Conference decided that the children should be returned to the parents. It also recommended that Miss Lorrington was to be encouraged to attend the clinic monthly, and the Health Visitor to visit fortnightly. This was not challenged by Miss Knowles or her supervisor. From the recorded visits it would appear that no effort was made to visit fortnightly. Monthly visits were, however, attempted.

Miss Knowles' visit in May 1982 was unsuccessful, but in June she saw Jasmine at home for the last time before handing over to Miss Leong. She recorded that Jasmine looked "pathetic and pinched," with little speech or concentration, and no interest shown in her by her mother. It is not apparent whether these observations, though recorded, were reported to Ms. Wahlstrom, the key worker. On 7 July 1982 Ms. Wahlstrom reported to Miss Knowles that the family was making good progress.

July 1982 – July 1984

Miss Knowles left her employment as a health visitor in July 1982 and handed over the case to Miss Leong, who remained the family's Health Visitor up to the time of Jasmine's death. Miss Leong was trained in 1978 as a Health Visitor and when she took over the case of the Beckford family she had a case load of 385 families from different social backgrounds. Of those families, only two were on the Child Abuse Register. She made monthly visits from July to October 1982.

A Case Conference was held by Area 6 Social Services on 9 November 1982 to remove the children from the Child Abuse Register. The Health Visitor was invited, but was unable to attend due to ill health. No-one else from the Health Service was in attendance.

Miss Leong made two visits following the Case Conference in November, but failed to gain access. She made nine visits to the home from January to December 1983; Jasmine was seen on two occasions – once in January and the other in April. Miss Leong was told on one other occasion that Jasmine was out shopping and on another that she was

140

at the grandmother's. The Panel heard in evidence that the grandmother had not seen Jasmine during 1983. No check had been made of the mother's statement.

In 1984 Miss Leong visited the Beckford household twice in February, twice in May and once in June, but had no reply on each occasion.

We are quite satisfied from the facts that we have examined that there has been no indication of lack of resources of any kind. It has not been borne out that any of the Health Visitors concerned had been adversely affected by an excessive case load. The three health visitors were well-equipped in terms of experience and training. They had a smattering of knowledge of child abuse. Miss Hindle had attended a multi-disciplinary course on child abuse in early 1979. Although Miss Knowles appears not to have undergone any training specifically on child abuse, it was she who was the keenest observer of signs of incipient child abuse. It was she who started the percentile chart; she reported generally on Jasmine's low weight; and she noted the understimulation of Jasmine. Miss Leong attended a course on child abuse in February 1982.

There is no evidence that, had more resources been available — in the form of lower case-loads and more time devoted to the child abuse cases, such as the Beckfords — the outcome would have been any different. What was sadly lacking was any sense of the proper use of the available resources. The resources were plainly ill-directed. There was an absence of vital decision-making in the Beckford case; misinterpretation of the indicators and warning signs of oncoming child abuse; a series of errors of judgment; and an inability on the part of Miss Leong to act as a member of a team in the child abuse system, a failure that is in part attributable to training and in part to the isolation of her work, for want of support through proper supervision. We trust that these criticisms are justified by the facts and comments related in chapters 8 and 10. We do no more here than examine some general issues that are prompted by our Inquiry.

Supervision

The aspect that has most troubled us has been the question of supervision. In his submission to us Mr. Nigel Pitt, on behalf of Miss Leong and the other community nurses, put the point crisply: "Supervision is essential in child abuse cases, even for experienced workers. It should bring an *objective* and *critical* view to bear on the case as well as the greater experience and knowledge of the supervisor. Without the benefit of adequate supervision in child abuse cases the inexperienced and inadequately trained field-worker may well miss the warning signs. That is what happened here." We agree. That summarises exactly what did happen here. Whatever criticism lies at Miss Leong's door, it is to be magnified in respect of those who were supposed to be supervising her. We do not want to elaborate unnecessarily, because readers of chapters 8 and 10 will, we think, find ample material to justify our view. But we think it will help the reader if we look at just one aspect of the problem of supervision (or the lack of it) following the April 1982 Case Conference — namely, ensuring medical examinations of the children while home on trial.

We have noted the non-attendance of Miss Knowles, unfortunate as it was. But one of the main recommendations of that Conference was that Miss Knowles, or her successor, Miss Leong, who was shortly to take over, should encourage Miss Lorrington to visit the clinic, and that the Health Visitor should visit the family fortnightly. From the records, it is evident that these recommendations were not followed through. It has been recorded that Miss Knowles established a monthly visiting pattern, but gave no indication that she had either informed her nursing manager, or that she had insufficient time in which to visit the family on a fortnightly basis. Miss Knowles did not continue with her percentile chart after September 1981. Also no reference was made by her regarding her liaison with Ms. Wahlstrom, the key worker. Nothing was passed on about exhorting the mother to take the children to the clinic.

Miss Knowles recorded an unsuccessful visit in May. In June, however, she recorded a home visit: "New home still sparsely furnished but couple making a great effort. Jasmine rather pathetic child, little speech or concentration although tried to go through books with her. Not interested if mother showed her either. Father came home and called up from downstairs. Jasmine refused to see him? Because I was there Louise making some normal responses to mother, walking well. A little speech heard. Both children reported to be eating well but Jasmine still looks *pinched* and *worried*." [the word was crossed out, but we decipher it as "worried"]. There is no indication that these matters percolated through to anyone, least of all to her supervisor. Miss Knowles left the Authority in July 1982 and handed over the case to Miss Leong. We were not told that Miss Leong's attention was drawn to the percentile chart. No evidence was offered to show that she had ever seen it, or that anyone else saw it. There is no evidence that the recommendation of the Case Conference was passed on. No supervisor was involved in the process of the hand-over.

Miss Leong recorded three successful home visits on 15.7.82, 3.8.82 and 20.8.82. On 6 October 1982 recorded home visit "Good vocabulary. Attends nursery a.m. wishes to apply for whole day. Good bonding with sister. Has a cold. Advised warmth and extra fluid. Mother now unemployed. Advised on mother and toddler group and under 5's centre. Mother wishes to extend nursery to whole day. Advised to contact S.W." There is no sign there that Miss Leong was encouraging or urging a visit to the clinic.

Brent Social Services held a Case Conference on 9 November 1982 to remove the children from the Child Abuse Register. The Health Visitor was invited but was unable to attend due to ill health. It was not recorded that the Nursing Officer was even alerted, let alone attended. No one else from the Health Service attended. The record shows that the minutes of the Case Conference were received by Miss Leong on 29 November, three weeks later. Again, with the exception to be described in the next paragraph, no supervisor appears to have been in play at any stage around the autumn of 1982, a period when, as we find, Jasmine suffered the earliest of her limb fractures while home on trial.

Miss Leong sent a copy of the Case Conference minutes together with the routine report on the family to Miss Tyler, the Nursing Officer, who then discussed both documents with the Senior Nursing Officer but not with the Health Visitor concerned. The normal procedure in Brent was that the Health Visitor should discuss with the Nursing Officer any new problems or information affecting the case between the reports. At this stage none of the staff directly involved, namely Miss Leong, Miss Tyler, and Miss Bateman, considered placing Jasmine or Louise on the Health Visitors Concern List.

Miss Leong was able to make two home visits following the case conference in November. Her records indicate that she did not gain access on 29 November 1982 and 30 November 1982. From January 1983 to December 1983 nine home visits were recorded. Jasmine was seen only twice, in January and again in April. On three other occasions when the Health Visitor did not see Jasmine, her records show that excuses were offered — once that Jasmine was out shopping, once that Jasmine was at her grandmother's and once that Jasmine was at school. In evidence, the grandmother told us that she had not seen Jasmine in 1983. When on 20 December 1983, Miss Leong's record showed that Jasmine was at school, not only was the school actually closed for Christmas — it had closed on 16 December — , but Jasmine had not attended school since 9 September 1983, nor did she ever again. None of this was discussed between Miss Leong and her supervisor. Miss Leong recorded further home visits on 13 February 1984, 17 February 1984 and 14 May 1984 — all failed visits.

Apart from attendance at the two Case Conferences of August 1981, no supervision of the two health visitors, Miss Knowles and Miss Leong, was effected, save in the limited sense that the supervisor was there, ever ready no doubt to be consulted as and when supervision was activated by the health visitor. Miss Tyler, Senior Nurse, told us that the health visitors under her supervision, which included Miss Leong, were expected to recognise their own areas of weakness and of doubt about their responses to individual cases, and to approach her for guidance and assistance. She considered that there was no obligation on her part to monitor the performance of a health visitor. The crux of supervision to her was self-monitoring by the supervised of his or her own performance; once problems were so identified, to seek help from the supervisor. We think this is a misconception of the true function of a supervisor. Supervision calls for initiative from the supervisor. It must be proactive, and not just reactive.

Miss Martin, Director of Nursing Services, told us that when she assumed her present post in September 1983 she was concerned about the absence of proper monitoring of health visiting. She encouraged regular interviews between Senior Nurse and Health Visitors, and she requested the constant checking of health visiting records by the Senior Nurse. We find it unnecessary to make any recommendation in this regard, because we are satisfied that the message about the importance of supervision had been absorbed by those in authority even before we began our Inquiry. **What we do recommend is that sometime in the near future Brent Health Authority should conduct an internal review of the present procedures to see whether the new broom has, as we confidently believe, swept away the dust gathered over years of inactive "supervision".**

Collaboration with Social Services

We have had an abundance of evidence all in favour of stressing the important contribution of health services in determining not merely whether a child has been abused by its parents but also in deciding the future management of the care of the child. The importance is heightened when the child is returned on a home on trial and the child's safety is at risk. It cannot be too strongly emphasised that the role of the health visitor in the management of a child abuse case is to cooperate fully with social workers. Given the importance of health services in the management of the child abuse system, we were initially tempted to consider whether the parental rights and duties assumed by a local authority under a Care Order should be jointly shared with the relevant health authority.

The responsibility for medical treatment clearly lies with the health authority and is performed by the provision of hospitals and a community health service. While having no direct statutory duties under the Care Order, the health authority is accountable to the Secretary of State in the event of failure to carry out any functions, being obligations and powers conferred or imposed on it: see Section 85(1), National Health Service Act 1977. This accountability to the Secretary of State is couched in terms similar to those imposed upon a local authority in respect of its functions. Is it necessary to impose further statutory obligations other than those running on parallel lines?

There is a temptation to say that when a death such as Jasmine's has occurred, the whole basis of caring for children must be altered radically rather than by tinkering with the existing system. One would give in to the temptation if the multi-disciplinary concept of the present child abuse system had been operating at its full potential, and still the tragedy had occurred. Where professional judgment must be applied, there is always some element of risk-taking, and it is fair to say that even with the most efficient system there may, and almost inevitably will be, tragic failures. What is required is a high level of commitment which must be engendered by good professional practice within a well-defined system which is followed by all agencies. We hope that our recommendations, if implemented, will greatly enhance the quality of professional judgment and action, and so improve the system. We have concluded that before we could contemplate recommending a joint order we would have to be satisfied that the present system, if operated fully and sensibly, was fundamentally unsound. We think that the system, with modifications, is basically sound. But while we reject the idea of a joint order, we do think that there are sound reasons for wanting to impose, by statute, some duties that will reflect the need to secure the collaborative efforts of Health Services and Social Services in the management by Social Services of the child abuse system.

At present the statutory duty to investigate and/or bring proceedings is imposed on the local authority. Section 2(1) of the Children and Young Persons Act 1969 provides that:-

> "If a local authority receive information suggesting that there are grounds for bringing care proceedings in respect of a child or young person who resides or is found in their area, it shall be the duty of the authority to cause enquiries to be made into the case unless they are satisfied that such enquiries are unnecessary."

Section 2(2) provides that:-

> "If it appears to a local authority that there are grounds for bringing care proceedings in respect of a child or young person who resides or is found in their area, it shall be the duty of the authority to exercise their power unless they are satisfied that it is neither in his interest nor in the public interest to do so or that some other person is about to do so or to charge him with an offence."

The *power* to bring care proceedings under Section 1, the Children and Young Persons Act 1969 is conferred on a local authority, police constables and authorised persons. Authorisation has only been extended to the NSPCC, in respect of whom there is no statutory duty to investigate. Statute does not confer on the Police or the NSPCC a duty to bring proceedings. Both Miss Howarth and Mr. Bedford were opposed to the extension of the duty to investigate and power to bring care proceedings to other public bodies, such as a health authority. While the power of the Police to act in certain situations is useful, it is rarely exercised in practice. It would, in our view, be an illogical and unhelpful duplication of resources to extend the power to bring care proceedings when the Care Order will be vested in the local authority. It is likely to result in confusion and further breakdown in the multi-disciplinary concept. There is little evidence that local authorities do not bring proceedings when necessary. An extension of the power to go before the court in such circumstances may serve only to intensify differences of opinion when the whole basis of a Case Conference should be to arrive at a consensus and make *recommendations*. It would be wrong to burden the local authority with the legal responsibility for a Care Order which it had not initiated, and which in the exercise of its duty under Section 2(2) of the Act it did not consider necessary in the interests of the child.

144

On the present framework of the legislation the statutory duty to investigate is, in the broad sense, *investigating whether there are grounds for bringing care proceedings.* As such, an extension of the duty to investigate is incompatible with the absence of power to bring proceedings which is neither necessary nor desirable. The duty to investigate, whether or not there are grounds to bring care proceedings, involves the investigation of a whole range of issues with which a health authority is not equipped to deal.

Duty to notify when child abuse is suspected
Within the ambit of the broader duty there is the duty to notify the Social Services Department when a health professional suspects that child abuse has occurred. Professor Greenland referred us to the statutory duty to inform, which is imposed in the Canadian legislation on child protection. Such a provision, being the expression of what must be good professional practice, would generally do little more than underline awareness of the duty, and avoid misinterpretation of professional duty and/or local policy.

We do not contend that there is evidence to suggest that the imposition of such a statutory duty would necessarily cure any current failure to notify. Nevertheless there is no doubt that there is a professional duty to inform the Social Services Department when a child is examined and is found to be physically injured in suspicious circumstances. In practice, the only situation where one could envisage a health professional not informing the Social Services Department is where he/she did not think that there were *reasonable grounds* for suspecting child abuse. Any statutory duty imposed would have to be so circumscribed. Even the statutory duty imposed on the local authority to investigate is qualified by reference to professional judgment as to whether such enquiries are necessary. Conceding that the statutory obligation might be no more than cosmetic, we do think, however, that the statutory declaration of the duty to inform would give expression to society's deep concern that health professionals should play their part in bringing child abuse cases to the notice of Social Services. **We recommend that the observations of the relevant professional bodies, whose members would be included in the categories specified as being under the obligation to inform, should be consulted. It may be that the consultative process should properly emanate from the Secretary of State for Health and Social Security.**

Duties to consult and to assist
During our Inquiry we investigated the need for a statutory duty on local authorities to consult health authorities and other agencies, whenever a major decision about the future of a child under a Care Order is about to be made, and a correlative duty on Health Authorities and other agencies to assist by providing relevant information and specialist advice. We noted that section 22(1), National Health Service Act 1977 already imposes a duty on health authorities and local authorities to cooperate with one another in the discharge of their respective functions. **We think there are powerful reasons why this duty should be made more specific, to include the duty to consult and the duty to assist by advice and the supply of information in the process of the management of the child abuse system. We so recommend.** Such a statutory duty would operate as a positive and practical step towards giving meaning to the multi-disciplinary concept both within the initial Case Conference and in the involvement of other agencies *after* the initial Case Conference. It would ensure consultation after a Care Order has been granted and during the management of the case. All our expert medical witnesses strongly favoured their involvement in the management of the child abuse system, in particular when vital decisions, such as home on trial, removal from the child abuse register and applications for revocation, are being made. Historically, all the emphasis has been placed on involving other agencies in *identifying* child abuse, rather than in the management of the child

145

abuse system in all its stages. It would be essential for the statute to spell out the fact that the duties involved are reciprocal. You cannot be under a duty to supply information unless you know of the existence of the Care Order, and that changes are about to be made in a child's future, i.e., rehabilitation, removal home to parents, deregistration, the revocation of the Care Order, and/or the seeking of a Supervision Order. It would be important to ensure that senior personnel on the medical side are informed. It would be insufficient if it were thought that the duty was simply to inform and consult a health visitor.

In Brent, the need for consultation of senior medical personnel has now been recognised in the Area Review Committee's Policy Memorandum. The Health Authority's new Internal Guidelines devised by Dr. Pelc and her committee provide clearer lines of communication within the health services. A statutory provision would reinforce and give teeth to this local practice and extend it nationally. Even though it would be necessary that the duty to consult would be at a level senior to the Health Visitor, it would immeasurably strengthen the Health Visitor's hand. We heard a good deal of evidence about their lack of assertiveness and of confidence. It is not a question of Health Visitors being indifferent to their responsibilities; far from it. But we did detect that on occasions they have thought that their contribution has been undervalued or regarded as unimportant. A statutory definition of a duty to consult and correlative duty to advise may improve the perception of *other* agencies as to their role, with a corresponding improvement in confidence in the Health Visitor herself.

In chapter 19 we deal extensively with the response of Brent Borough Council to the death of Jasmine Beckford on 5 July 1984. The response from Brent Health Authority, as the main other agency in the case, was an internal review that, we were told, evoked no cause for concern — and no communication to Brent Social Services — about the work of the Health Visitors with the Beckford family over the four and a half years since Jasmine Beckford was born, and more particularly since August 1981 when the incidence of child abuse occurred. Nor was there any communication to Brent Area Review Committee that the Health Visitors' role had been other than normal. Since there was little sign coming out of Brent Borough Council that the case required extensive investigation, it might be thought that Brent Health Authority could properly take its cue from the statutory agency responsible for managing the Care Order. The supervisor of Miss Leong certainly did not express any concern about the quality of community health service to the Beckfords at any time, least of all in the period after June 1983, which was the last occasion on which Miss Leong saw Jasmine.

That there should have been some concern emanating from Brent Health Authority is highlighted by a remarkable document that was disclosed to us. On 17 July 1984 Miss Baichoo wrote a memorandum to Miss Martin "personally" in which she passed on a report by Miss Leong, including a summary of Miss Leong's visits to the Beckfords, prepared with the assistance of a solicitor. Miss Baichoo added her observations in note form. They were so percipient in reflecting our conclusions about Brent Health Authority's involvement that we repeat them here as she wrote them and without any comment from us, save for inserting certain facts in square brackets.

1. *Poor liaison* — in house: HV, School Nurse, Clerical
 — out house: Social workers and HV;
               School Service and
               School Nurse and HV.

2. *Social Services*: little recognition of HV role and extent of involvement necessary in case discussions (I have found this with other social workers in Brent).

3. Relating to above, would child have been off register and consequently everyone more relaxed if HV rep. was present?? Should the conference of 9 November 1982 have made such a decision in absence of Health Dept. rep.?

4. Unclear guidelines – in-house – re removal from NAI register and transfer to HV Concern.
?? same lack of guidance advice at time. This is pure speculation. Certainly this was not on my files as HV Concern or one of the families that Miss Leong discussed with me; nor had I any indication it existed having been removed from register mid-November 1982.

5. Absence of "intended" new HV at handover Case Conference [of 5 April 1982]

6. *System failure*: Very unclear procedures guidelines re the way Brent files records, etc. The same old problem I keep harping about. No built-in safety nets, etc.''

We cannot end our critique of the Health Services without saying something about the development examinations undertaken at the clinic by the clinical medical officer. We have particularly in mind the developmental "check" on Jasmine as a 3-year-old, undertaken by Dr. Peiris in October 1982. He had available to him in the clinic files the percentile chart which had been raised by Miss Knowles, yet the report of the developmental examination did not make any reference to weight. We find it hard to understand the purpose of such examinations when they are performed in the absence of medical and social history of the child and without comparison of growth.

CHAPTER 13

Law and Administration Department of Brent Borough Council

The Law and Administration Department of Brent Borough Council had no involvement in, nor any knowledge of the Beckford case until after Jasmine's death in July 1984.

It is the practice in Brent for an officer from the Court Section of the Social Services Department (who has no legal qualifications) to attend case conferences when care proceedings are being contemplated, and to represent the local authority in the juvenile court, unless he considers that a solicitor from the Department of Law and Administration should be involved. He would seek such assistance if, in the words of the Director of Law and Administration to us, the case "raised any particular legal difficulties, or if there was a concern over the level of representation that was going to be faced in court." In short, his Department would be used in the same way as a private citizen might go to a solicitor in private practice.

Such assistance was not thought necessary in relation to the application for Care Orders in respect of Jasmine and Louise in August/September 1981, nor for the application for revocation of these Care Orders in the Spring of 1983; and, as we have seen, no consideration was given by anyone in the Social Services Department to the need for care proceedings in respect of Chantelle at any time before the death of her half-sister.

Neither Mr. Forster, the Director of Law and Administration, nor Mr. Damms, the Senior Solicitor who represented him at the meetings of the Social Services Committee felt, even in retrospect, that it would necessarily have been helpful if the local authority had been legally represented at the care proceedings on 9 September 1981. Mr. Damms said that he had never had any complaints, either from Willesden Magistrates' Court (the local juvenile court for Brent) or from the Social Services Department about the work of the Court Section, and Mr. Forster said that it was "perhaps a somewhat presumptuous assumption" that the involvement of a lawyer would have made everything perfect. Likewise, neither Mr. Forster nor Mr. Damms felt that it would have been desirable for the Social Services Department to have sought legal advice about the implications of the Magistrates' comments following the making of care orders on 9 September 1981.

Following Jasmine's death, the Director of Social Services immediately informed the Chief Executive and the Chairman of the Social Services Committee; and the Chief Executive, in his turn, informed the leaders of the Conservative and Labour groups on the Council. There was no formal notification to the Department of Law and Administration, although Mr. Forster was present at a weekend management course from 13 to 15 July 1984, which included Miss Howarth, and she felt that all her colleagues there knew of her distress about the death of a child in care. Also, Mr. Thompson, the Principal Court Officer in the Social Services Department had mentioned the matter on the telephone to Mr. Damms, but Mr. Damms stated to us that this was just in the course of a conversation on some other topic. However, like the Chief Executive, the Director of Social Services, and those councillors who were aware of Jasmine's death, neither Mr. Forster nor Mr. Damms felt any sense of urgency about arranging a Special Cases Sub-Committee meeting to discuss the case. (We deal more generally with the events at Brent Town Hall after 5 July 1984 in Chapter 19.)

Meanwhile, in Area 6, a multi-disciplinary Case Conference had been held on 12 July 1984, to discuss the implications of the death of Jasmine in relation to her two surviving half-sisters, Louise and Chantelle Beckford. No-one from the Department of Law and Administration was invited to this case conference, and Mr. Damms told us, that he felt that there should have been such an invitation, in view of the serious nature of the case. We agree. However, at the Case Conference it was decided that the children's future should lie outside their family, and that the advice of the legal section of the Department of Law and Administration should be sought on the questions of access and freeing for adoption, since legislation on these matters had only recently come into force. The omission to have legal advice at the Case Conference was, in the circumstances, venial.

We gather from the documentation which we were given that a meeting took place on 27 July 1984 between Mr. Jeremy Burns, Mrs. Diane Dietmann and a solicitor from the Department of Law and Administration, but we have seen no record of that meeting.

On 2 August 1984, Mr. Thompson, on behalf of the Local Authority, served notice of refusal of arrangements for access to Louise and Chantelle on Beverley Lorrington, and on 16 August 1984 Beverley Lorrington's solicitors gave notice of her intention to apply to the juvenile court for an order granting access to both children. It was agreed between the parties that this application should be heard at the same time as the care proceedings in respect of Chantelle. Despite the serious nature of the case, and the novelty of the access proceedings, the Social Services Department was again not legally represented. In the circumstances, they ought perhaps at least to have asked the Department of Law and Administration to represent them. In fairness to the Court Section of the Social Services Department, it is clear from the documentation that the case was competently and successfully handled. Again, no adverse consequence flowed from the absence of legal assistance.

Following the making of a Care Order in respect of Chantelle, and the refusal of the Court to make an Access Order, arrangements were made to apply to the County Court for a Freeing for Adoption Order. Very detailed advice on how to carry out this new procedure was given to Mrs. Dietmann by the Adoption and Foster Care Section of the Social Services Department. We were not told whether that section had been guided by the Department of Law and Administration, but Miss Carol Rogers, acting head of the Adoption and Foster Care Section, told us that "the support we get is mainly through the professional association for adoption and fostering matters, who are more able to offer advice and consultation on immediate issues, particularly relating to new legislation." While we accept Miss Rogers' attitude, we do think that the Department of Law and Administration should be involved in disseminating knowledge about new legislation affecting Social Services, if only because nowadays such legislation is often complex and needs a lawyer's exposition.

The legal section of the Department of Law and Administration is not staffed to deal with "run-of-the-mill" care cases – nor need it be. Moreover, although most of the Assistant Solicitors have had some experience in juvenile court work, none has specific expertise in this field. We were told by Mr. Damms that if advice on care proceedings was sought by a social worker, the enquirer would usually be referred to the Court Section of the Social Services Department. Both Mr. Damms and Mr. Forster told us that they recognised that the Court Section had a great deal of experience in the conduct of care proceedings and in juvenile court work in general.

It is, therefore, understandable that, although Mr. Forster told us, in reply to questions, that he regarded his legal staff as being "on tap" to give advice to the Social Services Department if and when asked, such advice was rarely sought. In the words of Miss Howarth, "the problem is that they (the Law and Administration Department) don't have enough staff to respond in time, and that causes friction, and people give up."

Miss Howarth told us that she would welcome the appointment of a solicitor in the Department of Law and Administration who would specialise in Social Services matters and work closely with the staff of the Social Services Department. She described the situation she had experienced in another local authority where "the person had enough level of detachment by belonging to the Director of Law and Administration to retain, if you like, their legal position, but had enough involvement to be able to come into the Department, take part in case conferences, if that was appropriate, and to give advice, and, indeed to talk with me about points of law where there was some confusion and share ideas, and to contribute to the thinking about how we should move forward generally in these areas.''

We endorse Miss Howarth's view that the assignment of a solicitor in the Department of Law and Administration to work in this way would be helpful. We take Mr. Forster's point that involving a lawyer does not necessarily make everything perfect, and we recognise that the training of lawyers, like that of social workers, covers a wide field, of which child care law is only a very small part. Nevertheless, most local authority solicitors, if their work consisted mainly of Social Services matters, would quickly acquire the knowledge and experience to enable them to make a valuable contribution in this field. The volume of child care work in Brent is sufficiently large to engage one member of staff of the Department of Law and Administration for a fair proportion of his working time.

In addition to its role as legal adviser to the other Departments of the Local Authority, the Department of Law and Administration has a relationship with them through its servicing of the council's committees. In addition to the Committee Clerk, a senior solicitor attends all meetings of the Social Services Committee and the Cases Sub-Committee, as the representative of the Director of Law and Administration.

During 1984, this task was the responsibility of Mr. Damms, but although he was notified by telephone of Jasmine's death shortly after it occurred, he had no direct involvement with the case until 29 October 1984, the date of the first Cases Sub-Committee meeting after Jasmine's death.

He saw the notes prepared by the Social Services Department for that meeting shortly before it took place. He told us that he did not normally see or discuss in advance reports prepared by Departments for the Committees at which he represented the Director of Law and Administration, unless the Department drew his attention to them. However, he said that he would have expected to have been consulted about this report and would have found this helpful, especially as he was asked in the Cases Sub-Committee to comment on whether the guardian ad litem's report which had been presented to the juvenile court in respect of Louise and Chantelle Beckford could be shown to members. (It is illustrative of the lack of expertise in the legal section of the Department of Law and Administration about Social Services matters that he did not know the answer to this question but had to discuss it subsequently with someone in the justices clerks' office at Willesden Magistrate's Court — an action which could equally well have been taken by the Court Section of the Social Services Department).

Like members of the Cases Sub-Committee, he felt that the report from the Social Services Department was inadequate, and he subsequently telephoned Miss Howarth to express his concern about the lack of consultation. He told us that, at that time, he was concerned about not receiving in advance copies of reports for committees at which he represented the Director of Law and Administration, particularly the Social Services Committee.

Miss Howarth invited him to attend a meeting in the Social Services Department on 19 November 1984, the purpose of which was to draft a further report on the Beckford case for the Cases Sub-Committee on 26 November 1984. He attended this meeting and contributed to the discussion, but was unable to amend or approve the final version of the report before its circulation to Sub-Committee members because he was away, representing the Council at a public inquiry.

He attended the stormy meeting of the Cases Sub-Committee on 26 November and, like the other officers present, attempted to help members to draft an appropriate resolution about the setting up of an Inquiry. Eventually, the Cases Sub-Committee recommended that there should be an internal inquiry, external to the Directorate of Social Services, and that the Chair of the Inquiry Panel should be taken by a representative (officer) of the Directorate of Law and Administration; the Panel of Inquiry should comprise the Principal Solicitor (chair), the Principal Race Relations Adviser, the Assistant Director (Residential and Day Care) of Social Services and the Principal Nursery Officer.

Following this recommendation the inquiry was set up and a good deal of preliminary work was undertaken by the Department of Law and Administration. This involved perusing all relevant files and arranging appointments to interview those involved. However, on 5 January 1985, the Social Services Committee reversed the recommendation of the Cases Sub-Committee and called for an inquiry under the auspices of the Area Review Committee. This proposal was, in its turn, overridden by the Policy and Resources Committee which, on 12 February 1985 resolved that the inquiry should be undertaken by an independent panel, to be serviced by the Department of Law and Administration.

We have indicated in our Preface our warm appreciation of the efficient and helpful way in which the staff of the Department of Law and Administration have serviced our Inquiry. We echo it here, and would observe that such efficiency indicates the value of the Department to the Social Services Department in the future.

The remaining aspect of the involvement of the Department in the Beckford case concerns the criminal trial of Morris Beckford and Beverley Lorrington. A representative of the Director of Law and Administration (our Secretary, Miss John-Phillip) attended at the Central Criminal Court throughout the trial, which took place from 25 to 28 March 1985. When it became known that the Common Serjeant wished officers from the Social Services Department and the Education Department to be present in Court, the matter was discussed with the Chief Executive, and the Director of Law and Administration himself accompanied them to Court. He believed, understandably, that the judge would confine his questions to the setting up of an Inquiry and to changes in procedure following Jasmine's death; he was not in a position to intervene when the judge unexpectedly took his questioning of Mr. Simpson further. He too was disturbed by the manner in which Mr. Simpson was treated by the Common Serjeant.

Conclusion

We have hinted at the need for a closer relationship between the Law and Administration Department and Social Services Department, and have supported Miss Howarth's desire for some lawyer input to the management of the child care (and particularly child abuse) system. We hesitate to make a positive recommendation, since the issue must be dictated largely by the availability of resources. We are alive to the frequency and rapidity with which lawyers in local government move to senior appointments elsewhere. We know, moreover, that both Mr. Forster and Miss Howarth are working towards the ideal that Miss Howarth expressed.

We would add only this. The lawyer in public service is not just a specialist: he has a claim to pre-eminence over all other specialists, for the simple reason that the law is a crucial instrument for governmental control and is a working discipline essential for daily activity in local government business. We are conscious that social workers do not always take readily, or kindly to legal intervention in the practice of social work (and lawyers have only recently specialised in child care law). But, as we have described in Chapters 1 and 2 and in Chapter 20 on Training, the law provides the basic framework in which social workers must operate. We would remind those in the administration of local government, and child care in particular, of what Sir Thomas Barnes, the Treasury Solicitor, said in 1943 in a memorandum to the Barlow Committee on legal departments of the Civil Service, words that are as applicable to local as to central government.

> "The Treasury have, I think, been accustomed to treat the lawyers as specialists and class them with scientists, architects, doctors, etc. I venture to submit that there is very little analogy between the functions of the lawyer in the public service and the functions of scientists and other specialists. It is true that some departments require the services of architects, doctors, surveyors etc. for special purposes but every department requires the services of its lawyers in its day-to-day work. Most departments administer important codes of the law and all administration has to a great extent a legal basis. Parliament itself spends a great deal of its time in making laws and the contacts between the executive and the subject are most tender whenever functions of the executive cut down or in any way infringe existing legal rights ... The truth is that the law is part and parcel of the functions of every department ...."

Social workers, in their turn, must be wary of being too ready to accede to strong legal opinion from their legal department. The lawyer must be ever-present, but he must never dominate.

CHAPTER 14

Education Department of Brent Borough Council

After two months' non-attendance at Mortimer Road Day Nursery from November 1982 to January 1983 Jasmine Beckford was registered at Princess Frederica Primary School in its nursery section. She first went there on 11 January 1983, attended spasmodically during the Easter and summer terms, started going in the autumn term but left within days, never to return. Ms. Wahlstrom spoke to Miss Cowgill on the telephone on 11 January 1983 in circumstances we have described in Chapter 10, and thereafter visited the school only once; she was never contacted by the school. The link between Social Services and Education Authority – in the case of Brent, both administered by Brent Borough Council – in respect of a child in care and on the Child Abuse Register was at best tenuous and at worst never forged.

There are two separate aspects to the role of the school in relation to the management of the child abuse system. The first is preventive: to act as a watchdog for the Social Services in spotting children who show signs of abuse. The second is as a monitor over children who are in care of the local authority and/or on the Child Abuse Register. The first aspect is a continuing function; the second is specific in time and relates to individual schoolchildren. Both aspects were in play in the Beckford case.

While it is true that the function of school is to educate, the actual *process* of educating the young does not take place in a vacuum. A child comes to school from home. Whatever the financial and economic circumstances, whatever the life style, each family is held together (or torn apart) by tensions which are unique and peculiar to the adults and children who are its members. A child ineluctably brings with him to school all the familial tensions. How does a child become numerate, master his reading skills or develop social skills if the world of home is slowly breaking up around him? How does the child behave if there is disharmony or parental illness? How does the child deal with death, sickness, poverty and crime when he has lived for only a few years and has seen nothing different? And how does the child deal with physical and psychological abuse inflicted on him or on his siblings by his parents?

The prime concern of the school is for the child, whose educational programme must take into account the child's particular and individual needs. The child's educational response can be evaluated accurately only if the teacher is aware, and can take account of the external (i.e. non-school) influences upon his performance. The retort from educationalists is that the teacher is not a social worker. The former's task, it is argued, is circumscribed by the relationship with the pupil in the school. Teachers should teach and social workers care for the child's welfare out of school.

Social workers concentrate upon the cases where child abuse or child neglect has been brought to their attention. In those cases the monitoring role of the school must be invoked, as we shall note. It is with the child that has not so far come to the notice of Social Services that the school has a vital role to play. Too many children, we suspect, have not been observed as potential victims of child abuse, either at all or soon enough, because no one is spotting the symptoms. Quite apart from Jasmine Beckford not having been identified as a child at risk, why did not the school alert Social Services to the fact of Jasmine's non-attendance after 9 September 1983? We think that this may have been due to its failure to appreciate that changes in the fabric of our society have brought the problems that were once the province of the priest, the doctor and the lawyer, into the teacher's sphere. Schools are now perceived as being run by people who are more receptive to a parent-teacher relationship and evince a willingness and a desire to understand the child, not just as the recipient of an educational programme but as a person undergoing the whole process of socialisation, of which education is an important ingredient.

What we have said is drawn from our own knowledge and experience of the educational scene. We suspect, however, that we have been describing rather than prescribing.

We are aware that there are some people in the field of education who would like to see an improved and strengthened Educational Welfare Service. They advocate that every school, primary and secondary, should employ a teacher with responsibility in the area of family counselling. The teacher-social worker would fulfil all the functions of the school welfare officer as well as some of the functions which are currently the responsibility of social workers employed by the local authority. The involvement of the teacher-social worker would start from the child's needs and provide a link within the school setting between each child and all those organisations and agencies currently responsible for the welfare of the child. It is not for us to argue here the case for such an innovation in the educational system, even if we had the expertise to do it. For what it is worth, we add our own two-penny worth to this ongoing debate. Such an appointment of a teacher-social worker might improve the child protection service that needs to be developed from its narrower base of Social Services onto a wider platform of social agencies involved in the care of children. Such a development would bring into play a multi-agency approach to an area characterised by a singular lack of cohesion, a direct result of the fear expressed by practitioners in disparate disciplines of crossing the vague boundaries which divide the social worker from school, and in consequence prevent educational welfare workers from engaging in anything more than a superficial involvement with their children. The distancing between the school and Social Services was glaringly evident from the lack of contact between the teachers of Princess Frederica Primary School and Area 6, Brent Social Services in the case of Jasmine Beckford. It was in stark contrast to the communications between the matron of Mortimer Road Day Nursery (run by Brent Social Services itself) and Area 6, which disclosed Miss Proudlock informing Ms. Wahlstrom on no fewer than seven occasions between June and November 1982 that Jasmine had not been attending the nursery. **We recommend that in every school there is one member of the educational staff who is designated as the liaison officer with Social Services in respect of every child who is in care of the local authority and/or is on the Child Abuse Register.** The designated teacher should have a direct line to the Social Services Department of the local authority, and vice-versa. The designated teacher would also become the repository of any information from fellow teachers about any case of suspected abuse of a child on the school register.

One matter has occurred to us, arising from our Inquiry. At one point in July 1983 the Educational Welfare Officer at Princess Frederica Primary School was requested to visit the Beckford household. This he did. And we have described it in Chapter 10. But since Jasmine was under the age of compulsory education, he was under no obligation to supervise her school attendance. **We recommend that consideration should be given to extending the statutory duties of the Educational Welfare Officer to those children under the age of 5 and attending nursery school.**

It is clear to us that had there been in 1983 such an arrangement at Princess Frederica Primary School Jasmine Beckford's non-attendance after 9 September 1983, continuing until she died ten months later, would have not gone unnoticed and unattended to. Although there was no question of compulsory attendance educationally, Ms. Wahlstrom would have been in a position to compel the Beckford parents to take Jasmine to school. But Ms. Wahlstrom never envisaged Jasmine's school as a device for monitoring her daily life. Her failure was all of a piece with her insistence on focusing her attentions exclusively on the parents, and not on the child, with the continuing need to protect her against the risk of renewed abuse by her parents. We sincerely hope that this case will have impressed on all the social agencies the value of the school as part of the management of the child abuse system.

CHAPTER 15

Metropolitan Police

Police forces occupy a unique role in the handling of child abuse cases. Together with general medical practitioners and hospital authorities similarly providing a 24-hour a day service, they share the distinction of having the likely earliest knowledge about domestic violence, and in particular physical injuries to children inflicted by their parents. Over and above that, the police exclusively possess optimum access to a range of information about the criminal backgrounds of individuals that can be invaluable to those agencies engaged in the assessment of child abuse. For social services and the allied agencies engaged in child care to dispense with the expertise of police officers is to indulge in self-denial that may have serious, sometimes fatal results for children at risk. We have kept these basic principles in the forefront of our assessment of the part played by the Metropolitan Police in the Beckford case.

The police were first alerted to the case on 4 August 1981 when Miss Knibbs at St. Charles' Hospital rang Women Police Constable McAree, employed in the Juvenile Bureau at Wembley Police Station (Miss McAree is now a Woman Police Sergeant at Paddington Green Police Station; apart from giving valuable evidence to us, she attended nearly every sitting of our Inquiry). Since both Jasmine and Louise Beckford had by then been taken to hospital, and a Place of Safety Order had been applied for, Miss Knibbs had no need to seek the assistance of the Police, with their statutory powers to remove children at risk from their homes. She telephoned Miss McAree to invite her to attend the proposed Case Conference on 6 August 1981. Miss McAree contacted the Detective Superintendent at Kilburn Police Station, in accordance with paragraph 4 of General Memorandum 7/77 of 22 September 1977 issued by the Commissioner for the Metropolitan Police, made pursuant to a joint circular from the Department of Health and Social Security and the Home Office, LASS L(76)28 of 18 November 1976 (The current instruction to the Metropolitan Police on *Non-Accidental Injury to Children – The Police and Case Conferences* is contained in General Memorandum 1/82 of 14 January 1982 which alters the rank of police officer to be informed, to Detective Sergeant Inspector). Detective Chief Inspector Strachan and Detective Sergeant Crocker were detailed to attend the Case Conference on 6 August 1981. These two detective officers attended in their role as investigators of crime, while Miss McAree performed the task of providing police liaison with Social Services in all aspects of child care. Miss McAree supplied the Case Conference with information that Morris Beckford and his sister had come to police attention in 1972 for stealing from their own home, which led to the beating of both children by their mother, a valuable piece of knowledge which was unfortunately never followed up by Brent Social Services as part of any psychiatric assessment of Morris Beckford. Detective Chief Inspector Strachan indicated that he would want to make further investigations of the injuries to the children, and would want to interview both parents. From what he had heard at the Case Conference, he added that "it was possible that charges of grievous bodily harm could be brought." In the light of that observation, we find it shocking that Mrs. Dietmann should have told us that she had not regarded the attacks on Jasmine and Louise by their father as indicating a "serious assault". Either Mrs. Dietmann did not listen, or she never read the minutes of the Case Conference subsequently, or she simply turned a blind eye to the obviously gross cases of child abuse. We tend to think it was the latter, another example of concentrating attention on the parents and of ignoring the degree of risk that predictively indicated future child abuse, were the children to be reunited with their parents. It is such examples of devaluing the nature of a crime that have in the past led the police justifiably to express dissatisfaction with the attitude of Social Services. Police officers have voiced their opinion – much less frequently since 1977 – that the attitude of Social Services is in practically every case to keep the family together at all costs, usually to the detriment of the child. (We indicate later why we believe that the mutual suspicion between Police and Social Services, so prevalent in the past, has been replaced by mutual trust.)

The Case Conference of 6 August 1981 decided that Detective Chief Inspector Strachan should interview the Beckford parents with a view to bringing further charges. At the subsequent Case Conference on 20 August 1981, attended by Detective Sergeant Crocker only out of the three police officers, he reported the outcome of his criminal investigation. Morris Beckford admitted to shaking Louise on 30 or 31 July 1981, which caused the retinal haemorrhage, but he made no admission with regard to the broken arm by any "yanking action". Beverley Lorrington made no admissions of abuse on Louise, and both denied causing the injury of a broken thigh to Jasmine, explaining that she had fallen down the stairs. Detective Sergeant Crocker before us said that he could recall being present at Willesden Magistrates' Court on 9 September 1981 and hearing the contents but not seeing the report of Dr. Levick. Subsequently an examination of his diary had indicated that he was then on leave. We find that he is mistaken about his attendance at Court on 9 September 1981 (We deal below with the question of police attendance at care proceedings). A copy of the report was never supplied to the police. As part of the stress of the DHSS/Home Office joint circular on the importance of close co-operation between the Police and Social Services, a copy should have been supplied. We blame Mr. Thompson for not ensuring that the Police were sent a copy.

Detective Sergeant Crocker took his cue from the conclusion of the Case Conferences that, while Louise was a clear case of non-accidental injury, the doctors could not rule out the possibility that Jasmine received her broken thigh accidentally, on the hypothesis that someone may have fallen on top of the child when she fell down some stairs. Since Morris Beckford confessed to causing the retinal haemorrhage to Louise, Detective Sergeant Crocker, on 19 August 1981 charged him with the less serious offence of an assault occasioning actual bodily harm. Morris Beckford was found guilty at Willesden Magistrates' Court on 19 November 1981 of that offence. He was sentenced to 3 months' imprisonment, suspended for two years, fined £250 plus £100 costs. He was ordered to pay at the rate of £15 a week; he paid £50 at court that day. Detective Chief Inspector Strachan disagreed with Detective Sergeant Crocker that the sole charge in respect of Louise's less serious injury was the appropriate outcome of his criminal investigation. He asserted that once it became tolerably clear that Jasmine's case was one of non-accidental injury – and that much was clear at the latest by 9 September when Dr. Levick's report demonstrated multiple abuse and not just a "one-off episode" with a barely plausible explanation of its cause – he would have wanted the two parents to be "re-interviewed very closely". That interview never took place. We do not question Detective Sergeant Crocker's discretion to proceed only on the charge to which he had Morris Beckford's admission. In the absence of any other admission, he would have had difficulties of proving, up to the criminal standard of proof, any other offence without some evidence as to which of the two parents had caused the injuries to Jasmine. Had the Police been more fully brought into participation by Social Services personnel of Area 6 of assessing the nature and degree of child abuse on the Beckford sisters, the Police might have carried out further investigation, not merely with a view to pressing criminal charges but also, more valuably for the purposes of child protection, to providing the necessary profile of the battering Beckford parents. It is here that we think that collaboration emanating from Social Services needs pointing up and emphasising.

The primary task of the Police to investigate crime and to initiate a prosecution where appropriate remains unaffected by the fact that the investigation is into child abuse. The police function is independent of the statutory powers and duties of Social Services departments; Social Services departments, for their part, perform their statutory functions independently, and are not subject to monitoring or supervision by the Police. Given their independent roles and a recognition of the differences of approach of the professions concerned, close co-operation is, however, to be encouraged. One aspect of such inter-disciplinary attitudes is the desirability or otherwise of prosecuting parents for child abuse. We think that a strict legalistic intervention by the Police whenever a parent physically abuses his or her child may not be the most helpful way to handle such cases. In an article in 1972 in the British Medical Journal, entitled *Neglect, Cruelty and Battery* Volume 3, 22 July 1972, pp. 224-6, Dr. Susan Isaacs wrote: "Punishment plays no part in curing the problem or preventing recurrences, so investigation by the police can be dangerously inappropriate. On the other hand, a juvenile court may be of great help, concerned as it is for the welfare of the child in its family as a whole." While we would not be so emphatic as Dr. Isaacs about the Police desisting from criminal investigation, we do think that the Police should consider their investigations, not only from the point of view of a law enforcement agency but also as an auxiliary to the need for a proper assessment of the child abuse situation. We think, moreover, that the Police should be circumspect in pressing any criminal investigation to the point of prosecuting the offender in the criminal courts. Paragraph 10 of Metropolitan Police General Memorandum 1/82 acknowledges as much. It states: "It is the aim of the Case Conference to agree a course of action and occasionally this may include a recommendation to police not to investigate or prosecute the offender(s). Insofar as the former recommendation is concerned, the members of a conference must be informed that the police are obliged to *investigate* [the italics appear in the 1982 memorandum for the first time] any alleged offences coming to their notice, although under certain circumstances they may decide not to prosecute. However, the police cannot undertake not to prosecute." We would generally endorse this instruction in relation to investigation. But we think that the dual purpose of investigation – criminal and social – needs to be emphasised. This seems implicit in paragraph 17 of the joint circular from the DHSS and the Home Office, when it states the hope that where a Case Conference has been held "chief officers of police (while retaining the capacity to take independent action) will take into account any views expressed by the conference about the effect of an investigation on the welfare of the child." We wholeheartedly approve of that governmental guideline, and would add that every Case Conference should specifically discuss the question of police investigation and indicate what would be most helpful to the handling of the case from the point of view of child protection. No such discussion took place at either of the Case Conferences of 6 or 20 August 1981. The police officers merely indicated what had been learnt from their inquiries and what action they proposed to take. There was furthermore no discussion about the limited prosecution of Morris Beckford for the assault on Louise, or the disinclination to proceed in respect of Jasmine's injuries.

Paragraph 16 of the joint circular from the DHSS/Home Office notes that the prosecution of offences is a matter which rests by law within the discretion of the prosecuting authority. In considering the exercise of their discretion "chief officers of police will no doubt take account so far as possible of any views expressed by Case Conferences on the question of prosecution." Paragraph 10 of the General Memorandum 1/82 is less restrictive upon any decision to prosecute. It unrevealingly states that "under certain circumstances" the police may decide not to prosecute. Since under the Prosecution of Offenders Act 1985 there will be a national independent prosecuting service in 1986 we take this opportunity of stating what we think the policy of the Director of

Public Prosecution and his senior staff should be.

Dr. Taitz told us that in the Sheffield area he and others at Case Conferences try and persuade the police not to prosecute the parents of abused children, and that in his experience the Police rarely do prosecute. We think that it is a sensible policy as a rule not to prosecute, but that exceptionally the prosecuting authority must exercise its undoubted discretion to prosecute in the wider public interest. Such a policy of generally withholding the power to prosecute can properly be sustained only so long as both Police and prosecuting authorities have confidence in the whole system of child abuse management. Too often in the past too many cases appeared to the Police to have gone wrong, and their reaction had been to ignore the pleas of social workers and doctors to desist from prosecuting.

Since 1977 (after the governmental circular was distributed among Police authorities) understanding and mutual trust between the Police and other agencies involved in Case Conferences clearly developed to the point where Police were generally accepted as active participants in the management of child abuse cases. The Police responded by a willingness to share their function of decision-making about criminal prosecutions without foregoing their right of independent action. This development, reducing the tensions among professional workers, was not reflected in practice in Brent during 1981 and 1982, as evidenced by the involvement of Police officers in the Beckford case.

We have already noted that three Police officers attended the Case Conference on 6 August 1981. Only Detective Sergeant Crocker attended the second Case Conference on 20 August 1981, there being no need to duplicate the C.I.D. representation by the attendance of Detective Chief Inspector Strachan. Miss McAree told us that at the first Case Conference it was intimated that the subsequent one would have nothing to discuss in the way of plans for the placement of the children but would merely want to know the results of the Police investigation and future Police action. The decisions of that Case Conference bear out Miss McAree's evidence. One of three decisions noted was that Area 6 would thereafter organise "any review Case Conferences" to which "only those will be invited that it is felt necessary should attend."

The interest of the C.I.D. ends with the conclusion of any criminal proceedings; the conviction of Morris Beckford took place on 19 November 1981. Thereafter the Police interest in the aspect of child care protection would be represented by the juvenile bureau, of which Miss McAree was a member. It was unfortunate that Miss McAree did not attend on 20 August 1981, but felt that the Police at least had a representative in the presence of Detective Sergeant Crocker. The minutes of the second Case Conference were distributed to only one non-attender, Dr. Mallik, but not to Miss McAree. Clearly the organisers of the Case Conference did not think her absence was of any note. At no time after 20 August 1981 was any Police officer invited to attend any of the Case Conferences or statutory reviews. More particularly, no invitation was extended to the juvenile bureau (or any other Police unit) to attend the Case Conference on 5 April 1982 (when the plan to return the children home was to be decided); to the Case Conference on 9 November 1982 (when it was decided that the children were no longer at risk and should be removed from the child abuse register); or to the statutory review on 18 April 1983 (when it was decided to apply to the Magistrates' Court for revocation of the Care Orders).

All our Police witnesses and our expert witnesses (Professor Greenland, Dr. Taitz, Mr. Alan Bedford, Miss Alix Causby, Dr. Euan Ross and Dr. Bridget Edwards) were adamant that, while it was unnecessary for the Police to attend all Case Conferences and statutory reviews, whenever an important step was being contemplated in the placement of children who had been abused by their parents, it was crucial for the Police to be present. Any decision to return a child to its parents, to remove the child from

162

the Child Abuse Register, or to apply for the revocation of a Care Order could only be properly arrived at after the Police have had an opportunity of supplying any relevant information and of airing their views as to the propriety or wisdom of such a significant stage in the process of child protection. We think that it is not necessary for us to make any positive recommendation in this regard, since it is axiomatic that, if only to retain the Police confidence in the child abuse management system, the Police should always be invited, and we would expect a representative from the juvenile bureau ordinarily to attend. **We would add only the recommendation that after October 1986, when the national independent prosecuting service comes into being, a representative from that service should also be invited.** It may be that the prosecuting service will arrange with the relevant Police authority that at least one person will attend on behalf of both services. But social Services Departments should regard the two services as having separate interests.

We have an added reason for not making any general recommendation about Police involvement in case conferences and statutory reviews. Mr. Bishop, as Area Manager, while he could give no satisfactory explanation for the Police not having been invited after August 1981, thought it reasonable to invite them, although he thought they might not have anything useful to contribute. We think that he would invariably do so now. Miss Howarth, Director of Social Services, was unequivocal in saying that Police participation in significant case conferences was extremely valuable. The British Association of Social Workers in its recent memorandum would go further in stating that "the Police should be invited to all Case Conferences called under child abuse procedures, and not just those discussing N.A.I." The Association added that this regular participation should lead to "greater teamwork and minimal unilateral action." We entertain no doubt that the Policy Memorandum on Non-Accidental Injury will reflect the Director's desire that Police participation should be firmly based in the Case Conference system. We were similarly impressed by the evidence of Superintendent Kemp, who was the Police Community Liaison Officer for the Boroughs of Brent and Harrow from May 1981 to March 1984, and of his successor, Superintendent Briggs. Whatever may have been the state of the relationship between the Police and Social Services in 1981 and 1982 – and Superintendent Kemp was decorously uncritical of Brent Social Services and Area 6 in particular – we are confident that Miss Howarth's rapprochement is entirely reciprocated. There should be no repetition of the self-denial by Social Services in Brent of Police expertise in the child abuse management system. Having expressed our criticism of this aspect of the handling by Social Services of the Beckford case, we cannot say positively that their omission contributed in any respect towards the failure to prevent the death of Jasmine Beckford.

We allude to only one other issue relating to Police involvement in Case Conferences. Paragraph 8 of the joint DHSS/Home Office circular of 18 November 1976 under the rubric, Release of Information to Chief Officers of Police, states that the Home Office recommends that they should make available to Case Conferences the details of any relevant previous convictions concerning a person involved in the care (or a member of the same household as) a child who is the subject of a Case Conference. Paragraph 15 adds that the Police may often have other relevant information about a family which will assist the work of a Case Conference, and if so this information should also be communicated to the Case Conference, under conditions of confidentiality that restrict the information to the participants at the Case Conference. Paras 2 and 8 of the Metropolitan Police Memorandum 1/82 state that criminal convictions, spent or otherwise, "will NOT be supplied to Case Conferences, although certain information relating thereto, if relevant, may be disclosed, verbally. Relevant information relates to assaults on or ill-treatment of a child or member of the child's household, but no details of the conviction will be supplied." We think that there are other convictions that may be relevant than those set out in the General Memorandum. A parent's criminal record as a child or young person may well be relevant; indeed Morris Beckford's theft offence in 1972 was revealed to the Case Conference on 6 August 1981. **We recommend that the Commissioner of the Metropolitan Police should call for a review of the General Memorandum, in the light of the governmental circular, whose guidelines we endorse.**

Because we initially assumed from Sergeant Crocker's evidence to us that he had been present in court on 9 September 1981, we canvassed the question of the propriety of Police officers being in a juvenile court hearing care proceedings. If Sergeant Crocker had been present (contrary, however, to what we find) he would have appeared to have been there as of right. But are Police officers, who are not parties to care proceedings, entitled to be in court?

Under section 47(2), Children and Young Persons Act 1933 "no person shall be present at any sitting of a juvenile court except

    (a)   members and officers of the Court;

    (b)   parties to the case before the Court, their solicitors and counsel, and witnesses and other persons directly concerned in that case;

    (c)   bona fide representatives of newspapers or new agencies;

    (d)   such other persons as the Court may specifically authorise to be present."

The Ingleby Committee on Children and Young Persons (1960: Cmnd. 1191) considered this statutory provision but only on the issue that too many people not directly concerned with sittings of juvenile courts were being allowed into court. The Committee's conclusion was that "if too many people are present they change the character of the Court." Superintendent Briggs told us that there was some doubt about the police officer's status in relation to care proceedings; he courteously invited us to express our view for the guidance of the Metropolitan Police and other police forces. We do so willingly, recognising that it is only our humble opinion.

Some of us, at first blush, thought that a police officer who had been in attendance at a Case Conference in a child abuse case was a person "directly concerned in that case" within section 47(2)(b). But the combined advocacy of Miss Dodson and Miss Scotland has persuaded us that the "first blush" should be regarded as the reddening of our faces in shame for adopting so readily that construction. Police officers who are interested in a child abuse case, and to that end attend Case Conferences, are *not* directly concerned in *that* case", that case being an application by a local authority for a Care Order in respect of a young person or child. At best police officers investigating a crime by the child's parents can be said to be *in*directly concerned with the case." Moreover the policy behind the statutory provision must be to remove any inhibitions on the part of the parents not to incriminate themselves. To exclude self-incrimination about abuse of a child would be to detract from the value of proceedings to determine care or control of the child. Police officers would be attending to hear what the parents say, for the purposes of criminal investigation and not directly for child protection purposes. We conclude that police officers are not entitled as of right to attend sittings of juvenile courts unless they are "parties to the case before the court" or are "witnesses" or "other persons directly concerned in that case." **We recommend that in any future legislation this should be made explicit.**

We are aware that there may be cases where police officers might think it profitable for their official purposes to attend and listen to care proceedings. If so, they must obtain special authority from the Court to be present, as section 47(2)(d) provides. **Whenever a police officer desires to attend care proceedings, he should give notice to the parties – local authority, parents and child (or his representative) – of such desire. If no objection is raised, the Court, subject to its overriding discretion to exclude anybody for** some such reason as space in the Courtroom or detraction from the informality of Juvenile Court proceedings, should give authority. If there is an objection, properly founded, the police officer should be excluded. We so recommend.

CHAPTER 16

The Juvenile Court

We have already indicated our view that the rider added to the Care Orders made on 9 September 1981 by the Willesden Magistrates was at best unhelpful to Social Services in deciding the future placement of Jasmine and Louise Beckford, and at worst was powerfully and tragically influential towards the return of the two children to their parents. We now deal with the deferred question of the propriety and wisdom of such a rider, with only a passing reference to the facts of the Beckford case. We also consider the other, related question of the absence of any reasoned judgment by magistrates when making Care Orders.

The questions we ask can be simply stated. What is the law and practice relating to the jurisdiction of a juvenile court on an application to make a Care Order? Have magistrates any legal power to say or do anything that relates to the execution of that Care Order by a local authority invested with the power to determine what shall happen to a child in care until it is aged eighteen (or, in the exceptional case of a 16 year old, nineteen)? If the law does permit a magistrates' court to make a pronouncement about how it thinks the local authority should enforce the Care Order, how far (if at all) does good judicial practice demand restraint upon the magistrates not to interfere or seek to interfere in the decision-making processes of local authorities? We attempt to answer these questions.

We start from the undoubted proposition that magistrates' courts are wholly the creatures of statute. Unlike the High Court, which has an inherent jurisdiction at common law and at least may control its own practice and procedure, magistrates must found anything they do, apart from matters that are strictly administrative and auxiliary to their legal powers, upon a specific statutory provision. In short, it is not possible to augment or adjust any power conferred by Parliament, by resort to some extrinsic legal power. It is the statute, and nothing but the statute that tells the magistracy what it can, and cannot do.

The starting point for determining the jurisdiction in care proceedings is the Children and Young Persons Act 1969. Those who are entitled to bring care proceedings must prove two things about the child. First, that the facts of the case fall within any one of a number of specific conditions (the primary conditions) which, broadly speaking, are lack of proper development, exposure to moral danger, being beyond control, truanting (the educational condition) and committing an offence (the offence condition). Second, the court must be satisfied that the child is in need of care or control which he is unlikely to receive without an Order (the care or control condition). Each of the primary conditions is backward-looking; they relate to the child's past or present behaviour or circumstances. The court must be satisfied whether or not the condition exists. The care or control condition involves the court considering the likely course of events if an Order is, or is not made. This will require evidence of past and present circumstances, and a predictive judgment. To that last extent the magistrates are engaged in a forward-looking exercise, and may for that purpose at least hear evidence about what plans (if any) the local authority has for the child, if and when an Order is made. It cannot be doubted, therefore, that magistrates in deciding what (if any) Order they are contemplating, may concern themselves with prospective issues.

Magistrates have, generally speaking, three options in disposing of the application in care proceedings. They can make a Care Order, which commits the child to the care of a local authority: Section 20(1), Children and Young Persons Act 1969(We have considered in Chapter 2 the legal effect of that provision). Alternatively, the court may make a Supervision Order which places the supervised child under the supervision of a designated local authority or of a probation officer: Section 11 of the 1969 Act. Unlike probation, no consent of the supervised child is required. The Supervision Order may be accompanied by certain conditions, and in care proceedings may require that the child be medically examined in accordance with arrangements made by the supervisor. Finally, the court may make no order, in which case the child remains in the custody and care of its parent or guardian, without any restriction from the local authority. We have set out these powers in outline to indicate that, with minor qualifications, the court is not in any way involved in the treatment of the child who is placed in care of a local authority or under supervision. The moment the court makes a Care Order it hands over the destiny of the child to the local authority, subject only to an application to revoke the Order and to hear disputes about parental access to the child, and to any proceedings for adoption and, after December 1985, for custodianship. But the day-to-day decision about the pattern and nature of the child's life lies with the local authority.

Parliament drew not only a boundary line between the judicial decision of intervention in a child's life and the treatment to be administered, once that intervention had been judicially sanctioned. It also determined that there should be no restriction upon the administration of the Care Order,short of its lapsing at the age of eighteen (or exceptionally, nineteen) or a prior revocation of the Order at the instance of the local authority or of the child's parents. There is no hint in the legislation of any legal power to limit the period of operation of a Care Order, or to monitor or supervise the administration of the Order. In short, everything points to a legislative intent to require a judicial determination before a local authority can be vested with parental powers via a Care Order, and for judicial intervention to cease at the moment of making such an Order, subject only to the power to revoke the Order, not on its own initiative but solely on application by the local authority or the child's parents.

Anything said by the court in making an Order which does more than explain its effect, however, goes beyond what is legislatively sanctioned. Rule 21 of the Magistrates' Courts (Children and Young Persons) Rules 1970 deals with the court's duty to explain both the manner in which it proposes to deal with the case before it and the effect of any order it is making. Rule 21(1) provides that "before finally disposing of the case ... the court shall inform the relevant infant, any person conducting the case on his behalf, and his parent or guardian, if present, of the manner in which it proposes to deal with the case and allow any of those persons so informed to make representations." There is then a proviso exempting the court from this duty to inform the child if the court considers it undesirable or impracticable, having regard to his or her age or understanding.

It is Rule 21(2) that is relevant to our discussion. This provides that *"on making any order* [our emphasis], the court shall explain to the relevant infant the general nature and effect of the order unless it appears to it impracticable so to do having regard to his age or understanding or, in the case of an order requiring his parent or guardian to enter into a recognizance, it appears to it undesirable so to do." We note that on a strict reading of this Rule there is no duty on the court to explain the general nature and effect of its order to anyone other than the "relevant infant". Where the child is too young to understand, the duty might be said to include the child's parents or guardian. **We recommend that the Rules Committee should make this explicit, since we do think that it is desirable that magistrates should explain in simple and appropriate language the effect of their decision.** And in practice we understand that magistrates so interpret the statutory duty to explain.

The Rule is based upon the recommendation of the Ingleby Committee's report on

Children and Young Persons, published in October 1960*. The recommendation was to the effect that the court should be at pains to explain to both parents and child just what it is doing and why, so that they will be able to accept the court's decision as reasonable and appropriate, and becoming willing to co-operate in carrying the decision out. Paragraph 24 of the Basic Training for Juvenile Court Magistrates, issued by the Lord Chancellor's Office, states that before finally disposing of the case the court "shall inform juvenile and parents of order it proposes (unless undesirable or impracticable in case of juvenile) and invite representations and shall explain nature and effect of order." We think this is an inadequate summary of the statutory duty. There are two stages of the statutory duty – one to inform the parties of the proposed Order and to provide the opportunity for the parties to make representations before the Order is made; and second, to explain the effects of the order once it is made. These should be kept quite distinct and separate.

We digress simply to observe that the Willesden Magistrates on 9 September 1981 did not comply with the first stage – namely, of indicating what they proposed and inviting representations. Question 3(ii) to the Magistrates asked whether the Bench indicated to the parties that it proposed to make a recommendation in advance of announcing its decision, to which the Magistrates answered that "the conduct of the proceedings was such that those present had expressly or by implication an opportunity at every stage of addressing the Bench on any matter." None of the evidence of the persons who were at court that day and appeared before us supports that statement. We conclude that the Magistrates did not comply strictly with Rule 21(1). We think also that what they said on making the Care Orders was a rider to that decision, which went beyond what is required by way of explanation of the nature and effect of the Orders.

We think it may be helpful if we set out what we think magistrates should say in compliance of Rule 21(1) and Rule 21(2), as we have interpreted them, or as they should be amplified by amendment. To comply with Rule 21(1) it may be thought necessary to indicate only whether the magistrates are proposing to make a Care Order or Supervision Order. Even if the parties are legally represented, there is still a need for the legal representatives to be provided specifically with the opportunity to make their submissions. If the parents or the child of age and understanding are unrepresented, then the effect of the proposed Order should be explained, as it will have to be explained on making the Order whether the parents or child are represented or not. We now suggest the formula to be used.

"In this case we propose to make [or are making] what is called a Care Order. It means that the London Borough of Brent, through its appropriate committee and its officers in the Social Services Department, will be responsible for looking after A [the child] until he [or she] is 18 [If the juvenile is 16 when the order is made it will continue until the age of 19]. It is for Brent Borough Council to decide where he [or she] shall live. He [or she] may or may not be allowed to come home, but if and when that is to happen the decision will be made by Brent Borough Council. If Brent Borough Council decides that the child should go home, it will be for social workers to visit him or her at home, and ensure that the child is well looked after. If at any time it is thought that the child is not likely to be treated properly the child may be removed from his home by the Council. It is very important that you, Mr. and Mrs. X, and A [if the child is old enough to understand] should know that you have a right at any time to apply to this court or to the court for the area where A may be living, to put an end to the Order we are now proposing to make [or are making]. And should you decide to take this step you are entitled

---

* Cmnd 1191, paras 111 and 112 at p. 42, and recommendation (14) at p. 155.

to apply to the court for legal aid in your application. We can make no promises that the court will grant your application. Brent Borough Council may also ask the court at any time to put an end to the Order, in which case it is more than likely that the court will agree with Social Services because they generally know when it is no longer necessary that your child should be away from his [or her] parents' home. Do you understand what I have said? [If it is at the stage of a proposed order, the words should be: 'Do you wish to say anything before we decide to make the Order?'].''

We revert to the point at issue. The juvenile court has, in our view, no jurisdiction either to make a recommendation or even to endorse the expectations of the local authority as revealed in the courtroom. Even if (which is *not* this case) the local authority's representative invites, either expressly or by implication, the court to repeat what are the local authority's placement plans, it is our view that the court should neither echo nor comment upon such utterances.

We deal with the two situations — a judicial recommendation and an endorsement or comment on the local authority's plans for the child while in care. If Parliament in 1969 had considered that it wished the juvenile court to have a voice in the future custody and care of a child under a Care Order, it could so easily have provided for it. There are at least three legislative provisions, contemporary with the Children and Young Persons Act 1969 that spring to mind. Under section 1(2), Murder (Abolition of Death Penalty) Act 1962 a High Court judge, when passing the mandatory sentence of life imprisonment for murder, may recommend the minimum period that the life-sentence prisoner should serve in prison. By section 61, the Criminal Justice Act 1967, the Parole Board, when a prisoner on parole has been recalled to prison, may recommend to the Home Secretary that the prisoner should immediately be released back on parole, and that recommendation is binding on the Home Secretary. The third example is in the Immigration Act 1971 (which was drafted in the Home Office almost simultaneously with the Children and Young Persons Act 1969). When a criminal court (including a magistrates' court) convicts a person, who has no right of abode in the U.K., of an imprisonable offence, it may recommend that person to be deported. None of these examples provides an exact parallel, or is even analogous to a recommendation as to how a Care Order should be administered. But what they all show is that in a variety of situations Parliament has deliberately given the judiciary some voice, by way of recommendation, as to how the Executive (in the form of central or local government) might think it appropriate to perform its statutory functions. Parliament is deafeningly silent about such a power being conferred on juvenile magistrates in relation to Care Orders. It is incidentally in sharp contrast to a Care Order being made in wardship proceedings in the High Court, where the judges retain a continuing judicial overseership of the life of a child so long as he or she remains a ward of court. We make no comment on the desirability of one or the other of the two disparate jurisdictions. We merely observe the distinct difference in approach that the law makes in relation to the two jurisdictions.

We would add one further comment. It is in our view a breach of etiquette for an advocate to invite magistrates to say anything which might be interpreted as influencing the making of a rider to a Care Order. In the days of capital punishment juries not infrequently made recommendations to mercy when announcing their verdicts of guilty of murder. The Court of Criminal Appeal laid down that it was professionally improper for defence counsel in his speech to the jury to allude to, never mind invite the jury to add such a rider to its verdict.* We think the same principle applies to the making of a Care Order.

---

* *R* v. *Larkin* [1943] 1 K.B. 174; *R* v. *Black* [1963] 1 W.L.R. 1311.

If the juvenile court (contrary to our view) does have jurisdiction to add a rider to the making of the Care Order, indicating the way in which local authorities should execute a Care Order, we think it is both unwise and unhelpful for magistrates to indulge what in any event can only be a discretionary power. Apart from breaking the principle of non-intervention by the court into the administration of a Care Order, there are powerful practical reasons why no indication should come from the Bench as to how the Care Order ought to be administered, at least not in front of the parents. We deal with the issue only in relation to recommendations for (or indications favouring) reuniting of the family where a child has been taken into hospital or removed to some other place of safety.

There is the overriding consideration of the effect of any recommendation to reunite the family upon the relationship between social workers and the parents. As Mr. Bishop put it (and it was endorsed by Mr. Bedford in his expert evidence on behalf of the British Association of Social Workers) social workers lose therapeutic control over the situation. They constantly face the parents invoking what the court says, in order to counter any action that thwarts the parents' desire to have their children back home. There is the more pressing problem that parents will the more readily seek the opportunity to apply for a revocation order, in which proceedings the local authority will have to defend any action that appears not to be pursuing the course advocated by the Bench. There is the further point that Mr. Thomas, on behalf of Miss Rogers of the Adoption and Foster Care Section, drew our attention to in respect of future applications for adoption by foster-parents of the child in care. If an adoption agency desires to apply to the court to make an order declaring the child "free for adoption", there may be an insuperable obstacle to the making of such an order. The court must be satisfied, in the absence of parental consent, that such consent may be dispensed with if the parent is withholding consent unreasonably. How could a court say such withholding was unreasonable if a juvenile court has been favourably disposed towards retaining the family unit?

We appreciate the desire of magistrates to impose some control upon the unbridled power of local authorities to determine the destiny of children. But unless and until Parliament decides that juvenile courts should perform the role of judicial control or supervision over the functioning of Care Orders, we are quire clear that the temptation to indulge that desire should be severely resisted. **We recommend that the Lord Chancellor, in his review of paragraph 24 of** *Basic Training for Juvenile Court Magistrates* **should consider adding a sentence to the effect that no rider of any kind should be attached to a Care Order. And we recommend that the Magistrates' Association likewise informs its members.**

* * * * *

We are strongly of the view that in care proceedings at least − we have no right to comment on any other type of magisterial proceedings − magistrates should be required to give full and adequate reasons for any decision relating to the care and supervision of children. We note that the Review of Child Care Law supports our view that magistrates should give their reasons in writing (paragraph 16.40). **We state** *our* **reasons for arriving at the recommendation that justices should be bound by statute to give reasons.**

We presume that magistrates do actually have reasons for all their decisions. Were it not so, it would be a blot upon our system of magisterial justice; we prefer not to contemplate the possibility that decisions are unreasoned, even if at times they appear unreasonable. The obligation to think out and articulate the reasons for a judicial decision, justifying them in a public manner, will always promote that intellectual and judicial discipline necessary to ensure sound decision-making. Since care proceedings are conducted behind closed doors, and the press is rarely present to report them, the obligation to give a reasoned decision is all the greater. The public needs to be reassured that justice is being amply done, the more so if it cannot see it being done. And the parties before the court themselves will be materially assisted to understand the whys and wherefores of decisions affecting the welfare of children, not just for the moment but for the lengthy periods of childhood and adolescence.

Where a person has a right of appeal, the facility of reasons enables him to judge whether he should appeal; and, if so, on what basis. In care proceedings this is particularly important since the decision will touch the most sensitive human rights. Quite apart from the appellate right, the giving of reasons will render a magistrates' court more sensibly amenable to the supervisory jurisdiction of the High Court by way of judicial review. The reasoned decision will expose, and provide assurance that the magistrates have in fact acted within their prescribed powers.

Nothing would promote public confidence in the judicial process more than the publicly-avowed acceptance of the principle of reasoned decisions. A good deal of the complaints made about the exercise of magisterial power in the care and supervision of children stems from a genuine sense of grievance that the parties and their legal advisers express at not being told why a particular decision has been arrived at. As Mr. Justice Chilwell observed in the New Zealand case of *Connell* v. *Auckland City Council**, "the failure to provide reasons will, in a modern community, result in a litigant who is not only 'disappointed' but also 'disturbed'."

Finally, reasons for a decision constitute a healthy check on the exercise of discretionary power. They prevent arbitrary action; and they provide guidance for future cases. Reasons for granting or refusing an application for a Care Order may materially assist a local authority, which frequently comes before a magistrates' court, to understand the policy of the magistrates, and thus lead to better understanding between Bench and social worker.

The statutory requirement on the magistrates to give reasons for their decision should also indicate the various factors that they must direct their minds to in arriving at their reasoned judgment and we so recommend. The idea is to provide the magistrates with a checklist against which they can measure the adequacy and completeness of their reasoning, to be publicly stated when announcing their decision. **We also recommend that Parliament should in the legislation indicate what is to be the legal effect of non-compliance with the statutory duty to give reasons.**

By our criticism of the Willesden Justices for having exceeded their jurisdiction on 9 September 1981, and in recommending that reasons always be given for decisions in care proceedings, we recognise that we are advocating a higher degree of professionalism in the administration of juvenile justice. We make no apology for wanting a higher degree of professionalism among the lay magistracy. When several of the legal representatives urged us, in their written and oral submissions, to add our voice to the growing chorus of support for a Family Court, we detected that their advocacy was likewise stimulated by a critical sense that too much in the juvenile justice system smacks of amateurism. To some extent we share that feeling. It is a lack of training and of understanding among many magistrates of the legal processes in which juvenile justice is couched that has led

* [1977] 1 N.Z.L.R. 630,634, cited approvingly by Kirby P. in the Court of Appeal of New South Wales in *Osmond* v. *Public Service Board of New South Wales and another* [1985] L.R.C. (Const) 1041,1058.

legal practitioners and other observers to express unhappiness at the quality of justice meted out to children, to parents and to local authorities in care proceedings.

We, therefore, greatly welcome the initiative of the Inner London Juvenile Panel in the new process of selecting from among existing juvenile magistrates those suitable to take the chair. The new rules for appointing who will take the chair, and the week-end selection board plus training, will clearly assist in the striving for professionalism in the juvenile magistracy. If and when a Family Court is established − and, we think, its advent is not too far distant − we are confident that there will be a corpus of highly professional juvenile magistrates (not by any means all legally qualified) who, together with circuit judges and stipendiary magistrates, will form the nucleus of chairmen of the Family Court.

CHAPTER 17

National Society for the Prevention of Cruelty to Children

Two voluntary agencies have been mentioned in the course of our hearings – the National Society for the Prevention of Cruelty to Children, which plays in some parts of the country a notable role in the management of the child abuse system, and the Family Service Unit, which in part operates as an auxiliary to the statutory Social Services. Since the Family Service Unit was not involved in any way with the Beckford family, indicating thereby no lack of resource in Area 6 such as to call for assistance from the voluntary sector of Social Services, and since we have nothing useful to say about what role, if any, Family Service Units could play in the management of the child abuse system, we say no more about that voluntary agency.

The National Society for the Prevention of Cruelty to Children (NSPCC) is a voluntary society founded in 1889 and incorporated by Royal Charter in 1895. Its purposes are: "To prevent the public and private wrongs of children, and the corruption of their morals; to take action for the enforcement of laws for their protection; to provide and maintain an organisation for the above object; to do all other such lawful things as are incidental or conducive to the attainment of the above objects." The Society has had long experience and distinguished service in its work to promote child welfare and to protect children from parental abuse. In recognition of its outstanding part as a voluntary agency in child care, Parliament has accorded the Society a unique statutory role.

Section 1, Children and Young Persons Act 1969 authorises a juvenile court to make certain Orders for the protection of children and young persons who are, *inter alia* being ill-treated or neglected. By sub-section (1), care proceedings may be brought only by a local authority, a constable, or an "authorised person". By the Children and Young Persons Act 1969 (Authorisation for the Purposes of Section 1) Order 1970, the Society is the only person authorised under the Act.* Although it is empowered to bring care proceedings, neither constables nor the Society, unlike a local authority, have any statutory duty to do so. By section 2(2), where it appears to the local authority that there are grounds for bringing care proceedings in respect of a child who resides or is found in its area, it is the duty of the local authority to bring such proceedings unless it is satisfied that it is neither in the child's interest, nor in the public interest, to do so; or that some other person is about to do so or to charge him with an offence. By section 2(3), constables and the Society are required to give notice to the local authority before bringing care proceedings themselves. A Care Order can be made only in favour of the local authority.

To assist the Society in its task of carrying out the purposes of the function of a person authorised to take care proceedings under Section 1, and generally in its work as an investigative agency, the Society invites the help of the general public in telling the Society's officers of any child they know who may be the subject of child abuse. In practice, the Society's main function is to receive information, evaluate it and take appropriate action. In only a small proportion of its cases does the Society take care proceedings; more often, it will liaise with the local authority's Social Services Department and leave the question of court proceedings to the latter. It frequently applies for Place of Safety Orders. Thus, as we described in Chapter 2, the Crown's overriding parental power over children in need of care has been statutorily devolved on local authorities;

---

* It had been an authorised person for the purpose of taking proceedings under the corresponding section of the earlier Children and Young Persons Act of 1933: Section 62.

the High Court retains its wardship jurisdiction in a limited number of cases. The Society is, however, clearly acknowledged as playing an important part in the process of child protection.

Apart from its countrywide service in the protection of children, the Society has in the last two decades engaged in significant research in the field of child abuse. Its publication in 1969 of the report, *78 Battered Children: a retrospective study*, was a landmark in the literature and forerunner of subsequent studies, the most recent of which is *Trends in Child Abuse: 1977-82*, the fourth report on the children placed on NSPCC Special Unit Registers, undertaken by Susan Creighton, and published in July 1984. In recent years, the Society has established special units in inner city areas where the incidence of child abuse is high. Some of the procedures of these units, which collaborate closely with the local authorities, are worthy of imitation.

The Society's offices had no direct involvement with the Beckford case. Mr. Raymond Jenkins, a senior field officer for the Society in West London (including the Borough of Brent) was contacted on 4 August 1981 by Miss Knibbs, informing him of Louise Beckford's admission to St. Charles' Hospital and inviting him to the Case Conference on 6 August 1981. Mr. Jenkins forthwith checked the Society's records and turned up a reference to Morris Beckford's involvement with the Police and Social Services when he was a child in June 1972. Mr. Jenkins told Miss Knibbs of this fact, and indicated that he would also convey the information to the Case Conference: Which he duly did. He even produced photographs of the injuries to Morris Beckford, then aged 13, together with photographs of the garden shed in which Morris and his sister had been kept by their parents. He supplied the dates of criminal court proceedings and of the making of a Care Order on Morris Beckford. Mr. Jenkins was not invited to the subsequent Case Conference on 20 August 1981. We think that he should have been invited. Mr. Jenkins told us that he would have wished to be invited, but did not criticise the omission, since it was a Brent and not an NSPCC case. He certainly would have expected to be invited to — and would have attended — any case conference that was deciding the return of the children home on trial, or where the Social Services department was deciding to remove the children from the child abuse Register. If it had been Area 1, he would almost certainly have been invited, since he had a personal relationship with the Area Manager. Quite apart from any personal relationship, we are firmly of the view that the local NSPCC officer should be invited. We say this for two reasons. The first is the obvious one, that the Society is often the repository of background information about the abusing parents, as the Society had been about Morris Beckford. Doubtless Mr. Jenkins' colleagues in the areas where Beverley Lorrington had lived as a child might have had relevant information on her childhood. But, as we have described in Chapter 8, Area 6 seemed wholly disinterested in investigating the social and medical history of the Beckford parents.

Second, we think that NSPCC officers have a unique expertise in the whole area of child abuse — a commodity sufficiently rare for it never to be spurned — and that they should automatically be present at case conferences and case reviews in serious child abuse cases where impending decisions of importance are under discussion. In a sense, this is acknowledged by the fact that Mr. Jenkins was a member of all 7 Area Review Committees covering the 7 London boroughs on his patch. The value of Mr. Jenkins' presence at the Case Conference of 6 August 1981 is exemplified by one incident. He told Dr. Supramaniam that he regarded the injuries on Louise as having possibly been inflicted on separate occasions — the spiral fracture of the humerus by a twisting jerk, the retinal haemorrhage by a violent shake. In this, he was in profound disagreement with Dr. Supramaniam. As it turns out, Mr. Jenkins is likely to have been more right than wrong. He would also have been able to tell any future case conference that 60%

of battering parents have, as children, been battered themselves by their parents. Again, this factor was never perceptibly put into the scales in the decision to return the children in April 1982 to their parents' home. We doubt, however, whether that fact would have had any impact on Mrs. Dietmann and Ms. Wahlstrom, who were oblivious to the indications of future child abuse.

We are aware that the organisation and work of the NSPCC is undergoing a thorough internal examination, and that the move is towards concentration on the special units and reducing the individual inspectorial role. **We think that the time has come for an independent review of the role of the NSPCC together with all the other voluntary bodies engaged in the work of child care and protection, with special reference to their future contribution to, and collaboration with the statutory agencies in the child abuse system. We so recommend.**

CHAPTER 18

Political Complexities of Brent Borough Council

For some years now local government in Brent has see-sawed in its political composition. As a consequence, there has not been any sustained, coherent policy-making. Individual decisions have suffered a vacillation from one end of the political spectrum to another. Internally, this can hardly have contributed to smooth or easy administration; officers have found that they were constantly being pulled in differing directions. To the public outside the town hall, the political dimension infects every aspect of the services provided by the local authority. These factors have played, and will continue to play an important role in government in Brent.

From May 1982 until December 1983 the Labour group on the Council maintained a tenuous hold on political power; it was in fact sustained by virtue of the Mayor's casting vote. At that time, one Labour Councillor crossed the floor and at a stroke deprived the Labour group of its control of the Council. Since then, no one group has had an overall majority. Three Liberal councillors have held the balance of power. (No formal coalition has existed between any of the three political groups). Significantly, the Conservatives have taken the chairs of all Committees. Thus, during the period under inquiry, the Social Services Department worked under a precarious Labour administration until the end of 1983, and thereafter under a Conservative administration with a hardly less slender hold on power. We give below the names of chairmen to the two Committees relevant to our Inquiry.

Chairmen of Social Services Committee
1980-1981	Councillor Dr. Rosen
1981-1982	Councillor G. Crane (Labour)
1982-1983	Councillor L. Nerva (Labour)
1983-1984	Councillor R. Stone (Conservative)
1984-1985	Councillor R. Stone (Conservative)
1985-	Councillor Greenaway (Conservative)

Chairmen of Cases Sub-Committee
The Cases Sub-Committee was set up in September 1983.

September/October 1983	Councillor L. Nerva (Labour)
1984-1985	Councillor Mrs. F. Rees-Hughes (Conservative)
1985-1986	Councillor Mrs. F. Rees-Hughes (Conservative)

The situation of a "hung" Council is believed by some to be a built-in suppressor to the more extreme policies that either of the two main political groups might otherwise pursue. Others take the view that the inherent political instability is not conducive to sound policy-making, particularly in the area of Social Services. Whatever the merits of these opposing arguments, there is little doubt that the political complexion of Brent induces a climate in which every issue is hotly debated, each side seizing the opportunity to score a political point. Predictably, given that climate, no one can tell at any time precisely what the outcome of any issue will be.

We give one example which is directly relevant to our Inquiry. We have referred in Chapter 3 to the issues of the cost of our Inquiry. Brent Councillors have variously expressed their disquiet about the size of the bill the Borough will have to foot, jointly with Brent Health Authority. The cost, however, is not as great as it might have been, since all the represented parties, with two exceptions, were backed by professional organisations or trade unions which funded their members' legal costs. These were not inconsiderable.

From the outset it was obvious to us that it was imperative that Mr. and Mrs. Probert, the foster-parents, should be legally represented. The Council acceded to our request that their reasonable costs should be paid by the local authority. At a later stage, when the hearings were well under way, it became apparent that the Principal Court Officer was the subject of criticism. We administered a "Salmon letter" to him, and indicated strongly that he and his deputy should be legally represented. We became aware, however, that neither of them belonged to a trade union or professional body. This meant that they would have to bear their own costs. Mr. Ian Duncan, a solicitor, who appeared for Mr. Thompson and Mr. Hobbs, approached us with a request that his two clients should be similarly funded by Brent Council. We considered that it was entirely appropriate that an employee of a local authority who was the subject of potential criticism before an independent public inquiry should not have to meet his own legal costs. We recommended to the Council that the legal costs incurred by the two members of staff in being represented before us should be reimbursed, to a maximum of £2,000 for the two of them.

On 16 July 1985 the Policy and Resources Committee considered a resolution to pay Mr. Thompson's and Mr. Hobbs' legal costs. (The resolution was, we notice, considered in the absence of the press and the public, the Committee considering that the nature of the business to be transacted was confidential, by virtue of Section 1(2), Public Bodies (Admission to Meetings) Act 1960. We find it hard to understand why this item was considered in secret, but we have not been told why, and therefore do not make any criticism).

At that meeting the Committee passed the resolution by 7 votes to 6. No doubt the two members of staff were told the good news. Subsequently, on 31 July 1985, the Council reversed the decision of its Policy and Resources Committee and substituted a decision that "no action be taken" in respect of the reimbursement of the legal costs of the two members of staff. Apparently two Conservative Councillors voted with the Labour opposition.

Ordinarily, we would have been highly critical of a decision that smacks of parsimony and unfairness. No self-respecting local authority would take away what its main committee had given by way of legal aid to two members of staff faced with adverse comment and seeking to defend their work. But this is Brent. The narrowness of the vote in the Policy and Resources Committee would indicate to any resident of Brent how insecure its fate would be before the full Council. Accordingly, while we deplore the denial of justice to Mr. Thompson and Mr. Hobbs, we cannot criticise the members of Brent Borough Council in the circumstances of the political make-up of the Council. We would add only that this minor episode is symptomatic of the chronic political instability that pervades local government in Brent with its inevitable effects on staff. Other issues face a similar uncertain fate in the councils of this local authority.

CHAPTER 19

Responses of Brent Borough Council

Initially, no one, except police officers, the forensic pathologist who conducted the post-mortem, and the senior officers of Brent Social Services Department, knew of the multiple abuse Jasmine had suffered over the last months of her life. Not until the trial at the Central Criminal Court at the end of March 1985 did the public become aware of the circumstances that gave cause for concern about the work of Brent Social Services. Throughout the months from July 1984 onwards, members and officers of Brent Borough Council were thus fortuitously free to consider at their leisure what responses they should make, unperturbed by the prospect of having to answer awkward questions from members of the public or from investigative journalists. While the officers of the Social Services Department immediately began to review their child abuse procedures and management of the Beckford case, there was no sign of urgency evinced by individual Councillors to the news supplied to them in the days immediately following Jasmine's death; and none was forthcoming in the weeks following the tragedy.

Meetings and reports of officers, 5 July – 29 October 1984
The officers of the Social Services Department lost no time in reacting appropriately to the sad news of Jasmine's violent and unnatural death. Mr. Bishop learned of her death late in the evening of July 5 from the duty officer, Miss June Griffiths. He in turn told Mrs. Dietmann and Ms. Wahlstrom, with whom he arranged to meet the next day. The Director of Social Services was told early in the morning of July 6 by Mr. Bishop who was scribbling her an urgent note in her office when she arrived for work. On that day, Area 6 arranged for Louise and Chantelle Beckford to be removed from the home of Mrs. Lorrington, their maternal grandmother, to whom the Police had taken the children the night before from the Beckford household where Jasmine had been killed that morning. The two children were taken by Social Services staff immediately for medical examination. This revealed multiple bruising to both children as a result of blows inflicted over several days. Each child had a full skeletal x-ray, but no fractured bones were disclosed.

Earlier that day, Mrs. Dietmann and Mr. Bishop had discussed the case between them, being joined later by the Director, Mr. Simpson, Mr. Thompson and Ms. Wahlstrom. Before the full meeting had begun, Mrs. Dietmann and Mr. Bishop had arranged with Mr. Thompson that he should obtain a Place of Safety Order in respect of Chantelle. An order for 28 days was obtained by Mr. Thompson from a Magistrate sitting at Willesden Magistrates' Court. He did not involve the Law and Administration Department.

At the full meeting, departmental officers agreed to the immediate steps to be taken in their plan of action: to remove Louise and Chantelle to foster placement, which was effected later that day; that Mr. Bishop should be in attendance when Morris Beckford and Beverley Lorrington were being interrogated, which was also done; that Mr. Thompson would liaise with the Police and keep the Department informed of the results of the autopsy on Jasmine; that Ms. Wahlstrom and Mrs. Dietmann should prepare a case synopsis for the following Monday, 9 July 1984; that all, except Ms. Wahlstrom who was going on leave, should review the situation at a meeting to be held with the Director on 10 July 1984; and, lastly, that the Director would liaise with the Chairman of Social Services Committee, Councillor Stone, and with the Chief Executive, Mr. Bichard. The Public Relations Officer had already been informed, in the event of having to respond to any publicity. He was untroubled until the deluge of press coverage in March 1985, when the criminal trial was concluded and the setting up of our Inquiry was announced. We defer our description of the communications between the Director and members of the Council, and the latter's responses. It is necessary here only to say that the Director told the Chief Executive, either on Friday, 6 July or Monday, 9 July; he passed on the information – as the Director confidently expected he would – to the Leader of the Conservative Group, Councillor Lacey, and the Leader of the Labour Group, Councillor Coleman.

Mrs. Dietmann and Ms. Wahlstrom duly produced their synopsis of events, dated 9 July 1984, for the scheduled meeting on 10 July 1984. It, in fact, did more than provide a general survey, by descending to some particularity. It summarised accurately the two Case Conferences of 6 and 20 August 1981; it set out the *ipsissima verba* of Mr. Thompson's memorandum of 16 September 1981; it noted, by date reference, every social worker action over 3 years, and set out the conclusions of all the subsequent Case Conferences and Statutory Case Reviews. It noted Ms. Wahlstrom's visit of 12 March 1984, and recorded Jasmine's irregular attendance at school, but omitted the reference to Ms. Wahlstrom's entry in her Social Worker's Report that all three children appeared "well and happy". The synopsis finally referred to the letter of 3 July 1984 announcing the visit which Mrs. Dietmann and Ms. Wahlstrom were due to make, and noted that the two social workers "would appear for review on 5.7.84 at 1.00"; it described in outline that abortive visit on the day Jasmine died.

The document ran to 14 1/3 foolscap pages of typescript. (By contrast, the information supplied to members of the Cases Sub-Committee on 29 October 1984 was a mere page and a bit, a matter to which we shall refer at some length). By no stretch of the imagination could it be said that the authors of the synopsis had either evaded or scamped their duty to disclose the main features of the case as they culled them from the files and from their personal recollection. Given the shortness of time in which to prepare the document, it was a model of instructive clarity.

Anyone reading that document could tell at a glance the general drift of social work over three years with the Beckford family, with its early intensive and extensive casework with the Beckford parents, the run-down in social work input from November 1982, and the infrequent supervision after September 1983. The reader would quickly be able to calculate that there had been 78 visits to the family from 19 April 1982, 37 of them until 9 November 1982, when the children were taken off the child abuse register; 18 visits (some unsuccessful) were made from that date until 22 June 1983, when the application to revoke the Care Orders was unsuccessfully made to the Magistrates' Court; there were five visits up to 8 September 1983, when Jasmine ceased going to school; and only 18 visits from then until 5 July 1984 (on 13 of which Ms. Wahlstrom received no reply, and on 5 of which actual visits, when she gained entry, she saw Jasmine only once). That bird's-eye view of the entire social work monitoring of the Beckford household was enough in itself to preclude the conclusion that there was no cause for concern.

The other overall impression that a quick read of that document would have conveyed was the infinite complexity of the case, unravellable only after a more detailed examination of the documentation and some questioning of the main actors in not merely the social work input but also, after a review of the work of other agencies involved in the case, the work of the health visitors.

From a confidential note composed by the Director on 9 July, it appeared that she had heard unofficially from the Police that the autopsy on Jasmine had revealed "10-12 fractures over the last two months." Although this piece of information did not specifically relate to any period when Ms. Wahlstrom had been visiting the Beckfords, and would not of itself have given rise to concern, it did provide the first clear indication to the

Director and her staff that Jasmine's death was not the result of a single, violent eruption on 5 July, but was the culmination of a pattern of severe child abuse.

At a meeting on 10 July, the Director and Mr. Simpson, Mr. Bishop, Mrs. Dietmann and Mr. Thompson considered the lengthy synopsis of events. The Director recorded in her contemporaneous note of that meeting that "some of the other injuries appear to be of various ages and one femur seems to have had four old fractures." Mr. Thompson, who had been keeping in close touch with the Police, also made a contemporaneous note of that meeting. Apropos Jasmine's medical condition, he wrote: "15 fractures: various parts of the body – no medical help." He further noted that Jasmine was "badly undernourished", to which he made a parenthetical annotation indicating that Jasmine's condition suggested an offence of child neglect under section 1, Children and Young Persons Act 1933. (Subsequently at their trial in March 1985 both Morris Beckford and Beverley Lorrington pleaded guilty to child cruelty during the period, September 1983 – July 1984: see Appendix D).

At that early stage of the inquiries into the Beckford case, it might have been reasonable to infer that the multiple fractures occurred *after* Ms. Wahlstrom's last sight of the children on 12 March 1984. But the reference in Mr. Thompson's notes to "undernourishment" must presumptively have led anyone to think that such a condition had persisted over many months. A child of four years does not become "badly undernourished" overnight.

Until that moment, the Director was fully entitled to believe that there need be no particular concern about the nature and quality of the social work service provided by her staff. What she had so far communicated to the Chief Executive and to the Chairman of the Social Services Committee was unexceptionable. But on 10 July the picture was very different. The Director had been told of, and had noted, the many earlier injuries to Jasmine; she had a detailed record of Ms. Wahlstrom's contacts with the Beckford family over the whole period of the home on trial, in particular the months during which Ms. Wahlstrom was failing, for whatever reason, to visit effectively a child in the care of Brent Borough Council; and the notion that the death of Jasmine on 5 July was a "one-off" episode could be wholly discounted.

Putting together the fact of persistent child abuse over an indefinitive period of time and the largely ineffectual supervision by Ms. Wahlstrom over many months, any reasonable person, we think, would have concluded that there *was* some cause for concern about the local authority's responsibility in failing to protect this child. Miss Howarth denies that there was, on 10 July, any general picture of protracted abuse; she asserts that that only became clear when the evidence of the autopsy was given in the criminal trial. We disagree. There was, in our view, glaringly such a picture on 10 July. If the Director did not see it – and we accept her evidence that she did not see it – she certainly should have done.

We arrived at our conclusion after lengthy deliberations among ourselves, when composing this chapter of our report. We were very conscious that while the issue of the Department's response in the days immediately following Jasmine's death was raised during the hearings in May and June 1985, it was not as fully canvassed as we would have liked. We have not heard the Director or the people who attended that meeting of 10 July fully on whether they concluded that there was, or was not cause for concern. We did not think it necessary to reopen the Inquiry to deal with an issue which was peripheral to our main task. In the absence of a fuller investigation and the disclosure of a reasonable riposte, we would have concluded that the Director was at fault after 10 July in not alerting the Chief Executive and the Chairman of the Social Services Committee to the fact that, in the light of the fresh information, there was now some cause for concern. They should not have been left oblivious of the changed perspectives of the Beckford case. But we do not make any positive finding of blame on Miss Howarth. So far as the mismanagement of the case goes, no harm ensued. There was always going to be an inquiry, and we have held it -- we hope with thoroughness. Unhappily, the Director's failure, on or shortly after 10 July, to apprise the Chief Executive and the Chairman of the Social Services Committee of the changed perspective fanned the flames of a later suggestion, made by some members of the Council, that she was covering up for the inefficiencies in, and deficiencies of her staff. There is, as we have found, no basis for any such suggestion.

Our criticism of the Director led us to consider what, if anything, was being communicated to central government about the death of a child in care in circumstances that, after 10 July, certainly should have aroused concern. On 18 July, in the absence of the Director on leave but on her instructions, given on 10 July, Mr. Simpson wrote to the Department of Health and Social Security's Social Work Service, London Region. We reproduce the letter verbatim.

RE: BECKFORD/LORRINGTON FAMILY

This is to let you know that Jasmine Beckford died on Thursday 5th July 1984. She was in care to Brent. Her date of birth was 2nd December 1979. She was previously on the Child Abuse Register. In April 1982 she and her siblings were returned home. In the Autumn of 1982 the child was removed from the Child Abuse Register.

At present both parents are in custody, and the father is being charged with murder. The Police investigations are continuing. Both Valerie and I will be away on annual leave for the next 2/3 weeks, and will then look at the incident in relation to our child abuse procedures.

I am informing you about the death of a child in care, and also to let you know that the young person concerned was previously on the Child Abuse Register.

Yours sincerely,

Dennis Simpson
Assistant Director
Family Services Division

cc: David Bishop – Area 6

We were initially concerned that this letter did not supply sufficient details of the Beckford case; in particular it did not refer to Jasmine's earlier injuries, nor to the fact that Ms. Wahlstrom had seen the child so infrequently in the months before her death. But it did contain the bald information that a child in care of Brent Borough Council had died.

There is no duty on a local authority to inform the Department of Health and Social Security of the death of a child in care. A Home Office circular in 1964 (28/1964) did ask local authorities to notify the Secretary of State of the death of any child in care who had been boarded-out with foster-parents. But it said nothing about other children's deaths. A less formal approach to local authorities came by way of a circular letter to Directors of Social Services on 25 May 1977, when the Chief Social Work Officer at the Department wrote: "Although there is no formal requirement that you should do so, we should find it helpful if you would also let us know if a child in your care dies in unusual or unexpected circumstances, or because equipment or safeguards may have proved defective or inadequate. Reports of this kind will enable us to decide whether there is a need for further central guidance or the revision of existing guidance so as to help prevent further deaths in similar circumstances." The letter ended: "Some Directors of Social Services have taken the view that the death of a child in care is so serious a matter that they have continued to tell us of all deaths. If you should choose to do this, we should appreciate the information. For the future, it would be helpful if notification could be sent to the Principal Social Work Service Officer in your region who will then send the information to me." We think that this guidance is far too indefinite. **We recommend that Directors of Social Services should invariably report to the Department of Health and Social Security any death of a child in care or under the supervision of the local authority, and such report should give full details of the circumstances surrounding the death.** In this case it would have been helpful if Mr. Simpson had simply enclosed the admirable synopsis of events with his letter of 18 July.

On Miss Howarth's return from leave, we understand that she discussed the Beckford case personally with Social Work Service Officers from the London Regional Office of the Social Work Service, with particular reference to the timing of any inquiry Following these discussions, the Principal Social Work Service Officer of London Region wrote to Miss Howarth, offering help and advice, and stating "whilst any detailed investigation of the case must be sub judice, I would assume that in the meantime you will be looking in general terms at the procedures which are at present operating in respect of the Child Abuse Register."

It does not appear to us that the paucity of information in the letter of 18 July in any way affected the course of events. The role of the Department of Health and Social Security in respect of deaths of children in care of a local authority is unclear. It is likewise unclear what accountability local authorities have to Central Government. **We recommend that, pursuant to our recommendation about reporting such deaths, the Department of Health and Social Security should consider issuing clearer guidance to local authorities.** The Consultative Paper of 4 July 1985 is defective in that regard.

Any apparent indecision on the part of the Director regarding the setting up of an inquiry is wholly explicable by the fact that at that time there was confusion among local authorities about how to handle child abuse inquiries (We have alluded to this in Chapter 3). The Department had for some time been giving informal advice to constituent agencies of child abuse Review Committees (both public bodies and voluntary organisations) on the action they should take when serious cases of child abuse occur. The Department had become aware, however, that many of those working in the field were anxious to receive formal guidance. The Department was sympathetic to entreaties for guidance. Because of the complexity of the issues involved – differing local organisational structures and the variety of cases that needed to be considered – the Department felt that it was impractical to produce detailed guidance. It was in the throes of proposing a local framework and basic general guidelines which could be used as the need arose. The ensuing consultative paper on Child Abuse Inquiries, for which the Director was pressing in the autumn of 1984, in the event did not appear until June 1985, long after it had been decided to set up our Inquiry. In that state of flux, it is hardly surprising that the Director was feeling her way forward in determining what kind of inquiry should be instituted. To some observers it might reasonably have appeared that she was holding back, hoping that the nasty smell might go away.

We can understand how her actions were misinterpreted as a desire not to have any inquiry. But we dismiss the suggestions from some Councillors that the Director was at best reluctant to have an inquiry, and at worst was being positively obstructive to those bent on having a fully independent inquiry external to Brent Borough Council. We are fortified in that conclusion by the fact that no such suggestion was in the minds of Councillor Rees-Hughes, the chairman of the Cases Sub-Committee, and Councillor Crane. The latter was emphatic that the only hesitancy on the part of the Director was the timing of the inquiry, dictated by the operation of the *sub judice* rule. Councillor Crane impressed us, to the point where we preferred his account of events in October and November 1984 to those who maintained the contrary. Of the officers whom we have heard, Mr. Simpson and Mr. Thompson had no doubt that the Director was working actively towards the kind of inquiry (after the trial) which we have held.

We pause here to record our findings on the Director's view towards an inquiry of the Beckford case, as it appeared to her five days after Jasmine's death. We have no hesitation in concluding that, on 10 July and from then onwards, the Director always envisaged that some kind of full-scale inquiry was both inevitable and desirable, even desired. The two questions that urgently remained to be answered were, what sort of inquiry would be appropriate, and when should it be held? The Director was anxious to elicit a good deal more information before she could decide what she should be recommending to the Chairman of the Social Services Committee. Her actions were dictated by two considerations: a sensitivity to the effect on the morale of her staff and an awareness that a thorough and fair inquiry had to be delayed until after the criminal proceedings. Her contacts with the Police, both directly and through her chairmanship of the Area Review Committee, had convinced her that the *sub judice* rule precluded any Police collaboration until after the trial, and that witnesses for the forthcoming trial could not properly be questioned. She was also anxious to hear from the Department of Health and Social Security what procedures should be followed in arranging a child abuse inquiry.

The Director went away on 13 July on a week-end management course with other Brent Directors, including the Director of Law and Administration. Before going on leave after that week-end the Director discussed with Mr. Simpson the further considerations that the case needed. The Director told us that Mr. Simpson, in addition to preparing the material for an expected meeting of the Cases Sub-Committee, volunteered to "do the investigation into the management aspect of the case." The Director was keen not merely to have a thorough check of the procedures but also to ascertain whether they had been followed, in order to reveal what lessons might be learned, with a view to amending the procedures and preventing anything similar happening again. She also expressed the desire to make sure that there had been no wanton conduct or gross negligence on the part of any member of the staff of the Social Services Department. Mr. Simpson did not fully accept the Director's evidence. He accepted that he was made responsible for the procedural review, but not for the management review as such, although he conceded that any procedural review would necessarily involve examining to some extent the managerial aspects. When he attended the Cases Sub-Committee on 29 October 1984, he was recorded contemporaneously by the Committee clerk as saying, in answer to a question from Councillor Haftel whether an inquiry was on foot: "Yes, full inquiry being made. Me and some people from Area have looked at the case file." Mr. Simpson further accepted that he and the Director discussed the management of the case after the Director's return from leave on 9 August 1984 and did so on numerous occasions during the late summer and autumn of 1984.

It is tolerably clear to us that the Director and Mr. Simpson felt that the child abuse procedures pertaining throughout the three years of social work with the Beckfords had not been breached, although they both now acknowledge that the procedures were in some respects couched in ambiguous terms. The prime example of obscurity was that Area 6 staff thought that the precise procedures for administering case conferences related only to the initial conferences prior to the obtaining of a Care Order, whereas they were intended, and should reasonably have been construed as operative for *all* case conferences and case reviews. Indeed, such non-observance of procedures as we have found stemmed mainly from not applying the procedures uniformly over the nine Case Conferences and Case Reviews. While the two senior social work administrators considered that there had been no breaches of procedure, they both thought that Area 6 staff had been much too sanguine about the progress in the Beckford family in the later stages of the social casework. Both were convinced that a longer and harder look at both the social worker and health visitor input was called for. The Director said – and we believe her – that she never doubted that at some stage it was vital to view the Beckford case in the wider context of social and health services. At that stage they had not seen the documentation of Brent Health Authority; in particular, they had not seen the impressive memorandum written by Miss Baichoo to her superiors on 17 July 1984 in which she revealed unerringly the serious questions that needed to be answered in any review of the health visitors' role in the child protection service for the Beckford children. (We have set out Miss Baichoo's memorandum at the end of Chapter 12).

The Director told us that throughout the weeks and months following 5 July she was deeply concerned that an internal inquiry would not involve agencies other than Social Services, and that she was convinced that a proper inquiry could not be so restricted in its task. We endorse that approach. We have ourselves seen how right the Director was in foreseeing the multi-agency responsibility for Jasmine's death – not just social services, but health, education and juvenile court. Whatever impression others may have had of the Director's approach to an inquiry, we think they misunderstood her. Her approach was impeccable – first, look at Social Services; then broaden out the inquiry to take in other agencies; the ultimate goal was to be a full-scale independent inquiry as soon as the criminal trial is out of the way. We do not merely acquit the Director of any fault; we applaud her foresight in anticipating the outcome of the Department's report on the case, and ensuring that everything was done to facilitate what has become our task.

Before we pass on to describe briefly the activities of the Social Services Department in the weeks between mid-July and the meeting of the Cases Sub-Committee on 29 October 1984, there is one matter to which we need to allude.

At the short meeting on 10 July 1984 the Director gave instructions that the Department of Law and Administration should be officially informed. The Director met the Director of Law and Administration at the week-end conference of Directors of Brent Borough Council and unofficially told him of Jasmine's death. Mr. Forster does not recall it, but he does not contradict Miss Howarth's recollection of telling him. We think it made no impact on Mr. Forster, because his Department did not become involved in the preparation of the synopsis and later documentation until Mr. Damms had attended on his behalf at the October meeting of the Cases Sub-Committee. Why the Department of Law and Administration was not informed and actively involved soon after 10 July remained unclear at first. We tended to think that there might have been a misunderstanding among those present at the Director's meeting of 10 July. Miss Howarth, however, told us that there was no misunderstanding on her part. She had made a note: "In addition, Bill Thompson will talk to Martin Damms officially." She went on to say that Mr. Thompson had already spoken to Mr. Damms – a note for file by Mr. Damms on 14 December confirms this – and told him about the situation, and that she insisted that he contacted Mr. Damms again "and say officially from the Department." Miss Howarth told us that Mr. Thompson said he would do it. Miss Howarth "believed he did." Mr. Damms told us that the case was not formally reported to his Department until just before the October meeting of the Cases Sub-Committee. The Director's absence on leave until the end of the month contributed to the failure to see that Mr. Thompson did what he was instructed to do. What had been unclear to us became clear once we heard from Miss Howarth and Mr. Thompson.

On 12 July 1984 a Case Conference was held at Area 6's office to discuss the implications of the death of Jasmine Beckford in relation to her two sisters. At that Case Conference, chaired by Mr. Bishop, personnel from other agencies attended. Miss Leong and Miss Tyler were there. The senior hospital officer (Paediatrics) from Central Middlesex Hospital, Dr. Morgan, was there; it was she who had examined the two sisters on 6 July 1984. The Police were there in force, three detectives from Kilburn Police and an officer from the Juvenile Bureau of Wembley Police. Dr. Morgan produced the results of her examination of the two sisters, including the full skeletal x-rays. Miss Leong gave an account of her involvement with the Beckford family from the time of Chantelle's birth in December 1983 onwards. Her account of her visits disclosed a similar pattern to that of Ms. Wahlstrom's – ineffective or abortive visits. While the focus of the Case Conference was properly on the future of Louise and Chantelle, the minutes of the meeting should have been fed into the reports being prepared for the ongoing inquiry into Jasmine's death. No one apparently thought of asking Miss Tyler to supply further information on the health visiting aspect of the case. (We note, incidentally, that the Case Conference ended with a rubric "Summary and Recommendations" and not "Decisions". Something at least had been learnt about the proper role of Case Conferences).

One of the recommendations of the Case Conference was that no direct parental or family access should be allowed. On 1 August an interim Care Order was made in respect of Chantelle, and on 2 August 1984 notices were issued under Section 12B, Child Care Act 1980, stating that Brent Borough Council was proposing to terminate any arrangements for parental and family access to Louise and Chantelle. The notices went out from the Court Section of the Social Services Department under Mr. Thompson's signature. Mrs. Dietmann took it upon herself to serve the notices on Beverley Lorrington at Holloway Prison. She was not allowed to see Beverley Lorrington alone, and was under some pressure from the psychiatric social worker at Holloway prison not to go ahead with denying a mother's access to her child. The Director commented to us that this was a typical example of the kind of pressures that social workers in the child care field have to operate under. When we suggested to the Director that it might be preferable for legal notices to be served by process servers and not by social workers, the Director countered with the strong view that social workers had to cope with difficult situations such as that which presented itself to Mrs. Dietmann. We think that our initial reaction was wrong, and that the Director was right. We were struck by a sentence in her evidence, which we have been echoing throughout this report. She said: "I don't think social workers can duck difficult situations that contain *authority* [emphasis supplied] problems." If the Director had ever been consulted about the Beckford case before 5 July 1984, we are confident that she would have said to Ms. Wahlstrom: "When you visit the Beckford household do not forget the authority you have as the parent of Jasmine; however much your work is with the Beckford parents, you must not duck the difficult situation of telling them that you are Jasmine's parent, and that your primary duty is to protect her."

On the same day that Mr. Thompson drew up the notices of termination of access, the Director wrote personally to the solicitors acting for Beverley Lorrington to explain her Department's reasons for applying for a Care Order in respect of Chantelle and stopping any access to both children. She continued to conduct the correspondence from the local authority's side, because she felt that it was important that on so sensitive an issue she should personally deal with the mother's solicitors. Had the Director not, quite understandably, taken upon herself that work, the Law and Administration Department would almost certainly have been brought into play, and Mr. Thompson's lapse would have been cured earlier.

On 29 August 1984 an interim Care Order was made in respect of Chantelle Beckford, and solicitors had indicated that Beverley Lorrington would be opposing both the full Care Order and the termination of access, to be heard on the same occasion. By that time Miss Alix Causby had been appointed as the *guardian ad litem*: her appointment had been made on 13 July 1984. A copy of her report, plus addendum, dated 18 September 1984 (Appendix F) was sent to Brent Social Services and became the subject of much discussion at the subsequent meeting of the Cases Sub-Committee. We note only two important factors for those at Brent Borough Council who were considering what action should be taken in terms of a child abuse inquiry. Jasmine's injuries represented "prolonged, protracted torture" of the child, indicating the consequence of a failure to see Jasmine over the last months of her life. Miss Causby noted that "in March 1984 the social worker began to have difficulties seeing the family." She noted also that "according to the health visitor, Jasmine and Louise were always small, thin children, below normal in weight." Ms. Wahlstrom put her report in to the juvenile court. On 26 September 1984 the hearing for a Care Order was adjourned for 28 days, the interim order being continued. On 2 October 1984 the Case Conference was reconvened, at which only the three social workers at Area 6 attended, together with the health visitor, Miss Vivekanandan and her supervisor, Mrs. Brown. Nothing relevant to the inquiry on Jasmine's death was discussed; the next meeting was fixed for 19 December 1984. On 24 October there was a further adjournment of the court proceedings to 21 November 1984. On 1 December 1984 Dr. Hugh Jolly made written reports on the two children at the request of solicitors acting for Miss Causby, the *guardian ad litem* (Appendix F). We draw attention to one observation of Dr. Jolly in his report on Louise: "Her foster mother told me that she [Louise] behaves well towards Chantelle so long as Chantelle is not crying. If she is crying she will hit her, put her fingers in her eyes and tell her foster mother to hit and to kick her": Such is the cycle of parental deprivation and child abuse. To round off the chronology of the court proceedings, the case was heard on 13 and 18 December 1984. A Care Order was made in respect of Chantelle.

Subsequently, in March 1985 orders were made terminating access and freeing Louise and Chantelle for adoption.

Actions, inactions and meetings of Brent Councillors, 5 July-29 October 1984
The Director of Social Services personally informed Councillor Stone, the Chairman of the Social Services Committee, of the death of Jasmine. She did so on or after 6 July 1984. But she overlooked informing the Shadow Chairman, Councillor Sealy. Ever since November/December 1983, when the political complexion of Brent Borough Council became so evenly balanced, it had been an unwritten rule that officers, when communicating any matter of importance or significance to the chairmen of their respective committees, likewise must inform the shadow chairmen. Before us, Miss Howarth acknowledged her error in failing to tell Councillor Sealy of Jasmine's death. It was an unfortunate slip, because Councillor Sealy would, in our view, have taken instant action to arrange for an urgent convening of an appropriate committee of the Council – either the Social Services Committee or the Cases Sub-Committee of the Social Services Committee. Councillor Sealy impressed us, along with Councillor Crane, in his

189

alacrity to acknowledge the prime and ultimate responsibility of the elected representatives of the Borough for anything that might have gone wrong in the child protection
service of the local authority. Councillor Sealy's persistence in pressing the demand for
an inquiry may have blunted his judgment about the facts of the case. It was wholly
admirable in its sense of political responsibility and answerability, although we are critical
of other aspects of his activity as a Councillor.

We think, however, that the Director is not to be blamed for the Council's failure,
through one or other of its committees, to meet urgently — at least before the end of
July — to consider the case of a child's death while in care of the local authority. The
chairman of the Social Services Committee who took no steps to call an urgent meeting
or to activate the chairmanship of the Cases Sub-Committee, Councillor Rees-Hughes,
with whom he had spoken on the telephone sometime in early July and had mentioned
Jasmine's death. That news evoked no response. Since the Cases Sub-Committee is a
small committee of some four members and it is, therefore, easy to call them to an urgent
meeting, it would have been sensible for Councillor Stone to tell Councillor Rees-Hughes
to call her members to such a meeting. We think that Councillor Stone is to be faulted
for not having taken some urgent action. We think that Councillor Rees-Hughes cannot
altogether escape criticism. She should have acted on her own initiative.

Miss Howarth's expectation that her report to the Chief Executive would be relayed
to the Leaders of the two main political groups was fulfilled. Councillor Coleman, Leader
of the Labour Group, and a close political associate of Councillor Sealy's, was told on
10 July. Councillor Lacey, the Conservative Group Leader, was told on 12 July. Both
Councillors were told in the course of one of the regular weekly briefings that the Chief
Executive has with the leading politicians on the Council. Councillor Coleman suggested
to us that he expected that he would receive such information in writing. In this respect,
Councillor Cribbin supported him. Mr. Bichard did not think it was necessary to communicate such information in writing. We entirely agree; a verbal communication sufficed to prompt any reasonable politician to seek more information and to consider
seriously convening an urgent meeting of the appropriate committee.

There was some suggestion that politicians were, by implication, dissuaded from taking appropriate political action by the manner in which Mr. Bichard communicated the
information. It was said that he reassured the Councillors to whom he spoke at that
time, and later, by saying that there was no cause for concern because the Social Services Department had handled the case in "an exemplary fashion." Mr. Bichard refuted
any such suggestion. He told us that he was not in the habit of using language that was
anything but cautious and temperate. His recollection was that he understood from the
Director, then in the very early days of investigating the nature and quality of the social
work with the Beckfords, that the facts were not such as to raise undue concern. Mr.
Bichard was not told, and did not pass on anything to the effect that there was no cause
for concern. We accept Mr. Bichard's evidence unhesitatingly. On what was known in
mid-July, and increasingly in the weeks ahead, no senior local government administrator
could conceivably have said anything other than that the fact of Jasmine's death, coupled
with the most tentative comment about the infrequency of visits in the last months of
Jasmine's life, was a matter for investigation. Had Mr. Bichard seen the synopsis of
events prepared on 9 July for the 10 July meeting, he would certainly have not allayed
any fears about the local authority's responsibility. It is a pity that the excellent summary produced by the Social Services Department was not seen by the Chief Executive.
Much of what followed in the acts of maladministration, leading up to a child abuse
inquiry, by the members of the Council would have been avoided.

In the event, neither Councillor Stone nor Councillor Coleman took any action; nor
did either of them prompt their respective political colleagues on relevant committees

to react to the fact that a child in care for 3 years had been killed by her step-father. Belatedly, the Cases Sub-Committee met on 29 October 1984, and again on 26 November 1984, in circumstances which we shall describe in detail. We anticipate our conclusion from our review of those two meetings and of subsequent action by the Council, by saying that the failure of the Council (or any committee of the Council) to meet and consider the case of Jasmine Beckford for nearly four months – even making due allowance for the holiday season and some minor disruptive industrial action by local government staff – was a grave dereliction of its duties owed to the citizens of Brent. Inaction is often worse than faulty action. **We recommend that whenever a child in care of a local authority dies, or is seriously harmed, that local authority's relevant Committee must meet to consider the case forthwith.**

Meeting of Cases Sub-Committee 29 October 1984

Mr. Simpson, who was the officer servicing the Cases Sub-Committee (although the Director attended its meetings from time to time) prepared the report for the Sub-Committee's meeting on 29 October 1984. Mr. Simpson had understood that the report had to be ready by 24 August 1984, on the assumption that the Sub-Committee would be meeting at the beginning, or in the middle of September. It is unclear as to what was the basis of that assumption. It matters not, since no one did convene a meeting for that date. The agenda for the meeting contained six items, the death of a child in care being the second item. The last item, ironically, was "any other urgent business." The first item dealt with at the meeting was the approval to an extension to the property of foster-parents to enlarge their premises to accommodate more foster-children. The report from the Department was contained in a page and a bit.

The report on the death of Jasmine Beckford was no greater in length. At the outset of the meeting, the Cases Sub-Committee – consisting of Councillors Rees-Hughes (in the chair), Crane, Cribbin and Haftel – seemed to show no greater interest or concern over the death of Jasmine than in respect of the other items on the agenda. But it could have been anticipated that, once the Sub-Committee got a snifter of the heady topic of a child dying while Social Services operated a Care Order, Councillors would want to imbibe a good deal more information than was contained in eight relatively short paragraphs. It was not as if the Social Services Department was in any difficulty about preparing a detailed report. Ever since 9 July, it had an admirably-compiled document which could either have been supplied *in toto* to the Sub-Committee, or at least tailored to the needs of Councillors who might not wish to wade through chronicled events of no great importance. But the highlights of that report, with one or two pointers about the effectiveness (or otherwise) of visits and the optimistic note sounded by the social workers in the late stages of the case, could have been included. Yet the Councillors were treated, almost cavalierly. It is little wonder that the meeting was stormy, and concluded with a demand that the Director of Social Services should present a fuller report on the case at a special meeting to be held on 29 November 1984. At last, by then, there was a sense among Council members of the grave importance in reviewing the case of the death of a child in care.

On the most charitable view of what Social Services had provided to the Cases Sub-Committee, the report was insufficiently informative. Mr. Simpson's lame explanation to us was that the report which was produced and finally despatched to the Sub-Committee was "comparable to other reports that had been sent to the Committee." Mr. Simpson conceded that, with hindsight, "perhaps a more complete report ought to have been provided"; and later, in answer to Miss Baxendale's question that by comparison with the document of 9 July the report for the meeting of 29 October was "woefully inadequate", Mr. Simpson said, "absolutely, yes, absolutely." We acquit Mr. Simpson of anything worse than ineptitude in his approach to what Councillors were entitled to expect from the Department. The paucity of information that Mr. Simpson supplied was exacerbated by an exchange between himself and Councillor Haftel. The latter declared that a general review of the case was needed, to which Mr. Simpson replied that the Beckford case was an isolated incident: "If there had been more, I'd share your concern." What Mr. Simpson was referring to was that the Jasmine Beckford case was the first of its kind in Brent, and that a review generally of child abuse cases did not seem to be indicated. Councillor Haftel thought that that was an indication on Mr. Simpson's part of resistance to an inquiry about the social work provided to the Beckford family. The consequence of Mr. Simpson's maladroitness was that it, not unreasonably, fed the suspicion thereafter, at least among the more vocal and articulate Councillors, that the Department was indulging in a cover-up. We have found that there is not a scintilla of evidence to support that unverified assertion by Councillors. But there is no doubt that the 29 October meeting generated a tension, if not hostility between some Councillors and both the Director and her staff involved in the Beckford case. If only the Council had met in mid- to late July and been supplied with the 9 July document, the unfolding of events leading to our Inquiry would have been conducted in a calm and rational atmosphere. As it was, the events that followed the meeting of 29 October, in particular the meeting of 26 November, were fraught and fractious; those are not our words, but Mr. Simpson's, endorsed by Councillor Crane.

The meeting of 29 October asked for details of changes made in child abuse procedure; of the sequence of events between Social Services and the Beckford family (which is what the document of 9 July did so comprehensively); of the type and intensity of social work intervention; and an explanation why the Willesden Magistrates had refused to revoke the Care Orders in June 1983. There was also a desire that the Director of Law and Administration should produce a copy of the "*guardian ad litem*" report on the case. This arose from a request from Councillor Crane who asked for the *guardian ad litem*'s report "prepared for [the Magistrates'] Court by independent social worker". That could have referred to Miss Joan Court's report of 8 September 1981, she being the independent social worker but not the *guardian ad litem*, that system not becoming operative until 27 May 1984. On the other hand, it could have referred to Miss Alix Causby's report to Court on 18 September 1984 in the care proceedings in respect of Chantelle Beckford. Miss Causby was the *guardian ad litem*, but not an "independent social worker".

Had the Cases Sub-Committee sat in July, the confusion could not have arisen. And even on 29 October, a fuller report would have clarified the two separate proceedings, involving the separate reports of Miss Court and Miss Causby. When Councillor Crane asked for the report (whichever one it was that he had in mind) Mr. Damms said that he would ask "if it can be made available." Had the Department of Law and Administration been officially informed, way back in July when the Director of Social Services instructed Mr. Thompson to contact Mr. Damms officially, another dose of suspicious conduct would not have been injected into the minds of certain Councillors looking for evidence that the Director was stalling on the question of an inquiry.

Interim between Cases Sub-Committee meetings, October-November 1984
On 5 November 1984 the Brent Area Review Committee on Child Abuse met at Brent Town Hall with the Director of Social Services in the chair. The Area Review Committee had last met on 2 July 1984, so that this was the first occasion the Committee had of responding to the death of Jasmine. Up until then, the Committee had been unaware of the application of the Care Orders of 9 September 1981; it had, therefore, never reviewed, let alone monitored the work of Social Services and Health Services with the Beckford

family. We comment on this aspect of the administration of the child abuse system, both generally and specifically in relation to Jasmine and Louise Beckford, in Chapter 24.

The Area Review Committee felt that it was inappropriate that it should discuss the case due to pending court proceedings. We have indicated that this reflects a misunderstanding of the *sub judice* rule and of the role of an Area Review Committee. The Committee went on to record that an inquiry would be held, and the chairman (the Director) answered that "a Social Services internal investigation was under way." This again negatives any question that the Director was opposing an inquiry in addition to the internal investigation.

On the following day, Mr. Simpson wrote a memorandum to Mr. Bishop confirming his oral conversation to the effect that the Cases Sub-Committee was calling for a further report to its specially arranged meeting on 26 November 1984. The memorandum also referred to a meeting of the Director and her staff, together with Councillor Rees-Hughes. Mr. Simpson added that before the Cases Sub-Committee met, the Director wanted to discuss "what form of 'full inquiry' might take place after the case has been heard in court. Members will ask questions about this." The meetings with the Director took place on 12 and 19 November 1984. The shape of the report for the Cases Sub-Committee was discussed. The Director was herself unhappy at the meagre contents of the report to the Cases Sub-Committee on 29 October 1984 and took charge personally of the preparations for the forthcoming special meeting, with a view to supplying all the material requested, which she regarded as an entirely reasonable request. She interpreted the request for the "*guardian ad litem*'s" report as being a reference to Miss Causby's report of 18 September 1984. Its unavailability hitherto was adequately explained by reference to the novelty of the *guardian ad litem* system post-May 1984. Councillor Rees-Hughes attended the meeting of 12 November, from whom the Director learned precisely what her Sub-Committee was seeking by way of a report.

No complaint whatsoever could be made about the report that was finally compiled for the Cases Sub-Committee. It contained a section on the record of Social Services Department's contacts with the Beckford family, which was a sensibly edited version of the document of 9 July, and it had a short section on the Department's plans in respect of Louise and Chantelle Beckford. Five appendices were attached: A copy of Miss Causby's report; a note on Case Conferences generally; the DHSS circular of August 1980 on Child Abuse: Central Register Systems; the Department's Child Abuse Policy and Procedures; and a note indicating proposed changes to improve the child abuse procedures in the light of the Beckford case.

Cases Sub-Committee meeting of 26 November 1984
Given the adequacy of the material put before the Cases Sub-Committee, the discussion and outcome of that meeting should have been helpful and fruitful. Had there not been a background of mutual misunderstanding and mistrust on the part of some Councillors, all would have been well. But the meeting quickly produced irrational statements, confusion as to what had to be discussed, and understandable frustration from the one member of the Sub-Committee, Councillor Crane, who tried desperately to get his colleagues to address themselves to the details of the report. He told us that he had great sympathy for the Director who was never given the chance to deal with members' queries.

The Sub-Committee was composed of Councillor Rees-Hughes (in the chair) and Councillors Crane, Haftel and Sealy, the last named having arranged to attend in place of Councillor Cribbin. Any Councillor is entitled to attend any committee of the Council, but he can vote only if he is a member of that Committee, or if he is standing in for a member of that Committee. Councillor Sealy had heard about the Beckford case only after the 29 October meeting. He had immediately taken the bit between his teeth and was pursuing a course of action that was prejudging the work of the Social Services Department, in particular that of the social workers directly involved.

Councillor Sealy had put down a motion calling for an internal inquiry "external to the Directorate of Social Services, and that the Chair of the Inquiry Panel be taken by a representative (officer) of the Directorate of Law and Administration." The Panel's terms of reference would have included the determination "whether any immediate steps should be taken arising from the internal inquiry and to advise what disciplinary action and/or disciplinary process should be taken and/or followed, if necessary, and recommend accordingly." Councillor Sealy had not shown, let alone discussed the motion with the Director before the meeting. Miss Howarth told us that she was perturbed particularly at the inclusion of disciplinary matters in the terms of reference of the Panel. We think she was entitled to be upset. We think that Councillor Sealy was at best thoughtless about its effect on staff; at worst he was pursuing a vendetta against social work staff without giving adequate consideration to what, on any showing, was a case of great complexity. After a preliminary discussion about the ineffectiveness of the social worker's visits to the Beckford home and related matters, Councillor Sealy pressed home his argument on the motion. The Director intervened, saying that she was not opposing any inquiry but that it could not be held until the criminal proceedings were concluded. She was quick to point out that there was a real danger that her staff would not cooperate in an inquiry, if disciplinary action was being held over their heads. Councillor Sealy intemperately said that he did not agree. If the officers did not want to cooperate, that was their affair. For his part he was not prepared to sit around till February or March before "we start looking at the case." At this point Councillor Haftel seconded the motion. Councillor Crane intervened to explore other options. Councillor Haftel proposed deleting references to "disciplinary process", which Councillor Sealy accepted. Other amendments were proposed to the terms of the motion; again Councillor Sealy accepted. The members then canvassed the names of persons to serve on the Panel. Councillors Rees-Hughes and Crane expressed their dis-ease at the apparent suggestion from Mr. Simpson that the proper forum for such a motion would be an early, special meeting of the Social Services Committee. On the motion, the vote was tied, with Councillor Rees-Hughes giving the chairman's casting vote against the motion.

Councillor Sealy then said that unless his motion was passed he would raise the matter, either in Council or before the Policy and Resources Committee, which meant that it would be heard in public. There was a heated exchange between him and Councillor Crane. Irrationality triumphed over an attempt to impose rational argument. The Director thought that the least dangerous outcome was to concede an immediate inquiry along the lines of the motion, and advised Councillor Rees-Hughes to alter her casting vote: Which she did. We deplore the bullying and hectoring style adopted by Councillor Sealy. In the gush of irrational argument he had, however, a fair point – namely, that some inquiry should be set in train before the criminal proceedings were concluded, with the thought that a full, independent inquiry might be necessary, to take place after the trial. Had Councillor Sealy been a little less hot-headed and listened to what others – both his colleague, Councillor Crane, and the Director – were trying to explain, there might have been a happier conclusion to an unruly meeting.

The Cases Sub-Committee could only recommend action to its parent body, the Social Services Committee, although there seemed to be a view that the Sub-Committee could, and was purporting to, pass a resolution setting up the Panel of Inquiry. The Panel was set up by the Director of Law and Administration and began its task. We see no need to discuss what happened, save to say that staff were expressing unhappiness, through their trade union representatives, at the prospect of appearing before the Panel. Their objection was not to an inquiry, only as to its form. At the Social Services Committee meeting on 8 January 1985 the recommendation of its Cases Sub-Committee was not accepted. The Committee decided that the internal inquiry into the death of Jasmine Beckford should not proceed any further. It ordered instead that an inquiry under the auspices of the Area Review Committee should be set up as soon as practically possible. It also confirmed that the review of child abuse procedures should meanwhile be reported to the Social Services Committee. (The modifications to the child abuse procedures were considered at a Cases Sub-Committee meeting on 16 January 1985). Councillor Crane's voice of moderation, advising this course of action, was not this time stifled by Councillor Sealy, who was away on holiday. On his return, however, he was not to be outdone. He objected to the idea that the inquiry be held under the auspices of The Area Review Committee, on the grounds that the Director of Social Services was its chairman and other staff members from Brent served on it, and this would produce a conflict of duties. We think that Councillor Sealy's point was a bad one (although the Director told us that she appreciated Councillor Sealy's feeling and gracefully did not oppose his view). The Area Review Committee is a large body with members from disparate agencies and professions. The Director herself would have taken no part in any of the decisions to set up the panel of inquiry and would have participated only to give evidence to it. (We set out our views about the role of Area Review Committees in Chapter 24.) We think that it is entirely appropriate that that body should be involved at every stage of the administration of child abuse inquiries, as supervisor of internal inquiries and, where necessary the promoter of independent inquiries. Councillor Sealy won his point. At a meeting of the Policy and Resources Committee on 12 February 1985 the advice of the Chief Executive that there should be an inquiry undertaken by an independent panel, the membership of which broadly reflects our composition, was adopted. The only modification to Mr. Bichard's helpful compromise solution was that the Council's Principal Race Relations Adviser was made only an adviser and not a member. In Chapter 3 we have explained why we think that individuals should either be members or not be participating with the panel. If it is thought that a Panel of Inquiry requires an expert on race relations, he should be a member and be drawn from outside the sponsoring local authority. This point was expressly taken up by members of the Area Review Committee when it met on 15 February 1985 to receive a report from its chairman, the Director of Social Services, on the latest developments for setting up our Inquiry. The Director explained that it would be useful to have someone from within Brent, not connected with the case, who could explain local circumstances. Our experience fully bears out the Director's point, but we nevertheless agree with the members of the Area Review Committee who expressed a "strong feeling that the inquiry should be seen to be totally independent." The police members on the Area Review Committee reiterated their view that they would be precluded from participating in the inquiry until after the trial was concluded, "including any appeal." We think that the extension of non-participation by the police beyond the trial (assuming conviction and no second trial) is quite unnecessary. The appellate process ordinarily involves no hearing of witnesses, and appellate judges are immune from the influences of public discussion and argument. Once the trial is over, there can be no proper objection to full participation by everyone whom the inquiry wishes to hear.

Conclusion

We attach no blame to the Director of Social Services for the manner in which she handled the case from 6 July 1984 (when she was told of Jasmine Beckford's death) onwards. We have alluded to her failure to alert the Chief Executive and the Chairman of the Social Services Committee to the implications of the 10 July meeting. We think it necessary, in view of our comments on this episode, to place on record our opinion that Miss Howarth is a high quality Director of Social Services.

The way in which the Cases Sub-Committee was treated on 29 October, in the shape of a meagre report, was less than satisfactory. For that Mr. Simpson must accept the blame; in the absence of the Director he had been deputed to prepare and present the Department's report. But we do not place much emphasis on his failure. He presented a report, that in length and content was comparable to all other items before the Cases Sub-Committee. The fact that the Committee had delayed meeting, unforgivably, for four months must have induced in Mr. Simpson the feeling that the Committee was not too perturbed about a child dying in the Council's care, and would not thank him for having to wade through a long report. Why Mr. Simpson did not simply provide the report of 9 July remains puzzling. The fact that he did not reach for the method of least work to himself and his colleagues only goes to show that he was not concealing anything, but was responding in the manner he thought was required by, and best suited to the needs of the Sub-Committee. He misjudged the mood of some members, and then mismanaged the Committee. His blame, therefore, is not trifling, but it is not very serious.

The failure of Mr. Thompson to carry out the Director's instruction to contact the Law and Administration Department formally was blameworthy. If he had done what he was ordered to do, some, if not all, of the irritation and confusion of later events might have been avoided. We have in mind the issue over the *guardian ad litem*'s report and even the disclosure of the document of 9 July. Lawyers have at least one virtue. They are good at sticking to the well-tried procedures and in organising material in a palatable and manageable form. They do not easily get caught out in sloppy administration. Mr. Thompson may properly mitigate his failure by observing that he was quite capable of advising the Social Services Department about legal matters. His expertise in child care, plus his experience as Court Officer, do go some way to substantiating his defence. The fact that we think that the Department should have at its elbow a solicitor from the Law and Administration does not affect Mr. Thompson's position. The Department had chosen the post of Court Officer, and he filled that post. At the end of the day we criticise him solely for not having done what the Director clearly instructed him to do.

For the inordinate dilatoriness in reacting to the death of Jasmine Beckford, and for the confused deliberations of the Cases Sub-Committee, we blame the Council exclusively. The Director and Mr. Simpson (subject to the one minor criticism relating to him) did their best to work with, and not against the elected members. They were loyally and properly supported by Councillor Crane, but he was overborne by Councillor Sealy in his uncontrolled enthusiasm to show Social Services in a bad light, aided and abetted by Councillor Haftel. We would hope that Brent Borough Council will learn from this experience that, hung Council or no, there is no room for scoring political points where the subject matter is, not money or property, but the death of a child placed in trust to a local authority.

CHAPTER 20

A. Training – Social Workers

It is not our function to review the education and training for the profession of social work in the United Kingdom, even if we were competent to carry it out – which we are not. It is our function, however, to discuss any defects or shortcomings in the education and training of social workers which have been pinpointed by what has been revealed in the course of our Inquiry into the death of a child who had been the subject of a Care Order for nearly three years and was in trust to the local authority Social Services Department, supported by auxiliary agencies; and to make recommendations. To that end we sought expert guidance of both a general and specific nature, always remembering to hammer the nail of expert testimony on the anvil of administration of the child abuse system.

The issues that spring to mind from any child abuse inquiry are to be found in the context of arrangements for existing training, with their origins based on the advice of the Seebohm Committee on Local Authority and Allied Personal Social Services (1968) (Seebohm)*. One is led on to analyse the current proposals of the Central Council for the Education and Training of Social Workers (CCETSW) for qualifying training in relation to contemporary child abuse inquiries, and not just to our inquiry. From the outset of this aspect of our deliberations we became acutely aware that social work training needs to be extended, specifically to provide for "specialist" areas of work. Our conclusion is that political commitment and support to this development, and generally, to educating and training social workers must carry a high priority in public spending. Before we develop this theme, we think it necessary to describe how we think that the profession of social work has arrived at the stage at which specialist skills have taken a back seat in the country's vehicle for effecting social policy and practice.

The profession of social work
In one sense it is only since Seebohm that there has been a beginning of a profession of social work. Before that there were specific social work services with related training courses. These were developed in the universities and by tertiary educational establishments. Each course focused on the specific future job, be it as a Child Care Officer, or other specialist service. Later, universities developed broader generic case work courses, which prepared students who would be taking up posts in a range of field work jobs. Students nevertheless opted for "specialist" classes within these courses, according to their intended career in one or other of the welfare services, e.g., as a child care officer. The Local Authority Social Services Act 1970 enacted the recommendations of Seebohm. Local Authority Welfare and Children's Services, together with some of the former local authority health services, were unified within each local authority into a single personal social service. The establishment of CCETSW with statutory functions "to promote education and training in social work for the Personal Social Services", provided the potential for a new unified social work profession to service the unified social services. It is unnecessary to describe in detail the remit of CCETSW. Suffice it to say, that between 1971 and 1974 CCETSW took over the work of six previous training Councils, covering all the work for which social work training had to provide, all the client-groups, all the settings – field, residential, day and community provisions – together with all the range of methods and skills each such work demanded.

---

* Cmnd. 3703

The Seebohm report

Much of contemporary social work originates from the guidance provided by Seebohm. It is useful, therefore, to be reminded of what Seebohm actually said. We can do no better than cite the relevant paragraphs.

A Unified Social Services Department

Para 139: "We believe the best way of achieving these ends is by setting up a unified Social Services Department which will include the present children's and welfare services together with some of the social services functions of health, education and housing departments."

Para 140: "Such a unified department will provide better services for those in need because it will ensure a more coordinated and comprehensive approach to the problems of individuals and families and the communities in which they live.

Para 161: "One of the arguments advanced against the integration of the personal social services is that progress has come through specialisation, which has enabled Children's Departments, e.g., to concentrate on caring for deprived children without the distractions of caring for other people in need....."

Paras 162 and 163 go on to refute this argument, and to maintain the Committee's belief in the desirability of a unified social services department.

During the time that Children's Departments were in existence and Children's Officers were not distracted from caring for deprived children by other tasks, there was, remarkably, only one major inquiry into the abuse of a child for whom a local authority had some responsibility. (That was in respect of a child in care of Dorset County Council in 1966). The Dennis O'Neill case of 1945 had been one of the factors leading up to the establishment of local authority Children's Departments under the Children Act 1948, which were then absorbed into the Social Services Departments in 1971. The first child abuse inquiry under the new Departments was Maria Colwell in 1973, since when there have been more than twenty such inquiries.

Although the misgivings expressed in paragraph 161 of the Seebohm Report may seem, sadly, to have been well-justified, it is often said that the development of the "generic" social worker has been founded on a misunderstanding or misinterpretation of what Seebohm really meant. The apologists of Seebohm have argued that what was being proposed was a unified Social Services Department, but that within the Department there would be retained the specialist social workers. At this juncture it is wise to go back to the Seebohm report. We, therefore, cite the relevant parts of the two chapters – Chapters XVII and XVIII – on "specialisation in social work" and "training" respectively.

Para 509(c): "...students could enter a common training in social work courses and the present pattern of specialisation in employment could be radically altered. We favour this last possibility."

Para 516: "there will be strict statutory requirements which the social services department must meet. Nevertheless subject to certain important provisos discussed later we consider that a family or individual in need of social

198

care should, as far as possible, be served by a single social worker ... with a comprehensive approach to the social problems of his clients....the basic aim of a social services department is to meet all the social needs of the family or individual together and as a whole.

Para. 520: "the new approach to specialisation which we suggest accords with the view that the common elements in the practice of social workers in different settings are much more important than the elements which distinguish them."

Para 521: The Field of Responsibility of Social Workers
"The range of work of the newly qualified social worker would normally be limited ... he would be expected soon to undertake a wider range of functions and to develop skill in them. He might develop interests in particular aspects of the work and it would be right for him to be enabled to pursue such concentration of interest, always provided that this did not conflict with the primary object of giving people the help they required at the right time."

Para 522: "Most workers in the present separate departments could undertake a substantially wider range of work than at present given the opportunity of suitable in-service training. .... We think it would prove a help to the social worker himself to have a range of cases, involving a variety of interests and opportunity for wider professional development."

Para 523: Service for institutions of various kinds
"Social workers should be attached on a fairly long-term basis to institutions such as schools, health centres, courts and hospitals, although they should continue to be based in the social service department."

Para 524: Specialisations in particular kinds of social work or in particular areas of knowledge.
"Specialisation will be necessary above the basic field level – not least to help in the advancement of knowledge ... Although we recognise that in the transitional period existing expertise should be used, we expect that as the service develops specialisations will cluster differently and new types of specialisation emerge to meet new problems and needs and fresh conceptions of how these might be tackled."

Para 525: "We do not wish the present kinds of specialisation to be accepted as necessary models for the future at any level in the social service department. The existing divisions are bound to influence the way the department works when it is first set up, but it will only work well if a serious effort is made to break down the divisions from the beginning."

Para 527: "There will undoubtedly be difficulties in the transition period over welding numbers of specialist workers into members of a comprehensive single service. *However the kind of social worker we expect to emerge will be one who has had a generic training aimed at giving him competence, after experience, to cope with a whole range of social need, provided he has the support of adequate consultation and other resources"* (emphasis supplied).

Chapter XVIII: Training
Para 558: "We consider there is room for experiment with a wider concept of generic training which aims to equip students to work as appropriate with individuals, groups and communities. The justification for this approach is the belief that the divisions between the different methods of social work are as artificial as differences between various forms of casework and that in his daily work, the social worker needs all these methods to enable him to respond appropriately to social problems which involve individual, family, group and community aspects.

Para 559: "Those who question this wider concept of generic training are, with some justification, afraid that in the *limited time available* (emphasis supplied), it may give the student only a superficial acquaintance with a range of social work methods..."

Para 560: "...We assume therefore that students should have the opportunity, by means of optional courses, of taking their studies and/or professional practice to greater depth in certain areas of knowledge and in one social work method and we also recognise the need to provide opportunities for students to develop skills to a higher level in subsequent training."

In its chapter on "Conclusions" the Seebohm Committee said:-

Para 134: "The present pattern of specialisation in employment should be radically altered."

Para 135: "As a general rule and as far as possible a family or individual in need of social care should be served by a single social worker."

Para 138: "Most workers in the present separate departments could undertake a substantially wider range of work than at present, given the opportunity of suitable in-service training."

Para 140: "Specialisation will be necessary above the basic field level. During the transitional period it will be based on existing expertise. As the service develops, specialisation will cluster differently and new types of specialisation emerge."

Our conclusion from all this is that the Seebohm Report *was* advocating that social workers at "basic field level" should undertake a wide range of work, and should accordingly be trained to do just that. Specialisation was seen as desirable, but desirable at a more senior level. Further training was envisaged for those specialist social workers. We agree with the implication in the report that the existing social work courses were, and are, too short. But we believe that, if their length cannot be increased, there should be some specialisation at the qualifying stage (as is now the case with the CSS training) and that wider training should be offered in the form of post-qualification modules.

Current Education and Training for the Personal Social Services

CCETSW promotes two forms of qualifying training leading to two qualifying awards, the Certificate of Qualification in Social Work (CQSW), and the Certificate in Social Service (CSS).

The CQSW is a "generic qualification", in that it qualifies the holder for any job for which a social work qualification is required, i.e., the certificate does not specify the content of the training programme completed, or the areas of the student's practice during the training period. It is thus considered as a qualification for all jobs, whether in a fieldwork, residential or day-care setting, for which a social worker is required. It in fact qualifies for all social work except, since the Mental Health Act 1983, the particular functions of "the approved social worker," in the speciality of mental health.

The CSS is a job-related education and training, and a CSS certificate is endorsed with the details of the training. For a variety of reasons it has come to be regarded as the main qualification for posts in the residential day care and domiciliary sectors. There are 140 CQSW courses and 29 CSS schemes covering the U.K.; approximately 90% of field work staff are qualified, but under 20% of those working in residential and day care settings.

CQSW Courses

CQSW courses are based in higher education, in Universities, Polytechnics and Colleges of Higher Education. They are of varying academic level, from postgraduate (some at Masters'degree level) through undergraduate (Bachelor degree level) to non-graduate diploma level. Their origins are various; some are based on the previous 'specialist' courses promoted by, for example, the Central Training Council in Child Care; others have developed from the University 'generic' casework courses; many others are more recent and are the product of the great expansion of the seventies.

The effective length of all CQSW courses is only two years. Students with 'relevant' social science degrees and a year's social work experience are eligible to take one year postgraduate courses; there are three-year 'extended' courses for students with 'family commitments' and one part-time course of that length; there are four year undergraduate programmes, but these combine social science first degree work, and the professional social work part of the course thus extends only over two years.

Two years is, we think, a very short period for professional education and training, especially in comparison with all the other professions – e.g., teachers, doctors, lawyers, and nurses. When one examines the range and depth of responsibilities of social workers it is astonishing that training for the profession is so limited in time, and hence in content. It is necessary only to summarise these responsibilities here. There is a continuing increase in the range and numbers of vulnerable people 'at risk' in the community, and social workers have statutory responsibilities in relation to all these vulnerable groups, children, mentally ill and handicapped, the aged, etc. Furthermore, social work is currently practised in a wide variety of settings; it involves work with client groups of different sizes, ranging from individuals to whole communities and requires inter-personal, inter-group and inter-professional understanding, skills in administration, management, planning and research and some aspects of habilitation, training and remedial activities.

The tragedies of child abuse have raised an additional, highly pertinent factor in the role of social workers. That is social work's dual mandate. We can do no better than cite the two paragraphs in CCETSW's Paper 10, Education and Training for Social Work, of November 1975 at page 18, paragraphs 3.6 and 3.7 which describe the two kinds of mandate for practice in social work:

"Social work practice has two kinds of mandate. The first is derived from society and its values and concerns which may in part be embodied in social policy and legislation. The second comes from the client or users of the social worker's services towards whom the social worker feels a contractual obligation for specific acts of intervention. In other words, social workers can only intervene with the authority conferred by society on their agency or with the agreement of clients. For the most part, the social worker does not determine the problems he must deal with; he is more often a 'reactor' than an 'initiator', and for this he is sometimes criticised."

"The social worker can legitimately intervene .... only in those areas where he is sanctioned to do so, but it is also part of the role of the social work profession to seek to extend this mandate where there are problems which could be reduced or overcome by social work intervention and where it can contribute to the continuously evolving process of formulating social policy."

Social workers are thus employed to provide help, assistance support and sympathy for their clients, and to promote and to make possible change in even the most unyielding of people. Therein lies the inevitable commitment to work that raises the expectation of change for the good to which we allude in our next chapter (Chapter 21). But social workers are also required by society to carry out certain duties and exercise powers, and these duties and powers are laid down in Acts of Parliament. These may require the social workers to implement decisions that go against the wishes of the client, and to exercise control if, in their professional judgment, the life and well-being of the client – who may often be a child – is at risk. The dual mandate thus imposes responsibility for both social care and social control.

It is hard to see how effective education and training for such formidable and demanding tasks can be achieved in two years. There is evidence that social work qualifying courses have been struggling with this complexity for a number of years. CCETSW's advice to course teachers, as laid out in CCETSW, Paper 10, is:-

(a) to provide a comprehensive framework within which the many tasks, functions and activities of practice may be ordered;

(b) to state the skills to be acquired, thus providing the rationale for the selection of teaching content for the course.

The dilemmas about what can be achieved within the two-year time-scale, however, remain; about the most appropriate framework, let alone the selection of content to be made within the framework. In social work there is a constellation of knowledge, values, skills, settings, methods, client groups; and debate continues about the proper ordering of these, about whether there is an inalienable 'core' element in all or some of these, which every social worker should cover. CCETSW has both encouraged courses to develop their own understanding of 'generic', and at the same time has sought to see that essential areas are covered. This approach has led, in our view, to too much being attempted in the time available, and the latter has suffered by concentration on the former.

In 1983 CCETSW revised its guidelines to courses. Its emphasis was placed, not so much on content, but on outcome, on the assessment of students at the end of the education and training period. In specifying the areas for assessment, CCETSW sought to reinforce some core areas, (e.g. social work statutory law) and to encourage specialist emphasis through introducing the notion of 'transfer' of knowledge and skills. CCETSW's new assessment guidelines thus require that students are able to demonstrate to the satisfaction of examiners a capacity to transfer learning and apply it in practice in respect of either a particular client-group or a particular context of practice. It was hoped that through 'transfer' the 'generic' nature of the CQSW qualification could be retained, while at the same time students could gain more specific competence in their practice.

CCETSW's report on the implementation of the new assessment guidelines indicates that the message of 'transfer' had not been sufficiently understood, and the new requirements had, if anything, increased the pressure on already very full college programmes. Nevertheless, this may be a way for potential development. It could enable courses to concentrate again on more specific areas, in relation both to knowledge and practice skills, and yet provide a basis for a professional education which must ever be capable of responding to new needs, and specialisms, new modes of service delivery.

CSS Schemes

In the early 1970s, with the growth of local authority Social Services Departments, and in order to provide further education and training opportunities for the many unqualified works in Social Services Departments, CCETSW promoted a new form of qualifying training, the Certificate in Social Service.

CSS is an in-service mode of education and training; it is modular; it comprises three units (Common, Standard and Special), and the college components are mainly based in colleges of further education. It is specific in terms of client-group; students choose for their standard option one client-group, e.g., children and adolescents, and in the following special unit there is opportunity for even greater specificity, related to the student's job. Students continue working while on training; their work provides the practice element of the course and there are requirements about the college components, required class contact and private study time, and requirements about adequate release from work. All students are allocated a study supervisor, and CCETSW appoints two external assessors (an academic and a practice assessor) to each of the 29 schemes. As with CQSW the minimum length is two years, but being modular, students are allowed a longer period up to five years in which to complete the qualification. Some schemes (about a third of them) extend for three years.

As originally envisaged, and endorsed in the Birch Report on Manpower for the Social Services (1976), CSS was to be the large number qualification for the Social Services, building up to intakes of 9,000 p.a., in relation to intakes of 3 to 4,000 CQSW. In the event, this development has not taken place, probably because CSS is quite a costly form of training and its development coincided with governmental cuts in public spending. Hence intakes are now around 1300, and instead of providing for a wide range of social service personnel, the CSS is mainly providing training for residential and day care workers.

There are anomalies in the existence of two training schemes, which both 'qualify' for residential work, but which in other respects allow almost complete movement to the CQSW holder, but none to the CSS holder. Such anomalies have been exacerbated by the failure to develop the CSS to the large number system for which it was envisaged and its concentration in the residential sector.

CCETSW's Review of Qualifying Training Policies

Since 1981 CCETSW has been reviewing its qualifying training policies (CQSW and CSS). We learned from the Director of CCETSW, who provided us with some helpful background material in her oral evidence and from CCETSW reports, that CCETSW

Council had decided that there would eventually be a unified system of qualifying awards in social work. At the time that the Director gave her evidence to us the Council had put forward six propositions as its preferred way of achieving such a unified system. These were outlined in its Paper 20.3, issued in January 1985, and the Council has just completed a process of consultation on these propositions. In the main there is support for ending the present divisive 'untenable' position. The employers have expressed it thus: The continued parallel qualification of CQSW and CSS no longer makes sense as service developments are merging the distinction between what were previously seen as separate modes of social work.

We understand that at this stage the CCETSW proposals for change have concentrated almost entirely on the structure, and further discussions and negotiations will be required on content and on the nature of the 'Single Award in Social Work.'

At CCETSW's special meeting at Harrogate on 20 September 1985 a resolution was passed that the minimum period of training prior to qualification in social work should normally be three years. We are very glad to note this development and urge that resources are soon found to implement the resolution.

Implications for the child abuse system

We apologise to our readers for having taken them, somewhat wearily, through the thickets of social work training. But we have not found it possible to frame our recommendations − particularly our main one − other than within the existing scheme of social work training which is unknown except to the *cognoscenti*. While most of what we have described is relevant to all aspects of social work, including the specialisms, it is likewise directly relevant to what we have to say about its applicability to a knowledge and handling of child abuse cases.

This case, in common with all child abuse cases, is an example of the power and correlative responsibility of social workers. After only two years' training, and scant acquaintance of child abuse in practice, a social worker has the power − of course, judicially sanctioned − to remove a child from its parents, for a long time, perhaps irrevocably. While magistrates may invest the local authority with all the powers of a parent, through the making of a Care Order, the social worker and his or her supervisor, and others in line management, thereafter become the arbiters of the child's pattern of life. Social workers decide if and when children in care should be returned to their natural families. So long as the Care Order persists, social workers have the awesome task of exercising those parental powers on behalf of the local authority.

These powers are no less, and in some respects greater than, those possessed by various medical practitioners. Yet their training is infinitely longer and more comprehensive. **We are convinced that nothing short of a period of three years is required for the professional training of social workers, of which a larger proportion than at present should be devoted to specialist areas of knowledge, and we have so recommended.** We are confident that a minimum of three years is what the informed public would expect; it is the very least that the profession itself should require in order that its members can shoulder the immense responsibilities which society puts upon them; and it should be supported by public administrators and politicians. There can be little hope of increasing the competence of social workers and of increasing the confidence of the public in social work so long as social work education remains sorely under-resourced.

Specialism in Child Care

We have concluded from what we have seen and heard in the course of our Inquiry, limited though it is to a single case, that social work training needs to produce a higher degree of proven competence in two ways:

(a)   in relation to particular "specialist" areas, like child care; and

(b)   in relation to the statutory duties imposed on social workers, in which the worker acts under mandate in a protective, inspectorial and controlling role.

(a) Specialist areas, like child care

There are many aspects of work with children that demand specialist skills. They cannot be undertaken by social workers unless they possess the necessary specialism. These skills range from the ability to communicate with children, to a proper understanding of the legislation which empowers the work with children (a feature of the work with the Beckford children that was lamentably absent), to the ability to work with clear objectives and goals in mind, and above all, to attend first and foremost to the welfare of the child and his/her development, both physical and psychological. That means that the social worker must (i) understand the child's health needs, and must monitor growth in the form of percentile charts for weight, height and head circumference; (ii) be able to influence that developmental growth through supporting parents in the care of their children and do so by enforcing contractual terms whenever the child in care is in the family household; (iii) possess the ability to work as the focal member of a multidisciplinary team; and (iv) *receive and accept* supervision that will supply the *objective* appraisal of the case. All these skills need to be sustained by an awareness, through knowledge of child development, of parental psychopathology and stress; of child abuse research findings to appraise those cases where the risk factors of abuse outweigh those of separating children from their parents. In short, the ability to detect the "high risk" cases. Such knowledge, skills and, quintessentially, the judgment must exist to balance the social worker's inevitable belief that what he is doing is for the best. These attributes of the good social worker in the management of the child abuse system can develop only over time and with appropriate specialist training, both professional and postqualifying, and supervised experience in handling child abuse cases.

We noted from an article, *Post-Qualifying Studies — Too Little, Too Late?* in March 1979 by Eileen Holgate and Tony Neill, lecturers in the diploma course in Applied Social Studies at Liverpool University, that students involved in the "children and adolescents" option began their course by reading the official inquiry reports on the deaths of Dennis O'Neill (1945) and Maria Colwell (1973), from which they learnt at least the important lesson of the social worker talking alone (out of sight and hearing of the child's parents) with children in care or under supervision, and at the end of their course spending time doing just that. Neither Mrs. Dietmann nor Ms. Wahlstrom had apparently ever read any of the growing literature on child abuse. And Mrs. Dietmann, with her American academic qualifications had not read Dr. Kempe's seminal work, *The Battered-Child Syndrome* (1962), although she did say she had heard of Dr. Kempe's name. For two social workers handling a difficult case of child abuse in the 1980s to have neither a nodding acquaintance with the relevant literature nor a smattering of social work knowledge on child abuse is eloquent testimony of a failure in those responsible for imparting knowledge and skills to practitioners who are required to provide a child protection service.

CCETSW and the organisers of courses in social work training must pay greater attention to these specialist matters during both qualifying and post-qualifying training. The history of the former, from Seebohm onwards, has disclosed how these "specialist" issues, except courses with "Probation options" for those entering the Probation Service, have been unhelpfully relegated by competing pressures from other aspects of curricular content. At post-qualifying level, the history discloses a different tale. Although many courses have been developed, few are viable. This is because of the lack of sufficient funding and of some backwardness in support from local authorities. We have noted that the CCETSW study group, convened after the Maria Colwell inquiry of 1974, produced in 1977, Study No. 1, "Good Enough Parenting", but did not feel able to distinguish between the kinds of learning experience appropriate at different stages of training – initial or post-qualifying studies, for example, or for those workers who undertook CSS training. These issues will need to be addressed by CCETSW as it develops its new qualifying award. The bringing together of the CQSW and the CSS into a "single award" will, we hope, bring about the confrontation of these issues. Minimum requirements for competence that local authorities, social workers' clients and the public are entitled to expect from holders of the new award will need to be stated. This, in turn, will generate changes in present training programmes based on the best from the two systems. Child abuse inquiries, like ours, should provide the spur to the debate on the content of courses and on specialist expertise.

(b) *The Statutory Mandate*
We have already alluded to the social worker's dual mandate from, on the one hand, the families and the public, and, on the other hand, Parliament in its statutory intent, the concomitant of which is the essential, but recognisably difficult task for the social worker of marrying care and control functions within the dual mandate. We have been at pains to point out at every twist and turn of this unhappy story, that the social workers – Mrs. Dietmann, foremostly as supervisor, and Ms. Wahlstrom, as the key field worker – displayed a total lack of understanding of, and indeed lack of commitment to, the statutory ingredient in the dual mandate. These deficiencies originate in a background of training and experience that has both relegated the specialist skills to a back seat role and allowed the generalised aspects of case-work to diminish the respect for statutory responsibilities.

Those responsible for contemporary reshaping of the training of social workers, through academic studies and practical learning, will need to reapportion the educational values. CCETSW's guidelines require approximately 50% of training to be in practical work on placements, but the practical work of the trainee is undertaken "as a student". We think this is to overlook the training value of internal professional experience. We, therefore, welcome CCETSW's consideration of the introduction of an additional method – "learning from employment" – to the existing methods. We note that "employment learning" is a central feature of the CSS training courses, and has proved itself as an educational tool of real benefit to practitioners. We understand from the report on the consultations that there was considerable support for the idea of "employment learning", but considerable reservation about the particular CCETSW proposals. These reservations derive from the relevant trade unions and in particular the National Association of Probation Officers, which have fears for the impact on conditions of service. We trust that CCETSW will develop its idea further. It should not be beyond the ability of the framers of these proposals to accommodate the reservations and seek means whereby students can undertake a period of accountable practice during their training. Such accountable learning could have a treble value for child care work. It could enable an employing local authority to test the employee's willingness and capacity to fulfil the demands of the statutory mandate – the ability to accept the authoritarian role implicit in the execution of a Care Order. It could further provide, through the experience of employment learning, an opportunity to test out the theoretical teaching. Third, the period of "employment learning" would supply time and experience to acquire and apply this learning in daily practical situations. This new concept in social work training is based on the model of the medical profession which has long since required doctors to undertake two pre-registration posts before being licensed to practise medicine. We hope that the model can be successfully adapted and applied to the profession of social work. We would envisage that it might involve attachment to health services as well as to general practitioners. We think that, moreover, this period should enable the development of specific competencies – for example, in child care. We think that consideration might be given to according recognition to those specialist qualifications by the award signifying as much. This will be designed to announce to employing local authorities whether the social worker has received special training in child care or child abuse.

We have deliberately avoided any discussion or comment on the content of social work training, in particular any treatment of training directly referable to the subject matter of our inquiry. We have no basis, other than our impressionistic views, to warrant any such discussion. But we cannot conclude this chapter without expressing a strong feeling that the aspect of the dual mandate – the statutory mandate – which calls for knowledge of the law has not been given the prominence in training that it undoubtedly warrants. We have relied for our bald assertion that the law – especially child care law – has been neglected in social work training, on a survey of social workers' opinion, conducted by Professor Martin Davies, Professor of Social Work at the University of East Anglia. In *Training: what we think of it now*, published in 1984 in *Social Work Today*,* Professor Davies wrote: "The social sciences were judged to have been well-taught and to have been enjoyed, but they were seen as having less practical usefulness than the course teaching on social work practice. The two courses scoring worst on the ranking scale were law (which was sometimes missing altogether from the curriculum) and social work literature theory, where the quality of teaching was seen as especially poor. The law teaching was held to be the least enjoyable course element". One of the six prescriptions that Professor Davies says emerges from this survey is: "Raise the quality and status of course teaching of law and welfare rights."

We can only say that what we have heard in the course of our Inquiry reflects generally the low status and quality of law teaching for social workers. We have described earlier how Mrs. Dietmann and Ms. Wahlstrom had no idea what the legal implications of a Care Order were, and certainly never appreciated them in their work with the Beckford children. Something has gone drastically wrong if the practitioners in the child protection service do not fulfil the edicts of relevant legislation. In July 1974 CCETSW published Paper 4, which was a study group's report on *Legal Studies in Social Work Education*, under the chairmanship of Professor Nigel Walker, then Director of the Institute of Criminology, University of Cambridge. That valuable report ended with the recommendation that a member of CCETSW's professional staff should devote part of his or her time to a regular review of the content of such studies. We understand that that has been carried out. The Walker study group thought, however, that it would be unrealistic to suggest that CCETSW should plan a further study of this kind after a specific period. In the light of the survey conducted by Professor Davies ten years later, **we recommend that such a further study by CCETSW should now be seriously considered as a matter of high priority.** Law is part and parcel of the functions of a social worker in all fields of his or her work, never more so than when engaged in the service of child protection. Training in legal studies must not be allowed to remain any longer the Cinderella of social work training.

We end by making one political (with a small "p") observation. There is currently

* Vol. 15 (20), 24 January 1984, pp. 12-16

no secure funding of social work training and education. Social workers operate within the framework of statutory powers and duties, and CCETSW itself is a statutory body called upon to promote training in social work. Yet there appears to us to be little or no promotion, or even protection of social work training as a priority in higher education, as there is for lawyers, doctors and teachers. The funding of students on training courses is also precarious. Mandatory grants, for example, are available only for undergraduates who form only 12% of CQSW intakes. Our Inquiry provides the opportunity for drawing the attention of the public and politicians to the lack of priority afforded to social work training. If, as we have had impressed upon us in the weeks and months that we have lived with this Inquiry, child abuse is a burning topic of acute public concern, then the public, through its political representatives, must will the means to administer effectively a service of child protection. The means call for resources to implement a policy of redressing the balance between "generic" and "specialist" training, in favour of the latter at qualifying and post-qualifying stages.

The profession of social work is still relatively young, whether or not one calculates its birth before or since Seebohm. It will come of age when the professionalism of its practitioners has been sharpened by better education, more sensibly directed training and an understanding that specialist treatment of the most socially vulnerable of our citizenry – children, old people, the physically handicapped and the mentally disordered – call for the development and deployment of specialist skills in social workers relevant to those classes of persons.

B. Training – Health Visitors

Health Visitors are required to be Registered General Nurses and to be qualified as midwives or have completed an approved 12 weeks' course on obstetrics before they enter training for health visiting. The Health Visitor course is of one academic year's duration plus nine to twelve weeks' supervised practice. The curriculum broadly covers the normal development of the individual, the social effects upon the individual's development, the unfolding of social policies, and the community aspects of health and disease as they impinge upon the principles and practices of health visiting. The statutory qualification is the Certificate in Health Visiting. The content of the courses run by individual colleges or institutions of education and training has to be approved by the English National Board for Nursing, a statutory body. Guidelines for the Health Visitor Course are set by the Board and interpreted and implemented by Course Teams in the educational institutions. Following the report of the Panel of Inquiry into the death of Lucy Gates (1982) the Board's predecessor, the Council for the Education and Training of Health Visitors, promoted a debate on the subject of child abuse, focusing on the Health Visitors' role. Professional studies included the functions of the Health Visitor and particularly the inter-working relationships with other disciplines, especially with social workers.

All the academic bodies providing the courses for the health visiting qualification reported that the predisposing factors of child abuse were taught, and lectures were delivered explaining the roles of other workers in a multi-disciplinary setting. But, as Ruth Sharman, the Education Officer with the English National Board for Nursing with particular responsibility for the Education and Training of Health Visitors suggested to us, education is rather like vaccination – you can apply it universally but it sometimes fails.

From the evidence that we have heard from a number of Health Visitors we have concluded that while there is a general and unspecified awareness among Health Visitors of children at risk of abuse, field workers are not always knowledgeable about specific factors relating to child abuse. If the work done by the two Health Visitors, Miss Knowles and Miss Leong with the Beckford family is anything to go by, there appears to be a serious shortfall in the education and training relating to child abuse acquired during the period of Health Visitor studentship. Furthermore, in this instance, the two Health Visitors' work revealed, in practice, an inability to interpret what had been learnt.

Five aspects of the training of the two Health Visitors who were principally involved in this case may indicate deficiencies in training.

First, there was imperfect, if any understanding of Care Orders and their implementation by both Health Visitors. A more serious cause for concern is that the social worker in this instance was also unable during the Inquiry to show her knowledge of care procedures. It can, therefore, be suggested that this lack of knowledge on the part of the Health Visitors was wholly shared, to the detriment of Jasmine Beckford.

It was noted in the report of the Inquiry into the death of Lucy Gates (1982) that both the social worker and the Health Visitor found themselves involved with a mother of immature personality who loved her children but was unable to cope in circumstances of poverty and was starved of companionship and love, thus rendering her incapable of providing a suitable physical and emotional environment for her children's development. The two workers both saw "the client" to be the mother rather than the child. They both used their respective skills towards sustaining the mother and child as a family unit to enhance the supposed therapeutic relationship between the workers and the mother. They did not perceive that in the case of a child at risk, the protection of the child is of paramount importance.

Second, we believe that as with social workers, so with Health Visitors, they are imbued with the same philosophical approach towards the operation of a Care Order. Those responsible for Health Visitor training will need to review their courses so as to apply the necessary corrective measures. We suspect that here also the knowledge of the law relating to child care is defective.

Third, there is the question how far the Health Visitor is able to work positively in a multi-disciplinary setting. Clearly, there is evidence of an inability of the two main Health Visitors involved to do this. If Health Visitors were to be educated and trained alongside general practitioner trainees, clinical medical officers and social workers, effective teamwork might be a by-product of such joint tuition. If interdisciplinary work for the protection of children at risk is to be effective, it is essential that some shared learning experience takes place at both qualifying and post-qualifying levels.

Multi-professional training for all those involved in child abuse, including police officers operating within juvenile bureaux, needs to be stimulated by central government departments, health authorities and local authorities. There must also be a clear commitment from the statutory educational bodies of the respective professions towards multi-disciplinary training.

Fourth, Health Visitor's courses should ensure that quantitative and qualitative education and training is given to students on all aspects of the development of children. This will not only enable them to carry out realistic surveillance of normal children but also to assess deviations from the normal; and hence the prevention, where possible, and early detection of child abuse.

Fifth, it is evident that there was poor communication between the Nursing Officer and the two main Health Visitors who were involved in this case. This is disconcerting, since at this level of functional management, these problems should not occur. The Nursing Officer should not only monitor the Health Visitor's work, but should also offer support – for example, continuously attending case conferences when any member of his/her staff are involved in such situations.

We are given to understand that Nursing Officers do monitor and assess student Health Visitors during the period of supervised practice, and that they also monitor and assess fieldwork teachers during part 2 of their course. It is expected that Nursing Officers would be sufficiently skilled not only in all aspects of child care, but also in matters relating to child abuse so that they could enhance the developing skills of these two groups of students.

Continuing education and training should be provided in the form of in-service and multi-disciplinary seminars with social workers, general practitioners, clinical medical officers and police officers. We think it is important that Health Authorities should ensure that all Health Visitors understand the policy for child abuse.

We are aware of the E.N.B. proposals on nurse, midwife and health visitor's education and training, and that those proposals represent a major change in the pattern of both the basic and post registration training. We would hope that the proposals lead to sufficient time for better education in those aspects of child care that at present cannot be dealt with in any great depth, and that these proposals represent a major change in the pattern of both the basic and post registration training.

C. Training – Magistrates

The juvenile court is the fulcrum of the child abuse system, and its prime power in proceedings involving children and young persons, the Care Order, preceded by the Place-of-Safety Order, and/or the interim Care Order, is the exclusive means by which State intervention in parental rights is authorised to protect the child. It is the lay magistracy which staffs the juvenile court – stipendiary magistrates seldom sit with lay magistrates in care proceedings – and has the responsibility for deciding whether to deprive parents of the care and control of their children. Not unnaturally, magistrates express reluctance to sanction the deprivation of parental powers; and if they do sanction it, they try to ensure that such deprivation is restricted to a minimum period consistent with immediate protection of the child. Hence the understandable temptation among magistrates to place some limits on the functioning of the Care Order, as we have described and commented on critically in Chapter 16.

Magisterial reluctance is not only an instinctive individual reaction to the power of the State over the family, but it also reflects a generalised attitude within a democratic society that values highly the family and the right of individual members of the family to resist any State intervention that would disrupt it by separation of its members, as acknowledged by Article 8(2) of the European Convention on Human Rights.* In recent years this generalised attitude has found expression in the activities of pressure groups, such as the family rights lobby, which has been immeasurably enhanced by sustained attacks in the media castigating, quite unjustifiably, social workers for daring to remove children from their parents. More and more, the magistracy has been under pressure to resist the applications by social workers for Care Orders, and social workers have experienced the same pressures emanating from magistrates. Potent as the arguments

---

* Similar international law provisions are to be found in Article 16(3) of the Universal Declaration of Human Rights; Principle 6 of the Declaration of the Rights of the Child adopted by the General Assembly of the United Nations, December 1951; Article 16 of the European Social Charter, October 1961; Article 10(1) of the International Covenant on Economic, Social and Cultural Rights, December 1966; Article 23(1) of the International Covenant on Civil and Political Rights, December 1966, which reproduces Article 16(3) of the Universal Declaration on Human Rights.

are for favouring strongly the claims of parents to their own children, unmolested by the powers of government, the unpalatable fact is that some parents cannot safely be left to look after their own children. Some children need to be protected from their own parents. The Beckford children were two of many such children. Studies over the past twenty years have identified a number of indicators, suggesting that children who have suffered non-accidental injury or preventible neglect, which in turn supply strong predictive factors, are likely to undergo further abuse if left in their parents' custody. The medical, nursing and social work professions are gradually becoming trained to recognise the signs of actual or potential child abuse, although they still have a long way to go, as we have become aware. Failure to thrive, for example, has long been an indicium of child abuse; yet it was not picked up in Jasmine's case. Likewise, it is imperative that the lay magistracy is made aware of the knowledge of child abuse. In terms of child protection, it is particularly important that magistrates can recognise the signs of child abuse, since their decisions may be the last word. While a child (through the guardian ad litem) or the parents can appeal against the making of a Care Order, the local authority has no right of appeal against the decision *not* to make a Care Order. A Supervision Order may not be enough to provide the requisite protection for the child. Professor Greenland, who has studied a large number of child abuse cases in England and in North America, told us "there have been a number of tragedies in the United Kingdom where children have been returned home [as a result of court decisions declining to make Care Orders] against the advice of Social Services." He added: "The training of magistrates and judges is enormously important. One area that seems to me particularly ripe for education and training is the notion of what is possible. It seems to me that courts and judges in particular have unrealistic expectations of what social workers can do. They will say 'increase the amount of supervision', as though supervision will necessarily protect the child."

Every juvenile court magistrate appointed since 1965 has had to undergo a course of training, details of which are to be found in the booklet, *Basic Training for Juvenile Court Magistrates*, issued by the Lord Chancellor's Department. The first stage, which must be completed before a magistrate is empowered to adjudicate in a juvenile court, consists of − a) three attendances at a Juvenile Court, to include, if possible, care proceedings; and b) three instruction sessions, usually given by the justices' clerk, one of which covers "an appreciation of the full range of social services and agencies available to the juvenile court, including educational, medical and psychological services and the provision of reports to the court." The second stage, which starts six months after appointment to the juvenile panel and must be completed within twelve months of appointment includes a series of instructional sessions which deal with the following matters:-

(a)   the exercise of the procedures and powers of the juvenile court in both civil and criminal proceedings;

(b)   the social, psychological and educational backgrounds of juveniles before the court and the environmental factors which put them at risk;

(c)   the role of the local authority services and the probation service in relation to the juvenile court and its Orders;

(d)   practical exercises to illustrate such matters as the use of the powers of the court, the reception and use of reports and the announcing and explaining of the court's decisions. Among sixteen examples of such practical participation exercises are included:- "An exercise in which a local authority social worker applies to a magistrate in his home for a Place-of-Safety Order. What action does the magistrate take and what tests does he apply before granting the Order." "An exercise to demonstrate that in care or control proceedings, both requirements must be satisfied."

Local Magistrates' Training Committees do arrange evening meetings, day courses and residential weekends for juvenile court magistrates, as does the Magistrates' Association; these may, and often do include talks from doctors, social workers and university teachers specialising in child abuse. In some areas, regular meetings between juvenile court magistrates and Social Services Area teams are held. These have proved useful in giving magistrates an understanding of the way in which their local Social Services Department handles cases of child abuse. To quote Professor Greenland again: "Some dialogue between the Social Services Department and the judiciary would not do much harm!"

We are ourselves aware that many juvenile court magistrates make a great effort to attend these training courses and meetings with social services personnel. Regrettably not all of them are as conscientious. **We recommend that the Magistrates' Association, through its branches, together with chairmen of benches and juvenile court panels and clerks to justices, should now communicate to justices and emphasise the importance of keeping up to date with contemporary knowledge about child abuse.** Their attention should also be drawn to existing and new publications. We would like to think that our report will become prescribed reading for every juvenile court magistrate in the country.

Like the courses for doctors, nurses and social workers, the basic course for training juvenile court magistrates covers a syllabus in which there is room for no more than the briefest of mentions of child abuse. The in-service courses do little more than "top up" inadequate basic training. Added to which, magistrates are busy people with full-time occupations, who are part-time judges and even more part-time students. Assiduous as they may be in equipping themselves to fulfil the function of adjudicators in the lives of parents and children, they are not seeking to obtain either a professional qualification or a professional status. They are amateurs who will become professional at their task only by long experience on the bench, attendance at relevant training sessions and lectures, and a willingness to read widely beyond the lecture room.

D. Training – Lawyers

Until the late 1960s it was rare for lawyers to appear in juvenile courts. Nowadays, in care proceedings, it is not unusual to see lawyers separately representing the parents, the child (usually through a *guardian ad litem*) and the local authority. On the role of the *parents' lawyer*, we again quote Professor Greenland. "Due to the adversary nature of the court proceedings, the child protection agency is likely to be challenged by the lawyer employed to represent the parents' interests .... in promoting the parents' rights, in opposition to the child protection agency, the lawyer, whether he is conscious of it or not, is waging an old ideological battle. This is concerned with asserting the primacy of the parents' right to care for and control their children, within the limits allowed by law and with the minimum of State intervention .... Within this concept, arbitrary interference by the State, however well-intentioned, is regarded as damaging to the child, the family and to society .... It is for this reason that the majesty of the court precludes the possibility of lawyers being held accountable for the death of a child who has been returned to the care of a successfully defended parent. Unlike lawyers, whose relationships to clients are by nature transitory and mercenary, child protection workers, as agents of social control have long-term commitments to families and lasting concerns for the welfare of children under their supervision."

We endorse Professor Greenland's observations and would add that the entry of the lawyer-advocate into care proceedings has injected into the process a dose of legalism that, for good or ill, has sharpened up the conflict of interests and given point to the assertion that children have rights and may need protection against both authority and their own parents.

This means that it is particularly necessary in the interests of the child that the lawyers representing the child, the *guardian ad litem* and the local authority should all have some understanding of the significance of evidence relating to child abuse, not only to satisfy the primary condition, but also in predicting the likelihood of continued abuse if the child is returned home, thus satisfying the secondary condition that the child is "in need of care or control which he is unlikely to receive unless an Order is made."

Regarding the *child's lawyer*, we welcome the action of the Law Society which, in response to a recommendation by the House of Commons Social Services Committee's report on "Children in Care" (April 1984), has established a panel of solicitors to act in child care cases. All solicitors included on this panel, which came into operation on 1 March 1985, must have satisfied the Law Society that they have at least 18 months experience of advocacy and have either:

a)   conducted at least five recent contested care cases; or

b)   (i)   attended an approved training course and

      (ii) successfully satisfied an interview panel of their suitability to be included

(Every interview panel includes a practising solicitor and a *guardian ad litem* with considerable experience in this field).

All members of the panel have undertaken normally to conduct personally child care cases referred to them as members of the panel. A client's choice of solicitor, however, need not be limited to those on the panel.

We recognise that, in the short term, the fact that a solicitor has conducted at least five recent contested care cases may have to be regarded as sufficient qualification for membership of the panel. However, we agree with the comment in "Justice of the Peace" (22.9.84) that care proceedings form "an area of work which requires a special sensitivity towards the needs, the language and the emotions of young people. By no means every solicitor has this combination of talents and the fact that he has been doing this type of work for some time is not necessarily a guarantee that he is competent at it." We hope that, as soon as possible, all members of the panel will have to satisfy the criteria outlined in (b) above. We trust, also, that the "approved training course" for membership of the panel will include a section on the factors which are now widely regarded as indicators of past child abuse and predictors of future abuse, if the child remains with his parents.

These observations apply likewise to the *guardian ad litem*'s solicitors, and we are sure that *guardians ad litem* will welcome the establishment of the Law Society's panel. (We deal shortly with the role of the *guardian ad litem* in Chapter 26). We have recommended elsewhere that, in view of the growing tendency for parties to be legally represented in care cases, the Social Services Department, when bringing care proceedings should also be so represented. If a solicitor in private practice is instructed for this purpose, we hope that he will, in future, normally be selected from the Law Society's panel. **If, as is more usual, a lawyer from the local authority's own legal staff is required to conduct the case, we recommend that similar criteria to those pertaining to the Law Society's panel should be applied.** Like solicitors in private practice, child care work forms only a very small part of their range of work. In the words of Dingwall and Eekelaar in their *Care Proceedings – a Practical Guide for Social Workers, Health Visitors and Others*'' (1982): "The appropriate place to look for legal advice is the legal department of the local authority. Unfortunately, these vary a good deal in the interest and status afforded to child care work. What should be remembered is that career advancement for solicitors in local government is related much more to their involvement with committees and councillors than to the sort of advocacy involved in child care. In some authorities, care cases are dealt with at arm's length."

Similarly, in *Understanding Child Abuse* – edited by David Jones (1982), we are told, "it is essential that the application is presented by a lawyer with experience of child care law. It is a matter of some concern that many authorities give child care cases to newly-qualified and inexperienced lawyers, for the issue at stake is the future welfare and liberty of a child until his eighteenth birthday." More recently, the House of Commons Social Services Committee said, in 1984: "At present the practice of child care law does not in general attract the calibre of lawyers which the subject deserves and, as a result, care proceedings are not always conducted as professionally as they should be .... local authorities often leave care proceedings to be dealt with by their most junior and inexperienced solicitors, who will be advanced to more financially and politically significant work just when they have gathered experience of child care law. **We recommend that the need to promote the skilled practice of child care law is reflected in legal education and that the child care content of legal education be kept under review.**"

We echo that recommendation and, in particular, **we recommend that the Law Society should extend its panel of solicitors to act in child care cases to include solicitors employed by local authorities, and that only those local authority solicitors who meet the criteria for membership of the panel should be allowed to represent their authority in care proceedings.**

CHAPTER 21

Supervision*

(a) *Social Workers*

From the start in 1971 of the newly-created Social Services Departments, it has been the practice for teams of four or five social workers to be under the supervision of a senior social worker acting both as their line manager and as their professional supervisor. This form of supervision was particularly necessary in those early days, when many basic grade social workers were untrained. Today, most local authority social workers are qualified, but supervision is still seen as valuable both for the field social workers and for social workers generally. Criticism of the standard of supervision given to social workers has been a feature of many earlier child abuse inquiries. It has figured prominently in this Inquiry.

Both the social worker and her supervisor act on behalf of their employing local authority in the task of protecting children at risk. The supervisor has line management responsibility for ensuring that the social worker is carrying out this task, although it is neither appropriate nor possible for her to direct in detail the activities of the individual social worker. To carry out this responsibility, the supervisor must not only be constantly available to the social worker so as to discuss problems as they arise; it is also essential that she should set aside a regular period each week for full, uninterrupted discussion with each social worker. Such an arrangement relieves the social worker of the fear that she may be taking up too much of her supervisor's time by referring specific problems to her; it also enables the supervisor to structure her own monitoring of the social worker's cases, and ensures that she does not forget those cases which the social worker may choose not to refer to her.

In working with the social worker who is dealing with a child at risk, the supervisor has four main functions:-

1) *To ensure that the social worker has the knowledge and skills to carry out her task.* The supervisor must be satisfied that the social worker is aware of the law relating to children at risk and be sensitive to the legal rights and civil liberties of children and their parents. The supervisor must further ensure that the social worker understands the legal powers and duties of other professionals in the field and the administrative frameworks within which they operate. She must ensure that the social worker can recognise the indications that a child has been abused and the predictive factors which suggest that abuse may continue if the child were to remain with his parents. She must satisfy herself that the social worker has the ability to relate to, and communicate with children.

2) *To monitor the activities of the social worker.* It is the supervisor's duty to ensure that a plan for treatment, based upon as complete an initial assessment as possible, is drawn up by the social worker as soon as possible after a child at risk has been referred, and that it is up-dated as appropriate. The plan should include a statement of objectives and such details as frequency of visiting; the need for health checks, (regular measurement of weight and height, developmental tests, medical examinations, etc.); and the need for the child to attend school or nursery. In particular contacts with the extended family of both parents should always be considered. It

---

* In writing this chapter we have relied heavily on BASW's *Code of Practice for Senior Social Workers Dealing with Children at Risk*

215

has been fairly pointed out to us that this is the more necessary to-day when working with black families.

The supervisor must ensure that the social worker is keeping up-to-date records of all work with a child at risk. Such records should include details of every visit, telephone call, message and discussion of the case, with dates; also all decisions relating to the case, and the reasons for them. The supervisor should read these records before each supervisory session, and this should enable her to ascertain whether the treatment plan is being carried out. If the records do not clearly show this, the supervisor should ask the social worker whether the specified frequency of visits, health checks and school or nursery attendance has been maintained and, if not, why not. In particular, she should check whether the social worker has actually seen the child; whether she has handled the child and/or had a conversation with him; whether or not this was in the presence of the parent(s); how the child and the parents reacted to each other. At all times the supervisor must ensure that the focus of casework is on the child.

3) *To be aware of the attitudes of the social worker towards the case and to correct, if necessary, the way in which they affect her handling of it.* It is almost inevitable that a social worker will become emotionally involved with a family with whom she is working closely. One of the most important tasks of a supervisor is to counteract any potential distortions of judgment. Dingwall, Eekelaar and Murray, in their work, *The Protection of Children – State Intervention and Family Life* (1983) note the rarity of allegations by social workers of mistreatment of children by their parents. They describe this attitude as the product of the "rule of optimism" that staff are required, if possible, to think the best of parents. The authors attribute this tendency in staff to two "institutional devices" – namely, (a) cultural relativism; and (b) natural love. The former is an intellectual position that all cultures are an equally valid way of formulating relationships between human beings and between human beings and the material world. Members of one culture "have no right to criticise members of another by importing their own standards of judgment". The latter is derived from the belief that parent/child life is "an instinctual phenomenon grounded in human nature". "If it is assumed that all parents love their children as a fact of nature, then it becomes very difficult to read evidence in a way which is inconsistent with that assumption". The authors argue that, as a result of these two devices, "front line workers are led either to an open acceptance of the client's justifications, if called for, or to concluding that the fault lies with them, for failing sufficiently to empathise with the alleged deviant".

Both these attributes were doubtless at play in the Beckford case. Indeed it has been suggested to us that Mrs. Dietmann and Ms. Wahlstrom over-compensated for the fact that they were highly-educated, middle-class, white social workers coming into the home of under-educated, working class Afro-Caribbean parents. While we have not been able to detect any such overt attitude, we confirm that there was a distinct unwillingness ever to be censorious of the Beckford parents' behaviour, which may be said to be a facet of over-compensation. Indeed, the most favourable interpretation was always put upon the behaviour of Morris Beckford and Beverley Lorrington. Second, there was abundant evidence from Ms. Wahlstrom's recorded notes that she invariably interpreted actions as displays of affection and of caring by Beverley and Morris for their children, in spite of past abuse and signs of repetition of abuse.

Throughout our Inquiry there has been frequent use by witnesses and legal representatives of the phrase, "rule of optimism". By "rule of optimism" no-one who appeared before us, however, intended the concept in the

216

Dingwall/Eekelaar/Murray sense. Their rule might be more aptly called "the rule of expectation". Our own notion of the phrase was derived and deployed from the way in which Professor Greenland explained it to us.

In his evidence, Professor Greenland said: "One of the problems in working with high-risk child abuse is what is called the rule of optimism. Because the problems are so complex, in order to develop enough enthusiasm and enough energy, the social workers tend to have a very optimistic view of what can be accomplished. They tend to exaggerate progress that has been made, and they may see progress where there is no progress. They do that to sustain their own morale, at least to some extent. For this reason, because of the loss of objectivity, professional supervision is vital, so that when the social worker reports that the marital relationship has improved enormously, it will be the job of the supervisor to say 'where is the evidence for this?' He must compel the front line social workers to examine their judgments in a critical way..... If it is felt that the judgment of the front line worker is faulty, it would be the duty of the supervisor to make a visit with the front line worker to see for himself or herself what the true situation is. The loss of objectivity is a common factor in the management of high risk cases."

Dr. Taitz made the same point when he told us: "There should be some objective assessment of the parent/child relationship other than by the Health Visitor or the Social Worker working with the family, because I find all too often with both the Health Visitors and the Social Workers, and I say this with the best will in the world because this has happened to me as well, so I do not want to exclude paediatricians from this, that they sometimes get emotionally involved with their clients and lose their judgment and, as they are providing the therapy, they are looking for evidence of improvement which is often not there."

Dr. Taitz felt that the ideal person to carry out such an objective assessment would be a properly trained clinical psychologist. In the absence of such a resource, we regard it as a vital function of the supervisor to distance herself emotionally from the case and to apply detached objective tests in judging the social worker's handling of the case. In short, the supervisor must constantly apply the suppressor to an unbridled rule of optimism.

4) *To support the social worker both practically and emotionally.* This support should include:-

(a) ensuring that the workload carried by the social worker does not reach a level which would prevent the social worker from visiting clients in accordance with the plan and timetable deemed appropriate;

(b) helping the social worker to establish proper priorities within her workload, and supporting her in maintaining these priorities in the face of pressure and criticism;

(c) trying to ensure that the employing authority makes available adequate clerical assistance, filing systems, dictating machines, etc. to enable the social worker to maintain up-to-date records.

(d) recognising the high level of anxiety aroused by working with children at risk, and offering all possible emotional support to the social worker, making joint visits with her, if necessary, and sharing in major decisions. In emphasising the importance of emotional support to the social worker, our attention was drawn by Professor Greenland to recent research which attributed the high rate of attrition among front line child protection workers to "burn-out", the symptoms of which included "emotional and physical exhaustion. A variety of frequent illnesses. Negative, cynical attitudes towards clients. Avoidance of seeing clients, or taking refuge in inaction because of various 'rules'. Reduced personal and professional esteem." (Falconer and Swift, 1983). McFadden (1983) observed that "child welfare brings one face to face with a particular concentration of anxieties and negative, hostile emotions ... The bureaucracy, rules and procedures inevitably associated with child welfare services also serve to generate stress and burn-out." Professor Greenland added that an even greater source of stress must be the assumption that social workers have the means to remedy the social conditions which precipitate child abuse and neglect.

Conclusion
The objectives of the supervisor in respect of a child at risk are basically the same as those of the front-line social worker, but the task is different. The supervisor must build up a relationship of trust between herself and the social worker, but she must also distance herself, to a certain extent, from the social worker so that she can offer the objective monitoring of the social worker's activities and attitudes so essential to protect the interests of the child. She must give emotional support to the social worker, but must also remember that the social worker is not her client, and that the support is given in order to help the social worker in carrying out the task of protecting the child and promoting his welfare — a task which is the joint responsibility of both social worker and supervisor.

We have dealt at some length with this topic because we consider that, in some vital respects, Mrs. Dietmann failed to give Ms. Wahlstrom adequate supervision. We think she did give emotional support and that, except when on leave, she was always approachable by Ms. Wahlstrom. (We certainly do not blame her for failing to ensure that adequate clerical help was available to social workers in Area 6, since her superiors, up to and including the Director, had been likewise unsuccessful in that respect!) We are doubtful whether she herself was sufficiently knowledgeable in the field of child abuse to ensure that Ms. Wahlstrom could recognise indicators and predictive factors relating to child abuse. We think that she signally failed to draw Ms. Wahlstrom's attention to the fact that Jasmine had not been seen for several months; nor did she enquire about health and developmental checks, or nursery attendance. We express some astonishment that, given her lack of experience in child abuse, she did not acquaint herself and Ms. Wahlstrom with the growing literature on the subject. No professional person ever knows everything about his subject, but does know where to find out about it and to that end instinctively repairs to the library. Mrs. Dietmann had not even guarded against this charge, by preparing herself in the weeks and months before she came to give evidence as ignorant of child abuse as she ever was. Regarding Ms. Wahlstrom's general attitudes to the case, notably the "rule of optimism", we consider that Mrs. Dietmann totally shared these attitudes; consequently, she was disabled from the essential duty to distance herself from Ms. Wahlstrom. She was incapable of applying the objective tests so tragically absent in the handling of this case. Ms. Wahlstrom's overweening sense of improvement in the personal behaviour of the Beckfords was never tested, let alone corrected by her supervisor.

(b) *Key Workers*
The DHSS Circular, "Non-Accidental Injury to Children: Area Review Committees" (LASSL(76)2/CMO(76)2/CMO(76)3) recommended "the practice of nominating one of the participants in a case conference as the 'key worker'. The professional most closely concerned with the case and responsible for the actual management of it is identified as the focal point through whom information is channelled, and is made responsible for ensuring that it reaches all the other participants. This arrangement does not relieve the other professionals of their own responsibilities, but it does facilitate the swift and ready exchange of information between those concerned." (We note, in passing, that

218

the term "key worker" is also used, in the field of social services, to describe the member of staff in a residential establishment who takes a particular interest in an individual resident and with whom that resident can form a close personal relationship. Thus, a child in the care of the local authority who has been the subject of abuse may have one key worker carrying out the functions described in the DHSS Circular and another key worker with whom he has a close personal relationship in the Children's Home in which he is living).

Following the publication of the DHSS Circular, it was, for a time, thought to be appropriate in some cases for the Health Visitor to be nominated by the Case Conference as key worker, i.e., when she was seen as "the professional most closely concerned with the case." This development caused some alarm within the nursing profession, and in December 1982 a joint report from the Nursing, Midwifery and Health Visiting Professions, entitled "Key Workers, Child Abuse and the Nursing Profession" was issued. In this document, it was argued firmly and at some length that "it would be an inappropriate use of professional skills and resources to combine the nurse's role with the essentially administrative duties of the key worker." "The professional who may have had the longest contact or who has the greatest knowledge of the family, or who may have the easiest or only access to the family is sometimes described as the 'Prime Worker' ..... when a member of the Health Service acts as Prime Worker the administrative duties should be undertaken by a senior social worker under the title of Case Manager." The report concluded: "The administrative duties which are necessary for the effective management of child abuse cases are essentially those of the co-ordination of the agencies, disciplines and professions. Therefore, in child abuse cases, the administrative and coordinative functions of the Key Worker are clearly the responsibility of the Social Services Departments, particularly as, with their central role for statutory care and protection, they need to be the centre for coordinating information, and it is inappropriate that these duties should be assumed by a member of the nursing profession."

Some of these arguments could be used to suggest that the field social worker dealing with a child abuse case should not undertake the "essentially administrative duties of the key worker." In practice, however, it is nowadays very usual for the initial case conference to nominate the social worker who will be working directly with the family as key worker — as was done in the Beckford case. Where the front-line social worker is also the key worker, the supervisor has the additional responsibility of ensuring that the social worker:-

(a) notifies all professionals involved in the case of her own position as key worker, and tells them how to contact her;

(b) records promptly, fully and accurately all oral messages about the case, giving the date and source of the information, and files all written communications;

(c) disseminates all such information promptly to other relevant professionals;

(d) keeps under review the involvement of other agencies concerned with the family;

(e) actively seeks information from, e.g., health visitors, school nurses, teachers, general practitioners and other professionals.

In the case of Ms. Wahlstrom, who was carrying out her first assignment as key worker in a child abuse case, we consider that Mrs. Dietmann did not give her sufficient guidance as to her duties as a key worker. Ms. Wahlstrom's contact with other relevant professionals appears to have been casual and unstructured. There is no evidence that Mrs. Dietmann ever monitored this aspect of her work. In mitigation, both Ms. Wahlstrom and Mrs. Dietmann were severely handicapped in carrying out these duties efficiently simply because the Area teams in Brent were deficient in the supply of clerical and secretarial support.

(c) *Health Visitors*

The relationship between the Health Visitor and her line manager is different from that between the social worker and her line manager for several reasons. In the first place, the Health Visitor occupies a much higher position in the nursing hierarchy than does the basic grade social worker in a Social Services Department. The qualified Health Visitor will have had at least four years professional nursing training, as against the qualified social worker's two years of training, and her position, on Grade 8, is higher than that of a ward sister in hospital. The Health Visitor is, therefore, regarded as a professional worker who is accountable for her professional practice and is fully competent to make clinical judgments.

Second, the Health Visitor has a very much higher caseload than that of the field social worker – 300 to 400 families as against the social worker's 20 to 30 cases. It would, therefore, be impossible for her senior nurse to monitor in detail her work with every case.

Third, each senior nurse is responsible for managing 10 to 15 staff, as against the senior social worker's 4 or 5. (We were told by Miss Tyler, Miss Leong's supervisor until December 1983, that she was responsible for managing between 50 and 60 staff but this was when there were unfilled vacancies for senior nurses in Brent.) We were told that, until recently, it was not the normal practice in Brent, nor in the neighbouring Health District of Harrow, for Health Visitors to have regular face-to-face interviews with their senior nurses. They did submit reports and they were given to understand that they could always approach their senior nurses if they felt that they needed advice or help over a particular case but we got the impression that such approaches were rare. However, the present Director of Nursing Services, (Primary Health Care Unit) in Brent told us that she is insisting that such regular interviews should take place. She considered that such monitoring was a top priority because of the importance of the nurse/client relationship. It had been suggested to her that a structured system of regular meetings between individual Health Visitors and their senior nurses was unrealistic in view of limited staff resources. Refreshingly, her reply was emphatic. It had been done in other areas, and she quoted Ealing, where the Director of Nursing Services expected Senior Nurses to meet with Health Visitors once a week.

One former senior nurse in Brent, Miss Baichoo, had introduced the practice of regular, structured meetings instead of continuing an *ad hoc* approach. This, in her opinion, enabled her to manage time more effectively for the following reasons:- time spent in personal interviews was undisturbed; matters could be explored more fully. Staff could more readily grasp the function of the interview as a means of facilitating their expertise. We were interested to learn that, once Miss Baichoo had introduced this system, the Health Visitors working to other Senior Nurses requested, formally, that they, too, should have regular interviews with their seniors.

We strongly recommend that the practice of planning regular discussions between Health Visitors and their Senior Nurses should be established, and that Senior Nurses should particularly ensure that they discuss all child abuse cases regularly with the Health Visitor involved, even if she herself does not consider that there is any problem with which she is unable to deal. Such regular monitoring is facilitated if the Senior Nurse always accompanies the health visitor to child abuse case conferences and we are glad to note that, in a document "Case Conferences in Relation to Child Abuse and the Nursing Profession" produced in March 1985 by the Nurses' Professional Organisations Working Party, it is recommended that "in relation to case conferences, the nurse manager should, ideally, arrange a meeting with the nurse(s) prior to the case conference. Discussion should take place regarding factual nursing information and professional opinion to be shared, ensuring that it is accurate and up-to-date. Confidentiality of information must also be discussed. The nurse manager will ensure that the nurse is aware of her professional responsibility to the family whether the child's name is registered de-registered or otherwise. The nurse manager should participate in the case conference.''

Such guidance, if followed, should do much to improve the level of supervisory support and monitoring given to Health Visitors dealing with cases of child abuse, and we wholeheartedly commend it.

CHAPTER 22

Documentation

Our terms of reference do not refer specifically to the methods or quality of social work, or of other agencies', recording. However, at the outset of our Inquiry and during the course of the hearings we have necessarily read and digested a vast amount of documentary material, the most important of which we have extracted and included in Appendices to this report, so that our readers can judge for themselves the quality of recording as well as assess the value of our comments on those documents.

Recording in social work is a topic arousing strong comment from professional workers. Such has been the feeling of dissatisfaction with case recording that a working party was set up in 1983 by the British Association of Social Workers to examine the topic. The working party concluded that "a radical reappraisal of the role and organisation of recording systems in social work is needed." Our encounter with the minutes of case conferences, statutory case reviews, and with other reports and case records covering a 3 year period of social work with the Beckford family impels us to contribute some thoughts, and to offer some suggestions on this ongoing debate about an important aspect of the management of the child abuse system.

We have taken as our starting point for good practice in recording, the code of practice for social workers and supervisors, the report, *Child Abuse Policy*, prepared by a Project Group of the British Association of Social Workers (1985). The code provides that social workers have a duty to record every visit, interview or phone call with, or about families involved in child abuse. This should include information passed on to supervisors, and any decisions made or instructions given, with signature and date. Good recording calls for a sharp distinction between unverified information, substantiated facts, observations and opinion. The source of any information should be noted. Plans, reviews and the reasons for decisions must be recorded by social workers dealing with child abuse. Inaction or indecision, particularly where it is due to lack of resources, should also be clearly recorded. Supervisors have a duty to ensure that the standards of recording laid down in the Code should be fully observed. Supervisors must sign and date records they have seen, and in particular ensure that any note of the social worker-supervisor discussions or instructions from the supervisor is accurately recorded. Supervisors have the additional duty to ensure that appropriate administrative tools for good recording is always available. The BASW code concludes that "accurate records are so crucial to child abuse work" that supervisors have a duty to bring failure to meet the appropriate standard to the attention of senior management.

Reviewing the reports of child abuse inquiries from 1973 to 1981 the Department of Health and Social Security in its pamphlet *Child Abuse* (1982),* concluded that a study of the reports demonstrated that "efficiency in recording, transmitting and storing information is an essential and integral part of professional practice." Given the importance attached to the communicating of information through documented social work in the field of child abuse, we considered it more appropriate and more helpful if we dealt with the topic under a separate rubric, instead of punctuating our unfolding of the events over three years with comments on documentation as it impinged on relevant incidents.

Before dealing with the specific documentation used by individual workers and social

* HMSO, para 2.66, p.49

agencies in relation to the case of Jasmine Beckford, we wish to make one general observation that has struck us forcibly during our Inquiry. Whatever the commitment to consistent noting of every facet of work in the management of the child abuse system, there is the overriding requirement that not merely should the social work always have a clear purpose, but also that the recording should be purposive so that readers of the information can immediately appreciate what was intended by the social worker in relation to each event. Miss Alix Causby put it to us accurately: "I am very concerned about workers going into families where the visiting is unfocused and where they are not clear, and the family is not clear, what the purpose of that particular visit is. So, to ensure that everyone is clear what work is being done and what the goals for that work are, I think it is extremely important that the case recording reflects this, and that if visiting is unfocused, that can be extremely dangerous in terms of work with families." When asked what she thought of the documentation in this case, Miss Causby said: "The elements of recording that I was asked to look at were not very clear in terms of purpose of the visit and what was being achieved at that particular visit." We entirely endorse that statement of principle about the essential duty of recording, and we shall demonstrate and substantiate Miss Causby's point. Miss Causby helpfully, in cross-examination by Mr. Bond, pointed to an instance where Ms. Wahlstrom had exceptionally observed the precept. On 11 April 1983 Ms. Wahlstrom recorded: "Collected Beverley and Louise and went to collect Jasmine. The purpose was for me to be able to find out from Jasmine's teachers how she progressed since she started", and she went on to record what the teachers thought – a matter we have dealt with in Chapter 10. That, Miss Causby said, was a classic way of indicating "clear overall goals as to what one is trying to achieve." Another example is Ms. Wahlstrom's letter of 3 July 1984 announcing the forthcoming visit on 5 July 1984, not for the purpose of seeing the children but "so that we can have the Review and hopefully apply to the court for the Care Orders to be discharged".

Our criticism, reinforced by what Miss Causby told us, is that while the individual workers working with the Beckford family may well have had clear objectives in mind when making visits, or otherwise contacting the family (and others involved) the records do not invariably reflect these objectives. The records further failed to indicate the overall objectives or context within which particular actions were set. Ideally, visits, telephone conversations, discussions and other activities would each have a purpose, and that particular purpose would be set within a single framework of overall goals and objectives. These overall goals and objectives would be known by all the agencies and individuals working with the family.

Applying these principles to the case of Jasmine Beckford, we conclude that such clarity of objectives was not then, and is not even now, apparent to the reader. Apropos overall goals and objectives, it is unclear, from the time of the original Case Conferences of August 1981 until April 1982, what the long-term plans for the children would be. While it is true that, necessarily, there might be some indecision about such plans, that indecision is gleaned, not from a clear statement in the documentation that no decision could be arrived at but only from the confusion of messages emanating from the principal participants in decision-making. The evidence given to us by these witnesses revealed their confusion about what they had in mind in 1981, even discounting their recall ability four years after the events.

With regard to the recording of particular visits or discussions, it is frequently not possible to discern from the recorded entries whether, for example, Ms. Wahlstrom was primarily concerned with improving the marital relationship of Morris Beckford and Beverley Lorrington, or effecting a change in the quality of parenting by the Beckfords of their children. It is also not clear whether, and to what extent, Ms. Wahlstrom and Miss Leong viewed, as part of the purpose of contact with the Beckford family, regular reviews of the children's development in terms of their health and general well-being. What is singularly lacking from both Ms. Wahlstrom's and Miss Leong's notes – particularly once the children had been returned home in April 1982 – is a record of either, or both of them having exclusively focused their attention on the children, in particular on Jasmine. There is not a single entry that either worker ever spoke to the child, either alone or in the presence of her parents; there is no entry that either was looking for, or saw any sign of possible further abuse. There is no entry that Ms. Wahlstrom ever took Jasmine out for a walk or saw her at school, other than on the one occasion in April 1983 when Beverley Lorrington was present. Miss Causby, in answer to a question from Mr. Courtnay Abel, what she would expect in the report of the social worker, replied that she would have expected regularly for her to have summarised how she viewed the children's progress. It is not a question only of recording what she saw of the children and heard from Jasmine. There was nothing recorded about the parents' perception of how they were coping with the children, and how the children were responding. Again, Miss Causby: "I have not seen any clear assessment of the children in terms of how the parents viewed the children, how they disciplined the children, how they say they treated the children on a day-to-day basis, or any details of what the interactions between the children and the parents were like." We have read and re-read Ms. Wahlstrom's notes, and we too could find nothing there from which we could determine the factors that would lead a reasonable reader of the notes to make any assessment of the risk (or lack of risk) of further child abuse. The one entry on the visit to the school stands out as a shining exception, instead of being just one more example. We would add that Miss Leong's notes are not entirely bereft of such information, but they are still barely adequate.

Had the objectives and purposes, generally and specifically, been spelt out clearly in the records it would have been immeasurably easier to determine to what extent those objectives and purposes had been achieved, and consequently to know what the next step in the process of rehabilitation should be. It is a matter of criticism that Mrs. Dietmann, as Ms. Wahlstrom's supervisor and herself as a not infrequent recorder of events in the Social Worker's Report, failed utterly to observe the cardinal principle that records should reveal the clarity of objectives and purposes. In the sense that Ms. Wahlstrom was the field worker and not in the line of management she may be excused for thinking that her recording, which was, at least until the last six months of Jasmine's life, meticulous in its adherence to detailing every action taken or incident occurring, complied with the standards demanded. That it palpably did not is her superior's failure.

It is impossible to say whether, had the objectives and purposes been recorded, the outcome would have been any different from what in fact happened. Clearly, the individuals involved with the family would have had a much clearer picture, and even a more objective view, of the developments and changes taking place. But the absence of declared objectives and purposes throughout the period of April 1982 to July 1984, together with the general skimpiness of any relevant information because of ineffective visits to the house during the last six months of Jasmine's life, makes it tolerably clear that nothing then could have deflected the social workers from an increasingly misplaced optimism about the Beckford family and a devaluation of the Care Orders. Had, of course, Mr. Bishop been apprised of what was happening, we are inclined to think that his initial pessimism might have reasserted itself to counter the growing confidence of Mrs. Dietmann and Ms. Wahlstrom that all was going swimmingly in the Beckford household. If Mr. Bishop had seen the recording of events – as perhaps he should have done at, or just after the birth of Chantelle in December 1983 -- he would have been unjustifiably reassured that his early pessimism had been allayed.

We strongly recommend that paragraphs 44(A)-8 and 52(B)-10 of the Code of Prac-

tice for Social Workers Dealing with Child abuse (1985) formulated by the British Association of Social Workers, should be prefaced by a statement that the primary obligation of social workers and their supervisors is to ensure that the clarity of objectives and purposes is a prerequisite to the proper standards of recording. And we recommend that Brent's Policy Memorandum on Child Abuse should likewise proclaim this principle.

We divide the remainder of this chapter into two main sections. The first section considers the documentation used by the individuals and agencies in Jasmine's case. The second section is devoted to the manner in which documentation should be gathered and collated whenever there is to be a child abuse inquiry, either by way of an internal inquiry or (as here) an independent public inquiry.

Documentation used in Jasmine Beckford's case
We have been provided with the Social Worker's Report and the Health Visitor's notes. The notes made by Mrs. Dietmann as the supervisor and by the Family Aide, were incorporated in Ms. Wahlstrom's Social Worker's Report; there is no objection to that so long as the persons making the entries are clearly indicated. This was not always the case in the reports. They consisted of a set of diarised entries recording visits for the Beckford family as a unit.

Ms. Wahlstrom recorded almost all of her visits, successfully or unsuccessfully accomplished, to the Beckford household (For some inexplicable reason four intended visits in March 1983 and three intended visits in February 1984 did not appear in the Report, although Ms. Wahlstrom had noted them in her personal diary). By contrast the Health Visitor's notes were helpfully individualised into the card for each child and a separate card for the whole family. Each card contained a series of diarised events. We do not think it necessary that the Social Worker's Reports should likewise be divided up, so long as each entry differentiates between data referable to each child and to the parents.

Each worker went her own way, and their respective records were never cross-referenced, or inspected by the other. This is what Dahl and Lindblom have described as "disjointed incrementalism".* **We recommend that periodically – preferably as and when the two agencies' representatives meet at case conferences or statutory case reviews – their records should be available to all the participants at those meetings for them to consult.** Exchange of information is vital, not merely orally but documentarily, in pursuance of the bi- and multi-disciplinary administration of the child abuse system. If only the two workers on this case had compared notes, they would have quickly discovered that they were being told different and contradictory stories by Beverley Lorrington.

The Health Visitor's records inevitably covered a more extensive period, from Jasmine's birth at Hammersmith Hospital on 2 December 1979. (Ms. Wahlstrom's notes begin with the events of 4 August 1981 onwards). The Health Visitor's records kept until Jasmine's admission to hospital in August 1981 were not revealed to the Case Conferences of 6 and 20 August 1981, including the tell-tale failure of Jasmine to thrive, evidenced by Miss Knowles' observation of 8 June 1981 that Jasmine was a "thin, miserable-looking child." Although Miss Knowles communicated verbally to the Case Conferences the purport of that and other of her recordings about Jasmine's weight, no documentary evidence was produced. It should have been. The percentile chart on which Miss Knowles started in October 1980 to record Jasmine's weight lay in the clinic's file, unseen and untouched by anybody else.

---

* *Politics, Economics and Welfare: planning and politico-economic system resolved into basic social processes*, University of Chicago Press (1976)

Hospital records

The clinical notes of St. Charles' Hospital on the two Beckford children in August 1981 were similarly not disclosed to the Case Conferences. They ought to have been. The clinical notes on Louise Beckford, which apparently included (according to Dr. Warner) a "number of acutely relevant entries" referable to both Louise and Jasmine, have gone missing. We are, therefore, in no position to comment on their relevance generally to child abuse beyond what they recorded about the orthopaedic and radiological aspects of Jasmine's injuries. We think that, where there is a suspicion of non-accidental injury, the hospital authorities should carefully note anything that might contribute to the general picture of child abuse, and that such documented information should be communicated to case conferences. In chapter 12 we have recommended that there should be a statutory duty on health authorities to supply information to the relevant local authority Social Services Department.

Format of social workers' records

The records produced were, as we have indicated, set out in diarised form, with space for dates and times, and with a portion for straight narrative. What is not immediately apparent on the face of the records is whether Jasmine had in fact been seen, or not. This is particularly true of the entries in the Social Worker's Reports, since they deal consistently and only with the family. The separation of comment on the child from that on her parents appears only in the course of reading the narrative, and is not highlighted in any way. We have contrasted with the Health Visitor's cards. Even this practice did not indicate clearly whether a child had been seen or not, because the information would be recorded on the child's separate card even though he or she had not actually been seen, but where someone else had supplied the information. The entry would not then state whether or not the child had been seen. If the value of separate cards is to be maximised, entries on any child's card should be made *only* where the child has *actually* been seen. In this way it would become immediately apparent whether the child has not been seen for some time. Alternatively, a system of regular review forms should be instituted (e.g. weekly, bi-weekly or monthly) in which the individual worker is required to undertake to state whether the child has been seen or not. this could conveniently be placed on the front cover of the file for the retriever of the file to notice instantly that the child has, or has not been seen. In Jasmine's case it is common knowledge that she had been seen only once in 1984 – on 12 March 1984. Between September and the end of 1983 she was seen once, fleetingly, when on 13 December 1983 Ms. Wahlstrom was delivering Christmas presents. A similar situation of a child in care not being seen for 10 months would have been starkly noticed at the time it was happening, if the facts had been highlighted contemporaneously.

Review of Records and information transference

It is obvious that records need not merely to be kept, but that they are accurate, referred to by those involved in the case and reviewed frequently to detect inconsistencies, and to have verified that which is unsubstantiated. If information is to be transferred from one record to another it must be done fully and accurately.

We give one example of an inconsistency in Miss Leong's notes. On 29 November 1983 she recorded: "School medical arranged. Jasmine removed from school on 25.11.83 'moved'." On 20 December 1983 a visit is noted as having taken place, "Jasmine not seen, reported as at nursery school". We have noted in chapter 10 the unforgivable inaccuracy of this entry. Princess Frederica Primary School shut down for the Christmas holidays on 16 December 1983. Finally, on an undated occasion in January 1984, it is noted that "Michael Jones (speech therapist) made school visit to Princess Frederica.

Informed child left on 7.10.83." These entries are clearly internally inconsistent with each other. Yet, while they are all recorded within a short space of time — 3 months — nothing seems to have been done by the Health Visitor's supervisor* to check the inconsistencies and to verify the facts. If records are never referred to or reviewed regularly, such inconsistencies will go unnoticed and the records are rendered useless. The mere fact that information supplied is contradictory may itself be an indication that the suppliers of it are telling different agencies different stories, as we have observed in the case of Beverley Lorrington telling Miss Leong one thing and Ms. Wahlstrom another. This in turn is an indication of something not quite right within the family.

Transferred information is likewise important. We give two instances of inaccurate and incomplete transferance within Brent Social Services Department's records. The first was on the occasion in November 1982 that it was decided that Jasmine and Louise should be taken off the non-accidental injury register. A form entitled *Change of Circumstances — Case Closure* was filled in by Ms. Wahlstrom and countersigned by Mr. Bishop. It had at the top two boxes marked Tier 1 and Tier 2, a reference to the category of child at risk used by Health Visitors. The tick was placed in the wrong box. The brief details said: "Parents have improved their marital relationship and are able to communicate with each other," and the details of decision or change in circumstances recorded "No signs of stress in the family." This form did not mention the fact that only a week prior to the decision there had been marital problems which were clearly noted by Ms. Wahlstrom in her Social Worker's Report, but nowhere else. Her entry for 4 November 1982 chronicled a build-up of matrimonial disharmony, and recorded that "Beverley talking about leaving him and taking the children with her," which incidentally would be a breach of a Care Order, if done without authority of Brent Social Services. While Beverley Lorrington and Morris Beckford might have been able to iron out their problems in the few days between the date of Ms. Wahlstrom's visit and the preparation of the form — which was a possibility, since Ms. Wahlstrom the next day (5 November) stated that "Beverley confident that she will be able to talk to Morris about the situation" — it was grossly inaccurate to record on the form on 12 November that there were "no signs of stress".

The second instance relates to a period in April 1983 when Social Services decided to apply to the magistrates for a revocation of the Care Order. At that time Beverley Lorrington had just become pregnant with her third child. On 19 April 1983, on a visit to the Beckfords, Ms. Wahlstrom records Beverley Lorrington's visit to hospital that day and the opinion that she probably had an infection, "but she might also be pregnant." The Statutory Case Review of the previous day (18 April) made no mention of this, although earlier that day Ms. Wahlstrom had arranged the next day's hospital appointment and added in her records the "possibility that B is pregnant." In the form sent by the Area Manager to the Principal Court Officer on 5 May 1983 no mention was made of the fact that Beverley Lorrington was expecting her third child. This form, which was signed by Mr. Bishop, contains headings requiring factual background to, and reasons for the application to revoke the Care Order. While it is true that the form's precise wording did not seek information about future additions to the family, it could hardly be argued that the pregnancy of a mother, whose two children under the age of 4 had been seriously abused less than two years earlier, was irrelevant. We have indicated earlier our view that the forthcoming addition to a family where the existing children are the subject of Care Orders is of supreme importance. That Beverley Lorrington's pregnancy was not recorded in the relevant documentation, leading up to the

---

* It is fair to note that it was in December 1983 that Miss Tyler was handing over to Miss Baichoo.

228

application to the court to revoke the Care Orders, only goes to show how unimportant, if not irrelevant, Area 6 staff thought that fact was. That apart, it was actually misleading both the Court Officer, Mr. Thompson, and the magistrates not to have mentioned the fact.

Here again, had the records been thoroughly reviewed by Mrs. Dietmann and the information in them been correctly transferred to their documents, the inconsistencies and misinformation would have been noticed and corrected.

The Health Visitor's family card

While Miss Leong's cards for the three children record beyond December 1983, the time of Chantelle's birth, information on the family card stops abruptly on 20 December 1983. In Brent the family card was not an obligatory document. It is up to each Health Visitor to decide whether or not to keep a separate card for recording information referable to the family. Miss Leong told us that she stopped writing up notes on the Beckford family card after 20 December 1983, because in her opinion there was nothing of any importance to record about that family after that date, notwithstanding the arrival of a newly-born baby, a potentially stressful period for any family and particularly the mother with three children under the age of 4, let alone for a mother handicapped as a parent in a household where child abuse had taken place. If family cards do have a use beyond the use of the individual children's cards, they should be made obligatory.

Sources of information

In BASW's Code of Practice (1975) and in their latest (1985) recommendations for revising that Code of Practice, emphasis has been placed on the duty to record every visit, telephone call, message, discussion with seniors or other workers, including the dates of these events. There is also a requirement that the source of all information and messages should be made absolutely clear in the case record. By these standards Ms. Wahlstrom's recording of the case was good, in so far as she does record clearly the persons with whom she had contact. But in one important respect she failed to comply with the standard of recording.

When Jasmine began to attend at Princess Frederica Nursery School, Ms. Wahlstrom telephoned the school. Her entry for 11 January 1983 recorded "T/C to Princess Frederica's Primary School. Jasmine *has* started school part-time. Left my name for school to contact Area 6 if there is a problem." The record does not indicate to whom Ms. Wahlstrom spoke. For all the world, it could have been the Head Teacher, the school secretary, a teacher, the Education Welfare Officer, or the School Caretaker. We now know, from Miss Cowgill's scribbled entry on the fly-leaf of her daily diary, that she took the call from Ms. Wahlstrom. No one else in Brent Borough Council, not even the staff of the school, knew that. Again on 11 April 1983, when Ms. Wahlstrom went with Beverley Lorrington and Louise to visit Jasmine's "teachers", she did not record the teachers she spoke to. The teachers at the school at the time gave evidence before us. They could recall no occasion when they spoke to Ms. Wahlstrom. Lastly, on 15 April 1984, when Ms. Wahlstrom again telephoned the school and was told that Jasmine had not attended school since September 1983, there is no record of the person who supplied that information.

While these are only three occurrences when Ms. Wahlstrom did not comply with the standard of recording, they all three occurred at crucial moments in Jasmine's life. Before she started attending Princess Frederica Nursery School, Jasmine had been going to Mortimer Road Day Nursery, run by Brent Social Services Department. As such, the Social Services Department were able to monitor Jasmine's record of attendance, and did so through the day nursery officer in charge, Miss Proudlock. Social Services Department

229

would not automatically be informed of any non-attendance of Jasmine at Princess Frederica Primary School (which is run by the Education Department of Brent Borough Council) and indeed Social Services were not informed. In these circumstances it would have been good practice for Ms. Wahlstrom to have recorded clearly the name of the person to whom she spoke on the telephone on 11 January 1983 and the names of the teachers whom she says she met on 14 April 1983. Furthermore, sound practice would dictate that Ms. Wahlstrom should have confirmed by letter the information she communicated on the telephone to Miss Cowgill. In that way the information would have been received by the school secretary and percolated to the teaching staff.

Brent Health Authority's records

There is one aspect of documentation that is peculiarly relevant to Brent Health Authority. We have stated that in the recording of child abuse cases information must be both accurate and effective. It is also important that the filing and keeping of records must be efficient and systematic. Systematic filing is essential if information is to be readily traced and identified. It is an insurance against records being lost, mislaid or overlooked. The filing system in Brent Health District (later Brent Health Authority) during 1981-1984 left a great deal to be desired. Miss Baichoo, who was the senior nurse for Health Visiting in Brent Health Authority from December 1983 to December 1984, impressed us greatly by her forthright manner and professional approach to the question. Her memorandum of 17 July 1984 on the health services' role in the Beckford case (which we have reproduced in Chapter 12), submitted to her superiors only 12 days after Jasmine's death, accords broadly with our view of the evidence concluded after 37 days of hearing witnesses, fully examined and cross-examined. We think that not only is it a remarkable document, but it displayed qualities of rare percipience and professional judgment. We unhesitatingly accept her judgment of the state of the filing system that she encountered in Brent.

The files relating to children on the non-accidental injury register were, Miss Baichoo said, "in a terribly cluttered state, which became overpowering as I went through them to sort them out." Not only were the files "cluttered", but Miss Baichoo also was not supplied with all the files at one time. After several months employed by Brent she received "a further set of bundles relating to children on the registers." We can support this statement by the fact that we too did not receive all the documentation we needed until Miss Goodrich was briefed by Brent Health Authority after we began our oral hearings. In order to familiarise herself with the work that was being carried out under her supervision, Miss Baichoo had to spend much time at home, out of working hours, sorting through the jumble of files. On top of all this she felt that there was no "set policy for transfer of notes within the unit itself."

The combination of these factors led to complaints being brought to Miss Baichoo from her staff. Her own words depict a deplorable state of affairs, which we hope has been remedied.

> "I got this impression [of no system of close liaison between the nursing personnel and administration personnel] from various complaints that I had been having from my staff, from various things that I had found out had gone wrong, from various dissatisfactions they set out to me about not knowing that the [Beckford] family had been moved or they had bits of records here and there and things have been lost generally."

230

The confusion was worse confounded by the fact that when documents were transferred, they were transferred from, and to administrative clerks, so that field workers were kept ignorant of what was happening. The problems which Miss Baichoo pinpointed were particularly acute in the case papers relating to Jasmine Beckford at the time when she stopped attending Princess Frederica Nursery School. When Jasmine ceased attending the school in the autumn of 1983 the school filled out a form A3, dated week-ending 25 November 1983. The entry was as follows:

2. *List of children who have left during the week*

Class	Name of child in full	Date of Birth	Address and also new address if removed to another address.	Reasons for leaving
N p.m.	BECKFORD Jasmine	2.12.79	57 College Road	Moved

The document, which contained the Delphic word "moved", was sent by the school to the clinic clerk, who affixed the Brent Health Authority date stamp of 28 November 1983. This form would, therefore, have bypassed the Health Visitors because of the detachment of administrative staff from nursing personnel, unless the clinic's clinical staff had thought to bring the matter to the attention of Health Visitors. Since the reason for leaving was given by the school as "moved", it had not been appreciated that, although Jasmine was supposed to have moved out of the school's area, her sister, Louise, had not. Miss Baichoo made the appropriate comment on this piece of inept administration: "That is not unusual. If you have records moving from clerk to clerk they will not necessarily know the numbers in the family and that was the reason why I had asked since February that field workers should be informed always in cases of transfer."

Yet a further difficulty that can arise if the filing system is not efficient is where several field workers are involved – there were at least four Health Visitors for Jasmine in her short life, Miss Hindle (1979-1980), Miss Knowles (1980-September 1981 and April-July 1982), Miss Bowden (September 1981-April 1982) and Miss Leong (July 1982-July 1984). A hand-over of a case to the next field worker is never easy. But to facilitate the transfer of relevant information there must be a sound system of availability of documentary material. This should not be difficult for intra-agency administrators to operate, even if it presents problems for inter-agency communication. In Jasmine's case it was rendered impossible for Miss Leong to tell Ms. Wahlstrom about Form A3, and what information it contained, simply because she did not herself possess the information.

By memoranda, dated 17 February and 18 July 1984, Miss Baichoo put forward proposals dealing with the transfer of records. These proposals were not accepted by her superiors, on the grounds that they were not considered viable. Undaunted, Miss Baichoo proceeded to take action and, supported by Miss Martin, who took up the post of Director of Nursing Services in September 1983, did effectively put her own proposals into action.

We conclude that the filing system in Brent Health Authority during Jasmine Beckford's life was pitifully inadequate. It was a contributory factor in the mismanagement of the child abuse system in Brent.

Minuting of Case Conferences
Social workers rightly value Case Conference minutes as a crucial working tool in the administration of the child abuse system, recording both the information supplied by the participants and opinions by professionals from various disciplines, and indicating

231

what actions are to be taken by field workers and others. The minutes provide the fulcrum, or springboard for all future work in child abuse cases.

Minute-taking is a skilled secretarial activity. In this case the minutes of both case conferences of 6 and 20 August 1981 were taken by Miss Knibbs' secretary, and we have no reason to doubt their quality. All the twelve witnesses we heard agreed that the minutes were a fair and broadly accurate record of what had been said. But one issue about the minutes attracted our attention, and we think it worthy of comment.

In the minutes of the Case Conference of 20 August 1981 a part of what Miss Carol Rogers said had been expunged by Tipp-ex after the minute-taker had drafted the typescript preparatory to distribution (At every conference subsequent to the initial one the accuracy of the minutes of the previous meeting should be checked and approved). The minute-taker had originally recorded Miss Rogers as saying that "both children could be fostered long-term in Harlesden, almost immediately moving onto adoption in due course." When distributed to the participants, it read, "both children could be fostered in Harlesden almost immediately." This erasure of part of what Miss Rogers said was never the subject of any checking or approval, other than that which we are about to describe. We note, incidentally, that one of the declared purposes of the Case Conference of 20 August 1981 was "to check the minutes [of the earlier Case Conference] for accuracy". The next Case Conference, on 5 April 1982, had no such declared purpose, and no check for accuracy was made.

During the Inquiry, we were able to establish that Mr. Bishop, as Chairman of the Case Conference had taken upon himself to remove the part indicated. He did so because he felt that the entry did not "reflect what [he] thought was decided at the Case Conference." After giving a rather tortuous and disingenuous explanation for having made the alteration without consulting anyone, Mr. Bishop conceded that it was bad practice. If what Mr. Bishop did was something out of the ordinary, we would not have thought it worthwhile mentioning such a venial offence in our report, but would have regarded the public revelation of his peccadillo quite sufficient. But we have reason to think that the practice of chairmen of case conferences altering minutes, unilaterally, is widespread.

Miss McAree said that if she discovered any discrepancy between what she had said at a case conference and what was later recorded in the minutes, she would ring up the person who had signed the minutes and arrange for a suitable correction. That suggested to us that from time to time there are discrepancies, which of course would not necessarily involve the chairman making any unilateral alteration of them. But Dr. Warner, who in the past has taken the chair at case conferences, was asked by Miss Baxendale whether he ever found in the minutes something with which he did not agree. Dr. Warner's answer was revealing: "Normally the case conference minutes are a reasonably accurate reflection of what has been said, because they are very carefully checked by the chairman; when I have been chairman, I have sometimes made some minor alterations but I have never actually suggested any changes when I have not been the chairman of the conference."

There are obvious practical difficulties about leaving the checking of the accuracy of minutes to a subsequent case conference, which may not occur for months after, and at which not all the original participants will be present; and there may even be no subsequent case conference at all. It may be that the individual whose remarks have been inaccurately recorded will not raise the matter either immediately with the chairman or at any subsequent conference. But we are convinced about one thing, and that is that it is improper for the chairman to delete, augment or in any material way amend what has been transcribed by the minute-taker, without at least first getting the consent of the relevant participant to any alteration. Strictly speaking, only the subsequent case conference could approve any alteration to the minutes of the previous case conference.

We recommend that BASW's Code of Practice and Brent Policy Memorandum should state clearly that those responsible for the preparation and signing of case conference minutes should observe the rule that only the reconvened case conference or, possibly, the relevant participant can authorise an alteration. What we suggest is the better practice, is that the transcription should be left unaltered, the chairman indicating by way of a footnote what he understands the participant to have said. The subsequent case conference can then resolve the matter, with the rival texts in front of them.

Princess Frederica Nursery School

The records disclosed to us concerning Princess Frederica primary school were the Nursery School Daily Register and Jasmine's Index Card. The index cards used by the school record the basic details about the children attending the school. They record whether or not any child has a social worker, or is under a Care Order. In the case of Jasmine Beckford nothing of that kind was noted on her index card, or about her having been subjected to child abuse, notwithstanding the fact that Miss Cowgill, the former headmistress, had noted the interest of Ms. Wahlstrom and Area 6 in Jasmine's welfare. This information should have been, but was not transferred onto Jasmine's index card; indeed, it got no further than the flyleaf of Miss Cargill's diary. If the index card system is to be of any value, it is necessary that each and every piece of pertinent information should find its way onto the cards. The extent to which the index card system used by Princess Frederica Primary School is actually of value in any child abuse case was questioned by Miss Cowgill's evidence that those cards would probably not record whether a child was on the Child Abuse Register, or was even subject to a Care Order. This was because, she said, the cards are "not exactly private and not exactly public, but they were there and anyone could pick them up." There does not appear to be any centralised system of recording such information at the nursery part of the primary school, according to a member of staff, Mrs. Ashley Player.

In 1977/8, Brent Area Review Committee produced a booklet entitled *Non Accidental Injury to Children: Guidelines for All Professional Agencies Involved in Child Care in Brent*, known as the Green Book (See Appendix H). Page 8 of this child's guide to child abuse cases is headed, *Teachers and Staff in School*, and outlines certain basic procedures. In November 1977, Miss Rickus, the then Director of Education for the London Borough of Brent, had sent a letter and instructions to all school heads in the area. These instructions, entitled *Non-Accidental Injury: Action to be Taken by Teachers in Staff in Schools in Cases of Suspected Non-Accidental Injury*, further outlined basic procedures. The letter requested schools to display these instructions for all staff to see. Neither the instructions, nor anything like them was affixed to any notice board at Princess Frederica Nursery School, and the Green Book was wholly unknown to the staff. Not one of the witnesses who gave evidence could recognise the Green Book when it was shown to him, nor had any one of them (Miss Cowgill, Mr. McErlean, Mrs. Felix, Mrs. Ashley Player or Miss Baines) seen it prior to the Inquiry. According to Mr. McErlean, the Deputy Head of the school, the Green Book had been "unearthed" during the period of our Inquiry.

If the Area Review Committee and the Education Department of the London Borough of Brent are desirous that their guidance to schools on the administration of the child abuse system should be disseminated and become part of education welfare, they must ensure that any documentation supplied to educational establishments is both seen and digested by staff, and is ready to hand when required. Preparing and publishing such documents is a thorough waste of time and effort, if the guidance they contain simply never percolates to those for whom it is intended. Otherwise the exercise is pointless.

Preparation of Documentation Pending an Inquiry
Where a child has died while in the care of the local authority, some kind of review or inquiry is likely to be undertaken, whether it is conducted by management within the local authority or by an independent review panel. Whatever form of inquiry is chosen, the documentation relating to the case needs immediately to be assembled. The files of the Social Services Department, including Social Worker's Report and Court Officers' reports and various internal memoranda and correspondence with parents and foster-parents, all need to be collated in suitable bundles. Additionally, the relevant documentation should include the relevant child care legislation and government circulars on implementation of the law in practice; agency and inter-agency policy and procedural manuals; reports of the individual agencies' case conferences and statutory case reviews; relevant parts of the transcript of any trial of those held criminally responsible for the child abuse; and previously published reports of child abuse inquiries.

In the case of Jasmine Beckford, the Social Services Department had extracted all the documentation from its files in the Autumn of 1984 and they were readily available to us. By the time our Inquiry was set up at the end of March 1985, it was possible for counsel to the Inquiry and panel members to read much of the documentation that ultimately constituted the totality of the material.

Brent Health Authority, however, had collected together only a fraction of the relevant documentary material when we began our hearings, and it became necessary to call for the full documentation when the Inquiry was well under way. While the trickle of health service documentation did not hamper our work, it made for untidiness in the assembled material and may have caused frustration among those legal representatives advising and acting for the parties to the Inquiry. We stress the importance that all relevant agencies should collate the material and hand it over to the panel of inquiry at the earliest possible opportunity. The relevant health authority ought also to be responsible for obtaining hospital records from its own medical institutions as well as from other hospitals that may have been involved in the child abuse case.

The Commissioner for the Metropolitan Police readily supplied us with all the statements in the proceedings, *R* v. *Beckford and Lorrington*, and provided us with the transcripts of the proceedings of trial at the Central Criminal Court. He also supplied us with the post-mortem report of the forensic pathologist to the Coroner, and gave us access to the post-mortem photographs. We record that we had nothing short of the optimum assistance from the Solicitors' Department of the Metropolitan Police.

If the inquiry is to be prompt, efficient and scrupulously fair to all those who are professionally and otherwise affected by the inquiry, *all* agencies which have handled the case must submit their documentation instantly the inquiry is set up. Even if at that time the documentation has not been neatly arranged, and has to be extracted from disparate files and locations, it is better that it should be supplied in that form than that its disclosure should be delayed. The inquiry team can readily organise the material in a way that best suits its method of conducting the inquiry.

CHAPTER 23

General Practitioners

The general practitioner has no statutory duties in relation to child care. Nevertheless, he occupies a unique position in the management of the child abuse system, since it is he who will frequently be the first to be made aware of the signs of child abuse occurring within the family, and, therefore, able to set in motion the child protection service. When a child is presented to the general practitioner, his primary duty is to diagnose the injury and to secure immediate treatment and care for the child. Often the doctor may suspect that the injury is non-accidental, but the comparative rarity of acquaintance with child abuse cases may lead a doctor not to refer the child to hospital. In the recent report of the Inquiry into the case of Reuben Carthy (September 1985) the Standing Inquiry Panel of Nottinghamshire Area Review Committee received evidence of recent, yet unpublished research by Dr. Peter Barbor that "of 82 diagnosed fractured ribs in 35 children under the age of 5 years, no fracture was diagnosed clinically and was only apparent following a skeletal X-ray survey."* These fractures were, with the exception of injuries resulting from an identifiable major incident (such as a road accident) the result of child abuse. These facts emphasise the difficulty of diagnosing serious child abuse and the need for doctors to refer a child for expert diagnosis. The problem lies in the fact that, unfortunately, far too many general practitioners still do not operate within the philosophy of the management of the child abuse system, which stresses the need for close co-operation between all the professionals working in the field of child care, despite precatory words from governmental authorities and responsible voluntary agencies. We endorse what the Derbyshire Area Review Committee said to general practitioners in its area: "It must, however, be stressed that medical practitioners have no statutory responsibilities and must act as members of a multi-disciplinary team in the management of child abuse rather than as individuals." (see annex to this chapter). In the case under Inquiry there was no obstacle to the immediate involvement of child abuse procedures, such as have occurred in other cases. But we did hear much evidence about the role of general practitioners in the functioning of the management of the child abuse system, both immediately before and after the making of the Care Orders, which lent support to the substantial body of opinion that suggests that many general practitioners isolate themselves, and are isolated from the efforts which other professionals devote to ensure good liaison and common action in order to protect children from abuse by their parents.

We have been told by many of our witnesses, both medical and non-medical, that it is rare for general practitioners to attend a case conference convened within the child abuse procedures. The evidence in the case of the Beckford children amply supported that view. None of the nine case conferences or statutory case reviews was attended by a general practitioner; on the three occasions when a general practitioner was invited, apologies for absence were sent. A major difficulty for many general practitioners, as was reported in LASSL(76)27, in attending conferences is the fact that that they work, not in group practices but single-handed. This is particularly so among general practitioners in inner city areas, where most child abuse cases come to the notice of the authorities. These general practitioners also often do not have an attached health visitor who could report to a case conference on their behalf.

---

* para 151, Report of the Inquiry into the case of Reuben Carthy (1985).

Dr. Debabrata Mallik was such a GP. In the summer of 1981 Beverley Lorrington and her daughters, Jasmine and Louise, were on Dr. Mallik's 'list'. On 1 August 1981 Beverley Lorrington took Louise to see Dr. Mallik because the child had a painful arm. Dr. Mallik thought that Louise had probably broken her arm and advised that she should be taken to St. Mary's Hospital. Louise was subsequently admitted to St. Charles' Hospital. On 4 August Beverley Lorrington and Miss McLean took Jasmine to see Dr. Mallik. Dr. Mallik formed the opinion that Jasmine had probably broken her left thigh and suggested that the child be taken to hospital straight away. He said Jasmine should go to St. Charles' where her sister was. Beverley objected, because St. Charles' "had asked a lot of questions which she didn't like" − Jasmine was taken to St. Charles'. Dr. Mallik did not see Beverley or the children again. Dr. Mallik told us that he had not considered that either Louise or Jasmine had been battered when he saw them. He also told us that, although he knew he had some fostered children in his practice − presumably because of receiving fees for the statutory examination − he was not aware that he had children who were 'in the care of the local authority', nor was he aware of any children who had been registered under the child abuse procedures. Dr. Mallik was invited to the Case Conference held on 6 August, to which he sent his apologies, but did not recall recall whether he had been invited to the Case Conference held on 20 August. He is recorded as having sent apologies (see Appendix G:2). He did say, however, that he had not been invited to any case conferences since that time, or before.

After spending some weeks in St. Charles' Hospital, Jasmine joined Louise in the care of Mr. and Mrs. Probert who, on 25 September 1981, registered both children on the 'list' of Dr. Elizabeth Price. On 17 November both children were taken by Ms. Wahlstrom to be seen by the Health Visitor and the GP in the Harrow area where the foster-parents resided. The doctor who saw the children was Dr. Justice, a partner of Dr. Price. He recorded briefly in the Family Practitioner Records that Jasmine was "being fostered long-term by Mrs. Probert. Sister also fostered. Past medical history: fractured left femur, query non-accidental injury, immunised Diphtheria, Tetanus, Polio x 3 and BCG". The wallet also contained the minutes of the Case Conference held on 20 August. This record was produced by Dr. Price at the Inquiry on 1 May 1985. It had been in her possession continuously from the time when Jasmine was registered with her. There was no record of the practice (Drs. Price and Justice) being consulted after 17 November 1981.

The children were returned to their parents in April 1982. Ms. Wahlstrom recorded in her notes for 8 April 1982, prior to the children going home: "Beverley has arranged to register with Dr. Khan"; on 20 April 1982 she recorded: "She (Beverley) had spent one and a half hours in Dr. Khan's surgery with the children crying of hunger". This was most probably the occasion when Dr. Kavarana (assistant to Dr. Khan) completed a temporary registration card for Jasmine, which came to be included in the records held by Dr. Price.

The Beckford/Lorrington family had quite clearly been permanently resident in Dr. Khan's practice area since they had been rehoused in March 1982. We were not presented with any evidence to suggest that Beverley Lorrington or Morris Beckford considered that their residence was temporary. The social workers clearly believed Dr. Khan to be the permanent family doctor, since on 20 October 1982 Ms. Wahlstrom recorded "telephone call to Dr. Khan/Kavarana to invite her to the Case Conference. Dr. Khan decided not to come to the Case Conference but would like minutes sent to her." (This is a reference to the Case Conference of 9 November 1982 when it was being proposed to remove the children from the child abuse register).

Dr. Kavarana told us that before the telephone call she did not know that "Louise and Jasmine were children at risk", nor was she able to know from the children's medical

236

records and the Case Conference record within. Because the family had been temporarily registered – wrongly – this crucial information remained unseen in the records at Dr. Price's practice. Dr. Kavarana told us that she did not take any particular steps to see the children after receiving the telephone call, because she thought they would have gone back to Dr. Mallik. However, Dr. Kavarana did not send the Case Conference notes to the Family Practitioner Committee, to be associated with the permanent record.

Temporary resident status means that the doctor providing 'temporary care' does not have any previous medical records. Morris Beckford and Beverley Lorrington remained as temporary residents until registered with Dr. Khan's practice "permanently with me (Dr. Kavarana) through the pregnancy". During Beverley Lorrington's pregnancy, which was described by Dr. Kavarana as "very tough", Dr. Kavarana did not seek extra help from the Health Visitor, although she initially discussed with Ms. Wahlstrom and Beverley Lorrington the difficulties the latter might have to face, – knowing she already had two children.

Dr. Kavarana gave no further thought to Louise and Jasmine during the pregnancy, and said she considered that when Beverley Lorrington was attending during pregnancy that "a partner might be looking after them or she might have left them at the day nursery. I didn't enquire." Dr. Kavarana told us that social workers had sometimes sent her a list of children who were 'in care', "especially when there is talk of mishandling or abuse; they always get in touch with us." Dr. Kavarana has never attended any case conferences, because of pressures on her time. She had not raised this issue with the Family Practitioner Committee, nor was she aware of the work of the Area Review Committee in connection with the Beckford case or anything else.

It is a matter of fact that when any patient is treated as 'temporary' the only records available will be those that were contemporaneously recorded on previous occasions that the patient had been treated by the same practice. Otherwise the patient's NHS notes will be contained within the wallet, maintained on behalf of the Family Practitioner Committee by the doctor with whom the patient is formally registered. These records will include hospital letters to the GP, and in the case of an abused child should include minutes of case conferences: There is no way that the patient's full medical history can be available to the doctor who is treating her as a temporary patient.

It must be unsound practice not to take steps to find out about a child's previous history when the question of non-accidental injury arises. If Dr. Kavarana believed the family was normally registered with Dr. Mallik, inquiries by the Social Services should have been directed to him, when Dr. Kavarana was approached with regard to attending the Case Conference.

The role of General Practitioners in non-accidental injury has been discussed in, and codified by many Area Review Committees. We append as an annex to this chapter the relevant advice included in the Derbyshire Area Review Committee's 1985 revision of its procedures. **We recommend that Area Review Committees take this as a model.**

ANNEX

GENERAL PRACTITIONERS

1) The immediate treatment and care of an abused child is essential. The need for accurate factual information is paramount in all cases, as it is often the absence of concisely documented information which leads to unnecessary difficulties.

2) In addition to the production of accurate medical information, the General Practitioner has an essential role in the subsequent discussion of the causes of the abuse whether or not the history given is compatible with the nature of the injuries, etc.

3) Where possible an assessment of the child's injuries or state of health should in-

clude a statement about its growth and development, both physical and mental for comparison against that of their peers. A similar assessment of the physical and mental state of the child's parents or other care givers is also advantageous.

4) *It must however be stressed that medical practitioners have no statutory responsibilities and must act as members of a multi-disciplinary team in the management of child abuse rather than as individuals.*

5) *Suggested Procedures to be followed by General Practitioners*

   5.1) Undress the child completely and examine it carefully.

   5.2) Record the nature, site and extent of injuries with diagrams if possible.

   5.3) Record any other findings from the physical examination.

   5.4) Record the height and weight where possible.

   5.5) Record the explanation given to you by the parents or other care givers at the time of examination, for comparison with any later statements which are made.

   5.6) The notes of the examination should be signed and dated.

   5.7) The names and designation of the medical practitioner should be clearly stated.

6) The cases you may see will probably fall into one or more of the following categories:

   6.1) Physical abuse – These need to be referred to the nearest Accident and Emergency Department or Paediatric Department with a letter.

   6.2) Suspected physical abuse – These should be discussed with the Social Worker and/or Health Visitor – referral should be made to the hospital for further diagnosis, if necessary.

   6.3) Severe failure to thrive – These should be discussed with the Social Worker and/or Health Visitor – most cases will require the opinion of a Consultant Paediatrician.

   6.4) Emotional abuse leading to behavioural and/or emotional disturbance - These require consultation with the Social Worker and/or Health Visitor, and in most cases psychiatric help should be sought.

7) It should be borne in mind that subsequent litigation is possible in all cases of child abuse and detailed notes should be kept for future reference. Procedural and practical guidance in cases of difficulty may be obtained from the Managers (Child Abuse).

CHAPTER 24

Area Review Committees

At no stage of the management of the Care Orders by Brent Social Services in respect of the two Beckford children was Brent Area Review Committee ever apprised of the case. It became fleetingly involved in the case only after Jasmine Beckford's death, when Brent Social Services Committee, at its meeting of 5 January 1985, in effect invited the Area Review Committee to take over the question of either conducting an inquiry itself or setting up an independent inquiry. But on 12 February 1985, three days before the Area Review Committee was due to meet at its quarterly meeting, Brent's Policy and Resources Committee reversed the decision of its Social Services Committee, and proceeded to set up this Inquiry.

Brent Area Review Committee had met three days before Jasmine Beckford died, on 2 July 1984, and only at its next meeting, on 5 November 1984, was it informed of the death, although some of its members were painfully aware of the tragedy. At the November meeting, members felt that it was inappropriate that the Committee should discuss the case "due to pending court proceedings." The minutes of that meeting went on to record: "An enquiry would be held and the Chairperson announced that a Social Services internal investigation was under way." We think it would, on the contrary, have been entirely appropriate, indeed essential, that the Area Review Committee should have discussed the case. Hereafter, we indicate that there should be machinery whereby the Area Review Committee takes on board, immediately after the event, the task of conducting an inquiry. Since, however, by the beginning of November Brent Borough Council was in the throes of setting up an inquiry, and because the Standing Inquiry Panel, to which we refer later, authorised by that same meeting of the Area Review Committee, was not in being, there were other sound reasons for leaving the matter to the local authority.

These bald facts impelled us to look at two separate and distinct aspects of the role of Area Review Committees – namely, a) the function of an Area Review Committee in relation to the management of individual cases of child abuse; and b) the role of an Area Review Committee to inquire into the death of, or serious harm to a child, arising from non-accidental causes. Before we deal with these two aspects, we set out briefly the history of Area Review Committees, and refer to some of the problems relating to their composition and status.

Background
Although there had been a move before 1974 towards the establishment of bodies to co-ordinate the various agencies working in the area of child abuse, it was not until after the Maria Colwell Inquiry in that year that official promptings led to the setting up of Area Review Committees. The Committees were established with the status of advisory bodies, with the specific task of advising local authorities and health authorities, as the two main agencies involved, on what measures would ensure the optimum co-operation between their varied groups of professional employees engaged in the management of the child abuse system. A series of circulars, beginning in April 1974, emanated from the Department of Health and Social Security. We cite them here, mainly with reference to the two issues we have selected for treatment in this report.

The first circular was LASSL(74)13-CMO(74)8 of 22 April 1974. The introduction to the circular stated: "Recent cases have underlined the need for regular joint reviews of these measures by all the agencies concerned." It outlined the procedures for care management and rehabilitation of abused children, and went on to make proposals with regard to the local organisation of services, including the establishment of Area Review Committees, together with comments on the nature of training and prevention. The circular set out the tasks of the Review Committees as follows:

(a) advise on the formation of local practice and procedures to be followed in the detailed management of cases;
(b) approve written instructions defining the duties of all personnel concerned with any aspect of these cases;
(c) review the work of case conferences in the area;
(d) provide education and training programmes to heighten awareness of the problem;
(e) collect information about the work being done in the area;
(f) collaborate with adjacent Area Review Committees;
(g) advise on the need for inquiries into cases which appear to have gone wrong and from which lessons could be learned;
(h) provide a forum for consultation between all involved in the management of the problem;
(i) draw up procedures for ensuring continuity of care when the family moves to another area;
(j) consider ways of making it known to the general public that e.g., health visitors, teachers, social workers, the NSPCC and police may be informed about children thought to be ill-treated.

We draw particular attention to paragraphs (c) and (g).

In a circular later that year – LASSL(74)27 of 6 November 1974 – the Director of Social Work Service at the Department wrote: "You will recall the memoranda issued on 22 April this year simply recommended the setting up of Area Review Committees in order to ensure the regular joint review of all aspects of the management of cases", and proceeded to request information of what had been accomplished. The information was analysed and communicated in a further circular in February 1976 – LASSL(76)2 – CMO(76)2. It offered guidance as to minimum standards or safeguards. We mention three features of that circular. First, the circular gave particular guidance with regard to the establishment of central registers. The reported arrangements showed that many registers were kept by Social Services Departments, a lesser number by Area Health Authorities, and in 9 areas they were kept by the local NSPCC unit.

Second, the circular gave detailed advice about case conferences, and described variations in the convening and holding of case conferences which Area Review Committees had agreed upon. We deal with these issues in the next chapter. Third, the question of the involvement of general practitioners was dealt with. Among the difficulties encountered by Area Review Committees was the fact that general practitioners faced the problem of finding time to attend case conferences. This we have dealt with in the last chapter.

Brent Area Review Committee
Brent Area Review Committee was established in 1975 under the Chairmanship of Mr. Whalley, then Director of Social Services. He was succeeded in June 1982, when he retired from being Director, by Miss Valerie Howarth. We are aware that towards the end of 1984 some members of Brent Borough Council had envisaged potential difficulties in having as chairman the Director of Social Services whenever there might be a challenge to the management of a child abuse case by Social Services. This unease surfaced at

the beginning of 1985. While not one of the several members of the Area Review Committee whom we heard in evidence had any complaint about Miss Howarth's chairmanship over the last three years — indeed they complimented her generally, and in particular as having rejuvenated the Committee — there was a feeling that perhaps it was not wise to perpetuate the apparent dominance of Social Services. The Committee had, at its meeting of 5 November 1984, resolved that the "Chairmanship of the Committee shall be the Director of Social Services or Deputy." But some pointed comments from members of Brent Borough Council, and the change of tack in early 1985 which led to the setting up of our Inquiry, have made some people think that a change is now due. We agree.

Dr. Euan Ross told us that he now favoured election of the chairman. He readily acknowledged that Social Services, being the prime agency involved, should provide the secretariat, but that **any member of the Committee, skilled in chairmanship and knowledgeable about the management of the child abuse system, should be an acceptable candidate for taking the chair. We agree, and so recommend.** While we take Miss Howarth's point that such an important office "should not be left to the vagaries of democracy", nevertheless we do think that the appearance, if not the reality of dominance of Social Services gives a bad impression to those who properly seek a truly multidisciplinary approach to the child abuse system. We do think, however, that as part of the servicing of the Area Review Committee the custody of the child abuse register should remain in the hands of a member of the Social Services Department. Mr. Thompson, as Principal Court Officer, has been the custodian. We see no reason to change that appointment in the immediate future.

We were told that in the early days of the Area Review Committee the membership was large — over 50 people — and consequently unwieldy. That led to the setting up of a two-tier system, the full Committee meeting annually and a smaller group coming together quarterly. In the late 1970s the Committee, according to Dr. Ross, "ran so efficiently that it did not quite have the element of debate or input" from other than the Social Services personnel. This was reflected in the ready acceptance of current practices of the Social Services Department, without discussion of its procedures and the belief that they remained unchallengeable. The Register was often referred to as "the Social Services Register" and not that of the Area Review Committee. At its November 1984 meeting, it was stated, for example, under the heading *Statistics*, "there are no longer two tiers of child abuse." There was apparently no discussion on this important topic. These matters seem trifling, but unless members of the Area Review Committee perceive that the established procedures are theirs, they will fail to regard their role on the Committee as significant. It is vital that members from the various disciplines make a pronounced contribution. Otherwise the Committee will merely be paying lip-service to the multi-disciplinary approach that is so loudly proclaimed as the desideratum of the child abuse system.

We think that the present composition of Brent Area Review Committee broadly reflects the varied interest groups and service agencies. We strongly support the additional advice contained in the DHSS circular LASSL(76)2 that there should be a representative of the Law and Administration Department of the local authority. Mr. Forster told us that there is now, although there has not always been in the past, a representative of his Departmenht on the Area Review Committee. We think it is imperative that there should always be a lawyer on the Committee.

Function of Area Review Committees
Superintendent Briggs told us that in his experience on the Area Review Committee it has never looked at individual cases, but has devoted its energies to reviewing procedural problems relating generally to case conferences or to deviations from established stan-

241

dards. Mr. Whalley confirmed this. During his Chairmanship, the Committee did not monitor case conferences. And Mr. Jenkins, the NSPCC representative, said that while the Committee could call for a case at any time and ask what the situation was, it was not written down that it would see certain cases. We think that in this respect Brent Area Review Committee has been wanting. Had any of the Case Conferences or Statutory Case Reviews in the Beckford case been subjected to scrutiny, some of the defects of those conferences to which we have alluded in Chapters 8 to 10 and in the next chapter might have been uncovered and corrected. The Beckford case, from its outset, presented difficulties in the management of the child abuse system. It would have been helpful, to say the least, had Mr. Whalley in 1981 or 1982 (in either his capacity of Director of Social Services or of Chairman of the Area Review Committee) called for a monitoring of the Beckford case. By the time Miss Howarth was in post, after June 1982, it was not too late to do anything in that direction, but we do not blame her, since she had other, more pressing matters to attend to. By the time she had got firmly into the saddle, it was too late. The Beckford children had been removed from the child abuse register within 6 months of Miss Howarth's arrival at Brent. **We recommend that Brent Area Review Committee set in train immediately a system for monitoring individual cases currently being handled by Social Services.**

Child Abuse Inquiries

On 5 November 1984 Brent Area Review Committee passed a resolution giving itself power to appoint a Standing Committee whose responsibility would be to investigate all cases of child abuse where death of, or serious injury to, a child occurs. The Standing Committee would advise the Area Review Committee. We applaud that initiative, and only hope that the power will now be exercised. We commend to Brent Area Review Committee the Standing Inquiry Panel set up in June 1982 by Nottinghamshire Area Review Committee. We are aware that it works well. We set out a model code for a Standing Inquiry Panel, as a variant on the Nottinghamshire one.

Standing Inquiry Panel

The Standing Inquiry Panel shall consist of:-

1. The Chairman of the Brent Area Review Committee.
2. A representative of the Director of Social Services.
3. A representative of Brent Health Authority.
4. A legal representative of the Law and Administration Department of Brent Borough Council.
5. A representative of the NSPCC.
6. The Consultant Community Paediatrician.
7. In cases involving the death of a child, a Chairman of a neighbouring Area Review Committee.

Where the case appears to involve criticism of Brent Social Services or of Brent Health Authority, the chairman of the panel shall be someone other than those members in 1 to 3 above; preferably it shall be the chairman from a neighbouring Area Review Committee or, even better, a legally qualified person. Where the case arouses public disquiet, the Area Review Committee shall itself order an independent inquiry.

Terms of Reference
The terms of reference of the Standing Inquiry Panel shall be:-

(1) To inquire into those cases in which the death of a child appears to have arisen from non-accidental causes, and

(2) To inquire into those cases which, although not involving the death of a child, concern child abuse in circumstances which may have arisen from a failure with regard to procedure

and to ascertain what, if any, lessons can be learnt from the case.

Procedure

(1) Any person may refer a case with a request that the issue raised be enquired into.

(2) A referral shall in the first instance be to the Director of Law and Administration of Brent Borough Council who will:-

    i. form a view as to whether the matters raised fall within the terms of reference of the Standing Inquiry Panel;

    ii. if the matters raised fall within the terms of reference, summon a preliminary meeting of the Panel which will decide the basis on which to proceed depending upon the nature of the case;

    iii. if not within the terms of reference, inform the person who referred the issue of any alternative appropriate procedures available and report to the Area Review Committee on the reason why an Inquiry is not taking place.

(3) The Area Review Committee is to be informed at the earliest opportunity that the Panel is undertaking the Inquiry.

(4) The head of the agency or agencies concerned with the issue shall be informed at the earliest opportunity.

(5) The conduct of the Inquiry shall be at the discretion of the Standing Inquiry Panel depending upon the circumstances of the case.

(6) Any persons requested to appear before the Standing Inquiry Panel shall be given the opportunity of legal, professional association, trade union or other representation as they wish but at their own cost.

(7) On completion of the Inquiry, the Standing Inquiry Panel shall produce a Report for the Area Review Committee with recommendations, as appropriate.

(8) The Area Review Committee shall decide whether it is appropriate that a Report should be forwarded to particular agencies and the form which any such Report should take. The Area Review Committee should consider what action it should take to inform participants of the decisions.

(9) The Chief Officer of any agency involved is to be informed by the Standing Inquiry Panel if it considers it appropriate that further enquiries should be made into matters which lie exclusively within the responsibility of that agency.

Had the Standing Inquiry Panel been in existence at the time of Jasmine Beckford's death, there need have been no delay whatsoever in the setting up of an inquiry. The Panel could have set about its task, irrespective of the criminal proceedings to come. If Brent Area Review Committee had concluded, either at the outset or after the Standing Inquiry Panel had sat and reported, that there had to be a more detailed and extensive inquiry it would have been empowered to set up an inquiry independent of itself.

Two matters occur to us as stemming from such a suggested procedure. The two main agencies within Brent Area Review Committee – Brent Borough Council and Brent Health Authority – will need to consider the funding of the Standing Inquiry Panel. **If ultimately there has to be an independent panel, we recommend that central government,if it does not set up the inquiry, as we have recommended in the Preface, should respond to a reasonable request to fund the inquiry.** For inquiries conducted by the Standing Inquiry Panel, the cost will have to be borne by the two authorities. A fund for this purpose should be set up forthwith.

We are alive to the problem that all inquiries involve busy professional people in giving up their ordinary work for varying periods of time. Inevitably the task tends to fall upon the shoulders of almost entirely one member of the panel. Because of his background and training, the lawyer (if there is one) tends to be more soundly equipped for the task. That is no doubt why independent inquiries are usually chaired by a Queen's Counsel. We think that within the Standing Inquiry Panel this ought to be recognised in any procedure. But a representative from the Law and Administration Department, even if he is a barrister or solicitor, is not sufficiently detached to be the chairman. A chairman of any multi-disciplinary Panel of Inquiry should be drawn from outside the agencies directly involved in the case under inquiry. **We recommend that Brent Area Review Committee immediately give effect to its resolution of 5 November 1984,** and does so along the lines we have indicated.

CHAPTER 25

Case Conferences and Statutory Case Reviews

Nine Case Conferences or Statutory Case Reviews were held in the course of the management of the Beckford case, starting with the initial Case Conference on 6 August 1981, within days of the two Beckford sisters being received into hospital, and ending with the Statutory Case Review of 6 December 1983, when it was decided to reapply for the revocation of the Care Orders. (The minutes of each of those meetings are contained in Appendix G:1-9). We think it may be helpful at the outset to summarise the meetings, with reference only to their structure and purpose. (We have dealt with the substance of those meetings in the context of the events discussed in Chapters 8, 9 and 10.)

6 August 1981   Case Conference, held at St. Charles' Hospital, to determine the cause of injury to the children, and to decide on the action to be taken. The meeting was chaired by Mr. David Bishop. The minutes were taken by Miss Knibbs' secretary.

                           Apart from the members of the Social Services Department, there were 3 police representatives, an NSPCC officer, a Health Visitor and her supervisor, a Nursing Officer, a Consultant and a Registrar in Paediatrics, two Senior House Officers, a Ward Sister and the Senior Social Worker at the hospital.

20 August 1981   Case Conference, held at St. Charles' Hospital, to review the decisions which were made at the original Case Conference, to check the minutes for accuracy, and to discuss the next move. Mr. David Bishop took the chair. The minutes were again taken by Miss Knibbs' secretary.

                           The same personnel attended, minus the NSPCC officer, two of the three police officers, the Registrar in Paediatrics and one of the Senior House Officers. Miss Rogers, a Senior Social Worker from the Adoption and Foster Care Section, attended for the first time.

9 December 1981   Statutory Case Review was held by Area 6, which it was intended to hold in two parts — one with the foster-parents and the other among staff. Due to weather conditions, the former did not take place.

5 April 1982   Case Conference at Area 6, to review situation regarding the children. "Given agreement re the degree of success of the rehabilitation programs, plan return home and input on return". The meeting was chaired by Mr. David Bishop, who also took the notes of the meeting as "minute-taker". No one, other than personnel from Social Services Department, was present, although the Health Visitor was invited to attend by, letter which never reached her. Apologies were received from Miss Rogers and Miss Proudlock.

25 May 1982   Statutory Case Review at Area 6. Itemised topics covered were

"finances, positive changes, Morris' feelings about SW intervention and procedure regarding revocation of the Care Order." The meeting consisted of Mrs. Dietmann in the Chair, Ms. Wahlstrom, Mrs. Ruddock and Morris Beckford. Mr. Bishop subsequently signed the Review Form with his comment, "Agree with foregoing".

30 September 1982   Statutory Case Review at Area 6. Itemised topics covered in review were "Case Conference planned for October; Day nursery for Louise; revocation of the Care Order; changes in the family; Morris' job; and finances." The same people attended, save that Beverley Lorrington replaced Morris Beckford, and brought Louise with her. Mr. Bishop simply appended his signature as Area Manager.

9 November 1982   Case Conference at Area 6, "to review Jasmine and Louise Beckford's inclusion on the N.A.I. register". Mrs. Dietmann took the chair, at which only Social Services personnel were present. The parents and the general practitioner sent their apologies. Mr. Bishop's signature was not appended.

18 April 1983   Statutory Case Review to consider the revocation of the Care Orders. Area 6 staff under Mrs. Dietmann's chairmanship only attended, plus Morris Beckford. Under "Area Manager's Comments" there appeared Mr. Bishop's signature, dated "4.7.83", the same date on which was entered for signature, "Chairperson. p.p. D. Dietmann."

6 December 1983   Statutory Case Review to discuss "finances, Christmas, and relationships within the family". Only Mrs. Dietmann and Ms. Wahlstrom attended. Apologies were received from the parents. The meeting decided to include in future reviews the Court Section and "school". Statutory visits were to continue and there would be a renewal of the application for revocation of the Care Orders. Mr. Bishop signified his agreement to "reapply for revocation of CO". The next review date was fixed for April 1984.

The next statutory review never took place. When Mrs. Dietmann and Ms. Wahlstrom were frantically searching for the Beckford parents on 5 July 1984, they were well out of time with conducting the review.

General

We think that there is substance in Mr. Bedford's evidence to us that there is confusion between the two different types of meetings. Like him, we favour all Case Conferences to be called "Child Abuse Case Conferences", so as to distinguish the function of the case conferences, which are directly linked to registration on the child abuse register, from the statutory reviews. We do not wish case conferences to be other than non-statutory, to be convened as and when appropriate agencies (normally, Social Services as the prime agency for managing a child abuse case) need advice preparatory to the making of important decisions about the welfare of a child. Once the child is off the register, the child abuse procedures drop away, the statutory case reviews fulfilling exclusively the function of review of a child in care. We have no views to offer specifically about the statutory reviews, which cover child care cases and not just child abuse cases.

The case conference has over the last few years become increasingly an essential feature of the management of a child abuse case. So long as it is well-organised and is clear about its purpose, it is an indispensable ingredient in the management of the child abuse system. We have indicated in our report where things went wrong in the Beckford case. Here we deal with the organisational aspects.

Who should attend?

We heard a considerable body of evidence about the proper composition of a case conference. All of our witnesses agreed that it is crucial that it should reflect the multi-disciplinary approach. But there was disagreement about which disciplines, other than social workers, should be involved. We deal with some of these "other" disciplines.

Police

Although in the past, the police were not always welcomed by social workers as participants in the management of the child abuse system, it is now the received wisdom that they must always be invited and expected to attend. It is in fact the policy of BASW that they should invariably be invited. We have indicated in Chapter 15 that, apart from the initial conferences when the question of prosecuting parents is being considered, it should be officers from the local juvenile bureau who should represent the police interest. Since it is the bureau that focuses on protection of the young, it is appropriate that officers from that unit of the police force should be present when important issues relating to the placement of children in care are being discussed.

Police officers should always attend when there is a proposal either to return children home on trial or to take them off the child abuse register. Neither on 5 April 1982, nor on 9 November 1982, were police officers invited to attend the respective Case Conferences. They should have been. **We recommend that the Area Review Committee should indicate the desirability of the attendance of police officers.**

Health Visitors

It is axiomatic that the relevant health visitor should attend every case conference dealing with an abused child under the age of 5 whom she is visiting. The health visitor's immediate superior should also usually attend. This had been the practice in Brent, which was dropped, but has now been revived. We applaud the revival of a sound practice. In the case of children at nursery school, the school nurse would be the appropriate person to be invited. We deal with children of compulsory school age under the heading of "teachers".

Paediatricians

It has never been doubted that paediatricians should attend Case Conferences. But, as we have noted in Chapter 7, it is not enough for paediatricians to attend for the sole purpose of advising medically on the nature and extent of child abuse. They must be involved in every aspect of the process of decision-making, in the sense that their clinical judgment must not only look backwards to past injuries but also forward to potential risk of further abuse. This means involvement in the follow-up of the case, after the child has been taken into, and kept in care. An example, taken from this case, is the percentile chart. Had it been brought to the attention of the case conferences or statutory case reviews at any time over 3 years, it would have loudly proclaimed both Jasmine's failure to thrive when she was in her parents' home before August 1981 and the dramatic upsurge in her development during fostering. It is to the follow-up reviews that paediatricians tend not to be invited. Dr. Warner was not invited to the Case Conference of 5

April 1982. He would have liked to have been; the failure to invite him was an error of judgment by Mr. Bishop, which he now acknowledges.

But there is one important point about inviting a paediatrician. Dr. Warner's special interests are children's chest complaints and allergies. It so happens that, working in inner London hospitals, he has been involved in a large number of child abuse cases. What in preference is needed is a paediatrician specialising in community health problems. Dr. Bridget Edwards should fulfil that role. She is the primary paediatrician to whom Brent Social Services should turn.

General practitioners
As a rule the general practitioner is likely to be an asset to any case conference, since it is he who is most likely to possess good information about the child's health. **We, therefore, recommend that the family's general practitioner should invariably be invited to case conferences.** We appreciate the difficulty that busy general practitioners have of attending case conferences which are frequently ill-timed, time-consuming and generally not well-suited to most medical practitioners. But we regard this aspect of the personnel who ought to be in attendance at a case conference as so important that it requires thorough discussion. We have dealt with it in Chapter 23.

Teachers
Where the child is in compulsory education, it is essential that his school be represented at every case conference, since his teacher may well be the person who will see him most after his parents, and will almost certainly be the person who will see him most regularly. He will, therefore, be in the best position to monitor his progress. Usually the school is represented at case conferences by the Head Teacher or his Deputy. This has the advantage that the Head Teacher can, we hope, be trusted by other members of the case conference not to misuse confidential information about the child; also, he is in a position to ensure that his staff monitor the child's progress and report to him any signs of injury, distress or failure to thrive and also any known changes in the home circumstances of the child. Class teachers rarely seem to attend case conferences, although a child's own teacher could probably provide more detailed information than the Head Teacher about the child and could·respond more fully to "supplementary questions" from other members of the conference. However, a class teacher might have difficulty in ensuring that all other relevant members of the school staff were aware of the necessity to monitor the child's progress. Also, professionals from other disciplines have a fear – sometimes, alas, well-founded – that the class teacher may use such information when addressing the child in front of other pupils. Consequently, they may be reluctant to share confidential information about the child with his class teacher.

On balance, we think that, if the choice is between the Head Teacher or the class teacher, it is desirable that the Head Teacher should attend the case conference. However, if our recommendation in chapter 14 that "in every school there is one member of the educational staff who is designated as the liaison officer with social services in respect of every child who is in the care of the local authority and/or is on the child abuse register" is implemented, then that designated teacher would clearly be the most appropriate person to represent the school at all case conferences.

Others
We turn now to the attendance of persons who are neither professionally nor occupationally involved in the management of the child abuse system. Employees of agencies who do not have professional status, such as home helps, family aides and social work assistants, may have considerable contact with families, and their attendance at case

conferences could be entirely appropriate. More contentious is the question whether, and in what circumstances, the abusing parents, the foster-parents and, moreover, the child of sufficient understanding should be invited to attend case conferences.

Abusing parents

We have had no expert evidence on whether the parents of an abused child should attend case conferences. In the instant case Morris Beckford and Beverley Lorrington attend case conferences or statutory case reviews only after their children were returned home on trial in April 1982. Morris Beckford was present at the Statutory Case Review on 25 May 1982, a month after Jasmine and Louise came home, and Beverley Lorrington attended the Review on 30 September 1982. They were both invited, but did not attend the Case Conference of 9 November 1982. But Morris Beckford attended the Review on 18 April 1983. No consideration appears to have been given to their attendance at the initial Case Conferences in August 1981, or at the reviews in December 1981 and April 1982 when the Beckford children were living with the Proberts.

We think this division reflects a generally sensible approach. While Social Services are deciding the long-term future of children in care, it is perhaps wise not to involve the parents too directly with the process of decision-making. Communication about what Social Services are planning should be confined to relaying information through the key social worker. Once the children are returned home on trial, the reverse situation applies. It is important that discussion about the experiment of reuniting the family should be by way of direct contact between the parents and those assessing the success or otherwise of the experiment. While we endorse the apparent division between the period when children are in care and away from their parents' home and when the children are at home on trial, we feel that local authority Social Services Departments should treat the issue flexibly. Circumstances of a case may indicate a variation on the theme we have expressed. The test must always be the best interests of the child. It may be that those interests cannot remain the objective focus of a case conference if parents are present throughout the meeting. Parents might properly be excluded for the last part of a case conference.

Foster-parents

We heard a great deal of evidence about the position of foster-parents in case conferences, not all of it consonant. The division of view focused on the issue of confidentiality. While all our witnesses favoured the attendance of foster-parents in principle, it was felt that the presence of foster-parents at case conferences could seriously inhibit professional people who would be willing to reveal confidences, but not if non-professionals were present. We see the force of this objection.

No problem arises with initial case conferences where the child is still in hospital or in a residential establishment. The first two Case Conferences in the Beckford case represented just such a situation. Once the child has been placed in a foster-home the foster-parents are an invaluable repository of information about how the child is coping with life and is developing. We agree with what Mr. Bedford told us, that the attendance of foster-parents should not in the early stages of fostering be automatic. Case conferences should, however, have a detailed report about how the child is faring in the foster-home. Once foster-parents have considerable experience of rearing and nurturing the child, then it should be possible to accommodate their presence at case conferences, at the very least, part of it.

Children

We are conscious that what follows did not arise from our Inquiry, since Jasmine was too young. But we did consider the issue of children's attendance at case conferences an issue that must be brought into relief when discussing, on a more general level, child abuse. This category is, therefore, applicable to children of school age whom we are aware are also at risk of being physically, psychologically or sexually abused.

We are aware that at any case conference, professionals from all agencies are there to protect and promote the welfare of the children. We are also aware that many professionals feel that the involvement of the child in his own case conference is inappropriate. Those professionals who favour the child being involved in his own case conference argue that it is his right to be there, it being his future that is exclusively and vitally at stake. A child who feels mature enough to verbalise his feelings and wishes ought to be afforded such an opportunity. The National Association of Children and Young People in Care (an association which has, as its members, children and young people who are, or who have been in care) supports the view that it is the child's right to choose whether to be involved in the decision-making and planning process concerned with his future.

Those who argue against the children's involvement generally do so for, what can be considered as, sound professional reasons. One of their main points is that children may be overawed by the group of professionals in attendance in case conferences. It is also argued that children who have been abused will often be too traumatised and emotionally entangled to be able to offer any realistic contribution to the decision-making process and the future planning of their lives.

We think that the answer must lie with the child. The child must be asked whether he wishes to be involved in a case conference. In short the child must be given the right to choose and decide after consultation with the social worker or personal advocate. If the child should opt to choose not to attend, then we consider it of paramount importance to have his views canvassed and represented at such conference. In order to obtain the views of the child himself, rather than those relayed by the social worker in the case, it might be appropriate to use a person of the child's own choosing, who canvasses the views and wishes of the child and ultimately passes them on to the case conference members.

Whatever decision is made concerning the child's attendance, the person chairing the conference should, as a matter of standard practice, consider the issue of whether the child should be involved or not. Whatever course is adopted, the minutes of the case conference should clearly record the child's views.

The overriding consideration of case conferences is that they should inject into the process of decision-making an objectivity that cannot be obtained by those directly involved in the management of a child abuse case. Even if all, or some of the professionals not directly involved in such management attend a case conference, there is no guarantee that there will be a clear objective view emerging from the discussion of the case. Bringing together a mixture of professional disciplines may not achieve the desired objectivity; indeed the larger the spread of disciplines the more unwieldy the case conference is likely to be, and the more muffled will be the message to Social Services. We, therefore, searched for some mechanism that might produce a coherent and objective judgment in the difficult task of assessing the degree of risk-taking with the lives of abused children.

We indicated in Chapter 8 that we strongly favoured case conferences being held either side of the care proceedings, particularly favouring a review soon after the juvenile court has made a Care Order. The other crucial case conference is the one that considers a proposal to reunite the family in a "home on trial". It occurs to us that the one really independent presence could be the *guardian ad litem*. Parliament, in the Children Act 1975, set up the system of *guardian ad litem*, for the expressed purpose of supplying the care proceedings with a voice for the child, by a person who would make an independent assessment which might come to a different conclusion from the local authority and thus best protect the safety and interests of the child. There seems to us to be no good reason why that independent voice should go mute, once the care proceedings are concluded. That voice should be heard as loud and clear in the post-judicial, administrative process as it is in the courtroom. We recognise that the guardian is *"ad litem"*, and acts under a legal aid certificate for the *"lis"* of the care proceedings. But the conclusion of legal services should not prevent the continuation of his services afterwards.

We, therefore, recommend that the local authority in possession of a Care Order should be under a statutory duty to consult the relevant *guardian ad litem* on the two occasions when the local authority considers convening a case conference — namely, after the hearing of the care proceedings and when it is contemplating reuniting the child with its family. Consultation with the *guardian ad litem* would carry the implied invitation to attend the case conference. If the *guardian ad litem*, in response to the consultative process, indicates that he or she desires to attend, and to that end needs to make further inquiries about the family, the local authority should be empowered to pay suitable remuneration for the service. In making this recommendation, we are conscious that there should be a trial period of *guardians ad litem* attending case conferences, and would urge that Brent Social Services take the initiative in this respect. We expect the experiment to support our recommendation.

We repeat here what we have said already in Chapter 8, that, apart from selecting the key worker and deciding to put a child on the child abuse register, the initial case conference should not make decisions, but only recommend what action should be taken by those who are legally responsible for action in pursuance of Care Orders. Likewise, subsequent case conferences should be advisory. We have heard it said that one of the besetting defects of case conferences is their indecisiveness. In part, that complaint stems from a misunderstanding of the role of case conferences. They do not, nor ought they to, make decisions. But, given that case conferences are advisory bodies, it may still be said that their recommendations should be decisive. There is in fact nothing wrong about a case conference being indecisive, so long as it knows why it is being indecisive. There is nothing untoward about a case conference saying, for example, that no long-term plan can be made until more information is to hand. Indecision is in that instance entirely appropriate.

Chairing

A good deal of attention has been paid to the important role of chairmanship of case conferences. Mr. Bishop told us that in his experience, case conferences were chaired by senior social workers rather than by Area Managers. In the Beckford case, he, as Manager of Area 6, was chairman of the early case conferences but ceased be do so on and after 25 May 1982, although he saw the minutes of the meetings and counter-signed them, except the crucial one of 9 November 1982, and thereafter. We are quite clear in our minds that it is wholly inappropriate for the Senior Social Worker, who is supervising the social worker primarily involved in the case, to chair the case conference. Although the supervisor should, as we have pointed out in chapter 21, distance himself emotionally from the case, and apply detached objective tests in judging the social worker's handling of the case, we feel that he is still likely to be too close to the case to be able to fulfil the role of chairman of the case conference by listening impartially to all members of the conference and giving due weight to their views.

The Area Officer, although managerially responsible for the case, is further distanced from it by one or, possibly, two tiers. He should, therefore, usually be less emotionally involved with it. By virtue of his senior managerial position, he is likely to be experienced in chairing meetings, and he should be able to regard the case objectively.

However, while we would not normally exclude an Area Manager from chairing a case conference on a child for whom he carries managerial responsibility, we recognise that, in some cases – especially the more serious cases – he may have had to become personally involved in day-to-day decision-making. In these circumstances, he may well not be able to retain sufficient objectivity to chair a case conference. We are mindful of Mr. Bedford's comments: "The emotional impact of serious cases is such that it can contaminate several levels of management who became emotionally involved and enmeshed with the case."

The question is, who appropriately should chair a case conference? We think that the prime qualification is the ability to steer and control a meeting of professionals from a variety of disciplines with objectivity, combined with a knowledge of child abuse. The most likely candidate will be the child abuse co-ordinator, where such a post exists. Alternatively, an Area Manager from another Area might fill the bill. Or it may be possible to obtain a Senior Social Worker, or Area Manager from a neighbouring Borough on a reciprocal basis. We make no recommendation about who shall take the chair, save to say that there is a range of potential candidates, some of whom we have indicated.

One thing is clear. The practice of the chairman also acting as "minute-taker" must cease. If there is no secretarial assistance to hand, then someone other than the chairman must volunteer, or be press-ganged into taking the minutes. Minute-taking is a skilled task and ought ideally to be performed by a trained secretary. Distribution of the minutes should be expeditious. It took 20 days for the minutes of the Case Conference of 9 November 1982 to reach Miss Leong. A week should suffice to compile and send out the minutes, particularly to those who could not attend the meeting. It is an aspect of documentation, on which we have laid stress in Chapter 22.

CHAPTER 26

Guardians Ad Litem

In 1975 Parliament enacted in the Children Act a provision (inserted as Section 32B of the Children and Young Persons Act 1964) whereby the juvenile court may, unless it considers it unnecessary to safeguard the child's interests, order separate representation of parents and children in care proceedings on grounds of conflict; and then appoint a *guardian ad litem* for the child. That provision did not come into force in respect of opposed proceedings until 27 May 1984. Previously, through the legal aid scheme, representatives for a child could, and often did employ an independent social worker to report on the family situation. That is what happened in August/September 1981 when the solicitor for the Beckford children, Mr. Simon Pollard, engaged the services of Miss Joan Court. We have described in some detail in Chapter 8 how that arrangement worked − or rather failed to work properly, in large part because of the attitude then prevailing in Brent Social Services Department towards the novel creature of "independent social worker", by a denial of access by Miss Court to the key social worker, to the foster-parents and to some documentation.

We say no more about what has now passed into the history of child care legal procedure. Independent social workers are still occasionally being employed, but they have been almost entirely replaced by *guardians ad litem*.

After Jasmine's death in July 1984, care proceedings were initiated in respect of her sister, Chantelle, and Miss Alix Causby was appointed her *guardian ad litem* − she was subsequently appointed for both Louise and Chantelle in relation to access proceedings. As a result of hearing Miss Causby in evidence, we have been able to study the system of the *guardian ad litem* in action, and accordingly we proffer one or two general observations on the new procedure.

We should like to highlight the value of the *guardian ad litem* in care proceedings. The essential feature of that role is that for the first time there is someone, other than a legal representative, whose concern is exclusively the welfare of the child, independent of both the child's parents and of the local authority which has the duty to protect the child. The *guardian ad litem* − who is a qualified social worker drawn from a local authority panel by the court − is definitionally possessed of the power and the expertise to investigate and comment objectively on all the circumstances surrounding the case. Unlike an independent social worker, who will be commissioned by a lawyer acting for the parents or the child, and whose report may or may not be used at the lawyer's discretion, if it does not appear to support the case being advanced by the lawyer, the *guardian ad litem* is appointed by the court and, reversing roles, instructs a solicitor to act for him. It is the *guardian ad litem* who is thus in control of the case for the child, and not the lawyer. Mr. Pollard himself acknowledged that in August/September 1981 he found himself in an ambiguous role in having to make decisions about how to conduct the case for the Beckford children.

We cannot say generally whether there would have been a different outcome to the care proceedings were there to have been a *guardian ad litem* appointed in August/September 1981. But one thing we are confident about. Dr. Levick's report would never have suffered the fate of courtroom confusion, or subsequent interment in a departmental file. A *guardian ad litem* would just as likely have obtained a radiological expert's opinion on the children's injuries, and would have incorporated its findings in a report to the court. It would have been in the court's own files and should certainly have been constantly in front of those who had the responsibility for managing the case.

That potentially ambiguous position of the independent social worker is now happily removed. We have noted already in Chapter 25 on Case Conferences that so valuable is the function of the *guardian ad litem* that we envisage him having a real part to play in the management of the child abuse system after the making of the Care Order.

The one substantial feature of the *guardian ad litem*'s function is his access to examine Social Services' and other records. Contrariwise, the independent social worker was at the mercy of the policy of Social Services Departments, which varied widely. We assume that since May 1984 there have been no hurdles put in the way of *guardians ad litem*; indeed if there were to be, doubtless the juvenile court could be asked unofficially to intervene to permit access to records, although the court possesses no powers to do so.

The one problem we envisage about the *guardian ad litem* system is the court's ability to identify those cases where there is in fact a conflict of interest between parent and child, or how courts are in practice exercising their discretion to make an order that the parent is not to be treated as representing the child. It is our view that in any case where there has been severe child abuse, the court ought presumptively to order separate representation. **We recommend that if the court does make a separation order, it will − as we have noted − ordinarily appoint a** *guardian ad litem* **whose duty it is then to safeguard the interests of the child as prescribed by section 32B(2) and (3), Children and Young Persons Act 1969.** But that may mean that the parents face an adversary in the shape of the *guardian ad litem*. Although the parents will be eligible for legal aid, they may still experience difficulty in putting forward their own point of view. The reality of the situation, in child abuse cases at least, is that the parents are "being put in the dock" to face allegations of a criminal nature. It is true, as Professor Cretney points out in his classic textbook, *Principles of Family Law** that the parents have been given the right to meet any allegations made against them in the course of proceedings by calling or giving evidence, and have also been given the right to cross-examine witnesses. They are, however, still not parties to the proceedings. Professor Cretney observes that the extent of their legal rights "remains, in a number of respects, obscure". The second report from the Social Services Committee,**recommended that **the court should be required to make a parent a party to care proceedings on the parent's application. We recommend similarly.**

This leads us to make a tentative proposal. Much of the difficulty about who is a party to care proceedings would be alleviated if the evidence from the local authority, the parents and the *guardian ad litem* was to be on affidavit, supplemented (if necessary) by oral evidence at the hearing. This is the practice in the High Court in wardship proceedings, and we see every advantage in adopting it in the juvenile court in care proceedings. In this way the imbalance in forensic armoury, by the introduction of the *guardian ad litem*, would be redressed.

Erratum: On page 253 Children and Young Persons Act 1964 should read Children and Young Persons Act 1969.

* 4th ed. 1984, p. 548.

** Session 1983-1984, *Children in Care* at para. 98.

CHAPTER 27

Place of Safety Orders

Three Place of Safety Orders figured in the period of events under inquiry. The first two were made on 5 August 1981 in respect of Jasmine and Louise Beckford when they were in hospital. We have commented on the fact of delay in obtaining the Orders, in our chapter on the medical evidence (Chapter 7). We do not repeat it here. Miss Knibbs obtained an order for 14 days from Mrs. Porteous, a Magistrate on the Inner London Juvenile Panel. The third Place of Safety Order was obtained in respect of Chantelle Beckford on the morning of 6 July 1984 from a Magistrate sitting at Willesden Magistrates' Court. Chantelle, with her sister Louise, who was still the subject of a Care Order, were later removed from the home of her maternal grandparents. She and her sister had been taken to the grandparents by police, the evening before, from their home where Jasmine had been killed. That Order was made for 28 days.

Three main issues arise out of those facts. First, what are, or ought to be the grounds for making a Place of Safety Order? Second, is the maximum period of 28 days for such an Order too long? Third, where a child is already in a place of safety, e.g., a hospital, in what circumstances should a Place of Safety Order be made? We deal with each in turn.

Grounds for making a Place of Safety Order

Section 28, Children and Young Person Act 1969 authorises the detention of a child or young person and his removal to a place of safety, if a magistrate is satisfied that the applicant has reasonable cause to believe that one of the seven primary conditions for making a Care Order is established. The magistrate may grant an application for a period of 28 days, beginning with the date of authorisation, "or for such shorter period". A constable may, without applying to a magistrate, detain a child if he has reasonable cause to believe that any one of the primary conditions in Section 1(2)(a)-(d) of the 1969 Act is satisfied, and on the authority of a senior police officer the child may be kept in a place of safety for 8 days. Any other person may apply to a magistrate for a Place of Safety Order, if he can satisfy the magistrate that one of four situations pertain. The main situation is the applicant's ability to satisfy the magistrate that one of the seven primary conditions in Section 1(2) (a)-(f) is established. (We think it unnecessary to set out the conditions here — they are set out in Appendix E. We only observe that the condition under (e) relates to the child of compulsory school age failing to receive efficient full-time education). The next situation relates to Section 1(2)(b) which allows the court to intervene in respect of a child of the same household as the child whose proper development is being avoidably prevented or neglected. (This would have been the situation if Miss Knibbs had applied for a Place of Safety order for Jasmine immediately after Louise had been brought in to hospital on 1 August 1981). The third situation is where the child is about to leave the United Kingdom in contravention of laws relating to the sending abroad of juvenile entertainers. The last situation is where the applicant has reasonable cause to suspect that the child is being assaulted, ill-treated or neglected.

Applications for Place of Safety Orders are usually made by a local authority social worker, or occasionally by an NSPCC officer. There is no requirement that the parents and the child be informed in advance of the application being made, and the magistrate is under no legal duty to see them or hear any representations on their behalf before making the Order. Section 28(3) requires the detaining authority to inform the parents of the reason for the detention as soon as practicable. There is no right of appeal against a Place of Safety Order, but since the Order is made *ex parte*, we regard it as axiomatic that **a parent or child could apply to the court for setting aside the Order.** We do not know of any such case, but **we think that the right to do so should be specifically stated in any future legislation. We so recommend.** The other possible remedy would be an application for judicial review but this would be directed at some procedural irregularity and could not challenge the decision on its merits.*

We remind ourselves that Parliament in 1969 obviously intended that the power to seek a Place of Safety Order is an emergency provision to ensure that a child in danger can immediately be taken and put in a place of safety. The section contemplates cases where children are already in a situation of danger calling for instant action. It is a draconian measure to meet a drastic situation. While it is a piece of public mythology that social workers on their own initiative "snatch" children away from the parents against the latter's wishes – the mythographers adding, for effect, "screaming and kicking" – it is in our view imperative that the power should be exercised with appropriate caution to ensure that there really is a danger to the child who is in instant need of protection. The Order is plainly an infringement of the liberty of the child and impinges upon parental rights. Recent researches have indicated that Place of Safety Orders are frequently made in circumstances that do not appear to be appropriate; these findings have been the subject of critical concern by those undertaking the Review of Child Care Law which followed the Select Committee on Social Services report on *Children in Care*. What we have to say is designed to tighten up the application of a necessary power in the system of child protection.

The successful applicant for a Place of Safety Order does not have the right to enter premises and search for and remove a child. But obviously it is a bold parent who resists the authority of the Order. If action is needed, a warrant has to be obtained, authorising a police officer to enter the premises, search for and remove the child.

To deal with a marginal issue, we find it difficult to understand why a Place of Safety Order should be available on the ground of the child's truanting (Section 1(2)(e) of the 1969 Act). It may be necessary that such child should be brought before a juvenile court, and perhaps be made the subject of a Care Order. But it scarcely follows that a child is in immediate danger if he remains at home, not going to school, until the court hearing. **We recommend that this ground should not in any event found an application for a Place of Safety Order.** Likewise, a child who is being neglected may need to be brought before the court, but unless the neglect is so serious that he is in danger, he should not be liable to be compulsorily removed from home, prior to the court hearings. On the other hand, immediate removal of a child from his home may be necessary to ensure his safety.

Examples of the misuse of the power have led some people to suggest that, instead of stating the grounds for a Place of Safety Order by reference to the primary conditions for care proceedings, some formula directly reflecting the immediacy of the need to protect the child would be preferable. We agree. **We recommend that the criterion for the Place of Safety Order should be that the applicant "has reasonable cause to believe that there is a real and present danger to the health or well-being of the child."** We prefer "real and present" to "imminent", since the latter is an insufficiently stringent test. The former phrase represents simpler and clearer language. A social worker might con-

---

* R. v. Lincoln (Kesteven) County Justice ex parte M. (A Minor) [1976] QB 957 is an example of a case where a parent unsuccessfully applied to the Divisional Court for an order of certiorari to quash a Place of Safety Order.

vince a magistrate that, based on suspicion, there will be physical abuse on the child in the near future. We think that the applicant should have to be more confident than that in thinking that the child is, at the moment of applying, at risk.

Duration of Place of Safety Orders

At present a single magistrate may make a Place of Safety Order for any time up to 28 days. We understand that in some parts of the country it has been, and is still the practice for applicants to ask for the full period, on the ground that this gives the local authority Social Services Department time to work with the family, in the fond expectation that the children can be returned home safely before the lapse of 28 days. The effluxion of time, it is argued, at least provides a breathing space to allow for the avoidance of the traumatic experience which the child and parents undergo in court proceedings. If there is a real hope that care proceedings can be obviated within 28 days, it would seem to us that the Place of Safety Order itself was inappropriately obtained. Moreover, we think that the execution of the Place of Safety Order is at least as traumatic as the appearance before the juvenile court.

We are convinced that 28 days is too long a period for a child to be removed from his parents, without the issue of removal being tested judicially − at a court hearing in which the parents and, if appropriate, the child can challenge the order by making representation to the juvenile court. In the course of recent discussions reviewing child care law, many organisations − including the Magistrates' Association, the Association of County Councils, the Association of County Court and District Registrars and the British Association of Social Workers − have recommended that, as a matter of good practice, a magistrate should make a Place of Safety Order only until the next sitting of the appropriate juvenile court. In metropolitan areas this would mean that 72 hours would cover almost every case. And we know of a number of justices on the Inner London Juvenile Court who ordinarily give only 72 hours. In more remote areas of the country, there will not be an appropriate juvenile court sitting almost daily.

We note that the Magistrates' Association and others are recommending the lowering of the limit of a Place of Safety Order from 28 to 8 days. We would go further. **We recommend that Section 28(1) of the 1969 Act be amended to fix the limit at 72 hours or where there is no relevant juvenile court sitting within the next 72 hours, up to a maximum of 8 days, beginning with the date of authorisation.**

Where the child is in a place of safety

Some magistrates are said to be reluctant to make a Place of Safety Order when the child is in a place of safety, such as a hospital, in which case the applicant does not need to "take" the child to a place of safety. We think that they are merely applying the law correctly. The only situation where a social worker would be entitled to apply for such an Order is where there are grounds for believing that the parents might remove the child from the hospital, thus placing the child in danger. Hospital staff also may believe that they will be in difficulty in persuading the parents to allow their child to remain in hospital, unless they have the backing of a Place of Safety Order. We think that, where there are grounds for suspecting that the child might be removed from hospital (or might remove himself) the law supplies the authority to "detain" the child. But short of that suspicion, there is no present authority for a Place of Safety Order. We doubt very much whether on 5 August 1981 there was a sufficient basis in fact for a Place of Safety Order in respect of Jasmine, who by then was in traction and could hardly have been in a position to be removed.

We think the position ought, in any event, to be as follows: If the sole ground for making a Place of Safety Order is (as we recommend) that the applicant has reasonable cause to believe that there is a present and real danger to the health or well-being of the child, then the applicant will have to satisfy the magistrate additionally that he (the applicant) has "reasonable cause to believe" that the allegedly abusing parent may remove the child from the hospital where he has been taken. It is worth pointing out in this context that parents who abuse their children are often labile. Even if they protest that they have no intention of removing their injured child from hospital, a mood swing can quickly lead to an insistence on removing their child, in defiance of advice from the hospital authorities; in such circumstances a Place of Safety Order is entirely justified in order to protect the child.

A more stringent test for detention and removal may have the effect of diverting the attention of social workers to the use of voluntary care. Parents, under the threat of a Place of Safety Order, may be willing to have their child received into care under Section 2, Child Care Act 1980. Such action will avoid resort to the court. That may not in practice provide the necessary protection for the child, because although the child is in care it will not prevent removal of the child from care. In those cases the social worker should be alive to the parents "buying off" the Place of Safety Order. It may be in the child's interests that the Place of Safety Order should be sought.

Pending changes in the law along the lines we have indicated, **we recommend that social workers and magistrates should respectively apply for, and grant applications only where there is a present and real danger to the health and well-being of the child.** Short of that test for a Place of Safety Order, social workers should be directed to initiate care proceedings.

CHAPTER 28

Court Officers

Our criticism (in Chapter 8) of Mr. Thompson in his handling of the care proceedings in August/September 1981 must be tempered by the fact that his post of Court Officer was created in circumstances very different from those pertaining today. The job specification for a Court Officer had been tailored to a different legal scene. Even after the Children and Young Persons Act 1969 came into force in 1971, it was rare for any of the parties appearing in the juvenile court in care proceedings to be legally represented. Local authorities, responding to that situation, appointed persons as Court Officers, to conduct the cases before juvenile courts, who were not legally qualified. Many were former police officers (both Mr. Thompson and Mr. Hobbs had been policemen, the former also having been a probation officer). In 1981, and even more so today, lawyers have become involved in the conduct of care proceedings in ever-increasing numbers. Some local authorities have found already that they too need to employ legally-qualified persons. We set out below our views about the relationship between a Social Services Department and the Magistrates' Court as represented by the Court Officer system. And we state our views of the future of Court Officers.

Whenever a juvenile court sits to exercise any one of its jurisdictions over children and young persons, it is necessary for a representative of the local authority to be present, or readily available. There are six separate situations when the assistance of the local authority will be required.

1. To prepare and present social inquiry reports composed by the local authority's social workers. There may be a requirement also for school reports.
2. To make arrangements for the placement of a juvenile who has been remanded to the care of a local authority, or is made the subject of an interim care order.
3. To note requests emanating from the Bench for action to be taken by the Social Services Department in respect of juveniles whose cases are adjourned, so that field workers can take appropriate action.
4. Where neither parent, nor guardian can be brought before the court, to act *in loco parentis*, and to sit beside the juvenile who is appearing before the court.
5. To provide a link with other local authorities whenever juveniles from other areas are brought to court.
6. To conduct care proceedings on behalf of a local authority.

All but the last of these six situations can be performed more than adequately by staff from the Social Services Department. But to be an advocate in care proceedings calls for the skills associated with the legally qualified person. The muddle that occurred before the Willesden Justices on 9 September 1981 (and perhaps the confused picture of what took place on 22 June 1983, on the application to revoke the Care Orders) was in part produced by Mr. Thompson's inability to deal with the two main legal problems presented by a) the admissibility of Dr. Levick's report; and b) his ready compliance to communicate the impermissible rider to the Magistrates' decision. A lawyer experienced in child care law appearing for Brent Borough Council on 9 September 1981 would have handled Dr. Levick's report in a lawyerly fashion, such as would have led to its absorption into the documentary material; and he would have responded instantly and adversely to the Magistrates' rider:

During the period when local authority Children's Departments were in existence from 1948 to 1971, it became the practice for a specific officer from the Children's Department to undertake the duty of attendance at juvenile courts. In areas where juvenile court sittings were infrequent, a social worker or administrative officer would carry out this work in addition to his other duties; where there were several juvenile court sittings per week, one or more full time court officers might be appointed. The attendance of a specialist Children's Department Court Officer at a juvenile court enabled him to get to know, and be known by the magistrates, the court clerks and officers from other services, such as police and probation, who regularly attended the court. This system facilitated good communication between the court staff and the Children's Department which could be told in advance when a child was about to appear before the court and might need an immediate residential placement.

Because of his regular contact with the juvenile court, the Children's Department's Court Officer tended to advise social workers on whether grounds existed for court proceedings and on the likely attitude of the juvenile court to an application from the local authority. He was regarded as the most suitable person to represent the local authority when applying for a fit person order in respect of a child in need of care and protection. He would prepare the statutory notices, interview witnesses, including the social workers who had investigated the case, and arrange for them to be present in court, and would then conduct the case in court, on behalf of the local authority.

Before 1969 it was rare for a qualified lawyer to be present in a juvenile court in either criminal or care cases. The child was very seldom legally represented; the prosecution in criminal cases would be undertaken by a police officer; the court clerk would often not be legally qualified. Indeed, if a lawyer did appear in a juvenile court he would often be noticeably uneasy in dealing with procedures which were quite unfamiliar to him, and in communicating with children. If the proceedings had the aura of the courtroom, the procedure was sufficiently informal to perplex the legally-minded visitor. In such circumstances it was natural that the local authority should not perceive a need to be legally represented when applying to the court for fit person orders.

In the past fifteen years, however, there has been a growing tendency for children to be legally represented in both criminal and care proceedings. This has led to a corresponding tendency for the prosecution in criminal cases to be undertaken by a lawyer and for court clerks to be more frequently qualified in law.

In this changed climate the non-lawyer appearing for a local authority is at a disadvantage in the face of parties with legal representatives. We, therefore, consider it desirable that the Social Services Department, also, should be legally represented when bringing care proceedings to a Juvenile Court. There is still a place for an unqualified Court Officer − but with a ranking below that of present Court Officers − to carry out the liaison functions described earlier, but **we recommend that the legal departments of local authorities should arrange for one or more of their solicitors to specialise in juvenile court work.** These solicitors would be expected to attend case conferences in order to advise social workers on the appropriateness of care proceedings and also to familiarise themselves with the background to the case, so that they may present it competently in court. To quote "Understanding Child Abuse" (1982), edited by David Jones,

> "The local authority has no right to appeal from care proceedings, but only the child (or somebody acting on his behalf, usually the parents), so that application must be right first time, and it is essential that the application is presented by a lawyer with experience of child care law. It is a matter of some concern that many authorities give child care cases to newly qualified and inexperienced lawyers, for the issue at stake is the future welfare and liberty of a child until his eighteenth birthday.

We share this concern. Some solicitors in private practice who appear in juvenile courts are now tending to specialise in this field and to acquire expertise in it. We welcome the establishment in March 1985 by the Law Society of panels of solicitors to act in child are cases. We ourselves benefited considerably from hearing some of those who spend a good deal of their professional time in juvenile courts, and indeed this chapter owes much to their submissions.

We specifically do not advocate the replacement of a non-lawyer with immense experience in the field of child care law (as Mr. Thompson undoubtedly is) by a lawyer inexperienced in the field of child care law. If we had to choose, we would prefer the former. A local authority lawyer inexperienced in child care law will lack credibility both with the social workers whom he is advising and with the magistrates, and the outcome may be disastrous for the child who is before the court. By contrast, as we were told by Miss Howarth, **a local authority solicitor who specialises in social services matters can make a very valuable contribution to the work of the Social Services Department. We recommend that consideration be given to making such an arrangement.**

CHAPTER 29

Options on Placement: Residential Care, Fostering, or Home on Trial?

When Brent Social Services became involved initially with the care of the Beckford children in August/September 1981 no consideration was apparently given to the possibility of making use of the limited residential care at their disposal. The immediate and exclusive response to the urgent need to place the two children on their discharge from hospital – Louise within a month of reception and Jasmine, six weeks – was to request the Department's Adoption and Foster Care Section to find a suitable foster-home. No appropriate foster-parents were to be found within the Borough, certainly not within the foreseeable future. The only feasible placement was with Mr. and Mrs. Probert who were residents in the neighbouring Borough of Harrow and were then being assessed as approved foster-parents by the head of Brent's Adoption and Foster Care Section, Mr. Jeremy Burns. While there was some hesitancy about the suitability of the Proberts' fostering as anything more than a stop-gap arrangement, the placement was made with them, with all the ensuing difficulties which we have described in Chapter 9. It never seems to have occurred to anyone in Area 6 that the two children might have been placed in residential care for a short time, while a suitable long-term foster-home was found. The ostensible reason was the innate hostility to residential care among social workers. To understand the reasons for this hostility one has to examine the general attitude of social workers to the placement of children in care.

Residential institutions for children have a long history. But, as early as the nineteenth century, when boarding-out from workhouses occurred, fostering became a preferred option. Modern fostering had its spur during the last war, when large numbers of children were evacuated from the areas of the country vulnerable to wartime bombing. The Dennis O'Neill case in 1945 was the first public parade of the outcry of bad fostering which prompted public concern for the fate of children who, for whatever reason, could not be (or were not being) reared in their own families. Modern fostering in fact began with the recommendations of the Curtis Committee (1946) and the ensuing Children Act 1948. From that legislative prompting there grew the belief that children could invariably be cared for in a substitute family environment better than in an institution. The 1950s and 1960s heralded a growing concern that youngsters raised in institutional settings were at a grave disadvantage to those in substitute families. It was the absence of any refined process of matching the substitute family to the particular needs of the child that led to a high proportion of fostering breakdowns, and not any inherent defect in the concept of fostering. The response predictably was for children's departments of local authorities not to turn away from fostering but to improve the techniques of finding the right family to take the child in need.

Until the amalgamation of local authority health, welfare and children's services into a single Social Services Department, following the Seebohm report and the 1970 Act implementing its proposals, child care had been carried out by individual workers who were not involved in caring for other needy groups, such as the aged, the handicapped or the mentally ill. The child care specialist gradually disappeared from the scene and was replaced by the generic social worker whose role encompassed all groups under the umbrella of a broad social worker service. They soon began to handle the social problems of all needy groups. We have observed in Chapter 20 on Training that the emergence of the generic social worker relegated the specialist skills of the children's officer to a subsidiary role. This development had the effect of entrenching a generalised antipathy towards residential care for children. Hitherto, there had never been anything approaching a total ban on residential care, only a restricted use of it because of its known limitations and potential risk that children would never be moved on, but simply left to shrivel emotionally and psychologically.

The Children and Young Persons Act 1969 removed the powers of the courts to commit children to Approved Schools. Instead children who were made the subject of Care Orders could, at the exclusive discretion of the local authority Social Services, be accommodated in Community Homes, which represented little more than a changing of the label. Social workers seized their opportunity to reduce the numbers that had gone into Approved Schools, by declining to fill up the Community Homes with children in care. The distaste for residential care was thus fed by the opportunity to spurn its use. Once again a more professional approach to fostering was the response. Social workers, not wishing to give any fillip to residential institutions, turned their attentions elsewhere. A few local authorities did try to improve the residential care of children, by bringing the parents into the residential homes every day to look after their offspring until the children were put to bed. But by the mid-1970s the use of residential care rapidly began to be seen as an expensive option which, on the whole, failed to turn out young people who were able to fit into wider society as "normal", reasonably adjusted adults. With the increasing success of placing the less difficult children into foster homes, Social Services turned their attention towards the problem of finding foster homes for the more difficult young children with behavioural problems. Foster-parents began to receive training of a more professional nature to provide them with the skills to cope with such youngsters. Thus the need for residential care establishments began to diminish. While there may well be some justification for feeling that residential care was not the most appropriate alternative for such children, there can be no doubt its long existence has meant that it played a role in the care of children and young people. The question remains: can, and should a residential establishment meet the very short term needs of particularly young children who have had a traumatic entry into care, due to their having been abused by one or both of their parents? Would a residential home have been a viable option for Louise and Jasmine Beckford in August 1981?

Writers on the needs of children and young people confirm the view that local authorities have long been opting for fostering as against residential care. Dr. John Bowlby, in his book "Child Care and the Growth of Love", printed in 1953 (later edition 1965) stressed the importance of the bonding process in the mothering of very young children and babies. "Bonding", he interpreted to mean as the normal attachment that takes place between the developing child and in normal circumstances their natural parents, who become the significant adults for providing for their everyday needs and supporting them throughout their development to young adulthood. Bowlby considered this an important and significant factor in the normal process of growing from childhood to adulthood. In the absence of the natural parent, it became a significantly important factor for social workers to provide for the child substitute adults who would become important figures on whom children could model themselves. In recent years, there has been a challenge to the belief that bonding for children is such a significant factor that it takes priority over all the other needs for the child. We heard, for example, from Dr. Taitz who put forward the view that very young children were capable of bonding with a number of adults; and that the blood-tie was not the only, nor, necessarily, the best bond. Since others can provide the overall needs of the child, it is safe to assume that for a short period of time children may be outwith the family setting, so that their total needs may be more thoroughly assessed before deciding where to place them – back with their parents or in a foster home.

We have referred to the importance of matching individual children's needs to the substitute family in which they are to be placed. A more professional approach has been taken in recent years to assessing families with a view to making sure this is the case. From the mid-1970s through to the present, residential establishments have been set up to provide short term care for children and young people whose needs are assessed with a view to placing them back home because the situation which caused their removal has altered. These establishments also, as an alternative, look for substitute family settings for children who cannot be returned home due to the inability of their parents to cope, regardless of resources that have been brought in to try to help them. It is indeed the case (as we have said) that, wherever possible, for very young children, substitute family settings will be a more realistic alternative to residential establishments. But we stress that the substitute family setting must be an "appropriate" and "approved" setting.

We were struck by a piece of evidence from one of our expert witnesses, Mr. Tony Hall, Director and Secretary of the British Agencies for Adoption and Fostering. He sympathised with the attitude of social workers who saw the negative aspects of taking a child into care. But he thought they tended to overlook the positive side. So long as coming into residential care is, he said, "part of a considered plan for the long-term care of the child, then it may be the best thing that could be done." We entirely agree. Most children are infinitely better cared for and brought up in a family, and everything should be done to keep the child at home with his parents, if possible. But that may not always be possible. Proven child abuse is an instance where it may not be possible. A substitute family, through fostering or adoption, is then the preferred option. While that transition is effected, however, residential care may have its place. But if it is used, the decision about the longer-term care must not be allowed to drift without constant concern about how and where the child will be brought up permanently. The temporary expediency of residential care must not turn into permanency. But that risk should not rule out the short-term use of residential care. If not, then a good professional child care establishment, geared towards short term care of children, must be the alternative provision. We think that is implicit in the statutory duty of the local authority under section 21, Child Care Act 1980. We would remind readers of what a recent report on the subject said:*

> "There will always be children who need residential care on a temporary basis and the value of the more recently developed rehabilitative work to prepare children in the short term, either for return home or fostering or adoption, cannot be denied but there are other children for whom residential care using positive skills and a healing environment, needs to provide continuing care over a longer period. These children are the children and young people for whom residential care would be the best option. It is the special needs of these children that will help to identify the necessary skills to be developed."

Though the latter part of the quotation specifically relates to children and young people who are in need of long term residential care, we believe that the paragraph as a whole aptly sums up the positives that can be gained for even very young children who have suffered the trauma of child abuse. Such traumata may be counteracted through pro-

* Residential Care for Children in London, a report by DHSS Social Work Service, London Region — July 1982

viding them with a professional, skilled and caring "healing environment" for at least the period immediately following the abuse.

We think it may be helpful if we now apply these principles to the case of Jasmine and Louise Beckford as at August 1981. On 1 and 4 August 1981, Louise and Jasmine were respectively admitted to hospital suffering from physical injuries resulting in broken bones. On 6 August, a fullCaseConference was held at which Jasmine and Louise were put on the child abuse register. From that moment, until January 1982, no consideration at all was given to the use of residential care for these children. Jasmine and Louise were placed straight from hospital to the foster-home. The couple chosen as foster-parents, at the time of placement, were not fully assessed as long term foster-parents for Brent; neither had they any previous experience of, or skills related to, working with children from abused families. On receiving the children into care, there was no stated firm conclusion that the children were to be committed to their care for the duration of their childhood, or whether efforts were going to be made to return them back to their parents after assessment of the total family circumstances. Not only was there a need to give serious consideration to the circumstances and reasons for the injuries to the children, but there was also a need to assess comprehensively the ability, coping skills and circumstances of the parents. The social workers involved with the case were very early on appraised of the fact that Beverley Lorrington lacked commitment to her children. This was evidenced during their stay in hospital, at which time, though encouraged to do so, the mother stayed only intermittently with her children. This information was noted at theCaseConference held on 20 August 1981. It was also noted at that time, and had previously been so, that neither parent was going to find it easy to co-operate with, or accept help from authority. All this was amply confirmed in Miss Joan Court's report to the Magistrates' Court on 9 September 1981.

We have stated in other chapters that the real role of the social worker with regard to the Beckford case was a duty laid down in section 20(1), Child Care Act 1980, which reads:

> "In reaching any decision relating to the child in their care, a local authority should give first consideration to the need to safeguard and promote the welfare of the child throughout his childhood and shall so far as practicable ascertain the wishes and the feelings of the child regarding the decision and give due consideration to them having regard to his age and understanding."

If that statutory duty had been adhered to, then all options of placement for the children would have been given due consideration, and those options should clearly have included residential care. We think that, bearing in mind the circumstances of the case outlined, and weighing up the positives for all types of placement available, the use of Green Lodge (which was the residential care establishment for Brent) would have clearly come out as the immediate, viable and short-term option. Miss Pamela Gordon, who was the residential social worker at the establishment, told us that Green Lodge offered a professional, short-term residential resource for children of various ages. The work carried out there included preparing children for fostering, or working with them with a view to returning them to the family. Their professional skills would also have been used to monitor the behaviour of the parents and the way in which they interacted with the children. This would have helped to confirm or deny any concerns that the other pro-

266

fessionals had regarding the risks of returning the children to their parents. There is indeed evidence to show that parents are more likely to co-operate with social workers if their children are not placed with foster-parents but are in fact in a residential establishment.*

Ironically, Green Lodge was eventually used. This was as a result of Area 6's concern about both the placement with the foster-parents and also the latter's ability to cope professionally with the plans for the children's future. With a view to allowing Beverley Lorrington and Morris Beckford time to get used to having the children for longer periods during the day, Green Lodge was used as a place where the children could reside; they moved to Green Lodge from the Proberts' home for one week on 13 April 1982. None of the staff at Green Lodge was used to work with the children, except to watch over them when they slept at night after the parents had gone home. Mrs. Dorothy Ruddock and Ms. Gun Wahlstrom did in fact continue to work with the family on a daily basis during the children's time in residence, thus providing a monitoring role and a continuation of their teaching of the parents to acquire parenting skills. During the whole of Miss Gordon's working experience at Green Lodge, this was a wholly unique use of Green Lodge. She informed others of the fact that the use of Green Lodge as a "bricks-and-mortar" base was only ever done in this case. All other children had been admitted to the establishment *prior* to the children being returned to their home, or going onward to a foster-home. If Green Lodge had been used in its normal way, i.e. in August/September 1981, at the very least the Social Worker and her senior would have been less open to criticism, had the children eventually been returned home from the Proberts. We conclude that Mrs. Dietmann and Ms. Wahlstrom were at fault in not having considered Green Lodge in August/September 1981, even if it was only to have ruled it out as an option, although we think it would have been the right option.

We are concerned about the fact that Green Lodge no longer exists. We accept, however, that to use it exclusively as a resource for serious non-accidental injury cases would not be economically justifiable. It would prove to be expensive to maintain, happily because such serious cases of this type rarely occur in one borough. We are aware, however, that professional resources of this nature are available, and we are able to cite as an example a residential resource of this nature that exists in the London area. This is an establishment run and staffed by Dr. Barnardo's and, complementary to this resource, there is a highly professional fostering team that works in harness with the residential establishment. We would hope that if the need arose in the future, social workers would unhesitatingly consider using such a resource.

We draw attention to a statutory power as offering one of the ways in which a local authority may discharge its duty to provide accommodation and maintenance for such a child in care. Under the rubric of Community Homes, section 31, Child Care Act 1980 provides: "(1) A local authority shall make such arrangements as they consider appropriate for securing that homes (in this Act referred to as "community homes") are available for the accommodation and maintenance of children in their care and for purposes connected with the welfare of children, whether in their care or not and, without

---

* J. Aldgate, (1980) in *New Developments in Foster Care and Adoption* edited by Triseliotis J., stated that "only 5% of parents whose children were in residential care said that they would have preferred a foster-home. In contrast to this 40% of the parents whose children were in foster-care thought that the children's home was a preferred placement." The important factor for parents here was that in their eyes "the professionalism of house parents prevented them from stealing children's affections and the attitude of house parents was generally more encouraging to parents than that of foster-parents."

prejudice to section 101(5) of the Local Government Act 1972, may do so jointly with one or more local authorities. (2) In making such arrangements, a local authority shall have regard to the need for ensuring the availability of accommodation of different descriptions and suitable for different purposes and the requirements of different descriptions of children.''

This statutory provision superseded similar provisions in the Children and Young Persons Act 1969, which also required the setting up of Children's Regional Planning Committees to organise the establishment of Community Homes. Regional planning was abolished by the substitution of a new section 31 (quoted above) by virtue of section 4(1), Health and Social Services and Social Security Adjudication Act 1983. **Section 31 invites local authorities to collaborate in setting up a specialist establishment in their region for children who have suffered abuse. We recommend that local authorities should consider exercising such powers.**

CHAPTER 30

Fostering (a) General – Selection and Management

The Curtis Report of 1946 stated that "If the substitute home is to give the child what he gets from a good normal home it must supply:

(i) Affection and personal interest; understanding of his defects; care of his future; respect for his personality and regard for his self esteem.

(ii) Stability; the feeling that he can expect to remain with those who will continue to care for him till he goes out into the world on his own feet.

(iii) Opportunity of making the best of his ability and aptitudes, whatever they may be, as such opportunity is made available to the child in the normal home.

(iv) A share in the common life of a small group of people in a homely environment."

It noted that the view expressed in nearly all quarters was that "boarding-out" (now known as fostering) was on the whole the best method, short of adoption, of providing the child with a substitute for his own home and it recommended:-

> "Boarding out is to be preferred to institutional care for children
> who are suitable for boarding out wherever entirely satisfac-
> tory homes can be found; and a vigorous effort should be made
> by local authorities to extend the system."

Section 13 of the Children Act 1948 listed the various ways in which children in care might be accommodated and maintained by a local authority and, according to the Home Office Circular (160/1948) which accompanied it, "Boarding-out has been placed first as being generally the most satisfactory method of providing a substitute home."

The efforts of Children's Departments in the 1950s to find substitute families for as many of the children in their care as possible were reinforced by research which pointed to the long-term emotional damage which could be caused if very young children were brought up in institutions. Absence of early experience of a close, loving relationship, it was said, could make it impossible for the individual to grow up into an adult capable of making such a relationship with anyone. This led to strenuous attempts on the part of local authorities to avoid placing small children in residential care; most residential nurseries were closed by the 1960s or 1970s and some authorities, including Brent, adopted a firm policy that no young child should be placed in a residential Home.

The belief in a good foster-home as the preferred form of placement for a child in care remains widespread and was echoed by the House of Commons Select Committee in its 1984 report on "Children in Care" – "Most children need the stability and love that only family life can offer." Foster-parents, like natural parents, fall short of perfection but, given this view of fostering, it is understandable that the qualities needed in a good foster-parent were seen to be those of a good natural parent. Indeed, the statutory form of agreement which a foster-parent has to sign still includes, as the first under-taking, "We/I will care for .... and bring him/her up as we/I would a child of our/my own."

In fact, it was never the case that a foster-home could be equated to a good natural family home. As one of our witnesses, Miss Christine Reeves, Director of the National Foster-Care Association, said in her evidence to the House of Commons Select Committee: "Foster-parenting obviously involves many parenting skills and qualities, but foster-parenting is something extra to that." Looking after a child who has other parents can never be the same as looking after one's own. He will, unless placed as a small baby, have memories of life with his own parent(s) and will probably be grieving for the loss of his own family, however unsatisfactory it may seem to the outsider. There may be plans to return him to his own family, and the foster-parents will have to understand that part of their task is to help him to retain his loyalty to his own parents and see them in a positive light. On the other hand, he may have undergone very distressing experiences in his early years and will need skilled therapeutic care if the physical and emotional damage which these have caused is to be overcome. (It does not take much imagination to realise that the foster-parents of Louise and Chantelle Beckford will not only need to give them love and good physical care, but will also have to carry out specialised therapeutic treatment, under the guidance of experts, if the children are to overcome the emotional damage resulting from their early life with their natural parents.)

As far back as 1970, it was suggested by V. George in "Foster-Care: Theory and Practice" that the term, "foster-parent" was a misnomer and that "foster-care worker" would be a better description. More recently, the House of Commons Select Committee observed that "the role of foster-parents has changed considerably." The Select Committee also points out that "in the last decade, almost 10,000 'new' foster-places have been found ..... it is not surprising that this expansion of foster-care has revealed some weaknesses in fostering practice, nor that the inadequate preparation of social workers for this kind of work has been exposed."

Selection of Foster-Parents

To quote the Select Committee yet again, "recruitment of foster-parents is still a pretty haphazard business." In assessing the suitability of applicants to become foster-parents, it is, of course, important to ascertain whether they have the parenting skills and qualities which are characteristic of good natural parents. It is also necessary to take up references, both from private referees and from statutory agencies, regarding the reputation, suitability and physical and mental health of the applicant. Much more than this is needed, however, in order to assess how the applicants are likely to cope with the problems which are likely to arise if they become foster-parents. As a guide to the kind of assessment needed, we commend the report form produced by British Agencies for Adoption and Fostering, which requires the social worker to produce a detailed account of the applicants' backgrounds; relationships with one another and with their children and extended families; philosophy of life; interests, hobbies and talents; parenting capacities; family lifestyle; expectations of the child to be placed. With the kind permission of BAAF, we reproduce this form in full as an annex to this section of the chapter.

The carrying out of such a detailed assessment will obviously involve several visits, extending over a number of weeks. In addition, it is often useful for prospective foster-parents to attend group discussions with social workers and existing foster-parents. The National Foster-Care Association has prepared a very useful training package, "Parenting Plus" which comprises six 2-hour sessions and is used by many Social Services Departments for this purpose. One of our witnesses, Miss Carol Rogers, then acting Principal Officer in the Adoption and Foster-Care Section of Brent Social Services Department, estimated that it would normally take three or four months to prepare prospective foster-parents for their task.

Clearly, the assessment of prospective foster-parents is a specialised task, for which the CQSW course does not provide adequate preparation. We are glad to know that many Social Services Departments, including Brent, now include specialist fostering/adoption sections which are responsible for assessing, training and supporting foster-parents. Social workers in such units should have the time to carry out thorough assessments of the capabilities of prospective foster-parents and should be able to judge the type of child whom they could foster successfully.

The Boarding-out of Children Regulations 1955, which are still in force, state that a child shall not be boarded out unless "the foster-parents and the dwelling where the child will live have been visited by a visitor who is personally acquainted with the child and his needs ..... and the visitor has reported in writing that the sleeping and living accommodation and other domestic conditions at the dwelling are satisfactory and that the household of the foster-parents is likely to suit the particular needs of the child." (Regulation 17(1)(a)). The selection of a foster-home for a specific child must, therefore, be shared between the social worker who has assessed the foster-parents and the social worker who is responsible for the child. The child's social worker should be able to indicate, in the words of Miss Rogers, "the circumstances surrounding the child(ren), what sort of physical and emotional care they needed, what the nature of the request was, whether it was likely to be short term or whether a longer term placement was needed and any circumstances surrounding such issues as contact from parents." The social worker from the fostering/adoption unit would then be able to suggest possible foster-parents who would be suitable for the child, or, if none was available to make a specific effort to recruit such people.

Unfortunately, when a child needs an urgent placement, the selection of suitable foster-parents for him is often scamped, and we have suggested in chapter 29 that it may sometimes be desirable for a temporary residential placement to be made, so that the process of finding suitable foster-parents, and preparing them to meet the needs of the child can be carried out more carefully. The selection of Mr. and Mrs. Probert as suitable foster-parents for Jasmine and Louise Beckford was clearly undertaken in haste. Mr. Burns was still in the process of assessing them when the need arose for a foster-home for the two girls and, although the Proberts were originally assessed as being suitable for one teenage girl, he suggested that they might take Jasmine and Louise, since no other suitable foster-home could be found, despite extensive enquiries in neighbouring London boroughs. Ms. Wahlstrom visited them with Mr. Burns and recorded that she "found both Mr. and Mrs. Probert to be very sensitive and caring people with a lot of affection for each other and their children. I believe that they are very suitable as foster-parents for Louise and Jasmine and have a lot to offer these children." On the basis of this assessment, Louise was placed with the Proberts two days later, with Jasmine following on her discharge from hospital.

Mr. Burns continued with his assessment of the Proberts and his report (on the BAAF form) was commendably thorough but, in fact, most of the assessment process, including a "second opinion visit" by Miss Rogers, took place after the Beckford children were already in the foster-home; indeed it had not been completed by the time the children were removed in April 1982! In particular, Mr. Burns had not had sufficient time to explore fully with the Probert family their feelings about foster-children continuing to have regular contact with their own parents and, possibly, returning to their parents in due course.

Management of Fostering
The House of Commons Select Committee pointed out that foster-parents are "now increasingly regarded less as applicants required to sign statutory undertakings and more as partners in providing substitute care." It welcomed "the development of ..... 'contract fostering' ..... foster-parents and the authority agree in writing the broad outlines of how a placement is to be managed − its length, arrangements for parental access, arrangements for termination of a placement, social worker and financial support and so on. Parents and children can also be included in this informal contract. This sort

of written agreement should become a general practice." We strongly support this recommendation. In the Beckford case, the existence of such a contract would have resolved much of the misunderstanding between the Probert family and the social workers, and we suspect that such misunderstandings between foster-parents and social workers about plans for the foster-children may not be uncommon. The absence of a clear understanding about what is involved is a recipe for the kind of misunderstandings that resulted in the Beckford case.

We consider, in principle, that foster-parents should, as a rule, be involved in case conferences and reviews concerning their foster-children, not only because they have an interest in the children, but, more importantly, because they know a great deal about the children and can contribute valuable information to the discussions. It has been argued that foster-parents should not have access to confidential information about the children but it seems strange to us that people who are being trusted to undertake full time care of the children cannot be trusted with confidential information about them. We have dealt with this issue in chapter 25.

The payment of fees to foster-parents, over and above the normal boarding-out allowances, which barely cover the cost of the child's maintenance, clothing etc., was, at one time, frowned upon, because it was felt that someone caring for a child for payment would give a lower standard of love and care than someone undertaking the task for some other motive. It is now generally recognised, however, that foster-parenting is a quasi-professional job, and most professional people are paid for their work and would be unlikely to carry it out more conscientiously if such payment were denied to them. We consider that payment of fees to foster-parents, particularly when they are caring for children with special problems, may encourage some very suitable people who could not otherwise afford to give up their existing jobs to become foster-parents. (We note, in passing, that the Proberts did receive payment over and above the normal boarding-out allowance since, on the recommendation of Ms. Wahlstrom, a double allowance was paid to them in respect of Jasmine. Ms. Wahlstrom wrote: "Jasmine is a very under-stimulated child and the period in hospital has contributed to her being a very frustrated little girl. In the past, she has been able to get things by screaming. Given the overall picture of this case and likely length of court hearings and the anxieties involved and the amount of care and stimulation that Jasmine will need, I request that double-boarding out rate be paid.")

We have mentioned earlier the very difficult nature of the tasks which many foster-parents are expected to undertake. In carrying out these tasks they, like other workers in the field of Social Services, need training, supervision and support. In this respect, as with the selection of foster-parents, we believe that a specialist fostering unit in a Social Services Department can be of great value. It may be difficult for the child's social worker to act also as a supporter for the foster-parents, and a social worker from the fostering unit, who will keep in touch with the foster-parents, perhaps through a number of different foster-placements, may perform a useful role in this respect. It is, of course, essential that the child's social worker and the foster-parents' social worker should keep in close touch with one another and should not be working in opposition, as apparently happened in the Beckford case.

We have become aware, during the course of this Inquiry, that the development of specialist skills and good practice in the field of fostering owes a great deal to two non-statutory organisations – British Agencies for Adoption and Fostering and the National Foster-Care Association. We have referred earlier to BAAF's work in producing model procedures for many of the functions connected with adoption and fostering and to NFCA's promotion of a training package for foster-parents and the staff who work with them. The influence of these two organisations is widespread throughout the field of foster-care and, to quote Miss Carol Rogers, "the support we get is mainly through the professional association for adoption and fostering matters, who are more able to offer advice and consultation on immediate issues, particularly relating to new legislation."

The two organisations are funded partly by central government, partly by fees from local authorities and partly through their own fund-raising activities. We were glad to learn that BAAF receives membership fees from every Social Services Authority in the country, bar one, and that the NFCA also receives membership fees from many Social Services Authorities. We were, however, very concerned to hear that, because of a recent increase in the membership fee, Brent Borough Council has withdrawn from membership of the NFCA, thus depriving staff and foster-parents of the valuable training material provided by that organisation. **We strongly recommend that the Authority should reverse this decision.**

We have emphasised throughout this chapter the immense demands which are made upon foster-parents, and we agree with the House of Commons Select Committee that "the nation owes a lot to the willingness and enthusiasm of foster-parents." The Committee mentions that it "had several opportunities to meet groups of foster-parents and some of the children they were fostering ..... it was always a refreshing experience." Those of us who have worked with foster-parents over the years wholeheartedly share this view.

Form F

Information on prospective substitute parent(s)

NOTES FOR GUIDANCE

Form F was designed to provide fostering and adoption agencies with a standard way of collecting and presenting information about prospective substitute parents. It aimed to cover all the areas which should be considered during an agency's preparation/assessment process and which would be needed both within the agency (for example, when the application was presented to the panel) and by other agencies (for example, when an Exchange placement was under consideration).

In response to comments about the original format, BAAF has looked again at the structure and content of form F with the aim of maintaining the comprehensive coverage of information while allowing for more flexibility in the presentation of the detailed descriptive material.

The redesigned form F now comprises two distinct sections:

Part I gathers all the factual information together in as concise a format as possible and provides for a brief summary of the skills and interests of the applicants as prospective substitute parent(s). On its own it should give a quick 'overview' of what the applicant has to offer both in general and for a particular child. However, more detailed descriptive information will be needed to give a full picture of the potential of the applicant(s) as foster or adoptive parent(s).

Part II contains guidelines for writing a descriptive report which is intended to enable agencies to record detailed information in whichever way best suits their needs while still maintaining comprehensive coverage. Agencies may find it helpful to use part II as a checklist of areas which need to be covered in the report.

Throughout, the expectation has been that applicants will be actively involved in the completion of form F, perhaps by writing parts of it themselves. In addition, agencies are increasingly making the completed report available to applicants for comment before it is presented to the panel or made available to other people. This practice, while very welcome, has implications for the confidentiality of some of the information provided by third parties such as medical and personal referees. Agencies will need to consider both what detail can be included from such sources and how best to discuss the inclusion of such information with those providing it. However, agencies must, of course, continue to strive to ensure that all the relevant information is made available to their panel when the application is being considered and to colleagues who become involved in placement discussions.

In completing form F and, in particular, when writing the descriptive report, it is vital that social workers include information which supports their statements and so rounds out the picture of the family rather than confining themselves to generalised comments such as 'home-loving': for example, the report should offer the evidence which leads to that conclusion and comment on the importance of this for the family and any child who may be placed with them.

Name of Agency..   Social Worker...

Address..   Senior ....

....   Address...

'Link person' (if any)..   ....

Telephone ....   Telephone ....

Date of completion ....

Updated ....

PART I
DETAILS OF PROSPECTIVE ADOPTIVE OR FOSTER FAMILY

1.   Male   Female

     Surname..(Maiden name if married)

     Forename(s)..

     Date of Birth ....

     Ethnic Origin ....

     Religion...

     Occupation (or previous occupation and when this ceased) ....

     ....

     Availability (e.g. hours of work, shift pattern, etc.)..

     Income (p.a.) ....

     Address ....

     .... Telephone ....

2.   **Children in the household**

Name	Sex	Date of birth	Relationship to applicant(s) (e.g. adopted, etc.)	Type of school

3.   **Other Children** (living elsewhere or deceased)

Name	Sex	Age (or age at death)	Relationship to applicant(s)	Whereabouts (or date and cause of death)

How much current contact do any of the above have with the family and what is their attitude to the proposed placement?

275

4.   **Other Adult Members of the Household** (including grown-up children living at home)

Name	Sex	Age	Relationship	Interviewed (Yes/No)

What is the attitude of these members of the household to the proposed placement?

Have they any particular attributes which could be of significant advantage to a child placed in this home?

---

5.   **Extended Family** (including also friends, neighbours, godparents)

Indicate the most significant relationships in the wider family and neighbourhood, frequency and form of contact and their attitudes toward the proposed placement. If hostile, how do the applicants plan to cope? Have you interviewed any of these people? Have they any particular attributes which could be of significant advantage to a child placed in this home?

---

6.   Has any member of the household or extended family a physical or mental or emotional handicap or difficulty (e.g. senility, asthma, bad heart, etc.)? If so, please name the person and give brief details, including significance for any children of the household.

---

7.   **Family Description** Attach recent photograph(s) of household members. Give brief physical description(s) of the applicant(s) and any children in the family, including height, build and colouring. Give general impression of personality, temperament and any special talents and needs. If any of the children are fostered or adopted, give brief details of their background, placement and present situation including any continuing contact with relatives and others from the past. Give date of placement (and adoption order if applicable). Describe briefly any special relationship between a particular child and a parent (e.g. Daddy's girl, Mother's big boy) or between children (e.g. is there a 'pecking order' or a 'protective' relationship?).   (NB. Detailed information as appropriate should be included in part II of this form.)

Male Applicant:

Female Applicant:

Children

276

8. **Marriage** Present marital status: Male applicant ....

   Female applicant ....

   If married to each other give: Date certificate seen ....

   Date and place of marriage ....

   Has either had a previous marriage? Yes/No. If yes, give details, how terminated and, if children involved, custody arrangements made. Specify documents seen.

9. **Health** (BAAF publishes standard medical forms for the examination of applicants)
   Name, address and telephone (if known) of family doctor(s) ....

   ....

	Date of medical examination and any significant comments by doctor(s)	Date report seen by agency medical adviser and any significant comments

   Male applicant:

   Female applicant:

   Children and other members of the household: any significant comments made by the doctor on their health or adjustment.

10. **Personal references** Number taken up .... Number interviewed ....

    State any particular significant comment by a referee ....

    ....

    ....

11. **Local authority enquiries** (incl. police checks): as required under Adoption Agencies Regulations and Boarding Out Regulations

    Dates reports received ....

    State any significant factor in reports:

12. **Legal information** To which court would adopters apply? ....

    Are any special difficulties likely to arise at this court? ....
    Are they domiciled in the UK, Channel Islands or Isle of Man? Yes/No

    If no give domicile(s) ....

    Nationality .... (Male) .... (Female)

13. **Application** When was application first made? .... When did preparation begin? ....

    State number of times seen: Together .... Separately .... Male applicant .... Female applicant

    Have applicants attended group meeting? Yes/No How Many? ....

    If there are already children in the household, what contact has social worker had with them?

    Date application presented to agency's panel ....

    Decision ....

277

14. **Accommodation, Neighbourhood, Mobility**

 Type and condition of accommodation (including whether rented or mortgaged), and attitudes to housework, e.g. casual, organised, chaotic, house-proud. Include number of living rooms, bedrooms, proposed sleeping arrangements for child, amount of playspace outdoors. Number and kinds of pets kept. Brief description of neighbourhood (include ethnic mix) and special amenities e.g. schools, medical resources, recreation and sports facilities. If family plan to move, give details. Indicate public transport facilities. Do the applicants have a car? (Who drives?) Could they travel for introduction? How do their work and social commitments affect this?

15. **Type of Resource** Please tick box(es) which apply

 PERMANENT ☐ Adoption with/without* contact with parents/wider family*

 ☐ Foster home a. able to adopt or continue fostering as appropriate for child*
 b. able to adopt if finances permit*
 c. with active parental contact*
 d. with wider family contact*

 TIME LIMITED ☐ Adolescents ☐ Mother & Baby
 ☐ Observation & Assessment ☐ Respite Care
 ☐ Short term ☐ Emergency

 ☐ Other (specify) ....

 Can they consider a child where legal situation is complex? Yes/No

 Age range ....

 Sex ☐ male number this ☐ 1
 ☐ female time ☐ 2
 ☐ either ☐ 3
 ☐ more than 3

 Can they consider a handicapped child?

 Physical handicap: No/mild/moderate/severe*
 Mental handicap: No/slow learner/ESN(M)/ESN(S)*
 Emotional handicap: Yes/No*

 Specify any ethnic backgrounds they cannot consider ....

 Specify any other background feature they cannot consider (e.g. mental illness in parent, epilepsy, incest, etc.) ....

 ....

 Special features, if any (e.g. skills, experience, facilities available, interest or proven capacity in working with natural parents) ....

 ....

 State language usually spoken at home, if not English ....

 * delete as appropriate

16. **Social Worker's Assessment**

Comment on the sorts of children this family could consider and the sort they would probably do best with. If there is any disagreement on this point between you and the applicants, it is important to record it so that they may be considered for the widest possible range of children. How did they impress you at first and on closer acquaintance? What use did they make of the preparation period, and how do they expect to use social worker(s), the agency and other 'helping' people such as parent groups, medical support staff, in future? What strengths do you think they have in working with the agency, with other officials, with natural parents and other contacts of importance to the child?

Completed by: Name . . . . Status . . . .

Agency . . . . Date . . . .

PART II

DESCRIPTIVE REPORT

Please give details of the following:

1. **INDIVIDUAL PROFILE ON EACH APPLICANT**

   a. **Background:** family of origin; childhood experiences; significant details of other family members.

   b. **Education:** type of school; any qualifications; attitude to school.

   c. **Employment:** work experience; attitude to work; present job and plans for future.

   d. **Interests/Talents:** what? when? who with?

   e. **Personality, Philosophy/Religion:** self-presentation; underlying values; religious observances; tolerance and expectations of other family members' philosophy/religion.

2. **PREVIOUS RELATIONSHIPS**

   Describe any previous significant relationships and their outcome. If there were children of this relationship, what difficulties did they experience, how did they cope, what present contact is there between the applicant and the child/children?

3. **PRESENT RELATIONSHIP**

   a. **For a single applicant**
   Are there significant relationships outside the home?
   What makes this situation stable and satisfying?
   What are the possible areas of strain? (Adjustments as a single parent if applicable.)

   b. **For two applicants**
   Include brief details of the development of the relationship; what makes it stable and satisfying to both partners? What are the possible areas of strain? How do they cope with problems? How much communication is there between them? How do they deal with disagreements/anger? What evidence is there of mutual support and understanding? How do they show feelings/tenderness? How are the roles distributed? Is there a dominant partner?

4. **PARENTING CAPACITY**

   For each applicant please describe:-

   a. actual and potential attitudes to children and child rearing;

   b. use of own childhood experience – what would he/she repeat with his/her own children and what would be changed?

   c. knowledge of child development;

   d. experience of children.

5. **CHILDLESSNESS/LIMITATION OF FAMILY SIZE**

   Are the reasons for childlessness known? If so, please give them. Give brief but specific details of when they first learned of it, how they have coped with it and the degree to which they have come to terms with it at present. Are they aware that they may never come to terms fully with childlessness or an inability to have more children and that their feelings about it will probably be revived at various times in their lives, for example when discussing an adopted child's origins? For couples that have made a conscious decision to limit the size of their family, please comment on how they arrived at this decision and whether both partners are equally committed to this plan.

6. **DESCRIPTION OF FAMILY LIFESTYLE**

   Indicate the sort of family life a child placed in this home would experience. It is especially important in the placement of older children where the child's previous lifestyle needs to be considered in choosing a family. Some things to include are whether they are open or controlled in expressing feelings; are cuddlers or touch-me-nots; do things as a family group or have separate activities; are very much involved with neighbours, friends, church, clubs, etc.

   What are their attitudes to money and food? What are their attitudes to health and ill-health? How important is school achievement and homework? Are there household rules and how strict are they? What sort of punishments are there and who decides them? How are birthdays and special occasions celebrated? What special roles exist in the family? Are sexual roles important, e.g. is there a stress on femininity for girls, toughness for boys?

What are the expectations of where and how another child will fit into the family patterns? If there are already children in the family, describe how they have been involved in the preparations, what views they have on the plan and their understanding of the implications for them.

Encourage the family to contribute particularly to this section, perhaps by describing a day in their lives. Include information on individual and family hobbies and interests.

7. **MOTIVATION/PREPARATION**

Comment on their expressed motivation to adopt/foster and indicate any factors you think significant (for example the applicants' own experiences of separation, deprivation or bereavement). Do they know other adopters/foster parents? How have they used the preparation offered by your agency? Comment on the applicants' development during the preparation period – in what ways, if any, do you and they think they have changed? If offering a permanent home, what plan have they for the child's future care if their present family structure is disrupted, for example, by serious illness or marital breakdown? How do you assess their present understanding of the tasks involved and their ability, willingness and understanding of the need to work in partnership with the agency?

8. **EXPECTATIONS OF PLACEMENT**

a. **Child's background**

What are the applicants feelings about heredity? Comment also on their attitude to various background factors such as mental illness and retardation. Can they accept a child where little is known about the father and/or the mother? If they are considering a child of a different ethnic origin, what evidence is there of their knowledge and acceptance of his or her ethnicity? What specific plans have they to help the child identify with his or her heritage, feel positive about origins and form a positive (ethnic) self-image? Have they an understanding of the problems involved in coping with a cross-cultural identity? How do they hope to help the child cope with the individual racism he/she will encounter? How will the family cope with the racial prejudice they will meet in a dominant white society?

b. **Child as he/she is**

Do the applicants have expectations of the child's appearance, educational achievement, behaviour, etc? What is their understanding of possible areas of disturbance such as delayed or excessive affection, testing, acting out, attention seeking, rivalry, bullying, bed wetting, stealing, etc? What behaviour would be intolerable to them? What is their attitude to medical problems, physical and mental handicap? Do they have any special skills, experience or local facility to offer to a child with special needs?

For families interested in taking an adolescent: what is their attitude to emerging independence, peer group pressures, mood swings, sexual development, regression, etc? For baby adopters: are they prepared for the possibility of a baby being placed with them directly from hospital? What is their attitude to this and their understanding of the implications?

c. **Contact with natural family/people from the child's past**

What are their expectations of contact with natural parents and other relatives? If adopting or offering a permanent family, how far are they prepared to maintain a child's links with natural parents, relatives, or other people from his or her past?

If offering a shorter term home, what is your assessment of their capacity to:

1. work with the parents and the agency towards rehabilitation or other placement,

2. establish a caring relationship with the natural parents,

3. withstand the child's distress after visits,

4. be willing to offer visiting parents meals or over-night accommodation regularly/occasionally,

5. cope with difficult parental behaviour.

Describe any parental behaviour you and/or they think they would find particularly difficult or to which they feel particularly sympathetic.

(b) Trans-Racial Fostering

When the Beckford case first hit the headlines in March 1985 it was readily assumed in certain sections of the public that the Beckford children had been "snatched away" from the Proberts' home by social workers, by virtue only of the supposed philosophy among social workers which was hostile to trans-racial fostering. The Proberts were seen as "white" and the Beckford sisters were "black", and never the twain shall mix.

We have found, without much hesitation, that, given the inadequate assessment of the Beckford parents and the lack of appreciation of the available evidence (described in Chapter 8), the reuniting of the Beckford children with their parents would have taken place in April 1982 irrespective of where the children had been living after they left hospital in August/September 1981. Whether they had been in residential care, or had been fostered with families who were black, white or brown, they would have gone back home to their parents. It was strictly unnecessary for us, therefore, to examine, what has become a topic of intense argument, whether it is right to place black children in white families. But we felt we could not avoid examining the issue, and to that end we have heard four experts on the topic, reflecting the spectrum of informed opinion on the subject. This part of this chapter owes nothing to the facts of the Beckford case, and only a single allusion to the Proberts; it is a discussion of a topic that will no doubt occupy the professionals in social work for some time to come. We offer our observations, gleaned from our reading of the literature and advice from experts, as a contribution to that debate. We have also related our observations to the law as we find it.

Origins of the problem
While black children have been fostered and adopted by white families for many years, it has become a systematic practice only since the late 1960s. Faced with the growing numbers of immigrants from the black Commonwealth at that time, and correspondingly the numbers of black children in care, the British Adoption Project was established to answer the question: "Can families be found for coloured children?" The answer was yes; the follow-up studies showed the families and the children were "doing well". From then onwards, trans-racial adoption as the appropriate plan for black children without parents of their own became established practice. Although the study related to adoption, it clearly had implications for the closely associated process of fostering.

The social and demographic changes in Britain in the 1970s reduced the availability for adoption by strangers of healthy white babies from a peak of 14,000 in 1968 to less than 2,000 in 1974 and probably to less than 1,400 by 1984. Changes in the abortion law, increased availability and use of contraception, and changes in social attitudes which enabled, even encouraged, unmarried mothers to keep their children – all these contributed to the shift in adoption practice. Given the "shortage" of healthy white babies, many potential adopters considered taking into their homes "non-white" children. The practice of trans-racial placements with foster-parents, with a view to adoption, thus became commonplace by the beginning of this decade.

The demographic changes fitted comfortably with the contemporary philosophy of race relations. Crudely expressed, the idea was that race was irrelevant, and integration was best achieved by a mixture of races. Many of the trans-racial adopters believed that they were making a personal gesture towards a healthy, racially integrated society in which racial discrimination would wither and die. Today, it is the same people who feel angry, let down and distressed by a different philosophy of racial integration which challenges the basic assumption on which their own racially mixed families were created. This may supply the explanation for the unhelpful attitude of the Proberts, who in the

1970s had adopted two mixed-parentage children, when they agreed to foster the Beckford sisters in August 1981.

Fostering practice developed along parallel lines. Throughout the 1970s the overwhelming majority of black children in care who were boarded-out, was placed with white families. Mr. Tony Hall, Director and Secretary of the British Agencies for Adoption and Fostering (BAAF) told us that unfortunately, owing to an initial reluctance on the part of many organisations to collect data on the racial origins of their clients, there has been no systematic monitoring of issues, such as the effect of trans-racialism. As a result, service planning and development of trans-racial fostering has been seriously hampered. In the absence of research results, policy has been left largely to the politicians. The battleground was the growing political awareness and activity of the ethnic minorities. The immediate engagement was centred on the research begun in 1976, and the publication of the results in 1983, of *Adoption and Race*, a major research financed by the DHSS and conducted under the auspices of the Association of British Adoption and Fostering Agencies.

The ambivalence of its findings, if not its conclusions, spawned a variety of responses from a variety of sources. Trans-racial parents and the national press criticised the researchers for failing adequately to emphasise the positive findings that black children in white homes seemed to do well at home, in school and within the community. Black observers and others criticised the research as having been conducted entirely by white researchers, who failed to take account of the children's racial identity. We quote from Mr. Hall's evidence to us:

"This controversy stemmed from the researchers' interpretation of two broadly conflicting sets of data. They did not find evidence of major behavioural problems. Far from it. Most of the children appeared to enjoy family life, got on well with parents, siblings and friends, were doing well at school and had a high self-esteem. They concluded, in carefully chosen language, that 'By and large, using conventional measures of adoption success, the children in the placements studied appeared to be doing well.' But — and it was a very big BUT — other data pointed to less obvious and immediate problems. Most of the children studied were the only black child in their class, or even in their school; most had few if any black friends; most of their parents had no black friends; most had little knowledge or understanding of their racial origins or little direct contact with their culture of origin. Few of the families had moved house during the study period, but those who had, had moved from mixed ethnic areas into predominantly white environments. The picture seen and described by the researchers was one of black children being brought up in racial and cultural isolation. Perhaps not surprisingly the children 'did not see themselves as black or show any real sign of having developed a sense of racial identity'. The children, while not directly denying their racial background, perceived themselves as white in all but skin colour.

On the strength of these findings, the researchers concluded that wherever possible black children needing a permanent substitute home should be placed in black rather than white families. To this end they made a strong plea for local authorities and adoption societies to put greater efforts into finding black families for black children in care, waiting to be adopted. To achieve this they argued for 'more black social workers in key agency posts that determine policy, more black social workers involved in family finding and child placement, and increased sensitivities on the part of social workers in general to the strengths of the black community as providers of alternative families'.''

Contemporary fostering of black children

The report was nevertheless severely realistic. For some time to come some trans-racial placements would need to be made, unless society was prepared to countenance leaving large numbers of black children doomed to remain for the rest of their childhood in residential care. Given that reality, and the comparative paucity of potential black foster-parents, it was hardly surprising that most local authorities' Social Services Departments did not abandon trans-racial fostering, while at the same time doubling their efforts to find more black foster-parents. A few local authorities, however, announced a policy of commitment to same-race placements.

The British Agencies for Adoption and Fostering Secretary has a policy that, wherever possible, children should be placed with families of the same cultural origin. Good matching of the child to its foster-parents, as professionally developed by fostering agents over the last 20 years, demands that the match-maker tries to find the best possible opportunities for the child to have all the advantages that a child has in any family, with the additional advantage of a black child being placed with black parents that the family does not have to struggle with coping with the problems of racial identity, because it is built into the family from the start. Just as an agency would look instinctively to place a Jewish refugee from Nazi Germany in the 1930s with an identifiably Jewish family in England, so an Afro-Caribbean child in care today would be likely to be placed with an Afro-Caribbean family settled in Britain in the 1960s. But placing black children with black foster-parents would never be automatic. Such placement would merely be the product of good matching, which takes account of ethnic origins as important, not conclusive, features of the cultural whole. So long as a white family displayed the willingness and capacity to enable a black foster-child to establish and maintain contact with the black community and to develop a real sense of his own racial identity and heritage, there should be no obstacle to that foster-placement, in the absence of suitable black foster-parents.

The essence of good child care planning is to find the best available situation for each individual child, and more individual black children ideally would be better placed with black families. To that end, we support a drive to recruit more black families to look after black children in care. We do not, however, support those who wish to place a complete ban on trans-racial fostering. Such a policy is the antithesis of the flexible approach that we favour. The policy is in any event, we think, unlawful.

Race Relations Law

Section 23(2) of the *Race Relations Act 1976* overruled the decision of the House of Lords in *Race Relations Board v. Applin** in which it was held that section 2 of the

---

* [1975] AC 259

Race Relations Act 1968 (the predecessor of section 20 of the 1976 Act) applied to foster-parents. Section 23(2) provides that section 20(1) (which makes it unlawful to discriminate against a person who seeks to obtain or use goods, facilities or services) does not apply to anything done by a person as a participant in arrangements under which he takes into his home, and treats as if they were members of his family, *inter alia*, children. The effect of section 23(2) is that discrimination on racial grounds in the choice of foster-children is not unlawful, so that a prospective foster-parent could properly stipulate that he or she was prepared to foster only white, or as the case may be, black children. It would appear that secion 23(2) would apply to a local authority, insofar as the local authority is a participant in arrangements within the meaning of that subsection. On the face of it, therefore, a policy of "same-race" placement, enforced by a local authority Social Services Department, does not contravene the race relations legislation. But we do think that there is a more fundamental argument that such a policy is unlawful.

It is clear that a local authority has a statutory duty to act in the best interests of a child's welfare. At all times, a local authority has to consider how to exercise its discretion in order to perform its duties. It must take the individual case and decide what is best for the child; it must not, in advance of such decision-making process, exclude any relevant factor. It must not, what the lawyers call, "fetter its discretion"; otherwise it acts unlawfully. There is a direct case law decision to that effect.

In *R. v. Wandsworth London Borough Council, ex p. Tilley*,* the Court of Appeal had to consider a case where the local authority had adopted a policy, that assistance with housing should not be provided under the Children and Young Persons Act 1963 if the child's parents had rendered themselves "intentionally homeless" within the Housing (Homeless Persons) Act 1977. The Council's policy was to consider receiving the children into care and not to provide housing assistance. The Court held that this policy was *ultra vires*, since it would prevent the Council considering whether on the facts of the particular case the child's welfare required that he remain with his parents, if accommodation could be found for the family. The fact that the parents had become "intentionally homeless" was a factor to be taken into account in deciding how the local authority's power could best be exercised in the interests of the child. But one thing the local authority could not do was to lay down a general policy without exceptions. Even if there were exceptions to the policy, Lord Justice (now Lord) Templeman thought that the decision of the local authority based on its policy would be struck down by the courts.

Conclusion

We do not favour any ban on trans-racial fostering. We recognise that techniques of good matching may indicate that black children in care may more often than not have a better opportunity in life if they are fostered with black families. But we stress that it is the replication of the child's cultural heritage to the prospective foster-parents' cultural life that matters. Race and colour are important, but not decisive components of such matching.

Each case of a black child in care must be considered on its own merits. There must be no policy laid down in advance as to where that child's best interests lie. **We recommend that a greater effort be made to recruit black families as prospective foster-parents in order to provide the greatest measure of choice to local authorities seeking to place for fostering and adoption black children in their care.**

* [1981] 1 W.L.R. 854

CHAPTER 31

Conclusions

On any conceivable version of the events under inquiry the death of Jasmine Beckford on 5 July 1984 was both a predictable and preventible homicide. Even if it was not predicted, it was certainly preventible at the instance of those public authorities – health, education, social services and magistrates' court – which since August 1981 had had in their disparate ways individual and collective responsibility for her welfare. The blame must be shared by all these services in proportion to their various statutory and other legal powers and duties, and to the degree of actual and continuing involvement with the Beckford family. To the extent that Ms. Wahlstrom and Miss Leong were the two workers in the front line of social and health services, they must take some personal responsibility for what happened. But in no sense was either Ms. Wahlstrom or Miss Leong callous or indifferent to Jasmine's welfare. They had little or no training to qualify them to undertake the task of providing a child protection service, and furthermore they were pitchforked by their superiors, respectively Mrs. Dietmann and Miss Tyler, into a specialty of case-work, with very limited, if any knowledge of, and minimal experience in dealing with child abuse, a subject (as we have painfully discovered) about which there is both much ignorance generally in the social work field and far too little expertise even among those whose disciplines are directly involved. Furthermore, we have found that far too little professional and moral support was given to the two workers in their difficult task of discerning the warning signs (of which there were many) of impending disaster, and particularly around Christmas 1983 when Chantelle Beckford was born.

* * * * *

The Magistrates' Court at Willesden had the least involvement of the four public authorities, but its significant intervention in the sequential events was earliest in time, and hence a crucial one. Had the Magistrates on 9 September 1981 exercised appropriate judicial restraint, and refrained from the understandable temptation to pronounce, in the presence of the parents and their legal representatives, their earnest hope that the children would soon be reunited with their parents, it is doubtful (to put it no higher) whether Jasmine (and her sister, Louise) would ever have been returned to her parents' home. At least the Area 6 manager, Mr. David Bishop, might have remained unpersuaded of the correctness of a home on trial for Jasmine and Louise.

We believe that, for the period of fostering, the Probert household would have provided a loving and caring environment for Jasmine and her sister, Louise, just as had been provided over the years for the Proberts' two adopted daughters. The only time in her short and distressing life that Jasmine consistently thrived and demonstrated not just the outward, but evident signs of happiness was the period of seven months, September 1981 to April 1982, when she was being fostered by the Proberts. Had Jasmine continued to be fostered, or been adopted, she would probably have developed normally, both the physical and psychological scars of her battered body healed.

While we acknowledge the quality of parenting provided by the Proberts, we cannot say the same for their behaviour, once it became clear to them that Jasmine and Louise were not to remain but were to be returned to the Beckford household. One can readily appreciate the attachment nurtured in those few months, in particular, the devotion shown to Jasmine by the younger of the adopted daughters, even if (as we conclude) the Proberts had unjustifiably thought that the placement of Jasmine and Louise was fostering for more than a few months. We have to record, with regret, that their behaviour, in early 1982, did nothing to assist the Social Services personnel of Area 6 in the delicate task of implementing the decision to return the children to the parents. The task of removing the children and resettling them in the Beckford household was made infinitely more difficult by the failure of the Proberts actively to promote the smooth transition. The Proberts' behaviour led to friction between themselves and the social workers, that spilled over into public allegations and recriminations, after Jasmine's death, that were never substantiated. The popular press, ever avid for sensationalism and for evidence to buttress its innate and irrational hostility to social workers, repeatedly stated that the children had been "snatched, screaming" from the Proberts' home (a phrase which had its most flagrant repetition in *The Spectator* of 25 April 1985). This gross distortion of what happened – there were a few tears from Louise and understandable distress from Mrs. Probert who remained indoors while the children were taken by Mrs. Dietmann and a locum family aide to the car – was never denied by the Proberts until they appeared before this Inquiry and, through their counsel, withdrew any suggestion of improper conduct by social workers. We have to say that much of the public anger directed at social workers, and generated by the popular press, should have been assuaged by a firm and prompt public denial from the Proberts of any inhumane or improper behaviour.

* * * * *

Dr. Kempe, the author of the concept, the battered-child syndrome, once wrote: "If a child is not safe at home, he cannot be protected by case work." Of our expert witnesses, Professor Greenland and Dr. Leonard Taitz unqualifiedly endorsed this statement, and Dr. John Warner and Dr. Hugh Jolly echoed the sentiment. Nothing that we have heard at our Inquiry or read in the reports of other inquiries and in the various studies and research findings detracts one iota from the profound wisdom of that statement. Indeed, we have come to the firm conclusion that once a high risk situation is identified by social services and is endorsed by a judicial process in the form of a Care Order, no amount of input from Social Services (even if fully supported by the other agencies) can provide adequate protection for the child. Our finding that Jasmine was severely abused in November 1982, when the input of Social Services was extensive, amply bears out the point.

To think in terms of rehabilitation for the high-risk child is, to quote Dr. Taitz, to indulge in "bonding with barbed wire" or, as we would put it, to tighten a ligature that strangles. We do not define "high risk", mainly because we think that it is not susceptible of definition. Like the concept of dangerousness in the criminal justice system generally, it may even be dangerous to define it, simply because any definition will enmesh many cases which should not be caught in the net. We have in mind the case of an abusing cohabitee who later ceases to cohabit with the child's mother. The abused child could then properly be reunited with his mother. But all those engaged in the multi-disciplinary process of managing the child abuse system will need to assess – and regularly to reassess so as to note any improvement that would indicate a home on trial – whether the risk to a particular child in its parents' home is so great as to warrant long-term removal of the child from potential abuse at the hands of its parents. The proportion of "high risk" cases out of all proved cases of persistent child abuse will be small, and the task of identifying them may not be easy. But the attempt to isolate such cases from the majority of child abuse cases must always be made. To the question, can "high risk" situations be identified in advance, Professor Greenland told us that he could give an answer, "a cautious yes – in some cases". He went on to say that it seemed prudent to classify all non-accidental injuries to young children as "high risk" cases, since 80% of all children unlawfully killed by their parents had been previously abused. **Research**

designed to refine the techniques for predicting accurately those children who will continue to be at risk is urgently required, and we recommend that such research should be undertaken by medical sociologists. We have particularly in mind predictive techniques of dangerousness. We have become aware of one very recent, as yet unpublished, study from the Department of Paediatrics at Sheffield University that indicates that where children show substantial "catch-up" growth in foster-homes (as in the case of Jasmine) it is very doubtful whether it is appropriate to effect an early return home of the children.

The Review of Child Care Law (a report to ministers of an interdepartmental working party, published on 4 October 1985) has stated (para 2.13) that "only where children are put at unacceptable risk should it be possible compulsorily to intervene. Once such a risk of harm to the child has been shown, however, his interests must clearly predominate." We entirely agree. We endorse the remark that "the child is not the child of the State", but where the child is seen to be clearly in need of protection from his parents, the State must be his prime protector. We think that the English concept of the sovereign as *parens patriae* is suitable to describe the nature of the protection. While we were writing our report the decision of 17 October 1985 in *Gillick* v. *West Norfolk and Wisbech Area Health Authority and the Department of Health and Social Security** was handed down. We take comfort from the proposition, expressed or implied in all five speeches of the Law Lords, that parental rights cannot be insisted upon by a parent who has abused those rights. A decision by a local authority, armed with a Care Order, to reunite a child with its parents who have severely abused it can be made only where there are substantial reasons for believing that there will be an improvement in parental behaviour, such that parental rights can be properly exercised. And even then there must be a protection plan as part of the home on trial, to which the parents must be contractually bound. Short of such reasons and a willingness on the part of the parent to be bound by a protection plan, the child should not be exposed to risk, at least not for the near future.

Rather than indulge in a massive investment of social resources, which at the optimum can minimise only marginally the risk of injury, fatal or serious, to the child at home, and which impoverishes other areas of social service provisions, society should sanction, in "high-risk" cases, the removal of such children for an appreciable time. Such a policy, we calculate, might save many of the lives of the 40 to 50 children who die at the hands of their parents every year, and at the same time would concentrate scarce and costly resources of Social Services Departments to the "grey area" of cases where something more than supervision, and something less than long-term removal, is indicated. It is on those children who are at risk – but where the risk is problematical – that Social Services should concentrate their efforts. Those are the children who, while living with their parents at home on trial, must remain in trust to the local authority. And we do mean "trust". A local authority in possession of a Care Order is a trustee-parent with duties appropriate to a standard higher than just the reasonable parent.

* * * * *

Properly evaluated, through a full Social Services' assessment and contributions from all the professionals who attended the Case Conferences on 6 and 20 August 1981, the evidence that was available, if only it had been assiduously culled from existing sources, should have led ineluctably to the conclusion that Jasmine and Louise Beckford presented a high risk situation. At least by the autumn of 1981, when the import of Dr. Levick's report should have been absorbed, together with a proper profile of the Beckford parents, there should have been no question of the children being returned to the Beckford household in the near future. There should have been, moreover, no hint to the Magistrates on 9 September 1981 that the local authority would be responding to any entreaty from parents, the children's legal representatives or the Bench that an early reuniting of the children with their parents could be anything more than the remotest possibility. We conclude that Mr. Thompson, the Court Officer of the Social Services Department, was at fault in not indicating forcefully to the Bench, either before or immediately after the remarks were made, that it would be unhelpful (to say the least) that hope should be instilled in the parents that they might get their children back. We do not think that Ms. Wahlstrom did more than indicate to the Magistrates that rehabilitation was still only an option. The failure to indicate that a return of the children was the least likely option facilitated the Magistrates' influential remarks, which in their turn prompted the engagement of a plan of rehabilitation. Had the local authority not responded to the Magistrates' expressed hope, there would have been a real risk of a successful application by the parents to have the Care Orders revoked. From the moment that Mr. Thompson passed on the Court's recommendation, without indicating (as we have found) his view that it had no legal effect whatsoever and could be ignored, there was a lemming-like movement towards the dénouement of 5 July 1984. Every step in the process over the next two and three quarter years was taken against the backcloth of an ill-conceived programme of rehabilitation. Every step taken was part of the social work mosaic which bore the brand of inevitable disaster upon its face. In that sense Ms. Wahlstrom and Miss Leong can be excused for their individual failings to prevent the oncoming homicide.

* * * * *

On the assumption (which we have concluded was unwarranted) that the Beckford children fell into what we call the "grey area" of child abuse and were not "high risk" cases, we now consider whether, and to what extent (if at all) the various agencies through their individual employees failed to monitor the Beckford children's lives for the period from 19 April 1982 to 5 July 1984, and to take appropriate emergency action by way of removal of the children. Short of evasive action to remove the children, we repeat our conclusion that no amount of casework in the Beckford household could have prevented the severe abuse of Jasmine that we find occurred in November 1982 and again, persistently, from September 1983 until 5 July 1984. And even if a massive input of casework could have improved the parental behaviour of Beverley Lorrington and Morris Beckford towards the children (and we doubt whether any significant change could have been effected), such improvement would have involved long-term therapy, and would have come far too late in the day for it to have been reflected advantageously in the children's development.

The crucial step towards the return of the children was the decision of the Case Conference of 5 April 1982. No doubt there was, by then, a high degree of commitment by Social Services to place the children back home for a trial period. We think that at least Mrs. Dietmann and Ms. Wahlstrom started down the road to rehabilitation as far back as September 1981. But we conclude that the decision was materially affected by a failure to make a proper appraisal. The participants in that appraisal were exclusively from Social Services and did not, as the policy memorandum of 1977 required, reflect the "team approach" with other agencies (particularly health) directly involved in the process of decision-making; the meeting was chaired, undesirably, by Mr. Bishop, who had direct line-management responsibility for the case; inadequate information had been obtained about the children's development (in particular the basic knowledge of Jasmine's abnormally low weight and the dramatic upsurge in her weight-gain while being fostered); and insufficient knowledge had been gleaned from the foster-parents generally about the children's welfare. Over and above those missing elements, there was no one present to supply an objective view of the case. Had those factors been injected into a rather perfunctory discussion, the children might not have been taken home, although we think that that meeting did no more than endorse the informal decision to reunite the family. Once that decision had been made, no criticism can be levelled at anyone in Social Services for the manner in which the removal of the children from the Proberts home was effected. A painful action was handled with care and sympathy.

From April 1982 until November 1982 the actual input of social work with the Beckfords was by any standards impressive and even then, with a reduction in casework, the actual visiting to the Beckford home was, by the standards of case work with a family not subject to a Care Order in respect of the children, adequate until September 1983. Although Miss Leong did not see Jasmine after June 1983, Ms. Wahlstrom and Mrs. Ruddock, the family aide, provided good support to the Beckfords. Mrs. Ruddock, however, carried on visiting voluntarily and not as part of the planned social work input of Area 6. We reserve one comment for Mrs. Ruddock. Her work as reflected in the documentation and in the testimony of others was first-class, and when she appeared before us this impression was more than amply justified.

There is evidence strongly suggesting — and we so find — that in November of 1982 Jasmine Beckford was being abused in her parents' home. The earliest of Jasmine's bone injuries, identified on the x-rays by Mr. Geoffrey Walker, a consultant orthopaedic surgeon, when he appeared before us, could have been inflicted, he thought, as early as September 1982. Given the significant fact that from 2 November 1982 Jasmine ceased altogether to attend Mortimer Road Day Nursery — and started nursery schooling only on 11 January 1983 at Princess Frederica Primary School — we have inferred that that early injury coincided with the Beckford parents keeping Jasmine at home during that period, deliberately screened from any public authority. The fact of non-attendance was reported by Miss Proudlock to Ms. Wahlstrom on 8 and 22 November 1982, and she told us that she had mentioned the fact at the Case Conference on 9 November 1982, although there is no mention of it in the minutes. Yet no one in Area 6 treated this well-recognised index of child abuse, coupled with the fact that Ms. Wahlstrom on 4 November 1982 had recorded serious disharmony between the Beckford parents, as putting a large question mark over the viability of the home on trial. Far from properly indulging in a discussion at the Case Conference of 9 November 1982 that led to the removal of the children from the child abuse register, Area 6 should have been actively considering whether to terminate the home on trial. Had Area 6 directed its mind to that issue, things might have been different.

A further piece of evidence suggests that physical abuse on Jasmine had re-started in about September 1983. This evidence involves the Education Department of the local authority. Jasmine had been placed by her mother at the nursery section of Princess Frederica Primary School in January 1983, just after Jasmine's third birthday. (We strongly suspect that this was deliberate in order to avoid the daily surveillance operating at Mortimer Road Day Nursery; it was interpreted, over-trustingly, by Ms. Wahlstrom as a sign of Beverley Lorrington's positive approach to the rearing of Jasmine). Although Ms. Wahlstrom had, by telephone, notified Miss Cowgill, the then headmistress of the school, of Jasmine having a social worker (without indicating that she was under a Care Order), and that she should be contacted "if there was any problem", that piece of information did not percolate into any record at the school; nor was any nursery teacher notified of it. Since Jasmine had by then been removed from the child abuse register, it is hardly surprising that Miss Cowgill was not told that Jasmine was at risk. When Jasmine came to school one day with bruising on her face, Beverley Lorrington's explanation that it had resulted from a fall from her bicycle was understandably accepted.

Had the system set up by Brent Education Department since 1977 operated as it should have done, Social Services would have been alerted. Another aspect of fault in the educational services was the failure to recognise the significance of the irregular attendance by Jasmine both before, and more significantly after June 1983. After all, Miss Cowgill was asked to contact Ms. Wahlstrom "if there was any problem". Jasmine returned to school for a few days at the beginning of the autumn term, but never again attended after 9 September 1983 (ironically the second anniversary of the Care Orders) round about which time, we conclude, the acts of child abuse had re-started. Again, the only notification by the school was a form to the Health Services, stating inaccurately, or at least ambiguously, that Jasmine had "moved". These failures contributed in some measure towards the absence of vital information in the process of monitoring Jasmine's welfare.

By the autumn of 1983, the Beckford children had been nearly a year off the child abuse register and would have been no longer subject to Care Orders, had the Magistrates in June 1983 acceded to the application to discharge them. It is our conclusion that the social workers nevertheless subconsciously downgraded the Care Orders and treated the case as one requiring nothing more than cursory supervision. This conclusion is underscored by the fact that no one in Social Services thought of obtaining a Care Order in respect of Chantelle in December 1983 to accompany the Care Orders in respect of her siblings, or at the very least of convening a case conference to consider such action. Had they regarded the monitoring appropriate to a continuing Care Order as subsisting, they would undoubtedly have replaced Mrs. Ruddock when she ceased to be the family aide, to go on a training course. To have left the key worker, Ms. Wahlstrom, without the supervision of her senior social worker, Mrs. Dietmann (who was herself on maternity leave from May to November 1983), minus Mrs. Ruddock, and with little or no help from Miss Leong, the Health Visitor, was not to put too fine a point on it, foolhardy. This was the more so since the Beckfords were expecting their third child. In short, the pregnancy of Beverley Lorrington presented such a potentially stressful period for the family – in particular in the immediate pre- and post-natal weeks of November, December and January – that far from lessening the input of Social Services support, it should have been considerably stepped up. It is this period that arouses our severest criticism of both Social Services and Health Services. The fact of Beverley's pregnancy was recorded in both Ms. Wahlstrom's Social Worker's Report and in Miss Leong's family and children's visiting cards. Neither Mrs. Dietmann (from November 1983 onwards) nor Miss Tyler (until she ceased to be the supervisor after December 1983), the respective supervisors of the two field workers, did anything during the winter of 1983/84 to exercise anything approaching the regular supervision that is expected of senior managers. It is still the inescapable fact that not just they, but most of the main actors contributed to the tragedy – social service personnel, medical staff, health visitors and their managers, schools and magistrates; some more than others.

There can be little doubt that by the Autumn of 1983 Jasmine and Louise were being exposed daily (even hourly) to physical abuse in the Beckford home (When Jasmine died, it was found that she had suffered blows to her legs and thighs going back many months (one of them, as we find, as far back as November 1982), and her siblings, Louise and Chantelle, born in December 1983, had similarly suffered physical injuries). One last chance of saving Jasmine was presented when Ms. Wahlstrom visited the Beckford home on 12 March 1984. We have described in detail in chapter 10 what took place during the 45-minute visit on that day. We have to conclude that Ms. Wahlstrom lamentably failed to see what was crying out to be seen, namely, a grossly undernourished, limping child who could not conceivably be described by the most undiscerning of visitors – let alone by a trained social worker – as "well and happy." That description, contemporaneously recorded by Ms. Wahlstrom, was not just a travesty; it was empty of meaning. Her substitute phrase at the Inquiry, "calm and contented" was no less vacuous. It was based on the most fleeting and cursory inspection that any social worker, armed with the full legal authority of a Care Order and possessed of the duty of a trustee of the child's welfare, could possibly make. There's the rub.

Throughout the three years of social work with the Beckfords Ms. Wahlstrom totally misconceived her role as the field worker enforcing Care Orders in respect of two very young children at risk. Her gaze was focused on Beverley Lorrington and Morris Beckford; she averted her eyes to the children to be aware of them only as and when they were with their parents, hardly ever to observe their development, and never to communicate with Jasmine on her own. The two children were regarded as mere appendages to their parents who were treated as the clients, although Ms. Wahlstrom did tell the Magistrates in 1981 that her "primary role is the welfare of the children." (In the meticulous record of nearly 100 pages of detailed notes kept by Ms. Wahlstrom and others in the Social Worker's Report there is not a single entry devoted exclusively to Jasmine and Louise). Even when Ms. Wahlstrom and Mrs. Dietmann searched, almost frantically, for the Beckford family on that fatal day in July 1984, their irritation at not being able to track the family down was aroused, not by an urgent need to see the children but by their desire to set in motion the overdue review procedure preparatory to reapplying to the court for the revoking of the Care Orders. Before us these two social workers failed to perceive that their prime, if not exclusive, duty was, whether urgently or not, to ensure that the children were fit and well after a period of nearly 4 months since they had last been seen. There was a total absence, both during the relevant three years and in their evidence to us, of any sense by either social worker of trustee-parenthood in play. If (as we find) Ms. Wahlstrom's approach to her task was fundamentally flawed, Mrs. Dietmann's attitude as the supervisor was no less so. As the senior social worker responsible for the field work in pursuance of the Care Orders she must bear a heavy responsibility for the failure to perceive the role of trustee-parent as paramount over the social work needs – no doubt pressing in their own right – of the Beckford parents. By her non-intervention in flawed social work she was grossly negligent. We would add only that the failure of the two social workers in performance of their statutory duties was the direct product of a misconception of what a Care Order is, a misconception which in turn must be traceable in large part to faulty or inadequate training in child care law as applied to professional social work, and in fact as the result of the adage that there is none so blind as he who goes about his business blinkered – blinkered in a professional sense, as a result of bad training, no proper supervision and a functioning of a Care Order in which, over time, the parental control of the local authority dwindled to minimal care on the part of the social worker.

There are two aspects of deficiencies in social work training peculiarly relevant to what went wrong in the execution of the Care Orders in respect of Jasmine and Louise Beckford. The first is that generic social work, by definition, has relegated to an ancillary position the specialist skills, knowledge, and social work appropriate to particular classes of persons in need – children (as in this case), the aged, the mentally disordered, and the physically handicapped. (Children in particular are seen exclusively in the context of the nuclear family). Added to which, there is an apparent unawareness (and perhaps even a lack of sympathy for) specific legislative directions in the treatment of some of these specialist groups. Neither Ms. Wahlstrom nor Mrs. Dietmann fully appreciated that the Care Orders handed parental obligations to Brent Borough Council, and that it was they, as servants of the local authority, and not the Beckfords, who were exercising the overriding parental powers.

The second aspect is that social workers are not trained (as they should be) to recognise clearly that in their work with children in care, it is the children and not the parents who are their primary concern. At an early stage of their training social workers learn that their task with a client is not to decide what is best for the client and advise accordingly (as a doctor or a nurse will do) but to help the client, in the light of realistic conditions, to decide for himself what he himself wants to do, and to assist him to achieve his aims.

The principles of "client self-determination", of a "non-judgmental" attitude, of "going at the client's pace", instilled in social work students, are entirely appropriate in case work with adults. But such an approach can be disastrous if applied to parents caring for children whom they have seriously abused. To treat the parents as the clients is fatally to misdirect the efforts of what is in essence a child protection service.

It is clear to us that throughout this case Ms. Wahlstrom, unchecked (and indeed encouraged) by Mrs. Dietmann, applied this principle to her work with Beverley Lorrington and Morris Beckford. Both social worker and her supervising senior went along with the parents' earnest desire to have their children back home; they accepted the parents' wish to become independent of the Social Services Department; they actively welcomed Miss Lorrington's proposal to transfer Jasmine from Mortimer Road Day Nursery to Princess Frederica Primary School, without perceiving that a valuable monitoring function was being displaced by one that required replacement by their own monitoring; they were only too eager to accept the parental explanations for the absence of the children from home when visits were made, reflected in the maddening phrase of Ms. Wahlstrom's that "she had no reason to disbelieve" the explanations; and finally on the fatal day the two workers were still concentrating their searches on the Beckford parents who had removed the children from the home without the authority of the social workers.

At no time did the two workers ever exercise that authority which, inappropriate as it may be for adult clients, is not only appropriate but also essential for children who are at risk of physical and emotional abuse at the hands of their parents. Jasmine and Louise were, even on the most charitable view of the improvement in the behaviour of the Beckfords, always at risk. At no time did the two workers insist on seeing the children; nor did they ensure that they were medically examined at the local clinic (They did not even follow up the recommendation at the Case Conference on 5 April 1982 that the Health Visitor should encourage the Beckfords to visit the clinic).

We fear that their attitude in regarding the parents of children in care as the clients, rather than the children in their own right, may be widespread among social workers. We say this circumspectly, because we have not been able, nor has it been our function, to review the training or practice of social workers in the field of child care. But we have listened to a number of social workers and expert witnesses, and in each case we have detected this attitude which is the negation of any authoritarian role in the enforcement of Care Orders. Indeed, we were somewhat surprised that such an attitude even infected so outstanding an expert in child abuse as Miss Joan Court in her written report to the Magistrates on 9 September 1981, when she was recommending rehabilitation of the Beckford family, although in her evidence to us Miss Court re-interpreted her report as merely directive to the local authority not to rule out the possibility of rehabilitation. It is axiomatic that the protection of the child can usually be best achieved by working with the family, of which the child is an integral part. But the *focus* must invariably be on the child. If and when a choice has to be made between the parents' wishes and the child's interests, the choice must be in favour of the child, even if it is against the parents. Jasmine's fate illustrates all too clearly the disastrous consequences of the misguided attitude of the social workers having treated Morris Beckford and Beverley Lorrington as the clients first and foremost.

294

"Authority" is not a dirty word. Indeed, it must be brought officially from behind the arras of social work training onto the public stage, not just of child care law but also into the practice of all social workers. We regard it as an essential ingredient in any work designed to protect abused children. At the same time one has to recognise that social workers have a difficult task to perform, but it will not be made easier by being deflected from a proper appreciation of what society is demanding of them in the protection of children at risk.

The Health Visitors' default was altogether of a different order. The Health Authority was not the prime authority responsible for executing the Care Orders, but was an auxiliary agency concerned with the health of the Beckford family. Miss Leong's health visiting to the Beckford household traditionally separated out her divided attention to each member of the family, three health visitor's cards being filled in for Jasmine, Louise and the family on the occasion of each visit. In so acting, Miss Leong was in no danger of not focusing her attention on each individual child, distinct from her parents; her entries on the Health Visitor's card dealt exclusively with the individual child (although these entries do not distinguish whether the information is drawn from Miss Leong's own sighting of the individual child or from information given to her by another person). Nevertheless she failed to provide any notion of child protection service.

Miss Leong took over in July 1982 from Miss Knowles who, despite her evident fondness for the Beckford parents, had been ringing the alarm bells before the serious abuses of August 1981. Only two months earlier Miss Knowles had described Jasmine as a "thin miserable-looking" and understimulated child. By April 1982, when the misguided experiment of rehabilitation was under way, Miss Knowles was on the point of handing over the case. She was entitled to be cautiously optimistic about the future, although two months later she might have been much less optimistic. She knew from Miss Bowden, the Health Visitor in Harrow, that Jasmine had made a dramatic upturn in her physical and emotional development during her time with the foster parents.

For the next year that Miss Leong was visiting the Beckford home she did so irregularly under her own steam, largely unprompted by any directions or specific requests from Social Services, and unsupervised by her superior, Miss Tyler. She had infrequent contacts, either telephonic or personal, with Ms. Wahlstrom, and she carried out her health visiting almost oblivious of the broader context of the operation of Care Orders in respect of two children who had been seriously abused by their parents. On the last occasion that she saw Jasmine, on 22 April 1983, Ms. Wahlstrom happened to be there at the same time, unarranged by the two workers. Miss Leong noticed nothing during that year that alerted her to any signs of oncoming child abuse. Had she read her predecessor's notes and studied the percentile chart compiled by Miss Knowles, she might have had the good sense to have weighed Jasmine to see whether the stark improvement of early 1982 was being maintained; or at least she should have carried out the recommendation of the April 1982 Case Conference that Beverley Lorrington should be encouraged to take the children to the clinic "monthly", and "the Health Visitor should "visit fortnightly". Although she did not attend that Case Confeence, due to illness, she received the minutes of the meeting. She should have read, digested and acted upon the recommendations that affected her work. She only too readily followed the Case Conference recommendation to take the children off the child abuse register, by removing the children from the replica register, without talking the matter over with anyone, let alone her superior, Miss Tyler. In April 1983 she made four visits, three of them abortive. The visit of 22 April, when Beverley Lorrington had just become pregnant, was the last time Miss Leong saw Jasmine. Miss Leong's irregular and infrequent visits thereafter partook of the same misconceived approach of the social workers. She displayed no concern for the fact that when she did visit the Beckford home Jasmine was either away from home or out somewhere in the vicinity of home.

Miss Leong in fact made only four visits before the year's end during the later stages of Beverley's pregnancy, and thereafter never got a reply to her ring at the door of the Beckford house. Miss Leong saw no significance in the birth of Chantelle in December 1983 in relation to the welfare of Jasmine and Louise. All through the first six months of 1984, when the child abuse started up and Jasmine had already received a broken thigh bone, repeatedly fractured, Miss Leong was never called to account by her supervisors in respect of the two children.

The developmental check at the Mortimer Road Nursery in October 1982 conducted by Dr. Peiris was defective. Although the percentile chart was in the file, no reference was made to it and no weight or height measurements were taken. We are critical of Dr. Peiris for having failed to carry out these basic requirements.

* * * * *

We end as we began, with the setting up of the Inquiry. When we set out on our task the focus of public concern and of those who within Brent Borough Council had had for some time more than an inkling of the proportions of blameworthiness for Jasmine's death, was exclusively on the Social Services Department and in particular on Ms. Wahlstrom. This narrow perspective of responsibility for the death of a child in care of a local authority, while not unnatural, was both crude and simplistic. As we quickly discovered, none of the statutory agencies involved in Jasmine's welfare over three years was blameless. In any future discussion of the Beckford case, the responsibility of Brent Social Services needs to be put into proper perspective.

The narrow perspective was notably reflected in the response of members of Brent Borough Council to the information that a child in care had died. When the Cases Sub-Committee of the Social Services Committee tardily reacted to the incident at the end of October (and again at the end of November) some members (not all from the Labour Opposition in a finely balanced local authority) accused the Administration, at staff officer level, of a cover-up. Any suggestion there might have been, that lack of resources was the source of trouble, must be discounted. While we acknowledge that over a long period the Social Services Department was depleted in senior social workers, we think that staff shortages played only a marginal part in the events under inquiry.

Apropos a cover-up, we think that there was no conscious attempt on anybody's part to hide the facts, either at member or officer level. But the actions of both groups was such as to excite suspicion of concealment. The Director of Social Services, as soon as she heard of Jasmine's death, promptly informed the Chief Executive (who in turn told the leaders of the two parties) and the Chairman of the Social Services Committee. She did not tell the Shadow Chairman. Since Brent became a "hung" Council in November 1983 officers have been instructed to tell both the Chairman and Shadow Chairman of any matter of interest to members. The Director frankly acknowledged to us that she ought to have told Councillor Sealy. If the latter had known early in July (instead of in the late autumn) we have no doubt that he would have called for an urgent meeting of the relevant committee. He, above all his political colleagues, acknowledged instinctively the members' answerability for the death of a child in care of the local authority. Councillor Coleman, the leader of the Labour Group on the Council, also acknowledged that fact, but took no steps himself in July 1984 to convene an appropriate Committee meeting. Councillor Crane, a member of the Cases Sub-Committee, impressed us in his evidence. Had he known in July 1984 of the tragic event, he would undoubtedly have expected an immediate response from himself and his political colleagues.

The members' failure to call an urgent meeting was partially excusable, due to the initial communication from the Director to the Chief Executive assuring him that all the procedures had been observed by her department. By implication it was assumed that the quality of work was also not in question. That first reaction was grossly optimistic. By 9 July the Department had produced a chronological synopsis of events that immediately disclosed the fact that Jasmine had been seen by Social Services only once in the ten months before her death, and on the last occasion in March, she must have been suffering from at least one fracture of her thigh bone.

The Director was given this information on 10 July. We think she ought to have given a warning to the Chief Executive and the Chairman of the Social Services Committee that her earlier statement, that all procedures appeared to have been observed, needed revision. We find that at all times the Director and her senior staff accepted that there would have to be an independent inquiry — but only after the criminal proceedings were concluded.

But, in the final analysis, it is the members and not officers who must bear the responsibility of the inordinate delay in responding to Jasmine's death. Councillor Coleman was forthright in stating that the Director was similarly at fault in not prompting a meeting urgently. We do not agree. The Director gave the bare information to which any reasonable Councillor should have reacted with promptness. No local government politician worth his salt should allow nearly four months to elapse before he and his colleagues are apprised by officers of sufficient details of the death of a child in care. It is not for officers to tell members where their duties lie. Had the members of Brent Borough Council reacted promptly, a limited informal inquiry could have been instituted in the early Autumn; and if the full independent inquiry, in public or in private, had to await the conclusion of the criminal trial of Morris Beckford and Beverley Lorrington, all the preparatory stages could have been arranged by early 1985. Had we begun our hearings a month earlier than we did, having already perused the voluminous documentation, we would have completed the report before the end of the summer. Expedition, as much as thoroughness, is of the essence of child abuse enquiries in order to avoid the prolonged anxieties of those whose professional conduct is necessarily under scrutiny.

* * * * *

Every child abuse inquiry sets itself a threefold task: to ascertain the true facts of the case; to outline critically the role and functions of the relevant agencies, considering more or less in depth the nature and quality of their work and collaborative effort; and to list a number of recommendations for future legislation, governmental guidelines and professional action. Ours has been no exception. But we have attempted further to address some of the problems of child abuse, beyond just the "management" of social services and other agencies. We were concerned throughout our deliberations to point to the need for better identification of the signs of child abuse, and to indicate improved methods of inter-agency and inter-professional collaboration. But we have gone further. We think in fact we have identified and isolated one fundamental aspect of professional response to child abuse that has been overlooked or discarded by modern social work training and practice. It is that the making of a Care Order invests Social Services with pervasive parental powers. By such a judicial act society expects that a child at risk from abuse by its parents will be protected by Social Services personnel exercising parental powers effectively and authoritatively on behalf of society. Such a child is a child in trust.

CHAPTER 32

Summary of Recommendations

This chapter is intended to provide a list of the recommendations, appropriately edited and classified, with reference to the relevant chapter in brackets.

General

Whenever a child in care of a local authority dies, or is seriously harmed, that local authority's relevant committee must meet to consider the case forthwith. (Chapter 19)

Whenever there is a decision to reunite abused children with their parents, there should be a requirement as part of a protection plan that, *inter alia*, parents take children under five to the clinic at least monthly. (Chapter 9)

The duty on a local authority to cooperate with a health authority should be made more specific, to include the duty to consult; the local authority should be under a duty to assist, by advice and the supply of information, in the process of the management of the child abuse system. (Chapter 12)

The observations of the relevant professional bodies, whose members would be included in the categories specified as being under the obligation to inform Social Services of any case of child abuse, should be consulted. The consultative process should properly emanate from the Secretary of State for Health and Social Security. (Chapter 12)

A review should be carried out by the Social Services Inspectorate of the Department of Health and Social Security to evaluate the processes of decision-making in the management of child abuse cases. (Chapter 1)

An independent review of the role of the NSPCC, together with all the other voluntary bodies engaged in the work of child care and protection, with special reference to their future contribution to, and collaboration with the statutory agencies in the child abuse system should be set up. (Chapter 17)

Directors of Social Services should invariably report to the Department of Health and Social Security any death of a child in care, or under the supervision, of the local authority, and such report should give full details of the circumstances surrounding the death. (Chapter 19)

Pursuant to the recommendation about reporting such deaths, the Department of Health and Social Security should consider issuing clearer guidance to local authorities. (Chapter 19)

Whenever a child in care of a local authority dies, or is seriously harmed, that local authority's relevant Committee must meet to consider the case forthwith. (Chapter 19)

Research designed to refine the techniques for predicting accurately those children who will continue to be at risk is urgently required. (Chapter 31)

A greater effort should be made to recruit black families as prospective foster-parents in order to provide the greatest measure of choice to local authorities seeking to place, for fostering and adoption, black children in their care. (Chapter 30)

All policy statements and guidelines for procedure in child abuse cases should contain standardised definitions in relation to the placement of children in care. (Chapter 8)

Local authorities should consider exercising the power under Section 31 of the Child Care Act 1980 to collaborate in setting up a specialist establishment in their region for children who have suffered abuse. (Chapter 29)

Child Abuse Inquiries

Where the Inquiry is, exceptionally, one of enormous public interest, and likely to involve such large financial cost that it is unreasonable for local government to bear, the Secretary of State should initiate the inquiry under his statutory powers given in section 98, Children Act 1975. (Preface)

If ultimately there has to be an independent panel, central government, if it does not set up the inquiry, should respond to a reasonable request to fund the inquiry (Chapter 24)

A statutory power should be given to the Secretary of State and to local authorities to direct that the whole or part of the costs incurred by any party to a local inquiry should be defrayed out of some specified fund. (Chapter 3)

All child abuse inquiries should incorporate in their membership all the major professional disciplines, and should not have advisers or assessors. (Chapter 3)

Sufficient time must be allowed for the parties to a child abuse inquiry to be able to prepare their respective cases for the hearing. (Chapter 3)

Child Abuse procedures

Social Services

Paragraphs 44(A)-8 and 52(B)-10 of the Code of Practice for Social Workers Dealing with Child Abuse (1985), formulated by the British Association of Social Workers, should be prefaced by a statement that the primary obligation of social workers and their supervisors is to ensure that the clarity of objectives and purposes is a prerequisite to the proper standards of recording. Brent's Policy Memorandum on Child Abuse should likewise proclaim this principle. (Chapter 22)

Periodically – preferably as and when the two agencies' representatives meet at case conferences or statutory case reviews – their records should be available to all the participants at those meetings, for them to consult. (Chapter 22)

BASW's Code of Practice and Brent's Policy Memorandum should state clearly that those responsible for the preparation and signing of case conference minutes should observe the rule that only the reconvened case conference or, possibly, the relevant participant can authorise an alteration. (Chapter 22)

The second Case Conference should take place only as and when the Magistrates' Court has conferred legal powers on the local authority. (Chapter 8)

Whenever social workers are engaged in a child abuse case, they must re-acquaint themselves with the Policy Memorandum and the procedures to be applied, as well as consult any relevant literature on the subject. (Chapter 7)

Health Services

The practice of planning regular discussions between Health Visitors and their Senior Nurses should be established, and senior nurses should particularly ensure that they discuss all child abuse cases regularly with the Health Visitor involved, even if she herself does not consider that there is any problem with which she is unable to deal. (Chapter 21)

The family's general practitioner should invariably be invited to case conferences. (Chapter 25)

The specialism of a radiological paediatrician, capable not merely of discerning the more obscure bone and other injuries but also of dating the various injuries, should invariably be sought by the relevant hospital authorities whenever serious non-accidental fractures occur. (Chapter 8)

Child abuse procedures should emphasise that where a child has been admitted to hospital as a result of abuse by its parent(s), immediate steps must be taken to protect any sibling in the household that may be at risk. (Chapter 8)

Schools

Consideration should be given to extending the statutory duties of the Educational Welfare Officer to those children under the age of 5 and attending nursery school. (Chapter 14)

In every school one member of the educational staff should be designated as the liaison officer with Social Services in respect of every child who is in care of the local authority and/or is on the child abuse register. (Chapter 14)

The Director of Education should periodically check that the Green Book (updated) should be known and made readily available to every member of the schools' staffs. (Chapter 10)

Whenever a child in care is attending any educational establishment, the local authority which has the child in its care must formally notify not only the local education authority but also the school or institution which the child is attending; and the notice should ask for information about non-attendance and any other relevant matter pertaining to the child's health and welfare. (Chapter 10)

Law

The law should state that a child in care is a child in trust. (Chapter 2)

The criterion for the Place of Safety Order should be that the applicant "has reasonable cause to believe that there is a real and present danger to the health or well-being of the child." (Chapter 27)

Failure to attend school should not in any event found an application for a Place of Safety Order. (Chapter 27)

A parent or child should be empowered to apply to the court for setting aside a Place of Safety Order. (Chapter 27)

Section 28(1) of the 1969 Children and Young Persons Act 1969 should be amended to fix the limit for a Place of Safety Order at 72 hours, or where there is no relevant juvenile court sitting within the next 72 hours, up to a maximum of 8 days, beginning with the date of authorisation. (Chapter 27)

Social workers and magistrates should respectively apply for, and grant applications for Place of Safety Orders only where there is a present and real danger to the health and well-being of the child. (Chapter 27)

A local authority in possession of a Care Order should be under a statutory duty to consult the relevant *guardian ad litem* on the two occasions when the local authority considers convening a case conference – namely, after the hearing of the care proceedings and when it is contemplating reuniting the child with its family. (Chapter 25)

Legislation should make it clear whether it is intended or not that preventive work has to be exhausted before care proceedings are initiated. (Chapter 2)

Juvenile Courts

The magistrates' court should be required to make a parent a party to care proceedings on the parent's application. (Chapter 26)

If the magistrates' court makes a separation order, it should ordinarily appoint a *guardian ad litem*, whose duty it is then to safeguard the interests of the child as prescribed by section 32B(2) and (3), Children and Young Persons Act 1969. (Chapter 26)

The Lord Chancellor, in his review of paragraph 24 of *Basic Training for Juvenile Court Magistrates*, should consider adding a sentence to the effect that no rider of any kind should be attached to a Care Order. The Magistrates' Association should likewise inform its members. (Chapter 16)

The Magistrates' Courts' Rules should be explicit in providing that magistrates should explain in simple and appropriate language the effect of their decision in care proceedings. (Chapter 16)

The Magistrates' Association, through its branches, together with chairmen of benches and juvenile court panels and clerks to justices, should now communicate to magistrates, emphasising the importance of keeping up to date with, contemporary knowledge about child abuse. (Chapter 20)

Magistrates should be bound by statute to give reasons for their decisions in care proceedings. (Chapter 16)

The statutory requirement on Magistrates to give reasons for their decision should also indicate the various factors that they must direct their minds to, in arriving at their reasoned judgment. (Chapter 16)

Parliament should in the legislation indicate what is to be the legal effect of non-compliance by a Magistrates' Court with the statutory duty to give reasons. (Chapter 16)

Legal profession

Legal departments of local authorities should arrange for one or more of their solicitors to specialise in juvenile court work. (Chapter 28)

The Law Society should extend its panel of solicitors to act in child care cases, to include solicitors employed by local authorities, and only those local authority solicitors who meet the criteria for membership of the panel should be allowed to represent their authority in care proceedings. (Chapter 20)

If a lawyer from the local authority's own legal staff is required, in child care proceedings to conduct the case, similar criteria to those pertaining to the Law Society's panel should be applied. (Chapter 20)

Any solicitor acting for children in care proceedings must see, and if possible talk to, or play with those children whose interests he is hired to protect and to promote. (Chapter 8)

Police and prosecution

Whenever a police officer desires to attend care proceedings, he should give notice to the parties – local authority, parents and child (or his representative) – of such desire. If no objection is raised, the court, subject to its overriding discretion to exclude anybody for some such reason as space in the courtroom or detraction from the informality of juvenile court proceedings, should give authority. If there is an objection, properly founded, the police officer should be excluded. (Chapter 15)

The Commissioner of the Metropolitan Police should call for a review of the General Memorandum relating to the supply of police information to case conferences. (Chapter 15)

In all child abuse prosecutions involving children in care of a local authority, where the public is almost certain to express disquiet about the handling of the case by Social Services and other relevant agencies, suggestive of fault by social workers and other professional people, the criminal trial should, other than for exceptional reasons, take place within 3-4 months of the homicidal event, and certainly not beyond six months. (Preface)

When the national independent prosecuting service comes into being, a representative from that service should also be invited to case conferences (Chapter 15)

Brent Borough Council

Brent Borough Council should discuss with Brent Health Authority the establishment, under joint financing arrangements, of a post of Child Abuse Training Coordinator. (Chapter 11)

Brent Borough Council should reverse its decision to withdraw from membership of the National Foster-Care Association. (Chapter 30)

Brent Borough Council should give urgent attention to the question of appropriate accommodation for Area 6, Social Services Department. (Chapter 11)

Adequate typing support should be provided in each Area office of Brent Social Services Department. (Chapter 11)

Brent Health Authority

In the near future Brent Health Authority should conduct an internal review of the present procedures to see whether the new broom has, as we confidently believe, swept away the dust gathered over years of inactive "supervision". (Chapter 12)

Brent Area Review Committee

Any member of the Area Review Committee, skilled in chairmanship and knowledgeable about the management of the child abuse system, should be an acceptable candidate for taking the chair. (Chapter 24)

Brent Area Review Committee should indicate the desirability of the attendance of police officers at case conferences. (Chapter 25)

Brent Area Review Committee should immediately give effect to its resolution of 5 November 1984 to set up a Standing Inquiry Panel. (Chapter 24)

Brent Area Review Committees should take as a model Derbyshire Area Review Committee's 1985 revision of its procedures. (Chapter 23)

Brent Area Review Committee should set in train immediately a system for monitoring individual cases currently being handled by Social Services. (Chapter 24)

Training

Nothing short of a period of three years is required for the professional training of social workers, of which a larger proportion than at present should be devoted to specialist areas of knowledge. (Chapter 20)

A further study by CCETSW of legal training for social workers should now be seriously considered as a matter of high priority. (Chapter 20)

The need to promote the skilled practice of child care law must be reflected in legal education, and the child care content of legal education must be kept under review. (Chapter 20)

This report has been unanimously agreed upon by the members of the Panel of Inquiry:

Dr. John Beal	MRCS,LRCP,FFCM,DPH. Community Medicine Specialist, York Health Authority. Chairman, Derbyshire Area Review Committee 1977-1982. Assessor to Inquiry into the death of Karen Spencer (1978).	
Louis Blom-Cooper Q.C. (in the Chair)	LL.B. (London); Dr. Jur. (Amsterdam) Bencher of the Hon. Soc. of the Middle Temple.	
Ben T. Brown	Ruskin College, Oxford 1975-1977. CQSW; Diploma in Social Studies. Assistant Divisional Director, Dr. Barnardo's.	
Patricia Marshall	S.R.N., S.C.M., R.S.C.N., H.V. Director of Nursing (Community) City and Hackney Health Authority.	
Mary R. Mason J.P.	M.A. (Cantab), DMA. Chairman, Juvenile Panel, Manchester City Magistrates' Court. Former Director of Social Services, Bolton Metropolitan Borough Council. Chairman, Panel of Inquiry into the death of Gerard Fenton (Cheshire) (1982) and member of Panel of Inquiry into the death of Maria Mehmadagi (Southwark) (1981).	

Dated this 2nd day of December 1985.

APPENDICES*

A: Representation of Parties

B: List of Witnesses

C: Documents relating to Care Proceedings on 9 September 1981 and 22 June 1983
    1.   Dr. Levick's report
    2.   Miss Joan Court's report
    3.   Mr. Thompson's note of Magistrates' Statement on making Care Order.
    4.   Magistrates' Q & A to Panel of Inquiry.

D: Proceedings before the Central Criminal Court, March 1985
    1.   Charges against Morris Beckford and Beverley Lorrington.
    2.   Questioning by the Common Serjeant, Judge Pigot QC, of officers of Brent Borough Council

E: Relevant Child Care Law

F: Miss Alix Causby's guardian ad litem report of 18 September 1984.

G: Case Conferences and Statutory Case Reviews
    1.   6 August 1981
    2.   20 August 1981
    3.   9 December 1981
    4.   5 April 1982
    5.   25 May 1982
    6.   30 September 1982
    7.   9 November 1982
    8.   18 April 1983
    9.   6 December 1983

H: Brent Borough Council's Green Book (1977).

I: Dr. Iain West's post-mortem report on Jasmine Beckford.

J: Chief Executive's report on complaint re advertisement to find a foster-home for Louise and Chantelle Beckford.

K: Selected bibliography

* Errors in the text of the appendices have not been corrected and are reproduced in their original form.

APPENDIX A

Counsel for the Panel of Inquiry were Miss Presiley Baxendale and Mrs. Helen Helston, instructed by the Director of Law and Administration, Brent Borough Council.

Party	Representative
Mr. David Bishop and Ms. Gun Wahlstrom	Mr. Richard Bond, instructed by Penelope Grant, Solicitors.
Mrs. Diane Dietmann	Miss Joanna Dodson, instructed by Wilfred McBain, Solicitors.
Ms. Valerie Howarth, Mrs. Dorothy Ruddock and British Association of Social Workers	Mr. John Trotter, solicitor of Bates, Wells and Braithwaite.
Miss Yeng Lai Leong, Miss Janet Bowden, Mrs. Nandani Vivekanandan and Mrs. Margaret Forde	Mr. Nigel Pitt, instructed by Kershaw, Gassman and Matthews, Solicitors.
Miss Mary Tyler, Mrs. Joyce Brown and Miss Judy Knowles	Mr. Charles Bott, instructed by Mr. Hopkins of Legal Department, Royal College of Nursing.
Miss Savitrie Baichoo	Mr. Patrick Lawrence, instructed by Kershaw, Gassman and Matthews, Solicitors.
Brent Health Authority	Miss Siobhan Goodrich, instructed by J. Tickle and Co., Solicitors.
Commissioner of Police for the Metropolis	Miss Sheila James and Mr. Ronald Coupland of the Solicitors' Department, Metropolitan Police.
Miss Carol Rogers and Mr. Dennis Simpson	Mr. Edward Thomas, Solicitor, of Brethertons, St. Albans.
Miss Susan Knibbs	Mr. Alan Muir, Solicitor of Royal Borough of Kensington and Chelsea.
Mr. and Mrs. Peter Probert	Miss Patricia Scotland and Miss Joy Okoye, instructed by Mr. William Ackroyd, solicitor.
Brent Young People's Law Centre	Mr. Courtnay Abel, Community Lawyer.
Mr. William Thompson and Mr. James Hobbs	Mr. Ian Duncan, solicitor of T.V. Edwards and Co.
Miss Adeline Martin	Mr. Patrick Sadd, instructed by Charles Russell Co., Solicitors.
Dr. John Warner	Mr. Roy Warne, instructed by Hempsons, Solicitors.

i

APPENDIX B

1. WITNESSES EXAMINED BEFORE THE PANEL

Miss Savitrie Baichoo
Miss Joy Baines
Mr. Michael Barry
Mr. Phillip Bennett
Mr. Michael Bichard
Miss Christina Birch
Mr. David Bishop
Miss Janet Bowden
Mrs. Gillian Boyle (née Hindle)
Superintendent Michael Briggs
Mrs. Joyce Brown
Mr. Jeremy Burns
Mr. Charles Cochand
Councillor Martin Coleman
Miss Joan Court
Miss Frieda Cowgill
Councillor George Crane
Councillor Mary Cribbin
Det. Sgt. John Crocker
Mr. Martin Damms
Mrs. Mary Davidson
Det. Insp. Selwyn Dickens
Mrs. Diane Dietmann
Mrs. Eris Felix
Miss Margaret Forde
Mr. Stephen Forster
Miss Angela Goban
Miss Pamela Gordon
Councillor Mark Haftel
Mr. James Hobbs
Miss Valerie Howarth
Mr. Raymond Jenkins
Mrs. Dorothy Johnson
Dr. John Justice
Supt. John Kempe
Mr. Roy Kerridge
Dr. Hosaima Kavarana Khan
Miss Sue Knibbs
Miss Judy Knowles

Miss Yeng Lai Leong
Miss Beverley Lorrington*
Miss Carol Lorrington
Dr. Debarata Mallik
WPC Carmel McAree
Mr. Sean McErlean
Miss Adeline Martin
Miss Elizabeth Mead
Mr. Adrian Parsons
Dr. Jeffrey Peiris
Mrs. Ashley Player
Mr. Simon Pollard
Det. Constable John Powell
Dr. Elizabeth Price
Miss Coral Probert
Mrs. Gay Probert
Miss Michelle Probert
Mr. Peter Probert
Miss Marjorie Proudlock
Councillor Frances Rees-Hughes
Miss Gwenneth Rickus
Miss Carol Rogers
Mrs. Dorothy Ruddock
Mrs. Pamela Scafardy
Councillor Philemon Sealy
Mr. Dennis Simpson
Miss Petula Smith
Councillor Roger Stone
Det. Supt. John Strachan
Dr. Ganesan Supramaniam
Mrs. Elizabeth Szwed
Mr. William Thompson
Miss Mary Tyler
Mrs. Nandani Vivekanandan
Dr. John Warner
Ms. Gun Wahlstrom
Mr. Harry Whalley

*Miss Lorrington was examined only by the Panel at H.M. Prison, Cookham Wood, Rochester, Kent.

ii

2. WITNESSES WHO GAVE EXPERT EVIDENCE BEFORE THE PANEL

Miss Elaine Arnold, M.A.

Mr. Alan Bedford, M.A. (Social Work), B.A. (Sociology), C.Q.S.W.

Miss Alix Causby, B.A. (Sociology), University of Carolina, M.A. (Social Work) University of Tennessee, Child Abuse Training Coordinator, City of Westminster

Mr. David Divine, B.A. (Edinburgh), Ph.D. Senior Social Worker, London Borough of Hackney

Dr. Bridget Edwards, B.M., B.Ch., D.C.H., M.R.C.P., Consultant Community Paediatrician

Professor Cyril Greenland, M.Sc. (London), Ph.D. Birmingham, P.S.W., Professor of Social Work, McMaster University, Canada and Visiting Professor of Criminology, University of Toronto, Canada

Dr. Richard Levick, M.B., Ch.B., FRCP, MRCRadiologists, Consultant Radiologist, Children's Hospital, Western Bank, Sheffield

Mr. Anthony Hall, Director and Secretary, British Agencies for Adoption and Fostering

Dr. Hugh Jolly, M.A., M.D., F.R.C.P., D.C.H., Physician in Charge of Paediatric Department, Charing Cross Hospital, London

Miss Christine Reeves, Director, National Foster Care Association

Dr. Euan Ross, M.D., F.R.C.P., D.C.H., Consultant Paediatrician, Charing Cross Hospital

Miss Ruth Sharman, M.A., Education Officer with the English National Board for Nursing

Dr. Leonard Taitz, M.D. (Witwatersrand University), F.R.C.P., Consultant Paediatrician, Children's Hospital, Sheffield

Mr. Geoffrey Walker, F.R.C.S., Consultant Orthopaedic Surgeon, Queen Mary's Hospital, Carshalton, Surrey

Dr. Iain West, M.B., Ch.B., MRCPath, D.M.J., Consultant Forensic Pathologist, Head of Department of Forensic Medicine, Guy's Hospital, London

Miss Priscilla Young, M.A., Director, Central Council for Education and Training in Social Work

3. STATEMENTS READ IN WHOLE OR IN PART BEFORE THE PANEL

Mr. Morris Beckford (two statements)   Ms. Ruby Radex
Dr. Elizabeth Pelc   Miss Sally Moore

APPENDIX C.1

REPORT BY DR. RICHARD KEITH LEVICK
ON THE RADIOGRAPH OF JASMINE & LOUISE BECKFORD

JASMINE BECKFORD dob 2nd Dec. 1979

Radiographs were taken on the following dates:-

4th August 1981 – 5 films

Left Femur

Andro posterial and lateral views shows a sub-trochantric fracture of the femur with varus deformity and cominution. No other injury is shown. The right femur is shown on the AP projection and also appears normal.

Skull

Andro posteria lateral and Towne views show no evidence of bony abnormality.

5th August 1981 – 5 films

Chest

Normal appearances. No evidence of recent or old rib fractures.

Left Upper Limb

Antro posteria view normal.

Right Upper Limb

Antro posteria view normal.

Both Lower Limbs

Antro posteria and lateral views. There is periostural reaction on the lateral surface of the right tibial shaft in its upper third. No definite fracture is seen in association with this.

Conclusion

The fracture of the right *femur indicates that considerable force was applied to this bone and it is important to corrolate this with any available statements as to how the injury was sustained. The type of accident which could possibly produce this injury for example would be a fall downstairs with the mother landing on top of the infant. The periostural reaction on the lateral aspect of the right tibia is not associated with a definite fracture and is probably due to sub periostural haemorage due to minor trauma. The fracture of the left femur is recent ie. within 4 or 5 days of the date of the radiograph the reaction on the right tibia is probably between 7 and 14 days old. Suggesting two separate incidents. A further chest ex-ray should be obtained as although no rib fractures are visible these occasionally are only seen when healing is taking place.

There was evidence of injury on two separate occasions, however these must be carefully matched with the account given by the parents or other persons in charge as to how bone damage was sustained.

*This was later corrected to "left"

LOUIS BECKFORD – dob 27th May 1981

Radiograph taken on the following dates:-

1st August 1981 – St. Mary's Hospital, Harrow Road
One film of left upper limb

Two fracture lines are shown in the left humoral shaft. The upper line suggest an old fracture which has almost completely healed and was probably sustained at least four weeks before the date on which the film was taken. Periostural reaction in casing the shaft of the humerus is almost certainly resulted from this injury. The lower fracture is of recent origin probably not more than 3 or 4 days old and has passed through the periostural reaction of the previous injury. There is clear evidence here of bone injuries on two separate occasions.

3rd August 1981 – 7 films
skeletal survey

Chest & Abdomin antro posterial view
No evidence of bony or soft tissue abnormality.

Right Upper Limb
There is a-metapofeel defect in the lateral condile of the humerous.

Lower Limbs
Antro posterial views – There is a metapofeel defect on the inner upper aspect of the right fibia.

Skull
Antro posterial lateral and Towne views – No evidence of bony abnormality.

Conclusion
The left humerous shows evidence of major fractures probably sustained with an interval of about four weeks between them. The metapofeel defects in the right humerous right tibia suggest minor trauma, these are visible to date but most be at least 3 or 4 weeks old.

An account of any accidental falls or other injuries sustained by this baby must be carefully matched to the evidence of two fractures of the humerous. The metapofeel injuries usual for minor trauma are consistent with rough handling but could have been sustained on the same occasion as the earlier humeral fracture.

R.K. LEVICK, MB, BCH, FRCB, FRCR,
Consultant Paediatric Radiologist,
Chairman Paediatric Radiology Group, Royal College of Radiologists,
Chairman, Radiology Group, British Paediatric Assn.

APPENDIX C.2

Miss Joan Court's independent social worker's report 8 September 1981.

On August 24th 1981 I was asked by Mr. Pollard, solicitor, to prepare an independent social work report in the case of **Jasmine** and **Louise Beckford** of 103a Harrow Road, London, NW10.

In order to prepare this report I first contacted the parents to ask if I might visit them and then arranged an interview with Brent Area 6 Social Services Department.

I had a formal interview on 27.8.81 with the Principal Court officer, Mr. William Thompson, the senior social worker Miss Diana Dietmann and the social worker with primary responsibility for the case Miss Gun Wahstrom. I asked if I might talk with Miss Wahstrom on her own, but this was not permitted, and I learnt very little about the Beckford family from this interview, but I was given a copy of the Case Conference notes. The area officer, Mr. David Bishop, who came in briefly, gave me some idea of the Departments' view of the case.

I asked Mr. Thompson if I might visit the foster mother and Louise before the Court Hearing, but I was told this was impossible.

I visited the parents later the same day and spent two hours with them and obtained their written consent to discuss their case with all the agencies concerned.

On 1.9.81 I interviewed Miss Sue Knibbs, senior social worker at St. Charles Hospital, and the senior registrar Dr. G. Supramaniam. I then spent an hour observing both parents as they washed and changed Jasmine and made her comfortable for the night. Later, while father stayed with Jasmine, I talked with mother alone for about another hour.

On 3.9.81 I observed mother and infant Louise for about an hour in the parental home in the presence of the social worker who had brought the infant over from the foster parents, and I saw mother alone before and after the visit.

I have written to Mr. Jeremy Burns, Principal Fostering the Adoption Officer on 30.8.81 to express my concern that the parents have only been allowed to see baby Louise once in eight days as this may weaken the attachment between parents and infant. I also asked why the parents are not allowed to know the whereabouts of their baby. I consider this is unnecessarily harsh to the parents and is likely to further harm their self esteem and so indirectly impair their confidence as parents.

My report is based on these interviews and my knowledge of the medical evidence. I would be better informed if I had seen the records, interviewed the foster mother and if the social worker with primary responsibility had been allowed to discuss the case with me. If there had been sufficient time I would also have liked to interview the health visitor. In spite of these deficiencies I consider that my very full discussions with the parents and observations of their interaction with the children have enabled me to understand the case and to form an opinion.

Confidential

INDEPENDENT SOCIAL WORK REPORT ON JASMINE AND LOUISE BECKFORD

Problems as seen by the Social Services Department

This is a diagnosed case of non-accidental injury as far as the younger child is concerned and the injuries to the older infant are inadequately explained. The Social Services seek a Care Order.

Problem as seen by the parents

Mr. Beckford, the father, admits that he shook baby Louise and so presumably caused the retinal (eye) haemorrhage. He denies twisting the baby's arm and neither parent can offer any explanation of how this fracture occurred, although they are quick to latch on to the various suggestions that have been made, and to suggest other possibilities.

Miss Lorrington, the mother, says that Jasmine must have broken her leg when she fell down stairs. Further details about these events which led to the admission of both infants to hospital are contained in the body of this report.

The parents see their main problem as one of housing. They are desperate about this, and have been for a considerable time.

Both parents know they are suspected of "battering" their children, and mother in particular is well informed on this subject.

Family Composition

Mother	Miss Beverley Lorrington	Born 2.11.59
Father	Mr. Lord Livingstone Maurice	
	Beckford	Born 30.6.59
	Jasmine	Born 2.12.79
	Lousie	Born 2.5.81

Childrens' Placement

The children are subject to an Interim Care Order. Jasmine is still in St. Charles' Hospital where she was admitted on 4.8.81 suffering from a fracture of the left femur. Louise was admitted on August 1st with a spiral fracture of the left humerus and retinal haemorrhage, and was discharged to the care of foster parents on

Home Conditions and Income

The parents moved to their present address three years ago and rent a double room with shared kitchen and bathroom on the second floor of a three storied building on the main road in a dilapidated multi-racial area, with many boarded-up shops and houses. The bed-sitting room is approximately 18 ft. × 12 ft. and the double bed and chairs occupy most of the available space. This leads out to a landing and a small kitchen and bathroom. There are steep stairs leading down to the hall and the stair carpet is not securely fixed.

The parents are disgusted by this accommodation. The walls are damp in winter and it is cold and draughty. There is nowhere for Jasmine to play. As both parents have very high standards it is particularly unpleasant for them to have to share the kitchen and bathroom with their landlord and his friends who, it is alleged, micturate in the bath and basin if the lavatory is angaged. Cats come through the skylight and defaecate outside the room, and beetles crawl in the baby's cot.

The parents are on the housing list but have now been told that they will never get a place if the children are in Care.

Both parents are quite desperate about these conditions, and although I do not think these are the only cause of the children's injuries, I suspect they played a considerable role in the mounting stress felt by Miss Lorrington during her recent pregnancy and following the birth of Louise. She said she thought it was wrong that the only way you could get rehoused was if the children were battered.

The present accommodation is totally unsuitable for rearing small children. It is overcrowded, uncomfortable and enforces a constant physical proximity between the parents and between parents and children. There is only a small back yard and the next door garden is used as a rubbish dump. The conditions would be a strain on any parents, but particularly to those who are emotionally vulnerable.

Mr. Beckford's income is £85.00 a week and the rent is £15.00. He gives Miss Lorrington adequate housekeeping and pocket money allowances.

Parents' Family Background, Education and Personality

FATHER – Mr. Lord Livingstone Maurice Beckford. Age 22

Mr. Beckford has been in the same job for seven years. He is a checker in a nearby scaffolding and cradle firm and does heavy manual work, loading and unloading, welding and wood cutting. He works from 7 am – 6 pm with a break at home for breakfast at 10 am and at lunchtime. Since two men have been redundant he often does the work of three men and cannot take time off without the work piling up, and this makes him anxious. He often goes all day without food as he does not like eating in cafes and is too embarrassed to take sandwiches.

Mr. Beckford was born in Jamaica and spent his first nine years there with his maternal grandmother, maternal aunt and two sisters. His mother came to England, where father was already working, soon after Mr. Beckford was born. He comments that she rejected him from birth.

He is the third of nine siblings and has three brothers and five sisters, but he rarely sees the two sisters domiciled in England or his mother. His father deserted the family and emigrated to America when Mr. Beckford was 15 years of age.

Mr. Beckford was the scapegoat of the family and brutally treated by his mother, physically and mentally – "she hardly fed me and kept me in the woodshed – I nearly froze to death". He missed a lot of schooling as his mother kept him at home to do the housework and "she hit me over the head too much, I thought I would crack up". Father attended Woodfields School for the educationally backward, but he is literate, and I consider may be of normal intelligence. He does not blame his mother, but wonders why she hated him and thinks she may change in her attitude one day. He has not considered why his father failed to protect him.

When Mr. Beckford was fourteen the NSPCC were called in and he was placed in Care at Barretts Green House where he was very happy. He took a course in mechanical engineering at Willesden Technical College where he was 18 years old, but at the end of the year became ill and did not sit the City and Guilds examination. He would still like to continue his education.

Mr. Beckford says his health is good, but he suffers from a painful and irritating condition which has affected his sexual life for the last two or three years and needs treatment.

Mr. Beckford has an open, warm and sensitive manner, and I believe him to be a genuine and truthful person. He can be moody and his anxiety is expressed in perfectionism. He is quite obsessional about everything being just right and on time. Miss Lorrington finds this difficult in the present circumstances or over-crowding.

MOTHER – Miss Beverley Lorrington. Age 22

Mother's parents also came from Jamaica, but she was born and bred in this area of London. Her mother deserted the family when she was six months of age and there is no contact between them. She has a younger step-brother and step-sister, and like Mr. Beckford she was the scapegoat in the family. She was beaten by both parents, right up to the time she ran away from home at 17, and was "picked on" by her step-mother whom she describes as moody and difficult. She attended a normal primary and secondary school, but as she was a slow learner she was transferred to an ESN school. She met Mr. Beckford in school and went to live with him when they were both nineteen years old, working as a seamstress in the intervening two years.

Miss Lorrington is an appealing, frail looking young woman, blind in one eye from a childhood accident. She is reserved and shy, and cannot easily show when she is angry or upset. I think she is devious and quick to 'catch on' and find reasons for what has happened or might have happened. For example, she said if she had broken Louise's arm by rough handling she would have heard it snap. On the other hand she says she may have forced the baby's hand into a sleeve as some of her clothes are too small. And, she said, if she was a battering mother she need not have taken the baby to hospital at all, as she knows how to set a fracture. She is also very frightened and ashamed. The shame is because she does not know what to say to people who ask where the children are. She is frightened because she thinks she may lose not only her children but Mr. Beckford.

Her long term aspirations are to have a nice flat, fix it up and then get married to Mr. Beckford. She desperately wants the children back and finds it very lonely without them. Later she would like to put the children in a day nursery and go back to work.

Marital relationship, Birth of the two children and Social Life.

The parents have lived together since they were nineteen and seem happy together. Mother says they were like children themselves at first but having babies has helped them to grow up. She says she sometimes finds Maurice difficult and moody and it is hard to cope with his demands for instant and perfect service but on the other hand she says he is good to her and gives her sufficient housekeeping and pocket money – "I would never find another like him". Both babies were born in Hammersmith hospital, Jasmine only weighed 5 pounds but the birth was normal and painless. The home conditions were worse then than they are now as there were then four other couples living in the house and mother could not keep the place clean.

Louise was conceived eight months later and mother felt quite depressed at times, and found the short labour very painful. She is very afraid of pain, and grew up unprepared for the physical side of life. She could not even consider breast feeding. Both parents wanted a boy and mother in particular was very disappointed to have another girl.

Neither parents have any support from the extended family and are now afraid of their criticism and do not know how to explain the absense of the children. They are socially isolated although father has a friend who lives locally. They have no-one to babysit for them as mother's only acquaintance, Olive, "is too much occupied with the church". It is Olive who took Jasmine to the doctor the day after she injured her leg.

Parents' account of the childrens' injuries.

Mother says she knows there are inconsistencies in their account of the injuries as they have both been questioned and interrogated so often they get confused.

In regard to Louise, Father says she cried constantly, though not in the night, and "sometimes you have both of them at you" and "there is nowhere to put the baby when she cries". He told me that he had never shaken Louise before but she kept on crying and it got on top of me. I picked her up and hugged her, then I shook her when the crying got on top of me".

Father is quite sure that he did not twist the baby's arm. In my opinion father lost his temper because he was hungry – he does not remember having any meal that day other than a cup of tea first thing. He came home at 6 pm and mother gave him his dinner on a tray but before he could eat it she asked him to give Louise her bottle. He did this and then was over-come with rage when she would not settle down. I think this may have been caused by a combination of physical exhaustion and low blood sugar.

Father was not at home when Jasmine broke her leg. Mother says she did not know that the child was out of the room until she heared her fall down the stairs. She says she nearly tripped on the stair carpet herself (perhaps she did?) The child was screaming at the bottom of the stairs but was able to stand up. Mother fetched her husband and they bathed the child's ankle thinking it was sprained. According to mother the child seemed all right that day, but next morning was obviously in pain. She did not want to take her to hospital as she knew she was suspected of "battering" Louise.

Parents' Interaction with the Infants

Father says that Jasmine is very active but "sometimes she does not like to be touched." He talks warmly and lovingly of both children and his face lights up when he describes them. Mother has difficulty in describing either baby, and does not seem to see them having personalities of their own. She says that Jasmine is "father's child", taking after him and always turning to him, and I think she may resent this a little.

I observed both parents with Jasmine in hospital while they changed her and made her comfortable. Both are very competent in their handling and care, but mother scarcely speaks to the child at all. She knows this may appear odd and told me she could not behave naturally when other people are around, but I was concerned at the passivity and stillness of the child when mother washed and changed her, and the way she watched her father and did not look at her mother or smile.

Her behaviour at this time was in marked contrast to what I observed when I first came into the ward, when Jasmine was rolling around the floor with the nurse in charge, giggling and playing happily and full of life and vitality, so that I know she can be responsive.

I have not seen father with baby Louise as he was not able to get time off when the social worker brought her round to the parental home. Mother was obviously happy to see the infant, and wept when she left, but she interacted very little with the baby and hardly talked to her at all. She was uneasy when the baby cried and kept shaking a rattle to try to distract her, but eventually changed her and gave her a bottle of orange juice. I am sure she felt uneasy and self-conscious, but I think the lack of communication between mother and baby is untypical of the average mother in similar circumstances.

SUMMARY

Both parents desperately want the children home, and mother wants to be "given another chance." But I have explained to her that it would not be safe for the babies, or indeed for the parents to have them home until more is understood about how they came to be injured.

I suspect that father's sudden rage with the baby may be a "one off" episode, but one cannot be certain about this. I am more concerned about the uncertainties surrounding mother's role, and I suspect she has been under intolerable stress in the last two years.

Neither parent has had any experience of a normal loving home and I think they need a sustaining and nurturing experience themselves to enable them cope with the demands and stresses of their own small children.

The events and circumstances surrounding the injuries to these children are typical of the classic cases of nonaccidental injury to small children which occur when severely deprived young parents are victims of social, environmental and emotional burdens which are beyond their capacity to bear.

The two babies were born within a period of two years to a young unmarried couple who have themselves experienced violence and rejection. They have no supportive relatives or friends and are socially isolated. Mother is alone with these demanding infants most of the day in a home which is a constant irritation to her, and where there is no room for Jasmine to play. There is no adult to share the burden or with whom she can talk openly. Although she is very loyal to her husband she does admit that his moods and high expectations under circumstances which make it impossible for her to fulfil them adequately makes life difficult. Bad housing is obviously the precipitating crisis behind the recent tragic events. It would matter less if the parents did not have high standards and want to bring up their children in a clean and comfortable home. They are desperate for re-housing.

I support the social services' view that the childrens' well being and safety can only ensured by a Care Order, but I consider the parents have many strengths and would expect that the family could be brought together again providing the environmental conditions are relieved, the older child placed in a day nursery, and the parents receive the skilled case-work help they so urgently need but have not so far experienced. Their medical problems should also be attended to by the health visitor.

Joan Court
Independent Social Worker
8.9.81

LONDON BOROUGH OF BRENT

date 16.9.81

MEMORANDUM from Mr W Thompson, Principal Court Officer

my ref: C/WGT

TO:- Mr D Bishop, Area Manager, Area 6

ext: 667

your ref:

Re: BECKFORD Children – Care Proceedings 9.9.1981

In giving their decision, the Willesden Magistrates, made the following comments which they requested be brought to the attention of the proper authorities.

"This has been one of the most difficult cases we have had to adjudicate. It has caused us much heartsearching and unhappiness.

We must make a Care Order in respect of both children to the London Borough of Brent. In making these orders it is our earnest hope that the Social Services Department will do it's utmost to carry out a rehabilitation programme to unite these children with their parents.

We hope you do your utmost to give both parents frequent contact with their children so that the bonding is not broken. We have therefore noted what counsel for the children and counsel for the parents have said and suggest access of at least once a week. We also note the remarks made by Mrs COURT, the Independant Social Worker.

It is our further hope that you, Mr THOMPSON will pass our comments to the right people who will put sufficient pressure on the Housing Department to get this family together as quickly as possible in a proper family situation."

Then directing her comments to the parents, the Chairman said,

"There are a lot of people helping you both – you must co-operate with them all. I am sure the Social Services will do everything to help you both and get your children back to you, however your children will be in Care until 18 years of age, unless you make application before hand.

Our experience is that Brent apply much earlier to discharge Care Orders. That will be the same in this case if you both co-operate."

I hope you find this report of adjudication of help.

Mr W G Thompson
Principal Court Officer.

c.c. to Mr J Dietman, Principal Assistant, F.S.D.
c.c. to Mr J Burns, Principal Officer, Adoption & Foster Care.

APPENDIX C.4

A. Hearing before the Willesden Magistrates' Court on 9th September 1981

1. **Evidence before the Court**

   a) **Dr. Levick's report**

Q.   (i) Was the Bench supplied with copies of Dr. Levick's report, and if so, at what stage and in what circumstances was it seen by the Bench? Was it an agreed document, or did the Bench have to rule on its admissibility?

A.   The Bench recollects not being supplied with copies of Dr. Levick's report.

Q.   (ii) Did the Bench hear any application that Dr. Levick should give oral evidence?

A.   The Bench recollects not hearing any application that Dr. Levick should give oral evidence.

Q.   (iii) Did the Bench understand Dr. Levick's report as indicating that the two children had each suffered two fractures inflicted in incidents separated in time – 3 or 4 days?

A.   The Bench cannot recollect what understanding they reached as to Dr. Levick's report.

   b) **Miss Joan Court's report and evidence**

Q.   (i) How did the Bench regard the report of Miss Joan Court? Was it an independent social worker's report to the court, or was it a report submitted on behalf of the children in furtherance of the children's welfare, irrespective of parental rights?

A.   The Bench recollects that the report of Miss Joan Court was submitted on behalf of the children in furtherance of the children's welfare, irrespective of parental rights.

Q.   (ii) Was the Bench aware that Miss Court had not been allowed to interview the foster-parents or to see to files of Brent Borough Council for the purpose of making her report?

A.   The Bench recollects not being aware that Miss Court had not been allowed to interview the foster-parents or to see the files of Brent Borough Council for the purpose of making her report.

Q.   (iii) Was the Bench aware that Miss Court's report was written prior to her seeing Dr. Levick's report?

A.   The Bench recollects not being aware that Miss Court's report was written prior to her seeing Dr. Levick's report.

c) **Other Documentation**

Q.   Was the Bench supplied with the minutes of the meetings of the Case Conference of the Brent Borough Council of 6th and 20th August 1981? Alternatively, was the Bench informed by Mr. Thompson, the Court Officer for Brent Borough Council, or by Miss Gun Wahlstrom, the social worker, of the decisions (if any) of these case conferences? In particular, was the Bench told of any plan by the local authority either to rehabilitate the children with their parents or to place them long-term with foster-parents?

A.   The Bench recollects not being supplied with minutes of the meetings of the case conference of the Brent Borough Council of 6th and 20th August 1981. The Bench recollects not being informed by Mr. Thompson, the Court Officer for Brent Council, or by Miss Gun Wahlstrom, the Social Worker, of the decisions (if any) of those case conferences. The Bench recollects being told of the plans by the local authority to rehabilitate the children with their parents and to place them long-term with foster-parents; both plans were put forward.

Q.   Did the Bench have any views about the nature of the representation before it – that is to say, Counsel for the parents and for the children and the Court Officer, Mr. Thompson, for the local authority?

A.   [Not answered].

2. The Recommendation

Q. (i) Did any of the parties – and if so, whom and in what circumstances – expressly or by implication, ask the Magistrates, in the course of making a Care Order, to make a recommendation indicating the Bench's view as to the management of the Care Order by the local authority?

A.   The Bench recollects that the only recommendation in the proceedings was made to the Court by Miss Gun Wahlstrom, the Social Worker, in terms that Care Orders be made with a view to both children being placed with the same foster-parents, to arrangements being made for the children to see their parents, to encouragement being given by the local authority for these visits to take place, to access being envisaged as one day a week at first, and to put the family back together again hopefully in the future; all of which the Bench reiterated on making the Care Orders.

Q. (ii) Did the Bench take advice from the Justices' Clerk as to its jurisdiction to make a recommendation? Assuming that the Bench concluded that it had jurisdiction, did it indicate to the parties that it proposed to make a recommendation in advance of announcing its decision? and if not, did the Bench give the parties an opportunity of addressing the Bench on the recommendation after it was announced in court?

A.   The Bench does not accept that it made a recommendation, merely an expression of hope following on the recommendation made to it by Miss Gun Wahlstrom, which it had accepted.

The Bench recollects that the conduct of the proceedings was such that those present had expressly or by implication an opportunity at every stage of addressing the Bench on any matter.

Q.   Did the Bench intend that its recommendation should be communicated not only to those present in court and to those in the Social Services Department of Brent Borough Council who would be concerned to administer the Care Order, but also the foster-parents, Mr. and Mrs. Probert?

A.   The Bench recollects expressing a hope to those present in Court.

Q. (iii) Did the Bench intend that its further suggestion of access of at least once a week be communicated to the foster-parents?

A.   The Bench recollects reiterating the recommendation of Miss Gun Wahlstrom, the Social Worker, and making it clear that the detailed operation of the Care Orders was in the hands of the London Borough of Brent.

3. Adjournment

Q. (i) Did any of the parties at any stage apply to the Court for an adjournment of the second stage of the Care Proceedings – namely, the statutory requirement of care and control?

A.   The Bench recollects no applications being made to the Court for an adjournment of the second stage of the Care Proceedings.

Q. (ii) Was the Bench informed by Counsel for the children that an appointment had been arranged for later that month for the parents to be psychiatrically assessed by a specialist at Great Ormond Street Hospital?

A.   The Bench cannot recollect whether Counsel for the children gave information that an appointment had been arranged for later that month for the parents to be psychiatrically assessed by a Specialist at Great Ormond Street Hospital.

B. Hearing before the Willesden Magistrates' Court on 22nd June 1983

Q. 1.   Was the composition of the Bench the same as that which had heard the application for the Care Order on 9th September 1981? If not, was any one of the justices common to both hearings.

A.   The Bench recollects that its composition was the same as that which heard the application for the Care Order on 9th September 1981, save for one Justice who was not common to both hearings.

2-5 The Bench recollects that this was an application made at the end of a morning list; that there may well have been other short applications for presentation additionally; that only Mr. Thompson, principal Court Officer for Brent, and the Clerk of the Court were present; that Mr. Thompson briefly related the current circumstances but not the history; that the Bench refused to discharge the Care Order; that the matter lasted for two or three minutes; and that in such circumstances the answers to the remaining questions are set out as below, namely:

Q. 2. Did the Bench have before it all the documentation that was before the Court on 9th September 1981; in particular, was the Bench aware of the earlier recommendation?

A. The Bench recollects not having before it all the documentation that was before the Court on 9th September 1981; and not being made aware of any earlier particular.

Q. 3. Was the Bench informed that in November 1982 the children had been taken off the NAI register?

A. The Bench recollects not being informed that in November 1982 the children had been taken off the NAI register.

Q. 4. Was the Bench informed that Miss Beverley Lorrington was at that time three months pregnant?

A. The Bench recollects not being informed that Miss Beverley Lorrington was at that time three months pregnant.

Q. 5. Was the Bench informed in detail of the manner in which Brent Borough Council had administered the Care Order since April 1982, in particular, what support the social services were giving to the parents and children?

A. The Bench recollects not being informed in detail of the manner in which Brent Borough Council had administered the Care Order since April 1982, in particular, what support the Social Services were giving to the parents and children.

The Bench further recollects that since no documents were put before the Court and no history of the case was given, they were unable to discharge the Care Order on the basis of insufficient information put before it.

SUPPLEMENTAL QUESTIONS

I. In relation to the proceeding for a Care Order on the 9th September 1981

    a. In so far as the Magistrates relied upon the evidence of Miss Wahlstrom as the basis for their statement when making the Care Order, would they point to the passage (or passages) in their notes of evidence or other documentation provided to them, as supporting the terms of their statement?

    In so far as the Bench relied upon the evidence of Miss Wahlstrom as the basis for their statement when making the Care Order, they would point to the totality of her evidence, as supporting the terms of their statement.

    b. Do the Magistrates have any independent recollection of Miss Wahlstrom's evidence other than what is contained in their notes and the other documentation provided to them?

    The Bench has no independent recollection of Miss Wahlstrom's evidence.

c. Did the Magistrates rely in any way on the report and/or the evidence of Miss Joan Court?

The Bench recollects taking into account the evidence of Miss Joan Court as part of all the evidence before them.

d. Do the Magistrates have any independent recollection of Dr. Levick's report and its method of presentation, other than what appears in their notes and the documentation provided to them? If so, could they outline their recollection.

The Bench has no independent recollection of Dr. Levick's report and its method of presentation.

e. Assuming copies of Dr. Levick's report were generally available in the Court-room.
   (i) did the Magistrates see such copies;
      The Bench recollects not being supplied with copies of Dr. Levick's report.
   (ii) were such copies (or copy) returned to the legal representatives;
      Not applicable.
   (iii) is it the Magistrates' practice to keep such a copy on their files?
      Not applicable.

f. Assuming the Magistrates did not see Dr. Levick's actual report, but only heard Dr. Warner repeat its substance, did they appreciate that Jasmine Beckford had suffered more than one injury? (It appears from their notes of evidence that Louise had suffered more than one blow at different times; did they appreciate Dr. Levick's report as indicating the same for Jasmine?)

The Bench cannot recollect what understanding they reached as to Dr. Levick's report.

g. Could the Magistrates indicate which of the following most accurately records their statement when making the Care Order.
   (i) Mr. Thompson's note;
   (ii) Miss P. Smith's note;
   (iii) Miss E. Sczwed's note.
      The Bench can add nothing further to the answers they gave in response to the original question, number 3.

h. Do the Magistrates have any independent recollection of what the Chairman said in making the Care Orders?

The Bench has no independent recollection of what the Chairman said in making the Care Orders.

i. If the Magistrates considered they were merely repeating from the statement of Miss Wahlstrom about the plans for reuniting the family, did they consider that those recommendations were her personal views, or those of the Social Services Department? If the latter, did they confirm that fact with the Local Authority's representative, Mr. Thompson?

The Bench cannot recollect what view it took as to whether Miss Wahlstrom's recommendations were her personal views, or those of the Social Services Department.

The bench has not been able to re-convene and will not be able to do so until 9th September 1985 at the earliest.

II. In relation to the application for revocation of the Care Order on the 22nd June 1983

a. Can the Magistrates recall what documentary material was in their files and available to them prior to the application taking place?

The Bench recalls that they had no such material prior to the application taking place.

b. What is the normal practice for an application for revocation, in the sense of what evidence, if any, is called?

The Bench's normal practice for an application for revocation, is to invite the applicant to present their case as they see it with such material as they have available, and likewise any other relevant persons or bodies.

c. Can the Magistrates recollect whether during the application they were told that the Beckford children had been taken off the N.A.I. Register?

The Bench recollects not being told during the application that the Beckford children had been taken of the N.A.I. Register.

APPENDIX D

1. CHARGES AGAINST MORRIS BECKFORD TO WHICH HE PLEADED GUILTY

1. Assault occasioning bodily harm to Jasmine between 1st September 1983 and 1st January 1984

    Sentence: 3 years' imprisonment

2. Cruelty to Jasmine, contrary to Section 1(1), Children and Young Persons Act, 1933, between 1st September 1983 and 1st January 1984

    Sentence: 1 year's imprisonment

3. Assault occasioning bodily harm to Jasmine between 31 December 1983 and 5th July 1984

    Sentence: 3 years' imprisonment

4. Cruelty to Jasmine, contrary to Section 1(1), Children and Young Persons Act 1933, between 31 December 1983 and 5 July 1984

    Sentence: 1 year's imprisonment

All these sentences were made consecutive to each other: total of 8 years' imprisonment.

CHARGES AGAINST MORRIS BECKFORD TO WHICH HE PLEADED NOT GUILTY

5. Murder of Jasmine on 5th July 1984
   Verdict: Guilty of Manslaughter

    Sentence: 10 years' imprisonment concurrent with total sentence of 8 years' imprisonment on other counts

CHARGES AGAINST BEVERLEY LORRINGTON TO WHICH SHE PLEADED GUILTY

1. Cruelty to Jasmine between 1st September 1983 and 1st January 1984

    Sentence: 9 months' imprisonment

2. Cruelty to Jasmine between 3rd December 1983 and 5th July 1984

    Sentence: 9 months' imprisonment consecutive to charge 1 above

CHARGE AGAINST BEVERLEY LORRINGTON TO WHICH SHE PLEADED NOT GUILTY

3. Cruelty to Jasmine on 5th July 1984

    Jury discharged from giving verdict. Charge not to be proceeded with, without leave of the Court.

2. TRANSCRIPT OF PROCEEDINGS ON 28 MARCH 1985 BEFORE THE COMMON SERJEANT, JUDGE PIGOT, Q.C., AFTER SENTENCES PASSED IN

R. v. BECKFORD AND LORRINGTON
MR. DENNIS SIMPSON: Sworn
Examined by the Court

THE COMMON SERJEANT OF LONDON:

Q. What is your present position?

A. My present position is Assistant Director of the Family Services Division within the Social Services Department.

Q. Is that Brent?

A. That is Brent, the London Borough of Brent.

Q. Well I know that you and your Council share my grave concern over what happened over Jasmine when she was in the care of your Authority. I understand that now you have instigated an enquiry?

A. That is correct.

Q. And, therefore, I propose to limit my remarks so as not to prejudice anything that may take place in that enquiry, but I am anxious to ensure that steps have been, or will be taken, to prevent events of this nature occurring again and it would perhaps be helpful if I could reiterate the bare facts.

On the 9th September, 1981, full Care Orders were made in respect of two children.

On the 19th November, 1981, the male defendant was prosecuted for cruelty to Louise.

On the 22nd June, 1983, the Willesden Juvenile Court refused to revoke a Care Order, and then on the 8th September, 1983, the Social Worker visited the children and saw Jasmine well and relaxed. Thereafter there were numerous calls, excuses were given and Jasmine was not seen until the 12th March, 1984. When she was seen then there was nothing to arouse anxiety. Thereafter a number of appointments were made but never kept.

On the 6th May I understand the Social Worker was told that Jasmine had not attended school since the 9th September of last year. So, in fact, over a period of ten months this child, for which you had assumed, or your Council had assumed parental custody, was only seen twice. Those would appear to be the facts, would they not?

A. Yes.

Q. Now is there any mechanism now to ensure that when a child is not produced by those in whose custody it is, it can be produced for your authority?

A. Yes, my Lord, two things have happened. First we have had a complete review of our child abuse procedures. Secondly, we propose to make amendments to our Child

Abuse procedures and extending the second point slightly, what we propose to do is to ensure that where children are subject to a Care Order the Social Worker will physically see the child and continuing from there, what we also propose to do is to build into our case review procedures the ability for the Social Worker or the key worker concerned, to call a Paediatric Specialist, because it is all very well the Social Worker physically seeing the child, but a Social Worker might not on all occasions be the best person to assess any internal injuries. So for child abuse situations, in particular, we propose to build that into our procedures, access to a Paediatric Specialist.

Q. Have any steps been taken to produce rather more cynicism in this case than has been present, in other words, more scepticism, because it does appear that the Worker was fobbed off time and time again by excuses which would not have deceived a child?

A. Yes, my Lord, I think this particular case has hit the Department quite hard, and I think there is a concern felt by all people within the Department that we should be aware of the importance of child abuse situations.

Q. Well it is well known, isn't it, there is abundant child abuse. What I want to know is what steps can be taken to produce the child? Usually school is a good place for that, because the child goes to school and any marks can there be observed, but in this case there seems to have been a lack of communication between school and you?

A. If a child is at school or in the nursery, then as part of the case conference procedure, people from school and from a day nursery would obviously be present at the review and, therefore, it is incumbent upon people to actually express any concern they might feel about the child and, in particular, if the child is absent from that facility –

Q. Yes, I would have thought in loco parentis you should have required a notification by the Authorities, or somebody else – is that not the practice?

A. It is the practice, indeed, and it is presently part of our procedures.

Q. Well what went wrong in this case, was it the human element, or –

A. I think that is as much for the external enquiry to assess. I think it would be a mistake for me to talk about that here in open court.

Q. Well, you see the enquiry may not be brought for some time and it is already nine months from these occurrences. I want to know what has been done in the meantime?

A. The external enquiry is due to begin on the 11th April, and that is in two weeks' time. All I can say is what I have said previously, that we have had a complete review of our child abuse procedures and we have made alterations to those procedures. The two points I think that are particularly pertinent and important are that the key worker will on every occasion physically see the child and, secondly, we will have access to a Paediatric Specialist in terms of assessing any internal injuries; that will be built into our review procedures which we have frequently, so steps have already been taken, yes.

Q. Thank you very much, unless you wish to add anything?

A. No.

(The witness withdrew)

THE COMMON SERJEANT OF LONDON: Is Miss Tuck here?
MR. ANTHONY FARRINGTON RISLEY: I represent Miss Tuck.

ANTHONY FARRINGTON RISLEY: Affirmed
Examined by the Court

Q. What is your position?

A. Education Officer, Special, with the London Borough of Brent.

Q. Are you familiar with the facts of this case, perhaps you are by now, are you?

A. Over the last two days I have read the newspaper reports. I know very little more than that.

Q. It does appear that Jasmine attended the Princess Frederica School as late as the 9th September, she attended it several days before that, the 9th September, 1983.

A. I made enquiries yesterday afternoon and I was told that was so.

Q. And I assume that the School Authority would know that the child was under a Care Order?

A. On this occasion I am told – and is that admissible – I have no direct evidence, that the school did not know.

Q. The school did not know that. I merely enquire this. Is there any obligation under five to attend school?

A. No, the obligation is for the child to commence schooling at the beginning of the term after the fifth birthday.

Q. That is what I thought, so there would be no offence committed by the parents who failed to send their child to school?

A. No, but on this occasion there was pressure on the school, a waiting list, and the school enquired, therefore, whether or not the parents intended to take up the place which was reserved for the child.

Q. Yes, I can understand that, and the parents indicated that they did not wish to take –

A. The parents indicated that at that time they wished to withdraw Jasmine from the school, which was their right. They also asked if she could remain on the Admissions List to join the school at a later time, perhaps when she reached statutory school age.

Q. Well, thank you very much for coming. It is quite clear that no blame whatsoever can be attached to the School Authorities.

A. Thank you, my Lord.

(The witness withdrew)
(The Court Adjourned)

APPENDIX E

RELEVANT CHILD CARE LAW

CHILDREN AND YOUNG PERSONS ACT 1933, sections 40 and 47

Special Procedure with regard to Offences specified in First Schedule

40 Warrant to search for or remove a child or young person

(1)   If it appears to a justice of the peace on information on oath laid by any person who, in the opinion of the justice, is acting in the interests of a child or young person, that there is reasonable cause to suspect–

(a)   that the child or young person has been or is being assaulted, ill-treated, or neglected in any place within the jurisdiction of the justice, in a manner likely to cause him unnecessary suffering, or injury to heath; or

(b)   that any offence mentioned in the First Schedule to this Act has been or is being committed in respect of the child or young person.

the justice may issue a warrant authorising any constable *named therein* to search for the child or young person, and, if it is found that he has been or is being assulated, ill-treated, or neglected in manner aforesaid, or that any such offence as aforesaid has been or is being committed in respect of him [to take him to a place of safety, or authorising any constable to remove him with or without search to a place of safety, and a child or young person taken to a place of safety in pursuance of such a warrant may be detained there] until he can be brought before a juvenile court.

(2)   A justice issuing a warrant under this section be the same warrant cause any person accused of any offence in respect of the child or young person to be apprehended and brought before a court of summary jurisdiction, and proceedings to be taken against him according to law.

(3)   Any constable authorised by warrant under this section to search for any child or young person, or to remove any child or young person with or without search, may enter (if need be by force) any house, building, or other place specified in the warrant, and may remove him therefrom.

(4)   Every warrant issued under this section should be *addressed to and* executed by a constable, who shall be accompanied by the person laying the information, if that person so desires, unless the justice by whom the warrant is issued otherwise directs, and may also, if the justice by whom the warrant is issued so directs, be accompanied by a duly qualified medical practitioner.

(5)   It shall not be necessary in any information or warrant under this section to name the child or young person.

47 Procedure in juvenile courts

(1)   Juvenile courts shall sit as often as may be necessary for the purpose of exercising any jurisdiction conferred on them by or under this or any other Act.

(2)   A juvenile court shall [not sit in a room in which sittings of a court other than a

juvenile court are held if a sitting of that other court has been or will be held there within an hour before or after the sitting of the juvenile court]; and no person shall be present at any sitting of a juvenile court except–

(a) members and officers of the court;
(b) parties to the case before the court, their solicitors and counsel, and witnesses and other persons directly concerned in that case;
(c) bona fide representatives of newspapers or news agencies;
(d) such other persons as the court may specially authorise to be present.

CHILDREN AND YOUNG PERSONS ACT 1963, Sections 23(I) and 26

23 Children and young persons detained in places of safety

(1) A court or justice of the peace–

(a) ...
(b) issuing a warrant under section 40 of [the principal Act] authorising a constable to take a child or young person to a place of safety; or
(c) ordering the removal of a child or young person to a place of safety under [section 12 of the Foster Chldren Act 1980] or *section 43 of the Adoption Act 1958;*

shall specify in the warrant, . . . or order a period, which shall not exceed twenty-eight days, beyond which the child or young person must not be detained in a place of safety without being brought before a juvenile court; and accordingly the child or young person shall be brought before a juvenile court not later than the end of that period unless he has been released or received into the care of a local authority.

26 Medical evidence by certificate

In any proceedings, other than proceedings for an offence, before a juvenile court, and on any appeal from a decision of a juvenile court in any such proceedings, any document purporting to be a certificate of a fully registered medical practitioner as to any person's physical or mental condition shall be admissable as evidence of that condition.

CHILDREN AND YOUNG PERSONS ACT 1969, Sections 1, 2, 11-16, 21(2) & (2A), 27(4), 28, 32A and 32B.

1 Care proceedings in juvenile courts

(1) Any local authority, constable or authorised person who reasonably believes that there are grounds for making an order under this section in respect of a child or young person may, subject to section 2 (3) and (8) of this Act, bring him before a juvenile court.

(2) If the court before which a child or young person is brought under this section is of opinion that any of the following conditions is satisfied with respect to him, that is to say–

(a) his proper development is bing avoidably prevented or neglected or his health is being avoidably impaired or neglected or he is being ill-treated; or

(b) it is probable that the condition set out in the preceding paragraph will be satisfied in his case, having regard to the fact that the court or another court has found that that condition is or was satisfied in the case of another child or young person who is or was a member of the household to which he belongs; or

[(bb) it is probable that the conditions set out in paragraph (a) of this subsection will be satisfied in his case, having regard to the fact that a person who has been convicted of an offence mentioned in Schedule 1 to the Act of 1933, including a person convicted of such an offence on whose conviction for the offence an order was made under Part I of the Powers of Criminal Courts Act 1973 placing him on probation or discharging him absolutely or conditionally is, or may become, a member of the same household as the child or young person;]

(c) he is exposed to moral danger; or

(d) he is beyond the control of his parent or guardian; or

(e) he is of compulsory school age within the meaning of the Education Act 1944 and is not receiving efficient full-time edcucation suitable to his age, ability and aptitude [and to any special educational needs he may have); or

(f) he is guilty of an offence, excluding homicide.

and also that he is in need of care or control which he is unlikely to receive unless the court makes an order under this section in respect of him, then, subject to the following provisions of this section and sections 2 and 3 of this Act, the court may if it thinks fit make such an order.

(3) The order which a court may make under this section in respect of a child or young person is–

(a) an order requiring his parent or guardian to enter into a recognisance to take proper care of him and exercise proper control over him; or

(b) a supervision order; or

(c) a care order (other than an interim order); or

(d) a hospital order within the meaning of [Part III of the Mental Health Act 1983]; or

(e) a guardianship order within the meaning of that Act.

(4) In any proceedings under this section the court may make orders in pursuance of paragraphs (c) and (d) of the preceding subsection but subject to that shall not make more than one of the orders mentioned in the preceding subsection, without prejudice to any power to make a further order in subsequent proceedings of any description; and if in proceedings under this section the court makes one of those orders and an order so mentioned is already in force in respect of the child or young person in question, the court may discharge the earlier order unless it is a hospital or guardianship order.

(5) An order under this section shall not be made in respect of a child or young person–

(a) in pursuance of paragraph (a) of subsection (3) of this section unless the parent or guardian is question consents;

(b) in pursuance of paragraph (d) or (e) of that subsection unless the conditions which, under [section 37 of the said Act of 1983], are required to be satisfied for the making of a hospital or guardianship order in respect of a person convicted as mentioned in that section are satisfied in this case so far as they are applicable;

(c) if he has attained the age of sixteen and is or has been married.

(6) In this section "authorised person" means a person authorised by order of the Secretary of State to bring proceedings in pursuance of this section and any officer of a

society which is so authorised, and in sections 2 and 3 of this Act "care proceedings" means proceedings in pursuance of this section and "relevant infant" means the child or young person in respect of whom such proceedings are brought or proposed to be brought.

2 Provisions supplementary to s 1

(1) If a local authority receive information suggesting that there are grounds for bringing care proceedings in respect of a child or young person who resides or is found in their area, it shall be the duty of the authority to cause enquiries to be made into the case unless they are satisfied that such enquiries are unnecessary.

(2) If it appears to a local authority that there are grounds for bringing care proceedings in respect of a child or young person who resides or is found in their area, it shall be the duty of the authority to exercise their power under the preceding section to bring care proceedings in respect of him unless they are satisfied that it is neither in his interest nor the public interest to do so or that some other person is about to do so or to charge him with an offence.

(3) No care proceedings shall be begun by any person unless that person has given notice of the proceedings to the local authority for the area in which it appears to him that the relevant infant resides, or, if it appears to him that the relevant infant does not reside in the area of a local authority, to the local authority for any area in which it appears to him that any circumstances giving rise to the proceedings arose; but the preceding provisions of this subsection shall not apply where the person by whom the notice would fall to be given is the local authority in question.

(4) Without prejudice to any power to issue a summons or warrant apart from this subsection, a justice may issue a summons or warrant for the purpose of securing the attendance of the relevant infant before the court in which care proceedings are brought or proposed to be brought in respect of him; but [subsections (3) and (4) of section 55 of the Magistrates' Courts Act 1980] (which among other things restrict the circumstances in which a warrant may be issued) shall apply with the necessary modifications to a warrant under this subsection as they apply to a warrant under that section and as if in subsection (3) after the word "summons" there were inserted the words "cannot be served or".

(5) Where the relevant infant is arrested in pursuance of a warrant issued by virtue of the preceding subsection and cannot be brought immediately before the court aforesaid, the person in whose custody he is–

(a) may make arrangements for his detention in a place of safety for a period of not more than seventy-two hours from the time of the arrest (and it shall be lawful for him to be detained in pursuance of the arrangements); and

(b) shall within that period, unless within it the relevant infant is brought before the court aforesaid, bring him before a justice;

and the justice shall either make an interim order in respect of him or direct that he be released forthwith.

(6) [Section 97 of the Magistrates' Courts Act 1980] (under which a summons or warrant may be issued to secure the attendance of a witness) shall apply to care proceedings as it applies to the hearing of a complaint.

(7) In determining whether the condition set out in subsection (2) (b) of the

preceding section is satisfied in respect of the relevant infant, it shall be assumed that no order under that section is to be made in respect of him.

(8) In relation to the condition set out in subsection (2) (e) of the preceding section the references to a local authority in that section and subsections (1), (2) and (11) (b) of this section shall be construed as references to a local education authority; and in any care proceedings –

(a) the court shall not entertain an allegation that the condition is satisfied unless the proceedings are brought by a local education authority; and
(b) the said condition shall be deemed to be satisfied if the relevant infant is of the age mentioned in that condition and it is proved that he –
    (i) is the subject of a school attendance order which is in force under section 37 of the Education Act 1944 and has not been complied with, or
    (ii) is a registered pupil at a school which he is not attending regularly within the meaning of section 39 of that Act, or
    (iii) is a person whom another person habitually wandering from place to place takes with him.

    unless it is also proved that he is receiving the education mentioned in that condition;

but nothing in paragraph (a) of this subsection shall prevent any evidence from being considered in care proceedings for any purpose other than that of determining whether that condition is satisfied in respect of the relevant infant.

(9) If on application under this subsection to the court in which it is proposed to bring care proceedings in respect of a relevant infant who is not present before the court it appears to the court that he is under the age of five and either –

(a) it is proved to the satisfaction of the court, on oath or in such other manner as may be prescribed by rules under section 15 of the Justices of the Peace Act 1949, that notice of the proposal to bring the proceedings at the time and place at what the application is made was served on the parent or guardian of the relevant infant at what appears to the court to be a reasonable time before the making of the application; or
(b) it appears to the court that his parent or guardian is present before the court

the court may if it thinks fit, after giving the parent or guardian if he is present an opportunity to be heard, give a direction under this subsection in respect of the relevant infant; and a relevant infant in respect of whom such a direction is given by a court shall be deemed to have been brought before the court under section 1 of this Act at the time of the direction, and care proceedings in respect of him may be continued accordingly.

(10) If the court before which the relevant infant is brought in care proceedings is not in a position to decide what order, if any, ought to be made under the preceding section in respect of him, [the court may make–

(a) an interim order, or
(b) an interim hospital order within the meaning of [section 38 of the Mental health Act 1983],

in respect of him; but an order shall not be made in respect of the relevant infant in pursuance of paragraph (b) of this subsection unless the conditions which, under [the said section 38], are required to be satisfied for the making of an interim hospital order in respect of a person convicted as mentioned in that section are satsified in his case so far as they are applicable].

(11)   If it appears to the court before which the relevant infant is brought in care proceedings that he resides in a petty sessions area other than that for which the court acts, the court shall, unless it dismisses the case and subject to subsection (5) of the following section, direct that he be brought under the preceding section before a juvenile court acting for the petty sessions area in which he resides; and where the court so directs–

(a) it may make an interim order in respect of him and, if it does so, shall cause the clerk of the court to which the direction relates to be informed of the case;

(b) if the court does not make such an order it shall cause the local authority in whose area it appears to the court that the relevant infant resides to be informed of the case, and it shall be the duty of that authority to give effect to the direction within twenty-one days.

(12)   The relevant infant may appeal to [the Crown Court] against any order made in respect of him under the preceding section except such an order as is mentioned in subsection (3)(a) of that section.

(13)   Such an order as is mentioned in subsection (3)(a) of the preceding section shall not require the parent or guardian in question to enter into a recognisance for an amount exceeding [£1,000] or for a period exceeding three years or, where the relevant infant will attain the age of eighteen in a period shorter than three years, for a period exceeding that shorter period; and [section 120 of the Magistrates' Courts Act 1980] (which relates to the forfeiture of recognisances) shall apply to a recognisance entered into in pursuance of such an order as it applies to a recognisance to keep the peace.

(14)   For the purposes of this Act, care proceedings in respect of a relevant infant are begun when he is first brought before a juvenile court in pursuance of the preceding section in connection with the matter to which the proceedings relate.

11   Supervision orders

Any provision of this Act authorising a court to make a supervision order in respect of any person shall be construed as authorising the court to make an order placing him under the supervision of a local authority designated by the order or of a probation officer; and in this Act "supervision order" shall be construed accordingly and "supervised person" and "supervisor", in relation to a supervision order, mean respectively the person placed or to be placed under supervision by the order and the person under whose supervision he is placed or to be placed by the order.

[11Aa   Local authority functions under certain supervision orders

The Secretary of State may make regulations with respect to the exercise by a local authority of their functions in a case where a person has been placed under their supervision by an order made under section 1 (3) (b) or 21 (2) of this Act.]

12   Power to include requirements in supervision orders

(1)   A supervision order may require the supervised person to reside with an individual named in the order who agrees to the requirement, but a requirement imposed by a supervision order in pursuance of this subsection shall be subject to any such requirement of the order as is authorised by the following provisions of this section.

[(2) Subject to section 19(12) of this Act, a supervision order may require the supervised person to comply with any directions given from time to time by the supervisor and requiring him to do all or any of the following things –

(a) to live at a place or places specified in the directions for a period or periods so specified;

(b) to present himself to a person or persons specified in the directions at a place or places and on a day or days so specified;

(c) to participate in activities specified in the directions on a day or days so specified;

but it shall be for the supervisor to decide whether and to what extent he exercises any power to give directions conferred on him by virtue of this subsection and to decide the form of any directions; and a requirement imposed by a supervision order in pursuance of this subsection shall be subject to any such requirement of the order as is authorised by subsection (4) of this section.

(3) The total number of days in respect of which a supervised person may be required to comply with directions given by virtue of paragraph (a), (b) or (c) of subsection (2) above in pursuance of a supervision order shall not exceed 90 or such less number, if any, as the order may specify for the purposes of this subsection; and for the purpose of calculating the total number of days in respect of which such directions may be given the supervisor shall be entitled to disregard any day in respect of which directions were previously given in pursuance of the order and on which the directions were not complied with.]

(3A) Subject to subsection (3B) of this section, this subsection applies to–

(a) any supervision order made under section 7(7) of this Act in respect of a child or young person found guilty as there mentioned; and

(b) any supervision order made in respect of a person under section 2(2) of this Act by a court on discharging a care order made in respect of him under the said section 7(7).

(3B) Subsection (3A) of this section does not apply to any supervision order which by virtue of subsection (2) of this section requires the supervised person to comply with directions given by the supervisor.

(3C) Subject to the following provisions of this section and to section 19(13) of this Act, but without prejudice to subsection (4) below, a supervision order to which subsection (3A) of this section applies may require a supervised person–

(a) to do anything that by virtue of subsection (2) of this section a supervisor has power, or would but for section 19(12) of this Act have power, to direct a supervised person to do;

(b) to remain for specified periods between 6 p.m. and 6 a.m. –
    (i) at a place specified in the order; or
    (ii) at one of several places so specified;

(c) to refrain from participating in activities specified in the order–
    (i) on a specified day or days during the period for which the supervision order is in force; or
    (ii) during the whole of that period or a specified portion of it.

(3D) A requirement under subsection (3C)(b) of this section is referred to in this section as a "night restriction".

(3E) The total number of days in respect of which a supervised person may be subject to requirements imposed by virtue of subsection (3C)(a) or (b) of this section shall not exceed 90.

(3F)   The court may not include requirements under subsection (3C) of this section in a supervision order unless–

- (a) it has first consulted the supervisor as to–
    - (i) the offender's circumstances; and
    - (ii) the feasibility of securing compliance with the requirements, and is satisfied, having regard to the supervisor's report, that it is feasible to secure compliance with them;
- (b) having regard to the circumstances of the case, it considers the requirement necessary for securing the good conduct of the supervised person or for preventing a repetition by him of the same offence or the commission of their offences; and
- (c) the supervised person or, if he is a child, his parent or guardian, consents to their inclusion.

(3G)   The court shall not include in such an order by virtue of subsection (3C) of this section–

- (a) any requirement that would involve the co-operation of a person other than the supervisor and the supervised person unless that other person consents to its inclusion; or
- (b) any requirement requiring the supervised person to reside with a specified individual, or
- (c) any such requirement as is mentioned in subsection (4) of this section.

(3H)   The place, or one of the places, specified for the purposes of a night restriction shall be the place where the supervised person lives.

(3J)   A night restriction shall not require the supervised person to remain at a place for longer than 10 hours on any one night.

(3K)   A night restriction shall not be imposed in respect of any day which falls outside the period of three months beginning with the date when the supervision order is made.

(3L)   A night restriction shall not be imposed in respect of more than 30 days in all.

(3M)   A supervised person who is required by a night restriction to remain at a place may leave it if he is accompanied–

- (a) by his parent or guardian;
- (b) by his supervisor; or
- (c) by some other person specified in the supervision order.

(3N)   For the purposes of this section a night restriction imposed in respect of a period of time beginning in the evening and ending in the morning shall be treated as imposed only in respect of the day upon which the period begins.]

(4)   Where a court which proposes to make a supervision order is satisfied, on the evidence of a medical practitioner approved for the purposes of [section 12 of the Mental Health Act 1983], that the mental condition of a supervised person is such as requires and may be susceptible to treatment but is not such as to warrant his detention in pursuance of a hospital order under [Part III] of that Act, the court may include in the supervision order a requirement that the supervised person shall, for a period specified in the order, submit to treatment of one of the following descriptions so specified, that is

to say–

(a) treatment by or under the direction of a fully registered medical practitioner specified in the order;

(b) treatment as a non-resident patient at a place specified in the order; or

(c) treatment as a resident patient in a hospital or mental nursing home within the meaning of [the said Act of 1983], but not a special hospital within the meaning of that Act.

(5)   A requirement shall not be included in a supervision order in pursuance of the preceding subsection–

(a) in any case, unless the court is satisfied that arrangements have been or can be made for the treatment in question and, in the case of treatment as a resident patient, for the reception of the patient.

(b) in the case of an order made or to be made in respect of a person who has attained the age of fourteen, unless he consents to its inclusion;

and a requirement so included shall not in any case continue in force after the supervised person becomes eighteen.

13   Selection of supervisor

(1)   A court shall not designate a local authority as the supervisor by a provision of a supervision order unless the authority agree or it appears to the court that the supervised person resides or will reside in the area of the authority.

(2)   A court shall not insert in a supervision order a provision placing a child under the supervision of a probation officer unless the local authority of which the area is named or to be named in the order in pursuance of section 18(2)(a) of this Act so request and a probation officer is already exercising or has exercised, in relation to another member of the household to which the child belongs, duties imposed [on probation officers by paragraph 8 of Schedule 3 to the Powers of Criminal Courts Act 1973 or by rules under paragraph 18(1)(b)] of that Schedule.

(3)   Where a provision of a supervision order places a person under the supervision of a probation officer, the supervisor shall be a probation officer appointed for or assigned to the petty sessions area named in the order in pursuance of section 18(2)(a) of this Act and selected under arrangements made by the [probation committee]; but if the probation officer selected as aforesaid dies or is unable to carry out his duties . . . , another probation officer shall be selected as aforesaid for the purposes of the order.

14   Duty of supervisor

While a supervision order is in force it shall be the duty of the supervisor to advise, assist and befriend the supervised person.

[14A   Refusal to allow supervisor to visit child or young person

Where a supervision order has been made in a case where a condition set out in paragraph (a), (b), (bb) or (c) or section 1(2) above is satisfied, a refusal to comply with a requirement imposed under section 18(2)(b) below–

(a) that the supervisor of a child or young person shall visit him; or

(b) that a child or young person shall be medically examined.

shall be treated for the purposes of section 40 of the Children and Young Persons Act 1933 (under which a warrant authorising the search for and removal of a child or young person may be issued on suspicion of unnecessary suffering caused to, or certain offences committed against, the child or young person) as giving reasonable cause for such suspicion.]

15 Variation and discharge of supervision orders

(1) If while a supervision order is in force in respect of a supervised person who has not attained the age of eighteen it appears to a juvenile court, on the application of the supervisor or the supervised person, that it is appropriate to make an order under this subsection, the court may make an order discharging the supervision order or varying it by–

(a) cancelling any requirement included in it in pursuance of section 12 or section 18(2)(b) of this Act; or

(b) inserting in it (either in addition to or in substitution for any of its provisions) any provision which could have been included in the order if the court had then had power to make it and were exercising the power,

and may on discharging the supervision order make a care order (other than an interim order) in respect of the supervised person; but the powers of variation conferred by this subsection do not include power to insert in the supervision order, after the expiration of [three months beginning with the date when the order was originally made], a requirement in pursuance of section 12(4) of this Act, unless . . . it is in substitution for such a requirement already included in the order [or power to insert in the supervision order a requirement in pursuance of section 12(3C)(b) of this Act in respect of any day which falls outside the period of 3 months beginning with the date when the order was originally made].

(2) If on an application in pursuance of the preceding subsection, in a case where the supervised person has attained the age of seventeen and the supervision order was not made by virtue of section 1 of this Act or on the occasion of the discharge of a care order, it appears to the court appropriate to do so it may proceed as if the application were in pursuance of subsection (3) or, if it is made by the supervisor, in pursuance of subsections (3) and (4) of this section and as if in that subsection or those subsections, as the case may be, the word "seventeen" were substituted for the word "eighteen" and the words "a magistrates' court other than" were omitted.

[(2A) If while a supervision order to which section 12(3A) of this Act applies is in force in respect of a person who has not attained the age of eighteen it is proved to the satisfaction of a juvenile court, on the application of the supervisor, that the supervised person has failed to comply with any requirement included in the supervision order in pursuance of section 12 or section 18(2)(b) of this Act, the court may, whether or not it also makes an order under subsection (1) of this section–

(a) order him to pay a fine of an amount not exceeding [£100]; or

(b) subject to section 16(10 of this Act, make an attendance centre order in respect of him].

(3) If while a supervision order is in force in respect of a supervised person who has attained the age of eighteen it appears to a magistrates' court other than a juvenile

court, on the application of the supervisor or the supervised person, that it is appropriate to make an order under this subsection, the court may make an order discharing the supervision order or varying it by–

(a) inserting in it a provision specifying the duration of the order or altering or cancelling such a provision already included in it; or

(b) substituting for the provisions of the order by which the supervisor is designated or by virtue of which he is selected such other provisions in that behalf as could have been included in the order if the court had then had power to make it and were exercising the power; or

(c) substituting for the name of an area included in the order in pursuance of section 18(2)(a) of this Act the name of any other area of a local authority or petty sessions area, as the case may be, in which it appears to the court that the supervised person resides or will reside; or

(d) cancelling any provision included in the order by virtue of section 18(2)(b) of this Act or inserting in it any provision prescribed for the purposes of that paragraph; or

(e) cancelling any requirement included in the order in pursuance of section 12(1) or (2) of this Act.

(4) If while a supervision order is in force in respect of a supervised person who has attained the age of eighteen it is proved to the satisfaction of a magistrates' court other than a juvenile court, on the application of the supervisor, that the supervised person has failed to comply with any requirement included in the supervision order in pursuance of section 12 or section 18(2)(b) or this Act, the court may–

(a) whether or not it also makes an order under subsection (3) of this section, order him to pay a fine of an amount not exceeding [£100] or, subject to subsection (10) of the following section, make an attendance centre order in respect of him;

(b) if it also discharges the supervision order, make an order imposing on him any punishment which it could have imposed on him if it had then had power to try him for the offence in consequence of which the supervision order was made and had convicted him in the exercise of that power;

and in a case where the offence in question is of a kind which the court has no power to try or has no power to try without appropriate consents, the punishment imposed by virtue of paragraph (b) of this subsection shall not exceed that which any court having power to try such an offence could have imposed in respect of it and shall not in any event exceed imprisonment for a term of six months and a fine of [£2,000].

(5) If a medical practitioner by whom or under whose direction a supervised person is being treated for his mental condition in pursuance of a requirement included in a supervision order by virtue of section 12(4) of this Act is unwilling to continue to treat or direct the treatment of the supervised person or is of opinion–

(a) that the treatment should be continued beyond the period specified in that behalf in the order; or

(b) that the supervised person needs different treatment; or

(c) that he is not susceptible to treatment; or

(d) that he does not require further treatment.

the practitioner shall make a report in writing to that effect to the supervisor; and on receiving a report under this subsection the supervisor shall refer it to a juvenile court, and on such a reference the court may make an order cancelling or varying the requirement.

(6)   The preceding provisions of this section shall have effect subject to the provisions of the following section.

16   Provisions supplementary to s 15

(1)   Where the supervisor makes an application or reference under the preceding section to a court he may bring the supervised person before the court, and subject to subsection (5) of this section a court shall not make an order under that section unless the supervised person is present before the court.

(2)   Without prejudice to any power to issue a summons or warrant apart from this subsection, a justice may issue a summons or warrant for the purpose of securing the attendance of a supervised person before the court to which any application or reference in respect of him is made under the preceding section; but [subsection (3) and (4) of section 55 of the Magistrates' Courts Act 1980] (which among other things restrict the circumstances in which a warrant may be issued) shall apply with the necessary modifications to a warrant under this subsection as they apply to a warrant under that section and as if in subsection (3) after the word "summons" there were inserted the words "cannot be served or".

(3)   Where the supervised person is arrested in pursuance of a warrant issued by virtue of the preceding subsection and cannot be brought immediately before the court referred to in that subsection, the person in whose custody he is–

(a)   may make arrangements for his detention in a place of safety for a period of not more than seventy-two hours from the time of the arrest (and it shall be lawful for him to be detained in pursuance of the arrangements); and

(b)   shall within that period, unless within it the relevant infant is brought before the court aforesaid, bring him before a justice;

and the justice shall either direct that he be released forthwith or–

(i)   if he has not attained the age of eighteen, make an interim order in respect of him;

(ii)   if he has attained that age, remand him.

(4)   If on an application to a court under subsection (1) of the preceding section–

(a)   the supervised person is brought before the court under a warrant issued or an interim order made by virtue of the preceding provisions of this section; or

(b)   the court considers that it is likely to exercise its powers under that subsection to make an order in respect of the supervised person but, before deciding whether to do so, seeks information with respect to him which it considers is unlikely to be obtained unless the court makes an interim order in respect of him,

the court may make an interim order in respect of the supervised person.

(5)   A court may make an order under the preceding section in the absence of the supervised person if the effect of the order is one or more of the following, that is to say–

(a)   discharing the supervision order;

(b)   cancelling a provision included in the supervision order in pursuance of section 12 or section 18(2)(b) of this Act;

(c)   reducing the duration of the supervision order or any provision included in it in pursuance of the said section 12;

(d)   altering in the supervision order the name of any area;

(e)   changing the supervisor.

(6)   A juvenile court shall not–

(a)   exercise its powers under subsection (1) of the preceding section to make a care order or an order discharing a supervision order or inserting in it a requirement authorised by section 12 of this Act or varying or cancelling such a requirement except in a case where the court the satisfied that the supervised person either is unlikely to receive the care or control he needs unless the court makes the order or is likely to receive it notwithstanding the order;

(b)   exercise its powers to make an order under subsection (5) of the preceding section except in such a case as is mentioned in paragraph (a) of this subsection;

(c)   exercise its powers under the said subsection (1) to make an order inserting a requirement authorised by section 12(4) of this Act in a supervision order which does not already contain such a requirement unles the court is satisfied as mentioned in the said section 12(4) on such evidence as is there mentioned.

(7)   Where the supervised person has attained the age of fourteen, then except with his consent a court shall not make an order under the preceding section containing provisions which insert in the supervision order a requirement authorised by section 12(4) of this Act or which alter such a requirement already included in the supervision order otherwise than by removing it or reducing its duration.

(8)   The supervised person may appeal to [the Crown Court] against–

(a)   any order made under the preceding section, except an order made or which could have been made in the absence of the supervised person and an order containing only provisions to which he consented in pursuance of the preceding subsection;

(b)   the dismissal of an application under that section to discharge a supervision order.

(9)   Where an application under the preceding section for the discharge of a supervision order is dismissed, no further application for its discharge shall be made under that section by any person during the period of three months beginning with the date of the dismissal except with the consent of a court having jurisdiction to entertain such an application.

(10) In [paragraph (b) of subsection (2A) and] paragraph (a) of subsection (4) of the preceding section "attendance centre order" means such an order to attend an attendance centre as is mentioned in subsection (1) of section [17 of the Criminal Justice Act 1982]; and the provisions of that section shall accordingly apply for the purposes of [each of those paragraphs] as if for the words from "has power" to "probation order" in subsection (1) there were substituted the words "considers it appropriate to make an attendance centre order in respect of any person in pursuance of [section 15(2A) or (4)] of the Children and Young Persons Act 1969" and for references to an offender there wre substituted references to the supervised person and as if subsection [(13)] were omitted.

(11) In this and the preceding section references to a juvenile court or any other magistrates' court, in relation to a supervision order, are references to such a court acting for the petty sessions area for the time being named in the order in pursuance of section 18(2)(a) of this Act and if while an application to a juvenile court in pursuance of the preceding section is pending the supervised person to whom it relates attains the age of the seventeen or eighteen, the court shall deal with the application as if he had not attained the age in question.

21 Variation and discharge of care orders

(2) If it appears to a juvenile court, on the application of a local authority to whose care a person is committed by a care order or on the application of that person, that it is appropriate to discharge the order, the court may discharge it and on discharging it may, unless it was an interim order and unless the person to whom the discharged order related has attained the age of eighteen, make a supervision order in respect of him.

[(2A) A juvenile court shall not make an order under subsection (2) of this section in the case of a person who has not attained the age of 18 and appears to the court to be in need of care or control unless the court is satisfied that, whether through the making of a supervision order or otherwise, he will receive that care or control.]

27 Consequential modifications of 1948 c 43 ss 11 and 12

(1)-(3) . . .

(4) *Without prejudice to their general duty aforesaid, it shall be the duty of a local authority who have at any time had a child in their care throughout the preceding six months and have not during that period held a review of his case in pursuance of this subsection to review his case as soon as is practicable after the expiration of that period and, if a care order is in force with respect to him, to consider in the course of the review whether to make an application for the discharge of the order.*

28 Detention of child or young person in place of safety

(1) If, upon an application to a justice by any person for authority to detain a child or young person and take him to a place of safety, the justice is satisfied that the applicant has reasonable cause to believe that–

(a) any of the conditions set out in section 1 (2) (a) to (e) of this Act is satisfied in respect of the child or young person; or

(b) an appropriate court would find the condition set out in section 1 (2)(b) of this Act satisfied in respect of him; or

(c) the child or young person is about to leave the United Kingdom in contravention of section 25 of the Act of 1933 (which regulates the sending abroad of juvenile entertainers).

the justice may grant the application; and the child or young person in respect of whom an authorisation is issued under this subsection may be detained in a place of safety by virtue of the authorisation for twenty-eight days beginning with the date of authorisation, or for such shorter period beginning with that date as may be specified in the authorisation.

(2) Any constable may detain a child or young person as respects whom the constable has reasonable cause to believe that any of the conditions set out in section 1(2)(a) to (d) of this Act is satisfied or that an appropriate court would find the condition set out in section 1 (2)(b) of this Act satisfied or that an offence is being committed under section 10(1) of the Act of 1933 (which penalises a vagrant who take a juvenile from place to place).

(3) A person who detains any person in pursuance of the preceding provisions of this section shall, as soon as practicable after doing so, inform him of the reason for his

detention and take such steps as are practicable for informing his parent or guardian of his detention and of the reason for it.

(4) A constable who details any person in pursuance of subsection (2) of this section or who arrests a child without a warrant otherwise than for homicide shall as soon as practicable after doing do secure that the case is enquiried into by *a police officer not below the rank of inspector or by the police officer in charge of* a police station, and that officer shall on completing the enquiry either–

(a) release the person in question; or
(b) if the officer considers that he ought to be further detained in his own interests or, in the case of an arrested child, because of the nature of the alleged offence, make arrangements for his detention in a place of safety and inform him, and take such steps are are practicable for informing his parent or guardian, of his right to apply to a justice under subsection (5) of this section for his release;

and subject to the said subsection (5) it shall be lawful to detain the person in question in accordance with any such arrangements.

(5) It shall not be lawful for a child arrested without a warrant otherwise than for homicide to be detained in consequence of the arrest or such arrangements as aforesaid, or for any person to be detained by virtue of subsection (2) of this section or any such arrangements, after the expiration of the period of eight days beginning with the day on which he was arrested or, as the case may be, on which his detention in pursuance of the said subsection (2) began; and if during that period the person in question applies to a justice for his release, the justice shall direct that he be released forthwith unless the justice considers that he ought to be further detained in his own interests or, in the case of an arrested child, because of the nature of the alleged offence.

(6) If while a person is detained in pursuance of this section an application for an interim order in respect of him is made to a magistrates' court or a justice, the court or justice shall either make or refuse to make the order and, in the case of a refusal, may direct that he be released forthwith.

[32A   Conflict of interest between parent and child or young person

(1)   If before or in the course of proceedings in respect of a child or young person–

(a) in pursuance of section 1 of this Act; or
(b) on an application under section 15 (1) of this Act for the discharge of a relevant supervision order or a supervision order made under section 21(2) of this Act on the discharge of a relevant care order; or
(c) on an application under section 21(2) of this Act for the discharge of a relevant care order or a care order made under section 15(1) of this Act on the discharge of a relevant supervision order; or
(d) on an appeal to the Crown Court under section 2(12) of this Act; or
(e) on an appeal to the Crown Court under section 16(8) of this Act against the dismissal of an application for the discharge of a relevant supervision order or against a care order made under section 15(1) on the discharge of–
    (i) a relevant supervision order; or
    (ii) a supervision order made under section 21(2) on the discharge of a relevant care order; or
(f) on an appeal to the Crown Court under section 21(4) of this Act against the dismissal. of an application for the discharge of a relevant care order or against a

supervision order made under section 21(2) on the discharge of–

(i) a relevant care order; or

(ii) a care order made under section 15(1) on the discharge of a relevant supervision order,

it appears to the court that there is or may be a conflict, on any matter relevant to the proceedings, between the interests of the child or young person and those of his parent or guardian, the court may order that in relation to the proceedings the parent or guardian is not to be treated as representing the child or young person or as otherwise authorised to act on his behalf.

(2) In an application such as is referred to in subection (1)(b) or (c) of this section is unopposed, the court, unless satisfied that to do so is not necessary for safeguarding the interests of the child or young person, shall order that in relation to proceedings on the application no parent or guardian of his shall be treated as representing him or as otherwise authorised to act on his behalf; but where the application was made by a parent or guardian on his behalf the order shall not invalidate the application.

(3) Where an order is made under subsection (1) or (2) of this section for the purposes of proceedings on an application within subsection (1) (a), (b) or (c) of this section, that order shall also have effect for the purposes of any appeal to the Crown Court arising out of those proceedings.

(4) The power of the court to make orders for the purposes of an application within subsection (1) (a), (b) or (c) of this section shall also be exercisable, before the hearing of the application, by a single justice.

(5) In this section–

"relevant care order" means a care order made under section 1 of this Act;
"relevant supervizion order" means a supervision order made under section 1 of this Act.]

[32B Safeguarding of interests of child or young person where section 32A order made

(1) Where the court makes an order under section 32A (2) of this Act the court, unless satisfied that to do so is not necessary for safeguarding the interests of the child or young person, shall in accordance with rules of court appoint a guardian ad litem of the child or young person for the purposes of the proceedings.

In this subsection "court" includes a single justice.

(2) Rules of court shall provide for the appointment of a guardian ad litem of the child or young person for the purposes of any proceedings to which an order under section 32A (1) of this Act relates.

(3) A guardian ad litem appointed in pursuance of this section shall be under a duty to safeguard the interests of the child or young person in the manner prescribed by rules of court.]

LOCAL AUTHORITY SOCIAL SERVICES ACT 1970 Sections 1, 2, 3, 6

1   A local authority may delegate to their social services committee any of their functions matters relating to which stand referred to the committee by virtue of section 2

of this Act or this section (hereafter in this Act referred to as "social services functions") and, before exercising any of those functions themselves, the authority shall (unless the matter is urgent) consider a report of the committee with respect to the matter in question.

2 Local authority to establish social services committee

(1)   Every local authority shall establish a social services committee and, there shall stand referred to that committee all matters relating to the discharge by the authority of–

(a) their functions under the enactments specified in the first column of Schedule 1 to this Act (being the functions which are described in general terms in the second column of that Schedule); and

(b) such other of their functions as, by virtue of the following subsection, fall within the responsibility of the committee.

(2)   The Secretary of State may by order designate functions of local authorities under any other enactment for the time being in force as being appropriate for discharge through a local authority's social services committee other than functions which by virtue of that or any other enactment are required to be discharged through some other committee of a local authority; and any functions designated by an order under this section which is for the time being in force shall accordingly fall within the responsibility of the social services committee.

3   (1) The local authorities for the purposes of this Act shall be the councils of non-metropolitan counties, metropolitan districts and London Boroughs – the common council of the City of London.

(2) Nothing in section 2 of this Act or this section prevents a local authority from referring to a committee other than their social services committee a matter which by virtue of either of those sections stands referred to the social services committee and which in the authority's opinion ought to be referred to the other committee on the ground that it relates to a general service of the authority; but before referring any such matter the authority shall receive and consider a report of the social services committee with respect to the subject matter of the proposed reference.

3A   (1) A local authority may refer to their S S Committee any matter which in their view may appropriately be referred to that committee, but which would not otherwise stand referred to that committee by virtue of this Act, and may delegate to that committee any of their functions relating to a matter so referred.

6   The director of social services

(1)   A local authority shall appoint an officer, to be known as the director of social services, for the purposes of their social services functions.

(2)   Two or more local authorities may, if they consider that the same person can efficiently discharge, for both or all of them, the functions of director of social services, concur in the appointment of a person as director of social services for both or all of those authorities.

(5)   The director of social services of a local authority shall not, without the approval of the Secretary of State (which may be given either generally or in relation to a

particular authority), by employed by that authority in connection with the discharge of any of the authority's functions other than their social services functions.

(6) A local authority which have appointed, or concurred in the appointment of, a director of social services, shall secure the provision of adequate staff for assisting him in the exercise of his functions.

(8) Section 41 of the Children Act 1948 (appointment of children's officer) shall cease to have effect.

GUARDIANSHIP ACT 1973 Section 1

1 Equality of parental rights

(1) In relation to the [legal custody] or upbringing of a minor, and in relation to the administration of any property belonging to or held in trust for a minor or the application of income of any such property, a mother shall have the same rights and authority as the law allows to a father, and the rights and authority of mother and father shall be equal and be exercisable by either without the other.

[In this Act "legal custody" shall be construed in accordance with Part IV of the Children Act 1975.]

(2) An agreement for a man or woman to give up in whole or in part, in relation to any child of his or hers, the rights and authority referred to in sub-section (1) above shall be unenforceable, except that an agreement made between husband and wife which is to operate only during their separation while married may, in relation to a child of theirs, provide for either of them to do so; but no such agreement between husband and wife shall be enforced by any court if the court is of opinion that it will not be for the benefit of the child to give effect to it.

(3) Where a minor's father and mother disagree on any question affecting his welfare, either of them may apply to the court for its direction, and (subject to subsection (4) below) the court may make such order regarding the matters in difference as it may think proper.

(4) Subsection (3) above shall not authorise the court to make any order regarding the [legal custody] of a minor or the right of access to him of his father or mother.

(5) An order under subsection (3) above may be varied or discharged by a subsequent order made on the application of either parent or, after the death of either parent, on the application of any guardian under the Guardianship of Minors Act 1971, or (before or after the death of either parent) on the application of any other person having the [legal custody] of the minor.

(6) Section 15 (1) to (3) and section 16 of the Guardianship of Minors Act 1971 jurisdiction and procedure) shall apply for the purposes of subsection (3) to (5) above as if they were contained in section 9 of that Act, except that section 15 (3) shall not exclude any jurisdiction of a county court or a magistrates' court in proceedings against a person residing in Scotland or Northern Ireland for the revocation, revival or variation of any order under subsection (3) above.

(7) Nothing in the foregoing provisions of this section shall affect the operation of any enactment requiring the consent of both parents in a matter affecting a minor, or be taken as applying in relation to a minor who is illegitimate.

(8)   In the Sexual Offences Act 1956 there shall be substituted for section 38 the provisions set out in Schedule 1 to this Act . . .

[(9) Nothing in this section shall be taken to affect the provisions of the Mental Health Act 1983 as to the person who is 'the nearest relative' for the purposes of that Act.]

CHILDREN ACT 1975 Sections 12, 13, 14 and Schedule 3 para 71.

12   Parental agreement

(1)   An adoption order shall not be made unless–

(a)   the child is free for adoption; or
(b)   in the case of each parent or guardian of the child the court is satisfied that–
> *(i)   he freely, and with full understanding of what is involved, agrees unconditionally to the making of the adoption order (whether or not he knows the identity of the applicants), or*
> *(ii)   his agreement to the making of the adoption order shall be dispensed with on a ground specified in subsection (2)*

(2)   The grounds mentioned in subsection (1)(b) (ii) are that the parent or guardian–

(a)   cannot be found or is incapable of giving agreement;
(b)   is withholding his agreement unreasonably;
(c)   has persistently failed without reasonable cause to discharge the parental duties in relation to the child;
(d)   has abandoned or neglected the child;
(e)   has persistently ill-treated the child;
(f)   has seriously ill-treated the child (subject to subsection (5)).

(3)   Subsection (1) does not apply in any case where the child is not a United Kingdom national and the application for the adoption order is for a Convention adoption order.

(4)   Agreement is ineffective for the purposes of subsection (1)(b)(i) if given by the mother less than six weeks after the child's birth.

(5)   Subsection (2)(f) does not apply unless (because of ill-treatment or for other reasons) the rehabilitation of the child within the household of the parent or guardian is unlikely.

(6)   A child is free for adoption if he is the subject of an order under section 14 and the order has not been revoked under section 16.

13   Religious upbringing of adopted child

An adoption agency shall in placing a child for adoption have regard (so far as is practicable) to any wishes of the child's parents and guardians as to the religious upbringing of the child.

14   Freeing child for adoption

(1)   Where, on an application by an adoption agency, an authorised court is

satisfied in the case of each parent or guardian of the child that–

    (a) he freely, and with full understanding of what is involved, agrees generally and unconditionally to the making of an adoption order, or

    (b) his agreement to the making of an adoption order should be dispensed with on a ground specified in section 12(2),

the court shall, subject to subsection (5), make an order declaring the child free for adoption.

    (2) No application shall be made under subsection (1) unless–

    (a) it is made with the consent of a parent or guardian of the child, or

    (b) the adoption agency is applying for dispensation under subsection (1)(b) of the agreement of each parent or guardian of the child, and the child is in the care of the adoption agency.

    (3) No agreement required under subsection (1)(a) shall be dispensed with under subsection (1)(b) unless the child is already placed for adoption or the court is satisfied that it is likely that the child will be placed for adoption.

    (4) An agreement by the mother of the child is ineffective for the purposes of this section if given less than six weeks after the child's birth.

    (5) (Applies to Scotland only).

    (6) On the making of an order under this section, the parental rights and duties relating to the child vest in the adoption agency, and subsections (2) and (3) of section 8 apply as if the order were an adoption order and the agency were the adopters.

    (7) Before making an order under this section the court shall satisfy itself that each parent or guardian who can be found has been given an opportunity of making, if he so wishes, a declaration that he prefers not to be involved in future questions concerning the adoption of the child; and any such declaration shall be recorded by the court.

    (8) Before making an order under this section in the case of an illegitimate child whose father is not its guardian, the court shall satisfy itself in relation to any person claiming to be the father that either–

    (a) he has no intention of applying for custody of the child under section 9 of the Guardianship of Minors Act 1971 or under section 2 of the Illegitimate Children (Scotland) Act 1930, or

    (b) if he did apply for custody under either of those sections the application would be likely to be refused.

Schedule 3

71 In section 27 –

    (a) in subsection (3), for the words "their general duty aforesaid" there are substituted the words "their general duty under section 12(1) of the Children Act 1948";

    (b) the following subsections are substituted for subsection (4)–

    "(4) Without prejudice to their general duty under the said section 12, it shall be the duty of a local authority to review the case of each child in their care in accordance with regulations made under the following subsection.

    (5) The Secretary of State may by regulations make provision as to–

    (a) the manner in which cases are to be reviewed under this section;

(b) the considerations to which the local authority are to have regard in reviewing cases under this section; and

(c) the time when a child's case is first to be reviewed and the frequency of subsequent reviews under this section.

CHILD CARE ACT, 1980 Sections 1-3, 5-7, 10, 12 (A-G), 16, 18, 20-22, 31(1) & (2)

PART I

POWERS AND DUTIES OF LOCAL AUTHORITIES IN RELATION TO THE WELFARE AND CARE OF CHILDREN.

General duty of local authorities to promote welfare of children

1   Duty of local authorities to promote welfare of children

(1)   It shall be the duty of every local authority to make available such advice, guidance and assistance as may promote the welfare of children by diminishing the need to receive children into or keep them in care under this Act or to bring children before a juvenile court; and any provisions made by a local authority under this subsection, may, if the local authority think fit, include provision for giving assistance in kind or, in exceptional circumstances, in cash.

(2)   In carrying out their duty under subsection (1) above, a local authority may make arrangements with voluntary organisations or other persons for the provision by those organisations or other persons of such advice, guidance or assistance as is mentioned in that subsection.

(3)   Where any provision which may be made by a local authority under section (1) above is made (whether by that or any other authority) under any other enactment, the local authority shall not be required to make the provision under this section but shall have power to do so.

(4)   In this section "child" means a person under the age of eighteen.

2   Duty of local authority to provide for orphans, deserted children etc

(1)   Where it appears to a local authority with respect to a child in their area appearing to them to be under the age of seventeen–

(a) that he has neither parent nor guardian or hs been and remains abandoned by his parents or guardian or is lost; or

(b) that his parents or guardian are, for the time being or permanently prevented by reason of mental or bodily disease or infirmity or other incapacity or any other circumstances from providing for his proper accommodation, maintenance and upbringing,; and

(c) in either case, that the intervention of the local authority under this section is necessary in the interests of the welfare of the child,

it shall be the duty of the local authority to receive the child into their care under this section.

(2)   Where a local authority have received a child into their care under this section, it shall, subject to the provisions of this Part of this Act, be their duty to keep the

child in their care so long as the welfare of the child appears to them to require it and the child has not attained the age of eighteen.

(3)   Nothing in this section shall authorise a local authority to keep a child in their care under this section if any parent or guardian desires to take over the care of the child, and the local authority shall, in all cases where it appears to them consistent with the welfare of the child so to do, endeavour to secure that the care of the child is taken over either–

(a)   by the parent or guardian of his; or
(b)   by a relative or friend of his, being, where possible, a person of the same religious persuasion as the child or who gives an undertaking that the child will be brought up in that religious persuasion.

(4)   Where a local authority receive into their care under this section a child who is then ordinarily resident in the area of another local authority–

(a)   that other local authority may at any time not later than three months after the determination (whether by agreement between the authorities or in accordance with the following provisions of this subsection) of the ordinary residence of the child, or with the concurrence of the first mentioned authority at any subsequent time, take over the care of the child; and
(b)   the first mentioned authority may recover from the other authority any expenses duly incurred by them under Part III of this Act in respect of the child (including any expenses so incurred after he has ceased to be a child and, if the other authority takes over the care of him, including also any travelling or other expenses incurred in connection with the taking over).

Any question arising under this subsection as to the ordinary residence of a child shall be determined by the Secretary of State and in this subsection any reference to another local authority includes a reference to a local authority within the meaning of the Social Work (Scotland) Act 1968.

(5)   In determining for the purposes of subsection (4) above the ordinary residence of any child, any period during which he resides in any place–

(a)   as an inmate of a school or other institution, or
(b)   in accordance with the requirements of a supervision order or probation order or of a supervision requirement, or
(c)   in accordance with the conditions of a recognisance, or
(d)   while boarded out under this Act, the Children and Young Persons (Scotland) Act 1937 or Part II of the Social Work (Scotland) Act 1968 by a local authority or education authority.

shall be disregarded.

(6)   Any reference in this section to the parents or guardian of a child shall be construed as a reference to all the persons who are parents of the child or who are guardians of the child.

3   Assumption by local authority of parental rights and duties

(1)   Subject to the provisions of this Part of this Act, if it appears to a local authority in relation to any child who is in their care under section 2 of this Act–

(a)   that his parents are dead and he has no guardian or custodian; or

xlv

(b) that a parent of his–
  (i) has abandoned him, or
  (ii) suffers from some permanent disability rendering him incapable of caring for the child, or
  (iii) while not falling within sub-paragraph (ii) of this paragraph, suffers from a mental disorder (within the means of [the Mental Health Act 1983], which renders him unfit to have the care of the child, or
  (iv) is of such habits or mode of life as to be unfit to have the care of the child, or
  (v) has so consistently failed without reasonable cause to discharge the obligations of a parent as to be unfit to have the care of the child; or
(c) that a resolution under paragraph (b) of this subsection is in force in relation to one parent of the child who is, or is likely to become, a member of the household comprising the child and his other parent; or
(d) that throughout the three years preceding the passing of the resolution the child has been in the care of a local authority under section 2 of this Act, or partly in the care of a local authority and partly in the care of a voluntary organisation,

the local authority may resolve that there shall vest in them the parental rights and duties with respect to that child, and, if the rights and duties were vested in the parent on whose account the resolution was passed jointly with another person, they shall also be vested in the local authority jointly with that other person.

[(2) If the local authoirty know the whereabouts of the person whose parental rights and duties have vested in them by virtue of a resolution passed under subsection (1)(b), (c) or (d) above, they shall forthwith after it is passed serve notice in writing of its passing on hm.].

(3) Every notice served by a local authority under subsection (2) above shall inform the person on whom the notice is served of his right to object to the resolution and the effect of any objection made by him.

(4) If, not later than one month after notice is served on a person under subsection (2) above, he serves a counter-notice in writing on the local authority objecting to the resolution, the resolution shall, subject to the provisions of subsections (5) and (6) below, lapse on the expiry of fourteen days from the service of the counter-notice.

(5) Where a counter-notice has been served on a local authority under subsection (4) above, the authority may not later than fourteen days after the receipt by them of the counter-notice complain to a juvenile court having jurisdiction in the area of the authority, and in that event the resolution shall not lapse until the determination of the complaint.

(6) On hearing a complaint made under subsection (5) above the court may if it is satisfied–

(a) that the grounds mentioned in subsection (1) above on which the local authority purported to pass the resolution were made out, and
(b) that at the time of the hearing there continue to be grounds on which a resolution under that subsection could be founded, and
(c) that it is in the interests of the child to do so.

order that the resolution shall not lapse by reason of the service of the counter-notice.

(7) Any notice under this section (including a counter-notice) may be served by post, so however that a notice served by a local authority under subsection (2) above

shall not be duly served by post unless it is sent by registered post or recorded delivery service.

(8)   Where, after a child has been received into the care of a local authority under section 2 of this Act, the whereabouts of any parent of his have remained unknown for twelve months, then, for the purposes of this section, the parent shall be deemed to have abandoned the child.

(9)   The Secretary of State may by order a draft on which has been approved by each House of Parliament amend subsection (1)(d) above by substituting a different period for the period mentioned in that paragraph (or the period which, by a previous order under this section, was substituted for that period)

(10)   In this section–
"parent", except in subsection (1)(a), includes a guardian or custodian;
"parental rights and duties", in relation to a particular child, does not include–

(a)   the right to consent or refuse to consent to the making of an applciation under section 18 of the Adoption Act 1976 (orders freeing a child for adoption in England and Wales) or section 18 of the Adoption (Scotland) Act 1978 (orders freeing a child for adoption in Scotland), and

(b)   the right to agree or refuse to agree to the making of an adoption order or an order under section 55 of the Adoption Act 1976 (orders in England and Wales authorising adoption abroad) or section 49 of the Adoption (Scotland) Act 1978 (orders in Scotland authorising adoption abroad).

5   Duration and rescission of resolutions under s 3

(1)   Subject to the provisions of the Part of this Act, a resolution under section 3 of this Act shall continue in force until the child with respect to whom it was passed attains the age of 18.

(2)   A resolution under section 3 of this Act shall cease to have effect if–

(a)   the child is adopted;

(b)   an order in respect of the child is made under section 18 or 55 of the Adoption Act 1976 or section 18 or 49 of the Adoption (Scotland) Act 1978; or

(c)   a guardian of the child is appointed under section 5 of the Guardianship of Minors Act 1971.

(3)   A resolution under section 3 of this Act may be rescinded by resolution of the local authority if it appears to them that the rescinding of the resolution will be for the benefit of the child.

(4)   On a complaint being made–

(a)   in the case of a resolution passed by virtue of section 3(1)(a) of this Act, by a person claiming to be a parent, guardian or custodian of the child;

(b)   in the case of a resolution passed by virtue of section 3(1)(b), (c) or (d) of this Act, by the person who, but for the resolution, would have the parental rights and duties in relation to the child,

a juvenile court having jurisdiction where the complainant resides, if satisfied that there was no ground for the making of the resolution or that the resolution should in the interests of the child be determined, may by order determine the resolution, and the resolution shall thereupon cease to have effect.

6 Appeal to the High Court

An appeal shall lie to the High Court from the making by a juvenile court of an order under section 3(6) of 5(4) of this Act or from the refusal by a juvenile court to make such an order.

7 Guardians ad litem and reports in care proceedings

(1) In any proceedings under section 3(6) or 5(4) or 6 of this Act a juvenile court or the High Court my, where it considers it necessary in order to safeguard the interests of the child to whom the proceedings relate, by order make the child a party to the proceedings and appoint, subject to rules of court, a guardian ad litem of the child for the purposes of the proceedings.

(2) A guardian ad litem appointed in pursuance of this section shall be under a duty to safeguard the interests of the child in the manner prescribed by rules of court.

(3) Section 6 of the Guardianship Act 1973 shall apply in relation to complaints under section 3(6) or 5(4) of this Act as it applies in relation to applications under section 3(3) of the said Act of 1973.

10 Powers and duties of local authorities with respect to children committed to their care

(1) It shall be the duty of a local authority to whose care a child is committed by a care order or by a warrant under section 23(1) of the Children and Young Persons Act 1969 (which relates to remands in the care of local authorities) to receive the child into their care and, notwithstanding any claim by his parent or guardian, to keep him in their care while the order or warrant is in force.

(2) A local authority shall, subject to the following provisions of this section, have the same powers and duties with respect to a person in their care by virtue of a care order or such a warrant as his parent or guardian would have apart from the order or warrant.

(3) A local authority shall not cause a child in their care by virtue of a care order to be brought up in any religious creed other than that in which he would have been brought up apart from the order.

(4) It shall be the duty of a local authority to comply with any provision included in an interim order in pursuance of section 22(2) of the Children and Young Persons Act 1969 and, in the case of a person in their care by virtue of section 23 of that Act, to permit him to be removed from their care in due course of law.

[(5) This section does not give a local authority–

(a) the right to consent or refuse to consent to the making of an application under section 18 of the Adoption Act 1976 or section 18 of the Adoption (Scotland) Act 1978; or

(b) the right to agree or refuse to agree to the making of an adoption order or an order under section 55 of the Adoption Act 1976 or section 49 of the Adoption (Scotland) Act 1978.]

[PART IA
ACCESS TO CHILDREN IN CARE]

[12A Children to whom Part IA applies

(1) Subject to subsection (2) below, this Part of this Act applies to any child in the care of a local authority in consequence–

(a) of a care order (including an interim order);

(b) of an order under section 2(1) of the Matrimonial Proceedings (Magistrates' Courts) Act 1960;

(c) of committal under section 23(1) of the Children and Young Persons Act 1969;

(d) of an order under section 2(2))b) of the Guardianship Act 1973;

(e) of an order under section 17(1)(b) of the Children Act 1975 or section 26(1)(b) of the Adoption Act 1976 (order on refusal of adoption order);

(f) of an order under section 36(2) or (3)(a) of the Children Act 1975 (order on revocation of custodianship order);

(g) of an order under section 10(1) of the Domestic Proceedings and Magistrates' Courts Act 1978; or

(h) of a resolution under section 3 above.

(2) This Part of this Act does not apply to a child in the care of a local authority in consequence of an order made by the High Court.]

[12B Termination of access

(1) A local authority may not terminate arrangements for access to a child to whom this Part of this Act applies by its parent, guardian or custodian, or refuse to make such arrangements unless they have first given the parent, guardian or custodian notice of termination or refusal in a form prescribed by order made by the Secretary of State.

(2) A notice under this section shall contain a statement that the parent, guardian or custodian has a right to apply to a court for an order under section 12C below.

(3) A notice terminating access shall state that access will be terminated as from the date of service of the notice.

(4) A local authority are not to be taken to terminate access for the purpose of this section in a case where they propose to substitute new arrangements for access for existing arrangements.

(5) A local authority are not to be taken to refuse to make arrangements for access for the purposes of this section in a case where they postpone access for such reasonable period as appears to them to be necessary to enable them to consider what arrangements for access (if any) are to be made.

(6) A notice under this section may be served on a parent, guardian or custodian either by delivering it to him or by leaving it at his proper address or by sending it by post.

(7) For the purposes of this section, and of section 7 of the Interpretation Act 1978 in its application to this section, the proper address of a person shall be his last known address.]

[12C Access order – general

(1)   A parent, guardian or custodian on whom a notice under section 12B above is served may apply for an order under this section (in this Part of this Act referred to as an "access order").

(2)   An application under subsection (1) above shall be made by way of complaint to an appropriate juvenile court.

(3)   An access order shall be an order requiring the authority to allow the child's parent, guardian or custodian access to the child subject to such conditions as the order may specify with regard to commencement, frequency, duration or place of access or to any other matter for which it appears to the court that provision ought to be made in connection with the requirement to allow access.

(4)   A juvenile court is an appropriate juvenile court for the purposes of this Part of the Act if it has jurisdiction in the area of the authority serving the notice under section 12B above.

(5)   An appeal shall lie to the High Court against any decision of a juvenile court under this Part of this Act.]

[12D Variation and discharge of access orders

(1)   Where an access order has been made–

(a) the parent, guardian or custodian named in the order; or
(b) the local authority.

may apply for the variation or discharge of the order.

(2)   An application under this section shall be made by way of complaint to an appropriate juvenile court.]

[12E Emergency orders

(1)   A qualified justice of the peace may make an order under this subsection where he is satisfied that continued access to a child by its parent, guardian or custodian in accordance with the terms of an access order will put the child's welfare seriously at risk.

(2)   Subject to subsection (3) below, an order under subsection (1) above shall be an order suspending the operation of the access order for 7 days beginning with the date of the order under subsection (1) above, or for such shorter period beginning with that date as may be specified in that order.

(3)   If during the period for which the operation of the access order is suspended the local authority make an application for its variation or discharge to an appropriate juvenile court, its operation shall be suspended until the date on which the application to vary or discharge it is determined or abandoned.

(4)   An application for an order under subsection (1) above may be made ex parte.

(5)   A justice of the peace is a qualified justice of the peace for the purposes of this section if he is a member of a juvenile court panel formed under Schedule 2 to the Children and Young Persons Act 1933.]

[12F   Safeguarding of interests of child

(1)   A court–

(a)   to which an application for an access order or any other application under this Part of this Act is made; or

(b)   to which an appeal under this Part of this Act is brought.

shall regard the welfare of the child as the first and paramount consideration in determining the matter.

(2)   In any proceedings before a court under this Part of this Act the court may, where it considers it necessary in order to safeguard the interests of the child, by order make the child a party ot the proceedings.

(3)   If the court makes the child a party to the proceedings, it shall in accordance with rules of court appoint a guardian ad litem of the child for the purposes of the proceedings unless it is satisfied that to do so is not necessary for safeguarding the interests of the child.

(4)   A guardian ad litem appointed in pursuance of this section shall be under a duty to safeguard the interests of the child in the manner prescribed by rules of court.]

[12G   Code of practice

(1)   The Secretary of State shall prepare, and from time to time revise, a code of practice with regard to access to children in care.

(2)   Before preparing the code or making any alteration in it the Secretary of State shall consult such bodies as appear to him to be concerned.

(3)   The Secretary of State shall lay copies of the code and of any alteration in the code before Parliament; and if either House of Parliament passes a resolution requiring the code or any alteration in it to be withdrawn the Secretary of State shall withdraw the code or alteration and, where he withdraws the code, shall prepare a code in substitution for the one which is withdrawn.

(4)   No resolution shall be passed by either House of Parliament under subsection (3) above in respect of a code or alteration after the expiration of the period of 40 days beginning with the day on which a copy of the code or alteration was laid before that House; but for the purposes of this subsection no account shall be taken of any time during which Parliament is dissolved or prorogued or during which both Houses are adjourned for more than four days.

(5)   The Secretary of State shall publish the code as for the time being in force.]

Provisions relating to children in care of local authorities by virtue of care order etc

16   Recovery of children subject to care order etc

(1)   If any child–

(a)   who is committed to the care of a local authority by a care order or by a warrant under section 23(1) of the Children and Young Persons Act 1969 (which relates to remands to the care of local authorities); or

(b)   who is in the care of a local authority in pursuance of arrangements under section 29(3) of that Act (which relates to the detention of arrested children).

is absent from the premises at which he is required by the local authority to live at a time when he is not permitted by the local authority to be absent from the premises, he may be arrested by a constable anywhere in the United Kingdom or the Channel Islands without a warrant and shall if so arrested by conducted, at the expense of the authority, to those premises or such other premises as the authority may direct.

(2) If a magistrates' court is satisfied by information on oath that there are reasonable grounds for believing that a person specified in the information can produce a child who is absent as mentioned in subsection (1) above, the court may issue a summons directed to the person so specified and requiring him to attend and produce the absent child before the court; and a person who without reasonable excuse fails to comply with any such requirement shall, without prejudice to any liability apart from this subsection, be guilty of an offence and liable on summary conviction to a fine not exceeding [level 3 on the standard scale].

(3) Without prejudice to its powers under subsection (2) above a magistrates' court may, if it is satisfied by information on oath that there are reasonable grounds for believing that a child who is absent as mentioned in subsection (1) above is in premises specified in the information, issue a search warrant authorising a constable to search the premises for that child.

(4) A person who knowingly compels, persuades, incites or assists a child to become or continue to be absent as mentioned in subsection (1) above shall be guilty of an offence and liable on summary conviction to imprisonment for a term not exceeding six months or to a fine not exceeding [level 5 on the standard scale] or to both.

(5) The reference to a constable in subsection (1) and (3) above includes a reference to a person who is a constable under the law of any part of the United Kingdom, to a member of the police in Jersey and to an office of police within the meaning of section 43 of the Larceny (Guernsey) Law 1958 or any corresponding law for the time being in force.

(6) In the application of subsections (2) and (3) above to Northern Ireland, "magistrates' court" means a magistrates' court within the meaning of the [Magistrates' Courts (Northern Ireland) Order 1981].

18 General duty of local authority in relation to children in their care

(1) In reaching any decision relating to a child in their care, a local authority shall give first considertation to the need to safeguard and promote the welfare of the child throughout his childhood; and shall so far as practicable ascertain the wishes and feelings of the child regarding the decision and give due consideration to them, having regard to his age and understanding.

(2) In providing for a child in their care a local authority shall make such use of facilities and services available for children in the care of their own parents as appears to the local authority reasonable in his case.

(3) If it appears to the local authority that it is necessary, for the purpose of protecting members of the public, to exercise their powers in relation to a particular child in their care in a menner which may not be consistent with their duty under subsection (1) above, the authority may, notwithstanding that duty, act in that manner.

20 Review of care cases

(1) Without prejudice to their general duty under section 18(1) of this Act, it shall

be the duty of a local authority to review the case of each child in their care in accordance with regulations made under subsection (2) below.

(2) The Secretary of State may by regulations make provision as to–

(a) the manner in which cases are to be reviewed under this section;
(b) the considerations to which the local authority are to have regard in reviewing cases under this section; and
(c) the time when a child's case is first to be reviewed and the frequency of subsequent reviews under this section.

21 Provision of accommodation and maintenance for children in care

(1) A local authority shall discharge their duty to provide accommoation and maintenance for a child in their care in such one of the following ways as they think fit, namely,–

(a) by boarding him out on such terms as to payment by the authority and otherwise as the authority may, subject to the provisions of this Act and regulations thereunder, determine; or
(b) by maintaining him in a community home or in any such home as is referred to in section 80 of this Act; or
(c) by maintaining him in a voluntary home (other than a community home) the managers of which are willing to receive him;

or by making such other arrangements as seem appropriate to the local authority [and shall secure, subject to section 18 of this Act, that any accommodation which they provide is, so far as practicable, near the child's home].

(2) Without prejudice to the generality of subsection (1) [but subject to section 20A of the Children and Young Persons Act 1969 (power of court to add condition as to charge and control),] a local authority may allow a child in their care, either for a fixed period or until the local authority otherwise determine, to be under the charge and control of a parent, guardian, relative or friend.

(3) The terms, as to payment and other matters, on which a child may be accommodated and maintained in any such home as is referred to in section 80 of this Act shall be such as the Secretary of State may from time to time determine.

22 Regulations as to boarding out

(1) The Secretary of State may by regulations make provision of the welfare of children boarded out by local authorities under section 21(1)(a) of this Act.

(2) Without prejudice to the generality of subsection (1) above, regulations under this section may provide–

(a) for the recording by local authorities of information relating to persons with whom children are boarded out under section 21(1)(a) of this Act and persons who are willing to have children so boarded out with them;
(b) for securing that children shall not be boarded out in any household unless that household is for the time being approved by such local authority as may be prescribed by the regulations;
(c) for securing that where possible the person with whom any child is to be boarded out is either of the same religious persuasion as the child or gives an undertaking

that the child will be brought up in that religious persuasion;

(d) for securing that children boarded out under section 21(1)(a) of this Act, and the premises in which they are boarded out, will be supervised and inspected by a local authority and that the children will be removed from those premises if their welfare appears to require it.

PART IV
COMMUNITY HOMES

[31 Arrangements for provision of homes for children

(1) A local authority shall make such arrangements as they consider appropriate for securing that homes (in this Act referred to as "community homes") are available for the accommodation and maintenance of children in their care and for purposes connected with the welfare of children, whether in their care or not and, without prejudice to section 101(5) of the Local Government Act 1972, may do so jointly with one or more other local authorities.

(2) In making such arrangements, a local authority shall have regard to the need for ensuring the availability of accommodation of different descriptions and suitable for different purposes and the requirements of different descriptions of children.

BOARDING-OUT OF CHILDREN REGULATIONS 1955 (SI 1955 NO 1377)

1 September 1955

PART 1

GENERAL

1   Scope of the Regulations

(1) Subject to the provisions of paragraphs (2) and (3) of this Regulation, these Regulations shall apply to the boarding of a child –

(a) by a local authority in whose care the child is, or

(b) by a voluntary organisation in whose charge the child is otherwise than under an approved school order,

with foster parents to live in their dwelling as a member of their family, and the boarding of a child to which these Regulations apply as aforesaid is hereinafter referred to as 'boarding out', and 'board out' and 'boarded out' shall be construed accordingly.

(2) For the purposes of these Regulations a child who is delivered into the care and possession of persons or a person proposing to adopt him under the Adoption Act 1950, shall not be regarded as boarded out.

(3) For the purposes of these Regulations a child shall not be regarded as boarded out by reason only that he stays in the dwelling of any person for a holiday if –

(a) the period of his stay does not exceed twenty-one days, or

(b) he is sent there by a voluntary organisation in whose charge he temporarily is for the sole purpose of the arrangement of that holiday.

(4)   Nothing in these Regulations shall require, for the purpose only of complying with any provision thereof relating to a child before he is boarded out, his temporary removal from a household in which he is already living.

2   [Revoked]

3   Restriction on boarding-out outside England and Wales

A child shall not be boarded out outside England and Wales unless the special circumstances of his case make such boarding-out desirable, and if a child is boarded out outside England and Wales, steps shall be taken to ensure that the like requirements as are specified in Regulations 2, 7 and 9 and, as the case may be, Regulations 19, 21, 22 and 23 or Regulation 28 or Regulation 29 of these Regulations are observed in relation to that child as would have had to be observed under these Regulations if he were boarded out in England or Wales.

4   Duty of placing authority to terminate boarding-out

A care authority or voluntary organisation who have arranged the boarding-out of a child shall not allow him to remain board-out with any foster parents if it appears that the boarding-out is no longer in his best interests.

5   Power of supervising visitor to remove child

(1)   Where a visitor whose duty it is under these Regulations to supervise the welfare of a child considers that the conditions in which he is boarded out endanger his health, safety or morals, that visitor may remove him from the foster parents forthwith.

(2)   Where a child who is boarded out by a local authority with foster parents whose dwelling is outside the area of that authority is removed under paragraph (1) of this Regulation by a visitor of the care authority, the area authority shall forthwith be notified by the care authority of the reason why he was removed and, if the child is so removed by a visitor of the area authority who are performing any of the supervisory duties in respect of him under Regulation 13 of these Regulations, the care authority shall forthwith be given the like notification by the area authority.

(3)   Where a child who is boarded out by a voluntary organisation is removed from foster parents under paragraph (1) of this Regulation by a visitor of the voluntary organisation, the area authority shall forthwith be notified by the organisation of the reason why he was removed and, if the child is so removed by a visitor of the area authority who are performing the supervisory duties in the place of that organisation shall forthwith be given the like notification by the area authority.

6   Medical examination before boarding-out

Except in a case of emergency, a child shall not be boarded out with foster parents unless he has within three months before being placed with them been examined by a duly qualified medical practitioner and the practitioner has made a written report on the physical health and mental condition of the child.

7   Medical examinations during boarding-out

(1)   A local authority or voluntary organisation who arrange the boarding-out of a child shall ensure that he is examined by a duly qualified medical practitioner –

    (a)   within one month after being boarded out unless the child has attained the age of two years and has, under Regulation 6 of these Regulations, been so examined within three months before being boarded out; and *(b)* at least once in every six months if he has not attained the age of two years or at least once a year if he has attained that age.

(2) Arrangement shall be made for a written report on the physical health and mental condition of the child to be made by the practitioner after each such examination as aforesaid.

8 Arrangements for medical and dental attention

Adequate arrangements shall be made for a child who is boarded out to receive medical and dental attention as required.

9 Reports by visitors

Whenever, in pursuance of these Regulations, a visitor sees a child who is boarded out, he shall after considering the welfare, health, conduct and progress of the child and any complaint made by or concerning him, made a written report about the child, and whenever a visitor so visits the dwelling of foster parents he shall make a written report about its condition.

10 Case records to be kept by local authorities and voluntary organisations.

(1) A local authority shall compile a case record in respect of –
  (a) every child boarded out by them;
  (b) every child boarded out by another local authority in respect of whom they perform any of the supervisory duties under Regulation 13 of these Regulations; and
  (c) every child boarded out by a voluntary organisation in relation to whom they perform the supervisory duties;

and the said record shall be kept up-to-date.

(2) A voluntary organisation shall compile a case record in respect of every child boarded out by them and the said record shall be kept up-to-date.

(3) Every case record compiled under this Regulation or a microfilm recording thereof shall be preserved for a least three years after the child to whom it relates has attained the age of eighteen years or has died before attaining that age, and [such microfilm recording or, where there is none, such case record,] shall be open to inspection at all reasonable time by any person duly authorised in that behalf by the Secretary of State.

10A Microfilming of case records

A local authority or voluntary organisation may make a preserve a microfilm recording of any case record compiled under Regulation 10 of these Regulations and may destroy any case record of which they have made a microfilm recording.

11 Registers to be kept by local authorities

(1) A local authority shall, in respect of every child boarded out in their area, whether by them or by another local authority or by a voluntary organisation, enter in a register to be kept for the purpose the particulars specified in paragraph (2) of this Regulation, and so much of the particulars specified in paragraph (3) of this Regulation as may be appropriate.

(2) The particulars to be so entered in the case of every such child are his name, sex, date of dirth and religious persuasion, the name and religious persuasion of each foster parent and their address, the name of the authority or organisation by whom he is ~~arded~~ out, the dates on which boarding out on each occasion begins and ceases, and ~~son~~ why it ceases.

~~shall also be so entered –~~

(a) in the case of a child in respect of whom arrangements have been made under Regulation 13 of these Regulations, a note of those arrangements;

(b) in the case of a child in the care of a local authority boarded out by a voluntary organisation, the name of the care authority; and

(c) in the case of a child boarded out by a voluntary organisation in relation to whom the area authority are, under Regulation 14 of these Regulations, performing the supervisory duties, a note of that fact.

(4) Every register kept under this Regulation shall be preserved for at least five years after every child particulars about whom are entered therein has or would have attained the age of eighteen years, and shall be open to inspection at all reasonable times by any person duly authorised in that behalf by the Secretary of State.

12 Information to be given to or by area authorities in certain circumstances

(1) Where a child who is boarded out with foster parents in the area of a local authority by another local authority or a voluntary organisation ceases to be boarded out in a household, the authority or organisation by whom the boarding-out was arranged shall inform the area authority thereof and of the date on which the boarding-out ceased, the reason why it ceased and whether it is intended to board out another child in that household.

(2) If, while a child is boarded out with foster parents in the area of a local authority by another local authority or a voluntary organisation, any reason becomes known to the area authority whereby it appears that boarding-out with those foster parents may have ceased to be in the best interests of the child, the care authority, or, as the case may be, the voluntary organisation shall be informed thereof forthwith.

13 Arrangements in certain cases as regards children boarded-out by one local authority in the area of another

A care authority may make arrangements with an area authority, either in respect of a child boarded out by the one in the area of the other or generally in respect of all children who may from time to time be so boarded out, for the area authority to perform any of the supervisory duties and to furnish a report as often as may have been agreed on the welfare, health, conduct and progress of each child in respect of whom such arrangements have effect.

14 Duty of local authority as regards children boarded out by voluntary organisations

(1) In this Regulation and in Regulation 15 of these Regulations a reference in relation to a voluntary organisation to the supervisory duties is a reference to those duties in respect of children boarded out by that voluntary organisation in the area of a particular local authority, and a reference to the voluntary organisation being in a position to discharge the supervisory duties is a reference to that organisation having the requisite facilities, and having made adequate arrangements, for the discharge of those duties in that area.

(2) It shall be the general duty of an area authority to satisfy themselves as regards any voluntary organisation having children boarded out in their area whether or not that organisation are in a position to discharge the supervisory duties, and if satisfied that they are not, the area authority shall, except as otherwise provided in these Regulations, perform the said duties and that organisation shall be relieved of those duties.

(3) As soon as may be after a voluntary organisation board out a child in the area of a local authority in which there is not already a child boarded out by that organisation the area authority shall, for the purpose of carrying out their duties under paragraph (2) of this Regulation, cause investigation to be made into, and shall consider, the question

whether that organisation are in a position to discharge the supervisory duties, and for the said purpose, in any period during which that organisation continuously have any children boarded out in the area of that authority, shall cause investigation to be made into, and shall consider, the said question at least once in every three years.

(4) If while an area authority are performing the supervisory duties in the place of a voluntary organisation, they are satisfied that that organisation are in a position to discharge those duties, the area authority shall be relieved thereof as from such date as the organisation have notified the area authority as that upon which they will resume the discharge of those duties.

(5) Notwithstanding anything in paragraph (2) of this Regulation, an area authority shall not except with the written consent of a voluntary organisation take over from that organisation the supervisory duties until one month has elapsed after notice of their intention so to do has been sent to that organisation, and if within that period the area authority receive from that organisation a copy of representations made by them to the Secretary of State under the next following paragraph, they shall not take over the said duties unless the Secretary of State so directs under that paragraph.

(6) If a notice has under the last preceding paragraph been sent by an area authority to a voluntary organisation and that organisation are of opinion that they are in a position to discharge the supervisory duties, they may within the said period of one month make representations to that effect to the Secretary of State, and the Secretary of State, after considering those representations and any representations made to him on behalf of the area authority, may direct either that the organisation shall continue to discharge those duties or that the area authority shall, from such date as may be indicated in the direction, take them over, and the said duties shall continue to be discharged or be so taken over accordingly.

(7) If, after an area authority have under this Regulation performed the supervisory duties in the place of a voluntary organisation for a continuous period of not less than one year, that organisation are of opinion that they are then in a position to discharge those duties, and the area authority, after representations to that effect have been made to them on behalf of that organisation, are not satisfied that that organisation are in such a position, the organisation may make representations to the Secretary of State accordingly; and if the Secretary of State, after considering those representations and any representations made to him on behalf of the area authority, so directs, the organisation shall, from such date as may be indicated in the direction, resume the discharge of those duties and the area authority shall cease to perform them.

(8) Where an area authority take over the supervisory duties from a voluntary organisation, that organisation shall supply to the area authority full information about every child boarded out by them in the area of that authority.

(9) While an area authority perform the supervisory duties in the pace of a voluntary organisation, the area authority shall supply to the organisation the information in every relevant case record compiled by them.

15 Children in the care of a local authority who are boarded out by a voluntary organisation

(1) As soon as may be after the child who is in the care of a local authority and in the charge of a voluntary organisation is boarded out, the organisation shall notify that authority of the boarding-out and of the names and address of the foster parents, and as soon as may be after that child ceases to be boarded out with those foster parents, the organisation shall notify the authority of the reason therefor.

(2) Where such a child is boarded out with foster parents whose dwelling is outside the area of the care authority, and the area authority either –

(a) are, under Regulation 14 of these Regulations, for the time being performing the supervisory duties in the place of the organisation by whom he is boarded out; or

(b) subsequently, while the child is so boarded out, take over those duties from that organisation,

notice of the facts shall forthwith after the boarding-out, or, as the case may be, when the area authority take over those duties, be sent by the area authority to the care authority.

(3) Where notice under the last preceding paragraph is recevied by a care authority, then, notwithstanding anything in paragraph (2) of Regulation 14 of these Regulations, so long as the area authority continue to perform the supervisory duties in the place of the organisation by whom the child is boarded out, these Regulations shall have effect as if he were boarded out by the care authority.

PART II

PROVISIONS APPLICABLE TO BOARDING-OUT FOR A PERIOD EXCEEDING EIGHT WEEKS

16 Application of Part II

This Part of these Regulations shall have effect only with regard to the boarding-out of a child as a member of a household wherein he is expected to remain for a period exceeding either weeks, or, as the case may require and subject to the proviso to Regulation 30 of these Regulations, he has remained for a period exceeding eight weeks.

17 Prior visits to and reports about foster homes

(1) A child shall not be boarded out unless –

(a) the foster parent and the dwelling where the child will live have been visited by a visitor who is personally acquainted with the child and his needs, or, when that is not practicable, by a visitor who has been fully informed thereof, and the visitor has reported in writing that the sleeping and living accommodation and other domestic conditions at the dwelling are satisfactory and that the household of the foster parents is likely to suit the particular needs of the child;

(b) information has been obtained by a visitor and a written report made by him –

(i) on the reputation and religious persuasion of the foster parents and their suitability in age, character, temperament and health to have the charge of the child,

(ii) as to whether any member of the foster parents' household is believed to be suffering from any physical or mental illness which might adversely affect the child or to have been convicted of any offence which would render it undesirable that the child should associate with him, and

(iii) on the number, sex and approximate age of the persons in that household;

(c) where a local authority propose to board out a child with foster parents whose dwelling is outside the area of that authority, and where a voluntary organisation propose to board out a child (except in either case if it is a matter of urgency or if within the preceding three months another child has been boarded out by them with those foster parents in that dwelling), the area authority have been asked to report within fourteen days if any reason is known to them why

boarding-out with those foster parents might be detrimental to the child's welfare; and

(d) the available history of the child and the relevant reports indicate that boarding-out in that household would be in the best interests of the child.

(2) For the purposes of sub-paragraph (c) of paragraph (1) of this Regulation the area authority shall be notified of the name, sex, date of birth and religious persuasion of the child and the names and address of the foster parents.

18   Particulars to be given to a local authority about children boarded out in their area
Where –
(a) a local authority board out a child with foster parents whose dwelling is outside the area of that authority; or
(b) where a voluntary organisation board out a child,

the authority or organisation, as the case may be, shall notify the area authority, as soon as may be, of any particulars not already sent to them which are required under Regulation 11 of these Regulations to be entered in a register.

19   Religious persuasion
Where possible a child shall be boarded out with foster parents who either are of the same religious persuasion as the child or give an undertaking that he will be brought up in that religious persuasion.

20   Undertaking to be given by foster parents
(1) A local authority or voluntary organisation shall require foster parents to sign an undertaking in respect of any child boarded out with them in the form set out in the Schedule to these Regulations, or in a form to the like effect.

(2) The said undertaking shall be kept by the care authority, or, as the case may be, the voluntary organisation, and a copy thereof shall be left with the foster parents.

21   Visits during boarding-out
(1) In the case of a child who is boarded out with one person as a member of a household which does not include any other person, the local authority or voluntary organisation who have arranged the boarding-out of the child shall ensure that a visitor sees the child and visits the dwelling of the foster parent –
(a) within two weeks after the commencement of the boarding-out and within the two weeks next following those two weeks;
(b) thereafter as often as the welfare of the child requires, but not less often than –
(i) in the case of a child boarded out with a foster parent in whose household he has been less than two years, once in every six weeks, or
(ii) in the case of a child who has been in the household of the foster parent more than two years, once in every three months.
(c) within one month after any change of dwelling by the foster parents and
(d) forthwith after the receipt of a complaint by or concerning the child, unless it appears that action thereon is unnecessary.

(2) In any other case, a local authority or voluntary organisation who have arranged the boarding-out of a child shall ensure that a visitor sees the child and visits the dwelling of the foster parents –
(a) within one month after the commencement of the boarding-out;
(b) thereafter as often as the welfare of the child requires, but not less often than –
(i) in the case of a child boarded out with foster parents in whose household he has been less than two years, if the child has not attained the age of five

years, once in every six weeks, or, if he has attained that age, once every two months, or

(ii) in the case of a child who has been in the household of the foster parents more than two years, once in every three months.

(c) within one month after any change of dwelling by the foster parents; and

(d) forthwith after receipt of a complaint by or concerning the child, unless it appears that action thereon is unnecessary.

22 Review of welfare, health, conduct and progress

(1) A local authority or voluntary organisation shall ensure that a review of the welfare, health, conduct and progress of every child who is boarded out by them is made in the light of the reports written about him in pursuance of these Regulations:–

(a) within three months after the child is placed with any foster parents; and

(b) thereafter, so long as he remains boarded out with those foster parents, as often as is expedient in the particular case, but not less often than once in every six months.

(2) The said review shall be made, so far as is practicable, by persons who do not usually act as visitors, and a note thereof shall be entered in the case record relating to the child, with particulars of any action recommended as a result.

23 Special provisions as to children who have ceased to be of compulsory school age

(1) Nothing in Regulation 20 or 21 of these Regulations shall apply in relation to the boarding-out of a child who has ceased to be of compulsory school age.

(2) Where a child has already ceased to be of compulsory school age when boarded out with foster parents with whom he was not boarded out when he so ceased, the local authority or voluntary organisation who arrange the boarding-out shall require them to sign an undertaking in respect of him containing such parts of the form of undertaking set out in the Schedule to these Regulations, with or without modifications, as appear appropriate to his case.

(3) Where a child over compulsory school age is boarded out the local authority or voluntary organisation who have arranged the boarding-out shall ensure that a visitor sees the child –

(a) (i) in the case of a child who is already boarded out when he ceases to be of compulsory school age, within three months after so ceasing, or

(ii) in the case of a child who is already over that age when boarded out with foster parents, within one month after the commencement of the boarding-out;

(b) thereafter no less often than once in every three months,

(c) within one month after any change of dwelling by the foster parents; and

(d) forthwith after the receipt of a complaint by or concerning the child, unless it appears that action thereon is unnecessary.

PART III

PROVISIONS APPLICABLE TO BOARDING-OUT FOR PERIOD EXPECTED NOT TO EXCEED EIGHT WEEKS IN ALL

24 Application of Part III

This Part of these Regulations shall have effect only with regard to the boarding-out of a child as a member of a household wherein he is expected not to remain for a period exceeding eight weeks in all.

25 Prior visits to and reports about foster homes
A child shall not be boarded out unless the foster parents and the dwelling where the child will live have been visited by a visitor who has reported in writing that the boarding-out of the child with those foster parents would be suitable to the needs of the child for a period not exceeding eight weeks.

26 Particulars to be given to a local authority about children boarded out in their area
Where –
   (a) a local authority board out a child with foster parents whose dwelling is outside the area of that authority, or
   (b) a voluntary organisation board out a child,
the authority or organisation, as the case may be, shall notify the area authority as soon as may be of the fact that the child has been so boarded out and of the particulars required under Regulation 11 of the Regulations to be entered in a register.

27 Undertaking to be given by foster parents or notification in lieu
In the case of a child who is not over compulsory school age, a local authority or voluntary organisation shall either –
   (a) comply with the provisions of Regulation 20 of these Regulations as if that Regulation were included in this Part of these Regulations; or
   (b) send a letter to the foster parents stating the religious persuasion of the child and specifying the obligations which they would have been required to undertake in respect of the child if the provisions of the said Regulation 20 had applied to the case.

28 Visits during boarding-out
(1)   A local authority or voluntary organisation who have arranged the boarding-out of a child who is not over compulsory school age shall ensure that a visitor sees the child and visits the dwelling of the foster parents –
   (a) within two weeks after the commencement of the boarding-out, and
   (b) thereafter not less often than once in every four weeks, and
   (c) forthwith after the receipt of a complaint by or concerning the child, unless is appears that action thereon is unnecessary.
(2)   A local authority or voluntary organisation who have arranged the boarding-out of a child who is over compulsory school age shall ensure that a visitor sees the child –
   (a) within one month after the commencement of the boarding-out, and
   (b) forthwith after the receipt of a complaint by or concerning him, unless it appears that action thereon is unnecessary.

29 Boarding-out at intervals with same foster parents
Where a child who is receiving full-time education has been boarded out with foster parents and within four months of ceasing to be boarded out with them is again boarded out with them, Regulations 6, 7, 25, 27 and 28 of these Regulations shall not apply to that boarding-out, but the local authority or voluntary organisation who arranged it shall ensure that a visitor sees the child and visits the dwelling of the foster parents –
   (a) within one month after the commencement of the boarding-out, and
   (b) forthwith after the receipt of a complaint by or concerning the child, unless it appears that action thereon is unnecessary.

30 Provisions where boarding-out extends beyond eight weeks

If, while this Part of these Regulations has effect with regard to a boarding-out, it becomes expedient that the child boarded out should remain for a period longer than eight weeks in all in the household of which he is already a member, then at the expiration of the said period this Part of these Regulations shall cease to have effect with regard thereto and the provisions of Part II thereof shall have effect as if the child were about to be, or, as the case may required, were, boarded out in that household in such circumstances that the said Part II applied, so however that anything done under this Part of these Regulations which satisfies any requirements of the said Part II shall be deemed to have been done thereunder:

Provided that, if it appears to the care authority, or, in the case of a child boarded out by a voluntary organisation, to the organisation, that the period in excess of eight weeks during which the child will remain boarded out as aforesaid will not exceed four weeks, then this Regulation shall not take effect unless the expiration of that further period of four weeks.

PART IV

SUPPLEMENTARY

31 Transitional provisions

(1) Nothing in Regulation 2, in paragraph (1) of Regulation 15 or in Regulation 20 of these Regulations shall have effect in relation to the boarding-out of a child with foster parents with whom he is boarded out at the date when these Regulations come into operation, so long as he remains boarded out with them.

(2) Where at the date when these Regulations come into operation –

(a) a child is boarded out by a local authority with foster parents whose dwelling is in the area of another local authority and there are in force immediately before the said date administrative arrangements between those authorities made under Rule 18 of the Children and Young Persons (Boarding-Out) Rules 1946, in respect of that child, those arrangements shall, so far as they are consistent with these Regulations, continue in force and have effect as if they were arrangements made under Regulation 13 of these Regulations;

(b) a child is boarded out –

(i) by a local authority with foster parents whose dwelling is outside the area of that authority, or

(ii) by a voluntary organisation

the authority or organisation, as the case may be, shall within one month of the said date notify the area authority of the fact that the child is so boarded out and of the particulars required under Regulation 11 of these Regulations to be entered in a register.

(3) Notwithstanding anything in Regulation 14 of these Regulations, a local authority shall not take over from a voluntary organisation the supervisory duties except with the written consent of that organisation until the expiration of one year from the date when these Regulations come into operation, but, save as aforesaid, the said Regulations shall have effect as if any child boarded out by a voluntary organisation immediately before the said date had been first so boarded out on that date.

(4) Where, before the date when these Regulations come into operation, anything has been done under the Children and Young Persons (Boarding-out) Rules 1946, or is deemed by virtue of sub-paragraph (3) of paragraph 4 of the Second Schedule to the Children Act 1948, to have been done under those Rules, it shall be deemed to have

been done, as far as it could have been so done, under the corresponding provisions of these Regulations.

32 Interpretation

(1) In these Regulations –

'area authority', in relation to a child, means the local authority within whose area is the dwelling of the foster parents of that child;

'care authority', in relation to a child, means a local authority –
- *(a)* in whose care the child is under section one of the Children Act 1948, either because he has been received into their care under that section or under subsection (4) of section six of that Act or by virtue of paragraph 1 of the Second Schedule to that Act, or
- *(b)* to whose care as a fit person the child is committed under the Children and Young Persons Act 1933.

and reference to a child in the care of a local authority shall be construed accordingly;

'child' has the meaining assigned to it by section 87(1) of the Child Care Act 1980;

'foster parents' means persons or a person with whom a child is for the time being or is proposed to be boarded out;

'local authority' has the meaning assigned to it by section 87(1) of the Child Care Act 1980;

'supervisory duties' means the duties imposed by Regulations 7 and 8 and, as the case may be, Regulations 21, 22 and 23 or Regulation 28 or Regulation 29 of these Regulations;

'visitor' means a person carrying out on behalf of a local authority or voluntary organisation any of the duties under these Regulations to see children who are boarded out and to visit the homes of foster parents;

'voluntary organisation' means a body whose activities are carried on otherwise than for profit, but does not include a public or local authority.

(2) The Interpretation Act 1889, shall apply to the interpretation of these Regulations as it applies to the interpretation of an Act of Parliament.

34 Extent

These Regulations shall not apply to Scotland.

35 Citation and commencement

These Regulations may be cites as the Boarding-out of Children Regulations 1955, and shall come into operation on the first day of January 1956.

SCHEDULE   Regulations 20, 23 and 27

FORM OF UNDERTAKING TO BE SIGNED BY FOSTER PARENTS

We/I, AB [and BB], of   having
on the   day of   , 19   , received from
[the council of [the county/county borough/London borough/City of London)
of   (hereinafter
called 'the council')] [*name of voluntary organisation* (hereinafter called 'the
organisation')] CD, who was born on the   day of
            19,   , and whose religious persuasion is
                    , into our/my home as a member of our/my family undertake
that –

1.   We/I will care for CD and bring him/her up as We/I would a child of our/my
own.
2.   He/she will be brought up in, and will be encouraged to practise, his/her
religion.
3.   We/I will look after his/her health and consult a doctor whenever he/she is ill
and will allow him/her to be medically examined at such times and places as [the council]
[the organisation] may require.
4.   We/I will inform [the council] [the organisation] immediately of any serious
occurrence affecting the child.
5.   We/I will at all times permit any person so authorised by the Secretary of State
or by [the council] [the organisation] [or by the council of[the county/county borough/
London borough/City of London] where we/I live] to see him/her and visit our/my
home.
6.   We/I will allow him/her to be removed from our/my home when so requested
by a person authorised by [the council] [the organisation] [or by the council of [the
county/county borough/London borough/City of London] where we/I live].
7.   If we/I decide to move, we/I will notify the new address to (the council] [the
organisation] before we/I go.

                              (Sgd.) ....
                              (Sgd.) ....
Dated ....

CHILDREN AND YOUNG PERSONS ACT 1969
(AUTHORISATION FOR THE PURPOSES OF SECTION 1)
ORDER 1970
(SI 1970 No 1500)
7 October 1970

1   This Order may be cited as the Children and Young Person Act 1969
(Authorisation for the purposes of Section 1) Order 1970 and shall come into operation
on 1 January 1971.

2   The National Society for the Prevention of Cruelty to Children are hereby
authorised to bring proceedings in pursuance of section 1 of the Children and Young
Persons Act 1969 (care proceedings in juvenile courts).

MAGISTRATES' COURTS (CHILDREN AND YOUNG PERSONS) RULES 1970
(SI 1970 No 1792)
27 November 1970

20 Procedure after applicant's case has been proved

(1) Where the court is satisfied that the applicant's case has been proved –

   (a) where a guardian ad litem has been applinted, the court shall take into consideration his written report to the court, which may be received and considered by the court without being read aloud, and copies of which shall in any case be given by the court to the applicant and the respondent and to any parent or guardian of the relevant infant who attends the hearing or requests it before the hearing or to their legal representatives, except that if the relevant infant is not legally represented a copy of the report need not be given to him unless the guardian ad litem considers it desirable to do so;

   (aa) where a guardian ad litem has been appointed, he shall in addition be entitled to make oral representations to the court;

   (b) the court shall take into consideration such information as to the relevant infant's general conduct, home surroundings, school record and medical history as may be necessary to enable it to deal with the case in his best interests and, in particular, shall take into consideration such information as aforesaid which is provided in pursuance of section 9 of the Act of 1969.

   (c) if such information as aforesaid is not fully available, the court shall consider the desirability of adjourning the case for such inquiry as may be necessary;

   (d) any written report of a probation officer, local authority, local education authority or registered medical practitioner may be received and considered by the court without being read aloud, and

   (e) if the court considers it necessary in the interests of the relevant infant, it may require him or his parent or guardian, if present, to withdraw from the court.

(2) Where, in pursuance of paragraph (1) *(a)* or *(d)*, a report has been considered without being read aloud or where the relevant infant, his parent or guardian has been required to withdraw from the court in pursuance of paragraph (1) *(e)*, then –

   (a) the relevant infant shall be told the substance of any part of the information given to the court bearing on his character or conduct which the court considers to be material to the manner in which the case should be dealt with unless it appears to it impracticable so to do having regard to his age and understanding, and

   (b) the relevant infant's parent or guardian, if present, shall be told the substance of any part of such information which the court considers to be material as aforesaid and which has references to his character or conduct or to the character, conduct, home surroundings or health of the relevant infant;

and, if such a person, having been told the substance of any part of such information desires to produce further evidence with reference thereto, the court, if it thinks the further evidence would be material, shall adjourn the proceedings for the production thereof and shall, if necessary in the case of a report, require the attendance at the adjourned hearing of the person who made the report.

21 Duty of court to explain manner in which it proposes to deal with case and effect of order

(1) Before finally disposing of the case or before remitting the case to another court in

pursuance of section 2(11) of the Act of 1969, the court shall inform the relevant infant, any person conducting the case on his behalf, and his parent or guardian, if present, of the manner in which it proposes to deal with the case and allow any of those persons so informed to make representations:

Provided that the relevant infant shall not be informed as aforesaid if the court considers it undesirable or, having regard to his age and understandzing, impracticable so to inform him.

(2) On making any orders, the court shall explain to the relevant infant the general nature and effect of the order unless it appears to it impracticable so to do having regard to his age and understanding or, in the case of an order requiring his parent or guardian to enter into a recognizance, it appears to it undesirable so to do.

GUARDIANS AD LITEM AND REPORTING OFFICERS (PANELS) REGULATIONS 1983 (SI 1983 No 1908)
19 December 1983

1   Citation, commencement and interpretation
(1) These regulations may be cited as the Guardians Ad Litem and Reporting Officers (Panels) Regulations (1083) and shall come into operation on 27th May 1984.

(2) Any reference in these regulations to any provision made by or contained in any enactment shall, except insofar as the context otherwise requires, be construed as including a reference to any provision which may re-enact or replace it with or without modification.

2   Panels of guardians ad litem and reporting officers
(1) There shall be established in the area of each local authority a panel of persons appointed in accordance with the provisions of regulation 3 of these regulations from whom guardians ad litem and reporting officers may be appointed for the purposes specified in section 103(1) (a) of the Children Act 1975.

(2) A local authority shall ensure that the number of persons appointed to the panel eestablished in its area is sufficient for the purposes specified in t he said section 103(1) (a) in the area in which the panel is established.

3   Appointments to panels
(1) Members of a panel shall be appointed by the local authority in whose area the panel is established.

(2) Before appointing a person to be a member of a panel the local authority shall invite nominations from –
- (a) any probation committee established in its area by virtue of Schedule 3 to the Powers of the Criminal Courts Act 1973,
- (b) the clerk of each magistrates' court in its area.
- (c) any local authority whose area adjoins its area and
- (d) any other person as it considers appropriate.

(3) The local authority shall decide whether the qualifications and experience of any of the bodies referred to in paragraph (2) or by itself are suitable for the purposes of that person's appointment as a guardian ad litem or reporting officer.

(4) Before making an appointment to the panel, the local authority shall consult such

organisations and persons from whom nominations were invited under paragraph (2) above as it thinks fit, in respect of those persons whom it proposes to appoint to the panel.

(5) The appointment of a person to a panel shall be for a period not exceeding three years, so however that the local authority may terminate that person's membership of the panel at any time where the local authority considers that he is unable or unfit to carry out the functions of a guardian ad litem or reporting officer.

(6) A local authority shall maintain a record of those persons whom it has appointed to be members of the panel established in its area.

4 Expenses, fees and allowances of members of panels

(1) Local authorities shall in respect of the purposes specified in section 103(1)(*a*) of the Children Act 1975 defray expenses incurred by members of the panels established in their areas and pay fees and allowances for members of such panels.

(2) No expenses, fees and allowances as referred to in paragraph (1) shall be defrayed or paid by local authorities by virtue of paragraph (1) in respect of a member of a panel who is employed by a local authority or probation committee.

APPENDIX F.1

Confidential

REPORT OF GUARDIAN AD LITEM, Miss Alix Causby, 18 September 1984

MATTER BEFORE THE COURT
Chantelle Lorrington/Beckford, DOB 11.12.83, is subject of an Interim Care Order to the London Borough of Brent. The matter before the Court on 26th September 1984 is a Full Hearing of the case. I was appointed Guardian Ad Litem in this matter on 13th July 1984.

REPORT BY
Alix Causby, Guardian Ad Litem, City Hall, Victoria Street, SW1.

FAMILY COMPOSITION
Beverly Lorrington, Mother, DOB 2.11.59, 91 Bilton Road, Perivale, Middlesex.

Morris Beckford, Father, DOB 30.6.59, Her Majesty's Prison, Brixton.

Chantelle Beckford, DOB 11.12.83, subject to an Interim Care Order to the London Borough of Brent, currently placed with foster parents.

Louise Beckford, DOB 27.5.81, subject of a Care Order to the London Borough of Brent (9.9.81), currently placed with foster parents.

Jasmine Beckford, DOB 21.12.79, deceased on 5.7.84.

IN PREPARING THIS REPORT I HAVE SEEN THE FOLLOWING:
Beverly Lorrington on 2 occasions.

Chantelle Beckford/Lorrington.

Louise Beckford/Lorrington.

Foster Mother

Mr and Mrs Clifton Lorrington, Father and Stepmother to Beverly Lorrington.

Carol Lorrington, Beverly Lorrington's stepsister.

Gun Wahlstrom, Social Worker, London Borough of Brent.

Diane Dietman, Senior Social Worker, London Borough of Brent.

Miss Leong, Health Visitor, Brent Health Authority.

S. Baichoo, Senior Nurse, Health Visiting, Brent Health Authority.

Sue Knibbs, Senior Social Worker, Kensington and Chelsea Social Services Department, St. Charles Hospital.

Morris Beckford has refused to see me. Mr Beckford's solicitor, Ian Duncan, took instructions from his client. Mr Duncan told his client that he had no objection to his client seeing me but he (Mr Duncan) wished to be present during the interview. I have informed Mr Duncan that I will see Mr Beckford if he changes his mind. I regret that I am unable to present Mr Beckford's views in this report.

I HAVE SEEN THE FOLLOWING DOCUMENTS
Files of the London Borough of Brent's Social Services Department:

    Including –

    Case Conference records.

Report of Independent Social Worker, Joan Court.

Files of the Kensington and Chelsea Social Services Department, St. Charles Hospital.

Medical statement by Dr Kathryn, A.E. Morgan, following examination of Chantelle and Louise Lorrington/Beckford on 6.7.84.

I HAVE SPOKEN TO THE FOLLOWING ON THE TELEPHONE

Detective Inspector Dickens, Kilburn Police Station.

Dr D.K. Brooks, Consultant in Accident and Emergency, St. Mary's Hospital, Harrow Road.

Dr A.M.A. Khan, General Practitioner.

Dr Kathryn A.C. Morgan, formerly of the Casualty Department, Central Middlesex Hospital.

MEDICAL INFORMATION REGARDING CHANTELLE

Examination of Chantelle on 12.7.84 revealed five bruises on her lower back, a small bruise on her right shoulder, and three small bruises on her upper spine.

MEDICAL INFORMATION REGARDING JASMINE LORRINGTON/BECKFORD

I feel that it is important that the Court be in no doubt as to the severity of injuries to Jasmine Beckford. Dr D.K. Brooks, Consultant in Accident and Emergency, St. Mary's Hospital, Harrow Road, gave me the following information.

Jasmine was brought to his Department at 5.39 p.m. on 5.7.84. She had been dead for some time, probably since early morning. She had bruises over her forehead, nose, and both cheeks, many grazes on her face; cut lips both upper and lower internally, a linear laceration at the junction of the upper ear and scalp, grazes, probably old, over the back of the head, small grazes on the chest and right forearm, old scarring and four ulcers (probably cigarette burns) on the left thigh and left hip; swelling and discolouration of the abdomen with bruises in the left upper part, two ulcers (fresh cigarette burns) on the upper aspect of the left ankle with much scarring of the ankle, a fresh ulcer (cigarette burn) on the right heel, multiple old fractures of the left femur, cigarette burns down the back, and haemorrhages inside the skull.

Dr Brooks view is that these injuries represented prolonged, protracted torture of Jasmine.

MISS LORRINGTON'S VIEW ABOUT WHAT SHOULD HAPPEN TO CHANTELLE

Miss Lorrington simply views the Juvenile Court proceedings as a confirmation of whether or not she gets the children back. It is difficult for her to understand the legal complexities and for her to separate the Care Hearing in relation to Chantelle from the access hearing in relation to Louis and Chantelle. She does oppose the Care Order in relation to Chantelle as she feels that Chantelle has never been injured or neglected.

Miss Lorrington expresses great morose and guilt about what has happened to her children. She also professes great love for them. She begs for another chance to prove that she can care adequately for them.

Miss Lorrington naturally expresses much anger toward Mr Beckford. She says that she never wants to see him again and she has written him to this effect. She says she never wants anything to do with men, and that she will never again let anyone 'use here'. If given the children she will allow social workers to visit her at any time. She proposes to live with her parents initially but would like to be on her own at some time in the future.

THE SOCIAL SERVICES DEPARTMENT'S VIEW

The Social Services Department of the London Borough of Brent are requesting a Care Order in relation to Chantelle. They envisage that she and Louise will remain together in their current foster home until a long term placement can be arranged for them. They would like to place them permanently as soon as possible. They see no prospect of rehabilitating the children with their mother.

BACKGROUND INFORMATION OF PARENTS

Miss Lorrington

Miss Lorrington is a slim, attractive girl who talks in a soft voice. It is difficult at times to be sure that she has understood what has been said to her. She appeals to one's mothering instincts as she presents as a helpless, fragile, victimised young woman.

Miss Lorrington's natural mother left the family when she was six months old. Her father cared for her at weekends, and she was boarded out during the week. When she was two, her stepmother joined the family. Miss Lorrington has a stepsister, aged 22, and a stepbrother, aged 21. When Miss Lorrington was 8 or 9 a neighbourhood boy shot her in the eye with a bow and arrow and she has an artificial eye. She was called 'cross-eyed' at school and has always been self conscious about her eye. She was never interested in reading at school. She attended a school for the educationally sub-normal, where she met Mr Beckford when she was 14. Miss Lorrington always thought she was treated differently by her family to her half brother and sister. When an adolescent she was not allowed to go out and felt that she was 'the wife', having to do most of the housework. She left home soon after leaving school at 17 (her sister said she 'ran away' from home). She was working as a seamstress in a factory at that time. She soon cohabited with a man who was violent and cruel towards her. She became pregnant by this man and had a termination. Soon after, she became pregnant for the second time. She left this cohabitee because of his ill treatment and because he did not want their child. When she was six months pregnant, Morris Beckford asked her to move in with him. At that time they lived in one cramped room. When Jasmine was born, Mr Beckford suggested registering her in his name.

Mr Beckford

My information about Mr Beckford is based on the reports I have read and the information given me by Miss Lorrington. Mr Beckford was rejected and physically abused by his own parents. When he was almost 13, the NSPCC received a referral relating to Mr Beckford and his sister. Investigation revealed that both children had received injuries from a beating and that Mr Beckford had been living in a small space in a garden shed. The parents were charged with assault. Mr Beckford and his sister were committed to the care of the local authority. Mr Beckford attended a school for the educationally sub-normal. After leaving school at 17, he worked in the same employment, for a scaffolding company, until his arrest. On the 5th July, 1984, he was charged with murder in relation to the death of Jasmine Beckford.

BACKGROUND OF JASMINE AND LOUISE BECKFORD

On August 1st, 1981 Louise Beckford, two months old, was admitted to St. Charles Hospital with a spiral fracture of her left upper arm and with hemorrhages of her right eye. These injuries were felt to be non-accidental, and Mr Beckford was convicted of assault.

On 4th August 1981 Jasmine Beckford was admitted to St. Charles Hospital with a fractured left femur, felt by doctors to be caused by a strong blow. The parents denied inflicting this injury. Miss Beckford now tells me that she saw Mr Beckford break

Jasmine's leg by kicking her. There was concern at this time also about Miss Lorrington's relationship with the children, i.e. lack of stimulation of them.

On 9th September 1981 Jasmine and Louise Beckford were made subject of a Care Order to the London Borough of Brent. When discharged from hospital, both children were placed in a foster home. An active programme of rehabilitation to the parents was begun. Workers with the family were Gun Wahlstrom, Social Worker, and Dorothy Ruddock, Family Aid. On 22nd March 1982 the children were moved to a Local Authority childrens home to allow the parents increased opportunity to care for the children. In March 1982, the parents were rehoused into a three bedroom council property. They had previously blamed their problems on being cramped in one small room. On 19th April 1982 Jasmine and Louise were placed home on trial with close supervision by the Social Services Department. On 9th November 1982 the childrens names were taken off the Borough's Child Abuse Register. In November 1982 a Social Services note indicated that social work visits had increased due to marital problems. In April 1983 Miss Lorrington was having problems in relation to her pregnancy with Chantelle and there was increased social work visiting. On 25th May 1983 the Local Authority asked the Willesden Juvenile Court for revocation of the Care Order in relation to Jasmine and Louise. They had no concerns about the family's care of the children at that point and they had never seen any physical marks on the children. The Court refused revocation. In September 1983 the Family Aid left the employment of the local authority and the Beckford family was not allocated a new family aid. Visits to the family were cut down at this time.

In March 1984 the social worker began to have difficulties seeing the family. On 5th July 1984 the Social Services Department was informed of Jasmine's death by the Kilburn CID. Both Mr Beckford and Miss Lorrington have been charged with murder in relation to Jasmine's death.

MISS LORRINGTON'S VIEW OF HER RELATIONSHIP WITH MR BECKFORD AND HIS RELATIONSHIP WITH JASMINE AND LOUISE

Miss Lorrington appears to have a very ambivalent relationship with Mr Beckford. On the one hand, he provided for her and the children financially, he helped her around the house, he at times spoiled her by buying her presents of clothes or household appliances. On the other hand, Mr Beckford was obsessed with cleanliness and could not bear a speck of dirt in the house. For example, a new cooker he had purchased had a speck of dirt on the oven door, and he smashed the door in. Miss Lorrington felt pressure to clean the house and fix meals on time. She felt tied to the house.

Also, Mr Beckford disagreed with Miss Lorrington about care of the children. For example, he viewed the attention she tried to give to the children as 'spoiling' them. He was strict with the children, expecting that they instantly obeyed him. He wanted to teach them things that were too advanced for them (i.e., alphabet, numbers) and would become extremely angry if they could not learn. From the time Jasmine and Louise came home on trial, they were both subject to physical abuse by their father. There was constant bruising on the children, mainly on their buttocks, legs, lower back. Sometimes there was facial bruising including black eyes. Miss Lorrington suspects that not a week went by without one or the other children having a bruise. Mr Beckford would hit them hard, like they were adults; and sometimes he kicked them. Miss Lorrington spent much time covering up bruises from the outside world. She finally removed Jasmine from Princess Frederica School in September 1983 because of bruising. When Miss Lorrington intervened on behalf of the children, Mr Beckford would hit her and tell she did not know how to look after the children because she was stupid. Miss Lorrington lied and covered up for Mr Beckford because she 'loved him' and 'I love my children'. She knew that the children would be removed from her if she told what Mr Beckford was doing.

She also felt frightened of Mr Beckford. She told Gun Wahlstrom at one point that she wanted to leave Mr Beckford, but she could not tell him why. A part of her wished that someone would see the bruises and protect the children. Miss Lorrington denied that she was aware of fractures to Jasmine, or injuries that cause prolonged pain or difficulty in walking.

Both Jasmine and Louise were frightened of their father. Louise, particularly, would cry when he came home from work and Mr Beckford would hit her for crying. However, Miss Lorrington feels that the abuse of Jasmine was more severe because Jasmine was not Mr Beckford's child. He was always reminding Miss Lorrington of this.

On the morning of 5th July, Mr Beckford was in Jasmine's bedroom when Miss Lorrington awoke. She went into the bedroom and was told by Mr Beckford that Jasmine was resting as she was too tired to get up. Miss Lorrington thought this was unusual, but she went downstairs to prepare breakfast for Louise and Chantelle. When she returned to Jasmine's bedroom, she touched Jasmine, who was cold. Miss Lorrington thought that Jasmine was dead. She begged Mr Beckford to take Jasmine to the hospital, but he refused. Miss Lorrington telephoned her sister Carol, asking her to come to her parent's house where Miss Lorrington took Louise and Chantelle. She and Carol returned to her home and convinced Mr Beckford to go with them to take Jasmine to hospital. She thinks that they went to hospital at about 2.00 p.m. but she was in a state of shock, unable to remember adequately.

Miss Lorrington feels that her relationship with the children was good. She never needed help in knowing how to care for them. She enjoyed talking to and playing with them, and when Mr Beckford was at work she says she had a lovely life with the children. Miss Lorrington says she never physically injured the children. If they were naughty, she occasionally smacked them on the bottom or hand.

According to the Health Visitor Jasmine and Louise were always small, thin children, below normal in weight, and she advised Miss Lorrington about their nutrition. The Health Visitor never saw evidence of physical injury to the children.

CHANTELLE BECKFORD'S BACKGROUND

Miss Lorrington planned the pregnancy with Chantelle without discussing it with Mr Beckford. She had a difficult pregnancy, as she had had with the first two, vomiting, losing weight, and being generally ill. She described Chantelle as a lovely baby. She was quiet and easy going. She only cried when she was hungry and she had a very good appetite. She smiled, laughed aloud, rolled over, and was beginning to sit alone. Miss Lorrington says that to her knowledge Chantelle was never injured by Mr Beckford. She denies knowing about any bruising on Chantelle at the time of the Place of Safety Order.

The Health Visitor tells me that she had never had cause to worry about the care of Chantelle. She was aware that Miss Lorrington had been under some stress since Chantelle's birth. She attributed this to the normal stress of new motherhood and the demands of three children. Of all the children, Chantelle's growth and development seemed the best, i.e., her weight and developmental milestones were normal.

Miss Lorrington's Family

From the time Miss Lorrington left home, she did not maintain regular contact with her father and stepmother. They had never seen the children on a regular basis and had not visited Miss Lorrington at her home. They did talk to her by telephone and she did visit them on occasions. They did not know that Jasmine and Louise were subject to Care Orders.

Mr Clifton Lorrington, 51, is a redundant (Sept. 83) Ford car worker. In 1981 he was treated at the National Hospital for Neurological Diseases for a shoulder problem.

He has since been treated at Ealing Hospital for a dpressive breakdown. He is still on medication and has regular follow up. Mrs Lorrington, 60, is a Care Assistant in a London Borough of Brent Old Peoples Home. Both Mr and Mrs Lorrington are shocked and dismayed by what has happened to their grandchildren and their daughter. They feel guilty about the lack of contact with the children. Miss Lorrington is now living with them. Miss Lorrington said she is surprised by the love her family has shown her and their willingness to stand by her during this difficulty.

Mr and Mrs Lorrington would like Miss Lorrington to be given 'a chance' with Louise and Chantelle. They would take her and the children into their home and would help her care for the children. They would not like to see the children remain outside the family.

Carol Lorrington, 23, is an office manageress for a data computer firm. She is the one family member who has maintained contact with Miss Lorrington and the children. From the time Miss Lorrington left home, Carol Lorrington visited her in her home on a regular, if not frequent, basis. She has always felt close to her half-sister. She knew that there were times when Miss Lorrington was unhappy and depressed, but she was never told why. She had also seen Louise and Jasmine with bruises. She feels extremely guilty that she did nothing.

Miss Carol Lorrington lives with her 5 year old daughter, Tania, in her parents house, which consists of three bedrooms, a through lounge, kitchen, toilet and back garden. Miss Carol Lorrington feels that Miss Lorrington should be given a chance to care for Louise and Chantelle. She describes Miss Lorrington as a patient mother who cares for her children well. While Miss Lorrington is simple in terms of reading and writing, she shows common sense with the children. Carol Lorrington proposes that she and Beverly Lorrington can share a house, and that she could help Beverly Lorrington look after the children.

MY OBSERVATIONS OF CHANTELLE AND LOUISE IN THEIR FOSTER HOME ON THE 9.8.84

Chantelle and Louise were placed in a foster home on 6.7.84. They had been with their maternal grandparents overnight. At the end of July, the foster mother went on holiday, and the children had to be moved to another foster home for a month. They have now been placed back with the original foster mother. I visited the children in the interim foster home with Gun Wahlstrom who left after 15 minutes. It is most regrettable that the children had to be moved.

Chantelle – is a well-nourished baby. The foster mother told me that she eats very well and cries when her feed is finished. She has had some stomach upset which the foster mother relates to change in diet and the emotional upset that she has experienced. Chantelle is a quiet, easy going baby who only cries when she wants a feed. When Chantelle was taken to the foster home she could not roll over or sit up. In the week prior to my visit he had begun to do both. She will sit alone well if placed in a sitting position. She reaches for toys with either hand and exchanges them. She will laugh out loud when played with. When she came to this foster home her legs seemed tight and were always bent. The foster mother massages and stretches her legs. The foster mother feels that she is a bit slower in development than other children she has known.

Louise – shows little interest in Chantelle although she did kiss her when encouraged to do so. She appeared as a small, thin 3 year old. She seemed bright and cheerful. She recognised Gun Wahlstrom. She appeared indiscriminate in her relationships with adults (as one might expect from a child with her history), and as soon as Mr. Wahlstrom left was crawling unsolicited onto my lap wanting cuddles. The foster mother said that Louise demands a lot of attention. The previous week Louise had an upset stomach and did not sleep well and the foster mother experienced a difficult week. However, Louise is very good and obedient and has settled very well. She calls the foster mother "mummy" – initiated by herself. Louise did not talk much to me and her speech did not seem clear. She enjoyed playing 'games', i.e., pointing to parts of her face, counting to ten. The foster mother said that Louise sometimes talks about her father when she is having her morning bath. As the foster mother is washing her back or face she will say that her father hit her there. She does not talk about her mother or about Jasmine.

SUMMARY IN RELATION TO THE APPLICATION FOR A CARE ORDER IN RESPECT OF CHANTELLE LORRINGTON/BECKFORD

In this section I talk about both Chantelle and Louise Lorrington/Beckford as I feel that Louise's life experiences are relevant to decisions about Chantelle's future. I would also like to see the children remain together, if possible.

Chantelle Lorrington/Beckford is the youngest sister to two children, Jasmine and Louise Lorrington/Beckford who were made subject of Care Orders to the London Borough of Brent on 9.9.81. The children were returned to their parents on 18th April 1982. Their mother tells me that they were subject to systematic abuse by their father until Jasmine's death on 5.7.84. Injuries to Jasmine at the time of her death support that she had been subject to continuous abuse. We have no way of knowing who perpetuated these injuries, and it is my understanding that both parents have been charged with murder. Unfortunately I have been unable to interview Mr Beckford. I have also been unable to obtain little objective or detailed information regarding Miss Lorrington's day to day care of the children. I have been unable to observe Miss Lorrington with Louise and Chantelle.

Assuming that Miss Lorrington's descriptions of what happened to the children are accurate, she was unable to protect Louise and Jasmine and actively covered up longstanding injuries to them. In addition medical examination of Chantelle revealed that she had bruises on her lower back, right shoulder and upper spine. Louise also had bruises and healed cuts in the skin. Miss Lorrington denied knowledge of these injuries but said that she frequently was unaware when injuries occurred to the children. My opinion is that she also minimised the extent of injuries to the children.

Miss Lorrington is making a desperate and understandable plea for the return of Louise and Chantelle. She points out that her circumstances have now changed in that:

1) she has ended her relationship with Mr Beckford,

2) she has never injured her children and has always provided adequately for them,

3) she will be able to prove that she can adequately care for the children on her own,

4) she now has the support of her family.

Unfortunately the above issues relate to new resolutions by Miss Lorrington and cannot be tested out. My opinion is that Miss Lorrington would be unable to maintain changes in her situation. Despite Miss Lorrington's current protestations of hate towards Mr Beckford, I feel that her relationship with him has been an extremely strong one in which she protected him rather than her children. My experience would lead me to feel that this type of powerful relationship is not easily severed. In addition Mr Beckford was Miss Lorrington's second violent relationship and this pattern of establishing relationships with violent men is again one that is not easily broken.

Miss Lorrington says that she did not protect her children because of fear of losing them and because of fear for herself. In my experience, most mothers in similar situations and with similar fears do, at least, seek hospital treatment for their injured children as a means of asking for help. Miss Lorrington did not do this or talk to those offering her help, this magnifying the element of collusion between her and Mr Beckford.

Miss Lorrington seems to be a very dependent person who would find it extremely difficult to cope on her own. She has in the past been offered a tremendous amount of support and help by the Social Services Department. She was unable to use this help to establish more positive relationships with her children, to gain awareness of her childrens physical and emotional need or to protect the children. She also finally rejected this help.

Miss Lorrington's family has now offered her help and support. They have been unable to offer help in the past, partly because of their own personal problems, including the problems with Mr Lorrington's health and partly because of their poor relationship with Miss Lorrington. Even Carol Lorrington, who maintained contact with her sister, was not trusted with information about Miss Lorrington's situation. Miss Lorrington has rejected her family in the past, as she has, in fact, felt rejected by them. It seems that this pattern of rejection of help makes it unlikely that the current supportive relationship can be maintained.

Chantelle and Louise Lorrington/Beckford are children who have been part of a very violent and disturbed family. Their experiences of parenthood are of a physically abusive father and a mother who colluded with the abuse and was unprotective of them.

Louise is already showing extremely worrying signs i.e. shallow, indiscriminate relationships, settling too well after very traumatic experiences, being too good and obedient.

I am pleased that the Social Services Department is seeking expert help to look at Louise's needs and how to help her with the recent traumatic events. It is difficult to gauge at this point how successfully Louise will be able to overcome the trauma of her early years.

Chantelle, fortunately is of an age that provides her with a better chance of overcoming the traumatic events of her first months. To do this, however, she now needs to be given as much stability as can possibly be provided.

In my view both Chantelle and Louise Lorrington/Beckford need a chance to develop long term relationships in a stable, warm, and caring family who are in tune to each child's special emotional needs. This placement needs to occur as soon as possible with a view that the children may eventually be offered the stability of adoption by this family. The family chosen would need to accept that Louise, particularly, may need long term therapeutic intervention to help her overcome the emotionally damaging experiences she has endured.

I am afraid that Miss Lorrington's previous care and, at the least, lack of protection of the children, her own dependent personality, patterns of relationships and her inability to use help, do not provide a foundation to allow me to recommend any kind of rehabilitation programme. I do not feel that she would be able to provide the physical and emotional care and safety, or the degree of stability that these children need. Nor do I feel that the children have the time for us to take a chance on their mother's ability to change. I know that Miss Lorrington will be devastated by my views, and I have not reached these recommendations without a great deal of consideration.

In the above circumstances I must respectfully submit to the Court that a Care Order in respect of Chantelle Lorrington/Beckford is necessary to protect her safety and emotional development.

ADDENDUM TO GUARDIAN AD LITEM REPORT
REGARDING LOUISE LORRINGTON/BECKFORD, DATE OF BIRTH 27.5.81., AND CHANTELLE LORRINGTON/BECKFORD, DATE OF BIRTH 11.12.83.

REPORT BY: ALIX CAUSBY, CITY HALL, VICTORIA STREET, LONDON SW1

MATTER BEFORE THE COURT
Appeal against Notice of Refusal of Arrangements for Access issued by the London Borough of Brent Social Services Department in relation to Chantelle and Louise Lorrington/Beckford.

MISS LORRINGTON'S VIEW
Miss Lorrington is understandably distressed by not seeing her childern. She is eager for news of them and how they are. The Social Services Department has sent her photographs of the children. Miss Lorrington feels that the children should be returned to her and that the Social Services Department is being unreasonable in not allowing her access.

THE SOCIAL SERVICES DEPARTMENT'S VIEW
The Social Services Department has denied Miss Lorrington access to Louise and Chantelle Lorrington/Beckford since 6th July 1984, when they were placed in a foster home. They believe that access for Miss Lorrington would serve no useful purpose in relation to the children. They feel that the traumatic circumstances prior to the children's removal from the family could mean that the children would be further traumatised by contact with their mother. As the Department has no plans to rehabilitate the children to their mother and as they hope to place the children long-term outside the family, they felt that access would not be in the children's best interest. The Social Services Department are seeking expert professional consultation regarding Louise's needs and how to work with her about the losses she has suffered. They have requested that the family help them by giving them photographs of family members for the children and they plan to prepare a life book for the children.

GUARDIAN AD LITEM'S VIEW ABOUT ACCESS
I have supported the Social Services Department's view about long-term, secure placement of Chantelle and Louise outside their family of origin. If the children are to have any chance of repairing the damage they have already suffered, they need a fresh start in a family especially selected to meet their particular needs. This placement would hopefully lead to adoption of the children. Access would only serve to confuse them and hamper their ability to settle into their new family. I feel that Louise and Chantelle's best interests would not be served by access with their mother.

I, therefore, respectfully recommend to the Court that the Refusal of Arrangements of Access be upheld. I know that Miss Lorrington and her family will feel understandably distressed and devastated by my view. If the Court agrees with my view, I hope that Miss Lorrington can be offered help to come to terms with the loss of her children.

APPENDIX F.2

ADDENDUM TO GUARDIAN AD LITEM REPORT

26th October 1984 – Visit to Louise and Chantelle Lorrington/Beckford in the foster parents home.

Because of the re-scheduling of the Care Hearing in respect of Chantelle Lorrington/Beckford, and the Hearing of the Appeal against Termination of Access in respect of both Chantelle and Louise Lorrington/Beckford on 26th September 1984, I decided to visit the children again in their foster home and to discuss the childrens progress with their foster mother. The children had originally been placed in this foster home, but had been moved to another foster home for a month while this foster family was on holiday. The following is a description of the important points that came out of this visit.

Chantelle now shows attachment to the foster mother. She showed concern at being approached by a stranger (the Guardian) and she turned to the foster mother to be picked up by her. The foster mother confirms that Chantelle is wary of strangers and is becoming attached to the foster family. Chantelle has a temper which can be triggered by anything. The foster mother feels that Chantelle is slower than other children her age. She turns from back to front and back again. She sits for long periods. She does not crawl but slides on her back. She will not pull herself up but will stand when placed in a standing position. She babbles and attempts to mimic words.

Louise has become much more communicative than when I saw her previously. She talks more and her speech is clearer. The foster mother says that Louise is no longer "too good" but is now "normally naughty". Louise also has a temper. Louise still does not talk much about her past. On one occasion she told the foster mother that "mummy hit her on her fanny". (The foster mother says that Louise swears a lot). The foster mother said, "you mean me?" (Louise calls the foster mother mummy). Louise became very agitated and said, "no, my real mummy." On another occasion Louise was naming the members of the foster parents household, saying that each one loved her. She then said that "Jasmine killed me".

Another example of Louise's distress occurs when Chantelle either cries or wets herself. Louise becomes very agitated and attempts to hit Chantelle. She tells the foster mother to "hit Chantelle's back side". In addition, Louise tells Chantelle to "shut your bleedin' mouth". The foster mother has to be very careful to watch Chantelle and Louise when they are together. In my opinion, Louise's treatment of Chantelle reflects how she saw Chantelle being treated within the family, and how she herself was treated.

The foster mother seems to provide a lot warmth to both the children. I feel that she could benefit from further help in knowing how best to respond when Louise mentions her family. I would also suggest that Louise could benefit from continued play sessions with her social worker to help her express and understand some of the worrying things that have happened to her.

APPENDIX F.3

REPORT OF DR HUGH JOLLY MA MD FRCP DCH
HONORARY CONSULTANT PAEDIATRICIAN
CHARING CROSS HOSPITAL

CHANTELLE BECKFORD (born 8.12.83)

At the requests of Messrs. Hodders, Solicitors, I examined this child on 14th November, 1984, having previously studied relevant documents relating to her family history and herself. She was accompanied by her social worker, Miss Gun Wahlstrom, since her foster mother was unable to come. This meant that she was in the care of a relative stranger and not the foster mother who has cared for her day and night for approximately five months.

Although Miss Wahlstrom handled her very sympathetically, Chantelle took a long time to settle and spent much of the time crying. I am, therefore, unable to give a true picture of the child and her state of development on that occasion, although I undertook a full physical examination.

Because of the unsatisfactory nature of the examination on 14th November, I saw Chantelle again on 20th November, 1984, this time with her foster mother as well as her social worker, Gun Wahlstrom, and her sister Louise. Her foster mother told me that she came to her on 6th July, 1984 at the age of seven months. She seemed small for her age and never smiled. She constantly sucked two fingers. At this time she vomited repeatedly at any time of day or night.

Her foster mother stated her to be slow in all areas of development. She was unable to sit and kept wanting to be fed.

Her foster mother went on holiday for one month about three weeks after Chantelle's arrival and in that time she had shown improvement in her state of development. She started to read, to grasp objects and began to make sounds. She also became happier and would smile.

During the four weeks her foster mother was away she stayed with another foster mother. Her permanent foster mother found she had regressed while she was away and would scream for the first two weeks when she attempted to get her to walk.

Since this time she has made steady improvement in her developmental progress so that she now sits up and can stand holding on. She is also able to crawl. She answers in her own way when called but has a strong temper if she is not allowed to get her own way. She is not yet walking but has improved in her attempts to do so.

My **examination** showed Chantelle to be a cheerful healthy looking child who gurgled with laughter, banged objects to create sounds (evidence of hearing) and placed toys in her mouth in a normal manner for her age.

Weight 8.53 kg — 50th percentile
Height 72 cm — 25th percentile
Head circumference 46.6 cm — Mean

She is, therefore, of normal weight, but less than normal height.

She manipulated objects well, was ambidextrous (normal for age) and passed them with normal skill from one hand to another.

She sat well on her own and could be pulled to stand, though she was a long way from standing on her own. However, with her foster mother behind her holding her hands she made what were early attempts at walking.

On the first occasion she had a snuffly nose, but this had cleared by the second visit. The anterior fontanelle is closed. A large Mongolian blue spot covered much of both buttocks and there were numerous smaller Mongolian blue spots on the back. This is a normal racial characteristic in a black child.

In summary, Chantelle is a normal child though somewhat below the average in height and in her motor development. She is, however, within the limits of normal in both aspects and, given optimal opportunities for living, I believe that she will continue to catch up.

OPINION

Chantelle Beckford is a child who comes from a violent background and has suffered severe child abuse – both physical and emotional. This statement is based on the written reports of Miss Alix Causby (Guardian ad Litem) and Dr Kathryn Morgan; and conversations with her foster mother, Miss Gun Wahlstrom (Social Worker) and Miss Causby.

She has now spent nearly six months in the warm atmosphere provided by her foster mother and family which has caused her development to catch up, although she is still a clinging, insecure child who is shorter than the average for her age.

Both her parents come from deprived and violent backgrounds and have suffered greatly. This accounts for their physical and emotional abuse of their children. In view of the length of time they were deprived and abused and their subsequent behaviour to their children, I see no chance of a change.

Miss Lorrington states that she has broken her relationship with Mr Beckford but that does not mean that there is no risk that Mr Beckford will seek out Miss Lorrington and her children.

Miss Lorrington has already had relationships with two violent men and I would expect her to choose similar men in the future because this pattern is seldom broken. She failed to protect her children from Mr Beckford's attacks nor did she ask for help from that available. Particularly unusual is that she did not take the children to hospital when she knew the risk to their lives.

Miss Lorrington is clearly a very dependent person and I do not believe she could cope on her own with the children nor protect them from future attacks should these occur.

In view of the extreme risks and the suffering Chantelle has already undergone, I consider a Care Order is needed to protect her safety and her emotional development. It is essential that she is brought up with her sister Louise and I hope that both children can be adopted by parents who can provide for these needs.

REPORT OF DR HUGH JOLLY MA MD FRCP DCH
HONORARY CONSULTANT PAEDIATRICIAN
CHARING CROSS HOSPITAL

LOUISE BECKFORD (born 27.5.81)

On the instructions of Messrs Hodders, Solicitors, I examined this child on 20th November, 1984, in the presence of her foster mother and her social worker, Miss Gun Wahlstrom. I had previously studied the relevant documents relating to her family history and herself which I will not repeat since they are available to the Court.

I found Louise to be undersized with the following measurements.

Height 92.5 cm (50th percentile − 96.8 cm)
Weight 13.7 kg (50th percentile − 15.2 kg)
Head circumference 52.1 cm (Mean 50.1 cm ± 1.45)

These figures place her height and weight to be well below the 25th percentile and nearer the 10th percentile.

Her speech was immature but she was friendly and active in a superficial manner. She tended to flit from one toy to another without evidence of being able to concentrate in her play for the length of time one would expect in an average child of this age.

Her general health was satisfactory, the mouth and throat being clear and the heart, lungs and abdomen normal.

Louise is retarded in her development and her behaviour is of a superficial nature. Her foster mother told me that she behaves well towards Chantelle so long as Chantelle is not crying. If she is crying she will hit her, put her fingers in her eyes and tell her foster mother to hit and to kick her.

This very pathological behaviour is rare and is evidence of the emotional and physical trauma to which both children have been subjected.

Louise is in urgent need of a permanent and loving home. It is most important that she remains with her sister and is helped to love and to react normally to her. If she were separated from Chantelle she might never achieve a normal relationship with her so that both children would continue to interact abnormally.

It is my hope that the children will be adopted by a family who can be helped to supply these needs.

APPENDIX G:1

RECIPIENT ....

THE ROYAL BOROUGH OF KENSINGTON AND CHELSEA SOCIAL SERVICES DEPARTMENT

MINUTES OF NON-ACCIDENTAL INJURY TO CHILDREN

CASE CONFERENCE ON   LOUISE AND JASMINE BECKFORD

HELD ON   6th August 1981 AT   ST CHARLES HOSPITAL, Exmoor St, W10

FAMILY STRUCTURE

Mother – Miss Beverley Lorrington, age 22
Father – Mr Lord Livingstone Maurice Beckford, age 21
Jasmine – d.o.b.   2.12.79
Louise – d.o.b.   21.5.81

Address: 1030, Harrow Rd, Kensal Green NW10

PRESENT

Mr David Bishop, Area Manager, Area 6 Brent Health Social Services (Chairman)
Mrs Diane Dietmann, Senior Social Worker, Area 6 Brent Social Services
Miss Gunn Whalstron, Social Worker, Area 6 Brent Social Services
Mr J Hobbs, Court Officer, Brent Social Services
Detective Sergeant Crockor, CID Kilburn Police
Mr John Stachan, Detective Chief Inspector, Kilburn Police
Miss MacAree, WPC, Juveile Bureau, Wembley
Mr K D Jenkins, G.O., N.S.P.C.C.
Miss J E Knowles, Health Visitor, Mortimer Road Clinic
Miss Muriel Broad, NO/HV, Crawford Avenue Health Clinic
Dr Nicola Wood, SHO Paediatrics, St Charles Hospital
Dr G Supramaniam, Senior Registrar, Paediatrics, St Charles Hospital
Dr A F Abdulla, SHO Orthopaedics, St Charles Hospital
Miss M P Richie, Ward Sister, Peter Pan, St Charles Hospital
Dr Warner, Consultant paediatrician, St Charles Hospital
Miss Sue Knibbs, Senior Social Worker, St Charles Hospital

APOLOGIES

Dr Malik G.P.
A.H.A. Child Health Specialist

PURPOSE OF CONFERENCE

To determine the cause of injury to the children, and to decide on the action to be taken.

PRESENT SITUATION

LOUISE BECKFORD

DR NICOLA WOOD said that on Saturday 1st August, Louise Beckford was brought to Casualty by her mother. The child had a severe swelling of the left upper arm and Dr Wood admitted her straight away to Peter Pan Ward. Her mother said that she had first noted the swelling on the previous Wednesday 29th July on getting Louise up in the morning. She could offer no explanation for the swelling.

DR SUPRAMANIAM says that he examined the child on Monday 3rd August. The X-Ray examination showed a spiral fracture of the left humerus. On further examination he also saw haemorrhages in the right eye. The presence of these haemorrhages was subsequently confirmed by the ophthalmologist. There were no other njuries or bruising on the rest of the body and a skeletal survey showed no abnormalities. The mother stuck to the story that she had not noticed the swelling until 29th July. She had bathed the arm with cold, salt water but the swelling had become worse and eventually she had decided to seek medical advice bringing the child to St Charles. DR SUPRAMANIAM says that he thought the injury would most likely have been caused by a yanking, twisting action.

JASMINE

DR. ABDULLA said that the child had been brought to Casualty by both parents at about 3.30 pm on Tuesday 4th August. The parents stated that they had noticed swelling of the child's left upper leg that morning on getting her out of bed. The child had been able to stand on her leg but could not walk. X-Ray showed a subtrochanteric fracture of the left femur. There was some bruising over the site of the facture but no other injuries. He could not tell exactly when the injury had occurred as it was difficult to tell with an injury of this type exactly when it might have happened. The injury could have been caused by a fall downstairs, but, at the same time the parents had said that the child was playing after the fall which could not have happened with an injury of this type.

SISTER RITCHIE stated that she had that morning, received a verbal report from the Radiologist saying that there was no sign of any other bone injury to Jasmine.

DR SUPRAMANIAM said that this type of injury was unusual for a child of this age and thought it was most unusual for two children to be brought into hospital with such injuries at the same time. He thought that Jasmine's injury would require a very strong force, stronger than a kick. DR WARNER said that the injuries to both children were major with considerable force being needed to cause them. He said that the retinal haemorrhage in Louise would have occurred with shaking and he confirmed that there was no doubt that the injuries to Louise were non-accidental.

SUE KNIBBS said that she had interviewed Miss Lorrington, the mother of the children with Dr Supramaniam on Monday 3rd August at about 4.30 pm. It seemed that Miss Lorrington had not visited very much since Saturday, and when she had come had only stayed briefly. The concern of hospital staff over the injury to Louise was explained to Miss Lorrington. She again gave the explanation of finding Louise with a swollen arm on the morning of the 29th July and repeated the assertion that she thought that the child had 'slept on it badly'. She had tried bathing the arm but as the swelling had become worse she had brought the child into the hospital.

She had complained about the housing situation, about being in one room, and said that she had made efforts to do something about this. SUE KNIBBS had said it was essential that the father of the children should come to the hospital and Miss Lorrington was quite willing to arrange to bring him the following day, 4th August at 5 pm.

Miss Knibbs said that on the 4th August the parents were somewhat late for the interview but explained that they had been in the Casualty Department with Jasmine who had broken her leg. This was the first that Sue Knibbs and Dr Supramaniam had heard of the injury to Jasmine. The parents were not able to give any very clear account of any incident but mother did say that the child had been playing on the stairs while Miss Lorrington had been in the kitchen. She heard the child cry and found that she had fallen down the stairs. SUE KNIBBS said she asked both parents whether Jasmine had been playing after her fall and they had said that Jasmine had been playing quite happily that evening and that they had not noticed anything wrong with her until they had seen the swelling the following morning. The parents had complained at considerable length about the housing, stating that they were in one room which was very unsatisfactory. DR SUPRAMANIAM had asked the parents whether they had played with Louise in a rough manner and Mr Beckford had said that he would sometimes play with Louise throwing her up and catching her. He seemed to seize on this idea and stated that he was certain that this was how the injury to Louise must have happened, he said that as far as Jasmine was concerned he had not been there when she had had the fall down the stairs.

The family live in a privately rented bed-sitter in Harrow Road. The parnets have said that they had to share kitchen, bathroom and toilet facilities with the other residents in the house, but in fact there was only one other resident in the house at the time (the Landlord). Miss Lorrington commented rather bitterly that when she was pregnant with Louise she had been told by the Housing Department that she would be re-housed once the baby was born, but that nothing had happened.

SUE KNIBBS said that Miss Lorrington told her that her own mother had left the family when Miss Lorrington was very young, and she was brought up by her father and step-mother whom she described as 'a hard woman'. She has a half-sister and a half-brother. Miss Lorrington ran away from home when she was seventeen and set up house with Mr Beckford when she was nineteen. She has no contact with her family who live in Perivale. Mr Beckford is the third child in a family of eight, he came to this country in 1969 from Jamaica when he was nine years old. Mr Beckford said that his father left home when he was fourteen and he then went into care as he said that his mother was unable to manage the children. Mr Beckford said that his father is now in America but his mother lives in Neasden and he has contact with her.

SUE KNIBBS said that her impression of the parents was that their story was rather vague and a little uncertain. For instance, when she had pressed Mr Beckford as to the date when Louise's injury had been noticed he had said it was on Monday and Lorrington quickly corrected him to Wednesday. Sue Knibbs thought that Miss Lorrington was brighter than Mr Beckford and felt that Miss Lorrington probably manipulated him.

SUE KNIBBS said that in view of the concern of the medical staff and herself about the causes of the injuries to the two children, she took a place of safety order on the evening of Tuesday 4th August. This order runs for fourteen days.

JUDY KNOWLES confirmed the very poor housing conditions of the family. She had first met Miss Lorrington in October 1980 and had felt then Miss Lorrington was emotionally very flat. However, she attended the clinic regularly and appeared to appreciated the support received. JUDY KNOWLES said that Jasmine was of normal development mentally but that her weight was low and she felt that the child was under-stimulated. Judy Knowles said that she had noticed that Miss Lorrington was very impatient with her boyfriend, Mr Beckford, and she also seemed to be impatient with

Jasmine on occasions. She did not seem to have much idea on how to handle the child emotionally.

MR JENKINS said that the family of Mr Beckford became known to the N.S.P.C.C. on 13th June 1972. The case was referred by the police because of an excessively severe beating of Mr Beckford and his sister. This had been caused by the mother beating the children with wire. Investigations showed that Mr Beckford was, at that time, living in the shed in the garden of the family house where he had only a small space to occupy. Both children were taken into care and police action was taken against the parents.

WPC MACAREE said that on 10th May 1972, both Mr Beckford and his sister Angela were remanded for stealing from their own home. It was possible that this incident had caused the mother to beat the children.

MR JENKINS passed round photographs of the injuries to Lord Livingstone Maurice Beckford and Angela Beckford, together with photographs of the garden shed in which Mr Beckford was living at that time.

GUNN WHALSTRON said that Miss Lorrington had telephoned her the previous day, 5th August, and had come to see her on the afternoon of that day. She was asking for help with her housing problem. She seemed rather unemotional and did not mention Louise or Jasmine. Gunn Whalstron pointed out that those children were in hospital with serious injuries and that there was to be a case conference and the police would be involved. Miss Lorrington became very upset at the mention of police involvement and began to cry when she was told that a place of safety order had been taken. She still maintains that the injuries were accidental.

MR RITCHIE said that mother appeared to have quite a good relationship with Jasmine while Jasmine had been in hospital, but that she had not visited very frequently or for very long.

DAVID BISHOP asked if the injuries to Louise had been caused on the same or separate occasions. Dr Supramaniam said it was unlikely to be two separate injuries as there would most probably be other evidence of bruising, which there was not. On the other hand the child was dark skinned and bruising was therefore difficult to see.

In reply to a question from the Chairman, DR WARNER said that medically Louise was ready to return home but that Jasmine would need to stay in hospital on traction for several weeks. In reply to a further question he also said that no fear had been indicated by either child towards the parents.

DETECTIVE CHIEF INSPECTOR STACHAN said that the police would want to make further investigations of the injuries to the children and would want to interview both parents. From what he had heard it was possible that charges of grievous bodily harm could be brought.

It was agreed that the injuries to Louise were certainly non-accidental. There was some doubt about the injury to Jasmine as this could have been caused by an accidental fall. However the occurrence of the two injuries so close in time was extremely worrying, and, in view of this and the disturbed histories of both parents and their inability to give adequate explanations for the injuries, the children should not be returned home pending further investigations.

DECISIONS

ACTION BY

(1) The names of both children should be placed on Brent Social Services child abuse register.

GUNN WHALSTRON

(2) The children should be retained in hospital pending further investiaton.

(3) An interim care order should be sought by Brent Social Services, at the Inner London Juvenile Court on Monday 17th August

MR J HOBBS

(4) The police to interview the parents with a view to bringing further charges

DCI STACHAN

(5) The key working in the case will be Gunn Whalstron

GUNN WHALSTRON

(6) The case conference will re-convene on Thursday 20th August at 9.30 am at St Charles Hospital

(7) The mother should be encouraged to live in hospital with the children so that her relationship with them could be observed

GUNN WHALSTON/ SISTER RICHIE

Signature: ....
CHAIRMAN

APPENDIX G:2

RECIPIENT ....

THE ROYAL BOROUGH OF KENSINGTON AND CHELSEA SOCIAL SERVICES DEPARTMENT

MINUTES OF NON-ACCIDENTAL INJURY TO CHILDREN

2nd CASE CONFERENCE ON   LOUISE AND JASMINE BECKFORD

HELD ON   20th August 1981 AT   ST CHARLES HOSPITAL, W10

FAMILY STRUCTURE

> Mother – Miss Beverley Lorrington, age 22
> Father – Mr Lord Livingstone Maurice Beckford, age 21
> Jasmine – d.o.b.   2.12.79
> Louise – d.o.b.   21.5.81

Address: 1030, Harrow Rd, NW10

PRESENT

> Mr David Bishop, Area Manager, Area 6 Brent S.S.D. 27 Harlesden Rd, NW 10 (Chairman)
> Miss M J Tyler, Nursing Officer, Health Visiting, Craven Pk H/C, Shakespeare Cres. NW10.
> Miss Gunn Wahlstron, Social Worker, Brent Area 6, 27 Harlesden Road, NW10
> Mrs Diane Dietmann, Sen. Social Worker, Brent Area 6, 27 Harlesden Road, NW10
> Mr Jim Hobbs, Court Officer, Brent House, 349 High Road, Wembley, Middx.
> Mrs. Carol Rogers, Sen. Social Worker, Adoption & Foster Care, 349 High Road, Wembley, Middx.
> Mr J H Crocker, Police Officer, Kilburn Police Station, Salusbury Road, NW6
> Dr John Warner, Consultant Paediatrician, St Charles Hospital, W10
> Miss Sue Knibbs, Senior Social Worker, St. Charles Hospital, W10
> Miss Judy Knowles, Health Visitor, Mortimer Road Clinic, NW10
> Miss M.P. Ritchie, Ward Sister, St. Charles Hospital, W10
> Dr. N. Wood, Senior House Officer, Paediatrics, St. Charles Hospital, W10.

APOLOGIES

> Dr D. Mallik, 45 St. Johns Avenue, NW10

PURPOSE OF CONFERENCE

To review the decisions which were made at the original case conference, to check the minutes for accuracy, and to discuss the next move.

PRESENT SITUATION

MR BISHOP: Said that the children were both placed on register NAI.1. Both Louise and Jasmine have stayed in hospital. An interim care order was sought and obtained, and the hearing for a full care order will be heard at Willesden Juvenile Court on the 9th September, 1981, at 10.00 a.m.

DET. SGT. CROCKER: Had visited the flat, which he found relatively neat, though the building was dirty. Photographs which were taken are not yet available. When he spoke to Miss Lorrington on the 1st August about Jasmine, she mentioned a missing bannister at the top of the half flight of stairs, wide enough for a child to get through. It would have been possible for her to have fallen through. The stairs themselves, however, are well carpeted with underlay, and should not therefore have caused injury.

Det. Sgt. Crocker spoke to both parents about Louise, who admitted that on the 30th or 31st July Mr. Beckford had shaken her, holding her around the ribs, and both said they thought her arm had been broken by the shaking. When told this was not possible, neither could offer another explanation – Louise has not been in the care of anyone else except to say that Mr Beckford has thrown her up in the air, and held her on his knees by the wrists. He seemed not to comprehend the lack of muscle control in a baby's neck. Miss Lorrington took Louise to Dr. Malik, GP, on 1st August, who referred them to St Mary's, W9, from where they were sent to St. Charles. With regard to Jasmine Miss Lorrington repeated her original story that she thought she fell down the stairs; Mr. Beckford was not at home at the time. Det. Sgt. Crocker spoke to Miss Lorrington's friend, Olive Maclean, yesterday morning, who is also godmother to Louise. She visited the parents on the 2nd August, and believes Jasmine to have had the injuries then. The parents, however, say it happened on the Monday, 3rd August, but deny slapping her on the leg; they say she fell or jumped down the stairs. In view of this Mr Beckford was charged last night with causing actual bodily harm to Louise. He is on bail and will be appearing at Willesden Magistrates Court on 28th August, represented by Paddington Law Centre. Dr Malik saw Jasmine in his surgery on August 4th, and it was obvious to him then that her leg was broken. According to Olive, Miss Lorrington had said "Please don't send them to St. Charles, because that lot down there accuse us of baby-bashing".

DR. WARNER: Said that with regard to Louise's retinal haemorrhages, these do not harm the vision, although there might be underlying haemorrhages within the skull.

SISTER RITCHIE: Said she felt that both parents had spent the normal amount of time visiting the hospital that could have been expected of them, but obviously felt over-powered by the doctors and nurses. However, Miss Lorrington seems to have little understanding of very small children, and makes no attempt to play with Jasmine or cuddle Louise.

MISS WAHLSTROM: Saw Miss Lorrington after the first case conference, and encouraged her to say at the hospital as much as possible. She also found the flat to be neatly kept and very well furnished. Both parents said if they had had better housing the accidents would not have happened. Miss Lorrington spoke about her background, repeating much that she had told Miss Knibbs previously. It also emerged that at the age of 4 a boy had shot an arrow at her injuring her eye which was replaced by a glass one, and she had never forgiven her father for not having obtained better treatment for her. She had attended Woodfield School in Kingsbury for the educationally sub-normal when aged 14, and it was there that she wet Mr. Beckford. He found the flat in Harrow Road and Miss Lorrington moved in about 2½ years ago. She had worked as a machinist and her last job lasted two years when she left to have Jasmine. Mr. Beckford has held his job for seven years. Miss Wahlstrom said that both parents say the other cares for the child well, that they love them and want them back, but they do not seem to have grasped the seriousness of what has happened. There are no relatives or friends around to give them any help and support.

MR HOBBS: Said that proceedings have been commenced on Louise and Jasmine on the grounds that they were ill-treated, and he thinks it will be possible to obtain care orders on both children. The parents can immediately appeal against a care order, however, if one is made, and can apply for a discharge after a period of time, and then every three months if they wish.

DR. WARNER: Said that Louise was ready to be discharged from hospital, although Jasmine would have to remain for a maximum of six weeks from the time of injury. Although he was happy for both children to remain, it would be desirable for Louise to leave hospital, due to the ever-present risk of infection to a young baby in a children's ward.

CAROL ROGERS: Said that both children could be fostered in Harlesden almost immediately

Louise to be discharged from hospital as soon as possible, preferably into the home where she is going to be on a long-term basis, and where Jasmine can join her. There were a number of reservations expressed about the suitability of the proposed Harlesden foster home, which is known to Area 6.

DECISIONS	ACTION BY
1. Miss Wahlstron will speak to the parents to acquaint them with the decisions of today's meeting	G.W.
2. Brent, Area 6, to organise any review case conferences from now on. A smaller meeting will be adequate, and only those will be invited that it is felt necessary should attend.	
3. Jasmine will be followed up from an orthopaedic point of view. Subsequent follow-ups for Louise could be done at the local Health Centre.	

DISTRIBUTION

Mr. Bishop
Miss Tyler
Mr. Hobbs
Mrs. Rogers
Det. Sgt. Crocker
Dr. Warner
Miss Kibbs
Miss Knowles
Dr. Mallik

Signature ....
CHAIRMAN

APPENDIX G:3
STATUTORY CASE REVIEW HELD ON 9th DECEMBER 1981
LONDON BOROUGH OF BRENT – SOCIAL SERVICES DEPARTMENT

REVIEW FORM

1.   Louise BECKFORD   2.   Date of Birth: 27.5.81   Section: 1 1969 Act

2.   Since 26.8.81   Placed at: Mr & Mrs Probert
12a Primrose Close,
South Harrow, Middx

4.   Date received into care and reason: 4.8.81 5.   Reason why now in care, if different
Development prevented and ill-treated

6.   Previous placements (type and number): St. Charles Hospital

7.   School/Employment: N/A   8.   Wages, if employed: N/A

9.   Progress at school or in employment: N/A

10.   Health and physique: Has put on weight and developed very well.

11.   (a) Date last medical examination   17.11.81   12.   Date last dental
(b) Were any comments made?   examination:

13.   Interests, leisure activities and friends:

14.   Reglious upbringing: Baptized R.C; parents Rastafarians.

15.   (a) Condition of home Very Good   (b) fireguard, etc.: N/A
(c) Any change in sleeping accommodation since last review (if first review, describe)
Louise sleeps in a cot in Mr. & Mrs. Probert's bedroom.
(d) Any change in household since last review (if first review, please list occupants overleaf)

16.   Clothing: Good   17.   Pocket money: N/A

18.   General observations on progress and behaviour, suitability of present placing, and
information about contact with (a) parents, (b) brothers and sisters, (c) any other relatives:
Louise is a happy child who enjoys her own company as well as adult attention. She recognises
her sister Jasmine and there is a close bond between them.

a) Contact with parents has been once a week for two hours at Treetops, Under 5's centre.
Louise has been crying a great deal during these visits for various reasons – tired, hungry, wet,
constipated, change of routine.

19.   Date of visit: 2.12.81   Was child seen? Yes   Date of previous visit: 24.11.81

20.   Have statutory requirements and committee instructions regarding visits and
reviews been fulfilled?

Date   7.12.81   Signed   Gun Wahlstrom
Supervising Officer

Name: Louise BECKFORD

21. General observations, present family situation and plans for future:

Both Mr. Beckford and Miss Lorrington have met with Jasmine and Louise at Treetops Under 5's Centre, once a week as arranged. Apart from this Miss Lorrington has spent an hour or so with the Family Aide at Treetops. Miss Lorrington has made few friends and there appears to be no close friend with whom she can confide in. Mothers at the Under 5's Centre have made efforts to communicate with Miss Lorrington, but she has responded inappropriately.

Mr. Beckford is still employed and works longer hours than previously. He is now responsible for locking up after the cleaners have left the premises in the evening.

Mr. Beckford has still very high expectations of his children as well as of his co-habitee.

Miss Lorrington finds it difficult to talk to and play with her children and rarely sees to both children at once.

Jasmine and Louise are very well settled with the foster parents, Mr. & Mrs. Proberts. The children have developed well.

Date   9.12.81   Signed   Gun Wahlstrom

                                   Designation   Social Worker

22. Review: Action recommended, if any:

1) To continue with parental contact once per week but change the venue from Treetops to parental home; visits to last for four hours; Gun Wahlstrom or Dorothy Ruddock to supervise.

2) Miss Lorrington to spend Wednesday and Thursday mornings at Treetops with Dorothy Ruddock in order to develop skills in parenting as well as relationships with other adults.

3) Gun Wahlstrom to meet with Mr Beckford and Miss Lorrington once a fortnight to try to enable them to talk about their relationship, parenting, why the children are in care and other problems.

Date: 19.1.82   Signed: David Bishop
                                   Supervising Officer

REVIEW FORM

1.   Jasmine BECKFORD   2.   Date of Birth: 2.12.79   Section: 1 1969 Act

2.   Since 14.9.811   Placed at: Mr & Mrs Probert
                                        12a Primrose Close, South Harrow, Middx

4.   Date received into care and reason: 4.8.81 5.   Reason why now in care, if different
     Development prevented and ill-treated

6.   Previous placements (type and number): St. Charles Hospital

7.   School/Employment: N/A   8.   Wages, if employed: N/A

9.   Progress at school or in employment: N/A

10. Health and physique: Good, has developed very well; put on weight

11. (a) Date last medical examination   17.11.81   12.   Date last dental
     (b) Were any comments made?   examination:

13. Interests, leisure activities and friends:

14. Reglious upbringing: Baptized R.C; parents Rastafarians.

15. (a) Condition of home Very Good   (b) fireguard, etc.: N/A
     (c) Any change in sleeping accommodation since last review (if first review, describe)
     Jasmine sleeps in a cot in the same room as Michelle (Mr & Mrs Probert's adoptive 13 year old
     daughter)
     (d) Any change in household since last review (if first review, please list occupants overleaf)

16. Clothing: Good   17.   Pocket money: N/A

18. General observations on progress and behaviour, suitability of present placing, and
     information about contact with (a) parents, (b) brothers and sisters, (c) any other relatives:
     Jasmine has changed a great deal since her stay in hospital. She is no longer frustrated and
     jealous of her younger sister. Jasmine is eager to help with chores and does not forget what
     she is asked to do. She enjoys playing with her toys. She is very close to Louise and makes sure
     that she is alright.

     a) Contact with parents has been once a week for two hours at Treetops, Under 5s Centre. At
     first Jasmine showed signed of distress when she saw her father. This is no longer so.

19. Date of visit: 2.12.81   Was child seen? Yes   Date of previous visit: 24.11.81

20. Have statutory requirements and committee instructions regarding visits and
     reviews been fulfilled?   Yes

     Date   7.12.81   Signed   Gun Wahlstrom
                                   Supervising Officer

Name: Jasmine BECKFORD

21. General observations, present family situation and plans for future:

Both Mr. Beckford and Miss Lorrington have met with Jasmine and Louise at Treetops Under 5's Centre, once a week as arranged.

Miss Lorrington has also spent one hour a week with a Family Aide at Treetops. Apart from the hours Miss Lorrington has been asked to spend at Treetops she has arrived with the minibus in the mornings and spent several hours there. However, she has made few friends and there appears to be no close friend with whom she can talk. Mothers at the Centre have made efforts to communicate with Miss Lorrington, but she has responded inappropriately.

Mr. Beckford is still employed but he works longer hours and is now responsible for locking up after the cleaners have left in the evening.

Date   Signed   Gun Walhstrom

                              Designation   Social Worker

22. Review: Action recommended, if any:

1) To continue with parental contact once per week but change the venue from Treetops to parental home; visits to last for four hours; Gun Wahlstrom or Dorothy Ruddock to supervise.

2) Miss Lorrington to spend Wednesday and Thursday mornings at Treetops with Dorothy Ruddock in order to develop skills in parenting as well as relationships with other adults.

3) Gun Wahlstrom to meet with Mr Beckford and Miss Lorrington once a fortnight to try to enable them to talk about their relationship, parenting, why the children are in care and other problems.

Date: 19.1.82   Signed: David Bishop
                              Supervising Officer

APPENDIX G:4

CASE CONFERENCE ON LOUISE & JASMINE BECKFORD
ON 5th APRIL 1982

Present: Jim Hobbs, Court Section   **Apologies:** A.F.C.S
            Dorothy Ruddock, Family Aide   Mortimer Road, D.N.
            Pamela Gordon, Green Lodge
            Diane Dietmann, S.S.W.
            Gun Wahlstrom, S.W.
            David Bishop, Area Manager

Purpose:

To review situation regarding the children. Given agreement re the degree of success of the rehabilitation programme, plan return home and input on return.

Gun:

Gave historical background. First known to Social Services Department July '81 – referred by Health Visitor and M.P. – housing problems. Little input by S.S.D., supported housing application then closed.

August '81 referred by St. Charles Hospital. Louise admitted to hospital with fractured L. arm and eye damage. Jasmine with fractured femur admitted a few days later. S.S.D. became involved again.

Louise in hospital for 3 weeks – Jasmine 6 weeks. Jasmine very miserable in hospital. Mother did not avail herself of opportunity to stay in hospital with the children; did not seem to know how to play with kids or mother them in this setting.

9.9.81   Care Order obtained. Magistrates emphasised their concern that every effort should be made to rehabilitate the children with their parents. Children placed with foster parents. Plan made for weekly access at Under 5s Centre (Treetops). Morris stiff in his handling of the children and Beverley also unrelaxed. They improved through taking advice from Dorothy (F.A.) and Gun (S.W.) about play and general handling of children. Key influence was the F.A. They tended to avoid Gun. Gradually Beverley unfroze and began talking about her problem, relationship with Morris etc. They both responded eventually to the encouragement to discuss things.

Review in December agreed to supervise home access weekly for 4 hours per visit. Gun shared supervision with Dorothy. Visits very much better. Parents relaxed, shared in the child care - changing nappies, feeding, playing with the children. Morris' change in attitude is particularly remarkable. He previously was restrained, treated them as property. Now appears to enjoy them and treating them as individuals, doing things with them, talks to them. Both parents do this now. Jasmine much more settled. Foster parents have helped Jasmine to relate to the baby and this has been carried on by the parents.

Dorothy:

Beverley now talking to the baby, now sees the sense in this.

Gun:

Beverley now realises the limitations of the child's understanding.

Dorothy:
Morris also has learned to talk to Jasmine as a child.

Gun:
Beverley and Morris have visitors so are not as isolated as they were previously. Also are communicating with each other.

Family Aide has encouraged them to talk to each other, and Beverley has learned through relating to Family Aide to talk to others.

David B:
Summary of Changes

Diane:
Beverley enjoying life more now.
Morris changing too and improving.
Rehoused into very adequate 3 bedroomed house with garden last month to College Road.

Gun:
Morris' boss is very helpful.
Morris very patient recently over delays in getting attention at Housing Department.
Beverley and Morris able to communicate. Beverley able to tell Morris how she feels. Less isolated; friends call in and Morris and Beverley go out at times.

Gun & Diane:
Asked if they have any reservations . . . Diane – "they do not have the kids 24 hours per day, 7 days per week so their behaviour cannot be predicted."

Diane:
They are aware that the children would come home under strict supervision.
Morris – his expectations may still be unrealistic under certain circumstances.
Rehabilitation to continue with adequate safeguards.
NEXT STEP – The children are placed with foster parents in S. Harrow and there needs to be an opportunity for Beverley and Morris to get to know the kids more intensively and the foster parents relationship to be terminated.
Suggested plan. Transfer from foster parents to Green Lodge residential day nursery where Beverley can spend most of the day caring for them there.
Need for Family Aide and Social Worker to work with family while children are at home.
At the end of first week decision will be made about next step in the return process which will be overnight stay and return home.
Both parents aware of difficulties the children will have in re-adjusting.
Place at Mortimer Road D.N. 5 mornings per week for Jasmine. She will be seen by speech therapist there.
Beverley will be expected to go to Treetops which she is likely to look forward to.

1.
N.A.I. – to remain on register.

2.

Key workers – Family Aide & Social Worker who will organise intensive visiting with children return home.

3.

H.V. to be Judy Noble who will continue to liaise with key workers. Judy will have to transfer them to Miss Leong in July when she leaves. Beverley to be encouraged to attend Clinic monthly and H.V. to visit about fortnightly.

4.

Children to go to Green Lodge on Tuesday 13th April and will be reviewed the following Monday (19th April).

5.

N.A.I. review 1 month after the children go home.

6.

If the plans fail in the short term children will go to S/T foster parents with a view to eventual L/T placement with foster parents which may lead to adoption. (Not present foster parents).

DAVID BISHOP
6/DGB/JR

APPENDIX G:5

STATUTORY CASE REVIEW HELD ON 25th MAY 1982

LONDON BOROUGH OF BRENT – SOCIAL SERVICES DEPARTMENT

REVIEW FORM (CHILDREN IN CARE)

(Pages 1 & 2 to be completed by Area or AFCS prior to review case conference and circulated to all present at review).

1. Name: Louise Beckford   2. Date of Birth   27.05.81
         Jasmine Beckford   2.12.79

3. Date received into care: Act, section & reason (include previous care episodes) 1969 Sec. 1
   9.9.81 Sec. 1, 1969 Act; Development prevented and ill-treated

4. Current legal status & reason why now in care, if different from above:

5. Currently boarded-out or placed with: N/A   Since:

6. ALL previously placements, with dates:
   26.8.81 to 13.4.82 Fosterparents
   13.4.82 to 19.4.82 Green Lodge, Barretts Green Road, London NW10

Social Worker   G. Wahlstrom   Since 5.8.81

Senior Social Worker   D. Dietmann   Since 5.8.81

Record of visits by social worker since last review:

Dates	Venue	Who was seen (including child)			
5.4.82	57 College Road	Morris Beckford & Beverley Lorrington			
8.4.82	"	Beverley Lorrington + Jasmine + Louise			
13.4.82	Green Lodge	"	"	"	
14.4.82	"	"	"	"	
19.4.82	57 College Road	"	"	"	
20.4.82	57 College Road	"	"	"	+M.B.
21.4.82	"	"	"	"	
22.4.82	"/D.N.	"	"	"	
23.4.82	57 College Road	"	"	"	
24.4.82	"	"	"	"	+ M.B.
29.4.82	"	"	"	"	
4.5.82	"	"	"	"	
5.5.82	Mortimer Rd, D.N.	Jasmine not in			
5.5.82	57 College Road	Beverley Lorrington + Jasmine + Louise			
10.5.82	"	"	"	"	
10.5.82	Mortimer Rd, D.N.	"	"	"	

...../... P.T.O.

4.5.82	57 College Road	Beverley Lorrington + Jasmine + Louise
5.5.82	Mortimer Rd, D.N.	Jasmine not in
5.5.82	57 College Rd	Beverley Lorrington + Jasmine + Louise
10.5.82	"	" " "
10.5.82	Mortimer Rd, D.N.	" " "
20.5.82	"	Jasmine
20.5.82	57 College Rd.	Beverley Lorrington, Morris Beckford, Jasmine + Louise
21.5.82	57 College Rd.	Beverley Lorrington + Louise

7. Progress on recommendations from last review   5.4.82

1. Louise & Jasmine remained on N.A.I. Register.
2. Keyworkers (Family Aide + S.W.) did organize intensive visiting when children went home.
3. Judy Knowles (H/V) and S.W. have liaised and Judy Knowles has started to see Miss Lorrington and children.
4. Children moved to Green Lodge on the 13th April. Reviewed on the 19th April. Children moved home-on-trial.
5. N.A.I. review one month after the children moved home – 25/5/82.

LONDON BOROUGH OF BRENT – SOCIAL SERVICES DEPARTMENT

REVIEW FORM (CHILDREN IN CARE)

(Pages 1 & 2 to be completed by Area or AFCS prior to review case conference and circulated to all present at review).

1. Name: Jasmine Beckford   2. Date of Birth   02.12.1979

3. Date received into care: Act, section & reason (include previous care episodes)
   9.9.81 Sec. 1, 1969 Act; Development prevented and ill-treated

4. Current legal status & reason why now in care, if different from above:

5. Currently boarded-out or placed with: N/A   Since:

6. ALL previously placements, with dates:
   14.9.81-13.4.82: Foster Parents
   13.4.82-19.4.82: Green Lodge, Barretts Green Road, London NW10

Social Worker   G. Wahlstrom   Since   5.8.81

Senior Social Worker   D. Dietmann   Since   5.8.81

Record of visits by social worker since last review:

Dates	Venue	Who was seen (including child)			
5.4.82	57 College Road	Morris Beckford & Beverley Lorrington			
8.4.82	"	Beverley Lorrington and Jasmine and Louise			
13.4.82	Green Lodge	"	"	"	
14.4.82	"	"	"	"	
19.4.82	57 College Road	"	"	"	
20.4.82	57 College Road	"	"	"	+M.B.
21.4.82	"	"	"	"	
22.4.82	" /D.N.	"	"	"	
23.4.82	57 College Road	"	"	"	
24.4.82	"	"	"	"	+ M.B.
29.4.82	"	"	"	"	
4.5.82	57 College Road	Beverley Lorrington + Jasmine + Louise			
5.5.82	Mortimer Rd, D.N.	Jasmine not in			
5.5.82	57 College Road	Beverley Lorrington +Jasmine + Louise			
10.5.82	"	"	"	"	
10.5.82	Mortimer Rd, D.N.	"	"	"	

.../...P.T.O.

7. Progress on recommendations from last review

5.4.82

1. Louise & Jasmine have remained on N.A.I. Register.
2. Keyworkers (Family Aide + S.W.) did organize intensive visiting when children went home.
3. Judy Knowles (H/V) and S.W. have liaised and Judy Knowles has started to see Miss Lorrington and children.
4. Children moved to Green Lodge on the 13th April. Reviewed on the 19th April. Children moved <u>home-on-trial.</u>
5. N.A.I. review one month after the children moved home – 25/5/82.

8 Social Workers' view of present situation & future plans. Specify any areas of concern.

Both Jasmine and Louise well settled and cared for at home. Jasmine enjoying the Day Nursery – No problem when arriving or leaving. Jasmine's speech is still very poor but Speech Therapist will see her when she has settle in a bit longer.

Financial commitments worrying – must be reduced to alleviate stress.

Morris Beckford and Beverley Lorrington have worked extremely hard to improve the housing situation. Morris' attitude to social work help and the children has changed in a very positive direction.

M. Beckford and B. Lorrington able to relate to each other and now enjoying each others company.

9. Parental view of present situation & future plans.

Children happy at home – Parents wish to be left to cope, with support, but without the 'Authority'·

10. Child's view of present situation & future plans.   N/A

Social Worker   G. Wahlstrom   Date   28.6.82

Senior Social Worker   D. Dietmann   Date   25.6.82

c

11   Childs name

12   Religion: Specifying practising or non-practising

13a Name of school/employment

13b Progress at school/employment

14a Wages/pocket money
 b Savings
 c Board & Lodge contribution

15   Health & physical developments: State handicaps, medication, treatments.

16a Date of last medical
 b Were any comments made?

17a Date of last dental examination
 b Were any comments made?

18   What is the quality of contacts and relationships

a   With peers:

b   With adults in the home:

c   With family of origin: State whether contact has increase/decreased and outline parental attitude to placement.

d   With others outside the home: (For example, former foster parents, residential or field staff.)

19   Significant events & developments since last review.

20   Child's view of present situation & future plans.

21   Establishment's/foster parents'/AFCS view of present situation & future plans Outline attitude to support given by Area or AFCS.

22   Are present financial arrangements satisfactory. List any special needs which may arise before the next review (e.g. holidays, clothing, equipment, etc)

Foster parent/O-in-C/
AFCS Social Worker .... Date ....

Residential Care Manager/
AFCS Senior Social Worker .... Date ....

Childs name Jasmine Beckford   Area/~~Section~~ 6
             Louise Beckford

Venue of review Area 6

Date: 25.5.82   Date of last review: 5.4.82

Name and status of all persons attending

D. Dietmann	S S W
G. Wahlstrom	S W
D. Ruddock	F A
M. Beckford	Father

23 Itemised topics covered at review

1. Finances
2. Positive changes
3. Morris' feelings about S.W. intervention.
4. Procedure regarding revocation of the care order.

24 Summary of discussion: (Describe the process of reaching decisions.)

The discussion was must less a process of reaching a decision on specifics than an opportunity for Morris to publicly announce his resentment and humiliation of the social services intervention in his 'private' life, and an attempt to set a long term goal of revocation of the care order. Morris was given time to vent his feelings and spadework done for future working relationships. Stress was laid on Beverley and Morris being involved in the decision making process of Social Services and allowing Social Services to be privy to their decision making proceesses. There were may specifics that need to be taken up with Beverley and Morris during the next 6 months as there was neither the time nor appropriate atmosphere to tackle all of Morris' feelings and Beverley was unable to attend. I felt Morris left with the idea that there was some positive reasons for what Social Services was doing and it was not just a series of irrational spying exercises. There is no concern over the care of the children nor it is felt that they are at risk in their home-on-trial.

25 Should child's legal status be changed? if so, how?   No

25a Should placement at home (Home on Trial) be considered? N/A

26 Is an "Independant Person" (Section 11, Child Care Act, 1980) required? N/A

27 Comment on child's Personal Album   N/A

28 What did the child contribute to the review?   N/A

29   Objectives (short & long term) to be pursued.

The long term objective is revocation of the care order.
Short term is to help Morris and Beverley to make rational decisions rather than emotional reactions.

30.   What action must now be taken?   By Whom?

1. Willingness to negotiate fortnightly visits   Morris Beckford
2. Weekly support   G. Wahlstom.
                                                                            D. Ruddock

31   Next Review Date: Time: Venue:

6 months time   College Road

                                                                         Date   25.4.82
Chairperson   D Dietmann

Area Manager's comments: Agree with foregoing
                                             D. Bishop

ciii

APPENDIX G:6

STATUTORY CASE REVIEW HELD ON 30th SEPTEMBER 1982
LONDON BOROUGH OF BRENT – SOCIAL SERVICES DEPARTMENT

REVIEW FORM (CHILDREN IN CARE)

(Pages 1 & 2 to be completed by Area or AFCS prior to review case conference and circulated to all present at review).

1. Name: Jasmine Beckford   2. Date of Birth   02.12.1979
           Louise Beckford   27.05.81

3. Date received into care: Act, section & reason (include previous care episodes)
   9.9.81 Sec. 1, 1969 Act; Development prevented and ill-treated

4. Current legal status & reason why now in care, if different from above:
   As above

5. Currently boarded-out or placed with: N/A   Since:

6. ALL previously placements, with dates:
   26.8.81 to 13.4.82 Fosterparents
   13.4.82 to 19.4.82 Green Lodge, Barretts Green Road, London NW10

Social Worker   G. Wahlstrom   Since   5.8.81

Senior Social Worker   D. Dietmann   Since   5.8.81

Record of visits by social worker since last review:

Dates	Venue	Who was seen (including child)
3.6.82	57 College Road	Beverley Lorrington and Louise
3.6.82	Mortimer Rd, D.N.	Jasmine
10.6.82	57 College Road	Morris Beckford and Beverley Lorrington, Louise & Jasmine
24.6.82	"	Beverley Lorrington, Louise and Jasmine
29.6.82	"	Morris Beckford, Beverley Lorrington, Louise
6.7.82	"	Beverley Lorrington, Louise and Jasmine
8.7.82	"	Morris Beckford, Beverley Lorrington & Louise
15.7.82	"	Morris Beckford, Beverley Lorrington & Louise
22.7.82	"	Beverley Lorrington, Louise and Jasmine
12.8.82	"	Beverley Lorrington, Louise and Jasmine
13.8.82	Mortimer Rd, D.N.	Jasmine
19.8.82	57 College Road	No reply
26.8.82	"	Beverley Lorrington and Louise
9.9.82	"	Beverley Lorrington
16.9.82	Mortimer Rd, D.N.	Morris Beckford, Beverley Lorrington & Louise
27.9.82	"	Jasmine
27.9.82	57 College Road	Morris Beckford, Beverley Lorrington & Louise

7. Progress on recommendations from last review

    25.5.82

    1. S.W. met with Morris Beckford and/or Beverley Lorrington on a fortnightly basis
    2. S.W. helping Morris Beckford and Beverley to make rational decisions rather than emotional reactions.
    3. Family Aide has visited on a weekly basis to give support.

8. Social Workers' view of present situation & future plan.
    Specify *any* areas of concern.

    Children well settled and cared for at home. Jasmine enjoying the Day Nursery – happy when she arrives and pleased to leave midday. Jasmine has been seen by Speech Therapist. Jasmine is behind with her speech but there is no concern.

    Financial commitments have been worrying but Morris Beckford and Beverley Lorrington now able to save money to buy essentials when needed, rather than using catalogues and HP. Court fines paid off in full.

    Morris Beckford and Beverley Lorrington have worked hard to improve their house. They are now able to relate to each other and enjoy each others company. They have outside contacts are are able to go out occasionally. Morris Beckford not happy with employers at present. Must keep job until suitable alternative work can be found.

9. Parental view of present situation & future plans.

    Parents feel that children are happy and that they are a family for the first time. Parents able to cope but grateful for support. Children to be discharged from Care at the earliest opportunity.

10. Child's view of present situation & future plans.   N/A

Social Worker   G. Wahlstrom   Date   29.9.82

Senior Social Worker   D. Dietmann   Date   28.10.82

11   Childs name

12   Religion: Specifying practising or non-practising

13a Name of school/employment

13b Progress at school/employment

14a Wages/pocket money
   b Savings
   c Board & Lodge contribution

15   Health & physical developments: State handicaps, medication, treatments.

16a Date of last medical
   b Were any comments made?

17a Date of last dental examination
   b Were any comments made?

18   What is the quality of contacts and relationships

  a With peers:

  b With adults in the home:

  c With family of origin: State whether contact has increase/decreased and outline parental attitude to placement.

  d With others outside the home: (For example, former foster parents, residential or field staff.)

19   Significant events & developments since last review.

20   Child's view of present situation & future plans.

21   Establishment's/foster parents'/AFCS view of present situation & future plans Outline attitude to support given by Area or AFCS.

22   Are present financial arrangements satisfactory. List any special needs which may arise before the next review (e.g. holidays, clothing, equipment, etc)

Foster parent/O-in-C/
AFCS Social Worker .... Date ....

Residential Care Manager/
AFCS Senior Social Worker .... Date ....

Childs name   Jasmine Beckford   Area/Section   6
                      Louise Beckford

Venue of review   Area 6

Date: 30.9.82   Date of last review: 25.5.82

Name and status of all persons attending

Diane Dietmann	Senior Social Worker
Gun Wahlström	Social Worker
Dorothy Ruddock	Family Aide
Beverley Lorrington	Mother
Louise Beckford	Child

23   Itemised topics covered at review

1. Case Conference planned for October
2. Day Nursery for Louise
3. Revocation of the care order
4. Changes in the family
5. Morris' job
6. Finances

24   Summary of discussion: (Describe the process of reaching decisions.)

Morris was unable to attend the review because his boss did not tell him he had spoken to Gun and he could go. This led to a discussion about the job and how the manager had become much stricter lately and leaving just as much work as ever. Beverley would like a Day Nursery place for Louise because she feels that she ought to get a full time job in order to help out. It was explained to Beverley about the priority assessment for a day nursery place and why Jasmine was originally given one. Essentially we were saying she is doing too well to be allocated a place for Louise but Dorothy and Gun would help her look at child care possibilities. One idea being to wait until Jasmine goes to school, which lead to a discussion about enrolling Jasmine on a waiting list.

Explained to Beverley that a case conference was being organised for late October to review the children being on the NAI Register and we would be asking that they be removed. Beverley felt she was worried about things being said behind her back and she was offered the option to come. Beverley talked about the changes that have occurred in herself, Morris and the marriage. They feel a family and are looking forward to their first christmas as a family of four.

Beverley asked about having to continue paying back to the Council the debt for the children's care assessment. This is to continue even though one recognizes how difficult it is for them to pay £10 per week.

Beverley asked when the children could come out of care and the process and timing was explained to her.

25 Should child's legal status be changed? if so, how?   Not at this time

25a Should placement at home (Home on Trial) be considered? NA

26 Is an "Independant Person" (Second 11, Child Care Act, 1980) required? NA

27 Comment on child's Personal Album   NA

28 What did the child contribute to the review?

29 Objectives (short & long term) to be pursued.

Short term goal is to promote and continue to positive changes that have occurred in this family long term goal is revocation of the care order.

30. What action must now be taken?   By Whom?

1. Fortnightly Social Worker visits to continue   GW, MB, BL
2. Weekly family aid visits to continue   DR, MB, BL
3. Jasmine's school to be looked at   DR, BL
4. Childcare arrangements and job possibility to be looked at.   GW, DR, BL
5. Playgroup/mother's and Toddlers to be organised for Louise   DR, BL
6. Case Conference Planned   GW, DD
7. Council to be paid weekly   BL, MB

31 Next Review Date: Time: Venue:

March   To be discussed with Morris to enable him to attend.

Chairperson   D Deitmann   Date   20.9.82

Area Manager's comments: D. Bishop

32a This question is designed to monitor the need for different types of placements.
Please tick row A to indicate current placement.
Please tick row B to indicate the preferred type of placement.

	Family Group Home	Foster-ing	Specialised Adolescent Unit	Working Boys/Girls Hostel	Home for Children under 10	CH(E)	Home for Mentally Handicapped Children under 12	over 12
A Current Placement								
B Preferred Placement								

Additional comments on placement
(including placement not described above)

Placed at home.

Please tick if
current placement
is a private/
voluntary home ☐

32b This question is designed to monitor the fostering/adoption placement needs

	Permanent Substitite Care		Relief Care (Short-term Fostering)	Contract Placement	Location		
	Foster Home	Adoptive Home			Brent	Other London Borough	Outside London
A Current Placement							
B Preferred Placement							

APPENDIX G:7

CASE CONFERENCE ON 9th November 1982

re: Louise and Jasmine BECKFORD
57 College Road
London, N.W.10

****

PRESENT:

Miss Proudlock	– Matron, Mortimer Road Day Nursery
Ted Gadsten	– Court Officer, Court Section
Gun Wahlstrom	– Social Worker, Area 6
Dorothy Ruddock	– Family Aid, Area 6
Diane Dietmann	– Senior Social Worker, Area 6

APOLOGIES:

Beverley Lorrington
Morris Beckford   } – Parents
Dr. Kahn   – G.P.

The purpose of the the case conference was to review Jasmine and Louise Beckford's inclusion on the N.A.I. register. The original case conferences were on the 6th and 20th August 1981 at St. Charles Hospital, where both children were, due to their injuries. The decision of these case conferences was that both children should be placed on the register, care orders sought and long-term fostering arranged. This was all done and Morris Beckford was charged and found guilty and fined. He has since paid off his fine.

From placement at the end of August, the parents had access once a week, first at Treetops and then from December 1981 at their original home on the Harrow Road. They were reliable about these visits and showed a consistent and keen intertest in, and love for their children. The parents began to work with the social worker and the Family Aid to learn parenting, communication skills and improve their marital relationship.

In March 1982, the family were offered and accepted a 3-bedroom terraced house in College Road. They worked very hard by themselves, and in conjunction with Social Services staff to redecorate, budget for household expenses and organise the care of a house versus a room.

As housing had been considered a major factor in the original stressful situation and because of the parents cooperation and improvement, a further case conference was called on 5.4.82 to discuss a home-on-trial placement. It was agreed to do this using an intensive assessment/therapeutic interlude of up to 2 weeks at Green Lodge. Both parents to begin to resume full time care of the children in a neutral environment. This was very successful and both parents coped well beyond anyone's expectations.

The children were placed home under supervision on 19.4.1982 and Jasmine was given a part-time Day Nursery place at Mortimer Road Day Nursery.

Since that time, the family as been seen at least once a week by the Family Aide and once a fortnight by the Social Worker.

The parents have:
1) Matured.
2) are coping with all aspects of parenting.
3) are no longer isolated.
4) have maintained their financial situation without current arreas.
5) have improved their marital relationship and communciation.
6) are now able to identify problems or needs and seek help appropriately.

The children have:
1) responded well to the parenting provided and no longer accept adults indiscriminately.
2) Jasmine's speech as improved and she can articulate sentences.
3) always appears well cared for.

There are no longer any signs of ongoing stress in the family. They have made enormous strides in all areas since coming into contact with this department. As no worker saw any indicators of potential problem areas, any cause for concern about the physical or emotional care of the children and the parents were continuing full co-operation with this department, it was agreed that the children could now be removed from the register as they are no longer at risk.

Diane Dietmann
Senior Social Worker.

APPENDIX G:8

STATUTORY CASE REVIEW HELD ON 18th APRIL 1983

LONDON BOROUGH OF BRENT – SOCIAL SERVICES DEPARTMENT

REVIEW FORM (CHILDREN IN CARE)

(Pages 1 & 2 to be completed by Area or AFCS prior to review case conference and circulated to all present at review).

1. **Name:** Jasmine Beckford   2.   Date of Birth   02.12.1979
   Louise Beckford   27.05.81

3. Date received into care: Act, section & reason (include previous care episodes)
   9.9.81 Sec. 1, 1969 Act; Development prevented and ill-treated

4. Current legal status & reason why now in care, if different from above:
   As above

5. Currently boarded-out or placed with: N/A   Since:

6. ALL previously placements, with dates:
   26.8.81 to 13.4.82 Fosterparents
   13.4.82 to 19.4.82 Green Lodge, Barretts Green Road, London NW10

Social Worker   G. Wahlstrom   Since   5.8.81

Senior Social Worker   D. Dietmann   Since   5.8.81

Record of visits by social worker since last review:

Dates	Venue	Who was seen (including child)
7.10.82	57 College Road	No Reply
21.10.82	"	No Reply
28.10.82	"	No Reply
1.11.82	"	Morris Beckford
4.11.82	"	Beverley L, Morris Beckford, Jasmine & Louise
5.11.82	"	Beverley L, Jasmine & Louise
12.11.82	"	Beverley L, Morris Beckford & Louise
22.11.82	"	Beverley L & Jasmine & Louise
3.12.82	"	Beverley L, Jasmine, Louise & Morris Beckford
21.12.82	"	"
10.1.83	"	No Reply
11.1.83	"	Beverley Lorrington & Louise
20.1.83	"	No Reply
26.1.83	"	Beverley Lorrington, Louise & Jasmine
15.2.83	"	Beverley Lorrington, Jasmine, Louise & Morris Beckford
21.3.83	"	Beverley Lorrington & Morris Beckford

7. Progress on recommendations from last review

   1. S.W. has continued to visit on a regular basis

   2. Weekly visits by Family Aid now stopped.

   3. Miss Lorrington organised for Jasmine to start at Princess Fredericka Primary School in January 1983

   4./5 Louise no longer clinging to mohter so Miss Lorrington no longer asking for relief from Louise

   6. Case Conference held on 9 November 1982. Decision made to remove Jasmine & Louise from NAI register.

   7. Committee agreed to waive repayments of maintenance charges.

8. Social Workers' view of present situation & future plans.
Specify *any* areas of concern.

Children well settled and cared for at home. Jasmine now attending Primary School part-time. She is progressing well but her speech is still slow – no concern.

Financial commitments no longer a worry. Morris Beckford has had a pay rise. Mr Beckford happy in his job and not thinking of leaving.

Morris Beckford and Beverley Lorrington have many friends in the area who visit regularly. Family not isolated. Beverley Lorrington does not feel a pressure to have to go out to work full-time to supplement Mr Beckford's income.

However, Miss Lorrington would like a part-time job in the evenings to have a break from the house and the children.

The family making very good progress. The children have been at home on trial for one year. In view of this plans would now be made to revoke the Care Order.

9. Parental view of present situation & future plans.

Both Morris Beckford and Beverley Lorrington feel that they have cared well for their children during the last year. They see themselves as a family unit.

Mr Beckford and Miss Lorrington now wish the Care Orders to be discharged as soon as possible.

10. Child's view of present situation & future plans.   N/A

Social Worker   G. Wahlstrom   Date   15.4.83

Senior Social Worker   D. Dietmann

11   Childs name

12   Religion: Specifying practising or
non-practising

13a Name of school/employment

13b Progress at school/employment

14a Wages/pocket money
b Savings
c Board & Lodge contribution

15   Health & physical developments: State handicaps, medication, treatments.

16a Date of last medical
b Were any comments made?

17a   Date of last dental examination
b   Were any comments made?

18   What is the quality of contacts and relationships

a   With peers:

b   With adults in the home:

c   With family or origin: State whether contact has increase/cecreased and outline
parental attitude to placement.

d   With others outside the home: (For example, former foster parents, residential or
field staff.)

19   Significant events & developments since last review.

20   Child's view of present situation & future plans.

21   Establishment's/foster parents'/AFCS view of present situation & future plans
Outline attitude to support given by Area or AFCS.

22   Are present financial arrangements satisfactory. List any special needs which may
arise before the next review (e.g. holidays, clothing, equipment, etc)

Foster parent/O-in-C/
AFCS Social Worker .... Date ....

Residential Care Manager/
AFCS Senior Social Worker .... Date ....

Childs name   Jasmine Beckford   Area/Section 6
                    Louise Beckford

Venue of review   Area 6

Date: 18.4.83   Date of last review: 30.9.82

Name and status of all persons attending

D S Dietmann   SSW Area 6
G Wahlström   SW Area 6
D Ruddock   Family Aid Area 6
J Hobbs   Court Officer SS
Morris Beckford   Father

23   Itemised topics covered at review

Revocation of Care Order.

24   Summary of discussion: (Describe the process of reaching decisions.)

Briefly went over the past history and discussed the changes since the last review. Jasmine has moved from the Council Day Nursery to the Nursery class at the local infants school. Beverley organised this herself and Jasmine is doing very well. They have also stopped buying things on H.P. and now save and pay cash. They are very good at saving and budgeting. Morris and Beverley have always made it clear that they want all legal ties to SS dissolved and need this last vote of confidence and gesture toward their being a total independent family. There are no causes for concern and no reason to oppose revocationof the Care Order. Jim Hobbs satisfied himself that Morris and Beverley would seek help if they needed it without our legal responsibility so it was agreed to approach the Court immediately. The children have now been placed at home for a year, off the NAI register for 6 months.

25   Should child's legal status be changed? if so, how?   Yes, Revocation of Care Order

25a   Should placement at home (Home on Trial) be considered? NA

26   Is an "Independant Person" (Second 11, Child Care Act, 1980) required? NA

27   Comment on child's Personal Album   NA

28   What did the child contribute to the review?

29   Objectives (short & long term) to be pursued.

Revocation of Care Order

30. What action must now be taken?   By Whom?

   1. Court Report   GW
   2. Presentation   Jim H

31 Next Review Date: Time: Venue:

    Not scheduled unless Court Application,

Chairperson   D Deitmann   Date   20.9.82

Area Manager's comments: D. Bishop

32a This question is designed to monitor the need for different types of placements.
     Please tick row A to indicate current placement.
     Please tick row B to indicate the preferred type of placement.

	Family Group Home	Foster-ing	Specialised Adolescent Unit	Working Boys/Girls Hostel	Home for Children under 10	CH(E)	Home for Mentally Handicapped Children under 12	over 12
A Current Placement								
B Preferred Placement								

Additional comments on placement   Please tick if
(including placement not described above)   current placement
                                     is a private/
                                     voluntary home   ☐

32b This question is designed to monitor the fostering/adoption placement needs

	Permanent Substitite Care		Relief Care (Short-term Fostering)	Contract Placement	Location		
	Foster Home	Adoptive Home			Brent	Other London Borough	Outside London
A Current Placement							
B Preferred Placement							

STATUTORY CASE REVIEW HELD ON 6th DECEMBER 1983
LONDON BOROUGH OF BRENT – SOCIAL SERVICES DEPARTMENT

REVIEW FORM (CHILDREN IN CARE)

(Pages 1 & 2 to be completed by Area or AFCS prior to review case conference and circulated to all present at review).

1. Name: Jasmine Beckford 2. Date of Birth 02.12.1979
         Louise Beckford   27.05.81

3. Date received into care: Act, section & reason (include previous care episodes)
   9.9.81 Sec. 1, 1969 Act; Development prevented and ill-treated

4. Current legal status & reason why now in care, if different from above:
   As above

5. Currently boarded-out or placed with: N/A   Since:

6. ALL previously placements, with dates:
   26.8.81 to 13.4.82 Fosterparents
   13.4.82 to 19.4.82 Green Lodge, Barretts Green Road, London NW10

Social Worker   G. Wahlstrom   Since   5.8.81

Senior Social Worker   D. Dietmann   Since   5.8.81

Record of visits by social worker since last review:

Dates	Venue	Who was seen (including child)
19.4.82	57 College Road	Beverley L. and Jasmine and Louise
20.4.83	"	Beverley L. and Morris B. & Jasmine and Louise
21.4.83	"	"
22.4.83	"	Beverley L. and Jasmine and Louise
26.4.83	"	Beverley L.
27.4.83	"	Beverley L.
28.4.83	"	Morris B and Jasmine and Louise
11.5.83	"	Morris B and Beverley L.
26.5.83	"	Beverley L. and Jasmine and Louise
24.6.83	"	"
12.7.83	"	"
24.8.83	"	"
8.9.83	"	"
17.10.83	"	No reply
21.10.83	"	Beverley L.
22.11.83	"	No reply
23.11.83	"	No reply

7. Progress on recommendations from last review

    1.   Application made to revoke Care Order. Application refused.

8. Social Workers' view of present situation & future plans.
Specify *any* areas of concern.

Beverley and Morris coping very well and the children happy and settled.

Beverley pregnant and expecting baby middle of December. Morris will take annual leave when Beverley goes into hospital. Morris will have about 2 weeks leave over Christmas as usual and will be able to give Beverley a lot of support. Beverley has been able to have some rest over the past months with the help of relatives and friends.

Morris and Beverley will need some support in the near future to be able to involve Louise and Jasmine with the new baby.

Morris and Beverley have proved that they are willing and able to contact SSD when there is a problem.

9. Parental view of present situation & future plans.

Morris and Beverley believe that they have cared very well for Louise and Jasmine since they returned home in April 1982. They see themselves as a family and are looking forward to the new arrival.

Both Morris and Beverley now wish the Care Orders to be discharged as soon as possible.

10. Child's view of present situation & future plans. N/A

Social Worker   G. Wahlstrom   Date   5.12.83

Senior Social Worker   D. Dietmann   Date   5.12.83

11   Childs name

12   Religion: Specifying practising or non-practising

13a Name of school/employment

14a Wages/pocket money
  b Savings

13b Progress at school/employment

  c Board & Lodge contribution

15   Health & physical developments: State handicaps, medication, treatments.

16a Date of last medical
  b Were any comments made?

17a   Date of last dental examination
  b   Were any comments made?

18   What is the quality of contacts and relationships

a   With peers:

b   With adults in the home:

c   With family or origin: State whether contact has increase/cecreased and outline parental attitude to placement.

d   With others outside the home: (For example, former foster parents, residential or field staff.)

19   Significant events & developments since last review.

20   Child's view of present situation & future plans.

21   Establishment's/foster parents'/AFCS view of present situation & future plans Outline attitude to support given by Area or AFCS.

22   Are present financial arrangements satisfactory. List any special needs which may arise before the next review (e.g. holidays, clothing, equipment, etc)

Foster parent/O-in-C/
AFCS Social Worker .... Date ....

Residential Care Manager/
AFCS Senior Social Worker .... Date ....

Childs name   Jasmine Beckford   Area/Section   6
                 Louise Beckford

Venue of review   Area 6
Date: 6.12.83   Date of last review: 4.7.83
Name and status of all persons attending

D S Dietman   SSW
G Wahlström   SW
Apologies from reception for Bev. and Morris's absence, an unfortunate mix-up.

23   Itemised topics covered at review

     1. Finances
     2. Christmas
     3. Relationships within the family.

24   Summary of discussion: (Describe the process of reaching decisions.)

Morris is still employed at the same local job. The family budgets very well and no longer uses H.P. They are very independent and may accept a gift at Christmas from Gun but still wish to leave the statutory relationship with Social Services, having proved that they can contact this department when they need help – such as Beverley's illness at the beginning of this pregnancy. The baby is due quite soon. Morris has been extremely helpful to Beverley, shares the care of the children and household tasks. Both parents now encourage their children's development.

There is no cause for any concern and we feel strongly that this family ought to be relieved of the legal ties to Social Services and will reapply to the Court in the Spring, when the children have been at home 2 years.

25   Should child's legal status be changed? if so, how?   Yes, revocation of Care Orders

25a   Should placement at home (Home on Trial) be considered? NA

26   Is an "Independant Person" (Second 11, Child Care Act, 1980) required? NA

27   Comment on child's Personal Album   NA

28   What did the child contribute to the review?   NA

29   Objectives (short & long term) to be pursued.

     To let this family maintain an independent life.

30. What action must now be taken? By Whom?

Review to include Court Section and School
Statutory visits GW
Revocation of Care Order

31 Next Review Date: Time: Venue:

April

Chairperson D Dietmann Date 5.1.84

Area Manager's comments: Agree to reapply for revocation of CO.
D. Bishop

32a This question is designed to monitor the need for different types of placements.
Please tick row A to indicate current placement.
Please tick row B to indicate the preferred type of placement.

	Family Group Home	Foster-ing	Specialised Adolescent Unit	Working Boys/Girls Hostel	Home for Children under 10	CH(E)	Home for Mentally Handicapped Children under 12	over 12
A Current Placement								
B Preferred Placement								

Additional comments on placement
(including placement not described above)

Please tick if current placement is a private/ voluntary home ☐

32b This question is designed to monitor the fostering/adoption placement needs

| | Permanent Substitute Care | | Relief Care | Contract | | Location | | |
	Foster Home	Adoptive Home	(Short-term Fostering)	Placement	Brent	Other London Borough	Outside London
A Current Placement								
B Preferred Placement								

APPENDIX H

NON-ACCIDENTAL INJURY TO CHILDREN

GUIDELINES FOR ALL PROFESSIONAL AGENCIES INVOLVED IN CARE CARE IN BRENT

Brent Area Review Committee on Non-Accidental Injury to Children

INDEX

1. Introduction
2. The Injured Child
3. Case Conference
4. General Practitioners
5. Hospital Staff
6. Clinic and School Medical Officers
7. Community Nursing Staff (including Health Visitors and School Nurses)
8. Teachers and Staff in Schools
8A. Education Welfare Officers
9. Social Workers
10. N.S.P.C.C.
11. Probation and Aftercare Service
12. Dental Surgeons
13. Brent Family Service Unit
14. Police
15. Housing Service Staff
16. Other Non-Statutory Agencies
17. Addresses and Telephone Numbers

INTRODUCTION

This booklet, prepared by the Brent Area Review Committee on Non-Accidental Injury to Children, is intended to give guidelines to workers in all disciplines and agencies who in the course of their normal duties are brought into contact with children who may be at risk.

It is further hoped that the information contained herein will promote co-ordination and mutual understanding in dealing with any suspected or reported incident of child abuse.

Guidelines set out, are those agreed by the Brent Area Review Committee on Non-Accidental Injury to Children, and do not replace detailed procedural instructions maintained by individual agencies.

The Local Authority's intention in Brent is to provide as a 'prime objective' the safety of any child or young person involved in child abuse and the preservation of "the family" where appropriate.

THE INJURED CHILD

Recognition and Management

A rigid definition of a non-accidentally injured child and a list of signs and symptoms can only serve to narrow the vision and sensitivity of those who are involved in the care of children. Of paramount importance is a constant alertness to the risk of child abuse in any difficult or unhappy family situation or where a child is presented with physical or emotional damage. The professional can do no more than bear this in mind in the difficult process of assessment and diagnosis.

IF YOU SUSPECT – ACT

Signs and symptoms are many and varied and the Brent Area Review Committee, through its regular instruction courses, imparts knowledge to all persons who during their work or profession come into contact with children.

It is essential that obvious incidents or suspicious circumstances of an injury are handled efficiently, sympathetically and confidentially with medical attention if necessary.

The welfare of any child is paramount and the use of good communication is essential. For these reasons the three primary agencies, i.e. Social Services Departments, N.S.P.C.C. and Police, have resources for dealing with child abuse.

IF YOU SUSPECT – ACT

CASE CONFERENCES

1. In all cases, whether or not Court Action has commenced, it will be the responsibility of the Social Services Area Manager concerned to decide which agency will handle the case. It will also be at the Area Manager's discretion whether or not to call a case conference. This discretion will not apply when a child has been removed under legislation.
2. The date of the case conference will be as soon as is possible after the removal and in any case not more than five days after the removal inception. The conference must not be delayed because specific persons cannot attend within five days.
3. When a case conference is held, the Police, any appropriate Agencies, and the Social Services Court Officer must be invited. The case conference will make recommendations regarding action to be taken, and ALL AGENCIES have agreed to be bound by reasonable decisions made. However where strong disagreement is evident this should be recorded in the notes of the case conference along with any immediate action plan by disagreeing parties. Disagreements should be notified immediately to the Assistant Director of Social Services, who may wish to involve the Director, with a view to taking up negotiations at the most senior level.
4. The case conference should have the following objectives (there may be others specific to individual cases).
   (i) The full and constructive exchange of relevant information, expertise, 'intuition' and anxieties.
   (ii) Agreement on the foundation and broad outline of the 'long term' treatment plan (where appropriate). This should include a consideration of resources

available and not available and attempt a prediction of stress periods, and circumstances which will increase the 'risk' factor.

(iii) Agreement on the 'key worker' and the agency with primary case responsibility. Guidelines for the roles and tasks of other workers and agencies should also be clearly stated.

(iv) Establishment of clear and direct channels of communication between appropriate individuals and agencies.

(v) Agreement method of case review and where appropriate agreement on a date for the next case conference, where progress can be reviewed and plans amended etc.

(The frequency of subsequent case conferences, is in the last analysis the responsibility of the Area Manager but he should take into account the views and needs of the client and other agencies involved.

5. Case conferences must be clearly and accurately written up and should record the decisions reached in (ii)-(v) above. Minutes of case conferences should be available to all appropriate individuals and agencies within five days of the date of the conference.

6. The result of the case conferences and subsequent significant events in the life of the case will be reported to the Court Section for the information of the Director of Social Services and the Assistant Director, Family Services Division.

GENERAL PRACTITIONERS

DISCUSS with Health Visitor who may provide valuable information.

CHECK the N.A.I. register to see if the child is already known.

CONSULT Paediatric Consultant personally if admission is indicated and ensure director admission under his/her care.

CONTACT the key agency if there is one, and, if not, contact one of the three primary child abuse agencies.

RECORD events fully for medico-legal purposes.

ATTEND case conference.

HOSPITAL STAFF

Accident Unit Doctors

RECORD precise description of injuries and how they are said to have been caused. Illustrate all injuries and clinical findings on charts.

CONSULT a Paediatric Consultant immediately and directly.

All other Hopsital Staff (nursing, medical, administrative and ancillary)

CONSULT a Paediatric Consultant or a Hospital Senior Paediatric Social worker immediately and directly.

Members of Paediatric Unit

CONSULT a Paediatric Consultant immediately and directly.

ARRANGE admission and full investigation (medical, social and where appropriate psychiatric).

RECORD a detailed history, a chart of all injuries, photographs, X-rays and relevant laboratory investigations.

CHECK the N.A.I. register to see if the child is already known.

CONTACT the key agency if there is one and, if not, contact one of the three primary child abuse agencies.

INFORM the General Practitioner.

ENSURE that all reports are sufficiently detailed, are completed, typed and appropriately distributed.

ATTEND case conference.

NOTIFY the N.A.I. register if appropriate.

CLINIC AND SCHOOL MEDICAL OFFICERS

If you suspect N.A.I. or child neglect.

1. RECORD accurately the history and the results of your complete clinical examination.
2. DISCUSS the case with the Health Visitor immediately, and the General Practitioner if available, or any other relevant agencies.
3. CHECK whether the child or siblings are on the N.A.I. Register.
4. TELEPHONE the Principal Physician (Child Health) or the Senior Medical Officer to inform them of all cases, or to discuss doubtful cases.
5. REFER all suspected or definite cases to the Social Services Department.
6. ARRANGE admission to hospital for all definite cases, or whenever it is thought desirable, try personally contacting the Paediatrician by telephone.
7. REPORT fully in writing the events and your findings, and send it to the P.P. (CH) with copies to the S.C.M. (CH) and Area Nurse (CH).
8. ATTEND the case conference if possible and ensure that the case is followed up as required.

COMMUNITY NURSING STAFF (including Health Visitors and School Nurses)

CONSULT immediately with Nursing Officer (or SNO in her absence) who will be responsible for:
1. ENSURING that the child is medically examined by a Hospital Paediatrician or a General Practitioner and, if necessary, admitted to hospital under the direct care of the Consultant Paediatrician (by personal contact).

2. CHECKING the N.A.I. register to see if the child is already known.
3. CONTACTING the named key agency if there is one, and, if not, contacting one of the three primary child abuse agencies.
4. ADVISING and supporting the Health Visitor or Nurse about her future role on the case.

INFORM the child's G.P.
    the Principal Medical Officer
    the Clinic Medical Officer or School Medical Officer
    the Head Teacher if appropriate, i.e. if the case comes to the notice of a school nurse.
RECORD events fully and make a written report to the Divisional Nursing Officer with a copy to the Specialist in Community Medicine (Child Health) and the Area Nurse (Child Heath).
ATTEND case conference.

TEACHERS AND STAFF IN SCHOOLS

Steps to be taken in cases of suspected Non-Accidental Injury.

1. Any staff seeing a child at school, and have reasonable grounds for suspecting non-accidental injury, should immediately inform the Head or the most senior member of staff available.
2. The Head should then immediately inform the London Borough of Brent Social Services Department, 01-903 1400 Extension 215.
3. The Head should inform the Education Welfare Officer for the school immediately and send a written report to him/her with a copy for the Chief Education Welfare Officer as soon as possible.
4. If there is evidence of injury requiring immediate diagnosis or treatment, the Head should arrange for the child to be seen by the school medical officer if immediately available, or at the accident and emergency department of the local hospital. Parents should be contacted before such a referral and if they are not available, Social Services should, except in extreme circumstances, be consulted before the medical referral is made.
5. Social Services will arrange a Case Conference to which all agencies concerned will be invited and Heads are requested to attend such Case Conferences and to allow relevant members of staff to attend.

EDUCATION WELFARE OFFICERS

Steps be to taken in cases of suspected Non-Accidental Injury.

1. Contact Social Services Department, Brent House, 01-903 1400 extention 215 (this section holds "At Risk Register") to see if family or child are known.
2. Refer by telephone immediately to Social Services Area Office and follow up by a referral in writing.
3. Copies of referrals to be send to Education Officer (Ch. E.W.O.) and N.S.P.C.C. (for their information in case they have knowledge of family).
4. Follow up with Social Services Department within 2 days.
5. Keep relevant school staff informed; school staff will be asked to keep E.W.O. informed.

6. As a child cannot be medically examined without parental consent, advice must be sought from the Social Services Department IMMEDIATELY.
7. Information regarding N.A.I. received out of normal working hours contact Social Services Duty Officer (903 1400).

SOCIAL SERVICE STAFF

Social Workers

1. CONSULT Duty Senior Social Worker – who will alert Area Manager who will remain the accountable officer. The Area Manager Senior Social Worker will exercise their discretion controlling the immediacy of response, together with the potential seriousness of any child abuse referral utilising the department's policy and priority allocation to these cases.
2. CHECK AND NOTIFY
   (a) Area Records
   (b) Court Section for N.A.I. Index and Central Index.
   (c) Contact G.P. appropriate school, appropriate Health Visitor for any information available. In consultation with Court Officer, any other agencies, i.e. Police, N.S.P.C.C., to ascertain any other referrals known or member of family.
3. SEE THE CHILD AND PARENTS. where appropriate, immediate steps to be taken to see child and parents and assessing the necessity for removal of the child under legal authorisiation.
4. RECORD events, promptly and in detail.
5. ENSURE that in all cases where injury or physical neglect is suspected, the Social Worker seeks parental co-operation in obtaining immediately medical examination. Where this is refused, urgent consideration should be given to taking statutory action.
6. COMPLETE form N.A.I. 1 in consultation with Area Manager/Senior Social Worker, and despatch to Court Section as soon as possible after referral is received. The N.A.I. 1 should reach Court Section not later than 48 hours after referral. Where appropriate convene case conference.

N.S.P.C.C.

On receipt of any allegation of possible non-accidental injury, neglect or any other case where there may be high risk to a child, the following procedure must be carried out:
1. A visit must be made to the family and the child actually seen without delay and in any case within a maximum of 24 hours. Inability to do so must be communicated to a senior officer immediately.
2. In any case where significant injuries or poor physical condition is found, the child must be medically examined.
3. If an inspector considers that acts serious enough or persistent enough to warrant legal consideration have been committed, even though it may not be clear by whom, the case must be discussed with a colleague of senior grade within the next 24 hours. This applies whether or not steps have been taken to remove the child to a Place of Safety.
4. Information must be sought from any local Child Abuse Register and appropriate cases must be placed on it.

5. If it is known or discovered that another social work agency is working with the family, wherever possible opportunity must be given for the officer to be accompanied on his visit by a worker from that agency.
6. Local procedures agreed by the Society with the Area Review Committee, e.g. calling of case conference etc, should be implemented.
7. Ongoing supervision and consultation must be ensured by use of procedure laid down in Memo 3/75 (High Risk Case form).
   The Case Record must be sent to the Casework Executive in the following circumstances.
   (a) When a child has been removed.
   (b) When there is doubt about the safety of a child in circumstances that could be described as high risk.
   (c) When it is recognised that there is some risk to a child but it is considered that persistent skilled work may be successful in giving the child opportunity for reasonable development at home.
   (d) In specific instances set down in the Inspectors Directory.

PROBATION AND AFTERCARE SERVICE

1. It is normal practice for probation officers to visit homes of clients during the ordinary course of their supervision of those cases.
2. Probation Officers are alerted to the emotional and environmental difficulties which may well precipitate situations whereby children of the family could be at risk.
3. In such cases, the probation officer would make regular home visits in order to check on the situation regarding the children of the family at first hand.
4. In cases where there is evidence of non-accidental injury, probation officers are instructed to:
   a.   obtain any necessary medical attention;
   b.   immediately to inform the Social Services Court Section, where the N.A.I. Register is held;
   c.   if necessary, request a case conference;
   d.   to consult with a Senior Probation Officer or the Regional Assistant Chief Probation Officer.
5. In cases where there is suspicion that a child is injured or is at risk, probation officers are instructed to:
   a.   discuss the case with their Senior Probation Officer on the same day, or, in his absence, with another Senior Probation Officer or the Regional Assistance Chief Probation Officer.
   b.   contact the Health Visitor or, where appropriate, the school
   c.   to contact the Department of Social Services with a request for a case conference to be called to decide on a plan of action.

DENTAL SURGEONS

1. Some of the earliest signs of non accidental injury to children are of facial damage in the form of bruises or other injuries in and around the mouth.
2. Dental Practitioners may, in the course of their work, see a child exhibiting injuries which may be suspected to be non accidental. It is emphasised that the number of cases a dental practitioner may see during the course of his career is likely to be very

small and the dentist will need to exercise great care and judgement before deciding that injuries to a child might be considered non accidental. When, however, a suspicion of non-accidental injury is aroused, rapid, effective action to safeguard the child is imperative and the following guidelines to procedures are advised.

3. IMMEDIATE ACTION

   3.1 (a) When injury to a child requires immediate medical attention you are encouraged to ensure that the child is seen immediately by a general practitioner or by a medical officer at a hospital. An explanation of the injuries from parents and other possible witnesses should be sought. Detailed enquiries into the background are however the province of skilled workers and should be left to the appropriate agencies.

      (b) Inform the Area Dental Officer or if he is not available, one of his senior staff. The Area Dental Officer will inform the Department of Social Services, if this has not already been done, and will confirm the referral in writing to the Director of Social Services.

      (c) Inform the child's general practitioner.

      (d) In the event of the parents refusing to allow a child to be taken to a doctor, make an immediate and urgent referral to the Social Services Department or the N.S.P.C.C.

4. SUBSEQUENT ACTION

   3.2 (a) Keep a carefully written record or observations, treatment and action taken and forward a copy marked 'private and confidential' to the Area Dental Officer.

      (b) To follow up (to make sure that the parent has taken the child to the medical practitioner) the dentist should contact the doctor again after 24 hours.

5. PROCEDURES FOLLOWING REFERRAL

   4.1 (a) The initial urgent procedure will be the convening of a case conference. The dental surgeon, who will not at this stage be named, may be requested, though the Area Dental Officer, to attend this Conference.

      (b) Whatever steps are taken, it is adivsed that the dentist should avoid talking about or discussing the case with anyone else who may approach him, other than medical or dental colleagues involved with the patient, unless or until he is asked to attend a case conference.

      (c) In any case where the dentist is in doubt about how to proceed he is advised to consult immediately either the Area Dental Officer or the Consultant Dental Surgeon at the District General Hospital or a member of their senior staffs.

      The Chairman or Secretary of the Local Dental Committee would also provide advice.

BRENT FAMILY SERVICE UNIT

Steps to be taken in Non-Accidental Injury

1. Ensure that any message received regarding an at risk family reaches a responsible worker without delay.
2. Every reported injury should be acted on the same day as the message is received. The appropriate action to be determined by consultation between the worker, the Unit Organiser and, or where appropriate the responsible senior officer in Social Services.

3. Efficient, accurate and up to date recording.
   This should include:
   (i) Factual information regarding incidents, communications, decisions and any action taken with dates and times. A clear distinction should be made between fact and opinion, which are each of value.
   (ii) Regular updated names, addresses, and telephone numbers required for communications, e.g. schools, G.P., etc.

POLICE OFFICERS

CONSULT the delegated Senior Detective Officer, who will:
INFORM the appropriate Social Services Area Office and ask them to take any other necessary action.
DOCUMENT by completing Police Form 78.
These are the routine Police Officer instructions. A senior representative for the Metropolitan Police (Detective Superintendent of "Q" Division) is a member of the Brent Area Review Committee on N.A.I. to children. The police are also represented on this Committee by the Division Community Liaison Officer and his/her deputy. Police policy is to co-operate as fully as possible with the other agencies involved. The delegated senior detective officer will ensure that consultation with the appropriate agencies has taken place before any decision to prosecute is reached.
Full consideration will be given to providing help and supervision for the family by other agencies. The final right to decide on prosecution obviously remains with the police.

HOUSING SERVICE STAFF

Cases of N.A.I. should be referred to one of the three primary child abuse agencies for discussion about what action should be taken. A carefully written record of events should be kept.

OTHER NON-STATUTORY AGENCIES

Cases of N.A.I. should be referred to one of the three primary child abuse agencies for discussion about what action should be taken. A carefully written record of events should be kept.

APPENDIX I

Iain Eric WEST, M.B., Ch.B., M.R.C.Path, D.M.J.
Over 21
Consultant Forensic Pathologist, Senior Lecturer in Forensic Medicine
St. Thomas's Hospital Medical School
London SE1 7EH
01-928 9292 Extension 2670

13th September 1984

At 11.00 a.m. on Friday 6th July, 1984, at Westminster Public Mortuary, Horseferry Road, London S.W.1, Det. Insp. Dickens showed me the body of:

Jasmine Christina BECKFORD o/w LORRINGTON, aged 4 years

Also present were:
D. S. Lilly (Laboratory Liaison)
D. S. King
D. C. Powell (Exhibits Officer)
SOCO Connell
Senior Photographer Palmer
Dr. M. S. Hadidi

The deceased was photographed clothed and unclothed and X-rays were taken of her unclothed body. I examined the X-rays prior to my examination.

I performed a post mortem examination.

EXTERNAL APPEARANCES

She was a thin little girl 3ft 5in in height and weighing 1 stone 9lbs. She was dressed in:

1. White dress with a red star pattern cut up at the front.
2. Blue vest cut up at the front.
3. Pink tubular bandage over left leg with two pieces of white lint over the skin on the left leg.
4. Blue pants rolled below the groin.
5. Pair of white socks.

Her abdomen was distended and there was green and black discolouration of the skin of the abdomen due to early decomposition.

MARKS OF PREVIOUS INJURY

1. Deformity of the left thigh with extensive scarring of the anterior aspect of the thigh and front and sides of the knee. There were punctate and linear scars on the back of the left thigh and lower left buttock and oval and linear scars behind the left knee. There was old scarring around the left ankle. There was a scar on the front of the left thigh which showed evidence of having been repaired by sutures.

2. Scarring over the front of the left side of the pelvis.

3. There were areas of ulceration of the skin in the regions of scarring with one ulcer over the front of the left side of the pelvis, four over the front of the left thigh and

knee, the largest measuring 1" by 1½", and two on the front of the left ankle. There was a healed ulcer on the outside of the left ankle and an ulcer measuring 1" x ½" behind the left heel but the left Achilles tendon was intact.

4. The left thigh was very hard and appeared to largely consist of a cylinder of thick bone surrounding the shaft of the left thigh bone. There was little soft tissue covering the left thigh bone (femur).

5. There was deformity below the left knee due to an old fracture.

6. Old scarring on the front of the right side of the pelvis, inside the right knee with deformity below the right knee due to old fracture of the upper part of the shin bones.

7. There were small scars on the back of the right upper arm, on the right forearm, on the outer aspect of the right wrist and multiple scars on the back of the right hand.

8. There was scarring behind the left elbow and punctate scars on the back of the left hand, similar to those seen on the back of the right hand. The scars on the back of the hands were consistent with old burn scars.

9. Scarring on the left side of the chest and over the right side of the small of the back. All these areas of scarring were small. Tiny scars over the base of the spine. Healed ulcer over the back of the left shoulder blade.

10. Three areas of scarring over the centre and right side of the forehead. Eight areas of linear and punctate scarring on the right cheek. Three punctate scars below the right ear. Four linear scars on the left cheek. Two scars on the right side of the upper lip. Two tiny scars on the point of the chin. Two round small scars on the undersurface of the chin.

MARKS OF RECENT INJURY

Head and Neck:

1. 1" x 1" pressure abrasion on the scalp situated 1" behind the upper pole of the right ear.

2. ½" pressure abrasion situated 2" behind the upper pole of the right ear.

3. Three punctate abrasions high on the back of the head.

4. ¾" pressure abrasion just above the point of the back of the head, in the midline.

5. Tiny abrasion on the scalp 1" above the top of the left ear.

6. Bruising and slight grazing on the upper part of the left ear, mainly behind the ear with an associated ½" split on the upper part of the back of the root of the ear.

7. There were eleven injuries on the left cheek and jaw outside the level of the mouth including two linear grazes, which were superficial, a deep linear graze in front of the ear, an area of bruising 1" by ½" situated 1¼" in front of the ear. The other injuries including a ½" bruise in front of the ear and small punctate bruises on the outer corner of the left eye, in front of the left ear, on the outside of the left nostril and outside the left corner of the mouth. There was a small laceration near to an old scar below the left eye.

8. Two ¼" bruises above the left eyebrow.

9. Bruising of the central forehead measuring 2½" by 1¼" with two superimposed

linear and three small punctate abrasions. The area of bruising and abrasion extended from the root of the nose to above the hairline. There was a small bruise ½" above the right eyebrow.

10. Bruising and abrasion of the right upper eyelid.

11. An irregular area of abrasion measuring ⅝" by ⅓" below the right lower eyelid.

12. Small abrasions outside the left nostril.

13. Triangular abrasion measuring 1⅜" by ¾" just outside the right eyebrow.

14. A group of irregular punctate and linear abrasions, consistent with fingernails, on the right cheek covering an area 2" x 1" and extending in a line down the cheek.

15. Slightly diffused bruising on the centre of the right cheek measuring 2" by 1¼".

16. Bruising in front of the root of the right ear measuring 1¼" by ¾".

17. Bruising and abrasion of the upper half of the right ear with punctate abrasion of the lower half of the same ear.
There was bruising of the back of the right ear, apparently in continuity with the injuries to the front of the ear.

18. ⅜" x ⅜" pressure abrasion over the top of the nose with separate small nail type abrasions on the bridge of the nose and on either nostril.

19. Abrasion on right upper lip near to opening of nostril.

20. Two tiny linear and punctate abrasions, consistent with fingernails, on the surface of the chin.

21. "T" shaped split on the inside of the upper lip running along the junction between the gum and lip on either side of the midline and extending down through the frenum of the upper lip.
One tiny and one ¼" laceration on the inside of the left corner of the mouth and cheek.
⅞" laceration inside right corner of mouth.

22. Two vertical lacerations inside the lower lip on either side of the midline. Bruising and laceration of the inside of the mouth at the level of the 1st lower right sided pre-molar tooth.

Trunk:

1. Five tiny punctate abrasions over the front of the lower left chest.

2. 1¼" x 1⅛" fresh bruise, just beginning to diffuse, over the right side of the chest, 1" from the midline and over the area of the 5th to 8th ribs.

3. 2½" by 2" bruising straddling the left sided rib margin at the front and composed of five coalescing bruises consistent with knuckle marks. The individual bruises measured between ½" and ¾" in diameter.

4. 3½" by 2¼" bruise on the left flank extending from the 10th rib to the side and back of the left side of the pelvis. The bruising was heavier on the upper end of this wound.

5. ¼" bruise on the front of the abdomen 2" above the umbilicus.

6. Group of three bruises on the right lower front rib margin, 3" from the midline. The outer bruise measured ¾" in diameter, the inner bruise ½" in diameter and the lower bruise ⅜" in diameter. All bruises were consistent with knuckle marks.

7. Two small bruises and grazes on the back of the right flank just below the tip of the 11th rib.

8. Two linear bruises on the right lower quadrant of the abdomen, the upper measuring 2¼", the lower 1½". The bruises were separated by a distance of ½".

9. On the back of the trunk there were scattered abrasions over the back of the right shoulder blade, over the back of the right 12th rib, on the back of the base of the spine with some pressure abrasion over the base of the spine.

Legs

1. Fresh abrasions on the outer aspect of the left hip.

2. Fresh abrasions middle of left thigh.

2. Fresh abrasions mid right thigh, and on outside of right foot.
    All the abrasions on the legs were small.

Arms:

1. Swelling on back of hand.

2. 1¼" bruise on the outer border of the left forearm just above the wrist.

3. 1¾" linear bruise extending around the inside of the left lower forearm from back to front.

4. Small bruise on the outside of the left elbow. Small puncture mark on the left elbow (possibly treatment).

5. Three tiny grip type bruises on the back of the left upper arm.

6. Healing grazes on the back of the right middle finger.
    Linear oblique bruises on the front of the right wrist and lower forearm, 2" in length.

7. Punctate abrasions on the inner border of the right forearm.

8. 2¼" by 1½" bruise extending around the outer border of the right forearm from back to front. There was blanching of the centre of this bruise.

9. Oval abrasion on the back of the centre of the right forearm.

10. Small bruises and grazes on the back of the right forearm and elbow.

11. Tiny scratch on the back of the right upper arm.

12. Small grip type bruises on the back of the centre of the right upper arm.

13. Scattered linear grazes on the front of the right upper arm.

14. Linear bruises on the back of the left hand, measuring 1½" in length.

INTERNAL EXAMINATION

Skeleton:
Recent fractures of the fronts of the left 6th and 7th fibs. Fractures of the left side of the pelvis and of the pubic bones on both sides.

Scalp:
Bruising in relation to the outer scalp injuries with an additional bruise on the undersurface of the scalp high on the right side of the forehead and temple.

Brain:
The left cerebral hemisphere was covered by a thin layer of fresh non adherent blood clot with a smaller quantity overlying the right cerebral hemisphere (30cc over left cerebral hemisphere, 20cc over right). There was contusion of the right lobe of the cerebellum. The brain was swollen with flattening of the gyral pattern, displacement of the left uncinate gyrus. There was splitting of the corpus callosum between the two cerebral hemispheres with visible contusions on the frontal poles, both subfrontal regions and traces of subarachnoid bleeding in the left temporal region. The brain was preserved for further examination after fixation.

Mouth:
Injuries to lips as described. No bruising of tongue.

Neck:
No evidence of compression of the neck.

Lungs:
Patchy slight basal collapse of both lungs. Froth in air passages. No evidence of natural disease in either lung.

Heart:
Healthy pericardium, myocardium, endocardium, valves, coronary arteries and aorta.

Stomach:
Brown mucoid material. No evidence of food. No tablet remains.

Intestines:
Distention of small bowel with gas. Impaction of faeces in lower colon and rectum. No foreign bodies in bowel.

Liver:
Congested.

Spleen:
Congested.

Kidneys:
Pallor of renal cortices. Congestion of medullae.

Bladder:
Empty. Not collapsed.

Generative Organs:
Normal infantile uterus. Congestion of vaginal mucosa with early autolysis and traces of blood stained material in lumen. No evidence of direct vaginal or volval injury. The hymen was intact and the clitoris normal. The anus was dilated but the rectum contained hard impacted faeces.

Other organs:
Healthy suprarenals, pancreas and thyroid.

Samples of organs were retained for further examination. I handed swabs taken from the front of the deceased's chest and from the deceased's anus, vulva and vagina to D. C. Powell.

The X-rays taken prior to my post mortem examination revealed multiple old fractures and periosteal damage affecting the child's lower limb and pelvis with old fractures of the thigh bones and shin bones. There was also old bone injury around both shoulders.

The X-ray appearances of the bones did not suggest that they were unusually brittle.

CONCLUSIONS

1. Jasmine Christina BECKFORD o/w LORRINGTON was a very thin little girl who has died as the result of severe head injuries. Natural disease appears to have played no part in her death.

2. The deceased was extremely thin and appeared emaciated due to chronic under nourishment.

3. There were mutliple old scars on the deceased's body consistent with repeated episodes of physical abuse.

4. There were numerous fresh injuries on the deceased's body consistent with the effects of a severe physical beating conducted within the period of a day or so leading up to her death. There were marks which included injuries such as might be left by slaps and punches and some of the injuries to the face are consistent with the effects of hard punches.

   The fatal brain injury had been caused by blows to the child's head.

5. The overall appearance are suggestive of the child being subjected to repeated episodes of severe physical violence and to chronic and severe neglect.

6. I give as a Cause of Death:

   1a   Cerebral contusions and subdural haemorrhage

APPENDIX J

CHIEF EXECUTIVE'S REPORT ON A COMPLAINT RE AN ADVERTISEMENT TO FIND A FOSTER HOME FOR CHANTELLE AND LOUISE BECKFORD

1. Following a complaint from Councillor Coleman (Leader of the Labour Group on Brent Council) regarding the placing of an advertisement relating to Chantelle and Louise Beckford in the Voice on 6 April, I have carried out an inquiry into the events leading up to the appearance of the advertisement. In doing so I have spoken to the Director of Social Services, the previous Assistant Director of Social Services the Area Manager, the Senior Social worker (the last two in the presence of the Union Representative) Councillor Coleman and the Director, the Assistant Controller of Personnel and Industrial Relations and Mrs. K. Way in the Personnel Division.

2. In February 1985, after various unsuccessful attempts had been made to place Chantelle and Louise Beckford – attempts which involved the Fostering and Adoption Panel, other London Boroughs, the Independent Adoption Agency, New Black Families and the British Association of Social Workers – a decision was taken at Area level to advertise the children to see if this produced a better response.

3. A draft advertisement was sent to the Assistant Director of Social Services. This was not normal practice, but was done in this case because of its sensitive nature. The draft was discussed by the Assistant Director and the Director who expressed anxiety about the advertisement. She instructed that the inclusion of a phrase indicating that the children had been subject to child abuse should be removed. She also rcalls instructing that the children should not be indentifiable and that the name of the Senior Social Worker should be deleted. The Assistant Director of Social Services does not, however, recall an instrcution to withdraw the Senior Social Worker's name, and this was not, therefore, relayed to the Area. With regard to the photo which forms part of the advertisement, a note of a telephone conversation between the Senior Social Worker and the Director, kept by the Senior Social worker, indicates that the use of the photo was agreed.

4. A request was, therefore, made to the Controller of Personnel who is responsible for advisement with the Nursing Times, Voice, Jamaican Weekly Gleaner and the Daily Mail. This request was made on 18 March and received by Personnel on 25 March.

5. The advertisements were placed with the Council's agent on 25 March and were due to appear in the various journals between 1 and 3 April.

6. Further discussions on the advertisement took place in the week commencing 25 March during the course of the trial of the parents of the two children. These discussions culminated in an instruction being given to the Controller of Personnel on 29 March to withdraw the advertisements on the grounds that it would be insensitive to place them so soon after the trial and the publicity which it had attracted.

7. The advertisements were withdrawn from the Daily Mail and the Nursing Times, but the other two journals had gone to press and the adverts appeared. They attracted eleven replies – five of which were considered worthy of serious consideration.

8. The complaint made relates to:

(i) The alleged insensitivity of displaying photographs of the children and giving the name of the Senior Social worker.

(ii) The failure to take speedier action to withdraw the advertisements given the trial publicity.

9. My conclusions from the facts set out above are:

(a) That Social Services retained a duty to do everything possible to place Chantelle and Louise Beckford, and having failed to achieve that in other ways were right to decide to advertise.

(b) That there was uncertainty regarding the precise contents of the advertisements and the instructions which were given. If the intention was not to include the name of the Social Worker or a photograph, then that should have been made clearer.

(c) That it would have been better had the advertisement been withdrawn as soon as the trial commenced. One must, however, take into account the pressure placed on the Department and the personal pressure placed on senior officers during that period. In those circumstances it is not surprising that the advert which had last been discussed at the beginning of February was overlooked.

(d) The response to the advertisement was good and provided for more possible placements than all the other attempts had, taken together.

(e) That there is no evidence of deliberate insensitivity on the part of Social Services.

24.vi.1985

APPENDIX K

SELECTED BIBLIOGRAPHY

British Association of Social Workers, CHILD ABUSE POLICY, a report prepared by a Project Group, June 1985.

Caffey, J. MULTIPLE FRACTURES IN THE LONG BONES OF INFANTS SUFFERING FROM CHRONIC SUBDURAL HAEMATOMA, Am. J. Roentgenol, 56:163, 1946.

Central Council for Education and Training in Social Work, LEGAL STUDIES IN SOCIAL WORK EDUCATION, report of a study group, CCETSW Paper 4, July 1974.

Clarke Hall and Morrison on THE LAW RELATING TO CHILDREN (10th edition, 1985), edited by Brian Harris Q.C. and Richard White.

Cretney, PRINCIPLES OF FAMILY LAW (4th ed. 1984) Sweet & Maxwell

Committee on the Care of Children, THE CURTIS REPORT, Cmd. 6922, (London: 1946).

Committee on Children and Young Persons (1960), THE INGLEBY REPORT, Cmnd. 1191 (London: HMSO)

Committee on Children and Young Persons, Scotland (1964), THE KILBRANDON REPORT. Cmnd 2306 (Edinburgh: HMSO)

Committee on Local Authority and Allied Personal Social Services (1968) THE SEEBOHM REPORT, Cmnd 3703 (London: HMSO)

Davies, Martin, SOCIAL WORK, THE STATE AND THE UNIVERSITY, inaugural lecture, Br. J. Social Wk. (1981) 11, 275/288.

Davies, Martin, THE ESSENTIAL SOCIAL WORKER (2nd ed.) Gower, 1985.

Department of Health and Social Security, CHILD ABUSE: A study of Inquiry Reports 1973-1981. (London: HMSO: 1982)

Department of Health and Social Security, REVIEW OF CHILD CARE LAW, Discussion Papers 1-12, (London: January 1985)

Department of Health and Social Security, CHILD ABUSE INQUIRIES, a consultative paper (London: June 1985).

Eekelaar, John, FAMILY LAW AND SOCIAL POLICY, Wiedenfeld and Nicolson, 1978.

Geach (Hugh) and Szwed (Elizabeth) eds., PROVIDING CIVIL JUSTICE FOR CHILDREN, Edward Arnold, 1983.

Goldstein (Joseph), Freud (Anna) and Solnit (Albert), BEYOND THE BEST INTEREST OF THE CHILD, The Free Press, 1973.

Graham Hall (Jean) and Mitchell (Barbara), CHILD ABUSE – PROCEDURE AND EVIDENCE IN JUVENILE COURTS. (Barry Rose, 1978).

Kempe, C. Henry, et al. THE BATTERED CHILD SYNDROME, J.A.M.A. 7 July 1962, 181, 1:17-24.

Leeding, A.E. CHILD CARE MANUAL FOR SOCIAL WORKERS (4th ed. 1982) Butterworths.

Martin F.M. and Murray, Kathleen, eds. THE SCOTTISH JUVENILE JUSTICE SYSTEM, Scottish Academic Press, 1982.

Morris (Alison) and Giller (Henri), Szwed (Elizabeth) and Geach (Hugh), JUSTICE FOR CHILDREN, Macmillan, 1980.

National Society for the Prevention of Cruelty to Children, 78 BATTERED CHILDREN: a retrospective study by Skirmer, Aryela, and Castle, Raymond. 1969.

Parton, Nigel, THE POLITICS OF CHILD ABUSE, Macmillan, 1985.

Renvoize, Jean, CHILDREN IN DANGER, Routledge & Kegan, Paul, 1974.

Report of a Committee of Inquiry into the Care and Supervision provided in relation to Maria Colwell (1974) London: HMSO

Report of an Independent Inquiry into facts regarding the Care and Services provided by the relevant authorities and the communications between them and within those authorities in the case of Maria Mehmedagi and her family, to London Borough of Southwark, the Lambeth, Southwark and Lewisham Area Health Authority (Teaching) and the Inner London Probation and After-Care Service (London: June 1981)

Report of an Independent Inquiry into the provision and co-ordination of services to the family of Carly Taylor by the relevant local authorities and health services and by the persons or agencies to Leicestershire County Council and Leicestershire Area Health Authority (Teaching 1985).

Report of Professor J. D. McLean concerning Karen Spencer, Derbyshire County Council and Derbyshire Area Health Authority (Sheffield: 1978)

Report of Sir Walter (later Viscount) Monckton on the circumstances which led to the boarding out of Dennis and Terence O'Neill at Bank Farm, Minsterley, and the steps taken to supervise their welfare, (1945) (London: HMSO: Cmd. 6636)

Report of an Inquiry Panel into the examination of the implications of the death of a child, to Cheshire Central Review Committee for Child Abuse (July 1982)

Report of the Standing Inquiry Panel into the case of Reuben Carthy, to Nottinghamshire Area Review Committee (1985).

Report of the Panel of Inquiry into the death of Lucy Gates, to London Borough of Bexley and Bexley Health Authority (London: July 1982)

Sharman, Ruth, CHILD ABUSE, a discussion paper, Council for the Education and Training for Health Visitors, 1983.

Sinclair, Ruth, DECISION-MAKING IN STATUTORY REVIEWS ON CHILDREN IN CARE, Gower, 1984.

Social Services Committee Report: Second Report from the Social Services Committee Session 1983-84, CHILDREN IN CARE, Vol. 1 (H.C. 360-1)

Thoburn, June CAPTIVE CLIENTS – SOCIAL WORK WITH FAMILIES OF CHILDREN HOME ON TRIAL, Routledge and Kegan Paul, 1980.

time for, 122, 149
case conferences on. *See* Case
conferences (Beckford children)
child abuse
  evidence of, 181, 292
  register, entry on, 59
  Dr. Jolly's report on, 88,
  189, App. F:3
foster home, transfer to, 42, 59, 88, 181
grandparents, stay with, 42, 59, 181
place of safety order, 42, 59, 181, 255
Beckford, Jasmine
assaults on. *See* Child abuse; injuries,
below
birth of, 41, 57
care proceedings
  generally, *See under* Willesden
  Juvenile Court
  interim orders, 57, 79
child abuse
  August 1981
    medical evidence, 65-69
    police, reaction of, 159, 160
    social services, reaction of, 159, 160
  commencement of, 96
  lack of development indicating, 69-75
  November 1982
    finding of Inquiry, 74, 117, 119,
    288, 291
    health visitor's failure to detect, 119
    medical evidence, 117, 291
    non-medical evidence, 118, 291
    social worker's failings, 119
  preventability, 290
  psychological abuse, 2
  September 1983 onwards
    educational authority's failings,
    121, 291, 292
    finding of Inquiry, 290-292
    health services, failings of, 295, 296
    social services, failings of, 121,
    182-184, 292-294
child abuse register
  entry on, 41, 57
  removal from, 58, 116-118, 120, 142
death of. *See* Death of Jasmine
development
  fostering, during, 2, 70, 114, 287
  lack of, 69-75, 139, 140, 211, 295, 296
fostering. *See* Fostering; Proberts
general practitioner, visits to, 236, 237

Green Lodge, transfer to, 58, 115,
135, 267
home on trial. *See* Home on trial
hospitalisation, 41, 57, 68, 236
injuries to
  August 1981
    Levick Report. *See* Levick Report
    medical evidence, 65-69
    nature of, 41
    police investigation, 159, 160
    social workers' reaction, 159
  child abuse, as. *See* Child abuse,
  above
  healing during fostering, 287
  home on trial period, during, 69
  post mortem examination, 69, 182,
  183, App. 1
nursery
  day, attendance. *See* Mortimer Road
  Day Nursery
  school, attendance. *See* Princess
  Frederica Primary School
parentage, 41, 84-86
place of safety order, 57, 65, 68, 77,
255, 257
placement of, options on, 263-268
post mortem examination, 69, 182, 183,
App. 1
speech therapy, 136, 137
weight of
  April 1982, after, 73, 75, 295, 296
  death, at, 2, 73
  early months, during, 2, 72, 140
  fostering, during, 2, 70, 114, 139
  recording of, 70-75, 140, 295, 296
See also Beckford case; Beckford family
Beckford, Louise
access by parents to. *See* Beckford
parents
adoption, freeing for, 150, 189
birth of, 41, 57
care proceedings
  generally, *See* Willesden Juvenile
  Court
  interim care order, 57, 79
case conferences on. *See* Case
conferences (Beckford children)
child abuse
  August 1981
    medical evidence, 65, 75, 78, 81
    prosecution, 42, 77, 160, 161

autumn of 1983 on, 181, 292
child abuse register
  entry on, 57, 59
  removal from, 41, 58, 116-118, 120
Dr. Jolly's report on, 88, 189, App. F:3
fostering. *See* Fostering
general practitioner, visits to, 236
grandparents, stays with, 41, 42, 181
Green Lodge, transfer to, 58, 115,
135, 267
guardian ad litem, 253
home on trial. *See* Home on trial
hospitalisation, 41, 57, 77
injuries to, in 1981
  child abuse, as. *See* Child abuse,
  above
  social worker's reaction to, 159
place of safety order, 57, 65, 68,
77, 255
Beckford, Morris
  assault
    Jasmine, on
      August 1981, 65, 159, 161
      charge at trial, App. D
    Louise, on, conviction of, 42, 57, 77,
    160, 161
  biographical details, 42
  case conferences, attendance at, 249
  childhood of, 42, 79, 83, 86, 159, 176
  cruelty, charge of, 183, App. D
  evidence from, 6, App. B
  fastidiousness of, 109
  Jasmine, relationship to, 2, 41-42, 84-86
  Lorrington, relationship with, 42
  manslaughter, conviction of, 2, 59, 183,
  App. D
  murder, charge of, 59, App. D
  psychiatric assessment of, 87, 159
  statutory case reviews, at, 249
  trial at Central Criminal Court. *See*
  Central Criminal Court
  *See also Beckford family; Beckford
  parents*
Beckford case
  Area Review Committee's role. *See*
  Brent Area Review Committee
  Brent Borough Council and. *See* Brent
  Borough Council
  case conferences. *See* Case conferences
  (Beckford children)
  documentation. *See* Documentation

Education Dept, and. *See* Brent
Education Dept.
fostering. *See* Fostering
Health Authority, role of. *See* Brent
Health Authority
inquiry
  Independent Panel of. *See* Panel of
  Inquiry
  type of
    Cases Sub-Committee decision, 59,
    152, 194
    Director of Social Services' views,
    185-187, 193
    Policy and Resources Committee
    decision, 59, 152, 195, 239
    Social Services Committee decision,
    59, 152, 194-195
Law and Administration Department
and. *See* Brent Law and Administration
Dept.
NSPCC, role of, 176
placement of children, options on,
263-268
police involvement in, 159-164
persons involved in, details of, 41-55
political background, 7, 179
publicity, 2, 25-28, 181, 182, 288
racial dimension to, 1, 7, 8
records, *See* Documentation
Social Services Dept. and *See* Brent
Social Services Dept.
statutory case reviews. *See* Statutory
case reviews
summary of events, 57-60
Willesden Juvenile Court. *See* Willesden
Juvenile Court
Beckford family
  accommodation, 65, 134
  ethnic origin, 1
  Family Aide, *See* Ruddock, Mrs.
  financial resources, 134, 135
  health visits to
    Bowden, by. *See* Bowden, Miss
    Hindle, by. *See* Hindle, Mrs.
    Knowles, by. *See* Knowles, Miss
    Leong, by. *See* Leong, Miss
  rehousing of, 58, 91, 109
  social worker's visits to
    Dietmann. *See* Dietmann, Mrs.
    Wahlstrom. *See* Wahlstrom, Ms.
Beckford parents

access to children
death of Jasmine, after
proceedings as to, 150, 189, 253
proposed termination of, 150, 188
Proberts, whilst with, 107-109
attitude towards children, 290
behaviour of, 216, 290
case conferences, at, 249
casework with, 182, 287, 290 *et seq*
death of Jasmine, events immediately
following, 181
disharmony between, 118, 291
health visitor's attitude towards, 82, 295
hospital visits to children, 78, 80, 84,
92, 107
independent social worker's views, 92,
97, 98
psychiatric assessment, 87, 159
return of children to. *See* Home on trial
social workers' attitude to, 116, 159, 294
statutory case reviews, attendance, 107,
108, 116, 246, 249
trial of. *See under* Central Criminal
Court
Willesden justices views on, 100
See also Beckford, Morris; Beckford
family; Lorrington, Beverley
Bedford, Mr. Alan
expert evidence
case conferences, as to, 162, 246,
249, 252
child abuse inquiries, as to, 26
magistrates' rider, as to, 101
qualifications, App. B
Bibliography, App. K
Bichard, Mr. Michael
Chief Executive Officer, 49
death of Jasmine
notice of, 49, 182
response to
details of, 181, 183, 184, 190, 195
summary of, 49
qualifications, 49
report re foster home advertisement, 50,
App. J
Bishop, Mr. David
Area 6 team. *See under* Brent Social
Services Dept.
Beckford case, summary of role as to, 45
biographical details, 45
case conferences

chaired by, 45, 79, 110, 245, 251
invitations to attend, 248
minutes, taking of, 110, 232
change of circumstances form, 228
clerical support, lack of, 133, 134
death of Jasmine
notice of, 45, 181
role following, 181, 183, 188, 193
evidence before Inquiry, 33, 81
inattention to Knowles' statement, 83
independent social worker's report, 93
legal costs, 37
Proberts, approval of, 45, 92
psychiatric assessment of Beckford, 87
rehabilitation of Beckford children,
views on, 90, 91, 287
statutory case reviews, 45, 246
unapprised of events, 225
Willesden Magistrates' rider
impact of, on, 101, 287
Mr. Thompson's memorandum on,
45, 90, 98, 104, App. C:3
Black children, trans-racial fostering. *See*
Trans-racial fostering
Boarding out children
Brent, in, 63
history of, 263 *et seq*
regulations as to, 20, App. E
See also Fostering
Bowden, Miss Janet
biographical details, 54
health visitor, as, 73, 114, 231
Boyle, Gillian. *See* Hindle, Mrs.
Brent, London Borough of
care orders in favour of, 2
children
boarding out, 63
care, in, 64
housing, 61
population statistics
age and social services area, by, 61-63
ethnic group, by, 61, 63
unemployment, 61
Brent Area Review Committee
Beckford case
inquiry, setting up, 152, 195, 239, 244
involvement in, 192, 239, 242
Chairman
Beckford case, at time of, 43, 240
choice of, 240, 241, 304
Director of Social Services as, 240, 241

death of Jasmine
  notice of, absence of, 189, 296
  role following, 189, 193-196
Cllr. Sealy as. *See* Sealy, Mr.
Brent Social Services Department
  accommodation, 135, 304
  Adoption and Foster Care Section
    Area 6 team, relations with, 106,
    108, 109
    Beckford children, fostering
    arrangements, *See* Fostering; Proberts
    foster parents, selection of, 263, 271
    legal advice, 150
    Principal Officer.
      Mr. Burns as. *See* Burns, Mr.
      role of, 106
    work of, 106
  Area Review Committee, role of, 192,
  193, 242, 304
  Area 6
    accommodation for, 135, 304
    Adoption and Foster Care Section,
    collaboration with, 106, 108, 109
    Area Manager. *See* Bishop, Mr.
    clerical help, 133, 135, 218, 219, 304
    conclusions of Inquiry as to, 287,
    290-294
    death of Jasmine, response to,
    181 *et seq*
  Area 6 team
    Family Aide, Beckford case. *See*
    Ruddock, Mrs.
    placement of children, options on, 105
    police, links with, 160
    Proberts, relations with, 110, 288
    resource constraints, 134-136
    senior social workers
      deficiency of, 135, 136, 296
      Mrs. Dietmann. *See*
      Dietmann, Mrs.
      role of, 131-134
    Statutory case reviews. *See* Statutory
    Case review
    social workers
      generally. *See* Social workers
      health visitor, liaison with, 119, 295
      role of, 131-133
      senior. *See* senior social workers
      above
      statutory duty, 266
      Wahlstrom. *See* Wahlstrom, Ms.

  structure of, 131-133
  Assistant Directors
    Mr. Bishop. *See* Bishop, Mr.
    role of, 129-131
  assumption of responsibility for
  Beckford case, 57
  budget, 44
  care proceedings
    Chantelle Beckford. *See* Beckford,
    Chantelle
    generally. *See* Care proceedings
    Jasmine and Louise Beckford *See*
    Willesden Juvenile Court
  case conferences. *See* Case conferences
  child abuse
    procedures, review of, 44, 181,
    186-187, 195
    register, custody of, 241
    specialist in, 131, 136, 303
  Common Serjeant's remarks relating to,
  38, 39, App. D:2
  Court Officer
    Assistant. *See* Webbs, Mr.
    Principal. *See* Thompson, Mr.
    role of, generally. *See* Court Officer
  death of Jasmine
    blameworthiness as to, 287-294,
    296, 297
    response to, 181, *et seq*
  decision making in Beckford case, 135
  Director of Social Services
    Miss Howarth as. *See* Howarth, Miss
    Mr. Whalley as. *See* Whalley, Mr.
    role of, 129 *et seq*
  documentary evidence for Inquiry, 234
  Education Department, links with, 48,
  155-157, 292
  Family Services Division
    Adoption and Foster Care Section *See*
    Adoption and Foster Care section,
    above
    Area 6 team. *See* Area 6 team, *above*
    responsibilities of, 130, 131
    structure of, 130, 131
  Green Lodge. *See* Green Lodge
  Residential Day Nursery
    independent social worker, attitude
    towards, 253
    judicial criticism of, 38, 39
  Law and Administration Dept., relations
  with, 131, 149-153, 261

management team
  composition of, 129
  meetings of, 129
Mortimer Road Day Nursery. *See*
Mortimer Road Day Nursery
personnel on Beckford case
  conclusion of Inquiry, 287-294, 296
  names and detaiĺs of, 43-48
  role played by, generally. *See under
  individual's name*
police, liaison with, 159 *et seq*
Principal Social Worker, creation of
post of, 136
Proberts and, 105-114, 288
records. *See* Documentation
resource constraints, 296
schools, links with, 156, 229,
230, 291, 301
shortage of staff, 135, 136
size of, 44
social workers
  Area 6 team. *See* Area 6 team, *above*
  generally, *See* Social workers
time spent on Beckford family, 134, 135,
290, 291
training courses for staff, 135
Tree Tops, use of, by, 107, 134, 135
See also generally Social Services
Departments
Brent Young People's Law Centre, 35
Brewer, Wayne, case of, 28
Briggs, Superintendent, 163, 241, App. B
British Adoption Project, 282
British Agencies for Adoption and
Fostering, 270, 272, 273, 284
British Association of Social Workers
Code of Practice, records. *See*
Documentation
place of safety order recommendations,
257, 302
representation before Inquiry, 37
social workers' costs at Inquiry, 37
Brown, Mrs. Joyce M., 51, 189, App. B
Brown, Paul, case of 14, 16, 23
Burns, Mr. Jeremy
  Adoption and Foster Care Section, role
  in, 47, 105, 106, 108
  Area 6 team, relations with, 106,
  108, 109
  biographical details, 47-48
  death of Jasmine, meeting after, 150

dual role in Beckford case, 106, 107
Proberts
  assessment of 105, 108, 109, 263, 271
  dealings with, 106, 111-113, 271
Care order
  administration of, 19-21
  analysis of, 19, 20
  appeal against, 211, 260
  Chantelle Beckford. *See* Beckford,
  Chantelle
  health authority role following, 143
  Jasmine Beckford
    generally. *See under* Willesden
    Juvenile Court
    interim order, 41, 57, 79
  jurisdiction to make, 18, 167-171
  justices' duty on making, 168-171, 302
  Louise Beckford
    generally. *See under* Willesden
    Juvenile Court
    interim order, 41, 57, 79
  revocation of
    application for, 163
    jurisdiction, 168
  rider to
    invitation to add, 170
    jurisdiction to add, 168-171
    recommendation as to, 171, 302
    Willesden Justices'. *See under*
    Willesden Juvenile Court
  social workers' role after, 204
  text of relevant law, App. E
  trustee relationship created by, 16, 21,
  297, 301
  use of term, 19, 20
  wardship proceedings, in,
  distinguished, 170
  See also Care proceedings; Child
  care law
Care proceedings
  care order. *See* Care order
  case conferences before and after, 89,
  250, 251, 301
  Chantelle Beckford. *See* Beckford,
  Chantelle
  child, representation of, 103, 213, 253,
  260, 303
  composition of court, 210
  grounds for, 144, 145
  guardian ad litem, role of, 253, 254, 302
  independent social workers' role, 253

Child abuse inquiries
  funding of, 244
  involvement in, 195
  setting up, 242
  Standing Inquiry Panel, 242-244, 304
child abuse procedures
  general practitioners, for, 237, 238, 304
  Green Book. *See* Green Book
  revision of, 237, 304
case conferences
  monitoring of, 242
  police attendance, 245, 304
composition of, 195, 240, 241
health services, function as to, 192, 239, 242
Social Services, monitoring of, 192, 193, 242, 304
See also, generally, Area Review Committee
Brent Borough Council
  Chief Executive Officer, *See* Bichard, Mr.
  child abuse inquiries, funding of, 244
  Child Abuse Training Coordinator, 131, 303
  Conservative Group. *See* Conservative Group
  Education Department. *See* Brent Education Department
  Housing Department, 91, 92
  Labour Group. *See* Labour Group
  Law and Administration Department. *See* Brent Law and Administration Department
  Liberal Councillors, 179
  members
    death of Jasmine, response to, 181, 189 *et seq*, 296, 297
    generally, *See under individual's name*
    names and details of, 50, 51
  National Foster-Care Association, membership of, 273, 304
  officers
    death of Jasmine, response to, 181 *et seq*, 296, 297
    generally, *See under individual's name*
    names and personal details, 43-50
  Panel of Inquiry
    appointment of, 1
    costs arising, 36,37, 179-180

documentary evidence, supply of, 5, 234
representation before, absence of, 35
political complexion of
  outline of, 7, 179
  relevance to Inquiry, 35, 179-180
Policy and Resources Committee. *See* Brent Policy and Resources Committee.
Probert's allegations, 113-114
race relations, advice on, 1, 7-8, 29, 195
report of Ms. Wahlstrom, circulation of, 115
Social Services Committee. *See* Brent Social Services Committee
Social Services Dept. *See* Brent Social Services Department
Standing Inquiry Panel, funding of, 244
See also, generally, Local Authority
Brent Education Department
  Beckford Case, role in
    conclusions of Inquiry, 287, 291, 292
    summary of, 155-157
  child abuse guidelines to schools. *See* Schools (Green Book)
  Common Serjeant's questions, 38, App. D
  Director of Education
    Green Book, duties as to, 120, 301
    Miss Rickus as. *See* Rickus, Miss
    Mr. Parsons as, 48
  educational welfare officers
    Beckford Case, 49, 121, 156
    duties of, extension of, 156, 301
    Green Book, guidance in, App. H
    personnel, details of, 48, 49
    Princess Frederica Primary School. *See* Princess Frederica Primary School
  schools, links with
    Beckford case, *See* Princess Frederica Primary School
    generally, *See* Schools; Teachers
  Social Services Department, links with, 48, 155-157, 292
Brent Health Authority
  Area Review Committee and, 192, 193, 239, 242
  case conferences, attendance at. *See* Case conferences
  child abuse inquiries, 244, 300
  child abuse procedures, review of, 143, 304

Child Abuse Register, 139
Child Abuse Training Coordinator, 131, 303
communications within, 146
death of Jasmine
  blameworthiness as to, 287, 295, 296
  response to, 146, 147
decision-making in Beckford case, 141
Director of Nursing Services. *See* Martin, Miss
errors of judgment, 141
filing system, 230, 231
former name, 65, 139
health visitors
  child abuse, knowledge of, 141
health visitors
  Concern List, 139
  conclusions of Inquiry about, 295, 296
  experience and training, 141
  liaison with key workers, 119
  Miss Hindle. *See* Hindle, Miss
  Miss Knowles. *See* Knowles, Miss
  Miss Leong. *See* Leong, Miss
  Mrs. Vivekanandan. *See* Vivekanandan, Mrs.
  records, 230, 231
  resource constraints, 139
  supervision of, 141-143, 220-221, 304
  visits to Beckfords, summary of, 57-59, 139-141
legal costs, 36
Mortimer Road Clinic. *See* Mortimer Road Clinic
Panel of Inquiry
  appointment of, 1
  documentary evidence for, 5, 234
  representation before, 35
  personnel involved in Beckford case, 51, 52, 139, 231
reorganisation of health service, 139
resource constraints 139, 141
Secretary of State, accountability to, 143
senior nurses
  Miss Baichoo. *See* Baichoo, Miss
  Miss Tyler. *See* Tyler, Miss
  Mrs. Brown. *See* Brown, Mrs.
  supervision of health visitors, 141-143, 220, 221, 304
Standing Inquiry Panel, funding of, 244
warning signs of child abuse, 141
See also, generally, Health authority;

Health services
Brent Health District. *See* Brent Health Authority
Brent Housing Department, 91, 92
Brent Law and Administration Department
  Area Review Committee, representation on, 241
  Beckford case, involvement in, 50, 149-152, 186-188, 192
  council committee meetings, attendance at, 151
  Court Officer, role of
    generally. *See* Court Officers
    Mr. Thompson as. *See* Thompson, Mr.
  Director of, Mr. Forster as. *See* Forster, Mr.
  Panel of Inquiry, services to, 8, 152
  role of, 149-153
  Senior Solicitor, Mr. Damms as. *See* Damms, Mr.
  Social Services Dept., relations with, 131, 149-153, 261
Brent Policy and Resources Committee
  Beckford case inquiry decision, 59, 152, 195, 239
  Legal costs, resolution as to, 180
Brent Policy Memorandum
  case conference minutes, 233, 300, 301
  health visitors, direction to, 146
  social workers
    acquaintance of, with, 74, 301
    records of, 225, 226, 300
  See also Green Book
Brent Social Services Committee
  Cases Sub-Committee. *See* Cases Sub-Committee
  Chairman of
    Cllr. Stone as. *See* Stone, Mr.
    death of Jasmine
      notice of, 189, 296
      role following, 181, 183-184, 189-190, 192
  chairmen of
    list of, 179
  Inquiry, decision as to, 59, 152, 194, 195, 239
  Law and Administration Dept.
    representation of, on, 151
  shadow chairman

Jasmine
literature on, 7, 74, App. K
Louise Beckford. *See* Beckford, Louise
management of system. *See* Child abuse
system
medical evidence. *See* Medical evidence
normal social responses to, 24
parental disharmony as sign of, 118, 291
police investigation, 4, 161, 162
procedures. *See* Child abuse procedures
prosecutions, 3, 4, 161, 162, 303
psychopathology of, 86-88
register. *See* Child Abuse Register
suspected
   initial approach, 24
   inquiry. *See* Child abuse inquiries
   reporting of, 145
system. *See* Child abuse system
training in relation to. *See* Training
use of term, 9, 10
weight as indicator of, 74
See also Abused child
Child abuse cases
Brent Area Review Committee's
guidelines. *See* Green Book
care proceedings. *See* Care proceedings
case conferences. *See* Case conferences
co-operation between authorities,
143-147, 277, 299
documentation. *See* Documentation
expert radiological opinion, need for,
68, 81, 82, 301
health visitors. *See* Health visitors
"high risk" cases, 288
Key workers. *See* Key workers
NSPCC, role of. *See* NSPCC
nursing profession and, 219-221, 301
place of safety orders. *See* Place of
safety orders
police
   prosecution by, 3, 4, 161, 162, 303
   role of, 159, 161
procedures. *See* Child abuse procedures
professional bodies, consultation with,
145, 299
rehabilitation of child. *See* Home on
trial
"rule of optimism," 33, 216-218
schools, monitoring role of, 136, 137,
155-157, 301
social workers. *See* Social workers

statutory case reviews. *See* Statutory
case reviews
supervision of field workers. *See*
Supervision
training in relation to. *See* Training
See also Child abuse; Child abuse system
Child abuse inquiries
advisers, 29, 30, 300
Area Review Committees' role, 28, 195,
239, 242
assessors, 29, 30, 300
Beckford case
   independent panel. *See* Panel of
   Inquiry
Beckford case
   type of inquiry, decision. *See*
   Beckford case
case review preceding, 24
chairman of, choice of, 28, 29
Colwell case, 3, 14, 23
composition of panel, 28-30, 300
costs. *See* Costs
counsel for inquiry, role of, 5, 6
D.H.S.S. consultative paper, 1, 23, 185
documentation, preparation of, 226, 234
enormous public interest, of, 3, 300
expedition, need for, 297
form of, public or private, 25-28
function of, 26, 27, 34, 297
health visitors, attendance by, 27
issues arising from, 197
kinds of - examples of, 23-24
legal representation at, 35
non-statutory, 25, 28
observers, presence of, 30
parties
   cost to, 37, 38, 300
   time to prepare cases, 31, 300
police participation, 195
private inquiry, reasons for and
against, 25-28
procedure, determination of, 25, 30
public inquiry, reasons for and
against, 25-28
publicity. *See* Publicity
review of reports of, 223
setting up
   Beckford case, in. *See* Beckford case
   local authority, by, 3, 23, 28, 300
   modes of, 23, 28
   Secretary of State, by, 3, 25, 200

social workers, attendance by, 27, 30
Standing Inquiry Panel. *See* Standing Inquiry Panel
Child abuse procedures
    case conferences. *See* Case conferences
    documentation of social work. *See* Documentation
    hospitals, at, 79, 81, 82, 301
    policy statements and guidelines
        Brent's Green Book. *See* Green Book
        social workers' acquaintance with, 74, 301
        standardised definitions, 80, 300
    review of
        Brent Health Authority, by, 145, 304
        Brent Social Services Dept., 44, 181, 185-187, 195
    schools. *See* Schools
Child Abuse Register
    custody of, 131, 136, 244
    placement of Beckford sisters on, 57-59, 140
    removal of children from
        Beckford sisters, 58, 59, 118, 142
        police, advice of, 163
    schools' role as to children on, 156, 301
Child Abuse System
    Area Review Committees' role. *See* Area Review Committees
    case conferences. *See* Case conferences
    Colwell case, lessons of, 14-16
    documentation, importance of, 223-234
    Family Service Units, 175
    general practitioners' role, 235-238
    guardian at litem's role, 253, 254
    health services' role, 143-147, 299
    juvenile court's role, 210
    Law and Administration Department's role, 152, 153
    local authority's duties, 145, 299
    NSPCC's role, 175-177, 299
    placement of child, options on, 263-268
    police, role of, 159 *et seq*, 303
    professional bodies, consultation with, 145, 299
    recommendations of Inquiry, 299-304
    residential care, use of. *See* Residential care
    schools, role of, 136, 155-157, 301
    social services, links with health services, 143 *et seq*, 299

statutory case reviews, role of, 245-247
voluntary agencies' role of, 175-177
Child Abuse Training Coordinator, 131, 136, 303
Child care law
    care orders. *See* Care orders; Care proceedings
Child care law
    compulsory care, 18 *et seq*
    court officers, role of. *See* Court officers
    custodianship orders, 80, 168
    general duty of local authority, 17
    health visitors, 209
    legal education, 212-214, 304
    parental rights and duties. *See* Parental rights and duties
    place of safety orders. *See* Place of safety orders
    review of, 1, 256, 289
    skilled practice of, promotion of, 214, 304
    statutory case reviews, 18
    social workers, training of. *See* Training
    supervision orders. *See* Supervision order
    text of relevant law, App. E
    training as to. *See* Training
    voluntary care, 17, 18
Child in care
    access by parents, 19, App. E
    accommodation, 17, App. E
    administration of care order, 171
    adoption of. *See* Adoption
    black, fostering and adoption, 282-285, 300
    case conferences. *See* Case conferences
    child in trust, as, 16, 21, 297, 301
    contact between worker and child, 124 *et seq*
    death of
        committee meeting to follow, 185, 299
        publicity, 13, 14
        reporting of, 184, 185, 299
    duties of local authority, 17 *et seq*, 285
    education of. *See* Education; Schools
    fostering. *See* Fostering
    guardian at litem, consultations with, 251, 302
    health authority, consultation and advice, 145, 146, 299
    judicial supervision, 167-171

Jasmine Beckford
  generally. *See under* Willesden
    Juvenile Court
  interim care order, 57, 79
  jurisdiction of court, 167-171
  Law Society panel of solicitors to act in,
    213, 214, 303
  legislation relating to
    recommendation as to, 18, 302,
    text of, App. E
  local authority, representation of,
    212-214, 259, 303
  Louise Beckford
    generally. *See* Willesden Juvenile
      Court
    interim care order, 57, 79
  manner of dealing with, 168 *et seq*
  parent
    party, making a, 254, 302
    representation, 89, 212, 253, 302
  persons entitled to bring, 18, 144, 175
  police attendance at 160, 164, 165, 303
  reasons for decision
    factors to be considered, 172, 303
    failure to give, legal, effect of,
      172, 303
    need to give, 7, 171, 172, 302
  separate representation of parent and
    child, 253, 254, 302
  solicitor acting for child in, 103, 213,
    214, 259-261, 303
  supervision orders, power to make, 168
  time for bringing, 18, 302
  See also Child care law
Carthy, Reuben, case of, 23, 24, 235
Case conferences
  abusing parents at, 249
  Beckford children, as to. *See* Case
    conferences (Beckford children)
  Brent Policy Memorandum
    amendment of, 233, 300, 301
    text of, App. H
    minute taking by, 88, 134, 252
    selection of, 135, 251, 252
  children, attendance by, 250-251
  composition of, 247-252
  foster parents at, 249, 272
  function of, 88, 89, 144, 161,
    246, 247, 251
  general practitioners at, 235, 248
  guardian ad litem

    attendance by, 250, 251
    consultation by local authority,
      251, 302
  health visitors
    attendance by, 247
    records of, availability of, 226, 300
  initial, function of, 89, 251
  key worker, nomination of, 218, 219
  local authority solicitors at, 260
  minutes
    alteration of, 88, 233, 300, 301
    taking of, 88, 134, 252
  monitoring by Area Review
    Committee, 242
  multi-disciplinary concept, 145
  national independent prosecuting service
    representation at, 163, 303
  nursing profession and, 219, 220, 247
  paediatricians at, 247, 248
  police
    attendance by, 161-164, 247
    information, supply of, by, 163,
      164, 303
  second, timing of, 89, 301
  senior nurses at, 220, 221
  social workers
    attendance by, 247
    records of, availability, 226, 300
  statutory case reviews distinguished,
    246-247
  structure of, 88
  teachers at, 248
  use of term, 246
Case conferences (Beckford children)
  6 August 1981
    chairmanship, 232, 245
    composition of, 81, 140, 176, 236, 245
    evaluation of, 289, 290
    health visitors' records, 226
    hospital records, 227
    minutes of, 232, 245, App. G:1
    purpose of, 79, 245
    substance of, 79-83, 140, 160
  20 August 1981
    chairmanship, 232, 245
    composition of, 140, 160, 162, 245
    evaluation of, 289, 290
    health visitors' records, 226
    hospital records, 227
    minutes, 232, 245, App. G:2
    purpose of, 245

substance of, 88-91
5 April 1982
  chairmanship, 110, 245, 290
  composition of, 83, 89, 110,
    136, 245, 247
  conduct of, 89, 110, 290, 291
  decisions taken, 91, 110, 140, 290, 291
  health visitor's absence, 73, 140, 246
  minutes, 110, 245, App. G:4
  purpose of, 110
  timing of, 89, 90
  views expressed, 90, 91
9 November 1982
  chairmanship, 117, 137, 246
  composition, 117, 140, 246, 247
  crucial features of, 117, 118, 137, 291
  decision taken, 58, 118
  minutes, 117, 137, 252, App. G:7
  purpose of, 140, 246
12 July 1984
  chairmanship, 188
  composition of, 188
  legal advice, absence of, 149, 150
  minutes, 188
  purpose of, 149
  recommendations of, 59, 150, 188
2 October 1984,
  composition of, 189
  result of, 59
Brent's Green Book, App. H
  monitoring of, 242
  See also, generally, Case conferences
Cases Sub-Committee
  chairmen, list of, 179
  establishment of, 179
  Law and Administration Dept.
  representation, 151
  meeting on 29 Oct. 1984
    events leading to, 181-191
    report on death of Jasmine, 59,
     151, 191
    summary of, 192
    tardiness in calling, 296
  meeting on 26 Nov. 1984
    composition of, 193
    events prior to, 192, 193
    internal inquiry recommendation, 59,
     152, 194, 195
    summary of, 193
  meeting on 16 Jan. 1985, 195
  reaction to death of Jasmine, 296

reports for meetings of, 151
Causby, Miss Alix
  child abuse training programmes, 131
  expert evidence, 162, 224, 225, App. B
  guardian ad litem
    appointment as, 189, 253
    report, 189, App. F
Central Council for Education and
Training of Social Workers
  establishment of, 197
  functions of, 197, 208
  qualifying awards
    courses for, 201-203
    two types of, 201
  review of training policies, 203-207, 304
Central Criminal Court
  Beckford/Lorrington trial
    Law and Administration Dept., role
    of, 152
    charges, pleas, verdicts, etc., 2, 183,
    App. D
    Common Serjeant's remarks
    following, 31, 38, 39, 152, App. D
    transcripts of proceedings, 234
Central government
  child abuse inquiries
    costs of, 37, 38, 244, 300
    setting up, 3, 23, 25, 300
Certificate in Social Service, 201, 203-204
Certificate of Qualification in Social
Work, 201-204
Chantelle Beckford. *See* Beckford,
Chantelle
Chief Executive Officer, Brent. *See*
Bichard, Mr.
Child abuse
  cases of, generally. *See* Child abuse cases
  Chantelle Beckford. *See* Beckford,
  Chantelle
  child at risk from, protection. *See* Child
  abuse system
  death of child
    generally. *See* Death of child
    inquiry. *See* Child abuse inquiries
    Jasmine Beckford. *See* Death of
    Jasmine
  expert witnesses on, 7, App. B
  historical background, 9-16
  identification of signs of, 297
  inquiries. *See* Child abuse inquiries
  Jasmine Beckford. *See* Beckford,

legislation as to, text of, App. E
maintenance, 17, 267
medical examination, 20, 21
number of, 44, 64
nursery school. *See* Nursery schools
parental rights and duties. *See* Parental
rights and duties
placement of
definitions relating to, 80, 300
options on, 105, 263-268
racial considerations, 282-285, 300
residential care. *See* Residential care
reunion with parents
condition of, 111, 299
grounds for, 289
schooling. *See* Schools
serious harm to
committee meeting to follow, 191, 299
publicity, 13, 14
statutory case reviews. *See* Statutory
case reviews
voluntary care, 17, 18
See also Child care law
Child in trust, child in care as, 16,
21, 297, 301
Children's Departments
court officers, 259, 260
fostering arrangements, 269
history of, 259, 260
Chronological summary of events 57-60
Clerks to justices, 212, 302
Cochand, Mr. Charles M.
Beckford case, role in, 52, 95-97
qualifications, 52
Coleman, Mr. Martin
biographical details, 50
complaint about foster home
advertisement, 49, 50, App. J
death of Jasmine
notice of, 50, 149, 182, 190
role after, 50, 190, 191, 296
evidence at Inquiry, 33
Colwell case
Area Review Committees, setting
up, 239
Beckford case, comparison with, 11
criminal proceedings, 4
inquiry, 3, 11-14, 23
social work, effect on, 12-16
weight of child, relevance, 74
Common Serjeant

Beckford/Lorrington trial
generally. *See* Central Criminal Court
remarks following, 31, 38, 39, 152,
App. D
Community child health, 75
Community homes, 264, 267, 268
Confidential information, access to
foster parents, 249, 272
independent social worker, 93, 98
Conservative group
Leader, notice of Jasmine's death, 149,
182, 190
members of
chairmanship of committees, 179
details of, 50, 51
numbers on Council, 179
Consultations between authorities, need
for, 145, 146, 299
Coroner's inquest, role of, 24
Costs
Brent Standing Inquiry Panel, 244
child abuse inquiries, generally, 28,
36-38, 244, 300
Panel of Inquiry, of, 36, 37, 179, 180
parties, of
Beckford case, 37-38, 180
child abuse inquiries, 37, 38, 300
Council for the Education and Training of
Health Visitors, 208
Counsel for Panel of Inquiry, 5, 6, App. A
Court, Miss Joan
access to information 93, 98, 253
case conference after care proceedings,
89, 90
Dr. Levick's report and, 97, App. C:4
hospital visit by, 92
independent social worker's report, 93,
97, 98, 102, 294, App. C:2; 4
previous work done by, 10
psychiatric assessment of Beckfords, 87
Court officer
Brent Social Services Dept.
Assistant Court Officer. *See*
Hobbs, Mr.
Principal Court Officer. *See*
Thompson, Mr.
role of
current, 130, 131, 259, 260
future, 260-261, 303
Cowgill, Miss Frieda
care order, ignorance of, 49, 120, 291

Green Book, ignorance about, 49, 120, 233, 291
  head teacher, appointment as, 49
  social worker, contact with, 49, 120, 155, 233, 291, 292
Crane, Mr. George
  biographical details, 50
  death of Jasmine, role following, 50, 186, 189-196
  evidence at Inquiry, 33, 186, 296
Cribbin, Miss Mary
  biographical details, 50
  death of Jasmine, role following, 50, 190-193
Crocker, Detective Sergeant, 160, 162, App. B
Crown as *parens patriae*, 21, 175, 289
Curtis Committee Report, 3, 16, 263,, 269
Custodianship orders, 80, 168
Damms, Mr. Martin
  Beckford case, involvement in, 50, 149-151, 187, 188, 192
  biographical details, 50
Davidson, Mrs. Mary, App. B
Death of child in care
  committee meeting to follow, 185, 299
  Jasmine Beckford. *See* Death of Jasmine
  publicity, 13, 14
  reporting of, 184, 185, 299
Death of Jasmine
  Beckford trial. *See under* Central Criminal Court
  date of, 41, 59
  Inquiry. *See* Beckford case; Panel of Inquiry
  persons notified of, 149, 181, *et seq*
  post mortem examination, 69, App. I
  preventability
    education services, role of, 287, 291, 292
    health services, role of, 287, 292, 295
    magistrates' court, role of, 287
    social services, role of, 287, 289-294, 296
  publicity relating to, 2, 25-28, 182, 288
  response to
    Brent Borough Council, of, 181-196, 296, 297
  response to
    Brent Health Authority, of, 146, 147
  summary of events after, 2, 59, 60

Dental surgeons, App. H
Department of Health and Social Security
  child abuse
    inquiries
      consultative paper, 1, 23, 185
      review of reports of, 223
    procedures, guidance on, 185, 299
  child care law, review of, 1
  Colwell case, effect of, on, 14
  death
    child in care, of, reporting, 184, 185, 299
    Jasmine, of, notice of, 59, 184
  research financed by, 283
  Secretary of State. *See* Secretary of State
  Social Services Inspectorate, 1, 14, 299
Derbyshire Area Review Committee, 235, 237, 304
Dickens, Det. Insp., App. B
Dietmann, Mrs. Diane
  assaults on Beckford sisters, reaction to, 159
  biographical details, 45-46
  care orders, reactions to, 45, 84, 101, 207, 293
  case conferences, role at, 45, 90, 91, 110, 117, 136, 137
  child abuse
    experience as to, 45, 135
    indications of, 119, 159, 177
  death of Jasmine, role following, 46, 181, 183, 188
  evidence at Inquiry, 33
  fostering of Beckford sisters, role as to, 105-109, 113, 150, 206
  legal costs, 37
  monitoring of, 135
  records, 226, 227, 229
  rehabilitation of Beckford Children, 90, 91, 98, 107, 114, 115, 225
  statutory case reviews, 45
  supervision of Wahlstrom, 46, 79, 118, 119, 206, 287, 292, 293
  training and qualifications, 45, 135, 205, 293, 294
  visits to Beckford family, 46, 59, 127
Director of Education
  Miss Rickus as. *See* Rickus, Miss
  Mr. Parsons as, 48
  Green Book, duties as to, 120, 301
Director of Law of Administration Dept.

See Forster, Mr.
Director of Nursing Services, Brent. *See*
Martin, Miss
Director of Social Services
appointment of, 17
Brent
Area Review Committee,
chairmanship of, 240
Miss Howarth as. *See* Howarth, Miss
Mr. Whalley as. *See* Whalley Mr.
death of child in care etc., reporting,
185, 299
Divine, Mr. David, expert witness, App. B
Doctors, generally. *See* General
practitioners
Documentation
BASW Code of Practice
case conference minutes, 233, 300, 301
duties of social worker, 223, 226,
229, 300
proper standard of recording, 225,
226, 300
Beckford case
Brent Health Authority's records,
230-231
health visitor's records, 226, 229
hospital records, 227
information transference, 227-229
minuting of case conferences, 231
preparation in, pending inquiry,
5, 234
Princess Frederica Nursery
School, 233
review of records, 227-229
social worker's records, 224,
226 *et seq*
sources of information, 229-230
standard of recording in, 224-225
Brent Policy Memorandum, 226, 233,
300, 301
case conferences, 225, 226, 300, 301
general observations, 223-226
preparation of, pending an inquiry, 234
Dorset County Council case, 13, 198
Education
Brent Education Dept. *See* Brent
Education Department
child under compulsory school age. *See*
Nursery schools
educational welfare officers
Beckford case, 49, 121, 156

duties of, extension of, 156, 301
legal. *See* Legal education
medical checks on children, 21
nursery. *See* Nursery schools etc.
schools, generally. *See* Schools
training, and, generally. *See* Training
Educational welfare officers
Brent Education Dept., 49, 121, 156
duties of, extension of, 156, 301
Edwards, Dr. Bridget, 81, 248, App. B
English National Board of Nursing,
208, 210
Ethnic
communities in Brent, 61, 63
origins of Beckford family, 1
Evidence of Inquiry
documentary
Beckford/Lorrington trial, as to,
App. D
Brent's Green Book. App. H
care proceedings, as to, App. C
case conferences, as to, App. G
Chief Executive's report, App. J
guardian ad litem's report, App. E
post mortem report, App. I
preparation pending Inquiry, 5, 534
statutory case reviews, as to, App. G
See also Documentation expert
generally. *See* Expert witnesses
medical. *See* Medical evidence
oral, generally. *See* Witnesses at Inquiry
Expert witnesses
child abuse, on, 7, App. B
list of, App. B
medical evidence. *See* Medical evidence
order in which called, 33
trans-racial fostering and adoption,
7, 33
See also under names of individuals
Family aides
Beckford family. *See* Ruddock, Mrs.
Brent Social Services Dept., 132
case conferences, attendance at, 248
Family Court, establishment of, 172-173
Family Service Unit
Brent, guidelines to, App. H
role in child abuse system, 175
Felix, Mrs. Eris
Beckford case, involvement in, 49
evidence of, 121, 233
Forde, Miss Margaret, App. B

Forster, Mr. Stephen
  Area Review Committee, representation on, 241
  biographical details, 50
  Director of Law and Administration, period as, 50
  Inquiry, role as to, 8, 152
  involvement in Beckford case, 50, 149, 152, 186, 187
  training, views on, 151
Foster parents
  black, 284, 300
  boarding-out allowances, 272
  case conferences, 249, 272
  confidential information, access to, 249, 272
  'contact fostering', 271-272
  fees, payment of, to, 272
  natural parent, claims by, 80
  Proberts as. *See* Proberts
  prospective
    assessment of, 270-271
    group discussions, 270
    Jasmine and Louise, for. *See* Proberts
    racial discrimination by, 285
    report from, 270, 274-281
  statutory case reviews, at, 272
  supervision and support, 270, 272
  training, 270, 272
  use of term, 270
  See also Fostering
Fostering
  alternatives to, 105, 263-268
  British Agencies for Adoption and, 270, 272, 273, 284
  Chantelle and Louise
    advertisement for foster home, 50, App. J
    arrangements for, 59, 181
    report, 88
  history of, 263 *et seq*
  Jasmine and Louise
    access arrangements, 107-109
    alternatives to, 105
    long or short term fostering, 88, 105, 106
    function in, 109-110
    rehabilitation
      case conference decision (5/4/82). *See* Case Conference (Beckford Children)

  hand-over of children, 114, 287, 288
  Proberts views as to, 111-114
  See also Proberts
  long-term: definition, 80
  Louise Beckford
    death of Jasmine, after. *See* Chantelle and Louise, *above*
    Proberts, with. *See* Jasmine and Louise, *above*
  management of, 271-273
  National Foster-Care Association, 270, 272, 273, 304
  selection of foster parents, 270-271
  short-term: definition, 80
  trans-racial. *See* Trans-racial fostering
  See also Foster parents
Freeing for adoption
  Beckford children, 150, 189
  generally, 17, 150, 171
Gates, Lucy, case of, 23, 30, 31, 209
General Practitioners
  Beckford case, involved in, 53, 236, 237
  Brent, in, guidelines to, App. H
  case conferences, at, 235, 248, 301
  child abuse system, role in, 235-238
Generic social workers
  emergence of, effect of, 263, 264
  training, 197, 201 *et seq*
Goban, Miss Angela, App. B
Gordon, Miss Pamela
  biographical details, 48
  case conference, attendance at, 48, 110
  Green Lodge, work at, 48, 266, 267
  witness, as, App. B
Green Book
  Brent Area Review Committee, by, 233
  health visitors, directions to, 146
  hospital staff, directions to, 77
  Princess Frederica School's ignorance of, 49, 120, 233, 291
  social workers
    acquaintance of, with, 74, 301
    records of, 225, 226, 300
  schools
    Director of Education's duties, 120, 301
    issue to, 48, 233
    text of, App. H
Green Lodge Residential Day Nursery
  Miss Gordon's role at. *See* Gordon, Miss
  transfer of Beckford sisters to, 58, 110,

135, 267
work carried out at, 266, 267
Greenland, Professor Cyril
expert evidence, 162, 212, 217, 288
qualifications, App. B
Guardians ad litem
appointment of, 253, 254, 302
care proceedings, role in, 211,
253-254, 302
case conferences
attendance at, 250, 251
convening of, consultation about,
251, 252
Chantelle Beckford, for. *See*
Causby, Miss
independent social workers and,
253, 254
legislation relating to, App. E
Louise Beckford, for. *See* Causby, Miss
solicitors for, 213
text of relevant law, App. E
training, 213
Haftel, Mr. Mark
Beckford case
evidence at Inquiry, 33
role in, 50, 191, 192, 196
biographical details, 50
Hall, Mr. Anthony
expert witness, App. B
residential care, views on, 265
trans-racial fostering, views on, 284, 285
Harrow Health Authority, 54, 139, 220
Head teachers
case conferences, at, 248
Princess Frederica Primary School
Miss Cowgill. *See* Cowgill, Miss
Mrs. Baines, 121, 233, App. B
Health Authority
accountability to Secretary of State, 143
Brent. *See* Brent Health Authority
consultation by local authority, 145, 299
general practitioners. *See* General
practitioners
Harrow, 54, 139, 220
health visitors. *See* Health visitors
hospitals. *See* Hospitals
North-West Thames Regional, 139
senior nurses. *See* Senior nurses
Social Services Dept., links with,
143-147, 227, 299
See also Health services

Health services
child abuse procedures
case conferences, 248, 301
health visitors and senior nurses,
220, 301
hospital admission, following, 79, 81,
82, 301
social services, collaboration, with, 143
et seq, 299
See also Health authority
Health visitors
Beckford case, involved in. *See* Brent
Health Authority
case conferences, at, 226, 247, 300
child abuse inquiries, at, 27
key worker, nomination as, 219
qualifications for, 208
records, etc., keeping of. *See*
Documentation
senior nurses, discussions with, 220, 301
social workers
collaboration with, 143-145, 227
role of, comparison, 220
statutory case reviews, at, 226, 300
supervision of, 209, 210, 220, 221, 301
training of, 208-210
Helston, Mrs. Helen, role of, 5, 6
"High risk" cases, 288-289
Hindle, Mrs. Gillian
biographical details, 52
role in Beckford case, 52, 231
visits to Beckfords, 57, 86, 139, 140
Hobbs, Mr. James
Beckford case, role in, 47, 90
biographical details, 47, 259
legal costs, 37, 180
Home helps, 248
Home on trial
case conference, importance, of,
250, 251
guardian at litem, role of, 250, 251, 302
Jasmine and Louise
bonding process, 116-118
case conferences whilst. *See* Case
conferences
child abuse
evidence of, 117-119, 182-184,
290-293
register, removal from, 118, 120
decision as to
case conference of 5/4/82, by. *See*

Case conferences
  inevitability of, 282
  hand-over by Proberts, 114, 287, 288
  health visits after, 116 *et seq* 295, 296
  justices' rider to care order. *See*
  Willesden Juvenile Court
  Miss Court's views, 97, 98, 294
  Proberts' views, 109-114, 288
  protection plan, 87, 115, 116
  schools' role, 116-118, 120, 121,
    291, 292
  social workers
    attitude of, regarding, 90-92,
      94, 177
    visits, by, 58, 115 *et seq*, 182,
      290-294
  statutory case reviews. *See* Statutory
    case reviews
  stresses, 122-124
  protection plan, 87, 11, 115, 299
Hospitals
  child abuse procedures
    admission of child, following, 79, 301
    Green Book, App. H
    radiological expertise, call for, 81,
      82, 301
    St. Charles's Hospital, at, 65, 77
  child in, place of safety order, 257,
    258, 302
  St. Charles's Hospital. *See* St. Charles's
    Hospital
House of Commons Social Services
Committee, 213, 256, 269, 270
Howarth, Miss Valerie
  Area Review Committee, chairmanship
    of, 43, 240-242
  biographical details, 43-44
  death of Jasmine
    notice of, 44, 59, 181
    role following, 44, 181-186, 189-196,
      296, 297
  Director of Social Services
    period as, 49, 129
    qualities as, 196
  evidence before Inquiry, 26, 27, 163
  Law and Administration Dept., links
    with, 149-152
  legal costs, 37
Independent Panel of Inquiry
  Beckford case. *See* Panel of Inquiry
  costs. *See* Costs

generally. *See* Child abuse inquiries
Independent social worker
  access to confidential information, 93,
    98, 254
  guardian at litem and, 253-254
  Miss Court. *See* Court, Miss
  Mr. Burns, appointment of, 47
Ingleby Committee's Report, 164, 168
Inner London Juvenile Panel
  chairman, selection of, 173
  interim care orders, 57, 79
  place of safety orders, 68, 79, 255
Inquiries
  child abuse
    Beckford case. *See* Beckford case
    generally. *See* Child abuse inquiries
  function of, 34
  preparation of documentation
  pending, 234
Jasmine Beckford. *See* Beckford, Jasmine
Jenkins, Mr. Raymond, 83, 176,
  242, App. B
John-Phillip, Rosamond, role of, 8
Johnson, Mrs. Dorothy, App. B
Jolly, Dr. Hugh
  evidence of, 73, 189, 288
  qualifications, App. B
  report on Chantelle and Louise, 88,
    App. F:3
Judges, comments by, at criminal trials,
  31, 39
Justice, Dr. John, App. B
Juvenile court
  care proceedings. *See* Care proceedings
  chairman, selection of, 173
  child abuse system, role in, 210
  criminal proceedings in, 260
  Kensington and Chelsea, 79
  place of safety orders. *See* Place of
    safety orders
  procedure in, App. E
  right to attend, persons having, 164
  social services departments, contact
    with, 259, 260
  staffing, 210
  summary of recommendations as to,
    302, 303
  supervision orders. *See* Supervision
    orders
  training of magistrates, 210-212, 302
  Willesden. *See* Willesden Juvenile Court

Kavarana, D. Hosaima, 53, 236, 237
Kempe, Dr., work of, 9, 10, 87, 88, 205
Kempe, Supt. John, 163, App. B
Kensington and Chelsea Juvenile Court, 79
Kerridge, Mr. Roy, App. B
Key worker
  Beckford case. See Wahlstrom, Ms.
  nomination of, 218, 219
  supervision, 218, 219
  use of term, 218, 219
Khan, Dr. H.K., 117, 236, App. B
Knibbs, Miss Susan
  biographical details, 54
  case conferences, attendance at,
  54, 79, 90
  decisions and actions of, 78, 79
  NSPCC, contact with, 176
  place of safety order, application for,
  65, 68, 79
Knowles, Miss Judith
  Beckford parents, fondness for, 295
  biographical details, 52
  case conferences, attendance at, 52, 73,
  140, 141
  child abuse, warnings of, 295
  doctors' attitude towards, 82, 83
  handover to Miss Leong, 52, 140, 295
  health visitor for Jasmine, as, 231, 295
  percentile charts, use of, 72, 140, 141,
  147, 226
  rehabilitation of Beckford sisters, views
  on, 90, 110, 116
  supervision of, 143
  training, deficiencies in, 209
  visits to Beckfords, 57, 58, 74, 118-119,
  140-142
  weighing of Jasmine, 52, 72, 73, 226
Labour Group
  Leader of
    biographical details, 50
    complaint about foster home
    advertisement, 49, 50, App. J
    death of Jasmine
      notice of, 149, 182, 190
      reaction to, 50, 190, 191, 296
    evidence at Inquiry, 33
  members of
    chairmanship of committees, 179
    details of, 50, 51
  Panel of Inquiry, suggestions to, 8
  political power, 179

Lacey, Cllr. 149, 182, 190
Law, child care
  generally. See Child care law
  recommendations as to, 301, 302
  text of relevant, App. E
  training in. See Training
Law and Administration Dept. of Brent
Borough Council. See Brent Law and
Administration Department
Law Society
  child care cases, panel for
    establishment of, 213
    extension of, 214, 261, 303
Lawyers
  Area Review Committees, on, 241
  Brent Law and Administration Dept.
  See Brent Law and Administration
  Dept.
  local authority, employed by, 213-214,
  260-261, 303
  panels of inquiry, on, 28, 29, 36, 244
  training of, 212-214, 304
  See also Solicitors
Lay magistrates
  juvenile court, in, 210
  training. See Training
Legal education
  lawyers, 212-214, 304
  magistrates. See Training
  social workers, 207, 304
Legal representation
  care proceedings, in
    generally, 89, 149, 212-214, 303
    Willesden Justices, before, 52,
    53, 68, 149
  Independent Panel of Inquiry, 5,
  6, 35, App. A
Legislation
  child care
    recommendations as to, 301-303
    text of relevant, App. E
Legal profession
  generally. See Lawyers
  solicitors. See Solicitors
Leong, Miss Yeng Lai
  biographical details, 52
  case conferences, 117, 142, 188, 252
  conclusions of Inquiry about, 287,
  295, 296
  death of Jasmine, role following, 188
  failings of, 119, 141, 290, 295, 296

hand-over of case to, 58, 73, 118, 119, 140
health visits to Beckfords, 118-120, 140-142, 146, 295, 296
last visit to Jasmine, 146, 295
notification of removal from child abuse register, 52, 119
records of, 224, 225, 227-229, 231, 295
responsibilities of, 140
supervision of, 119, 141-143, 287, 295
training, 52, 140, 141, 209, 287
Levick, Dr. Richard
qualifications, 68, App. B
report on Jasmine and Louise Beckford. *See* Levick Report
Levick Report
circumstances in which sought, 68
contents of, 68, App. C:1
Court Officer and, 95-98, 259
fate of, 89, 94-98, 253
guardian ad litem, value to, 253
questions to justices about, App. C:4
Liberal councillors, 179
Local authority
Brent. *See* Brent Borough Council
care proceedings
duty to bring, 18, 114, 175
generally. *See* Care proceedings
investigation of whether grounds for, 144, 145
representation in , 212, 214, 259, 303
representation in, 212, 214, 259, 303
case conferences, convening of, 251, 302
child abuse inquiries. *See* Child abuse inquiries
child care law. *See* Child care law
child in care of. *See* Child in care
Children's Departments, history of, 259, 260
court officers. *See* Court Officers
Director of Social Services, appointment of, 17
Education Departments. *See* Education; Schools
guardian ad litem, consultations with, 251, 302
health authority, cooperation with, 143-146, 299
housing assistance, provision of, 285
legal department, 213, 214, 259-261, 303
schools. *See* Schools

social services departments. *See* Social services departments
special establishments for abused children, 268, 300
Welfare and Children's Services, unification of, 197, 198
Long-term fostering
definition, 80
generally. *See* Fostering
Lord Chancellor
advice to Willesden magistrates, 6
recommendations to, on riders, 171, 302
Lorrington, Beverley
access to children. *See under* Beckford parents
biographical details, 42, 43
care proceedings
evidence at, 100
representation in, 52
case conferences, at, 116, 246, 249
charges against, 2, 183, App. D
child abuse
evidence as to. *See* Beckford case
fear of being accused of, 78
childhood, 42, 83, 86
clinic, visits to, 140, 141
concealment of assault, 77
description of, 42
general practitioners, visits to, 77, 78, 236
hospital visits to children, 78, 80, 84
injuries to Jasmine, explanations for, 29, 78, 121
Morris Beckford, relationship with, 42-43
nursery school
contact with, 121, 122
excuses offered to, 121, 291
transfer of Jasmine to, 120, 291, 294
Panel of Inquiry, evidence before, 6
paternity of Jasmine, 42, 84, 85
pregnancy of, 121, 122
psychiatric assessment, 87
social workers, contact with,
Mrs. Dietmann. *See* Dietmann, Mrs.
Ms. Wahlstrom. *See* Wahlstrom, Ms.
statutory case reviews, attendance at, 249
Treetops, visits to children at, 107, 134
trial of. *See under* Central Criminal Court

teacher-social workers, 156
Thompson, Mr. William
  biographical details, 47, 259
  care proceedings, role in, 47, 95, 96,
  98-104, 259, 290
  child abuse register, 241
  child care law, experience of, 261
  Court officer, post as, 259
  death of Jasmine, role following, 47,
  159, 181, 186-188, 196
  independent social worker, and, 93
  Inquiry, costs at, 37, 180
  Law and Administration Department,
  and, 149, 150
  Levick Report, 94-96, 259
  memorandum to Mr. Bishop, 90, 98, 99,
  App. C:3
  revocation of care orders application,
  122, 228, 229, 259
  "Salmon letter" to, 180
Training
  foster parents, 270, 272
  guardians ad litem, 213
  health visitors
    child abuse, as to, 208-210
    continuing training, 210
    courses for, 208
    qualifications, 208
  lawyers, of, in child care law, 212-214,
  303, 304
  magistrates
    child abuse, as to, 211-212, 302
    courses for, 211-212, 302
    need for, 172
    publications, reading of, 212
  social workers
    Beckford case, 46, 205-207, 293, 294
    Central Council
      establishment of, 197
      functions of, 197, 208
      qualifying awards, 201-204
      review of training, 203-207, 304
    Child Abuse Training Coordinator,
    131, 136, 301
    current forms of, 201-204
    duration of
      current minimum, 201, 203, 204
      recommended minimum, 204, 301
    funding of, 208
    history of, 197-200
    law, knowledge of, 207, 304

Seebohm Report, 10, 197-200
  "specialist" areas, in, 197 et seq
Trans-racial fostering
  Beckford case, 7, 282
  conclusions as to, 285, 300
  contemporary fostering of black
  children, 284
  expert evidence, 7, 33
  race relations legislation, 284, 285
Tree Tops, use of, 107, 134, 135
Trial
  Beckford/Lorrington. See under Central
  Criminal Court
  inquiry distinguished, 30
Truancy from school, 256
Trust, child in, child in care as, 16, 21,
297, 301
Tyler, Miss Mary
  biographical details, 51
  case conferences, 90, 188
  evidence, 119
  responsibilities, 51, 220
  supervision of health visitors, 119, 142,
  143, 228, 287, 292, 295
Universities, social science courses,
201-203
V and G case (1968), 34
Vivekanandan, Mrs. Nadani
  Beckford case, involvement in, 52, 189
  biographical details, 52
Voluntary social services
  child care, role as to, 175-177, 299
  NSPCC. See NSPCC
Wahlstrom, Ms. Gun
  Beckford parents, attitude towards, 216
  biographical details, 46
  care proceedings, role in, 99, 189, 290
  child abuse
    experience of cases of, 46, 135, 206,
    219, 287
    indications of, 118, 119, 177, 291
    training as to, 46, 205-207, 293
  Common Serjeant's remarks about, 38
  death of Jasmine, role following, 47,
  181, 182
  key worker
    guidance on duties as, 219
    nomination as, 79
  last sighting of Jasmine, 47, 124
  parentage of Jasmine, knowledge of, 85
  records of, 46, 224-226

role in Beckford case
  conclusions of Inquiry, 287, 290-294
  summary of, 46, 47
schools, links with, 120, 136, 156, 229, 233, 294
supervision of, 46, 118, 119, 219, 292, 293
training, 46, 205-207, 293, 294
visits to Beckfords, 46, 47, 120-127, 134, 135, 183, 291, 292
witness at Inquiry, 5, 33, App. B
Walker, Mr. Geoffrey
  expert evidence, 69, 117, 137, 291, App. B
  qualifications, App. B
Warner, Dr. John
  biographical details, 53
  care proceedings, at, 72, 94, 96, 99, 100
  case conferences, attendance at, 73, 82, 110, 232, 247, 248
  child abuse cases, experience of, 248
  expert evidence of, 65, 288, App. B
  last contact with Beckford sisters, 53, 72
  qualifications, 53, App. B
  St. Charles's Hospital, at, 53, 65, 77, 107
Weight of child
  index of child abuse, as, 74
  Jasmine Beckford. *See* Beckford, Jasmine
  percentile charts, use of, 70-74
West, Dr. Ian E.
  expert evidence by, 2, App. B
  post mortem report by, App. I
  qualifications, App. B
Whalley, Mr. Harry
  biographical details, 43
  Brent Area Review Committee, chairmanship, 240, 242
  Director of Social Services, as, 43, 129
  evidence of, 89
Wilful neglect, Lorrington's conviction of, 59
Willesden Juvenile Court
  care proceedings (Jasmine and Louise)
    case conferences before and after. *See* Case conferences
    Court Officer, role of, 47, 95, 96, 98-104, 259, 290
    events leading to, 77-92
    legal representation, 52, 53, 68, 149

Levick Report. *See* Levick Report
Miss Court's report, 93, 97, 98, 102, 294, App. C:2:4
reasoned judgment, absence of, 167, 172
revocation of order, application for, 58, 122, App. C:4
rider to care order
  circumstances leading to, 77 *et seq*, 98-103
  impact of, 100, 101, 103, 104, 149, 287
  jurisdiction to add, 167-172
  note of, App. C:3
  questions to justices about, 6, 7, App. C:4
  witnesses, 99, 100
place of safety order (Chantelle), 59, 181, 255
role in Beckford case, conclusions as to, 287
Witnesses at Inquiry
  attendance of, 5
  Beckford parents, 6
  cross-examination, 6, 31
  examination-in-chief, 6, 31
  expert. *See* Expert witnesses
  list of, App. B
  order in which called, 33
  potential, statements of, 34
  silence, right of, 5
  statements
    circulation of, 34
    read in whole or in part, 6, App. B
  Willesden magistrates, position of, 6, 7
  See also under individuals' names